RCRA
Hazardous
Wastes Handbook

10th Edition

Crowell & Moring

Ridgway M. Hall, Jr.
Richard E. Schwartz
Nancy S. Bryson
Robert C. Davis, Jr.
Brian G. Donohue

 Government Institutes, Inc.

Government Institutes, Inc., Rockville, Maryland 20850

ISBN : 0-86587-355-0

Printed in the United States of America

TABLE OF CONTENTS

THE RCRA HAZARDOUS WASTES HANDBOOK

THE LAW: RCRA

The Resource Conservation and Recovery Act ("RCRA") hazardous waste program is the largest regulatory program ever undertaken by the U.S. Environmental Protection Agency ("EPA"). Although RCRA was enacted in October 1976, the first major wave of implementing regulations was not issued by EPA until May 19, 1980. These regulations went into effect on November 19, 1980, and carried with them a number of important compliance requirements for firms who were at that time generating or handling hazardous wastes. Since that time, Congress has amended RCRA (the statute is also known by its original name, the Solid Waste Disposal Act), in 1980 and again in 1984. As this edition goes to press in September, 1993, Congress is debating further amendments. To address the problems of uncontrolled releases of hazardous substances to the environment, primarily from inactive waste management sites, Congress passed the Comprehensive Environmental Response, Compensation and Liability Act, commonly known as "Superfund" or "CERCLA", in December, 1980 and substantially amended this law in 1986.

Meanwhile, EPA has continued to expand its RCRA hazardous waste program through numerous implementing regulations. These additions have included hundreds of technical amendments issued since November, 1980. Major additional regulations and revisions have emerged as a result of the 1984 amendments. The implementing regulations and related preamble material issued for this program cover several thousand pages of fine print in the Federal Register. Even a casual reading of them is a monumental task. Behind the regulations are lengthy preamble discussions regarding their basis and purpose, technical support documents (largely unpublished) and enforcement policy memoranda.

The purpose of this Handbook is to help the reader to gain a working knowledge of this massive hazardous waste management program. This book attempts to distill this bundle of interlocking regulations to make them easier to understand and apply. It also discusses liability and enforcement issues. The authors have had the benefit of being exposed to many questions presented by participants in the Government Institutes' seminars on hazardous waste laws and regulatory programs, as well as to the many practical and legal problems faced by those who must deal on a daily basis with the hazardous waste requirements, and which make up our practice of environmental law at Crowell & Moring.

This 10th Edition incorporates the major regulatory changes, as well as the input of recent case law, that have occurred since the last printing of this Handbook. These include, for example, new regulations regarding land disposal, corrective action, underground storage tanks, the disposal of waste in boilers and industrial furnaces, and municipal solid waste management. It also addresses the impacts of, and EPA's responses to, the D.C. Circuit's 1991 decision in <u>Shell Oil v. U.S. EPA</u> setting aside the "mixture" and "derived from" rules (Chapter 2). Recent trends in EPA's enforcement policy, including the implementation of its RCRA Civil Penalty Policy, are addressed in our chapter on Inspections, Enforcement and Liability.

With respect to liability arising out of hazardous waste management, there is a close relationship between RCRA and Superfund. Superfund is comprehensively discussed in our separate companion volume entitled <u>The Superfund Manual</u> (Government Institutes, 5th ed. 1993).

In fairness to the reader, the authors feel compelled to make two disclaimers. The first involves how one should view this Handbook. Sound legal advice requires a thorough understanding of the factual context of a question or problem and a careful application of the law and regulations to the operative facts - always with a view to the practical problems presented and the legal alternatives available. Such an understanding is necessarily beyond the scope of a handbook designed to be useful to a variety of readers who face questions and problems unique to their particular circumstances. Accordingly, this Handbook should not be viewed as a substitute for legal advice on any particular case.

The second disclaimer is that this Handbook does not answer every question about the RCRA hazardous waste regulatory program.

This is a rapidly evolving field. There are significant questions of interpretation remaining which will have to be dealt with both by those who implement and those who are regulated under the program. EPA will continue for some time to issue additional implementing regulations. There will be a lively interaction among the various sectors of the regulated community, EPA, the states, Congress and the courts for years to come. While the details of the regulatory program will change, the concepts which underlie the program should remain fairly constant.

All of the states have adopted their own hazardous waste laws. For many states these are similar to RCRA, but in some there are significant differences. This book does not purport to survey all those laws. However, they must be considered by the responsible corporate manager as well as the regulatory personnel.

In approaching this book and its complex subject matter, therefore, we encourage the reader to concentrate on the concepts of the program. The fine print will then tend to be more easily grasped when it is needed.

Finally, the authors wish to express their appreciation to others at Crowell & Moring whose assistance was invaluable in preparing this Handbook, including Timothy McCrum, Susan Koehn, Judy Reinsdorf, Bill Anderson, Richard Mannix, Michael Zoeller, Tom Stock, Doug Kendall, Michele Witten, Tina Lewallen, and the Crowell & Moring Word Processing staff. Grateful appreciation is also expressed to our partner Tom Watson, who was a co-author of the original Handbook and several successive editions, and to David Case, our former senior associate who contributed to each of the first seven editions.

Washington, D.C.   RIDGWAY M. HALL, JR.
September 1993   RICHARD E. SCHWARTZ
                                     NANCY S. BRYSON
                                     ROBERT C. DAVIS, JR.
                                     BRIAN DONOHUE

ABOUT THE AUTHORS

RIDGWAY M. HALL, JR.

Ridge Hall is a partner in the Washington, D.C. law firm of Crowell & Moring. Formerly Associate General Counsel of the U.S. Environmental Protection Agency, his practice includes all areas of environmental law and litigation. He appears before federal and state courts and agencies across the country. Mr. Hall has authored numerous articles on environmental law and is a prominent speaker at seminars and symposia on environmental law and regulatory programs.

A _magna cum laude_ graduate of Yale University, Mr. Hall received his law degree from Harvard Law School. He is a member of the Bars of the District of Columbia, Connecticut, and the Supreme Court of the United States, and a member of the American Law Institute.

RICHARD E. SCHWARTZ

Richard Schwartz is a partner at Crowell & Moring, where he specializes in all aspects of environmental law and litigation. He has handled complex cases arising under the major environmental statutes over the past 20 years including large hazardous waste cases. He also has extensive experience in settlement negotiations in multi-party and multi-media cases.

Mr. Schwartz received his college degree from Yale and his law degree _cum laude_ from the University of Michigan Law School. He is a member of the Bar of the District of Columbia.

NANCY S. BRYSON

Nancy Bryson is a partner at Crowell & Moring, where she specializes in environmental law. She is a former trial attorney and Assistant Chief of the Environmental Defense Section of the Environment and Natural Resources Division of the Department of Justice. In that capacity, she litigated many cases under all of the major environmental statutes. Prior to that time she was an appellate lawyer with the Occupational Safety and Health Administration. She has authored articles on environmental law and regulation under RCRA and Superfund.

Ms. Bryson received her B.A. from Boston University _summa cum laude_ and her J.D. from Georgetown University Law School. Ms. Bryson is a member of the District of Columbia Bar.

ROBERT C. DAVIS, JR.

Robert Davis is a partner with Crowell & Moring, practicing in all areas of environmental law with particular emphasis on hazardous waste cases. He was formerly Deputy Chief for Environmental Law for the U.S. Air Force, serving for two years at the Pentagon and one year at Air Force Headquarters in San Francisco, where he had major responsibility for environmental compliance at Air Force facilities. This included extensive negotiations with other federal and state agencies and private parties, as well as litigation arising under Superfund, RCRA, the Clean Air Act, and other federal and state environmental laws.

Mr. Davis graduated from the University of Oklahoma and received a masters in law from George Washington University with highest honors, specializing in environmental law.

BRIAN G. DONOHUE

Mr. Donohue is Of Counsel with Crowell & Moring, where he handles matters involving all areas of environmental law. Formerly he was Senior Attorney with the Environmental Enforcement Section of the Environment and Natural Resources Division of the U.S. Department of Justice in Washington, D.C. In that capacity, he was involved in many cases under all of the major environmental statutes. He also received extensive experience in settlement negotiations in hazardous waste cases involving the federal government.

Mr. Donohue graduated with honors from the University of Maryland and received his law degree from Georgetown University. He is a member of the bar of the State of Maryland and the District of Columbia.

CHAPTER 1

OVERVIEW OF SUBTITLE C OF THE
RESOURCE CONSERVATION AND RECOVERY ACT:
THE HAZARDOUS WASTE PROGRAM

1.1   The Hazardous Waste Problem

Phrases like "Love Canal", "Valley of the Drums", and "Rocky Mountain Arsenal" have become well recognized code words for environmental disaster. It is universally acknowledged today that past and current hazardous waste management practices give rise to potentially substantial environmental risks.   The management -- and especially the mismanagement -- of hazardous wastes also creates a variety of possible liabilities for companies and individuals for corrective action, penalties and fines, and damage to property and persons.   The country has come to realize that the hazardous wastes we have been generating as part of our modern, post-World War II economy pose problems that must be brought under control and soundly managed if we are to preserve our quality of life.

The United States produced more than 197.5 million tons of hazardous wastes in 1989.[1] That figure does not include wastes which were handled after generation by facilities exempt from RCRA permitting requirements.   EPA believes these unmonitored wastes constitute at least two-thirds of the actual annual total, which would therefore reach or exceed 600 million tons.[2] In fact, a 1991 EPA report estimated with 95% certainty that the total hazardous wastes volumes generated in 1986 were between 672 and

---

[1]   EPA, National Biennial RCRA Hazardous Waste Report, 1989 at 1 (1993).

[2]   Id. at 1-9.

822 million tons.[3] As it was inaugurating the RCRA program in 1979, EPA found that the mismanagement of hazardous waste causes the following types of environmental damage:

    (1)   pollution of ground water;

    (2)   contamination of surface waters;

    (3)   pollution of the air;

    (4)   fires or explosions;

    (5)   poisoning of humans and animals via the food chain; and

    (6)   poisoning of humans and animals via direct contact.[4]

EPA declared that there were (and probably still are) literally thousands of abandoned hazardous waste disposal sites -- "ticking time bombs" -- awaiting future discovery. While the scope of the problem remains to be determined, there can be little question that American businesses, municipalities, and federal and state agencies have in the past managed and disposed of hazardous wastes in ways that we now recognize were inadequate to fully protect public health and the environment.

---

[3]   EPA, National Survey of Hazardous Waste Generators and Treatment, Storage, Disposal and Recycling Facilities in 1986 at 4 (1991). This exceeds previous estimates by the Congressional Office of Technology Assessment in its report, Technologies and Management Strategies for Hazardous Waste Control at 8 (1983).

[4]   U.S. Environmental Protection Agency, "Hazardous Waste Fact Sheet," EPA Journal at 12 (February 1979).

1.2   Congressional Response To The Hazardous Waste
        Problem - RCRA and Superfund

Congress dealt generally with the problem of solid waste disposal in statutes enacted in 1965[5] and 1970[6] but it was not until passage of the Resource Conservation and Recovery Act of 1976[7] ("RCRA") that the first comprehensive, federal effort to deal with the problems of solid waste, and hazardous waste specifically, was begun. The legislative history of RCRA has been summarized as follows:

> In a last minute flurry of activity during the early Fall of 1976, the 94th Congress enacted a major new law, the Resource Conservation and Recovery Act. In June 1976 the Senate had enacted its version (S. 2150). The House held hearings on proposed legislation but seemed to be overwhelmed by the number of bills that were offered. Finally, in the closing weeks of the Congress a bill that represented a composite of many of the key concepts that had been proposed in the House was enacted. Since there was not sufficient time to have a Conference with the Senate, the House chose the expeditious route of enacting a bill with the Senate bill integrated. This House bill was enacted by an overwhelming majority: 367 to 8. It was then returned to the Senate for enactment and then was sent to the President for his signature.[8]

The legislative history of RCRA as enacted in 1976 is scant and largely unenlightening. As will be seen throughout this Handbook, many significant areas of interpretation of the statute are still being debated within EPA years after enactment. This was due at least in part to the broad statutory language in the 1976

---

[5]   Solid Waste Disposal Act, Pub. L. No. 89-272, 79 Stat. 99 (1965).

[6]   Resource Recovery Act, Pub. L. No. 91-512, 84 Stat. 1227 (1970), as amended, Pub. L. No. 93-14, 87 Stat. 11 (1973).

[7]   Pub. L. No. 94-580, 90 Stat. 2795 (1976), 42 U.S.C. §§ 6901 et seq. (1988).

[8]   T. Sullivan, "Solid Waste and Resource Recovery," in Environmental Law Handbook at 374 (1978).

RCRA, and to the dearth of helpful legislative history. In the amendments to RCRA added by the Quiet Communities Act of 1978,[9] and the Solid Waste Disposal Act Amendments of 1980,[10] Congress declined to address some of the major outstanding issues of interpretation. EPA was left largely on its own during the implementation of RCRA in making key decisions on the scope and substantive provisions of the hazardous waste regulatory program.

Congress took a firm hand, however, in redirecting and substantially amending major aspects of the RCRA program in the Hazardous and Solid Waste Amendments of 1984 ("1984 Amendments" or "HSWA").[11] That law, which passed both the Senate and the House in the waning days of the 98th Congress, reflected Congressional concern with perceived regulatory loopholes in the RCRA program. As a result, the law contains many so-called "hammer" provisions that require EPA to issue new rules by a statutory deadline or a Congressionally-fashioned requirement will automatically go into effect. Of the 72 major provisions of the 1984 Amendments, 52 required EPA to initiate studies and rulemaking actions during 1985-86. The detailed provisions of the 1984 Amendments are unprecedented in environmental law, and have significantly expanded both the scope and coverage of RCRA.

RCRA is a multifaceted approach to solving the problems associated with solid waste disposal in this country. This Handbook deals specifically with Subtitle C of RCRA -- the hazardous waste program -- and with Subtitle I ("eye") of RCRA which establishes the regulatory program for underground storage tanks. Nonhazardous solid waste is separately regulated under RCRA Subtitle D, which is addressed in Chapter 11 of this Handbook. The regulation of hazardous waste was the overriding concern of Congress in enacting RCRA because this legislation was seen as closing the

---

[9]   Pub. L. No. 95-609, 92 Stat. 3079 (1978).

[10]   Pub. L. No. 96-482, 94 Stat. 2334 (1980).

[11]   Pub. L. No. 98-616, 98 Stat. 221 (1984).

loop of environmental protection -- air pollution, water pollution, and now the disposal of hazardous wastes on and in the land.[12]

One aspect of the hazardous waste problem was not comprehensively addressed under RCRA, namely, the past disposal of wastes which took place before the effective date of the RCRA regulatory program (i.e., November 19, 1980).[13] To provide federal authority to respond to the environmental hazards posed by abandoned disposal sites, and to provide the resources to clean up those sites, Congress passed the Comprehensive Environmental Response, Compensation and Liability Act of 1980 ("CERCLA"), commonly known as Superfund.[14] This legislation also establishes reporting requirements for hazardous substance releases from active facilities, imposes liability for those releases and the cleanup of Superfund sites, and sets up a taxing mechanism for contributing to the federally managed "funds" to be used for cleaning up releases. CERCLA and its implementing regulations directly complement the RCRA hazardous waste program. CERCLA is comprehensively discussed in The Superfund Manual (Government Institutes, 5th ed. 1992).

1.3   The RCRA Hazardous Waste Program

The goal of the RCRA hazardous waste program is to regulate all aspects of the management of a hazardous waste from the time it is generated to the time it is finally disposed of properly. Persons managing solid wastes are required to identify the solid waste deemed to be "hazardous waste" by EPA, and then to manage

---

[12]   H.R. 94-1491, 94th Cong., 2d Sess. at 3-4 (1976).

[13]   RCRA does provide authority for EPA to direct cleanup of releases of hazardous wastes and constituents through corrective action (§§ 3004(u) and (v)), and to deal with imminent hazards (§ 7003), as discussed in Chapters 9 and 12 of this Handbook.

[14]   Pub. L. No. 96-510, 94 Stat. 2767 (1980), 42 U.S.C. §§ 9601 et seq. (1988).

that hazardous waste at a treatment, storage or disposal ("T/S/D") facility in accordance with regulatory requirements.

The hazardous waste program's statutory provisions are briefly described here to provide an overview and establish the essential vocabulary of RCRA. The individual statutory provisions are described in more detail in the subsequent chapters. The following diagram provides a schematic view of the major statutory sections of RCRA Subtitle C.

SCHEMATIC OF SUBTITLE C – HAZARDOUS WASTE MANAGEMENT –
RESOURCE CONSERVATION AND RECOVERY ACT, AS AMENDED

```
+-----------------------------+        +-----------------------------+
|           EPA               |        |      State Programs         |
|   (Implementation and       |        |   (replace federal          |
|     Administration)         |        |    program upon             |
|                             |        |    approval by EPA)         |
+-----------------------------+        +-----------------------------+

          +-----------------------------------------+
          |   Identification of Hazardous Waste     |
          |              § 3001                     |
          +-----------------------------------------+

          +-----------------------------------------+
          |   Notification of Hazardous Waste Activity |
          |              § 3010                     |
          +-----------------------------------------+

                +---------------------------+    +---------------+
                |    Generator Standards    |    |  Inspection   |
                |          § 3002           |    |               |
                +---------------------------+    |      and      |
                                                 |               |
                                                 |  Enforcement  |
                +---------------------------+    |               |
                |   Transporter Standards   |    |    § 3007     |
                |          § 3003           |    |               |
                +---------------------------+    |    § 3008     |
                                                 |               |
                                                 |    § 3013     |
 +-----------+  +---------------------------+    |               |
 | Permits   |  | Treatment, Storage and Disposal |  |    § 7003     |
 | § 3005    |  |  ("T/S/D") Facility Standards |  |               |
 +-----------+  |          § 3004           |    +---------------+
                +---------------------------+
```

The RCRA hazardous waste program is a major federal under-taking. It is administered by EPA, which was charged with developing a complete set of regulations implementing the program. Congress mandated that those regulations be promulgated by 1978, but EPA failed to make that deadline. After an action-forcing lawsuit which resulted in a court order,[15] EPA promulgated the basic regulations for the hazardous waste program on May 19, 1980. Those went into effect on November 19, 1980. Many other new and amending regulations have been issued practically every month since. As with every EPA program, nationally applicable regulations are prepared and implemented by EPA Headquarters staff. Field implementation and enforcement are carried out in the ten EPA Regional Offices, and by authorized states.

It is helpful to review briefly the important sections of RCRA Subtitle C which together make up the Congressionally mandated program. RCRA Section 3001 requires EPA to promulgate regulations for the identification of hazardous wastes. The statute provides that a hazardous waste may be identified by one of two mechanisms. First, EPA can "list" in regulations those solid wastes that are hazardous. Second, EPA can identify hazardous "characteristics", and if a solid waste then exhibits at least one of those characteristics it is a hazardous waste. Persons handling solid wastes are charged with the responsibility of ascertaining whether the wastes are hazardous wastes. The unsuspecting person may be surprised at the types of solid wastes that are listed, or upon testing exhibit a characteristic of a hazardous waste.

RCRA Section 3010(a) requires persons generating or managing a hazardous waste to file a notification with EPA of their hazardous waste activities. The first RCRA 3010 notifications were filed by the regulated community on August 19, 1980. If requested

---

[15]   State of Illinois v. Costle, 12 ERC 1597 (D.D.C. 1979), aff'd sub nom. Citizens for a Better Environment v. Costle, 617 F.2d 851 (D.C. Cir. 1980).

by EPA in the Federal Register, a notification must now be filed within 90 days of the time EPA first promulgates regulations that newly identify wastes as hazardous or management activities as RCRA regulated. In this way, EPA is made aware of the identity of the persons, companies and organizations that are regulated under the RCRA hazardous waste program.

RCRA Section 3002 requires EPA to establish standards for generators of hazardous wastes. A generator is a person whose act or process produces a hazardous waste. Generators are obligated to determine whether any of their solid wastes are hazardous and, once a positive identification is made, manage that waste in accordance with the generator standards. These standards include the preparation of manifests to track the hazardous waste from the time it leaves the generator's property to the time it arrives at its place of ultimate treatment or disposal. Another key obliga- tion is that generators must use only transporters and T/S/D facilities that have received an EPA identification number and which, consequently, are also regulated under RCRA.

RCRA Section 3003 requires EPA to establish standards for transporters of hazardous wastes. EPA's regulations, in conjunc- tion with the Department of Transportation ("DOT") regulations under the Hazardous Materials Transportation Act, mandate compli- ance with requirements dealing with recordkeeping, labeling of drums, placarding of trucks, and the delivery of hazardous waste shipments to designated T/S/D facilities.

RCRA Section 3004 requires EPA to establish regulatory stan- dards for T/S/D facilities. Because the improper treatment, stor- age and disposal of hazardous wastes throughout the country was a major concern of Congress, RCRA Section 3004 authorizes EPA to establish a wide range of design, location, construction, opera- tion and maintenance standards, as well as insurance and financial requirements, which regulate the operation of T/S/D facilities.

RCRA Section 3005 requires owners and operators of T/S/D facilities to obtain a permit. Permits are not required for gen- erators or transporters of hazardous wastes under the federal program. The permits for T/S/D facilities are based on the comprehensive standards promulgated by EPA under RCRA Section 3004. RCRA Section 3005(e) also establishes "interim status" which allows existing T/S/D facilities that were in existence as of the effective date of the regulatory program, i.e., November 19, 1980 (or the date of a change in the law that first made the facility subject to RCRA Subtitle C), to remain in operation until a site-specific RCRA permit has been issued. Owners or operators of interim status facilities must file a timely permit application, and eventually qualify for a RCRA permit. Pending receipt of a permit, they must comply with "interim status standards," issued under Section 3004, which are comparable in most respects to the permanent standards that are applied to T/S/D facilities through their permits.

In accordance with RCRA Section 3006, states are permitted to assume the responsibility for implementing a hazardous waste program that is at least equivalent to the federal program, although EPA retains ultimate oversight responsibility. State programs may be more stringent than the federal program, and in fact many are.

RCRA Section 3008 establishes both civil and criminal enforcement sanctions for violations of the RCRA hazardous waste program. These sanctions have been greatly increased by recent RCRA amendments enacted by Congress, and may be strictly enforced by the courts.[16] EPA recently revised the RCRA Civil Penalty Policy (RCPP),[17] which is addressed in Chapter 12 of this Handbook. The most significant changes in the new RCPP concern how

---

[16]   See, e.g., United States v. Hayes International Corp., 786 F.2d 1499 (11th Cir. 1986) (ignorance of permit requirement is no defense; knowledge that disposal site had no permit does not require certainty, and jurors may draw inferences from all of the circumstances, including the existence of the regulatory scheme).

[17]   Fact sheet, 1990 Revised RCRA Civil Penalty Policy, U.S. EPA Office of Enforcement.

multiday penalties are calculated. The RCPP establishes three classifications of violations for multiday penalties ("mandatory", "presumed", and "discretionary") based on the relative gravity of the violations. Further, for the first time, the RCPP will apply to civil judicial settlements, as well as administrative complaints and settlements.

The first major implementing regulations under RCRA, promulgated by EPA on May 19, 1980, established basic definitions, procedures for identifying hazardous wastes, and the basic standards for generators, transporters, and owners and operators of T/S/D facilities. At the same time, EPA issued permit regulations for T/S/D facilities as part of its consolidated permit regulations.[18] Those initial regulations took effect on November 19, 1980. Since that time literally thousands of regulatory amendments, many of major significance, have been issued. The following chart lists the regulations by topic and location in Title 40 of the Code of Federal Regulations which comprise the program established by EPA to implement all these statutory provisions (many states follow the same numbering system):

---

[18] In order to facilitate the RCRA permit application process, EPA has since "deconsolidated" two parts of the consolidated permit regulations which implement RCRA. 48 Fed. Reg. 14146 (April 1, 1983); 48 Fed. Reg. 30113 (June 30, 1983). See also the discussion in Chapter 8 of this Handbook.

40 CFR	Corresponding RCRA Section and Descriptive Title
Part 260	Definitions generally used in other parts and provisions generally applicable to other parts
Part 261	Section 3001: Identification and Listing of Hazardous Waste (characteristics and lists)
Part 262	Section 3002: Standards Applicable to Generators of Hazardous Waste
Part 263	Section 3003: Standards Applicable to Transporters of Hazardous Waste See also Department of Transportation regulations at 49 CFR Parts 171-179.
Part 264	Section 3004: Final Standards Applicable to Owners and Operators of Hazardous Waste Treatment, Storage, and Disposal Facilities
Part 265	Section 3004: Interim Status Standards Applicable to Owners and Operators of Hazardous Waste Treatment, Storage, and Disposal Facilities
Part 266	Standards for Management of Specific Wastes (including recyclable materials) and Types of Facilities
Part 267	Temporary Standards for Land Disposal Facilities (now superseded)
Part 268	Land Disposal Restrictions
Part 270	Section 3005: Permits for Treatment, Storage, and Disposal of Hazardous Waste
Part 124	EPA Permitting Procedure
Part 271	Requirements for State Programs
Part 272	Inventory of Approved State Programs
Part 280	Underground Storage Tanks

Citations in this Handbook to EPA regulations are to the Code of
Federal Regulations of (July 1, 1992), unless otherwise indicated.

1.4   EPA Interpretations of the Regulations

When EPA initially promulgated the RCRA hazardous waste program regulations in 1980, it launched a nationwide publicity and
education campaign.   EPA conducted public meetings in a number of
cities at which agency personnel answered questions on the new
regulations. From the questions raised by the public at these
meetings, as well as those posed directly to EPA officials by members of the regulated community and their counsel, EPA realized
that there was a need (and would be for a long time) for guidance
and clarification regarding this complex regulatory program.

At first, EPA adopted a formal procedure for issuing binding
interpretations of the hazardous waste regulations. These interpretations were called Regulatory Interpretative Memoranda
("RIMs"), and EPA also considered issuing Program Implementation
Guidelines ("PIGs") and Technical Amendment Regulations
("TARs").[19]   The RIM program could have been very helpful, especially in applying the complex hazardous waste program to specific
factual situations. EPA has largely abandoned this approach, however, preferring instead to explain and interpret its regulations
by issuing regulatory amendments.   Only a few RIMs have been
issued by the agency. EPA has also relied on technical guidance
documents, many prepared by outside contractors, to provide guidance in some areas of the regulations.   Frequently, EPA will
announce to the public the availability of these documents and
agency manuals, even though they may have been prepared for use by
its own personnel.[20]   These documents can then be obtained by

---

[19]   45 Fed. Reg. 55386 (August 19, 1980).

[20]   See, e.g., Notice of Availability of Permit Writers'
       Guidance Manual, 50 Fed. Reg. 5259 (February 7, 1985). See
                                              (footnote continued)

calling the RCRA Hotline at (800) 424-9346. For the most part, however, many of the key guidance and policy documents developed by EPA are not widely distributed to the regulated community.

EPA interpretations and clarifications have also been prompted by legal challenges to its regulations. As implementing regulations have been promulgated, the regulated companies and environmental groups have filed numerous lawsuits seeking judicial review. Under RCRA Section 7006, which provides for judicial review of RCRA regulations, a petition for review must be filed in the United States Court of Appeals for the District of Columbia Circuit within 90 days of the date regulations are promulgated. For example, the RCRA 3004 standards for land disposal facilities promulgated in July 1982 were challenged in the Consolidated Land Disposal Regulation Litigation, D.C. Cir. No. 82-2205. The issues raised in that lawsuit provided the impetus for many of the statutory amendments affecting land disposal facilities in the 1984 RCRA Amendments enacted by Congress. Other issues were settled by regulatory changes, and the two remaining issues (EPA's authority to issue permits for closure and post-closure care and to require monitoring of unusable aquifers) were finally decided by the Court of Appeals for the District of Columbia Circuit favorably to EPA on July 16, 1991. Thereafter, most of EPA's major regulations affecting T/S/D activity have been the subject of appellate litigation. While this has caused some uncertainty, the regulations remain in effect during the pendency of such litigation unless, in exceptional cases, the court stays them.

More recently, in Shell Oil v. U.S. EPA, 950 F.2d 751 (D.C. Cir. 1991), the D.C. Circuit Court of Appeals vacated several RCRA regulations promulgated in 1981. Final rules issued in May 1980 included in the definition of "hazardous waste" both the "mixture"

(continued)
> also RCRA Compliance/Enforcement Guidance Manual -- Policy Compendium (Government Institutes, 1985).

---

rule (45 Fed. Reg. 33119), which required classification as hazardous waste any mixture of a listed hazardous waste with any other solid waste, and the "derived from" rule (45 Fed. Reg. 33120), which so classified any residue derived from the treatment of hazardous waste. The Shell Oil court vacated and remanded both of these regulatory definitions. The court also held invalid the requirement of leachate monitoring at land treatment facilities (45 Fed. Reg. 33248). Each of these three regulations were vacated by the court on the basis of EPA's failure to comply with the notice-and-comment procedures required by RCRA and the Administrative Procedure Act, 5 U.S.C. § 553(b) (1988). The Shell Oil decision and EPA's response to the decision are discussed in Chapter 2 of this Handbook.

1.5   The 1980 Amendments

On October 21, 1980, the Solid Waste Disposal Act Amendments of 1980 ("1980 Amendments") were enacted into law.[21] Most of those amendments directly affected RCRA and the hazardous waste regulatory program. The significant amendments are highlighted below and described in more detail in later chapters of this Handbook:

> °   Interim status trigger date. The "in existence" deadline for qualifying for interim status was changed to allow more T/S/D facilities to continue operations. (See Chapter 6 of this Handbook.) RCRA Section 3005(e) originally required a T/S/D facility to have been "in existence" as of the date RCRA was enacted, i.e., October 21, 1976, to qualify for interim status. The amendment changed the "in existence" deadline to November 19, 1980, the effective date of the RCRA program. Without this amendment, many T/S/D facilities would have had to close down until EPA

---

[21]   See footnote 9, supra.

issued all the regulations necessary and obtained the agency resources required for a full scale RCRA permit program.

   ° <u>Generator duties</u>. Originally, a generator only had to utilize a manifest system to assure the proper transport, treatment, storage and disposal of its hazardous waste. RCRA Section 3002(a)(5) was amended to require that generators now also use "any other reasonable means necessary" in addition to compliance with the manifest requirements to accomplish this goal.

   ° <u>Waste exclusion</u>. Coal mining wastes already permitted under the Surface Mining Control and Reclamation Act of 1977 were exempted from RCRA Section 3005 permitting requirements.

   ° <u>Existing vs. new T/S/D facilities</u>. RCRA Section 3004 was amended to allow EPA to differentiate between new and existing T/S/D facilities in establishing requirements. This has proven to be an important amendment for those existing T/S/D facilities that might otherwise have required substantial modifications if EPA were required to impose identical regulatory requirements on both new and existing facilities.

   ° <u>Enforcement</u>. Criminal penalties were strengthened. (<u>See</u> Chapter 12 of this Handbook). For example, the maximum penalty for first violations was doubled. Explicit penalties were provided for knowingly failing to comply with material permit conditions. A new "knowing endangerment" offense for certain life-threatening conduct was also added.

   ° <u>State inventories</u>. RCRA Section 3012 was added to require each state to compile, as expeditiously as practicable, an inventory of hazardous waste sites within its boundaries. The inventory must cover both inactive and active hazardous waste sites, and

must include information related to the amount, nature
and toxicity of the wastes, the name, address, and corporate headquarters of the owner of the site, and other
information. If EPA determines that the site may
present a substantial hazard to human health or the
environment, it may order the owner or operator of the
site to conduct testing, analysis, and monitoring.

1.6   The 1984 RCRA Amendments

On November 8, 1984, President Reagan signed into law the
Hazardous and Solid Waste Amendments of 1984.[22] These amendments
significantly expanded both the scope of coverage and the detailed
requirements of RCRA. They were debated extensively by Senate and
House committees for more than two years. The detailed nature of
the amendments, together with the deadlines for action imposed not
only on the regulated community but on EPA, reflect a Congressional dissatisfaction with what the 98th Congress perceived as
less than vigorous administration and enforcement of RCRA by EPA.
Highlights of this law are summarized below, and the many detailed
provisions and EPA's implementing regulations are then discussed
throughout this Handbook.

> °   Small quantity generators. The 1984 Amend-
> ments greatly expanded RCRA's coverage of small quan-
> tity generators by requiring EPA to promulgate
> regulations for generators, transporters, and T/S/D
> facilities that handle hazardous wastes produced by a
> generator in a total quantity of 100 to 1,000 kg/month,
> and by generators of less than 100 kg/month, if neces-
> sary for environmental protection. These standards
> require use of the Uniform Manifest and disposal of
> small quantity wastes at an interim status or permitted
> T/S/D facility.

---

[22]   See footnote 10, supra.

° <u>Listed wastes</u>. EPA was required to add to the list of hazardous wastes, if appropriate, certain specified wastes. These wastes include solvents, oil refining wastes, inorganic chemical industry wastes, dioxin, dyes and pigments, paint production wastes, lithium batteries, and coal slurry pipeline effluent. EPA was also required to revise the characteristic which would identify as hazardous those solid wastes containing high levels of known toxic materials, <u>i.e.</u>, known carcinogens. Consistent with this statutory mandate, on March 29, 1990, EPA promulgated a rule that substitutes the more aggressive "Toxicity Characteristic Leaching Procedure" ("TCLP") for the "Extended Procedure" ("EP") Toxicity Characteristic.[23]

° <u>Delisting petitions</u>. The 1984 Amendments required EPA to take action on delisting petitions to delete wastes produced at a petitioner's facility from the hazardous waste lists within twenty-four months of submission. EPA was also required to consider hazardous constituents other than those for which the waste was originally listed when processing delisting petitions.

° <u>Used oil</u>. EPA was required to decide whether to identify used automotive and truck crankcase oil as a hazardous waste. The regulatory status of used oil has been the subject of ongoing debate.[24] If EPA decides that such used oil should be disposed of as a hazardous waste, generators, transporters, and operators of T/S/D facilities for used oil will become subject to the RCRA hazardous waste regulations, or to any different regulations EPA may promulgate.

---

[23] 55 <u>Fed</u>. <u>Reg</u>. 11798 <u>et seq</u>. The new TCLP rule is discussed in Chapter 2 of this Handbook.

[24] This subject is discussed in Chapter 13 of the Handbook.

°   <u>Waste-derived fuel</u>. Any person who distributes or markets any hazardous waste-derived fuel must place a conspicuous legend on the invoice or bill of sale that states:

WARNING: THIS FUEL CONTAINS HAZARDOUS WASTES
[followed by a list of the hazardous wastes]

This warning may be expected to discourage the burning of such fuels. In addition, anyone who produces, distributes, markets, or burns hazardous waste fuels must file a notification with EPA which gives the location, type of facility, and the hazardous waste that is used as a fuel. The 1984 Amendments required EPA to promulgate technical standards for the burning and blending of hazardous waste-derived fuel. These standards are now codified at 40 C.F.R. Part 266.

°   <u>Waste minimization</u>. The 1984 Amendments imposed "waste minimization" requirements on generators. Every generator must certify on manifests for hazardous waste shipments that he has a program in place to reduce the volume and toxicity of hazardous wastes to the extent that is economically practicable and that he has selected the method of treatment, storage or disposal currently available which minimizes the present and future threat to human health and the environment. The biennial reports filed by generators must describe the efforts made to reduce the volume and toxicity of hazardous wastes and the results actually achieved when compared to prior years. In addition, a generator that conducts T/S/D activities at the site of generation must make the above certification annually as a permit condition.

°   <u>Land disposal prohibitions</u>. In a far-reaching amendment to RCRA 3004, EPA was required to decide whether to prohibit the land disposal of all

RCRA hazardous wastes which are not pretreated using the best available demonstrated technology. To do this, EPA was required to address on a high priority basis spent solvents and dioxins, followed by a group of waste streams known as the "California List". Then EPA was directed to publish a ranking of all remaining hazardous wastes based on their intrinsic hazard and volume, with a schedule for determining whether to ban the land disposal of such untreated wastes. By August 1988, EPA was required to decide (and did) whether to prohibit land disposal of some or all of the first one-third of the highest priority hazardous wastes on the ranking list. EPA was required to issue (and did) land disposal restrictions for the second/one-third of the ranked hazardous wastes by June 1989. The remaining third was assigned a deadline of May 1990 for an EPA decision, which it made on June 1, 1990. EPA's land ban disposal restrictions are discussed in Chapter 7 of this Handbook.

°   Treatment methods before land disposal. Congress also took steps to promote the treatment of hazardous wastes in lieu of, or prior to, land disposal. When EPA promulgated the land disposal bans, it was required to issue (and did) regulations that specify the methods of treatment, if any, that substantially reduce the toxicity and the likelihood of migration of the wastes from land disposal facilities. Hazardous wastes that are treated in accordance with these methods of pretreatment are exempt from the land disposal ban.

°   Ban on liquids in land disposal facilities. Congress also banned the disposal in landfills of bulk or non-containerized liquid hazardous wastes, as well as hazardous wastes containing free liquids. In addition, EPA was required to issue regulations that minimize the disposal of containerized liquid hazardous wastes in landfills. These regulations are now codified at 40 C.F.R. §§ 264.314 and 265.314.

° <u>Minimum technology for landfills and surface impoundments</u>. The 1984 Amendments required that new landfills and surface impoundments, new or replacement units, and lateral expansions at existing landfills and impoundments be double-lined and have leachate collection systems. Ground water monitoring must also be required as a permit condition. Operators must notify EPA prior to receiving hazardous wastes in new, replacement, or expansion units and then file their final permit applications to expedite permitting of those facilities. Operators of interim status land disposal facilities had to certify to EPA by November 8, 1985, that all applicable ground water monitoring and financial responsibility requirements were being met.

° <u>Retrofitting of surface impoundments</u>. In one of the most controversial provisions of the 1984 Amendments, Congress mandated that all existing unlined surface impoundments be retrofitted with double liners, leachate collection systems, and ground water monitoring systems by November 1988.

° <u>Corrective action</u>. Congress gave EPA clear authority to require operators of T/S/D facilities to take corrective action for past releases, including releases that have migrated beyond the property boundary. EPA has amended its regulations to require such corrective action by operators of all permitted T/S/D facilities, and all existing landfill units, surface impoundment units, and waste piles that have received wastes after July 26, 1982.[25] Newly issued RCRA permits must require an operator to take corrective action for all releases of hazardous constituents at the T/S/D facility regardless of when the waste was placed in a unit, or whether a unit is currently active.[26]

° _Air emissions_. EPA was required to promulgate regulations for the monitoring and control of air emissions at T/S/D facilities. These regulations are now codified at 40 C.F.R. Parts 264 and 265, Subparts AA and BB.

° _Permitting_. Congress attempted in the 1984 Amendments to phase out interim status by accelerating the permitting of interim status T/S/D facilities. EPA, or an authorized state, had to issue permits for all land disposal facilities by 1988, for all incinerators by 1989, and must issue permits for all other T/S/D facilities by 1992. The life of a RCRA permit is limited to ten years. Land disposal permits must be reviewed every five years, and all permit renewals must reflect improvements in the state of control and treatment technology.

° _State authorization_. In states with final authorization, EPA retains authority to issue or deny the portions of permits affected by the 1984 Amendments, until such time as the state amends its program to incorporate the new requirements and EPA approves the changes. All new legal requirements in the 1984 Amendments with statutory deadlines will become effective in authorized states on the same day they take

---

[25]   40 CFR 264.101, 50 _Fed. Reg._ 28747 (July 15, 1985).

[26]   See Chapter 9 on Corrective Action.

effect for the federal program; EPA will then administer and enforce the requirement until the state amends its program.

° <u>Mandatory inspections</u>. Congress amended RCRA Section 3007 to require all privately-operated T/S/D facilities to be inspected at least every two years, and all federal, state and municipal facilities every year.

° <u>Criminal penalties</u>. The scope of criminal liability for violations under RCRA was further expanded. Criminal liability is imposed on generators who knowingly ship hazardous wastes either without a manifest or to an unpermitted T/S/D facility. Violations of federal or state interim status standards may now result in criminal penalties. The failure to file reports required under RCRA, or material omissions in such reports, may justify criminal penalties.

° <u>Citizen suits</u>. The citizen suit provisions of RCRA have been expanded to authorize suits for present or past management or disposal of hazardous wastes that have contributed to an imminent or substantial endangerment.

° <u>Underground storage tanks</u>. In a far-reaching new measure, the 1984 Amendments created RCRA Subtitle I ("eye"), which established a comprehensive program for underground storage tanks that contain "regulated substances". This includes all "hazardous substances" as defined in CERCLA 101(14) (but not RCRA hazardous wastes regulated under Subtitle C) and liquid petroleum substances. This regulatory program is discussed in Chapter 14 of this Handbook.

EPA promulgated the so-called "Codification Rule" implementing many of these statutory provisions on July 15, 1985,[27] and EPA has been developing additional changes to the RCRA regulatory program mandated by the 1984 Amendments. These changes have already had a profound impact. Since the land disposal ban has been in effect, for example, generators have had to turn to alternative treatment and disposal methods. Pretreatment to render hazardous wastes less mobile, toxic, and persistent prior to land disposal will spawn other new technologies. The requirements of waste minimization, and the practical difficulties and costs of disposal, will encourage industry to make significant changes to production processes in order to reduce the quantity and toxicity of hazardous wastes. At the same time, EPA has expanded the universe of solid wastes that are hazardous by broadening the toxicity characteristic. This together with greater regulation of recycling activities has significantly expanded RCRA's reach.

1.7   The Medical Waste Tracking Act of 1988

During the summer of 1988, substantial amounts of untreated medical and hospital wastes washed up on the shoreline areas of Connecticut, New Jersey, New York and other states, causing widespread public concern. These wastes included needles, syringes, blood bags, bandages and vials. There were also reports of incidents of careless management of medical waste, for example, by dumping it into open dumpsters or other locations affording potential human exposure. In response to this concern, Congress, on November 1, 1988, passed the Medical Waste Tracking Act of 1988 ("MWTA")[28], which added a new Subtitle J to RCRA.

---

[27]   50 Fed. Reg. 28702. This rule, which was promulgated without prior notice and comment because it purported merely to "codify" statutory amendments into the regulations, was substantially upheld in United Technologies Corporation v. EPA, 821 F.2d 714 (D.C. Cir. 1987).

[28]   Pub. L. No. 100-582, 102 Stat. 2950.

This law called for a two-year demonstration program among coastal states in the northeast and Great Lakes areas for medical waste tracking during a two year period. EPA designated certain general types or classes of medical wastes to be tracked under the demonstration program including: (1) cultures and stocks of infectious agents and associate biologicals; (2) pathological waste; (3) human blood and blood products; (4) used syringes, needles, and other sharp instruments; (5) contaminated animal carcasses; (6) surgery or autopsy waste; (7) laboratory waste; (8) dialysis waste; (9) discarded medical equipment; and (10) isolation wastes.

EPA is currently working on a report to submit to Congress evaluating the threats posed by medical waste, estimating the costs associated with the tracking and management requirements under the demonstration program, evaluating the success of the program, and discussing available or potentially available methods for managing and treating medical wastes on a broader scale. Two interim reports were submitted in May and December, 1990, respectively addressing generally the same subjects.

On March 24, 1989, EPA issued an interim final rule establishing the medical waste tracking and regulatory program pursuant to Subtitle J.[29] The effective date for these regulations was specified as June 22, 1989. However, the demonstration program, which ran from that date through June 22, 1991, has now expired.[30]

1.8   RCRA and Ground Water Pollution Control

One of the most important environmental issues for the next decade is the control of ground water pollution. According to the

---

[29]   54 Fed. Reg. 12326, amended at 54 Fed. Reg. 24310 (June 6, 1989), codified at 40 C.F.R. Part 259 (1990).

[30]   Because efforts to reauthorize the program have failed, the law is no longer effective. Still, forty-nine states each have their own medical waste program, which in some way attempts to address the hazards posed by mismanaged medical wastes.

National Groundwater Association, 53% of Americans get their drinking water from groundwater sources. That figure includes municipal water systems which depend on groundwater. EPA has identified ponds, lagoons, and impoundments where wastes have been disposed of and leaking underground storage tanks as major sources of ground water pollution. Because ground water is such a substantial source of drinking water supplies, its protection is particularly critical.

There is no one environmental statute that deals specifically and exclusively with ground water protection. Surface impoundments and other hazardous waste management facilities or sites can be regulated under RCRA; to the extent that they are active sites and inactive sites, they are generally addressed under Superfund. The RCRA Subtitle I ("eye") program addresses leaks from underground storage tanks, including cleanup and prevention. In addition, regulatory authority under the Clean Water Act and the underground injection control program of the Safe Drinking Water Act, and possibly the Toxic Substances Control Act, provide a variety of authorities for EPA to deal with ground water protection. These statutory authorities, and the regulatory burdens and liabilities that arise under them, need careful coordination. From time to time Congress has considered separate ground water protection legislation, but as of this writing such legislation has not been enacted.

EPA has created an Office of Ground Water Protection in its Office of Water Programs. In 1984, EPA also issued a Ground Water Protection Strategy document which outlines the nature and extent of ground water contamination in the United States and sets forth EPA's strategy to protect ground water. Later, in 1989, EPA created a Ground Water Task Force to review the Agency's ground water protection program. As a result of that effort, EPA has developed a policy as well as implementation principles that set forth an aggressive approach to protecting the Nation's ground water resources and direct the course of the Agency's efforts over the coming years.[31]

Although RCRA will be only one of several regulatory programs used to address ground water protection, it will be an important one. As the reader progresses through the following chapters which describe the RCRA hazardous waste regulatory program, it is worth keeping in mind that one of the principal purposes of the program is the protection of ground water.

1.9   EPA's RCRA Reform Initiative

On February 10, 1992, during the last year of the Bush Administration, the Office of Solid Waste and Emergency Response ("OSWER") proposed an "Environmental Growth Initiative" setting forth steps to restructure the RCRA regulatory program. The Initiative stated that because the RCRA program is perceived to be redundant, burdensome and overbroad, a reform plan is needed to make RCRA's prevention and cleanup programs more cost-effective and risk-oriented, in turn reducing RCRA's regulatory reach.

In the Initiative, OSWER recognized the need to establish a system which captures high-risk waste activities for environmental control, while excluding those that are low-risk. In this way, many wastes and cleanup actions can be freed from regulatory control. In addition, OSWER proposed to create a set of reduced, tailored management standards for groups of higher risk wastes warranting some control. Recycling will also be encouraged. OSWER believes that certain types of industries would benefit most from this approach, such as the metal recovery industry, building and related industries, and recyclers that store incoming materials prior to processing.

The Initiative specifically proposed the development of special rules for cleanup of "old waste sites" (as compared to

---

[31]   Protecting the Nation's Ground Water: EPA's Strategy for the 1990s, The Final Report of the EPA Ground Water Task Force, May 1991.

cleanups of ongoing, industrial chemical operations). These proposals include:

- adoption of concentration based levels such that little or no corrective action would be required;

- exemption of temporary storage and treatment at cleanup sites from the more stringent land disposal restrictions (which were designed with permanent disposal in mind);

- allowing stabilization in place of wastes from cleanup sites (along with removing permit impediments related thereto);

- recognition that technical impracticability exists at some sites;

- finalization of special, tailored treatment standards for cleanups involving contaminated debris and soil; and

- separate handling of petroleum contaminated media.

Moreover, EPA called for special rules regarding treatment, storage and disposal facilities, including:

- development of universal land disposal treatment standards based on constituent concentration, rather than the current situation in which the same constituents in different wastes are subject to different standards;

- development of risk-based, tailored management standards to replace current overbroad requirements;

- amendment of current technology based land disposal requirements to take into account the risks involved, and elimination of regulatory controls over wastes treated to below characteristic or delisting levels; and

- reduction of paperwork burdens associated with land disposal and permit requirements.

Further, EPA proposed to reduce permit requirements for low-risk facilities. These proposals include:

- adoption of class permits for low technology units (e.g., filtration, dewatering, etc.) conducting short-term cleanups;

- elimination of mandatory post-closure permits because many closed facilities do not need the level of oversight a post-closure permit entails;

- development of a class permit for R&D and experimental facilities;

- class permitting based on risk for storage prior to recycling; and

- reassessment of the 100 kg. limit on treatability studies for contaminated soils.

Another set of proposals in the Initiative related to Underground Storage Tanks ("USTs").   First, EPA indicated it would develop a rule to give States flexibility to extend the federal financial responsibility compliance date relating to USTs to 1999 on a case-by-case or group basis. It would also try to expedite issuance of a final rule to permit local governments to use alternative mechanisms to meet financial responsibility requirements. In addition, EPA hoped to correct a problem in which loans have been denied to UST owners who wish to use the money to make needed improvements in their facilities to meet regulatory requirements. (Some lenders have been unwilling to make such loans when they are secured by contaminated properties.)   EPA intends to clarify through an interpretation or rulemaking (similar to that issued under Superfund, see 57 Fed. Reg. 18344 (April 29, 1992)) the circumstances where a lender would incur liability regarding such properties.

The Clinton-Gore Administration, and Carol Browner as EPA Administrator, seem interested in pursuing these initiatives. They have also recognized the importance of a sound scientific foundation for regulatory action, and pledged to improve relations between EPA and the States. Finally, there is at least some expressed interest in trying to streamline the regulation in the interest of greater clarity and efficiency for all concerned, and a reduction in transactional costs. Whether these goals can be met over the next few years remains to be seen.

CHAPTER 2

THE IDENTIFICATION OF HAZARDOUS WASTE

The RCRA program applies to all persons who currently manage a "hazardous waste". RCRA Section 3001 and EPA's implementing regulations at 40 CFR Part 261 are the foundation of the RCRA regulatory program because they establish the mechanisms for identifying those wastes that are deemed hazardous.

2.1 Statutory Requirements of RCRA Section 3001

The scope of the RCRA program, like many other federal environmental programs, is delineated by the definitions of key terms. Commonplace words take on new and important meanings because of statutory definitions enacted by Congress or adopted by agency regulation. The scope of the hazardous waste regulatory program depends upon the definitions of two key terms: "solid waste" and "hazardous waste." These definitions are integrated directly into the regulations at 40 CFR Part 261 that implement RCRA Section 3001, rather than being set forth in the general definitions of Part 260.

The term "solid waste" first distinguishes between waste and all other materials such as products. The term "hazardous waste" then identifies those solid wastes that pose a danger to human health or the environment, and must be managed accordingly.[1] The starting place, therefore, for determining the applicability of the RCRA hazardous waste program is to decide whether a particular material is a solid waste. If the answer to this inquiry is "yes", the next question is whether that solid waste is deemed a hazardous waste.

---

[1] The terms "management" or "hazardous waste management" are defined to mean the "systematic control of the collection, source separation, storage, transportation, processing, treatment, recovery, and disposal of hazardous waste." 40 CFR 260.10.

A "solid waste" was defined by Congress as:

> [A]ny garbage, refuse, sludge from a waste treatment plant, water supply treatment plant, or air pollution control facility and other discarded material, including solid, liquid, semisolid, or contained gaseous material resulting from industrial, commercial, mining, and agricultural operations, and from community activities.[2]

Note especially that Congress stated that liquids and contained gaseous materials are to be considered "solid wastes".

This statutory definition of solid waste goes on to exclude solid or dissolved materials in domestic sewage, solid or dissolved materials in irrigation return flows, and industrial discharges that are point sources subject to permits under the Clean Water Act. It also excludes source, special nuclear, or byproduct material as defined by the Atomic Energy Act of 1954, as amended.[3] The 1980 RCRA Amendments also authorized EPA to study and decide how to regulate fly ash and other wastes from the combustion of fossil fuels; waste from the extraction, beneficiation, and processing of ores and minerals;[4] and cement kiln dust wastes.

---

2   RCRA § 1004(27).

3   Id. These statutory exclusions are discussed further in section 2.2.1.3 of this Chapter.

4   RCRA § 3001(b)(3). This provision prohibits EPA from regulating these wastes under RCRA until completion of certain studies and rulemakings. EPA submitted its Mine Waste Report to Congress on December 31, 1985. Based on that report, EPA issued its regulatory determination that mining wastes (chiefly waste rock, gangue and tailings) will not be regulated under the RCRA hazardous waste program. 51 Fed. Reg. 24996 (July 3, 1986), but under Subtitle D of RCRA instead. This decision was upheld by the Court of Appeals for the District of Columbia Circuit in Environmental Defense Fund v. United States EPA, 852 F.2d 1309 (D.C. Cir. 1988) ("EDF I").

EPA withdrew its proposed "reinterpretation" of the mining waste exclusion so that wastes from processing ores and minerals, particularly smelting wastes, are still within the
[footnote continued]

Congress then defined the term "hazardous waste" to mean:

[5] solid waste, or combination of solid wastes, which because of its quantity, concentration, or physical, chemical, or infectious characteristics may -

[continued]

RCRA exclusion. 51 Fed. Reg. 36233 (October 9, 1986). The D.C. Circuit Court held that the withdrawal of the proposal was arbitrary and capricious and that the so-called Bevill exclusion for mining wastes was not intended "to encompass all wastes from primary smelting and refining" but to apply to "only those wastes from processing ores or minerals that meet the 'special waste' criteria, that is, 'high volume, low hazard' wastes." Environmental Defense Fund v. EPA, 852 F.2d 1316, 1328-29 (D.C. Cir. 1988) ("EDF II") cert. denied, 489 U.S. 1011 (1989) (directing EPA to reinterpret the scope of the exclusion for Mineral Processing Wastes). In response to this decision, EPA promulgated a final rule setting forth specific mining wastes which meet these criteria. See 54 Fed. Reg. 36592 (Sept. 1, 1989). Only wastes specifically listed by this rule will be considered by EPA to be subject to the RCRA mining waste exclusion. The final rule designated 20 mineral processing waste streams for conditional retention pending further study. In a related rulemaking, on January 23, 1990, EPA permanently removed five of the 20 conditionally retained mineral processing wastes from the Bevill exemption. See 55 Fed. Reg. 2322 et seq. On June 13, 1991, EPA determined that the 20 special wastes were inappropriate for regulation under Subtitle C. Eighteen of the wastes will be regulated under Subtitle D. The remaining two wastes, phosogypsum oil process water from phosphoric acid production, will be regulated under the Toxic substance Control Act. 56 Fed. Reg. 27300.

In addition, on August 9, 1993, EPA issued a final determination in which it concluded that regulation under the hazardous waste management program was inappropriate for four of the waste streams from the combustion of fossil fuels -- fly ash, bottom ash, boiler slag, and flue gas emission control waste -- because of the limited risks posed by them. Instead, EPA will consider regulation of these wastes under RCRA's solid waste disposal program. EPA intends to make a final regulatory hazardous waste determination on the remaining fossil fuel combustion waste stream by April 1, 1998. 58 Fed. Reg. 42466 (August 9, 1993). EPA has not yet proposed any rules governing the other "special wastes" -- that is, fly ash, cement kiln dust, and drilling fluids.

(A)   cause, or significantly contribute to an increase in mortality or an increase in serious irreversible, or incapacitating reversible, illness; or

(B)   pose a substantial present or potential hazard to human health or the environment when improperly treated, stored, transported, or disposed of, or otherwise managed.[5]

From this definitional beginning, Congress directed EPA in RCRA Section 3001 to follow a two-step process leading to the identification of hazardous wastes. First, EPA was directed to establish "criteria" to be used to identify the characteristics of hazardous waste and to actually list hazardous wastes. Factors that EPA had to consider in establishing the criteria included:

(1)   toxicity, persistence, and degradability in nature;

(2)   potential for accumulation in tissue; and

(3)   other related factors such as flammability, corrosiveness, and other hazardous characteristics.[6]

Then EPA was required to promulgate regulations, based upon the criteria, which listed particular hazardous wastes and which identified the characteristics of other hazardous wastes.

Thus, both wastes that are listed as hazardous and wastes that exhibit a hazardous characteristic are included in the RCRA program, although listed hazardous wastes are subject to somewhat more extensive regulation.[7]

Congress has also directed EPA in a new provision in Section 3001 added by the 1984 Amendments to list additional hazardous

---

5   RCRA § 1004(5).

6   RCRA § 3001(a).

7   See, for example, the exclusion of sludges and by-products that are hazardous by characteristic only from regulation when reclaimed. 40 CFR 261.2; 50 Fed. Reg. 664 (January 4, 1985).

wastes. For example, EPA was required by the statute to decide whether to list a number of named substances and a variety of common industrial wastes including solvents, refining wastes, chlorinated aromatics, dyes and pigments, inorganic chemical industry wastes, lithium batteries, coke by-products, paint production wastes, and coal slurry pipeline effluent.[8] Significantly, Congress also directed EPA to promulgate new regulations identifying additional characteristics of hazardous waste (besides ignitability, corrosivity, reactivity, and EP toxicity -- the characteristics presently used by EPA).[9] Finally, EPA was also to undertake a regulatory effort to identify or list hazardous wastes solely because of the presence of certain constituents which have been identified as carcinogens, mutagens, or teratogens.[10] Besides illustrating Congress' propensity in the 1984 Amendments to write statutory provisions almost as detailed as regulations, these amendments caused EPA to greatly expand the universe of materials that are hazardous wastes under RCRA.

2.2 EPA Implementation of RCRA Section 3001

EPA has carried out Congress' directions in RCRA Section 3001 in the regulations promulgated at 40 CFR Part 261.

2.2.1 Regulatory Definition of "Solid Waste"

EPA's regulatory definition of "solid waste," which elaborates on Congress' definition particularly with respect to the meaning of "other discarded materials," has had a checkered history. EPA's 1980 definition was challenged in the original RCRA

---

[8]   RCRA § 3001(e).

[9]   RCRA § 3001(h).

[10] A carcinogen is a substance that causes cancer; a mutagen is a substance that causes the mutation of genes; a teratogen is a substance that causes abnormal development such as malformations.

regulation lawsuit, Shell Oil Co. v. EPA, (D.C. Cir. No. 80-1532) and in response to settlement negotiations EPA worked on developing a redefinition of solid waste for over three years.[11] That redefinition promulgated on January 4, 1985, has expanded the universe of materials regulated under RCRA, particularly with respect to recyclable materials, as discussed below.

2.2.1.1 EPA's 1980 Definition

EPA initially defined "solid waste" in its regulations as "any garbage, refuse, sludge or any other waste material" not expressly excluded by a statutory exemption in RCRA or in the regulations.[12] The phrase "any other waste material", based on the statutory phrase "other discarded material" in RCRA Section 3001, became the focal point of the definition. EPA elaborately defined that phrase to include, among other things, any material that had "served its original intended use and sometimes is discarded."[13] A material was "discarded" if it was disposed of or burned, except burning as a fuel for energy recovery.[14] A material was "sometimes discarded," according to EPA's interpretation,

---

[11] See proposed redefinition at 48 Fed. Reg. 14472 (April 4, 1983) and final rule at 50 Fed. Reg. 614 (January 4, 1985), as amended, 50 Fed. Reg. 14216 (April 11, 1985).

[12] 40 CFR 261.2(b) (1980) (superseded). See 45 Fed. Reg. 33084, 33093 (May 19, 1980). EPA's regulations do not define the terms "garbage" or "refuse." The term "sludge" is defined as "any solid, semi-solid, or liquid waste generated from a municipal, commercial, or industrial waste-water treatment plant, water supply treatment plant, or air pollution control facility exclusive of the treated effluent from a waste water treatment plant." 40 CFR 260.10.

[13] 40 CFR 261.2(b) (1980) (superseded) [emphasis added].

[14] Materials burned as a fuel for the purpose of recovering usable energy were exempted from the definition of solid waste, and thus from the RCRA program. 40 CFR 261.2(c) (1980) (superseded).

if any person or company within a particular industry ever discarded that material.

Thus, from the beginning of the RCRA regulatory program until EPA promulgated the 1985 redefinition of "solid waste", EPA's regulatory definition of solid waste was based on a specialized interpretation of the statutory phrase "other discarded material" in RCRA Section 3001. EPA had difficulty from the outset of the RCRA program excluding product intermediates and secondary materials from RCRA coverage, while at the same time ensuring that every conceivable material intended by Congress to be subject to RCRA as a waste was in fact brought within the regulatory program. Therefore, EPA focused on whether a material was "sometimes discarded" by anyone in a particular industry as the basis for whether the material was a solid waste. The result, however, was a definitional scheme that was fraught with confusion.

2.2.1.2 EPA's 1985 Redefinition

EPA promulgated a new and more expansive definition of "solid waste" on January 4, 1985.[15] Under this new definition, a "solid waste" is "any discarded material" which is not excluded by regulation or variance granted by EPA.[16] A "discarded material" is any material that is "abandoned", "recycled", or considered "inherently waste-like", as those terms are expressly defined in the regulations. The terms "recycled" and "inherently waste-like"[17] are significant only in determining which materials are

---

[15] 50 Fed. Reg. 614 (January 4, 1985).

[16] 40 CFR 261.2(a).

[17] Although defining a material as a solid waste if it is "inherently waste-like" appears to be inherently vague, EPA has narrowed the concept as a practical matter by expressly defining "inherently waste-like" materials as certain listed hazardous wastes (i.e. dioxin wastes) which are regulated when recycled, as discussed below. See 40 CFR 261.2(d).

solid wastes when used, reused, recycled or reclaimed, and there-fore are discussed in section 2.5 of this Chapter on EPA's new recycling regulations. At this point, the key concept in EPA's new regulatory definition of "solid waste" is the meaning of "abandoned." A material is "abandoned" if it is being:

> (1) disposed of; or
>
> (2) burned or incinerated; or
>
> (3) accumulated, stored, or treated (but not recycled) before or in lieu of being abandoned by being disposed of, burned, or incinerated.

40 CFR 261.2(b).

In general, "disposal" of a material means:

> the discharge, deposit, injection, dumping, spilling, leaking, or placing of any solid waste or hazardous waste into or on any land or water so that such solid waste or hazardous waste or any constituent thereof may enter the environment or be emitted into the air or dis-charged into any waters, including ground waters.[18]

The terms "burned" and "incinerated" are not defined. Note, how-ever, that a material is now a solid waste when burned, regardless of whether the purpose is to recover energy or to recover both material resources and energy.[19] Note also that a material that is being accumulated or stored before being disposed of is also defined as a solid waste. This could pose interpretive problems for a company that finds it is storing an unknown material which may be usable as a product, but otherwise could be a solid waste under the new definition.

---

[18] 40 CFR 260.10.

[19] See 50 Fed. Reg. at 627 (January 4, 1985). The special rules for solid wastes burned for energy recovery are discussed in section 2.5 of this Chapter on the recycling regulations.

When these interlocking definitions are put together, the basic concept is that a material is a "solid waste" if it is burned, incinerated, or disposed of in any manner, or if it is being stored or treated prior to or instead of those activities. The remainder of the regulatory definition of "solid waste" addresses which materials are wastes even when recycled. This is discussed below in section 2.5.

2.2.1.3 Exclusions

EPA's regulations implement two important statutory exemptions from the definition of "solid waste".[20] The first such exclusion is for "solid or dissolved material in domestic sewage."[21] EPA has decided that industrial wastes which are mixed with sanitary wastes in a sewer system leading to a publicly-owned treatment works ("POTW") are not "solid wastes."[22] EPA's rationale is that the POTW will prohibit or require adequate treatment of discharges to the sewer under the pretreatment requirements of the Clean Water Act. Industrial wastes introduced to a sewer system which leads to a privately owned treatment works instead of a POTW, however, are not exempted because they are not subject to the same Clean Water Act standards.

EPA has stated that the exclusion of mixed industrial and domestic sewage which passes through a sewer system to a POTW is

---

[20] The other RCRA statutory exclusions from the term "solid waste" for irrigation return flows and nuclear materials are implemented at 40 CFR 261.4(a)(3) and (4). There are also regulatory exemptions from the definition of "solid waste" for in situ mining materials, 40 CFR 261.4(a)(5); black liquor that is reclaimed in a Kraft pulping liquor recovery furnace and then reused in the Kraft paper process, 40 CFR 261.4(a)(6); and spent sulfuric acid used to produce virgin sulfuric acid, 40 CFR 261.4(a)(7).

[21] 42 USC § 6903(27).

[22] 40 CFR 261.4(a)(1)(ii). Domestic sewage, which by definition is also not a "solid waste," is defined as "untreated sanitary wastes that pass through a sewer system." Id.

based upon previous Congressional intent, and not the Agency's view of environmental protection. For example, if a company uses holding lagoons or polishing ponds to treat a hazardous waste before it enters the sewer system, then the treatment of that waste requires a RCRA permit. On the other hand, if the hazardous waste is discharged directly into the sewer system, because of the lack of a pretreatment standard or otherwise, where it mixes with domestic sewage, EPA's regulations exclude such waste from the RCRA program. Because of this incongruity, many states have decided not to incorporate the domestic sewage exemption into their state programs.

In the 1984 Amendments, Congress directed EPA to study the domestic sewage exemption and determine whether the regulations should be changed.[23] On February 7, 1986, EPA submitted the Domestic Sewage Study to Congress which examined the impacts of hazardous wastes discharged into POTWs, specifically describing the types, size and number of generators that dispose of hazardous wastes in this manner, the types and quantities of hazardous wastes so disposed, and the identification of significant generators and hazardous wastes that are not regulated in a manner sufficient to protect human health and the environment.[24] On July 24, 1990, EPA published a final rule implementing the recommendations of the Study by amending the General Pretreatment Regulations (40 CFR Part 403) and the NPDES Regulations (40 CFR Part 122) promulgated under the Clean Water Act to prohibit the discharge to POTWs of certain RCRA hazardous wastes (such as certain ignitable wastes, reactive wastes, listed solvents and used oil); to improve monitoring of discharges; and to impose more stringent local limits on industrial users.[25]

---

[23] RCRA § 3018.

[24] See 51 Fed. Reg. 29499 (August 18, 1986).

[25] See 55 Fed. Reg. 30082 (July 24, 1990).

The other major statutory exemption from the definition of "solid waste" is for industrial discharges that are point sources subject to regulation under the National Pollutant Discharge Elimination System ("NPDES") pursuant to Section 402 of the Clean Water Act.[26] Note that this exemption applies only to the actual point source discharge, and not to all wastes that are managed at a wastewater treatment facility subject to an NPDES permit. For example, wastes that are held in surface impoundments upstream from the actual point source discharge are solid wastes and thus potentially hazardous wastes. EPA originally proposed a limited set of special requirements to regulate "wastewater treatment units" at facilities subject to the NPDES permit program, while at the same time suspending RCRA regulation of such units.[27] However, before placement in or on the lands, these facilities generally aggregate/dilute waste streams during the treatment process, sometimes resulting in dilution below characteristic levels. Prior to August 8, 1990 (at which time land disposal restrictions for the "Third Third" wastes became effective[28]), there was no land ban on such management of characteristic wastes at these

---

[26] 40 CFR 261.4(a)(2); But see Inland Steel v. EPA, 901 F.2d 14119 (7th Cir. 1950) (holding that deep injection wells subject to state NPDES permits are not excluded from RCRA under 40 CFR 261.4(a)(2).)

[27] 45 Fed. Reg. 76074 (November 17, 1980). The RCRA requirements for wastewater treatment units are discussed in Chapter 6 of this Handbook.

[28] As described in Chapter 7 of this Handbook, Congress created a series of scheduled statutory land disposal prohibitions in Section 3004 of RCRA. Extensive regulations implementing these restrictions are contained in 40 CFR Part 268. The first of the phased prohibitions applied to solvent and dioxin wastes; the next phase prohibited land disposal of the so-called "California List" wastes. All of the remaining listed and characteristic wastes were addressed one-third at a time. The Third Third waste prohibitions became effective on August 8, 1990. 55 Fed. Reg. 22520 (June 1, 1990). The Third Third Rule addressed treatment standards for hundreds of hazardous wastes, including all characteristic wastes.

facilities. However, EPA recognized that this would change with the advent of the lands ban for Third Third characteristic wastes. Thus, EPA amended its regulations allowing permitted treatment systems to continue to aggregate or dilute characteristic waste streams. In a challenge to this rule, the District of Columbia Court of Appeals in Chemical Waste Management, Inc. v. EPA, 976 F.2d 2 (D.C. Cir. 1992), cert. denied, ___ U.S. ___ 61 U.S.L.W. 3731 (1993), concluded that such dilution was permitted when the waste is decharacterized prior to placement in a Clean Water Act surface impoundment.[29]

The exclusions set forth in the regulations include the so-called "laboratory exclusion," which states that waste samples and other samples collected for the purpose of testing to determine their characteristics or composition are not subject to RCRA. 40 CFR 261.4(d). EPA has expanded this exclusion to samples which are used for small scale "treatability studies" -- that is, analyses intended to determine whether the waste is amenable to a treatment process, how best to operate the process and what results can be achieved. See 53 Fed. Reg. 27290 (July 19, 1988). Under this provision, generators of such waste samples and operators of laboratories or testing facilities conducting such treatability studies will be exempt from RCRA Subtitle C requirements (including permitting) when certain specified conditions are met.[30]

2.2.2 Regulatory Definition of "Hazardous Waste"

Once a material is found to be a solid waste, the next question that must be asked is whether it is also a "hazardous waste".

---

[29] The Chemical Waste Management decision is discussed in greater depth in Chapter 7 of this Handbook.

[30] EPA has proposed expanding this provision to include larger-scale (e.g., up to 10,000 kg) treatability studies of contaminated soil and debris. 58 Fed. Reg. 36367 (July 7, 1993).

EPA's regulations automatically exempt certain solid wastes from being considered hazardous wastes. These exemptions include:

    (1)   household waste;

    (2)   agricultural wastes which are returned to the ground as fertilizer;

    (3)   mining overburden returned to the mine site;

    (4)   certain utility wastes from coal combustion;

    (5)   certain oil and natural gas exploration drilling waste;

    (6)   wastes from the extraction, beneficiation, and processing of ores and minerals, including coal;

    (7)   cement chromium-bearing wastes;

    (8)   cement kiln dust wastes;

    (9)   arsenical-treated wood wastes, generated by end users of such wood.[31]

Note that the household waste exemption is intended to apply to waste streams generated by people in their homes, but also includes waste streams from hotels, motels, mobile residences, and pumpings from household septic tanks.[32] The exemption has also been expanded to include wastes from bunkhouses, ranger stations, campgrounds, and recreation areas.[33]

---

[31]   40 CFR 261.4(b), as amended, 50 Fed. Reg. 28743 (July 15, 1985).

[32]   See 45 Fed. Reg. 33084, 33098-99.

[33]   49 Fed. Reg. 44978 (November 13, 1984). In the 1984 Amendments, Congress also clarified in a new RCRA Section 3001(i) that the household waste exclusion excludes resource recovery facilities that recover energy from the mass burning of municipal solid waste from treatment, storage or disposal regulations, but only if any waste from commercial or industrial sources does not contain hazardous wastes. EPA has
[footnote continued]

EPA has also provided a regulatory exemption for hazardous wastes that are generated in a product or raw material storage tank, transport vehicle, pipeline, or manufacturing process unit.[34] The hazardous waste is not regulated until such time as the waste exits the unit in which it is generated. The exemption does not apply if (1) the unit involved is a surface impoundment, or (2) the hazardous waste remains in the unit in which it is generated for more than 90 days after the unit ceases to be operated. Without such an exemption, product and raw material storage tanks, transport vehicles, pipelines, and processing units would be regulated as hazardous waste storage facilities from the point in time at which the hazardous waste is first generated.[35] Thus, the practical effect of the exemption is simply to postpone regulation of the wastes generated therein.

EPA has also exempted waste samples that are collected and sent to an analytical laboratory for testing. This exemption lasts only until the laboratory has completed its work and no longer requires storage of the samples.[36]

Special exemptions apply to spent pickle liquor from steel finishing operations (a K062 listed hazardous waste). First, EPA has exempted spent pickle liquor that is reused in wastewater treatment processes at a facility holding an NPDES permit. The exemption applies to generators and brokers of spent pickle liquor, transporters, and facilities that reuse the spent pickle liquor. Second, EPA amended its definition of hazardous waste to

------

[continued]
    implemented this provision in 40 CFR 261.4(b)(1). Note, however, that one count has held that this exclusion does not exempt such facilities from complying with generator standards for ash generated therefrom. Environmental Defense Fund v. Chicago, 985 F.2d 303 (7th Cir. 1993) (appeal pending).

[34]   40 CFR 261.4(c).

[35]   40 CFR 261.3(b).

[36]   40 CFR 261.4(d).

specifically exclude waste pickle liquor sludge generated by lime stabilization from the iron and steel industry (formerly a K063 listed hazardous waste).[37] Notwithstanding this exemption, the sludge may still be deemed to be hazardous if it exhibits a hazardous waste characteristic, and generators are required to make that determination periodically.[38] It should be noted that this exemption applies only to such sludge generated from the iron and steel industry, and not to steel finishing operations in other industries.

If a solid waste material does not qualify for one of the exemptions discussed above, it will be deemed a "hazardous waste" if it:

(1) is listed as a hazardous waste by EPA in 40 CFR Part 261, Subpart D, and has not been delisted;

(2) is a mixture of a listed waste and a solid waste and has not been delisted; or

(3) exhibits any of the four hazardous waste characteristics identified in 40 CFR Part 261, Subpart C.[39]

The development of listed and characteristic hazardous wastes will be discussed respectively.

2.2.2.1 Hazardous Waste Lists

In meeting its statutory responsibility to develop criteria for listing hazardous wastes, EPA developed the following three criteria:

(1) the solid waste exhibits a hazardous waste characteristic (ignitability, corrosivity, reactivity, EP toxicity);

---

[37] 40 CFR 261.3(c)(2).

[38] 49 Fed. Reg. 23284, 23285 (June 5, 1984).

[39] 40 CFR 261.3(a).

(2)   the solid waste has been found to be fatal in humans in low doses or, in the absence of human data, has been shown to be dangerous in animal studies; or

(3)   the solid waste contains any of the toxic constituents identified by EPA in Appendix VIII unless, after considering certain other factors, EPA concludes the waste is not capable of imposing a substantial present or potential hazard to health or the environment when improperly managed.[40]

The reference to Appendix VIII of 40 CFR Part 261 has proved to be a source of some confusion. Appendix VIII sets forth toxic constituents which, if found in a solid waste, will cause EPA to consider listing that waste as hazardous. But Appendix VIII is not a separate list of hazardous wastes. Therefore, the mere presence of a substance identified in Appendix VIII in a solid waste does not mean that the waste is deemed hazardous. Rather, the presence of an Appendix VIII constituent means that EPA may consider the solid waste to be a candidate for listing as a hazardous waste, but the waste is not a listed "hazardous waste" unless and until it is so listed.

Based upon the criteria referred to above, EPA established three hazardous wastes lists:

(1)   hazardous wastes from nonspecific sources (e.g., spent nonhalogenated solvents, toluene, methyl ethyl ketone), 40 CFR 261.31;[41]

---

[40]   40 CFR 261.11.

[41]   EPA has expanded the universe of spent solvents that are hazardous wastes to include spent solvents and all "spent solvent mixtures containing [before use], ten percent or more (by volume) of total listed solvents." 50 Fed. Reg. 53315 (December 31, 1985). All existing TSD facilities that have qualified for interim status or received a permit must have filed a revised part A permit application by January 30, 1986, in order to manage the listed spent solvent mixtures/ blends.

(2) hazardous wastes from specific sources (e.g., bottom sediment sludge from the treatment of wastewaters from wood preserving), 40 CFR 261.32; and

(3) discarded commercial chemical products, and all off-specification species, containers, and spill residues thereof, 40 CFR 261.33.

The first two lists are largely self explanatory. A company need only compare its solid waste stream to the lists to determine if it is a hazardous waste. The third list sets forth commercial chemicals which, if discarded, must be treated as hazardous wastes.[42] This hazardous waste list actually consists of two sublists. One sublist sets forth chemicals deemed toxic and, therefore, hazardous if discarded.[43] These are regulated like the other listed hazardous wastes. The second sublist sets forth wastes which EPA has identified as acutely hazardous.[44] These are subject to a more restrictive test for when such wastes will be excluded from RCRA regulation when produced by small quantity generators, as discussed in Chapter 3 of this Handbook. In addition, any residue of these acutely hazardous commercial chemicals

---

[42] Note that the regulations apply to commercially pure grades of the listed chemicals, all technical grades, and all formulated products in which the listed chemical is the sole active ingredient (but not products containing mixtures of listed commercial chemicals). See 45 Fed. Reg. 78524, 78539 (November 25, 1980). In addition, the regulations apply to an off-specification product which, if it met specifications, would be one of the listed chemicals, and to any residue or contaminated soil or debris from a spill of such a chemical. 40 CFR 261.33; 45 Fed. Reg. 78524, 78541 (November 25, 1980). Finally, the regulations also apply to any such chemicals when they are mixed with waste oil or used oil or other material and applied to the land for dust suppression or road treatment, or if in lieu of their original use the chemicals are distributed or burned as a fuel. 50 Fed. Reg. 28702, 28744 (July 15, 1985). For convenience, only the commercial products themselves are discussed in the text.

[43] 40 CFR 261.33(f).

[44] 40 CFR 261.33(e).

remaining in a container, or an inner liner removed from a container, is considered a hazardous waste if discarded, unless triple rinsing or other cleaning measures are taken.[45]

Hazardous waste regulation under the commercial chemical list will be triggered most often when a company decides to reduce inventory and discard a listed commercial chemical product in its pure form. Note that the mere presence of a listed commercial chemical in a solid waste stream does not automatically render that waste hazardous. If a company's solid waste contains one of the listed commercial chemical products as a result of the manufacturing process, the waste is not a listed hazardous waste unless the solid waste is otherwise included in one of the first two lists. To illustrate, if a company has a quantity of pure acetone which it decides to discard, then that quantity of acetone will be deemed a hazardous waste. See 40 CFR 261.33(f). On the other hand, if the company uses acetone in its manufacturing process and a waste from that process contains acetone, that waste stream will not be regulated as a hazardous waste unless it is listed or it fails one of the four hazardous waste characteristic tests.

Another common scenario that triggers the commercial chemical list is an accidental spill.[46] If a listed commercial chemical is spilled, the spilled chemical and any contaminated material, i.e. dirt and other residue, becomes a hazardous waste and must be managed as such. Therefore, even companies that generally do not discard or intend to discard any of the commercial chemicals on the list must be prepared to comply with the RCRA hazardous waste regulations in the event of an accidental spill.[47] As discussed in Chapter 3, this will involve, among other things, obtaining an

---

[45] 40 CFR 261.33(c). The provisions on "empty" containers are discussed in section 2.3 of this Chapter.

[46] 40 CFR 261.33(d).

[47] See 45 Fed. Reg. 76618, 76629 (November 19, 1980).

EPA Identification Number and complying with the generator standards.

Once it is determined that a solid waste is a listed hazardous waste, one must check to see if other solid wastes are "mixed" with that listed hazardous waste. Under EPA's original "mixture rule," mixtures of listed hazardous wastes and non-hazardous wastes were always considered hazardous, no matter how small the quantity of listed hazardous waste in the mixture. This often happened, for example, when the waste stream from a company's R&D lab was combined with the non-hazardous waste stream from the company's manufacturing operation prior to treatment. EPA has now eased that rule. See section 2.2.2.3 infra. Nevertheless, as a practical matter persons who have such mixtures may find it advisable to completely segregate listed hazardous wastes from other solid wastes to avoid unnecessary regulatory costs.

2.2.2.2 Hazardous Waste Characteristics

Assuming that a solid waste is not a listed hazardous waste, or a mixture of a listed hazardous waste and a solid waste, the final step is to determine if the waste exhibits a characteristic that makes it hazardous. RCRA Section 3001 authorized EPA to identify hazardous wastes by simply establishing hazardous characteristics. Thus, if an unlisted solid waste exhibits a hazardous characteristic, it is still regulated under the RCRA program.

EPA established two criteria for identifying the characteristics of hazardous wastes.[48] The first is that the characteristic must be one that causes a solid waste to be hazardous under the statutory definition of the term "hazardous waste", discussed above. The second is that the properties defining the characteristic must be measurable by standardized testing protocols

---

[48]   40 CFR 261.10.

which are reasonably within the capabilities of the regulated community. The second criterion has had the practical effect of hampering RCRA regulation of solid wastes that may be infectious, carcinogenic, teratogenic, mutagenic, or the like. EPA decided that reliable testing protocols for these characteristics are not generally available, although under Congressional direction EPA is working on developing appropriate protocols.[49] Some states have already extended RCRA regulation to such wastes in their state programs.

EPA has established four hazardous waste characteristics.[50] All persons who generate a solid waste have the responsibility to ascertain whether their wastes exhibit one or more of these characteristics:

- Ignitability
- Corrosivity
- Reactivity
- Toxicity

Each of these characteristics is discussed in more detail below.

Ignitability[51]

The hazardous waste characteristic of ignitability was established to identify solid wastes capable during routine handling of causing a fire or exacerbating a fire once started. A solid waste is deemed to exhibit the characteristic of ignitability if it meets one of the following four descriptions. First, it is a liquid, other than an aqueous solution containing less than 24 percent alcohol by volume, with a flash point of less then 60 degrees centigrade (140°F). Second, it is a nonliquid which under normal conditions can cause fire through friction, absorption of

---

[49] EPA must now address these considerations under the 1984 Amendments. RCRA § 3001(b)(1).

[50] 40 CFR 261.20.

[51] 40 CFR 261.21.

THE IDENTIFICATION OF HAZARDOUS WASTE

moisture or spontaneous chemical changes and burns so vigorously when ignited that it creates a hazard. Third, it is an ignitable compressed gas as defined by the DOT regulations at 49 CFR 173.300. Finally, it is an oxidizer as defined by the DOT regulations at 49 CFR 173.151.

Corrosivity[52]

The hazardous waste characteristic of corrosivity was established because EPA believed that wastes capable of corroding metal could escape their own containers and liberate other wastes. In addition, wastes with a pH at either the high or low end of the scale can harm human tissue and aquatic life and may react dangerously with other wastes. Therefore, EPA determined that any solid waste is deemed to exhibit the characteristic of corrosivity if it is (1) aqueous and has a pH of less than or equal to 2.0 or greater than or equal to 12.5, or (2) liquid and corrodes steel at a rate greater than 6.35 millimeters (.250 inches) per year under specified testing procedures.

Reactivity[53]

EPA established the hazardous waste characteristic of reactivity to regulate wastes which are extremely unstable and have a tendency to react violently or explode during stages of its management. The regulation lists several situations where this may happen which warrant specific consideration (e.g., the behavior of the substance when mixed with water, when heated, etc.). Instead of developing a precise scientific description of this characteristic, EPA has promulgated a descriptive, prose definition of reactivity because suitable test protocols for measuring reactivity are unavailable.

---

[52] 40 CFR 261.22.

[53] 40 CFR 261.23.

Toxicity Characteristic (TC)[54]

EPA decided that one of the most significant dangers posed by hazardous wastes is the leaching of toxic constituents of land-disposed wastes into ground water. Consequently, EPA designed the Extraction Procedure (EP) toxicity characteristic, the original test for toxicity, to identify wastes which are likely to leach hazardous concentrations of specific toxic constituents into ground water when improperly managed. The hazardous waste characteristic of toxicity is one of the most far-reaching and controversial elements of the RCRA regulatory program.

To implement the EP toxicity characteristic, EPA established a mandatory testing procedure which extracts the toxic constituents from a solid waste in a manner EPA believes simulates the leaching action that occurs in landfills. EPA made the assumption in establishing the EP testing protocol that non-domestic waste would be co-disposed with domestic waste in an actively decomposing municipal landfill situated over a ground water aquifer.[55]

In the 1984 Amendments, Congress directed EPA to revisit the EP toxicity characteristic, and the clear import of Congress' message was that EPA should expand the universe of hazardous wastes that are considered toxic.[56] The Senate Committee that drafted the new provision was concerned that "the extraction procedure toxicity characteristic may be insufficient to protect human health and the environment".[57] In particular, the extraction procedure test does not address potential air emissions or surface water contamination from runoff. In addition, certain wastes

---

[54] 40 CFR 261.24.

[55] For purposes of determining whether a solid waste is a hazardous waste using the EP toxicity test, it is irrelevant under EPA's regulations that a company does not, in fact, co-dispose of its industrial waste in a municipal landfill or in a landfill which overlies an aquifer.

[56] RCRA § 3001(g).

[57] S.Rep. 98-284, 98th Cong., 1st Sess. 35 (1983).

which are inherently of high alkalinity, or which are placed in highly alkaline sites, may exhibit higher levels of leaching than the extraction procedure would indicate. As a result, by March 1987 EPA was directed to:

> examine the deficiencies of the extraction procedure toxicity characteristic as a predictor of the leaching potential of wastes and make changes in the extraction procedure toxicity characteristic, including changes in the leaching media, as are necessary to ensure that it accurately predicts the leaching potential of wastes which pose a threat to human health and the environment when mismanaged.[58]

In response to this Congressional direction, EPA promulgated a new "Toxicity Characteristic" ("TC") rule to amend and broaden 40 CFR § 261.34 and replace the EP toxicity characteristic described above.[59] The effective date of the rule was September 25, 1990 for large quantity generators, i.e., 1000 kg/month or more, and March 29, 1991 for small quantity generators, i.e., more than 100 kg/month but less than 1,000 kg/month. EPA has issued several technical corrections and clarifications to the final rule.[60]

The TC rule requires use of a new Toxicity Characteristic Leaching Procedure (TCLP) that addresses the mobility of both organic and inorganic compounds. Like the EP, the TCLP is designed to identify wastes that pose a threat to human health or the environment resulting from ground water contamination by

---

[58]   RCRA § 3001(g).

[59]   55 Fed Reg. 11798 (Mar. 29, 1990); see Environmental Defense Fund v. Reilly, 31 Env. Rep. Cas. (BNA) 1046 (D.C. Cir. 1990) (where the court ordered EPA to issue the rule by March 15, 1990).

[60]   See, e.g., 55 Fed. Reg. 26986 (June 29, 1990); 55 Fed. Reg. 31387 (Aug. 2, 1990); 55 Fed. Reg. 32733 (Aug. 10, 1990); 55 Fed. Reg. 39409 (Sept. 27, 1990); 55 Fed. Reg. 40834 (Oct. 5, 1990); 56 Fed. Reg. 5910 (Feb. 13, 1991).

simulating the leaching process that occurs in a municipal landfill.[61] The rule adds 25 organic chemicals to the list of toxic
constituents of concern, which includes the 14 constituents previously regulated under the EP toxicity test method. If waste
leachate generated during the TCLP exceeds these regulatory
levels, then the waste is hazardous. The following list sets
forth the 25 new constituents included in the expanded Toxicity
Characteristic:

Benzene	Hexachloro-1,3-butadiene
Charbon tetrachloride	Hexachlorobenzene
Chlordane	Hexachloroethane
Chlorobenzene	Methyl ethyl ketone
Chloroform	Nitrobenzene
m-Cresol	Pentachlorophenol
o-Cresol	Pyridine
p-Cresol	Tetrachloroethylene
1,4-Dichlorobenzene	Trichloroethylene
1,2-Dichloroethane	2,4,5-Trichlorophenol
1,1-Dichloroethylene	2,4,6-Trichlorophenol
2,4-Dinitrotoluene	Vinyl chloride
Heptachlor	

As EPA explained, the "overall effect of [this] action will
be to subject additional wastes to regulatory control under
Subtitle C of RCRA . . . ." Id. The TC Rule does not, however,
apply to wastes which are already excluded from Subtitle C regulation under 40 CFR § 261.4(b).

The new rule establishes health-based regulatory levels for
the new constituents. The regulatory levels are based on "chronic
toxicity reference levels." Such reference levels include (i) the
currently available Maximum Contaminant Levels, (ii) Risk Specific
Doses for carcinogenic constituents which correspond to a 1 in
100,000 risk level, and (iii) Reference Doses for non-carcinogenic
toxicants without applicable MCLs based on No Observed Adverse
Effects Levels.

---

[61] The TC leaching procedure is described in detail in 40 CFR
Part 261, Appendix II.

To derive regulatory levels, chronic toxicity reference levels are multiplied by a dilution-attenuation factor ("DAF") to account for the reduction in hazardous constituent concentrations expected to occur during transport from the land disposal unit to the nearest drinking water source. EPA establishes DAFs for organic constituents using a ground water fate and transport model. The model assumes an unsaturated zone between the landfill and the aquifer and assumes that wells are located randomly throughout the contaminated plume. These assumptions increase the DAFs thereby resulting in less stringent regulatory levels. EPA's final DAF is 100, the same as the generic factor employed under the EP Toxicity characteristic.

Concentrations of waste extracted from the TCLP are measured against regulatory levels. If the extract from the TCLP testing procedure exhibits concentrations at levels 100 times or more above the chronic toxicity reference levels, then the waste will be deemed to exhibit the TC.

Under the TCLP, many solid waste generators were regulated as hazardous waste generators for the first time. To comply with Subtitle C regulations, such generators were required to submit Part A permit applications, thereby qualifying for interim status. Treatment, storage and disposal facilities that were already permitted and generated TC wastes had to submit permit modifications in accordance with recently promulgated permit modification procedures. See 53 Fed. Reg. 37934 (Sept. 28, 1988) (codified at 40 CFR 270.42).

Interim status facilities that manage TC wastes were required to file an amended Part A application to continue managing TC wastes. Facilities that did not file the necessary amendments by the effective date of the rule, did not receive interim status with respect to TC wastes. 55 Fed. Reg. 11849.

The TCLP has a significant impact on the following RCRA regulations and EPA regulatory programs:

    (a)   Under Section 3004(g)(4) of RCRA, EPA was required to issue land disposal restrictions for all TC wastes by September 29, 1990. The statute, however, does not provide for an automatic prohibition of the land disposal of such wastes if EPA fails to meet the deadline. On June 1, 1990, EPA promulgated land disposal restrictions for wastes that are hazardous under the TCLP test and exhibit EP toxicity at the point of generation. 55 Fed. Reg. 22520. EPA has not yet proposed treatment standards for TC wastes that exhibit one of the new 25 constituents of concern.

(b)   A waste identified as hazardous waste under the TC also qualifies as a hazardous substance under the Comprehensive Environmental Response, Compensation and Liability Act of 1980. Accordingly, the TC will apply to CERCLA remediation to the extent that TC wastes are generated during cleanup. 55 Fed. Reg. 11837. EPA does not intend for the TC to be used as a cleanup standard for corrective action under RCRA.

(c)   As discussed in Section 2.2.1.3 above, the discharge of wastewaters into navigable waters pursuant to an NPDES permit under the Clean Water Act is not subject to RCRA.[62] In addition, the domestic sewage exclusion exempts industrial wastewaters that are discharged to a public sewer system.[63] Industrial wastewaters that do not mix with domestic sewage and exhibit the TC would be subject to Subtitle C of RCRA.

At the time of promulgation of the TC rule, EPA made a determination to defer temporarily the applicability of the TC rule to media and debris contaminated with petroleum from underground storage tanks ("USTs") that are subject to corrective action requirements. The deferral was limited to the 25 newly listed organic chemicals under the TC rule. The Agency's rationale for the deferral was the lack of information available to evaluate the full impact of the TC rule on UST cleanups, particularly with

---

[62]   40 CFR 261.4(a)(2).

[63]   40 CFR § 261.4(a)(1)(ii).

respect to the amount of hazardous waste and the type of management feasible and appropriate for such wastes. EPA was also concerned that the imposition of Subtitle C requirements could delay UST cleanups. After further study, on February 12, 1993, EPA proposed an exemption of such wastes from certain portions of the TC rule.[64] The proposed action would be accomplished by maintaining the language contained in the deferral for UST petroleum-contaminated media and debris found at 40 CFR 261.4(b)(10).

2.2.2.3 Mixtures of Hazardous Wastes and Solid Wastes

It is important to note that EPA treats mixtures of a characteristic hazardous waste and a solid waste differently than it does a mixture of a listed hazardous waste and a solid waste. The entire volume of mixed waste that includes a listed hazardous waste is treated as hazardous, unless the mixture qualifies for the following exemption: (1) the listed hazardous waste in the mixture was listed solely because it exhibits a hazardous characteristic and the mixture does not exhibit that characteristic; or (2) the mixture consists of certain specified hazardous wastes and wastewater the discharge of which is subject to regulation under Sections 402 or 307(b) of the Clean Water Act, if the concentration of the specified hazardous waste does not exceed certain concentrations.[65] With respect to the second part of this exemption, the specified hazardous waste must be one of the following:

        (a) certain spent solvents listed in 40 CFR 261.31 if the maximum total weekly usage of the solvents, other than amounts which can be demonstrated not to be discharged to wastewater, divided by the average

---

[64] 58 Fed. Reg. 8504 (February 12, 1993). A summary of the findings of EPA's study regarding this issue may be found at 57 Fed. Reg. 36866 (August 14, 1992).

[65] See 40 CFR 261.3(a)(2); 46 Fed. Reg. 56582, 56588-89 (November 17, 1981).

weekly flow of wastewater into the head-works of the facility's wastewater treatment or pretreatment system does not exceed one part per million;

(b) mixtures containing certain other spent solvents listed in 40 CFR 261.31 if the maximum total weekly usage divided by the average weekly flow of the wastewater into the headworks of the facility's wastewater treatment or pretreatment system does not exceed 25 parts per million;

(c) heat exchanger bundle cleaning sludge from the petroleum refining industry;

(d) discarded commercial chemical products or chemical intermediates listed in 40 CFR 261.33 arising from de minimis losses of these materials from manufacturing operations in which the materials are used as raw materials or are produced in the manufacturing process; and

(e) wastewater resulting from laboratory operations involving listed toxic (T) wastes in small amounts.

With respect to (e) above, the annualized average flow of the laboratory wastewater may not exceed one percent of the total wastewater flow into the headworks of a facility's wastewater treatment or pretreatment system, or the wastes' combined annualized average concentration may not exceed one part per million in the headworks of the facility's wastewater treatment or pretreatment facility.[66]

On the other hand, a mixture including a characteristic hazardous waste and a solid waste will be deemed hazardous only if the entire mixture continues to exhibit the hazardous characteristic.[67]

---

[66] Id.

[67] See 45 Fed. Reg. 33084, 33095 (May 19, 1980).

EPA's application on the "mixture rule" was challenged in Shell Oil v. EPA, 950 F.2d 741 (D.C. Cir. 1991).[68] In Shell, the Court of Appeals for the District of Columbia vacated and remanded both the mixture and derived-from rules on the basis of EPA's failure to comply with the notice-and-comment procedures required by RCRA and the Administrative Procedure Act, 5 U.S.C. 553(b).

In response to the Shell decision, EPA reissued both the mixture and derived from rules. In the meantime, however, at least two court decisions have demonstrated the impact of Shell. For example, the Eighth Circuit invalidated the criminal conviction of two defendants which had been found to have violated the mixture rule. United States v. Goodner Brothers Aircraft, Inc., 966 F.2d 380 (8th Cir. 1992). The court ruled that since Shell vacated the mixture rule, the rule must be treated as never having been issued. In a state court action, Equidae Partners v. Oklahoma State Dept. of Health, No. C-91-532 (Dist. Ct. Okla. Jan. 16, 1992), the District Court of Oklahoma, without issuing a formal opinion, entered summary judgment against the state on the basis of the Shell decision with respect to the applicability of the derived-from rule.

2.2.2.4   EPA's "Contained-In" Policy

In addition to the mixture and derived-from rules, EPA has also developed what is known as the "contained-in" policy with respect to the identification of hazardous wastes. This policy applies to media (i.e., debris, soil, ground water, sediments), rags and wipers, personal protective equipment, wood pallets, etc., contaminated with RCRA hazardous wastes. The policy provides that such contaminated materials must be managed as if they

---

[68]   EPA's "derived-from" rule was also challenged in the same case. In general, the "derived-from" rule classifies as hazardous any residue derived from the treatment of a hazardous waste. 45 Fed. Reg. 33120 (May 19, 1980).

were hazardous wastes until they longer contain the waste (_i.e._, until decontaminated) or until the hazardous waste is delisted.[69]

The need for the contained-in policy, according to EPA, has to do with the reach of the mixture rule. That is, the contaminated materials listed above are not solid wastes because they are not abandoned, recycled, or inherently waste-like. Thus, the mixture rule (which, by its terms, involves the mixture of a hazardous waste with a solid waste, see 40 CFR 261.3(a)(2)(iv)) is inapplicable. The contained-in policy fills in this gap, applying same treatment, storage, and disposal requirements to the contaminated material as are applicable to the hazardous waste.

A question remains with respect to when such contaminated materials cease to be regulated, _i.e._, whether the policy requires complete removal of the hazardous waste (which, in some cases, might be impossible). EPA has yet to issue definitive guidance on the subject. Instead, in interpretive letters, EPA has repeatedly suggested that the EPA Regions or the States must be consulted on a case-by-case basis to determine when such materials contain such a de minimus amount of a hazardous waste that they can escape the hazardous waste management standards.

2.2.3   The Requirement of Self-Testing

A company must determine whether its solid wastes exhibit a hazardous characteristic by using the testing protocols EPA has established in the regulations, by using another testing protocol approved by EPA as an equivalent testing method, or by applying general knowledge of the solid waste and its constituents.[70] If general knowledge is the basis for a determination that a solid waste is not hazardous, a company should recognize that it thereby

---

[69]   See, e.g., 56 Fed. Reg. 55173 (October 24, 1991); 57 Fed. Reg. 47773 (October 20, 1992).

[70]   40 CFR 262.11(c).

assumes the risk of being wrong, possibly subjecting the company to enforcement sanctions.[71]

When testing for hazardous characteristics, it is important that a "representative sample of the solid waste" be obtained. A representative sample means "a sample of a universe or whole (e.g. waste pile, lagoon ground water) which can be expected to exhibit the average properties of the universe or whole."[72] Given the diversity of solid wastes, EPA has not promulgated mandatory representative sampling techniques. EPA has, however, identified techniques that presumptively yield a representative sample.[73]

2.3   Residues of Hazardous Waste in Empty Containers

When hazardous waste is removed from a container, it is likely that a residue of the waste will remain. EPA has decided that any hazardous waste residue remaining in an "empty" container, or in an inner liner removed from an "empty" container, is not subject to regulation under the hazardous waste program.[74]

The definition of the term "empty container" varies according to the type of hazardous waste in the container. If a container holds a hazardous waste that is a compressed gas, it is deemed empty when the pressure inside the container is equal to atmospheric pressure.[75] If a container or inner liner holds an acutely hazardous commercial chemical, it is deemed empty after it is triple rinsed with an appropriate solvent, or after it is cleaned using another method shown to achieve equivalent removal of any residue. Note that the rinsate will be a hazardous waste

---

[71]   See Chapter 10, infra, on Liability, Enforcement, and Inspections.

[72]   40 CFR 260.10.

[73]   40 CFR 261, Appendix I. See also 45 Fed. Reg. 33084, 33107-08 (May 19, 1980).

[74]   40 CFR 261.7(a)(1).

[75]   40 CFR 261.7(b)(2).

if it exhibits a hazardous characteristic or if it contains a listed hazardous waste. In addition, such a container is deemed empty when the inner liner is removed.[76]

If a container or inner liner holds any other type of hazardous waste, it is deemed empty when all wastes have been removed using practices commonly employed to remove materials from the specific type of container involved (e.g., pouring, pumping) and no more than one inch of residue remains on the bottom of the container or inner liner.[77] Alternatively, if the container is 110 gallons or smaller in size, it is deemed empty if no more than 3 percent by weight of the total capacity remains in the container; for containers larger than 110 gallons, the limit is 0.3 percent by weight of the total capacity of the container.[78]

If a container is deemed "empty" pursuant to one of these three definitions, the container and any remaining residue are not considered hazardous wastes. On the other hand, if the container does not meet one of these three regulatory definitions of "empty", any hazardous waste remaining in the container is subject to full regulation.

2.4 Delisting of Hazardous Wastes

EPA's regulations include a delisting mechanism whereby a person may petition EPA to amend the hazardous waste lists to exclude a waste generated at a particular facility.[79] These procedures are appropriate when a company's waste stream meets a

---

[76] 40 CFR 261.7(b)(3).

[77] 40 CFR 261.7(b)(1).

[78] Id.

[79] 40 CFR 260.20 and 260.22. RCRA § 7004 provides that any person may petition EPA for the promulgation, amendment or repeal of any regulation implementing RCRA Subtitle C, and the delisting mechanism is based on that statutory authority.

technical listing description for a hazardous waste, but the waste is not in fact hazardous.

Persons seeking to delist a waste must submit a petition to the EPA Administrator by certified mail which sets forth the facts required by the regulations demonstrating that the waste meets the criteria for delisting.[80] The petition must be signed and certified by a responsible corporate official attesting to the accuracy of the data.[81] It is important to note that a successful delisting petition is not an EPA determination that the facility's waste is not hazardous; it is only that the waste is not a listed hazardous waste. The company must still periodically analyze the waste for hazardous characteristics.

The factual basis for delisting which must be set forth in the petition can be summarized as follows. First, the petitioner must demonstrate that the waste produced at its facility "does not meet any of the criteria under which the waste was listed" as a hazardous waste. Second, where there is a reasonable basis to believe that factors other than those for which the waste was originally listed, including additional constituents, could cause the waste to be hazardous, EPA must determine that such factors do not warrant retaining the waste on the hazardous waste list.[82]

To overcome the first hurdle, a petition to delist a hazardous waste that was listed because it exhibits a hazardous characteristic (corrosivity, ignitability, reactivity or toxicity) must demonstrate that samples of the facility's waste do not exhibit that characteristic or any other characteristic. The test

---

[80] 40 CFR 260.20(b) and 260.22(a); 50 Fed. Reg. 28702, 28742 (July 15, 1985). This regulation implements Congress' directive in the 1984 Amendments for EPA to make the delisting procedure more restrictive. RCRA § 3001(f).

[81] 40 CFR 260.22(i)(12).

[82] 40 CFR 261.22(a); 50 Fed. Reg. 28702, 28742 (July 15, 1985).

THE RCRA HAZARDOUS WASTES HANDBOOK

protocols identified in the regulations defining the characteristic must be used to support the petition.[83] In addition, a petition to delist a hazardous waste that is listed because it contains one or more Appendix VIII constituents must demonstrate that samples of the waste do not contain those constituents, or that mitigating factors establish that the facility's waste does not pose a substantial present or potential hazard to human health or the environment when improperly managed. The test protocols outlined in Appendix III to 40 CFR Part 261 must be used to demonstrate the absence of hazardous waste constituents.[84] The test protocols must be performed on demonstration samples of the facility's waste stream, which means a sufficient number of representative samples of the waste (four is the minimum) taken over a period of time sufficient to indicate the variability or uniformity of the waste.[85]

In order to meet the second hurdle for delisting, a petitioner must submit sufficient information to EPA to demonstrate that other factors, including additional Appendix VIII constituents, would not cause the waste to be hazardous.[86] A petitioner may first submit a list of all raw materials, intermediates, by-products, and products used in the manufacturing process, and a description of each process which may contribute waste to the waste stream. EPA will evaluate this information to determine if any other Appendix VIII constituents are used or formed in the manufacturing process so that they are likely to be present in significant levels in the waste. If so, the petitioner

---

[83] 40 CFR 260.22(c).

[84] 40 CFR 260.22(d). A petition to delist a waste deemed acutely hazardous must also demonstrate that the waste does not meet EPA's acutely toxic criteria (e.g., the oral LD 50 toxicity of the waste is shown to be greater than 50 milligrams per kilogram). 40 CFR 260.22(e).

[85] 40 CFR 260.22(h).

[86] See 49 Fed. Reg. 4802 (February 8, 1984).

will have to perform additional analytical testing for those constituents. Alternatively, the petitioner may test the waste for any additional Appendix VIII constituents that may be present, and provide a written explanation for why any Appendix VIII constituents not tested for would not be present in the waste at levels that would pose a toxicological hazard. EPA will then evaluate all this information in light of the regulatory criteria for delisting.[87]

EPA has developed an analytical approach to evaluating delisting petitions based on a computer model known as the vertical and horizontal spread ("VHS") model.[88] The model estimates the dispersion of toxicants in an aquifer from the waste to be delisted assuming the waste is disposed of in a landfill located directly above an aquifer. The model incorporates a number of "worst case" assumptions such as no attenuation in the soil, continuous toxicant input to the aquifer, and no precipitation of metals. The overall approach is used to predict worst case contaminant levels in ground water at a hypothetical receptor well,

---

[87] See 50 Fed. Reg. 20239, 20240 (May 15, 1985) for a description of the EPA procedure.

[88] See 50 Fed. Reg. 7882, 7883-84 (February 26, 1985); 50 Fed. Reg. 20239, 20240-41 (May 15, 1985); 50 Fed. Reg. 48896 (November 27, 1985). In McLouth Steel Products Corporation v. Thomas, 838 F.2d 1317 (D.C. Cir. 1988), a steel company challenged EPA's denial of the company's delisting petition based on results from the VHS model. The Court of Appeals for the District of Columbia Circuit ruled that the VHS model was being used by EPA as a "binding norm" and, thus, was a legislative rule for which EPA had failed to follow the notice and comment procedures required by the Administrative Procedures Act, 5 U.S.C. § 563. The Court remanded the petition to EPA, and noted that EPA could treat the VHS model as a nonbinding policy rather than a legislative rule but, in doing so, the Agency must truly exercise its discretion in individual delisting cases by remaining open to all challenges to the VHS model in general as well as its application in particular cases. EPA has subsequently stated that it will treat the VHS model as nonbinding policy and will use it only where "appropriate". See 53 Fed. Reg. 21640 (June 9, 1988); 53 Fed. Reg. 28892, 28895 (August 1, 1988).

and then to compare those levels to health based standards such as the National Primary Drinking Water Standards. EPA is using this approach based on the VHS model as one factor in determining the potential impact of delisting a waste on human health and the environment. On July 18, 1991, EPA proposed to evaluate delisting positions with EPA's Composite Model for Landfills ("EPACML") instead of the VHS model. 56 Fed. Reg. 32993. The EPACML is a more sophisticated model which accounts for numerous waste factors.

EPA may grant a delisting petition only after following notice and comment rulemaking procedures and publishing a final decision on the petition in the Federal Register as a regulatory amendment.[89] A petition must be acted upon by EPA within 24 months of submission. EPA previously granted petitioners "temporary exclusions" if EPA thought upon initial review that there was a substantial likelihood the petition would ultimately be granted.[90] Congress directed in the 1984 Amendments, however, that this practice no longer be followed, and that all previously granted temporary exclusions be terminated by November 1986, when EPA was required to take final action on the underlying delisting petitions.

Since November 1984, EPA has taken back from authorized states the administration of the RCRA delisting program until each state is authorized for delisting under the new provisions of the 1984 Amendments.[91] Any final decisions by a state granting delisting petitions that were made prior to November 8, 1984, are not affected, although EPA has encouraged states to reconsider

---

[89] 40 CFR 260.22(e); RCRA § 3001(f).

[90] 40 CFR 260.22(m) (1984) (superseded); see RCRA § 3001(f) added by the 1984 Amendments; 50 Fed. Reg. 28702, 28743 (July 15, 1985).

[91] RCRA Reauthorization Statutory Interpretation No. 4: Effect of Hazardous and Solid Waste Amendments of 1984 on State Delisting Decisions, Jack W. McGraw, Acting Assistant Administrator, U.S.EPA (May 16, 1985).

those decisions in light of the new delisting criteria under the 1984 Amendments.

On March 3, 1988, EPA announced strategies and procedures applicable to its review of delisting petitions. 53 Fed. Reg. 6822. The strategies deal with a number of areas including the dismissal of certain incomplete petitions, petition review priorities and certification requirements. EPA hopes that these procedures will reduce the processing time for petitions and the backlog of petitions at the Agency.

2.5 Special Requirements for Hazardous Wastes That are Used, Reused, Recycled, or Reclaimed

On January 4, 1985, EPA issued final regulations extending RCRA regulation to many recycling activities that were previously exempt.[92] In those few states where EPA still administered the RCRA program, these requirements for recycling were effective on July 5, 1985. Authorized states generally had a year (or two years if a state statute needed to be amended) from the effective date to revise their state programs to incorporate the new recycling requirements.[93] Because of the complexity of the regulations, the particular facts of any potential recycling activity should be carefully analyzed to determine the steps necessary for compliance.

In the 1985 rulemaking, EPA abandoned its prior approach of exempting the recycling of characteristic non-sludge hazardous wastes from RCRA, and regulating only the storage and transportation of listed hazardous wastes and sludges prior to recycling.[94] For most discarded materials, the crux of EPA's new

---

[92] 40 CFR 260.10, 260.30-260.33, 260.40-260.41, 261.1-261.6, and related regulations, and Part 266, Subpart C-G; 50 Fed. Reg. 614 (January 4, 1985).

[93] 40 CFR 271.21(e).

[94] See 40 CFR 261.6 (1980) (superseded).

regulatory scheme requires a company to determine whether recycling will trigger RCRA regulation based on two factors: (i) the type of recycling activity, and (ii) the nature of the materials being recycled. EPA defines solid waste to include the following types of recycling activities:

(1) use in a manner constituting disposal (e.g., land application);

(2) burning for energy recovery;

(3) reclamation (i.e., regeneration or processing to recover a usable product); and

(4) speculative accumulation (i.e., less than 75% of the material is actually recycled or transferred to a different site for recycling in a calendar year).[95]

EPA defines the universe of recyclable materials as follows:

(1) spent materials ("any material that has been used and as a result of contamination can no longer serve the purpose for which it was produced without processing");

(2) sludges ("any solid, semi-solid, or liquid waste generated from a municipal, commercial, or industrial wastewater treatment plant [but not the treated effluent], water supply treatment plant, or air pollution control facility");

(3) by-products ("a material that is not one of the primary products of a production process and is not solely or separately produced by the production process", e.g., slags or distillation column bottoms);

(4) discarded commercial chemical products that are listed in Part 261.33; and

---

[95] 40 CFR 261.2(c)(4); 261.1(c)(8).

(5) scrap metal.[96]

Each of these materials when recycled using any of the recycling activities listed above is deemed to be a solid waste, with
certain exceptions discussed below.[97] Generally, spent materials,
sludges, by-products, commercial chemicals, and scrap metal which
are listed or exhibit a hazardous characteristic are RCRA
regulated when recycled in any manner described above. The
regulations set forth exceptions from the definition of solid
waste, however, for certain of these materials depending on the
manner of recycling.[98] Commercial chemical products, for example,
are not solid wastes when reclaimed but qualify as solid wastes if
burned for energy recovery.[99]

EPA exempts from the definition of solid waste materials that
are recycled by directly using or reusing discarded materials in
an industrial process.[100] In addition, other exempt activities

---

[96]   40 CFR 261.1(c). There are at present no substantive
requirements for scrap metal, however. 40 CFR 261.6(a)(3);
50 Fed. Reg. 614, 665 (January 4, 1985).

[97]   EPA has published a guidance document to help persons determine which materials when recycled are solid and hazardous
wastes. See 51 Fed. Reg. 26892 (July 28, 1986) ("The
Guidance Manual on the RCRA Regulation of Recycled Hazardous
Waste").

[98]   40 CFR 261.2(c), Table 1.

[99]   But see 40 CFR 261.2(d) (inherently waste-like materials are
solid wastes when they are recycled in any manner).

[100]   See 40 CFR 261.2(e)(1)(i) (use or reuse in an industrial process does not include materials being "reclaimed"); See
American Mining Congress v. EPA, 824 F.2d 1177, 1185 (D.C.
Cir. 1987)(excluding materials "destined for immediate reuse
in another phase of the industry's ongoing production
process. . . ."); Cf. American Mining Congress v. EPA, 907
F.2d 1179 (D.C. Cir. 1990)(holding that sludges from wastewater that are stored in surface impoundments are not part of
an ongoing treatment process); American Petroleum Institute
v. EPA, 906 F.2d 729 (D.C. Cir. 1990)(holding that slag that
is "discarded" before reclamation falls within the definition
of solid waste).

include (1) the use or reuse of secondary materials as effective substitutes for commercial products (40 CFR § 261.2(e)(1)(ii)); and (2) the return of secondary materials to the original primary production process in which they were generated without reclamation (i.e., a closed-loop production process that uses secondary materials as a return feed).[101] However, if the result of these otherwise exempted recycling processes is that materials are used in a manner constituting disposal, placed on land, burned for energy recovery, or speculatively accumulated, then the materials are solid wastes.[102]

Certain case-by-case variances are available from the EPA Regional Administrator or an authorized state.[103] For example, a variance may be obtained for materials that are being speculatively accumulated, provided the applicant can show that sufficient amounts of the material will be recycled in the following year. Another variance is available for materials that are reclaimed and then reused as feedstock within the original primary production process in which the materials were generated, if the reclamation operation is an essential part of the production process. The regulations set forth in detail the criteria and public notice procedures EPA will use to determine whether a variance will be granted.

EPA's redefinition of solid waste as it applied to certain recyclable materials was challenged in federal court by a number of parties. On July 31, 1987, the Court of Appeals for the District of Columbia Circuit ruled that the redefinition exceeded the scope of the statutory definition of solid waste to the extent that it regulated in-process secondary materials. See American Mining Congress v. U.S. Environmental Protection Agency, 824 F.2d

---

[101] 40 CFR 261.2(e)(1)(iii) ("The material must be returned as a substitute for new material feedstock. . . .").

[102] 40 CFR 261.2(e)(2).

[103] 40 CFR 260.30-260.31.

1177 (D.C. Cir. 1987). In response to this decision, EPA has proposed further amendments to the definition of solid waste which would exclude from regulation certain types of recycled materials specifically mentioned by the Court. These include certain in-process recycled secondary materials in the petroleum refining industry and certain other sludges, byproducts and spent materials that are reclaimed as part of continuous, ongoing manufacturing processes. However, EPA specifically noted that the Court's decision does not effect EPA's regulatory authority over recycled materials that involve an "element of discard" (such as used oil) and do not pass through a continuous, ongoing manufacturing process.[104] EPA issued these amendments as a clarification of its redefinition of solid wastes. They do not substantively alter EPA's program for regulating secondary materials as described above.

Generators and transporters of recycled hazardous wastes, i.e., "recyclable materials," should file a RCRA Section 3010 notification and must comply with Parts 262 and 263.[105] Storage facilities for recyclable materials must qualify for interim status by filing a Part A permit application and then comply with Part 265, Subparts A through L. A storage facility for recyclable materials will also need to qualify for permanent status by obtaining a RCRA permit that incorporates the applicable Part 264 standards.[106] These standards are discussed in detail in Chapters 5 and 6 of this Handbook. No permit or other requirements apply to the actual recycling operation.[107]

---

[104] See 53 Fed. Reg. 519 (January 8, 1988).

[105] 40 CFR 261.6(b), 50 Fed. Reg. 614, 665 (January 4, 1985). The notification was due April 4, 1985.

[106] Some of the materials expressly exempt from these general standards at this time include industrial ethyl alcohol that is reclaimed, used batteries returned to the manufacturer for regeneration, used oil, and scrap metal. 40 CFR 261.6(a)(3).

[107] 40 CFR 261.6(c)(1).

EPA has also established special Part 266 standards for (1) recyclable materials used in a manner constituting disposal, (2) hazardous wastes burned for energy recovery in boilers and industrial furnaces,[108] (3) used oil burned for energy recovery,[109] (4) recyclable materials utilized for precious metal recovery, and (5) spent lead-acid batteries that are reclaimed.[110] For the most part, these Part 266 standards also cross reference the applicable requirements for generators, transporters, and storage facilities in Parts 262-265. Persons who are engaged in the recovery of precious metals from recyclable materials, however, need only comply with the manifest system and certain recordkeeping requirements for storage facilities. Companies engaged in these particular recycling activities should refer to the discussion of Part 266 in Chapter 6 of this Handbook.

---

[108] These part 266 standards for hazardous waste derived fuels are reviewed in Chapter 6 of this Handbook.

[109] EPA's plans to regulate used oil under RCRA, the Used Oil Recycling Act, and possibly TSCA are discussed in Chapter 13 of this Handbook.

[110] See 40 CFR 266.20-266.80.

CHAPTER 3

GENERATORS OF HAZARDOUS WASTE

As the first link in the "cradle-to-grave" chain of hazardous waste management established under RCRA, generators initiate the overall RCRA hazardous waste regulatory scheme. As of September 1992, EPA has on record more than 262,000 large and small quantity generators in the United States which generate hazardous wastes subject to regulation under RCRA Section 3002. The failure of a generator to properly identify a hazardous waste may mean that the waste never enters the "cradle-to-grave" management program. Subtitle C[1] requires generators to ensure and fully document that the hazardous waste they produce is properly identified and transported to a RCRA treatment, storage, or disposal facility. A generator's failure to fully understand the regulatory requirements may cause the hazardous waste to be mismanaged or disposed of improperly, creating significant liabilities. Thus, the requirements for generators set forth in RCRA Section 3002 and EPA's regulations at 40 CFR Part 262 are of key concern.

3.1 Statutory Requirements Imposed Upon Generators

RCRA Section 3002 states that the EPA must promulgate regulations establishing standards applicable to generators of hazardous waste with respect to the following:

(1) recordkeeping that identifies the quantity, constituents, and disposition of hazardous wastes;

(2) labeling of containers used to store, transport, or dispose of hazardous wastes;

(3) use of appropriate containers for hazardous wastes;

---

[1]   40 CFR Part 262.

(4)   furnishing of information regarding a
        generator's hazardous waste to persons
        who transport, treat, store, or dispose
        of such waste;

(5)   use of a manifest system and any other
        reasonable means necessary to assure the
        proper disposal of hazardous waste; and

(6)   submission of reports to EPA or the au-
        thorized state agency that identify the
        quantity and disposition of hazardous
        wastes.

The 1980 RCRA Amendments added the requirement that the generator, in addition to complying with the manifest system, use "any other reasonable means necessary" to assure that his hazardous waste is managed at a designated T/S/D facility.[2] The 1984 Amendments further added the requirement to Section 3002 that generators undertake a program of "waste minimization" to reduce the volume and toxicity of wastes generated.[3] The waste minimization requirements could have a far-reaching impact on the way generators manage their hazardous wastes, as discussed below.

3.2   Who Is a "Generator" of Hazardous Waste?

In enacting RCRA, Congress did not provide a definition of the term "generator." Congress did define the phrase "generation of hazardous waste", however, to mean the "act or process of producing hazardous waste."[4] Accordingly, EPA's regulations broadly define the term "generator" to include any:

°   Facility or operator or person who first cre-
        ates a hazardous waste, or

°   Person who first makes the waste subject to
        the Subtitle C regulations (e.g., imports a

---

2   RCRA § 3002(a)(5).

3   RCRA § 3002(b).

4   RCRA § 1004(6).

> hazardous waste, initiates a shipment of haz-
> ardous waste, or mixes hazardous wastes of
> different DOT shipping descriptions by placing
> them into a single container).[5]

The definition of a "generator" refers explicitly to the particular site of generation. Thus, a corporation with several plants must evaluate and comply with the generator requirements individually for each facility. EPA's definition of "generator" does not provide any exemption for persons who produce hazardous waste infrequently or accidentally.

The words "act or process" also are not defined in RCRA or in the regulations. Obviously, "act or process" is a broad phrase which, through a literal interpretation, would arguably encompass almost any activity in which a person is involved which produces hazardous waste. EPA's definition of "generator" clearly covers those activities that produce hazardous wastes in process equipment, treatment units, raw material pipelines and storage tanks, and transport vehicles.[6]

A person who is not normally a generator, but whose act causes a hazardous waste to become subject to RCRA regulation for the first time, is also deemed a "generator." This would include, for example, a transporter who cleans out a tank truck and thus

---

[5] 40 CFR 260.10. RCRA § 1004(15) defines a "person" as:

> An individual, trust, firm, joint stock com-
> pany, corporation (including a government
> corporation), partnership, association, State,
> municipality, commission, political subdivi-
> sion of a State, or any interstate body and
> shall include each department, agency, and
> instrumentality of the United States.

[6] 45 Fed. Reg. 72028 (October 30, 1980), 45 Fed. Reg. 80287 (December 4, 1980). Note, however, that hazardous waste generated in a raw material storage tank, transport vehicle or vessel, pipeline or manufacturing process unit (other than a surface impoundment) is not subject to regulation until it is removed from the unit, unless the waste remains in the unit for more than 90 days after the unit ceases operation.

produces a hazardous waste residue that is subject to RCRA regulation. EPA has said that it will respect any arrangement between private parties which assigns generator duties, but the Agency reserves the right to hold the original generator and any other party whose act first causes the waste to become subject to regulation jointly and severally liable for compliance with the generator duties for each plant site.[7] This is discussed further in Chapter 4 on transporters.

3.3   Regulations Implementing RCRA Section 3002

EPA has promulgated standards for generators pursuant to RCRA Section 3002 at 40 CFR Part 262. The significant aspects of these standards are discussed below.

3.3.1   Responsibility to Identify Hazardous Waste

The initial duty imposed upon a generator is the obligation to determine whether any of his solid waste is "hazardous waste."[8] Although this requirement is not set forth in the statute, EPA has imposed it as part of the regulations so that a generator is liable for civil penalties and other sanctions if he fails to properly identify his waste as hazardous. The generator can employ outside consultants and testing laboratories to analyze his waste streams, but ultimately the regulatory liability is imposed on the generator. The procedures for ascertaining what materials are hazardous wastes, and whether any exclusion applies, are discussed in detail in Chapter 2 of this Handbook.

3.3.2.   Notification of Hazardous Waste Management Activities

RCRA Section 3010(a) requires that any person who manages a hazardous waste (i.e., generators, transporters, and the owners or

---

[7]   45 Fed. Reg. 72026 (October 30, 1980).

[8]   40 CFR 262.11.

operators of T/S/D facilities) must file a notification within 90 days after regulations are promulgated identifying the waste as hazardous.

On February 26, 1980, EPA published Form 8700-12 as the RCRA Section 3010(a) notification form.[9] The form requires minimal information, such as the company's name and address, and the EPA hazardous waste number for the hazardous waste it manages. The amount of hazardous wastes handled at a particular site or the activity that produces it need not be identified. The use of EPA Form 8700-12 is not required. Persons submitting their notice on a different form, however, must include all Form 8700-12 information.

Certain categories of persons who manage hazardous waste have been exempted from the notification requirement, including: (1) small quantity generators of less than 100 kg of hazardous waste per month;[10] and (2) persons who handle certain types of hazardous wastes which are recycled or reclaimed as expressly provided by regulation.[11] These categories are discussed in more detail below.

3.3.3 Requirement to Obtain an EPA Identification Number

One way that EPA monitors and tracks generators is to assign each generator a unique identification number. Every generator of a hazardous waste must obtain an EPA Identification ("ID") Number.[12] The generator is required to use his ID number on manifests and for all other RCRA regulated activities, and to have his

---

[9] 45 Fed. Reg. 12746 (February 26, 1980). EPA has not codified the notification form or instructions. Copies of Form 8700-12 can be obtained from EPA regional offices and most state agencies.

[10] 40 CFR 261.5(b).

[11] 40 CFR 261.6(a)(3).

[12] 40 CFR 262.12.

hazardous wastes transported, treated, stored, and disposed of by persons who also have obtained EPA ID numbers.[13] The EPA ID Number is designed to assist EPA in identifying all persons subject to the RCRA regulatory program. In particular, EPA has attempted to preclude anonymity (e.g., the "midnight dumper") in the management of hazardous wastes. Without this EPA ID number, the generator is barred from treating, storing, disposing of, transporting, or offering for transportation any hazardous waste. Furthermore, the generator is forbidden from offering his hazardous waste for transport to any transporter that does not have an EPA ID number, or from sending his hazardous waste to a T/S/D facility that does not also have an EPA ID number.

A generator receives an EPA ID Number by submitting EPA Form 8700-12. This is the same form used to satisfy the RCRA Section 3010(a) notification requirement discussed above. A person who began generating hazardous waste after the initial August 19, 1980, notification date under RCRA Section 3010(a), and who was not otherwise required to file a notification, should still use Form 8700-12 to obtain an EPA ID Number. A person who does not currently generate a hazardous waste, but who plans to do so at some future time, may also obtain an EPA ID Number in advance by filing Form 8700-12.

3.3.4 Manifest System

To ensure that hazardous waste destined for off-site treatment, storage or disposal actually reaches its destination, RCRA requires use of a manifest system. The manifest is a control and transport document that accompanies the hazardous waste at all times from the generator's facility to the final T/S/D facility. The regulations impose upon the generator the responsibility of ensuring that a manifest has been prepared before any hazardous

---

[13]   40 CFR 262.12(c).

waste is moved off-site.[14] In preparing the manifest, the generator must specify the name and EPA ID Numbers of each authorized transporter and the designated T/S/D facility which will accept the hazardous waste. Thus the manifest is both a record of all persons who handle a particular hazardous waste and a blueprint of accountability in the event of improper disposal of the hazardous waste. In addition to the manifest, generators who manage wastes restricted from land disposal must submit to the T/S/D facility a notice with each restricted waste shipment.[15] The notice must include the treatment standards for the restricted wastes, the manifest number and any available waste analysis data.[16] For waste that can be land disposed without further treatment, the generator must submit to the T/S/D facility a notice and certification stating that the waste meets applicable standards.[17]

Perhaps the most important aspect of the manifest system is the requirement that the generator designate a facility which is permitted to treat, store, or dispose of the hazardous waste described on the manifest.[18] The generator can also designate one alternate facility in the event an emergency prevents delivery of

[14]   40 CFR 262.20-262.23.

[15]   40 CFR 268.7.

[16]   40 CFR 268.7(1)

[17]   40 CFR 268.7(2)

[18]   40 CFR 262.20(b). Note that a "designated facility" is defined as an interim status or permitted T/S/D facility, under either an EPA or authorized state program, or a recycling facility subject to regulation under 40 CFR 261.6(c)(2) or 40 CFR Part 266, Subpart F (precious metal recovery facilities). 40 CFR 260.10, 50 Fed. Reg. 661 (January 4, 1985). For simplicity, the term "designated T/S/D facility" or simply "T/S/D facility" is used in the text, but the reader should keep in mind that a designated facility on a manifest may include a recycling facility.

the waste to the primary designated facility.[19] If the transporter cannot deliver the hazardous waste to either of the designated facilities on the manifest, the transporter must contact the generator, who may either designate another facility or request that the transporter return the waste.[20] If arrangements with another T/S/D facility can be made, the generator should make sure that the transporter amends the manifest accordingly.

EPA and DOT have published joint regulations requiring the use of a Uniform Hazardous Waste Manifest ("Uniform Manifest") for all regulated shipments of hazardous waste.[21] Previously, EPA and DOT regulations required certain information to be included on a manifest, but no standard form was required. As a result, states developed their own individual manifests. Generators shipping waste out-of-state were often required to complete several manifests with duplicative information in order to ensure that their wastes reached the designated T/S/D facility. Transporters were required to carry a different manifest for each state through which they travelled to comply with the various state manifest requirements. In addition, generators with sites in more than one state could not standardize their manifest procedures. The Uniform Manifest was intended to end this battle of conflicting state forms.

The information required on the Uniform Manifest can be divided into two categories: federally-required information and optional state-required information. In adopting the Uniform Manifest, EPA did not increase the federal information reporting requirements. The information that is required is the following:

---

[19] 40 CFR 262.20(c).

[20] 40 CFR 262.20(d).

[21] Form 8700-22, 49 Fed. Reg. 10490 (March 20, 1984). The Uniform Manifest form, which is an Appendix to 40 CFR Part 262, was revised and republished in the so-called "Codification Rule" which incorporated amendments required by Congress in the 1984 Amendments. 50 Fed. Reg. 28745 (July 15, 1985).

(1) the manifest document number; (2) the name, address, telephone number and EPA ID Number of the generator; (3) the name and EPA ID Number of each transporter; (4) the name, address, and EPA ID Number of the designated and alternate T/S/D facilities; (5) the DOT name and handling code of the hazardous waste being shipped; (6) the total quantity of each hazardous waste by weight or volume; (7) the type and number of containers used in transporting the hazardous waste; and (8) a certification that the hazardous waste has been properly classified, described, packaged, marked and labeled, and is in proper condition for transportation.[22] Note that RCRA Section 3008(d) provides that criminal penalties may be imposed on any person who knowingly makes a false material statement or representation on a manifest.

On February 16, 1989, EPA granted a six-month extension of the mandatory use of a new and somewhat revised manifest form, which requires the inclusion of the Office of Management and Budget's ("OMB's") burden disclosure statement.[23] On July 1, 1989,

---

[22] Appendix to 40 CFR Part 262. See 49 Fed. Reg. 10501-10503 (March 20, 1984). Note that EPA allows non-hazardous wastes to be included on the manifest, but the generator should then write in an additional hazardous materials column on the manifest in the space for the DOT waste description and designate which wastes are hazardous, as explained by EPA in the preamble to the Uniform Manifest at 49 Fed. Reg. 10495 (March 20, 1984). This procedure should also be used when shipping wastes that are defined as hazardous by either the generator's state or the consignment state, but not by EPA and DOT. Some states, however, have provided in their regulations that any wastes included on a Uniform Manifest will be deemed hazardous waste.

[23] 54 Fed. Reg. 7036-37 (Feb. 16, 1989). On November 8, 1988 EPA issued a Federal Register Notice renewing the Uniform Hazardous Waste Manifest for a three year period, and mandating the inclusion of an OMB burden disclosure statement. The notice stated that the compliance date would be December 31, 1988. The Office of Solid Waste ("OSW") realized that this December 1988, date put an undue hardship upon the regulated community and received from OMB a six-month extension on the compliance requirements.

use of the new manifest and the inclusion of the OMB burden disclosure statement became mandatory.[24]

In addition, generators must now certify on the manifest that
they have adopted a "waste minimization" program as provided by
Congress in the 1984 Amendments to RCRA.[25] The generator must
make the following certification:

> I have a program in place to reduce the volume
> and toxicity of waste generated to the degree
> I have determined to be economically practica-
> ble and I have selected the method of treat-
> ment, storage, or disposal currently available

---

[24] The Office of Management and Budget added § 1320.21 "Agency
Display of Estimated Burden" to 5 CFR Part 1320 on May 10,
1988. This regulation requires each agency to indicate on
each document requesting information the estimated average
"burden" hours required to fill out each document. Each
agency must also request comments concerning the accuracy of
the agency's estimate. The burden disclosure statement
required with each Uniform Manifest form is as follows:

> Public reporting burden for this collec-
> tion of information is estimated to average:
> 37 minutes for generators, 15 minutes for
> transporters, and 10 minutes for treatment,
> storage and disposal facilities. This
> includes time for reviewing instructions,
> gathering data, and completing and reviewing
> the form. Send comments regarding the burden
> estimate, including suggestions for reducing
> this burden, to: Chief, Information Policy
> Branch, PM-223, U.S. Environmental Protection
> Agency, 401 M Street, SW, Washington, DC
> 20460; and to the Office of Information and
> Regulatory Affairs, Office of Management and
> Budget, Washington, DC 20503.

The statement may either be: (1) printed on the form; (2) printed
in the instructions to the form; or (3) the statement can be
attached to the form.

[25] RCRA § 3002(b).

to me which minimizes the present and future threat to human health and the environment.[26]

This certification is required on all manifests used after September 1, 1985.

The Uniform Manifest was designed with a separate section for entry of certain optional information that states can require. This optional information is quite limited, and includes such things as the generator's, transporter's, and T/S/D facility's state identification numbers, a state manifest document number, state hazardous waste numbers, and a further description of the transported waste. These information requirements may be imposed on generators and T/S/D facilities by the state in which the generator is located and/or by the state in which the T/S/D facility is located, but not by states through which a waste shipment travels.

States may not require any forms other than the Uniform Manifest to accompany a waste shipment. They may, however, require generators or T/S/D facilities to submit additional information related to a waste shipment under separate cover, so long as there is no interference with the actual movement of the waste.

EPA has not printed copies of the Uniform Manifest for public use, but states may print and supply the form if they wish. States that choose to do so may preprint certain information directly on the Uniform Manifest.[27] Such information might include state emergency telephone numbers or state manifest numbers to aid in tracking shipments.

Generators disposing of hazardous wastes out-of-state must follow specific rules to determine whether to use a particular state's Uniform Manifest. If the state to which a shipment is manifested (consignment state) supplies a Uniform Manifest and

---

[26]   Appendix to 40 C.F.R. Part 262. See 50 Fed. Reg. 28744-45 (July 15, 1985).

[27]   Twenty-three states print their own forms. See 57 Fed. Reg. 24765 (June 11, 1992).

requires its use, the generator must use that Uniform Manifest.[28] If the consignment state does not supply a Uniform Manifest, then the generator must use the Uniform Manifest required by its own state.[29] If the generator's state does not supply a Uniform Manifest, the generator may obtain the Uniform Manifest from any source such as a commercial printing company.[30] If a generator prepares its own Uniform Manifest, the generator may preprint information on the form.

The generator must prepare a sufficient number of copies of the manifest so that all parties listed on the manifest as handling the hazardous waste will be provided with a copy and a complete copy will be returned to the generator from the T/S/D facility.[31] The generator must sign and date the manifest and obtain the signature of the original transporter.[32] The generator should retain one copy and give the remaining copies to the initial transporter.[33] The transporter must obtain the signature of the next transporter or the designated T/S/D facility upon delivery of the hazardous waste, retain a copy itself, and pass on the remaining copies. The T/S/D facility is required to sign and date the manifest and send a signed copy back to the generator.[34] Receipt by the generator of a completed copy of the manifest signed by the T/S/D facility and all other parties who handled the hazardous waste will signify to the generator that its hazardous waste has been properly handled. The return of an irregular manifest or the

---

[28] 40 CFR 262.21(a).

[29] 40 CFR 262.21(b).

[30] 40 CFR 262.21(c).

[31] 40 CFR 262.22. Some states also require that a copy of the manifest be sent to the appropriate state agency.

[32] 40 CFR 262.23(a)(1) and (2).

[33] 40 CFR 262.23(a)(3), (b).

[34] 40 CFR 264.71(a)(1) and (4).

non-receipt of a completed manifest by the generator within a specified time will trigger the need to file on exception report, as discussed below.

Generators transporting their wastes by rail or water must send three copies of the manifest dated and signed to the designated T/S/D facility or last water or rail transporter to handle the waste in the United States.[35] Signatures between intermediate rail or waste transporters are not required unless there is an intermediary nonrail or nonwater transporter involved. The T/S/D facility then has 30 days to sign and return the manifest to the generator after delivery of the hazardous waste.[36]

In November, 1992, EPA formed a Negotiated Rulemaking Advisory Committee to discuss proposed modifications to the hazardous waste manifest regulations. The goal of the Committee is to improve and standardize the manifest system by increasing uniformity among the states. To date, the Committee has not published any proposed modifications.

3.3.5 International Shipments of Hazardous Waste

Special manifest procedures must also be followed for international shipments of hazardous waste.[37] Persons who export hazardous waste to a foreign country must use the manifest, but they should identify the point of departure in the U.S. and substitute the foreign consignee for the designated T/S/D facility.[38] They must also comply with additional procedural requirements imposed in EPA's regulations.[39]

---

[35] 40 CFR 262.23(c), (d).

[36] 264.71(b)(1) and (4); 265.71(b)(1) and (4).

[37] 40 CFR 262.54.

[38] 40 CFR 262.54(a), (c).

[39] Additional requirements for exporters are found in 40 CFR Sections 262.41 (Biennial Report), 262.50 (Applicability),
[footnote continued]

A primary exporter of hazardous waste must now file a notice with EPA's Office of International Activities sixty (60) days before it ships waste to a foreign country.[40] The notice must include, among other things, the name and site address of the foreign consignee, a description of the means of transportation to be used, and a description of the manner in which the hazardous waste will be treated, stored or disposed of in the foreign country.[41] There is no prescribed form for the notice, although the notice is usually made in letter form.

EPA and the Department of State must provide the receiving country with the exporter's notification. When the receiving country consents in writing to the receipt of the hazardous waste, EPA must forward an EPA "Acknowledgment of Consent" to the exporter.[42] EPA will prohibit the export of hazardous waste unless notice is given, consent is obtained, and an EPA Acknowledgment of Consent accompanies the waste shipment and manifest.[43] For exports to Canada, an international agreement exists which allows for routine processing of notices of intent and consent by Canada unless objected to on an individual basis. The agreement provides that Canada will impose similar requirements such as special manifest, recordkeeping, and reporting requirements on the importation of waste from Canada into the United States. There are additional requirements relating to special manifests and recordkeeping and reporting

---

[continued]
    262.51 (Definitions), 262.52 (General Requirements), 262.53 (Notification of Intent to Export), 262.54 (Special Manifest Requirements), 262.55 (Exception Reports), 262.56 (Annual Reports), 262.57 (Recordkeeping), and 262.58 (International Agreements); see also 51 Fed. Reg. 28666 (August 8, 1986).

[40]   40 CFR 262.53(a), (b).

[41]   40 CFR 262.53(a)(2).

[42]   40 CFR 262.53(f).

[43]   40 CFR 262.52.

GENERATORS OF HAZARDOUS WASTE

requirements.[44]   EPA processes notices and consents as a fairly
routine matter.

On the other hand, persons who import hazardous wastes into
the U.S. must identify the foreign generator and the importer, and
the importer must sign the generator's certification on the
Uniform Manifest.[45]

3.3.6 Exception Reports

If the generator has not received a signed manifest from the
T/S/D facility within thirty-five (35) days, the regulations specifically provide that the generator must contact the transporter
and the designated T/S/D facility to determine the status of the
hazardous waste.[46] If the generator has still not received a
manifest with the proper signature from the T/S/D facility within
forty-five (45) days of the date the waste was accepted by the
initial transporter, the generator must submit an exception report
to the EPA Regional Administrator for the region in which the generator is located.[47]

The report must include: (1) a copy of the manifest for
which the generator does not have confirmation of delivery; and
(2) a cover letter which describes the efforts taken to locate the
waste and the manifest and the result of those efforts.[48]

The exception report requirements play an important role in
the enforcement of the hazardous waste program. EPA has focused a
significant part of its enforcement effort on generators who do

---

[44]   40 CFR 262.54, 262.56-262.57.

[45]   40 CFR 262.60(b).

[46]   40 CFR 262.42(a)(1). Special provisions for small quantity
generators are discussed below in Section 3.4.

[47]   40 CFR 262.42(a)(2). Some states prescribe a shorter period.

[48]   Id.

not exercise reasonable caution in selecting qualified transporters and T/S/D facilities. The requirement that a generator track down his hazardous waste when there is an irregularity involving the manifest is designed to promote self-enforcement of the RCRA requirements. The filing of a number of exception reports within a short time is a signal to EPA that a significant problem may exist, warranting further investigation and possible enforcement action.

3.3.7 The Temporary 90-Day Storage Provision

One of the most important provisions that EPA has included in the Part 262 regulations allows a generator to store his hazardous wastes on-site for a period of up to 90 days without having to obtain a permit as a storage facility, regardless of whether the wastes will be treated or disposed of on site or transported off-site to a T/S/D facility.[49] In addition, a generator may accumulate up to 55 gallons of hazardous waste, or one quart of acutely hazardous waste, at or near the point of generation ("satellite accumulation areas") for any amount of time without triggering the temporary 90-day storage provision, provided certain safeguards are taken.[50] These provisions are necessary because a generator cannot be expected to immediately ship or dispose of the hazardous waste he generates on a daily basis. EPA has, however, imposed significant requirements for temporary on-site storage.

---

[49] 40 CFR 262.34(a). The waste may be placed in containers or tanks, or the waste may be placed on drip pads. 40 CFR 262.34(a)(1) and (2), as amended by 55 Fed. Reg. 50483 et seq. (December 6, 1990).

[50] 40 CFR 262.34(c).

For example, the container must be labeled "Hazardous Waste" or otherwise suitably marked to identify its contents.[51] The container must be lined or constructed of materials that are compatible with the hazardous wastes accumulated in it, and the container must be maintained in good condition to prevent ruptures and leaks.[52] The container must be kept closed, except when wastes are added or removed.[53] If a container does begin to leak, the generator must immediately transfer the accumulated hazardous waste to another container or otherwise properly manage the waste.[54] If the 55 gallon (or one quart) limit is exceeded, the generator must mark the container with the date that the excess amount began accumulating and then remove at least that excess amount from the accumulation area within three days.[55] EPA has not expressly limited the total amount of hazardous wastes that can be accumulated at various satellite areas, or the number of such areas, at a generator's facility, but requires that a rule of reason be followed.[56]

Once hazardous wastes are removed to a central storage area, the generator may temporarily store the wastes for up to 90 days in approved containers or tanks.[57] The 90-day period commences the day on which accumulation of the hazardous wastes begins at

[51]   40 CFR 262.34(a)(3), (c)(1)(ii).

[52]   40 CFR 265.172; 265.173(b).

[53]   40 CFR 265.173(a).

[54]   40 CFR 265.171.

[55]   40 CFR 262.34(c)(2).

[56]   For example, accumulation areas located every five feet along a fence line would probably not qualify as a satellite accumulation area under the regulations. See 49 Fed. Reg. 49569 (December 20, 1984).

[57]   40 CFR 262.34(a).

the central storage area or when the amounts allowed at any satellite area are exceeded. EPA has taken the position that the 90-day period does not include any form of first-in, first-out accounting system. In other words, once a particular tank or container in a _central_ storage area begins to be filled, the date must be marked on the container and all of the hazardous waste which it contains must be transported off-site to a designated facility within the 90-day period, including hazardous waste that may be added to the tank or container on the 89th day.

EPA does not allow (storage) in surface impoundments or land storage facilities (e.g., waste piles) to qualify for the 90-day exemption. Hazardous waste must be stored only in "tanks" and "containers", or on drip pads which comply with Part 264 Subpart W.[58] Storage of hazardous wastes under this provision meet comply with the technical standards for "tanks" and "containers" set forth at 40 CFR 265, Subparts I and J. For example, tanks must be equipped with secondary containment systems in accordance with the Subpart J tank standards.[59] These requirements are discussed in more detail in Chapter 6 on the standards for specific types of T/S/D facilities. In addition, generators must comply with DOT marking and packaging requirements before the hazardous wastes are shipped off-site.

Most importantly, during this temporary storage period generators must comply with the personnel training, prevention and preparedness, contingency plan, and emergency response requirements in 40 CFR Part 265 that apply to interim status T/S/D facilities.[60] These standards include on-the-job or classroom instruction for facility personnel that provides training in hazardous

---

[58] 40 CFR 262.34(a)(1) and (2), as amended by 55 _Fed. Reg._ 50483 _et seq._ (December 6, 1990).

[59] 51 _Fed. Reg._ 25422 (July 14, 1986).

[60] 40 CFR 262.34(a)(4).

waste management and emergency procedures. The necessary equipment for responding to a fire, explosion, or release of hazardous
waste must be kept on hand, and arrangements must be made with the
local police, fire department, and hospital to familiarize those
local authorities with hazardous waste activities at the generator's facility. The generator must prepare a contingency plan,
which is a prepared set of responses to any emergency to be implemented by an Emergency Coordinator at the facility.[61] EPA's
rationale for imposing these requirements on generators is that
on-site storage of hazardous wastes for 90 days poses many of the
same hazards as longer term storage at a T/S/D facility. The generator does not, however, have to comply with the myriad of other
requirements that a permitted storage facility must satisfy, such
as providing a closure plan, financial responsibility, and third-
party liability insurance.

EPA has discretion to grant generators a 30-day extension of
the temporary accumulation period if hazardous wastes must be
stored for more than 90 days as a result of unforeseen, temporary,
and uncontrollable circumstances.[62] Otherwise, if hazardous
wastes are stored on-site for longer than 90 days, the generator
will be considered an operator of a storage facility, subject to
enforcement sanctions for failure to have a RCRA permit.[63]

EPA has published a Regulatory Interpretative Memorandum
("RIM") setting forth the conditions under which a generator may
qualify as an interim status T/S/D facility if and when the generator exceeds the 90-day limit and any extension.[64] Such a generator may qualify his storage facility as an interim status T/S/D
facility if:

---

[61] These standards are discussed in more detail in Chapter 5 of
this Handbook.

[62] 40 CFR 262.34(b).

[63] Id.

[64] 46 Fed. Reg. 60446 et seq. (December 10, 1981).

(1) the generator's storage facility was in existence on November 19, 1980, _i.e._, the generator was accumulating hazardous wastes at his facility on or before that date;

(2) a timely RCRA Section 3010(a) notification has been submitted to EPA; and

(3) Part A of the RCRA permit application is submitted within 30 days of the date the generator's wastes first become subject to the interim status standards, _i.e._, within 30 days of the date the 90-day accumulation time limit or any extension is exceeded.

3.3.8 Pretransport Requirements

Once a generator has prepared a manifest for hazardous waste, he must also properly package that waste for transportation off-site.[65] EPA has adopted by reference the DOT regulations with respect to the packaging, labeling, marking, and placarding of hazardous wastes.[66] These DOT regulations are discussed in Chapter 4 on Transporters.

In accordance with DOT regulations, EPA requires that any container of 110 gallons or less used in transporting hazardous waste must be specifically labelled with the generator's name, address, manifest document number, and the words:

HAZARDOUS WASTE Federal Law Prohibits Improper Disposal. If found, contact the nearest police or public safety authority or the U.S. Environmental Protection Agency.[67]

---

[65] 40 CFR 262.30.

[66] 40 CFR 262.30-262.33, cross-referencing 49 CFR Parts 172, 173, 178, 179.

[67] 40 CFR 262.32(b).

3.3.9   Recordkeeping Requirements

The recordkeeping and reporting requirements for generators provide EPA and the states with a method to track the quantities of waste generated and the movement of hazardous wastes. Generators are required to keep three types of records.[68] First, a copy of each signed manifest must be kept for a period of three years from the date of acceptance of the waste by the initial transporter.[69] Second, copies of reports required to be filed with EPA (e.g., exception reports and the biennial reports discussed immediately below) must also be kept for at least three years from the date each report was submitted.[70] The records of any test results, waste analyses, or other determinations that a solid waste is a hazardous waste must be kept for at least three years from the date the waste was last sent to a T/S/D facility.[71] Copies of notices, certifications, demonstrations and waste analysis data related to the determination that waste is restricted from land disposal, and related to the shipment of restricted waste, must be kept for at least five years from the date the waste was last sent to a T/S/D facility.[72] Although the regulation is not explicit on whether test results which reveal that a solid waste is non-hazardous need be kept, as a practical

---

[68]   40 CFR 262.40.

[69]   40 CFR 262.40(a).

[70]   40 CFR 262.40(b).

[71]   40 CFR 262.40(c). This requirement only applies to test results and waste analyses obtained for the purposes of the hazardous waste determination required by 40 CFR 262.11, using the EPA testing protocols set forth in Part 261 or an approved equivalent method. The regulatory requirement that a generator retain these records and make them available to EPA for inspection should not apply to other waste analyses a generator might obtain, such as a gas chromotography/mass spectrometry ("GC/MS") analysis of a waste stream made as a result of a self-initiated environmental audit.

[72]   40 CFR 268.7(7).

matter, generators should consider retaining all test results in order to defend against any EPA enforcement action challenging the generator's determination.

The retention periods for all of the above recordkeeping requirements are automatically extended either during the course of an unresolved enforcement action concerning a regulated activity or as requested by EPA.[73] A generator may expect that his records would be reviewed if EPA conducts an inspection at its facility. In view of the liability imposed by Superfund and other pertinent laws, generators should seriously consider maintaining RCRA reports for substantially longer than the minimum three-year period.

3.3.10 Biennial Reports

Generators must submit biennial reports to EPA, if EPA is the regulatory authority in the state, on March 1 of each even numbered year, covering hazardous waste management activities during the preceding year.[74] Thus, a report covering 1991 activities will have to be filed by March 1, 1992. The biennial report is submitted on EPA Form 8700-13A.[75] A great majority of states that have obtained authorization to administer the RCRA program have adopted an annual reporting requirement in their state programs.

---

[73] 40 CFR 262.40(d).

[74] 40 CFR 262.41. In its initial regulations, EPA established an annual reporting requirement, but EPA then proposed to reduce paperwork burdens on the regulated community by replacing annual reporting with a "spot check" survey of a statistically significant percentage of generators and T/S/D facilities. Commenters on the proposal argued that a survey approach would actually increase the regulatory burden, however, because states with authorized RCRA programs were likely to retain their annual reporting requirements. EPA was persuaded by these comments, and simply changed the annual report to a biennial report requirement.

[75] 40 CFR 262.41(a).

The biennial report filed with EPA must be certified by the generator or his authorized representative as true, accurate, complete and based upon personal familiarity with the information and personal inquiry of those responsible for obtaining the information.[76] The information called for includes: (1) the name, address and EPA ID Number of the generator; (2) the calendar year covered by the report; (3) the EPA ID Number for each transporter that was used during the calendar year; (4) the name, address and EPA ID Number of each T/S/D facility to which waste was sent; and (5) information on the hazardous wastes generated, including the DOT hazard class, the EPA hazardous waste identification number, and the quantity of the waste.[77]

In addition, every generator must now include in his biennial report a description of his "waste minimization" program, as required by the 1984 Amendments enacted by Congress.[78] Specifically, the generator must describe the efforts undertaken during the year to reduce the volume and toxicity of the waste generated, as well as the changes in waste volume and toxicity actually achieved in comparison to previous years.[79] EPA published guidance in June 1989 to assist hazardous waste generators in developing waste minimization programs.[80] More recently, EPA published an interim guidance for generators on what constitutes "waste minimization". 58 Fed. Reg. 31114. (May 28, 1993). EPA defined waste minimization as source reduction and recycling, but not treatment. EPA recommended the following six elements of an acceptable waste minimization program: (1) support by top management for waste minimization; (2) development of a waste

---

[76]   40 CFR 262.41(a)(8).

[77]   40 CFR 262.41(a).

[78]   RCRA § 3002(b).   40 CFR 262.41(a)(6) and (7).

[79]   40 CFR 262.41(a)(6) and (7).

[80]   See RCRA Orientation Manual 1990 Edition (EPA/530-SW-90-036).

accounting system to track the types, and amounts of hazardous wastes; (3) conducting waste minimization assessments to identify opportunities for reduction; (4) allocation of costs of waste management to the departments that generate the waste; (5) encouragement of technology transfer; and (6) periodic review of program effectiveness. EPA has not given any guidance on the term "economically practicable;" leaving it to interpretation by individual generators.

EPA is in the process of developing a strategy for institutionalizing waste minimization within the RCRA waste management framework. EPA is also developing strategies and priorities for encouraging source reduction and recycling of the nonhazardous solid waste stream regulated by Subtitle D of RCRA. There is also a new agency-wide, multi-media program to promote pollution prevention.[81]

In recent years, more and more states have established waste minimization programs to assist industry in waste minimization efforts. In many states, there are significant economic incentives to adopt waste minimization practices.

It should also be noted that a generator who treats, stores, or disposes of its hazardous wastes on-site must also submit the biennial report for T/S/D facilities, as discussed in Chapter 5 of this Handbook.[82]

3.4 The Special Requirements For Small Quantity Generators

Large quantity generators must (with a few exceptions) comply with all of the generator regulations developed under 40 CFR Part 262. Large quantity generators are defined as those facilities which generate over 1000 kilograms per month of hazardous waste, or over 1 kilogram per month of acutely hazardous waste. EPA has

---

[81]   Id.

[82]   40 CFR 262.41(b).

established somewhat less rigorous requirements for those generators that produce hazardous wastes in small quantities, however.
When the RCRA regulations were first promulgated in 1980, EPA
believed it would be administratively infeasible to immediately
regulate all generators of hazardous waste. EPA therefore
decided, at least initially, to impose minimum requirements on
generators that produced or accumulated less than 1,000 kilograms
of non-acutely hazardous waste per month so as not to unduly tax
agency resources.[83] In the 1984 Amendments, however, Congress
directed EPA to establish more extensive standards for small quantity generators of between 100 and 1,000 kg/mo, and to regulate
generators of less than 100 kg/mo if necessary to protect human
health and the environment.[84]

In response to Congress' mandate, EPA has established two
classes of small quantity generators. One class, consisting of
those small generators which produce less than 100 kg of hazardous
waste in a calendar month, remains "conditionally exempt" from
full regulation under RCRA.[85] These conditionally exempt generators must still determine whether any solid waste they produce is
a hazardous waste, and ensure that the waste is sent to a municipal or industrial solid waste facility licensed by a state, a T/S/
D facility, or a recycling facility.[86] A 100 kg small quantity
generator may still accumulate on-site up to 1,000 kgs of hazardous wastes without becoming subject to full RCRA regulation.[87]
However, conditionally exempt small quantity generators who exceed

---

[83] EPA Office of Solid Waste, Background Document on Specific
Requirements for Hazardous Waste Generated by Small Quantity
Generators (April 28, 1980).

[84] RCRA § 3001(d).

[85] 40 CFR 261.5(a).

[86] 40 CFR 261.5(g)(3).

[87] 40 CFR 261.5(g)(2).

the 100 kg per month hazardous waste cut-off are regulated as small quantity generators.

Another type of "conditionally exempt" small quantity generators consists of generators who may produce <u>and accumulate</u> only 1 kg/mo of acutely hazardous waste, and 100 kg/mo of any spill residue and contaminated soil or debris resulting from a spill of an acutely hazardous waste.[88] If the small quantity generator accumulates more than these threshold limits, the entire quantity of accumulated waste is subject to full RCRA regulation.[89] The small quantity generator must also treat or dispose of the acutely hazardous waste in one of the approved types of facilities identified above.[90]

The second class consists of (non-exempt) small quantity generators that produce between 100 and 1,000 kgs of hazardous waste at a site per month (and accumulate less than 6,000 kilograms at any one time). The rules require 100 - 1,000 kg/mo generators to comply with almost all of the part 262 standards for large generators.[91] These 100 - 1,000 kg/mo generators must now obtain an EPA identification number, use only RCRA regulated transporters and T/S/D facilities, and comply with DOT shipping requirements. EPA has established modified storage standards in 40 CFR 262.34 for these small quantity generators who accumulate up to 6,000 kgs of hazardous wastes on-site for up to 180 days, or for up to 270 days if the waste must be transported over 200 miles to a T/S/D facility. The standards include special emergency preparedness and response measures tailored to these small generators.

---

[88] 40 CFR 261.5(e), (f) (emphasis added).

[89] 40 CFR 261.5(e). "Full regulation" means those regulations applicable to generators of greater than 1,000 kg of non-acutely hazardous waste in a calendar month.

[90] 40 CFR 261.5(f)(3).

[91] 40 CFR 261.5; 262.34(d), (e), (f). <u>See</u> 51 <u>Fed</u>. <u>Reg</u>. 10146 (March 24, 1986).

EPA now requires these small quantity generators to use the full multi-copy manifest form and "round-trip" manifest procedures. There is a special exemption, however, for wastes shipped for reclamation under certain conditions. These small quantity generators must retain copies of their manifests for at least three years. EPA has also developed a modified "waste minimization" certification on manifests for these small quantity generators.[92] They must now certify that they have made a good faith effort to minimize waste generation and selected the best waste management method that was available and which they could afford.[93]

Until 1987, EPA's rules exempted 100-1000 kg/mo generators from the exception reporting requirement. In September, 1987, EPA promulgated rules requiring these generators to file an exception report when the generator does not receive confirmation of delivery of his hazardous waste shipment to the designated facility within 60 days.[94]

These small quantity threshold limits apply on a site-by-site basis.[95] Thus, a large corporation may qualify under the small generator provision on a plant-by-plant basis. However, EPA has interpreted the regulations as applying to the total of all non acutely hazardous wastes produced by a generator at each plant. Thus, if a generator produces three different hazardous wastes in monthly quantities of 300 kg, 600 kg, and 200 kg for a total of 1,100 kg, the small quantity generator provisions would not apply. On the other hand, the 1 kg limit for acutely hazardous wastes should be considered separately. Thus, if a company is over the 1 kg limit for the total of acutely hazardous commercial chemicals

---

[92] Appendix to 40 CFR Part 262. See 51 Fed. Reg. 35190 (October 1, 1986).

[93] Id. at 35191.

[94] 40 CFR 262.42(b). See 52 Fed. Reg. 35894 (Sept. 23, 1987).

[95] See 45 Fed. Reg. 76620-21 (November 19, 1980).

in a given month, but under the 1,000 kg limit for the total of all other hazardous wastes, then the company is subject to the full generator provisions for the acutely hazardous waste, but it is still within the small generator provisions for the other wastes. This might be expected to arise, for example, where there has been an accidental spill of a listed commercial chemical product.

Hazardous wastes that are subject to EPA's recycling regulations must be included in the small quantity generator determination.[96] This would not include, however, sludges and by-products that exhibit a hazardous characteristic and which are reclaimed, nor listed commercial chemical products that are reclaimed, since such materials are expressly excluded from the definition of "solid waste" in EPA's recycling regulations.[97] In addition, the following hazardous wastes are not counted in the quantity determinations if the wastes are recycled: used oil, spent lead-acid batteries that are reclaimed, industrial ethyl alcohol that is reclaimed, used batteries returned to the manufacturer for regeneration, scrap metal, and hazardous waste fuels that are spent materials and by-products which exhibit a hazardous characteristic.[98]

A company may move in and out of the small quantity generator provisions each month, as production rates and waste quantities change. This is permissible under the regulations, but a company should consider the advisability of adequately documenting such changes to avoid potential liability for non-compliance.

[96] 40 CFR 261.5(c). See discussion in Chapter 2 of this Handbook regarding EPA's recycling regulations.

[97] 40 CFR 261.2(c).

[98] 40 CFR 261.5(c); (40 CFR 261.6(a).

CHAPTER 4

TRANSPORTERS OF HAZARDOUS WASTES

4.1 Overview

Transporters of hazardous wastes play an important role in the RCRA regulatory scheme. Some 250,000 shipments of hazardous waste occur daily in the United States. The safe transport of hazardous wastes from generators to permitted T/S/D facilities is essential to the basic concept of cradle-to-grave management of hazardous wastes. Indeed one of the major concerns that prompted Congress to enact RCRA in 1976 was the need to prevent "midnight dumpers" from illegally transporting hazardous waste off-site and dumping it in fields, into lakes, and along highways.

In RCRA Section 3003, Congress attempted to prohibit such practices by regulating any person who transports hazardous wastes, whether in interstate or intrastate commerce. The reach of RCRA Section 3003 includes not only shippers and common carriers of hazardous wastes but also the private company that occasionally transports hazardous wastes on its own trucks solely within its home state. RCRA Section 3003 requires that EPA coordinate its transportation rulemaking activity with the requirements of the Hazardous Materials Transportation Act ("HMTA")[1] and any regulations promulgated by the U.S. Department of Transportation ("DOT") pursuant to HMTA.[2]

Under HMTA, Congress gave DOT broad powers to promulgate regulations for the transportation and handling of hazardous

---

[1]   49 app. U.S.C. §§ 1801-1819 (1988; supp. 1993).

[2]   DOT's regulations appear at 49 CFR Parts 171-180. They are administered by the Research and Special Programs Administration within DOT.

materials, including hazardous wastes and "reportable quantities" of hazardous substances.[3] Those regulations apply to the transportation of hazardous materials by, and their offering to: (1) carriers by rail, aircraft and vessel, (2) interstate and foreign carriers by motor vehicle, and (3) intrastate carriers by motor vehicle so far as the regulations relate to hazardous wastes and hazardous substances. They also apply to the manufacture, fabrication, marking, maintenance, reconditioning, repairing, or testing of packaging or containers which are represented, marked, certified, or sold for use in such transportation.[4]

As originally enacted, HMTA preempted state requirements that were "inconsistent" with DOT standards. However, if a state regulation afforded equal or greater protection when compared to the DOT standard, and if it did not unreasonably burden interstate commerce, it was not preempted.[5] In 1990, Congress clarified this matter of preemption by providing, in the Hazardous Materials Transportation Uniform Safety Act of 1990, Pub. L. No. 101-615, that various state requirements, including any that relate to classification of hazardous materials, their packing, handling, labeling, marking, and placarding, shipping documents, notification, recording, and reporting of unintentional releases, and the design, manufacture, etc. of packaging and containers, are preempted if they are "not substantively the same" as the federal

---

[3] Hazardous substances are substances designated as such under Section 101(4) of the Comprehensive Environmental Response, Compensation, and Liability Act (CERCLA), 42 U.S.C. §§ 9601 et seq. They are listed, together with their "reportable quantities," in an appendix to 49 CFR § 172.101.

[4] 49 CFR 171.1.

[5] See National Tank Truck Carriers v. Burke, 608 F.2d 819 (1st Cir. 1979).

requirements.[6] Under the new act, "[t]he Secretary shall issue regulations for the safe transportation of hazardous materials in intrastate, interstate, and foreign commerce."[7]

EPA, as required by RCRA Section 3003, promulgated its standards applicable to transporters of hazardous wastes at 40 CFR Part 263. These standards are closely coordinated with the DOT HMTA standards. For the most part, EPA's regulations incorporate and require compliance with the DOT provisions on labeling, marking, placarding, using proper containers and reporting discharges.

4.2 Statutory Requirements

RCRA Section 3003 requires EPA to promulgate regulations establishing standards applicable to transporters with respect to:

(1) recordkeeping concerning the source and delivery points of hazardous waste shipments;

(2) proper labeling of transported waste;

(3) compliance with the manifest system; and

(4) transporting waste only to T/S/D facilities designated on the manifest which hold a RCRA permit or have interim status.

It is important to know what the statute does not do with respect to transporters of hazardous waste. First, Congress did

---

[6] 49 app. U.S.C. 1804(a)(4)(A),(B). See 49 app. U.S.C. 1804(b)(4) (highway routing); 1811(a) (general preemption standard). States may apply to DOT for a waiver of preemption. Id. 1811(d). See 49 CFR § 171.3(c).

[7] Id. 1804(a)(1).

not directly impose any specific statutory requirements on trans- porters. Instead, Congress directed EPA to establish regulations respecting, but not limited to, the four aspects of transporter activities listed above. Thus, transporters must look to EPA's regulations for all applicable RCRA requirements, as well as to DOT regulations.

Second, Congress did not establish a RCRA permit requirement for transporters. Therefore, transporters do not have to receive advance permission to move hazardous waste, nor need they qualify in advance for transporter status by meeting any pre-established set of requirements.[8] As discussed in greater detail below, how- ever, a transporter of hazardous waste should have complied with the RCRA Section 3010(a) notification requirement and must obtain an EPA Identification Number.[9] (See Chapter 2 of this Handbook).

The 1990 amendments to HMTA do, however, require that DOT promulgate regulations establishing a safety permit program for common, contract, and private motor carriers engaged in shipment of certain hazardous materials.[10] Shipments requiring permits are currently limited to class A or B explosives, quantities of radioactive materials which require highway-routing, liquefied natural gas, and substances designated as "extremely toxic by inhalation."[11] The Secretary may expand the list of materials requiring permits.

The 1990 HMTA amendments also require the filing of registration statements by any shipper or carrier involved in

---

[8] A number of states, however, do require transporters of hazardous waste within state boundaries to be licensed or registered.

[9] 40 CFR 263.11(b).

[10] 40 app. U.S.C. § 1805(d).

[11] Id. § 1805(d)(5).

shipments of highway-route controlled quantities of radioactive materials, certain quantities of class A or B explosives, or materials designated as extremely toxic by inhalation; any hazardous material in bulk package of 3,500 gallons or more or more than 468 cubic feet; and any hazardous material in quantities of 5,000 lbs. or more which requires placarding.[12]

4.3 Transporter Obligations Under the Hazardous Waste Regulations
4.3.1 General Provisions

The terms "transporter" and "transportation" are not defined in RCRA. EPA, however, has defined both of these terms very broadly in its regulations. The term "transporter" is defined to mean: "any person engaged in the offsite transportation of hazardous waste by air, rail, highway or water."[13] Transportation means "the movement of hazardous waste by air, rail, highway, or water."[14]

Thus, anyone who moves a hazardous waste that is required to be manifested off the site where it is generated or the site where it is being treated, stored and disposed of will be subject to the transporter standards. The only persons not covered are gen-erators or operators of T/S/D facilities who engage in on-site transportation of their hazardous waste.[15] Once a generator or a T/S/D facility operator moves hazardous waste off-site -- which can be just a few hundred feet down a public road -- that

---

[12]   Id. § 1805(c). Regulatons implementing this safety permit program have been proposed at 58 Fed. Reg. 33418 (June 17, 1993) (to be codified at 49 CFR Part 397, Subpart B).

[13]   40 CFR 260.10.

[14]   Id.

[15]   40 CFR 263.10(b).

generation or operator then becomes a transporter and must comply with the Part 263 regulations.

All transporters subject to the regulations must obtain an EPA Identification Number prior to transporting any hazardous waste.[16] The EPA Identification Number should have been obtained by filing EPA Form 8700-12 in compliance with the RCRA Section 3010(a) notification procedure. If a person did not transport hazardous waste during the initial 90-day notification period (May 19, 1980, through August 18, 1980), an EPA Identification Number must nevertheless be obtained before a person engages in transportation activities. EPA has stated that in such a situation persons should still file EPA Form 8700-12, although information regarding specific wastes which are likely to be handled does not need to be included if the transporter does not have this information. This requirement has a counterpart in the generator standards, namely, that generators may not offer hazardous wastes for transportation off-site to transporters who do not have an EPA Identification Number.[17]

4.3.2   Compliance with the Manifest System

A transporter may only accept hazardous waste which is accompanied by a manifest signed by the generator. Upon receipt of the hazardous waste the transporter himself must sign the manifest and return one copy to the generator before leaving the generator's property. At all times the transporter must keep the manifest with the hazardous waste. When the transporter delivers the waste to another transporter or to the designated T/S/D facility, the transporter must (1) date the manifest and obtain the signature of the next transporter or the T/S/D facility operator, (2) retain

---

[16]   40 CFR 263.11.

[17]   40 CFR 262.12(c).

one copy of the manifest, and (3) give the remaining copies to the person receiving the waste.[18]

Note that there are special requirements which apply to rail or water transporters of hazardous waste, and those who transport hazardous waste outside of the United States.[19] In brief, railroads and maritime shippers, because they often use sophisticated computerized tracking and information systems in intermodal transportation, may use shipping papers rather than RCRA manifests and may waive signature requirements between intermediate carriers.

The entire quantity of hazardous waste which a transporter accepts from a generator or another transporter must be delivered in accordance with the instructions on the manifest. This means that the hazardous waste must be delivered to the primary T/S/D facility designated on the manifest. An alternate T/S/D facility may be used if it is designated on the manifest and a labor strike, fire, or similar emergency prevents delivery to the primary T/S/D facility. A transporter may deliver the waste to another transporter only if that is indicated on the manifest.[20]

If the transporter is unable to deliver the waste in accordance with the manifest, he must contact the generator for further instructions and revise the manifest accordingly.[21] If for any reason the generator cannot be contacted for further instructions, the transporter is expected to return the hazardous waste to the generator. In other words, the regulations specifically prohibit the transporter from undertaking on his own to redirect the hazardous waste. A solution to the problem, which this requirement

---

[18]   40 CFR 263.20(a)-(d).

[19]   40 CFR 263.20(e), (f) and (g) 263.22(b), (c) and (d).

[20]   40 CFR 263.21(a).

[21]   40 CFR 263.21(b).

may cause, may lie in working out advance written arrangements with the generator for cases in which normal delivery to a T/S/D facility cannot be made.

As noted in the preceding Chapter, EPA originally did not prescribe any particular form of manifest document. Any form could be used as long as the document included, at a minimum, the information required to be placed on it by the RCRA regulations. This was intended to allow generators and transporters maximum flexibility to adapt existing shipping documents which have been in use in connection with the DOT program or to generate their own manifest forms to suit their own circumstances.

Even good intentions sometimes go awry, however, and the lack of a uniform manifest caused confusion and unnecessary paperwork for shippers. Many states prescribed uniform manifests for their state programs and required that all shipments passing through the state be accompanied by the prescribed manifest. This meant that transporters passing through several states were often required to fill out and carry several different manifests for the same waste shipment.

At the behest of shipper groups, EPA and DOT, in a joint rulemaking, replaced the general information requirements for manifests with a Uniform Manifest form.[22] Now, states are not allowed to require transporters to carry any additional information on or with the Uniform Manifest.

---

[22] 49 Fed. Reg. 10490 (March 20, 1984). Instructions for completing the Uniform Manifest are found at 40 CFR Part 262, Appendix.

4.3.3   Recordkeeping Requirements

The regulations also impose certain recordkeeping requirements.[23] The manifest retained by the transporter will have been
signed by the generator, the transporter, and the owner/operator
of the designated T/S/D facility or the next transporter. The
transporter must keep this executed copy of the manifest for a
period of three years after the date it was accepted by the initial transporter. This three-year period is extended automatically during any unresolved enforcement action, or if the EPA
Administrator requests an extension.

4.3.4 Generator and T/S/D Facility Obligations Applicable to Transporters

Transporters of hazardous wastes may also become subject to
the Part 262 requirements for generators if, for example, the
transporter mixes hazardous wastes of different DOT descriptions
by placing them into a single container.[24] Moreover, EPA
regulations provide that a hazardous waste which accumulates in a
transport vehicle or vessel or a product or raw material pipeline
will trigger the generator standards when the waste is removed.[25]
As a direct result, the transporter who, for example, cleans out a
hazardous sludge from his tank car may qualify as a generator, and
thus may become subject to the applicable generator regulations in
Part 262.

Sludges, sediment and other residues are likely to be produced in tank cars, rail tank cars and the holds of ships and
barges that have carried products or raw materials which are not

-----

[23]   40 CFR 263.22.

[24]   40 CFR 263.10(c).

[25]   40 CFR 261.4(c).

themselves hazardous waste. Wastes may also accumulate in pipe lines used to transport crude oil, petroleum products, chemicals and other valuable products and raw materials. These sludges and wastes must be periodically removed through washing of the tanks of transport vehicles and vessels or flushing of pipelines. Where the sludges or residues are listed or exhibit the characteristics of hazardous wastes, they are subject to regulation at the point where they are generated -- that is, when they are removed from the transport vehicle, vessel or pipeline.

To facilitate this change, EPA amended its definition of "generator" to clearly cover persons who remove hazardous wastes from such units.[26] EPA also added definitions of "transport vehicle" and "vessel" which are the same as those in the DOT regulations.[27]

What happens when several different persons are involved in the removal of the hazardous waste? For example, a transport vehicle may be taken to a central facility for removal of sediment through tank washing or cleaning. This central facility will probably be owned by a person other than the owner of the vehicle. The owner of the product or raw material that produced the sediment is probably a third party still. In a given case, EPA may apply the definition of "generator" to all these parties since it is the "act or process" of each of them that produces the hazardous waste.

Accordingly, EPA has provided some guidance on who should be responsible for hazardous wastes that are generated in transport vehicles or vessels.[28] First of all, it is EPA's position that

---

[26]   40 CFR 260.10.

[27]   Id. See 49 CFR 171.8.

[28]   See 45 Fed. Reg. 72926-27 (October 30, 1980).

all parties who fit the definition of "generator," no matter how many are involved, must be responsible for compliance with the generator requirements. EPA reserves the right to enforce its requirements against any and all persons, jointly and severally, who are "generators." However, EPA has stated that it will initially look to the operator of the central facility where hazardous waste generated in transport vehicles or vessels is removed to perform the generator duties. Otherwise, EPA will look to the operator of the vehicle or vessel to assume the responsibilities of the generator. Given this situation, transporters would be well advised to clearly define their responsibilities in writing with the owners of transported products and the operators of central removal facilities to determine who will perform the generator duties.

It is important to remember that when two or more persons qualify as generators, the person who performs the duties of a generator must have and use an EPA Identification Number for each site at which hazardous wastes are removed from a tank, vehicle, vessel or pipeline. If removal takes place at several sites, and the transporter has assumed the generator duties, he must have and use a separate EPA Identification Number for each site. All the other generator duties discussed in Chapter 4 of this Handbook, including the 90-day accumulation provisions of 40 CFR 262.34, would also be applicable to the transporter.

Finally, it is also possible for transporters to become subject to the requirements for T/S/D facilities if hazardous wastes are treated or stored by the transporter. This may occur, for example, after cleanup of an accidental spill of hazardous waste during transport, a situation which is discussed more fully in Section 4.4.1 below.

EPA has made it clear that a transporter who holds a hazardous waste for a short period of time at a transfer facility should not be considered to be storing hazardous waste, and should not be required to obtain a RCRA permit or qualify for interim status.[29] Transporters may hold hazardous waste in the course of transportation for up to ten days at a transfer facility if the waste is accompanied by a manifest and remains in containers which meet the DOT packaging requirements. EPA has defined a "transfer facility" to mean:

> Any transportation related facility including loading docks, parking areas, storage areas, and other similar areas where shipments of hazardous waste are held during the normal course of transportation.[30]

If, however, a transporter uses his vehicle or vessel to actually store or treat hazardous waste, the Part 264 and 265 regulations may apply. In the special case of the transporter who uses his vehicle to neutralize corrosive hazardous waste prior to shipment, EPA has proposed to allow such a transporter to obtain a permit-by-rule without the need to apply for an individual RCRA permit if certain performance standards are met.[31]

4.4 Hazardous Waste Discharges

The regulations provide that if an accidental or intentional discharge of a hazardous waste occurs during transportation, the transporter is responsible for its cleanup. This is a requirement which DOT does not have authority to impose under the HMTA. A hazardous waste discharge is defined as the "accidental or intentional spilling, leaking, pumping, pouring, emitting, emptying

---

[29]   40 CFR 263.12, 264.1(g)(9), 265.1(c)(12), 270.1(c)(2)(vi).

[30]   40 CFR 260.10, 270.2.

[31]   40 CFR Part 266 (proposed), 45 Fed. Reg. 76076 (November 17, 1980).

or dumping of hazardous waste into or on any land or water."[32] Note that this definition is consistent with the regulations promulgated pursuant to Section 311 of the Clean Water Act concerning discharges of hazardous substances into navigable waters.[33] The RCRA definition applicable to transporters, however, extends to discharges on land as well as water.

In the event of a discharge, the transporter must take immediate action to protect human health and the environment, including treatment or containment of the spill and notification of local police and fire departments. Local authorities at the scene may temporarily suspend certain RCRA requirements while the emergency exists so that hazardous wastes may be removed by transporters without EPA Identification Numbers and without the need to prepare a manifest.[34]

A transporter may technically become a treater or storer of hazardous waste pursuant to his obligation to clean up an accidental or intentional spill. For example, he may use an absorption or neutralization technique to treat the spill or he may attempt to dike or otherwise contain the spilled materials.

EPA has recognized that transporters are not likely to have or want to obtain a RCRA permit to treat or store a discharge of hazardous wastes. Therefore, EPA has exempted the immediate containment and treatment activities taken in response to a discharge from the Part 264 and 265 regulations governing treatment and storage, and the Part 270 regulations dealing with RCRA permits and interim status.[35] Subsequent storage and disposal of the

---

32   40 CFR 260.10.

33   The Section 311 regulations appear at 40 CFR Parts 116-117.

34   40 CFR 263.30(b).

35   40 CFR 264.1(g)(8), 265.1(c)(11), 270.1(c)(3).

spilled materials or residue, however, fall outside the exemption. For this purpose an emergency permit might be available. (See Chapter 9 of this Handbook).

EPA has also established a special procedure for rapid issuance of EPA Identification Numbers in connection with spills and other unanticipated events.[36] A transporter who has not obtained an EPA Identification Number may obtain one over the telephone in an emergency by calling the EPA Regional Administrator, who will then send a notification form that must be filled out and returned within ten days confirming the Identification Number.

EPA has specifically incorporated DOT's discharge reporting requirements into the RCRA regulations.[37] The DOT regulations identify the situations in which telephone reporting of a discharge and the filing of a written report are required. Telephone reporting is required for incidents in which, as a direct result of hazardous materials:

(1) a person is killed;

(2) a person receives injuries requiring his hospitalization;

(3) estimated carrier or other property damage exceeds $50,000;

(4) fire, breakage, spillage, or suspected contamination occurs involving shipment of radioactive materials;

(5) fire, breakage, spillage, or suspected contamination occurs involving shipment of etiologic agents; or

---

[36]   45 Fed. Reg. 85022 (December 24, 1980).

[37]   45 CFR 263.30; see 49 CFR 171.15 and 171.16.

(6)   a continuing danger to life exists at the
       scene of the incident.[38]

The number to call is that of the National Response Center which
is 800-424-8802 or 202-426-2675. Notice involving etiologic
agents may alternatively be given to the Center for Disease Control in Georgia at 404-633-5313.

The caller will be expected to give the following information:

a.   name;

b.   name and address of carrier;

c.   phone number at the scene;

d.   date, time and location of incident;

e.   extent of injuries, if any;

f.   classification, name, and quantity of
     hazardous materials involved, if avail-
     able; and

g.   whether a continuing danger to life
     exists at the scene.[39]

Follow-up written reports must be filed with DOT in duplicate on
DOT Form F 5800.1 with a copy of the manifest attached to the
report.[40] Those reports should be submitted to: Information Systems Manager, Research and Special Programs Administration,
Department of Transportation, Washington, D.C. 20590. They are
required to be filed within 30 days of the incident.[41]

---

[38]   49 CFR 171.15(a).

[39]   49 CFR 171.15(b).

[40]   40 CFR 171.16(a).

[41]   Id.

Written reports are also required in the case of an unintentional release of hazardous materials from a package (including a tank) or the discharge of any quantity of hazardous waste during transportation.[42] The report must include an estimate of the quantity of waste removed from the scene, the name and address of the facility to which it was taken, the manner of disposition of any unremoved waste, and, of course, a copy of the manifest.[43]

4.5 DOT Hazardous Materials Regulations

As noted above, RCRA requires that EPA's regulations be consistent with DOT regulations under the Hazardous Materials Transportation Act. Therefore, EPA has specifically incorporated by reference the DOT regulations adopted under that Act.[44] These are codified at 49 CFR Parts 171-180. DOT's HMTA regulations fully encompass the transportation of hazardous waste. According to the DOT regulations, hazardous waste is any material subject to the manifest requirements of EPA's RCRA regulations.[45] This should assure consistency of coverage under the two programs.

In general, the DOT regulations cover packaging and labeling, proper identification of hazardous materials, basic vehicle safety, and driver training and qualification standards. The specific requirements for labeling, marking, placarding and the use of proper containers for hazardous waste are the same as those which apply to other hazardous materials.[46]

---

[42]   Id.

[43]   Id.

[44]   40 CFR 263.10(a).

[45]   49 CFR § 171.18.

[46]   49 CFR Parts 172, 173, 178 and 179.

The agency within DOT which is responsible for implementing and administering HMTA is the Research and Special Programs Administration ("RSPA"). Enforcement is split, depending on the mode of transportation, among the Federal Highway Administration, Federal Aviation Administration, Federal Railroad Administration, and the Coast Guard. RSPA has enforcement authority with respect to intermodal shipments and suppliers of packaging.

In Docket No. HM-181, RSPA issued a sweeping revision to its hazardous materials regulations under the title of "Performance-Oriented Packaging Standards." The final rule, which was issued on December 21, 1990, 55 Fed. Reg. 52402, and revised on December 20, 1991, 56 Fed. Reg. 66124, is intended to simplify and reduce the volume of regulation with respect to packaging standards as well as hazard communication and classification requirements. The revisions are based on the recommendations of the United Nations Committee of Experts on the Transport of Dangerous Goods. Among the major features of the final rule are the elimination of approximately 100 packaging specifications and their replacement by 20 performance test criteria for packaging.[47] Hazard class definitions and hazardous materials descriptions are aligned with the U.N. Recommendations and use the same numerical nomenclature.[48]

The final rule became effective on October 1, 1991. However, RSPA has provided several transition periods for various portions of the rule. A five year transition (until October 1, 1996) is permitted for continued use of DOT specification packaging which would otherwise be rendered obsolete by the rule, other than those

---

[47]   49 CFR Part 178, Subpart L (1992).

[48]   49 CFR Part 173, § 172.101 (1992).

for materials that are poisonous by inhalation.[49] A three year period is provided for continued manufacture of those packagings which will be rendered obsolete by the final rule, and a two year period is provided for other provisions of the final rule, such as classification, hazard communication, and packaging changes for materials poisonous by inhalation.[50] Shippers and transporters who are prepared to implement the new provisions earlier may elect to comply with either the applicable old requirements or the new requirements.[51]

Thus, during the transition period, transporters may receive and deliver shipments which comply with either set of regulations. RSPA urges that the 1990 edition of 49 CFR be retained for this reason. Shippers must, however, be consistent. If the material is described on the shipping paper in accordance with the 1990 CFR, then the package markings, labels and placards must also conform to the 1990 CFR. If the material is described on the shipping paper in accordance with the new requirements, then package markings, labels and placards must also conform to the new requirements.[52]

An important first step for the shipper of hazardous waste is to properly identify and classify the substances involved. DOT's Hazardous Materials Tables[53] provide the proper shipping names for hazardous materials, their hazard classes, and identification numbers, as well as a road map to the relevant packaging and labeling provisions in the regulations.

---

[49]   49 CFR § 171.14 (1992).

[50]   Id.

[51]   Id.

[52]   49 CFR § 171.14(c)(3) (1992).

[53]   49 CFR Part 172.

The generator or person who offers the substance for transportation is responsible for determining its composition and characteristics and for properly classifying it.

RSPA has established broad hazard classes or groupings of hazardous materials. There were 13 such classes under the old regulations. Under the new regulations there are 9 basic categories. These include various types of explosives; flammable, compressed and poisonous gases; flammable liquids and spontaneously combustible materials; oxidizers and organic peroxides; poisonous material; infectious substances; radioactive materials; and corrosive materials.[54]

The old regulations also contained five categories of "Other Regulated Material (ORM)" which were catch-all categories containing substances not otherwise regulated as hazardous materials, but were designated as such by EPA pursuant to RCRA or the Clean Water Act.[55] The categories used to be ORM-A, ORM-B, ORM-C, ORM-D, and ORM-E. A hazardous waste for which there is no specific appropriate entry in the Hazardous Materials Table and which does not meet a specific DOT hazard classification used to be classified ORM-E. That class was eliminated by the new regulations and such hazardous waste is now classed as miscellaneous Class 9 and the proper shipping name is "Hazardous Waste Liquid (or solid) n.o.s." where "n.o.s" refers to "not otherwise specified." See 55 Fed. Reg. 52438-39. The only ORM class retained by the new regulations is ORM-D, which are materials such as a consumer commodity. Although otherwise subject to the hazardous materials regulations, ORM-D materials present a limited hazard during transportation because

---

[54]   49 CFR Part 173, Subparts C and D (1992). A basic description of each hazard class and division is provided at 49 CFR § 173.2.

[55]   49 CFR Part 173, Subparts J-O (1990).

of their form, quantity and packaging.[56] Consumer quantities are generally packaged for retail sale in packages which do not exceed 66 pounds gross weight.

4.5.1 Shipping Paper

Hazardous materials which are offered for transportation must be properly described on a shipping paper, which must contain the information required by 49 CFR Part 172, Subpart C.[57] DOT prescribes no particular format for shipping papers, except that shipments of hazardous waste must be accompanied by the "Uniform Hazardous Waste Manifest."[58] The proper shipping name, hazard class, and identification number (preceded either by "UN" or "NA" as appropriate) must appear on the shipping paper. They are obtained from the Hazardous Materials Table. In the case of hazardous wastes, the word "waste" must precede the shipping name -- e.g.: "Waste Acetyl Chloride, Flammable Liquid, UN-1717."[59] Another important part of the description is, of course, the number of containers and the total quantity. Important additional description requirements are found at 49 CFR § 172.203. For example, special requirements apply to "hazardous substances." The letters "RQ" must appear either before or after the basic description. If the proper shipping name does not identify the hazardous substance by name, then one of the following must be indicated in parentheses immediately following the shipping name:

---

[56]   49 CFR § 173.144 (1992).

[57]   See 49 app. U.S.C. § 1804(g).

[58]   49 CFR § 172.205.

[59]   49 CFR § 172.101(c)(9).

    -- the name of the hazardous substance as shown in the appendix to § 172.101;

    -- for waste streams, the waste stream number assigned by EPA; or

    -- for wastes which exhibit EPA characteristics of ignitability, corrosivity, reactivity, or EP toxicity, the letters "EPA" followed by the appropriate characteristic or by the EPA "D" number.[60]

Thus, e.g. -- "RQ, Allyl alcohol, 6.1 UN 1098, I," where "G.1" is the hazard class and division, "UN 1098" is the United National identification number, and "I" is the packing group. As described below, the new regulations establish three packing groups: I, II, III. Materials posing the greatest hazard are assigned to Packing Group I. Each of the elements of the description will be found in the Hazardous Materials table entry for the particular substance. Other examples:

"RQ Waste Flammable Liquid, n.o.s., UN 1993, (EPA Ignitability)."

"RQ Waste Benzine, Flammable Liquid, UN 1115, "DOO1""

Generators of hazardous waste must certify that the waste is properly and accurately described, packaged, marked, and labeled and in proper condition for transport.[61] The Hazardous Waste Manifest provides the appropriate language.

---

[60] 49 CFR § 172.203(c).

[61] 49 CFR § 172.204. All shippers of hazardous materials must so certify.

Shippers of hazardous materials must have emergency response information immediately available at all times that the hazardous material is present. This information must be either on a shipping paper or a document that includes both the basic description and technical name of the hazardous material.[62]

4.5.2   Packaging

The Hazardous Materials Table should also be consulted to determine the proper packaging for the hazardous material. As noted above, the final rule promulgated by RSPA in Docket No. HM-181 comprehensively revises the Hazardous Materials Regulations to provide better hazard classification, hazard communication, and "performance-oriented" packaging standards, to promote innovations in packaging, and to facilitate international commerce. Many of the packaging requirements currently in the regulations are affected. Approximately 100 packaging specifications for non-bulk packaging in Part 178 of the old regulations are eliminated and replaced by 20 performance test criteria that will ultimately have to be met by different basic types of packaging, such as metal drums and plywood boxes. This eliminates the need for exemptions. Under the old regulations, shipments often moved in packaging authorized under a specific DOT exemption.[63].

The Table will indicate, for each type of material, the section or sections of 49 CFR Part 173 which prescribe the specific packaging requirements and any exceptions which apply to that material. Part 178 of the regulations provides detailed specifications for every type of shipping container. Shippers

---

[62]   49 CFR Part 172 Subpart G.

[63]   In such situations the shipping paper must bear the notation "DOT-E" followed by the exemption number -- e.g., "DOT-E4648".

must examine containers before offering them for transportation to insure that they still meet specifications, particularly if a container is being reused.

Under the new regulations, detailed materials specifications are not required. Packaging need only pass certain performance tests and be certified by its manufacturer. The new standards provide general requirements for materials, construction, and maximum capacity.[64] In addition to these general construction requirements, the strength and integrity of the packaging must be demonstrated by a series of performance tests which the packaging must either pass or be capable of passing before it can be authorized for use in transporting hazardous materials.[65] Authorization is indicated by markings that are to be placed on the packaging.

Materials listed in the Hazardous Materials Table are assigned to one of three packing groups. Packing Group I is for materials which pose the greatest hazard. Packaging for materials in this group must achieve more demanding test results. Packing Group III is for materials posing the least hazard. Packaging must pass some or all of the following types of tests: drop tests,[66] leakproofness test,[67] hydrostatic pressure test,[68] stacking test,[69] cooperage test,[70] and vibration test.[71] The new

---

[64] 49 CFR Part 178, Subpart L.

[65] 49 CFR Part 178, Subpart M.

[66] 49 CFR § 178.603.

[67] Id. § 178.604.

[68] Id. § 178.605.

[69] Id. § 178.606.

[70] Id. § 178.607.

[71] Id. § 178.608.

regulations specifically provide for periodic retesting by the manufacturer.[72] The manufacturer must mark every package with the U.N. symbol, an identification code which indicates the type of packaging and material of construction, the packing group, the year of manufacture, the materials for which it is intended, and the name and address of the manufacturer.[73] Shippers are responsible for selecting appropriate packaging.

Containers which are used more than once must continue to comply in all respects (including closure and cushioning materials) with the requirements of the regulations.[74] Any weak, broken, or deteriorated parts must be replaced. Manufacturers' markings must always be legible. Certain steel drums may be reused for shipments of flammable liquids, flammable solids, organic peroxides, oxidizers, poisons, radioactive materials, and corrosive materials only if they have been reconditioned by a reconditioner who is registered with DOT, tested with air pressure and water, and properly marked.[75]

4.5.3   Marking

Every package or container of a hazardous material must be marked as prescribed in 49 CFR Part 172, Subpart D. This includes the proper shipping name, identification number, the words "Inhalation Hazard" in the case of certain poisons[76] and in some

---

[72]   Id. § 178.601(e).

[73]   Id. § 178.503.

[74]   49 CFR § 173.28.

[75]   49 CFR § 173.28(m).

[76]   49 CFR §§ 172.301(a), 172.313.

instances the name and address of the consignee or consignor.[77] Specific requirements apply to liquid hazardous materials[78] and hazardous substances.[79] Other Regulated Materials must be marked with the appropriate ORM designation within a rectangle.[80]

Markings must be durable and in English, may be printed either on the package or a tag, must be displayed on a background of sharply contrasting color, and must be located away from other markings, such a advertising, which could obscure their effectiveness.[81] Under the 1990 amendments to HMTA, it is unlawful to represent, by marking or otherwise, that a hazardous material is present in a package if that hazardous material is not present, or to alter or remove any required marking.[82]

Finally, each vehicle transporting hazardous waste for which a manifest is required must be marked as follows:

Private Carrier[83] -- Name and business address of carrier,
Motor carrier identification number.
(Both sides of vehicle.)

ICC Carrier[84] ------ Company name,
ICC Docket Number.

---

[77]   49 CFR § 172.301(d).

[78]   49 CFR § 172.312.

[79]   49 CFR § 172.324.

[80]   49 CFR § 172.316.

[81]   49 CFR § 172.304.

[82]   49 app. U.S.C. § 1804(e), (f).

[83]   49 CFR § 390.21.

[84]   49 CFR § 1058.2.

4.5.4 Labels

Packages containing hazardous materials must bear the label specified for that material in column 6 of the Hazardous Materials Table. The labels, which are diamond-shaped graphics containing the hazard class name, class or division number, and a pictorial representation, are found at 49 CFR Part 172, Subpart E. Labels must be affixed near the shipping name.[85] Packages containing a hazardous material that meets the definition of more than one hazard class must be labeled for each class.[86]

4.5.5 Placards

Under certain circumstances, vehicles which transport hazardous materials must be placarded on both sides and at both ends. Placards are similar in appearance to labels. The regulations governing their use appear at 49 CFR Part 172, Subpart F.

In general, vehicles which contain any quantity of the following hazardous materials must be appropriately placarded: Class A or Class B Explosives (Explosives 1.1, 1.2, 1.3 under the new regulations), Poison A (Poison Gas 2.3 under the new regulations), Flammable Solids (Dangerous When Wet category 4.3 under the new regulations), Inhalation Hazards (category 6.1) Radioactive Materials requiring a yellow III label.[87]

Vehicles which contain 1,001 pounds or more aggregate gross weight of all other categories of hazardous materials, materials

---

[85] 49 CFR § 172.406.

[86] 49 CFR §§ 172.402(a), 172.404.

[87] 49 CFR § 172.504 (Table 1).

must also be appropriately placarded.[88] The only exceptions are ORM-D materials and infectious substances or etiologic agents.[89]

As with all of the requirements described above, the regulations should be consulted for special requirements and exceptions.

4.5.6   Highway Requirements

Finally, 49 CFR Part 177 contains additional requirements applicable to the acceptance and transportation of hazardous materials by motor vehicle.[90] In general, containers must be secured against movement and braced to prevent friction.[91] Poisons may not be carried with foodstuffs.[92] Some hazardous materials cannot be loaded, transported, or stored together. Section 177.848 of the regulations contains a "Segregation and Separation Chart" which must be consulted when cargoes of hazardous materials are mixed. For example, Corrosive Liquids cannot be transported with Flammable Solids.

---

[88]   49 CFR § 172.504 (Table 2).

[89]   Id.

[90]   Part 174 provides similar requirements for carriage by rail, Part 175 for carriage by aircraft, and Part 176 for carriage by vessel.

[91]   49 CFR § 177.834.

[92]   49 CFR § 177.841(e). On November 3, 1990, the President signed the Sanitary Food Transportation Act of 1990, Pub. L. No. 101-500, 49 app. U.S.C. §§ 2801 et seq., which requires DOT to issue regulations which will ensure that food, food additives, and cosmetics are not made unsafe by certain transportation practices, including the unsanitary backhauling of waste in vehicles used to carry food, the alternate carriage of food substances and chemicals in the same tanker truck, and the use of vehicles which carry food and consumer items to backhaul asbestos and hazardous waste. See 56 Fed. Reg. 6934 (Feb. 20, 1991).

Hazardous materials must be transported without unnecessary delay. If they cannot be delivered within 48 hours of arrival at their destination, they must be promptly disposed of by return to the shipper, by appropriate storage, by sale, or, when necessary for safety, by destruction.[93]

Many of these regulations are also incorporated into the RCRA regulations pertaining to generators.[94] For example, generators are required to mark hazardous waste in accordance with the above-described DOT Hazardous Materials Table which sets out the proper shipping name, hazard class, and the requirements to pack materials in appropriate containers.

4.6 Motor Carrier Safety Act of 1984

Transporters of hazardous waste are also subject to all of the Federal Motor Carrier Safety Regulations which DOT has adopted under the Motor Carrier Safety Act of 1984 ("MCSA"), 49 U.S.C. Sections 2501 et seq.[95] The Act was passed in order to "promote the safe operation of commercial motor vehicles" as well as to protect the safety of the drivers of those vehicles and is designed to reaffirm the scope of DOT's authority to regulate safety in this area.[96] It applies to all commercial motor vehicles, including those that transport hazardous waste.

These regulations contain alternative requirements relating to both the transport vehicle and the driver. There are detailed specifications for vehicle parts and accessories, including lighting devices, brakes, glazing and windows, fuel systems, tires,

---

[93]   49 CFR § 177.853.

[94]   40 CFR Part 262.

[95]   49 CFR 177.804, 49 CFR Parts 390 through 397.

[96]   S. Rep. No. 424 at 9, 98th Cong., 2d Sess. 1984.

horns, and other components.[97] There are requirements governing inspection, repair, and maintenance,[98] and there are special driving and parking rules which apply to the transportation of hazardous materials.[99]

Rules which relate to drivers establish minimum qualifications for such persons, including physical qualifications, background and character, and tests and examinations.[100] Subpart H of Part 391 prescribes controlled substances testing requirements to detect and deter the use by drivers of such substances as marijuana, cocaine, opiates, amphetamines and phencyclidine (PCP). Drivers covered by this program include those who operate vehicles which have a gross vehicle weight rating or gross combination weight rating of 26,001 or more pounds and drivers who operate vehicles which transport hazardous materials in a quantity requiring placarding, regardless of the size of the vehicle.[101]

On December 15, 1992, DOT issued a comprehensive series of proposed rules which were required under the Omnibus Transportation Employee Testing Act of 1991, Pub. L. 102-143, Title V, 105 Stat. 917, 952 (1991). 57 Fed. Reg. 59767 (Dec. 15, 1992). Among other things, that Act directs DOT to establish a program of alcohol testing for drivers who operate commercial motor vehicles and to apply that program, as well as the Subpart H drug testing requirements, to drivers and employers who operate in intrastate commerce. Commercial motor vehicles are defined to include

---

[97] 49 CFR Part 393.

[98] 49 CFR Part 396.

[99] 49 CFR Part 397.

[100] 49 CFR Part 391.

[101] 49 CFR §§ 391.81, 391.85.

vehicles which exceed 26,000 pounds GVWR and vehicles of any size which transport hazardous materials in a quantity or of a type requiring placarding. The proposed rule would establish a new Part 382 to Title 49 of the CFR, "Controlled Substances and Alcohol Use and Testing." Essentially, any driver who must obtain a commercial driver's license will be subject to drug and alcohol testing.

Other rules relating to drivers include standards for the driving of vehicles, stopping, fueling, the use of lamps,[102] rules governing the reporting of accidents,[103] and rules which provide for the monitoring and control of a driver's hours of service.[104] The Federal Highway Administration has an active inspection program at hazardous waste transporter facilities and on the highway to ensure compliance with the safety regulations.

Finally, the 1990 amendments to HMTA require that DOT establish federal standards and procedures that state would be required to follow if they establish, maintain or enforce highway routing designations for the highway transportation of nonradioactive hazardous materials.[105] The purpose is to ensure that such materials are moved safely and that commerce is not burdened by restrictive, uncoordinated or conflicting local requirements. These highway routing standards were proposed by the Federal Highway Administration on August 31, 1992, 57 Fed. Reg. 39522 (Aug. 31, 1992). For example, the proposed regulation would prevent local jurisdictions from imposing unreasonable routes or delays by prohibiting a forced deviation of over 100 miles from

---

[102]   49 CFR Part 392.

[103]   49 CFR Part 394.

[104]   49 CFR Part 395.

[105]   49 app. U.S.C. § 1804(b), (c).

the most direct route or an increase in trip length by more than 25%, whichever is shorter.[106] The amendments also prohibit local jurisdictions from levying fees which are intended to discourage hazardous materials tranportation through their region.[107]

4.7   Enforcement by EPA and DOT

As the foregoing discussion reflects, transporters are cautioned by EPA that they are subject to both DOT and EPA enforcement for potential violations of either set of regulations. EPA and DOT have executed a Memorandum of Understanding ("MOU") which delineates their respective compliance monitoring and enforcement responsibilities.[108]

Under the terms of the MOU, EPA is primarily responsible for monitoring compliance by generators and T/S/D facilities with the RCRA requirements. Meanwhile, DOT conducts an ongoing program of inspections of transporters to monitor their compliance with the HMTA regulations. DOT will immediately advise EPA of "any possible" violations of the RCRA transporter regulations so that EPA can take enforcement action. In addition, EPA intends to bring enforcement actions against transporters when the transportation of hazardous wastes is ancillary to treatment, storage or disposal of such wastes, such as the case of the "midnight dumper." When a transporter has allegedly violated both the HMTA and RCRA regulations, the MOU provides that one agency will "not normally" initiate an enforcement action if the other agency has already done so. In addition, the MOU provides for the extensive

---

[106]   57 Fed. Reg. at 39525.

[107]   49 app. U.S.C. § 1811(b).

[108]   45 Fed. Reg. 51645 (August 4, 1980).

exchange of information and compliance data between the two Agencies, including the results of inspections and investigations.

Transporters can thus expect that EPA and DOT will attempt to coordinate their inspection and enforcement efforts, particularly at the regional level, to obtain compliance with both the RCRA and HMTA regulations.

The enforcement options available under RCRA include compliance orders, civil penalties, injunctions, and criminal actions.[109] The statute provides criminal penalties for those who "knowingly" violate RCRA and for the more serious offense of "knowing endangerment," which is committed by a person who knowingly transports hazardous waste in violation of RCRA and who knows, at the time, that such transportation "places another person in imminent danger of death or serious bodily injury."[110]

Similarly, DOT's enforcement options include compliance orders,[111] civil actions against persons who "knowingly" violate the HMTA, criminal actions against persons who "knowingly" tamper with any marking, label, placard, description, package, container, or vehicle, or who "willfully" violates any other provision of the HMTA or DOT's regulations,[112] and "imminent hazard" orders or injunctions.[113] The 1990 amendments to HMTA provide that a person acts "knowingly" of such person has actual knowledge of the facts that you rise to the violation or if a reasonable person acting in the circumstances and exercising due cause would have been knowledge. 49 app. U.S.C. § 1809(a)(3).

---

[109] 42 U.S.C. § 6928.

[110] 42 U.S.C. § 6928(d), (e).

[111] 49 app. U.S.C. § 1808(a).

[112] 49 app. U.S.C. § 1809.

[113] 49 app. U.S.C. § 1810.

CHAPTER 5

THE REGULATION OF TREATMENT, STORAGE,
AND DISPOSAL (T/S/D) FACILITIES

By far the most detailed and complex regulations implementing
the RCRA hazardous waste program are the requirements imposed on
owners and operators (referred to collectively as "operators"
herein) of T/S/D facilities under RCRA Section 3004.[1] T/S/D
facilities range from the typical generator with a hazardous waste
drum storage area to the large, complex hazardous waste landfill.
EPA estimates that 80 percent of all generators also treat, store,
or dispose of their hazardous wastes and thus qualify as T/S/D
facilities. Over 30,000 T/S/D facilities notified EPA in 1980
that they would be subject to RCRA Section 3004 regulation.

As of 1989, there were only 3,078 T/S/D facilities -- half of
which were permitted only to store hazardous waste.[2] Of the 196.5
million tons of hazardous waste managed by T/S/D facilities in
1989, the predominant method of waste management was biological,
physical or chemical treatment, accounting for 76 percent of the
total. Underground injection wells (14%), landfills (1.2%), and
incineration (0.7%) were less often used as methods of hazardous
waste management. The vast majority of hazardous waste was
managed on-site. However, 8 million tons were shipped off-site to
484 T/S/D facilities, with 25 percent being disposed of in
landfills.

---

[1] "Owner" is defined as "the person who owns a facility" and
"operator" is "the person responsible for the overall operation of a facility." 40 CFR 260.10. In many cases the owner
of a T/S/D facility will not be the operator. EPA has stated,
however, that it deems owners and operators to be jointly and
severally responsible for compliance with RCRA Section 3004,
regardless of any arrangement existing between an owner and an
operator. See 45 Fed. Reg. 33169-70.

[2] U.S. EPA, National Biennial RCRA Hazardous Waste Report, 1989
(February 1993).

The term "T/S/D" is commonly used to refer to the three different hazardous waste management activities that are regulated
under RCRA Section 3004, and which thus require a permit under
RCRA Section 3005. All persons who handle a hazardous waste must
carefully consider the broad definitions of "treatment", "storage", and "disposal" to determine the applicability of RCRA Sections 3004 and 3005 and the implementing regulations.

5.1 Identification of T/S/D Facilities

A facility will be regulated as a "treatment" facility with
respect to the hazardous waste it handles if the operator utilizes:

> any method, technique, or process, including
> neutralization, designed to change the physical,
> chemical, or biological character or composition
> of any hazardous waste so as to neutralize such
> waste, or so as to recover energy or material
> resources from the waste, or so as to render
> such waste non-hazardous, or less hazardous;
> safer to transport, store or dispose of; or
> amenable for recovery, amenable for storage, or
> reduced in volume.[3]

This definition is obviously very broad, and will cover even the
most commonplace treatment activities such as neutralizing or dewatering hazardous wastes.

A facility will be regulated as a "storage" facility if it
engages in:

> the holding of hazardous waste for a temporary
> period, at the end of which the hazardous waste
> is treated, disposed of, or stored elsewhere.[4]

---

[3] 40 CFR 260.10. EPA does not include within the scope of
"treatment" for permitting and Part 264 purposes the combining
of wastes by a generator in an accumulation tank. See 515
Fed. Reg. 10146, 10168 (March 24, 1986), and 45 Fed. Reg.
72025 (Oct. 30, 1980).

[4] 40 CFR 260.10.

A facility will be regulated as a "disposal" facility if the
facility is used for:

> the discharge, deposit, injection, dumping,
> spilling, leaking, or placing of any solid waste
> or hazardous waste into or on any land or water
> so that such solid waste or hazardous waste or
> any constituent thereof may enter the environ-
> ment or be emitted into the air or discharged
> into any waters, including groundwaters.[5]

The term "facility" refers to "all contiguous land, and structures, other appurtenances, and improvements on the land."[6] The
narrower term "disposal facility" is defined as "a facility or
part of a facility at which hazardous waste is intentionally
placed into or on any land or water, and at which waste will
remain after closure."[7] This distinction is important. EPA
wanted to include unintentional acts such as spills in the definition of "disposal" in order to have jurisdiction over any facility
where such unintentional disposal and potential environmental harm
may occur.   It would be unworkable to require a permit for every
facility where an unintentional act constituting "disposal" might
occur. So, permits are required under RCRA Section 3005 for
"disposal facilities" rather than for "facilities" in general.

5.2 The RCRA Section 3004 Statutory Requirements for T/S/D Facilities

RCRA Section 3004 requires EPA to promulgate regulations
applicable to T/S/D facilities establishing such performance standards as may be necessary to protect human health and the environment. EPA is authorized to establish separate requirements for
new and existing facilities when appropriate. The standards promulgated under RCRA Section 3004 must include, but need not be
limited to, requirements respecting:

---

[5] Id.

[6] Id.

[7] Id. [emphasis added].

(1) maintenance of records of all hazardous wastes handled by the facility;

(2) reporting, monitoring, inspection, and compliance with the manifest system;

(3) operating methods, techniques, and practices for treating, storing, or disposing of hazardous wastes;

(4) location, design, and construction of the facility;

(5) contingency plans for unanticipated damage from hazardous waste treatment, storage, or disposal;

(6) maintenance and operation of the facility and such additional qualifications as to ownership, continuity of operations, training of personnel, and financial responsibility as may be desirable; and

(7) compliance with the requirements of RCRA Section 3005 relating to permits for T/S/D facilities.

In the 1984 Amendments, Congress extensively amended and added to Section 3004 to impose directly, or to require EPA to adopt, many additional requirements applicable to T/S/D facilities. Most of these new requirements apply to T/S/D facilities engaged in the land disposal of hazardous waste. These amendments are technical in nature and are discussed in detail in those portions of Chapter 7 on the specific standards for land disposal facilities.[8]

5.3 EPA's Two-Prong Approach To Regulating T/S/D Facilities

RCRA Section 3005 establishes initially two categories of T/S/D facilities: (1) interim status facilities that do not need individually-issued permits to continue operating while EPA puts

_____

[8] The 1984 Amendments, and particularly the amendments to RCRA § 3004 affecting land disposal of hazardous wastes, are also summarized in Chapter 1 of this Handbook.

the RCRA permit scheme in place; and (2) <u>permitted facilities</u> which include new T/S/D facilities and existing facilities that did not qualify for interim status, both of which must first obtain RCRA permits to begin or continue operations.

To qualify for interim status, a facility must satisfy the three-part statutory test in RCRA Section 3005(e) of:

> (1) being in existence on November 19, 1980 (or on the date a statutory change first makes the facility subject to RCRA);
>
> (2) notifying EPA pursuant to RCRA Section 3010(a) of its hazardous waste management activities; and
>
> (3) filing an application for a T/S/D facility permit.

As explained in Chapter 8 of this Handbook on RCRA permits, interim status facilities may be lawfully operated after November 19, 1980, even though a RCRA permit has not been issued to the facility.[9]

In 1980, EPA decided that many of the substantive standards issued under RCRA Section 3004 should be enforceable against interim status T/S/D facilities in order to protect human health and the environment during the many years it may take to issue a final RCRA permit to a facility. Dissatisfied with the efficacy of these standards and the slow pace of permitting, Congress in the 1984 Amendments imposed "minimum technological requirements" on interim status land disposal facilities, as described in Chapter 6. Congress also required EPA to process all permits for interim status T/S/D facilities on a specific timetable. Interim status for facilities not permitted by the statutory deadlines will lapse, unless a Part B application is timely filed.[10]

All other T/S/D facilities, including new facilities that were not "in existence" on November 19, 1980, and facilities that have

___

[9]   40 CFR 265.1(b).

[10] See discussion in Chapter 8, <u>infra</u>.

otherwise failed to qualify for interim status must obtain a site-specific RCRA permit. The operators of these facilities may not lawfully commence or continue hazardous waste treatment, storage or disposal activities until such time as the facility receives an effective RCRA permit.[11] They must then comply with the sometimes more extensive technical standards for permitted facilities, discussed in this chapter and Chapter 6.

5.3.1 Historical Implementation of the Program

On May 19, 1980, EPA promulgated the regulations that established most of the interim status requirements, as well as many of the general facility standards applicable during permanent status.[12] EPA designated this first set of T/S/D facility regulations as Phase I standards. They took effect on November 19, 1980. A second major set of T/S/D facility standards was promulgated on January 12, 1981, which included closure requirements, post-closure requirements and financial responsibility rules for interim status facilities.[13] In addition, a large portion of the Phase II technical regulations for permitted facilities were promulgated including requirements on the location of facilities, closure and post-closure care, financial requirements, use and management of containers and storage and treatment of hazardous

---

[11] RCRA § 3005(a). EPA has interpreted its authority under RCRA Section 3005 to include issuance of permits-by-rule. See 40 CFR 270.60. Permits-by-rule, which are granted only to certain types of T/S/D facilities are discussed in Chapter 8 of this Handbook.

[12] 45 Fed. Reg. 33066-258 (May 19, 1980), now codified at 40 CFR Part 265.

[13] 46 Fed. Reg. 2875-92 (January 12, 1981), codified at 40 CFR Part 265, Subparts G and H.

wastes in tanks, surface impoundments and waste piles.[14] On January 23, 1981, EPA also promulgated Phase II technical standards for incinerators.[15]

The technical standards for land disposal facilities were the most difficult for EPA to develop. On February 13, 1981, EPA issued so called "temporary" standards in Part 267 so that RCRA permits could be written for the first time for new land disposal facilities.[16] EPA, however, was pressed in a lawsuit filed by environmental groups to issue final design and operating standards for land disposal facilities.[17] Finally, on July 26, 1982, EPA complied with a court-ordered deadline and issued the Phase II technical standards that apply to all new and existing landfills, surface impoundments, waste piles, and land treatment units that are used to treat, store, or dispose of hazardous wastes.[18] These Phase II regulations became effective on January 26, 1983. As modified by the 1984 Amendments and the new implementing regulations EPA is required to issue, the Phase II regulations serve as the basis for site-specific RCRA permits issued to T/S/D facilities, including both new facilities and interim status facilities that intend to continue operations after their interim status has ended.

---

[14] 46 Fed. Reg. 2847-75 (January 12, 1981), codified at 40 CFR Part 264, Subparts B through L.

[15] 46 Fed. Reg. 7666-90 (January 23, 1981), codified at 40 CFR Part 264, Subpart O.

[16] 46 Fed. Reg. 12429 (February 13, 1981), codified at 40 CFR Part 267 (superseded).

[17] State ex rel. Scott v. Gorsuch, 530 F.Supp. 337, aff'd, 684 F.2d 1033 (1982).

[18] 47 Fed. Reg. 32274 (July 26, 1982).

5.3.2 Organization of the Regulations

The regulations applicable to interim status facilities and to permitted T/S/D facilities have been organized in separate parts. 40 CFR Part 264 sets forth the permanent program requirements that serve as the basis for issuing RCRA permits to T/S/D facilities. 40 CFR Part 265 sets forth the requirements applicable to T/S/D facilities operating under interim status.

Regulations in 40 CFR Part 266 establish requirements applicable to special types of T/S/D facilities and to the management of specific types of hazardous wastes and recyclable materials. In 1980, Part 266 standards were proposed for tanks and containers that are used as wastewater treatment units and elementary neutralization units. As of this writing the proposed standards have not been promulgated and those two types of units are exempt from permitting requirements. Some final management standards have also been issued at 40 CFR Part 266 for recyclable materials used in a manner constituting disposal, hazardous wastes burned for energy recovery, recyclable materials utilized for precious metal recovery, and spent lead-acid battery reclamation.[19] The Part 266 standards, which in many instances cross reference and incorporate the Part 264 standards discussed in this Chapter, are further addressed in Chapter 7.

Part 268 standards have been adopted to implement the land disposal restrictions of the 1984 RCRA Amendments.[20]

5.4 Scope and Coverage of the Regulations

The following T/S/D facilities or hazardous waste activities are exempted altogether from both the interim status and permanent program standards:[21]

---

[19] 40 CFR Part 266, Subparts C, D, F, and G.

[20] The land disposal restrictions are discussed in Chapter 8 of this Handbook.

[21] 40 CFR 265.1(c), 264.1(a)-(h).

(1) Facilities that dispose of hazardous waste by means of ocean disposal pursuant to a permit issued under the Marine Protection, Research, and Sanctuaries Act.

(2) The disposal of hazardous waste by underground injection pursuant to a permit issued under the Safe Drinking Water Act, Underground Injection Control Program.

(3) A publicly owned treatment work ("POTW") which treats or stores hazardous wastes which are delivered to the POTW by a transport vehicle or vessel or through a pipe.

(4) T/S/D facilities which operate under a state hazardous waste program authorized pursuant to RCRA Section 3006.

(5) Facilities authorized by a state to manage industrial or municipal solid waste, if the only hazardous waste handled by such a facility is otherwise excluded from regulation pursuant to the special requirements for small generators. (See 40 CFR 261.5.)

(6) The on-site accumulation of hazardous waste by generators for 90 days or less.

(7) Farmers who dispose of waste pesticides from their own use in compliance with 40 CFR 262.51.

(8) Operators of a "totally enclosed treatment facility." A totally enclosed treatment facility is one for the:

> treatment of hazardous waste which is directly connected to an industrial production process and which is constructed and operated in a manner which prevents the release of any hazardous waste or any constituent thereof into the environment during treatment. An example is a pipe in which waste acid is neutralized.[22]

----

[22] 40 CFR 260.10.

(9) Operators of elementary neutralization units and wastewater treatment units, as defined in the regulations.

(10) Persons taking immediate response actions to treat and contain an accidental or intentional discharge of hazardous wastes or an imminent and substantial threat of such a discharge. Note that after immediate response activities are completed, any hazardous waste discharge residue or debris is subject to full RCRA regulation.

(11) Transporters storing manifested wastes in approved containers at a transfer facility for 10 days or less.

(12) The acts of adding absorbent material to hazardous waste in a container and adding hazardous waste to absorbent material in a container, to reduce the amount of free liquids in the container, if the materials are added when wastes are first placed in the container.

In addition, certain recyclable materials are exempted from RCRA management standards including:[23]

(1) industrial ethyl alcohol that is reclaimed;

(2) used batteries returned to a battery manufacturer for regeneration;

(3) used oil that exhibits one or more of the characteristics of hazardous waste;[24] or

(4) scrap metal.

5.5 Standards of General Applicability

Both the interim status and permanent program regulations for T/S/D facilities include standards of general applicability (e.g., personnel training, security, financial responsibility) as well as

---

[23] 40 CFR 265.1(c)(6); 261.6(a)(3).

[24] Other types of used oil may be subject to regulation, as explained infra in Chapter 13.

specific technical standards for each different type of T/S/D facility (e.g., storage tanks, landfills, incinerators). This Chapter reviews all of the general standards applicable to T/S/D facilities. Chapter 6 of this Handbook reviews the specific design, construction, operating and other technical standards for each type of T/S/D facility. The interim status and permanent program standards are discussed together in each section below so that the reader can see in one place all of the requirements that apply to a T/S/D facility. For guidance on problems and for interpretations arising from specific hazardous waste treatment, storage, and disposal activities, the reader is encouraged to analyze carefully the actual language of the regulations.

Operators are largely left on their own to determine how to comply with the interim status standards, subject to EPA and state inspection oversight. Until a site-specific RCRA permit is issued, the operator of an interim status T/S/D facility is charged with the task of interpreting the regulations and applying them to his facility. Absent a specific request from an operator, EPA oversight during interim status will occur only by means of facility inspections and enforcement actions.[25] As the reader has probably already discovered, compliance with many of the interim

---

[25] Limited site-specific assistance may be available from EPA and state agencies upon request. The number of T/S/D facilities in interim status has prevented any widespread agency assistance on detailed matters. Indeed, one of the criteria for the interim status standards was that the regulations would not prompt the need for interpretation or negotiation with EPA. See 45 Fed. Reg. 33159.

status requirements is not a straightforward matter.[26] By contrast, the permanent program requirements applicable to an individual T/S/D facility will be derived from the Part 264 standards, with additions and modifications as needed, and specifically stated in the facility's permit.

5.5.1 EPA Identification Number and Required Notices

Under both the interim status and permanent programs, operators are required to have an EPA Identification Number, which is obtained by filing EPA Form 8700-12.[27] This number must be used by generators when designating that facility for receipt of hazardous wastes.

Certain required notices must be given, such as notice to the EPA Regional Administrator four weeks before receiving any hazardous waste shipments from foreign sources.[28] Operators must also, before transferring ownership or operation of a facility, notify the new operator in writing of the RCRA requirements that pertain to the T/S/D facility. This notice requirement points out the fact that the sale of a T/S/D facility has been greatly complicated by RCRA. Indeed, the drafting of a real estate sales agreement in light of the future RCRA obligations of the facility may prove very tricky. Moreover, if a T/S/D facility has not qualified for interim status, its value on the market may be impaired since any new owner will have to obtain a permit before

---

[26] Moreover, compliance with the interim status standards does not necessarily ensure immunity from enforcement actions. EPA retains authority under RCRA Section 7003 to seek injunctive relief against facilities if their hazardous waste management activities present an imminent and substantial endangerment to human health or the environment, regardless of whether they are complying with the RCRA regulations. 40 CFR 265.4, 264.4.

[27] RCRA § 3010(a); 40 CFR 265.11, 264.11.

[28] 40 CFR 265.12, 264.12.

commencing operations. It may take years to receive the permit, during which time the T/S/D facility would be closed.

5.5.2 Waste Analysis

In order to properly manage a hazardous waste, an operator of a T/S/D facility must have sufficient knowledge of the particular waste being handled. Consequently, the regulations require the operator to obtain or conduct a detailed chemical and physical analysis of a representative sample of the hazardous waste before the waste is treated, stored, or disposed of at the facility.[29] The waste analysis must be repeated as often as necessary for hazardous waste shipments received from a particular generator to ensure that it is accurate and up-to-date. In addition, operators are required to inspect and, if necessary, analyze each hazardous waste shipment delivered to the facility to determine whether it matches the identity of the waste specified on the manifest.

The procedures the operator intends to follow to comply with these requirements must be set forth in a written waste analysis plan maintained at the facility. The plan must be submitted as part of the facility's Part B permit application.

5.5.3 Security

To prevent unknowing entry, and to minimize the potential for unauthorized entry of people or livestock to the active portion of a T/S/D facility, operators must install a security system.[30] This may be either a 24-hour surveillance system or a barrier around the facility and a means to control entry and posted "Danger" signs. If the operator can demonstrate that unauthorized or unknowing entry will not result in injury to individuals, live-

---

[29] 40 CFR 265.13, 264.13.

[30] 40 CFR 265.14, 264.14.

stock, or to the environment, then an exemption from these requirements may be available.

5.5.4 Inspections

Operators are required to prepare and implement a self-inspection plan specifically tailored to the circumstances at their facility.[31] Inspection frequencies may vary depending on factors relating to a particular facility. However, EPA has specified that inspection frequencies should be based on the rate of possible deterioration of the equipment being used as well as the probability of harm if the deterioration, equipment malfunction, or operator error goes undetected between inspections. Areas subject to spills, such as loading docks, must be inspected daily.

Specific inspection requirements are also included in the regulations pertaining to particular types of facilities. For example, the regulations for storage tanks (discussed in Chapter 6) require, among other things, weekly inspection of the construction materials of the tank to detect corrosion or leaking of fixtures or seams. Inspection records must be made and kept on file at the facility for three years. A facility's inspection schedule will be reviewed by EPA during the permit process.

5.5.5 Personnel Training

T/S/D facility personnel are required to have expertise in the areas to which they are assigned, thus reducing the chances that a mistake due to lack of training might lead to an environmental accident.[32] The training may be by formal classroom instruction or on-the-job training, and must be directed by a person trained in hazardous waste management procedures. The content, schedule, and techniques to be used in the on-the-job training must be

---

[31] 40 CFR 265.15, 264.15.

[32] 40 CFR 265.16, 264.16.

described in personnel training records which must be maintained at the facility until closure.

The training program will also be subject to review by EPA during the permitting process. An outline of the program must be submitted with the Part B permit application, and it then becomes part of the final RCRA permit. Because of the variability in hazardous waste management processes and employee functions at T/S/D facilities, the regulations establish no rigid requirements concerning what courses are required, although appropriate topics are suggested. Personnel must be trained within six months after being employed or assigned to a new facility. Personnel may not work in unsupervised positions until they have completed training. All training must be reviewed and updated annually.

5.5.6 Special Handling

The requirement for analysis of hazardous wastes should provide operators with sufficient knowledge to safely handle reactive, ignitable, or incompatible wastes. The regulations also require that special precautions be taken to prevent accidental ignition or reaction of ignitable or reactive wastes (e.g., the posting of "No Smoking" signs where ignitable wastes are handled).[33] Any mixing of incompatible wastes must be conducted such that it does not:

    (1) generate extreme heat or pressure, fire or explosion, or violent reaction;

    (2) produce uncontrolled toxic mists, fumes, dusts, or gases in sufficient quantities to threaten human health;

    (3) produce uncontrolled flammable fumes or gases in sufficient quantities to pose a risk of fire or explosion;

    (4) damage the structural integrity of the device or facility containing the waste; or

---

[33] 40 CFR 265.17, 264.17.

(5) through other means threaten human health or
the environment.[34]

Other requirements for the handling of ignitable, reactive, and incompatible wastes are largely common sense practices.

Specific requirements regarding the mixing of ignitable, reactive, or incompatible wastes are also included in the regulations pertaining to specific treatment and disposal practices. For example, ignitable or reactive wastes cannot be placed in a landfill unless the waste is treated or mixed such that the resulting waste no longer is an ignitable or reactive waste.[35] The reader is referred to the regulations pertaining to each particular type of facility for the specific provisions pertaining to ignitable, reactive, or incompatible wastes.[36]

Operators of permitted facilities must document their compliance with the regulations concerning management of ignitable, reactive or incompatible waste.[37] The documentation may take the form of references to scientific literature or data acquired through experience with similar wastes under similar management operations.

5.5.7 Location Standards

Three types of location standards restrict siting of T/S/D facilities. These are the seismic, floodplain, and salt dome or underground mine location standards.[38]

---

[34] 40 CFR 265.17(b), 264.17(b).

[35] 40 CFR 265.312, 264.312.

[36] See 40 CFR 265.176, 265.177, 265.198, 265.199, 265.229, 265.230, 265.256, 265.257, 265.281, 265.282, 265.312, 265.313, 265.405, 265.406 for interim status facilities, and the parallel regulations in Part 264 for permitted facilities.

[37] 40 CFR 264.17(c).

[38] As required by RCRA § 3004(o)(7), EPA has also issued an interim final guidance manual entitled "Criteria for Identifying
[footnote continued]

Under the seismic location standard, portions of new facilities where treatment, storage, or disposal operations occur may not be located within 200 feet of faults which have moved in the recent geologic past (these faults are termed Holocene faults).[39] This regulation is intended to protect facilities from the deformation and displacement of the earth's surface which occurs when the fault moves. Political jurisdictions that have a history of seismic activity or a potential for faulting are listed in Appendix VI to Part 264. If a facility is located in a political jurisdiction located in Appendix VI, it must comply with the seismic location standard.

The second location standard limits the siting of T/S/D facilities in floodplains.[40] The environmental danger addressed by the standard is the exposure of surface waters, groundwaters, aquatic life and human health to waste contaminants when wastes are washed or flooded out of the active portion of a facility. Thus, the floodplain location standard prohibits the siting of a T/S/D facility in a 100-year floodplain unless the facility is designed, constructed and operated so as to prevent the washout of waste by a 100-year flood (i.e., a flood with a one percent chance of occurring in any given year). For example, dikes or flood walls may be constructed around the facility, or individual structures may be elevated with foundations sufficient to withstand flood effects. EPA considers the areas mapped by the Federal Insurance Administration ("FIA") as 100-year floodplains to be

[continued]
Areas of Vulnerable Hydrogeology Under The Resource Conservation and Recovery Act - Statutory Interpretive Guidance," which presents a technical method for determining groundwater vulnerability at hazardous waste surface impoundments, waste piles, and landfills.

[39] 40 CFR 264.18(a).

[40] 40 CFR 264.18(b).

determinative that a facility is in fact located within a flood-plain.[41] A limited exception from the floodplain location standard is allowed when the operator demonstrates to EPA that steps will be taken to remove the waste safely before flood waters reach his facility. The wastes must, of course, be removed to a facility authorized to manage hazardous wastes.

Unlike the seismic location standard which applies only to new T/S/D facilities, the floodplain standard will apply to existing facilities when they receive their RCRA permits. Thus, existing facilities located within 100-year floodplains should begin now to consider the cost and feasibility of complying with the standard. Extensive retrofitting of some facilities or other capital-intensive operational or structural modifications may be required to avoid forced closure.

The third location standard, adopted as a result of the 1984 Amendments, prohibits the placement of any non-containerized or bulk liquid hazardous waste in any salt dome formation, salt bed formation, underground mine or cave.[42] The interim status standard provides a flat prohibition on placement of _any_ hazardous waste in such a location. The permanent standard prohibits the placement of any non-containerized or bulk liquid hazardous waste in such locations. The statute permits EPA to lift this ban when issuing a Part 264 permit. However, at the current time EPA is not prepared to identify a process for lifting the ban and has, therefore, simply adopted a flat prohibition as part of the permanent standards.[43]

---

[41]   46 _Fed. Reg._ 2815 (January 12, 1981).

[42]   RCRA § 3004(b); 40 CFR 264.18(c), 265.18(c) 50 _Fed. Reg._ 28746, 28749 (July 15, 1985). A specific exemption is included in the statute and implementing regulations for the Department of Energy Waste Isolation Pilot Project in New Mexico.

[43]   50 _Fed. Reg._ 28717 (July 15, 1985).

5.5.8 Preparedness and Prevention

Regulations for preparedness and prevention have been promulgated to minimize the possibility and effect of an explosion, spill, or fire at a T/S/D facility.[44] Facilities must have, unless unnecessary due to the nature of the wastes handled, the following equipment:

> (1) an internal alarm or communications system;
>
> (2) a device capable of summoning emergency assistance from local agencies;
>
> (3) fire and spill control equipment; including water at adequate volume and pressure; and
>
> (4) decontamination equipment.

In addition, the regulations specify other requirements such as maintaining equipment in proper operating condition, routine testing of equipment, and providing adequate aisle space to allow unrestricted movement of emergency equipment to any area of the facility.

Operators of T/S/D facilities must attempt to make arrangements with local authorities (e.g., police and fire departments) to familiarize them with the layout of the facility, the properties of the hazardous wastes handled there and the places where facility personnel would normally be working.[45] In addition, local hospitals should be informed of the properties of the hazardous wastes handled at the facility, and the types of injuries or illnesses that could result from a fire, explosion, or accidental release. Where state or local authorities decline to enter into such arrangements, a T/S/D facility operator must document their refusal in the operating records of the facility. As with the other written plans required by the regulations, an operator's

---

[44] See generally 40 CFR 265.30-265.49, 264.30-264.49.

[45] 40 CFR 265.37, 264.37.

preparedness and prevention plan must be submitted with his Part B permit application and will become part of the final RCRA permit.

The arrangements with local authorities should be "appropriate" for the type of hazardous wastes handled at the particular facility. Showing EPA that the "appropriate" arrangements have been made may not be easy in some cases given the wide range of hazardous wastes regulated under RCRA. Complying with this requirement may also entail coordination of a company's policies under the Occupational Safety and Health Act ("OSHA"), state occupational safety laws and labor relations policies.

5.5.9   Contingency Plan and Emergency Procedures

Operators are required to have a contingency plan for the facility designed to minimize hazards to human health and the environment in the event of an actual explosion, fire, or unplanned release of hazardous waste.[46] The contingency plan is a prepared set of responses to an emergency. It should list the T/S/D facility's personnel who will serve as emergency coordinators and the emergency equipment that will be available. If an evacuation could prove necessary for the facility, an evacuation plan must be included. The plan must describe the arrangements agreed to by the local authorities pursuant to the preparedness and prevention requirements discussed above. The plan must be immediately revised if the applicable regulations are changed, the plan fails in an emergency, the facility changes (in its design, construction, operation or other circumstances), the emergency coordinators change or the list of emergency equipment changes.

Copies of the plan must be maintained at the facility and submitted to all local governmental units that might be called upon in the event of an emergency. The plan must also be available to EPA personnel during on-site inspections, and must be submitted as

---

[46]   See generally 40 CFR 265.50-265.56, 264.50-264.56.

part of the facility's Part B permit application. If the facility already has prepared a Spill Prevention, Control and Countermeasures ("SPCC") plan under the Clean Water Act, the SPCC plan may be amended to incorporate the hazardous waste provisions.

The contingency plan must be implemented immediately whenever there is a fire, explosion, or release of hazardous wastes which could threaten human health or the environment.[47] An employee of the facility designated as the Emergency Coordinator must be on call at all times to coordinate implementation of the contingency plan in the event of an emergency. The Emergency Coordinator must file a written report with the EPA Regional Administrator within 15 days after an incident that requires implementation of the plan.[48]

EPA has stated that it does not intend the contingency plan to be triggered when an insignificant amount of waste is released by small spills or leaking valves. This could be a point of practical significance, especially since EPA did not include such a de minimis provision in the regulations. Minor discharges which a plant manager considers routine may be viewed as within the scope of the contingency plan in the eyes of an EPA official.

5.5.10 Manifest System, Recordkeeping and Reporting

Upon receipt of a manifested shipment of hazardous wastes, the operator of a T/S/D facility must immediately sign, date, and give to the transporter a copy of the manifest prepared by the generator.[49] Within 30 days, the operator must return another copy of the manifest to the generator. Remember that if that copy is not received by the generator within 45 days, the generator must investigate and file an exception report with EPA. The original manifest, which will have been signed by all persons handling

---

[47] 40 CFR 265.51(b), 264.51(b).

[48] 40 CFR 265.56, 264.56.

[49] See generally 265.71-265.72, 264.71-264.72.

the waste, must be retained by the T/S/D facility operator for three years from the date of delivery of the waste. Special manifest provisions apply to shipments sent by rail or water transporters. (See Chapter 4).

Operators must annotate the manifest and notify EPA within 15 days if there is a "significant discrepancy" between the quantity or type of waste received from a generator and the information on the manifest, unless the discrepancy can be reconciled after contacting the generator or transporter. EPA has ruled that a "significant discrepancy" occurs when:

> (1) the weight of bulk shipments differs by more than 10 percent from that shown on the manifest;
>
> (2) there is any variation in the batch count (e.g., one less drum than indicated on the manifest); or
>
> (3) there are obvious differences in the waste type (e.g., waste solvents are received instead of waste acids).

A key provision of the regulations is the requirement that all T/S/D facilities maintain a complete operating record until closure.[50] The operating record must include the following information as it becomes available:

> (1) the type and quantity of each hazardous waste received and the method used to treat, store or dispose of that waste;
>
> (2) the location and quantity of each waste at the facility (for disposal facilities, the location must be recorded on a map);
>
> (3) waste analysis results;
>
> (4) incidents that require implementation of the contingency plan;
>
> (5) results of facility inspections carried out by the operator;

---

[50] 40 CFR 265.73, 264.73.

(6) monitoring, testing, or analytical data and corrective action records (monitoring data for disposal facilities must generally be kept through the post-closure period);

(7) notices to off-site generators that the facility has the appropriate permit(s) and will accept wastes being shipped;

(8) closure estimates and, for disposal facilities, post-closure cost estimates; and

(9) certifications attesting to compliance with the land disposal restrictions.

In addition, a permitted T/S/D facility that treats, stores or disposes of hazardous waste on the site where it was generated must also maintain, as part of the operating record, an annual certification that efforts were taken to minimize the amount and toxicity of the generated wastes.[51] Operating records must be available for inspection at reasonable times by EPA. As can easily be seen, the operating record constitutes a complete record of the facility's activities and thus is a "high visibility" item for enforcement purposes.

There are two basic reports which the T/S/D facility operator is obligated to file with the EPA Regional Administrator. The first is a biennial report to be filed by March 1 of every even numbered year covering hazardous waste management activities during the preceding odd numbered year.[52] EPA Form 8700-13B is used for this biennial report.

The second report is the "unmanifested waste" report which the operator must file within 15 days of accepting any hazardous waste that is not accompanied by the required manifest. This report

---

[51] 40 CFR 264.70 and 264.73(b)(9). EPA has published interim guidance on what constitutes an acceptable waste minimization program. 58 Fed. Reg. 31114 (May 28, 1993). EPA's recommended program contains six elements including the development of a waste accounting system and waste minimization assessments.

[52] 40 CFR 265.75, 264.75.

must include a description of the type and quantity of waste received, the method of treatment, storage or disposal and an explanation of why the waste was unmanifested, if known. There are, in addition, certain specialized reports that must be filed in specific circumstances.[53] For example, as discussed above, reports must be filed in the event of a hazardous waste release, fire, or explosion.

5.5.11 Releases from Solid Waste Management Units

Owners and operators of facilities with solid waste management units ("SWMU") must provide certain specified descriptive information on the units and all available information pertaining to any release from the units.[54] The regulations do not define the term "solid waste management unit." The term is explained in the preamble of the codification rule to include "any discernible waste management unit from which hazardous constituents may migrate, irrespective of whether the unit was intended for the management of solid or hazardous wastes."[55] The following types of units are therefore included in the SWMU definition: landfills, surface impoundments, waste piles, land treatment units, incinerators, injection wells, tanks (including 90-day accumulation tanks), container storage areas and transfer stations.[56]

The Regional Administrator may require the owner or operator to conduct sampling and analysis at SWMUs as necessary to determine whether a release has occurred.[57] Corrective action must be

---

[53] 40 CFR 265.77, 264.77.

[54] 40 CFR 264.90.

[55] 50 Fed. Reg. 28716 (July 15, 1985).

[56] Id.

[57] The release detection and groundwater monitoring requirements are discussed in Chapter 9 of this Handbook.

implemented whenever a release is discovered.[58] This requirement applies to all releases from a SWMU, including those that extend beyond the facility boundary.

EPA has stated that one time spills of wastes or constituents are subject to the corrective action requirement only if the spill occurred from a SWMU.[59] Thus, while cleanup may be necessary, a spill which cannot be linked to a SWMU (leaks from trucks, production processes, product storage, etc.) does not become part of the corrective action plan included in the facility permit.[60]

5.5.12 Closure and Post-Closure Care

T/S/D facilities which are closed must follow detailed closure and post-closure requirements under both the interim status and permanent standards.[61] "Closure" is the period after which hazardous wastes are no longer accepted by a T/S/D facility and during which time the operator completes treatment, storage or disposal operations. If the facility is a landfill, for example, the operator will close the facility by covering or capping the landfill. If it is a storage or treatment facility, equipment used in the facility must be decontaminated and the hazardous wastes must be removed from the facility. "Post-closure" is the 30-year period after closure when operators of _disposal_ facilities only must perform certain monitoring and maintenance activities. Properly closed treatment and storage facilities do not pose long-term environmental risks, and therefore the post-closure requirements do not apply to them.

---

[58] Corrective action requirements are discussed in Chapter 9 of this Handbook.

[59] 50 _Fed. Reg._ 28712 (July 15, 1985).

[60] RCRA §3008(h) gives EPA authority to compel corrective action for such releases.

[61] 40 CFR 265.110-265.120, 264.110-264.120.

The purposes of the closure requirements are to ensure that all T/S/D facilities are closed in a manner that minimizes the need for further maintenance, and minimizes, controls or eliminates post-closure escapes of hazardous wastes or their constituents into the environment. There are general closure requirements applicable to all T/S/D facilities and additional requirements for each specific type of facility.[62]

Operators must prepare a written closure plan for their facilities.[63] The closure plan must identify the steps necessary to completely or partially close the T/S/D facility at any point during the facility's intended operating life and to completely close the facility at the end of its operating life. At a minimum, this includes:

(1) a description of how each hazardous waste management unit at the facility will be closed;

(2) a description of how final closure of the facility will be conducted;

(3) an estimate of the maximum inventory of hazardous wastes on-site over the active life of the facility and a detailed description of the methods for removing, transporting, treating, storing or disposing of the wastes to be used during partial and final closure;

(4) a description of the steps needed to remove or decontaminate all hazardous waste residues and contaminated containment system components, equipment, structures and soils during partial and final closure;

(5) a description of other activities necessary during the closure period to ensure that all

---

[62] See 40 CFR 265.197, 265.228, 265.258, 265.280, 265.310, 265.351, 265.381, 265.404 for interim status facilities, and the parallel regulations in Part 264 for permitted facilities.

[63] 40 CFR 265.112, 264.112.

partial and final closures satisfy the closure performance standards;

(6) a schedule for closure of each hazardous
waste management unit and for final closure
of the facilities; and

(7) for certain facilities, an estimate of the
expected year of final closure.[64]

The closure plan for an interim status facility must be furnished
to EPA upon request and made available for on-site inspection.[65]

The closure plan for a permitted facility must be submitted
with the Part B permit application, and the approved plan will be
a condition of the RCRA permit. The closure plan may be amended
by the operator at any time. It must be amended within specified
time periods whenever changes in operating plans or facility
design affect the closure plan, whenever there is a change in the
expected year of closure or in conducting partial or final closure
unexpected events require a modification of the plan.[66] For a
permitted T/S/D facility, a modification to a material portion of
the plan is subject to the procedures for permit modifications in
40 CFR Part 270. (See Chapter 8.)

If an operator decides to close an interim status facility and
does not have an approved plan, the closure plan must be submitted
to the Regional Administrator for approval at least 180 days (45
days in the case of a facility with only tanks, container storage
or incinerator units) before closure is expected to begin. The
Regional Administrator may allow the submission of written comments and hold a public hearing on the plan. In order to assure
that inadequately operated facilities are closed expeditiously,
the operator of a T/S/D facility which has its interim status terminated or which is issued an administrative or judicial order

---

[64] 40 CFR 265.112, 264.112.

[65] 40 CFR 265.74, 264.74.

[66] 40 CFR 264.112(c).

directing that the facility cease receiving wastes must submit a closure plan within 15 days.[67] For a permitted T/S/D facility, because the closure plan is approved during the permitting process, it does not have to be resubmitted to EPA before closure can begin.

After initiating closure, the operator has only 90 days to complete the treatment, disposal or removal from the facility of all hazardous wastes. Moreover, closure must be completed within 180 days of receiving the last shipment of hazardous wastes. Both of these time limits may be extended by the EPA Regional Administrator if the operator can demonstrate need and entitlement, or if there is a reasonable likelihood that the operator or a new owner may recommence operations at the T/S/D facility within one year.[68] Also, under certain circumstances, a landfill, land treatment or surface impoundment unit may remain open to receive non-hazardous wastes, if the Regional Administrator approves. Finally, the owner or operator and a registered professional engineer must execute a certification that the facility has been closed in accordance with the approved plan.[69]

The operator of a disposal facility must also have a written post-closure plan.[70] The post-closure plan should identify the activities that will be carried on after closure. At a minimum it must include: (1) a description of the planned monitoring activities; (2) a description of the planned maintenance activities that will ensure the integrity of the final cover or containment structures used and the function of monitoring equipment; and (3) the name, address and phone number of the person to contact concerning the disposal facility during the post-closure care period.

[67] 40 CFR 265.112(d).

[68] 40 CFR 265.113, 264.113.

[69] 40 CFR 265.115, 264.115.

[70] 40 CFR 265.118(a), 264.118(a).

Like the closure plan, the post-closure plan for an interim status facility must be submitted to the EPA Regional Administrator for approval at least 180 days prior to commencement of closure.[71] This approval also includes public notice, an opportunity to submit written comments, and a public hearing on the post-closure monitoring plan. The post-closure plan for a permitted T/S/D facility will, of course, be approved at the time the RCRA permit is issued. Finally, not later than 60 days after completion of the post-closure care period for each unit, the owner or operator and a registered professional engineer must execute a certification that the post-closure care was performed in accordance with the plan.[72]

In addition to following the requirements for post-closure care set forth in the plan, the operator must comply with certain notice requirements.[73] Within 60 days after certification of closure, the operator of a disposal facility must submit a survey plat to the local zoning authority, or the authority with jurisdiction over local land use, and to the EPA Regional Administrator. The survey plat must show the location and dimensions of landfill cells or other disposal areas with respect to permanently surveyed benchmarks,[74] and a record of the types, location and quantities of hazardous wastes disposed within each cell or disposal unit.[75]

In addition the operator must, in accordance with state law, record a notation on the deed to the facility property, or some other instrument which is normally examined during a title search, that will in perpetuity notify any potential purchaser of the

---

[71] 40 CFR 265.118(e).

[72] 40 CFR 265.120, 264.120.

[73] 40 CFR 265.119, 265.120, 264.119, 264.120.

[74] 40 CFR 265.116, 264.116.

[75] 40 CFR 265.119(a), 264.119(a).

property that the land has been used to dispose of hazardous wastes, that its future use is restricted, and that a survey plat has been filed with respect to the location of hazardous wastes.[76] If and when all wastes, waste residues and contaminated soil are removed from the facility, the operator can request that the Regional Administrator either (1) remove any notations from deeds or instruments or (2) add a notation indicating the removal of the hazardous wastes.

The Comprehensive Environmental Response, Compensation and Liability Act (CERCLA or "Superfund") provided for the establishment of a Post-Closure Liability Trust Fund to assume a permitted facility's liability five years after closure provided certain criteria are met (e.g., post-closure care is conducted in compliance with the facility's permit). EPA was given discretion to use the Fund to pay the costs of post-closure care for qualifying facilities. However, the 1986 Superfund Amendments direct that the Post-Closure Liability Trust Fund not be used until a study can be conducted on the future role of the Fund and other options for managing liabilities associated with closed T/S/D facilities.

5.5.13 Financial Responsibility

The measures required in a facility's closure and post-closure plans could prove to be quite expensive. The closure and post-closure requirements would have little practical effect, however, if at the time of closure the operator did not have sufficient funds to implement the plans. Thus, financial responsibility requirements have been established in both the interim status and permanent standards to ensure that the funds needed to implement closure and post-closure plans for T/S/D facilities are available.[77] The financial requirements do not apply to states and federal agencies that are operators of T/S/D facilities because

---

[76]   40 CFR 265.119(b), 264.119(b).

[77]   See generally 40 CFR 265.140-265.150, 264.140-264.151.

EPA believes that such governmental units will always have adequate resources (i.e., we taxpayers) to cover closure and post-closure costs.

The regulations require the operator to have written estimates (based on the cost to the owner or operator of hiring an engineering firm or other third party to perform the closure or post-closure at the point in the life of the facility when final closure would be most expensive) of the cost of closing the facility and the annual cost of a post-closure monitoring and maintenance program for land disposal facilities.[78] The estimates must be changed whenever a change in the closure or post-closure plans would affect the estimate of closure costs or post-closure care. The operator must annually adjust the closure and post-closure cost estimates for inflation.

The operator must then adopt one of the financial instruments provided by the regulations to assure financial responsibility -- a trust fund, surety bond, letter of credit, insurance policy, or financial worth test. The trust fund is a mechanism that allows the full amount of closure and post-closure costs to be built up over the expected life of the facility or over a 20-year period, whichever is shorter. The 20-year period may be shortened when the facility is issued its RCRA permit to provide that any balance of the trust funds be paid over the term of the permit (a maximum of 10 years). The annual payment into the trust must be adjusted for inflation, changes in the closure and post-closure cost estimates, or changes in the value of any securities owned by the trust. During closure or post-closure, the operator is reimbursed from the fund for the costs incurred to accomplish closure and post-closure care.

Surety bonds and bank letters of credit made payable to the EPA Regional Administrator are administered like the trust fund, except they are not built up over a period of years. If an operator uses either of these mechanisms, he also must establish a

---

[78] 40 CFR 265.142, 265.144, 264.142, 264.144.

standby trust fund.[79] The terms of the letter of credit or surety bond must provide that any funds drawn must be placed into this trust fund by the institution making the payment. Without such a mechanism, any funds made payable to the Regional Administrator would have to be paid directly to the U.S. Treasury, and could not be used to pay for closure and post-closure costs directly. EPA has developed form agreements for the trust fund, surety bond and letter of credit, and the operator must use the identical wording in his agreements.

An operator may obtain an insurance policy from a qualified insurer with a face value at least equal to the full amount of its closure and post-closure cost estimates.[80] The policy must be non-cancellable except for non-payment of premiums. EPA has stated that an operator's failure to pay a premium when due will be considered a serious infraction of the regulations and possibly cause for revocation of the facility's RCRA permit. The face value of the policy must be increased if the operator's cost estimates increase. If the cost estimates decrease, the face value of the policy may be decreased with the written approval of the Regional Administrator. During closure or post-closure the insurer must be responsible for making payments out of the fund at the direction of the Regional Administrator to cover the costs.

An operator may satisfy the financial assurance requirements if the company owning the facility can meet a financial test designed to demonstrate the company's financial strength. To pass the test, the operator must meet four specific criteria set out in the regulations relating to assets/liabilities, net working capital, net worth, current bond rating and tangible assets in the U.S.[81] An operator may also obtain a guarantee from a parent corporation if the parent meets the financial worth test.

---

[79]   40 CFR 265.143(b)(3), 264.143(b)(3).

[80]   40 CFR 265.143(d), 264.143(e).

[81]   40 CFR 265.143(e), 264.143(f).

With limited exceptions, an operator is free to utilize more than one financial mechanism to provide financial assurance for a facility, to cover more than one facility with a single mechanism, and to use one mechanism for both closure costs and post-closure care.[82]

The 1984 Amendments reflect congressional approval of the EPA financial responsibility regulations, but dissatisfaction with the level of compliance and enforcement. Section 3005(e) provides that interim status for a T/S/D facility automatically expired as of November 8, 1985, unless the facility met these financial requirements and filed a certification to that effect with EPA. In addition, the 1984 Amendments now provide that a claim may be asserted directly against the guarantor of financial responsibility in cases where the T/S/D facility is in bankruptcy pursuant to the Federal Bankruptcy Code, or where court jurisdiction cannot be obtained over any owner or operator that is likely to be solvent at the time of judgement. The guarantor's liability is limited to the aggregate amount provided as evidence of financial responsibility to the owner or operator of the T/S/D facility under RCRA.[83]

5.5.14 Third-Party Liability Insurance

The regulations also require operators of T/S/D facilities to obtain liability insurance to provide coverage during the operating life of a facility for claims arising out of injuries to persons or property which result from hazardous waste management operations.[84] EPA must be notified of all valid claims against the insurance policy.

---

[82] EPA has also published a Guidance Manual on Financial Assurance for Closure and Post-Closure Care (May 1982), SW-955, which describes the various financial instruments in substantial detail.

[83] RCRA § 3004(t)(2) and (3).

[84] 40 CFR 265.147, 264.147.

All facilities must have third-party liability insurance for sudden and accidental occurrences in the amount of $1 million per occurrence with a $2 million annual aggregate. In addition, operators of landfills, surface impoundments, and land treatment units are required to obtain insurance for non-sudden and accidental occurrences (i.e., leakage and gradual groundwater contamination) in the amount of $3 million per occurrence with a $6 million annual aggregate. These liability limits must exclude legal defense costs. An operator may self-insure if the company owning the T/S/D facility can meet one of two sets of criteria which demonstrate the company's financial strength, similar to the financial worth test for demonstrating financial responsibility discussed in the preceding section.[85]

A T/S/D facility may use a letter of credit, a security bond assuring payment of liability claims, a fully funded trust fund, or a guarantee provided by a firm that is not the direct parent of the owner or operator to meet the third-party liability insurance requirement.[86] The requirements for these mechanisms parallel the financial mechanisms authorized for closure or post-closure care. Some provisions of the mechanisms differ, however, to address issues that arise only in the context of liability claims. Such differences include designation of the beneficiary, exclusions for categories of damages and obligations, the claims-payment trigger, the certification of validity and enforceability, and cancellation provisions. For example, letters of credit for third-party liability may use a standby trust with an independent trustee responsible for distributing funds when a claim is filed.[87]

A variance provision is contained in the regulations whereby an operator of a T/S/D facility can seek to adjust the required

---

[85] EPA has published a Guidance Manual on Liability Coverage (November 1982), SW-961.

[86] 40 CFR 264.147; 53 Fed. Reg. 33938 (September 1, 1988).

[87] 40 CFR 264.147; 57 Fed. Reg. 42832 (September 16, 1992).

level of liability coverage by demonstrating that the level is inconsistent with the degree and duration of risk associated with its facility.[88] In contrast, if a facility poses risks which warrant adjusting the required level of liability coverage upwards, the EPA Regional Administrator can require an increase and extend the non-sudden insurance requirement to treatment and/or storage facilities.

5.5.15 Current Developments Affecting Financial Responsibility and Third-Party Liability Insurance Regulations

Over the past several years, it has become increasingly difficult for operators of T/S/D facilities to secure the insurance required by EPA's financial responsibility and third-party liability insurance regulations. Few insurance companies offer such coverage and premiums for the policies that are available are very high and getting higher. A variety of reasons for these developments have been given. They include: losses due to low premiums and large claims; difficulty of assessing risk and setting accurate premiums; judicial interpretations of policies favoring insureds, and lack of compliance with liability requirements.[89] EPA maintains a list of companies providing such insurance.

EPA has recognized the controversy over the availability of insurance and the dilemma this caused T/S/D facilities that lost interim status on November 8, 1985, because they did not have insurance. For T/S/D facilities that are not in compliance due to the depressed state of the insurance market, EPA may exercise its enforcement authority to put the facility on a schedule of compliance to obtain insurance,[90] or to shut the facility down.

---

[88] 40 CFR 265.147(d), 264.147(d).

[89] 50 Fed. Reg. 33904 (August 21, 1985).

[90] See 50 Fed. Reg. 33906 (August 21, 1985).

In order to help companies cope with the difficulties of the insurance market, the regulations allow the use of a corporate guarantee.[91] The corporate guarantee can only be used if the guarantor is the parent corporation of the owner or operator of the T/S/D facility, directly owning at least 50% of the voting stock of the corporation that owns or operates the facility. This corporate guarantee differs from the corporate guarantee for closure or post-closure care in several ways; for example, the corporate guarantee for liability coverage is made to third parties, not EPA.

---

[91]   40 CFR 265.147(g), 264.147(g), 264.151(h)(2).

CHAPTER 6

STANDARDS FOR SPECIFIC TYPES
OF T/S/D FACILITIES

6.1 Overview

A T/S/D facility can range from a small drum storage area to a large commercial landfill, with a variety of other types of hazardous waste management facilities in between. In addition to the generally applicable standards discussed in Chapter 5 of this Handbook, EPA has promulgated specific standards for each of ten types of T/S/D facilities regulated under RCRA. These facilities include containers, tanks, surface impoundments, waste piles, land treatment facilities, landfills, incinerators, thermal treatment facilities, chemical, physical and biological treatment facilities, and underground injection wells.

The technical standards for interim status T/S/D facilities are set forth in 40 CFR Part 265, Subparts I through R; the standards for permitted T/S/D facilities are established in 40 CFR Part 264, Subparts I through 0 and X. In each section of this Chapter, the interim status standards for each type of T/S/D facility are discussed first, and then the permanent standards which will be incorporated into the RCRA permit issued to the T/S/D facility are discussed next. Because the groundwater protection standards in Subpart F of 40 CFR Parts 264 and 265 apply to surface impoundments, waste piles, land treatment facilities, and landfills, those standards are also discussed in this Chapter. In addition, the standards for other specific types of hazardous waste management facilities in 40 CFR Part 266, including facilities that burn hazardous waste as a fuel and facilities that recycle certain hazardous wastes, are discussed in this Chapter. The comprehensive land disposal restrictions of 40 CFR Parts 148 and 268 which affect virtually all T/S/D facilities are addressed in Chapter 7.

6.2 Use and Management of Containers

A container is defined as any "<u>portable</u> device in which a material is stored, transported, treated, disposed of, or otherwise handled."[1] Generally, the regulations for the management of hazardous wastes in containers at interim status T/S/D facilities mandate a level of care that corresponds to the nature of the risks posed by the hazardous waste stored in the container.[2] For example, containers are required to be in good condition and to be handled so that they will not rupture or leak. If the container does begin to leak, the waste must be transferred to another container or managed in some other approved way. Containers must be kept closed during storage. The operator must inspect containers on a weekly basis for leaks and deterioration. There are special requirements for reactive, ignitable, and incompatible wastes that are generally designed to prevent fires and explosions.

Containers are used normally for storage and not for disposal. Thus, during closure of a T/S/D facility, all hazardous wastes and residues held in containers must be removed. Such activities may in turn make the operator of the container storage facility undergoing closure a generator of hazardous waste, subject to the Part 262 standards discussed in Chapter 3 of this Handbook. Also note that the residue remaining in an emptied container is not considered hazardous waste under EPA's regulations if the container is "empty" as defined in 40 CFR 261.7, which is discussed in Chapter 2.

The regulations for the use and management of containers at permitted T/S/D facilities incorporate and build on the interim

---

[1] 40 CFR 260.10 [emphasis added].

[2] <u>See generally</u> 40 CFR 265.170-265.177. The handling of hazardous wastes in standard 55-gallon drums is likely to be a common activity for many companies. Remember that the interim status standards for containers also apply to generators that conduct temporary on-site storage of their hazardous wastes for up to 90 days. 40 CFR 262.34 (<u>see</u> Chapter 3).

status standards.[3] In addition to the requirements discussed above, the Part 264 regulations also require operators to maintain a secondary containment system under container storage areas.[4] The secondary containment system must be capable of holding and collecting any spills, leaks, or accumulated rainfall. Specifically, the containment system must be designed to include:

(1) a base underlying the containers which is sufficiently impervious to hold any wastes or accumulated precipitation for removal;

(2) a system to remove liquids from leaks, spills, and rainfall, unless the containers are elevated;

(3) sufficient capacity to contain 10 percent of the volume of all the containers, or the volume of the largest container, whichever is greater; and

(4) a method for preventing or removing run-on into the containment system, and for promptly removing accumulated liquids from spills and leaks.

If the collected rainfall and spillage inside the containment system exhibit a characteristic of hazardous waste, that contained liquid must be managed as a hazardous waste, for example, by pumping it into a drum for off-site disposal. Moreover, if the collected liquid is discharged through a pipe or other point source to a creek or other body of water, an NPDES permit under the Clean Water Act may be needed. If the collected liquid is discharged to a sewer system, a local or state permit program or ordinance may apply.

---

[3]   40 CFR 264.170-264.178.

[4]   40 CFR 264.175.

At closure, all hazardous wastes must be removed from the secondary containment system.[5] Any remaining containers, the containment base, contaminated soils, and other hazardous wastes must be removed or decontaminated.

6.3 Use and Management of Tanks

A "tank" is defined as a "stationary device, designed to contain an accumulation of hazardous waste, which is constructed primarily of non-earthen materials (e.g., wood, concrete, steel, plastic) which provide structural support."[6] This definition encompasses both covered and uncovered containment devices such as basins, as well as underground tanks. The standards for tanks apply to operators of T/S/D facilities that use tanks to either treat or store hazardous wastes. Tanks that are used to manage hazardous wastes containing no free liquids and that are located inside a building with an impermeable floor are exempted, however.[7]

The interim status standards recognize that the chemical properties of hazardous wastes will eventually affect the materials of which tanks are made.[8] Therefore, a tank must be capable of containing hazardous wastes during the intended useful life of the tank. A hazardous waste may not be placed into a tank if it will cause the tank or its secondary containment system to rupture, leak, corrode, or fail before the end of its intended life. Moreover, whenever a tank is to be used to chemically treat or store a

---

[5] 40 CFR 264.178.

[6] 40 CFR 260.10 [emphasis added].

[7] 40 CFR 265.190(a).

[8] See generally 40 CFR 265.190-265.201. These standards also apply to generators that store hazardous wastes on-site for up to 90 days. 40 CFR 262.34 (see Chapter 3).

hazardous waste which is substantially different from waste previously held in the tank (or if a substantially different treatment process is to be used), a waste analysis and trial tests must be conducted to ensure the continued integrity of the tank.

The interim status regulations also impose various operational requirements for tanks. For example, the tank must be operated using appropriate controls and practices to prevent spills and overflows. This may include equipment such as check valves and dry disconnect couplings to prevent spillage, alarms and automatic feed cutoffs to prevent overfilling, and maintenance of sufficient freeboard to prevent overtapping. Tanks must be inspected daily to detect spills, corrosion, leaks, and operator error.

Operators of both above-ground and underground interim status tanks, which do not already have secondary containment systems, were required to conduct a structural integrity assessment by January 12, 1988.[9] The rule required an independent registered professional engineer to prepare a written assessment of the structural integrity of the tank which addresses the age of the tank, cracks, leaks and corrosion protection. Most significantly, all interim status tanks had to be retrofitted with secondary containment systems which prevent releases to the environment.[10] Three types of secondary containment for tanks are recognized by EPA: (1) an external liner system (e.g. a synthetic liner or a diked concrete containment facility); (2) a vault; and (3) double-walled tanks.[11] The secondary containment system would have to include a leak detection mechanism, such as a sump that allows the system to be inspected for collected leakage or an automatic detection device.

---

[9]   40 CFR 265.191.

[10]   40 CFR 265.193.

[11]   40 CFR 265.193(d).

The deadlines for retrofitting interim status tanks with secondary containment systems are based on the age of the tank.[12] For those tanks that have a known and documented age, secondary containment must be installed before the tank is 15 years old, or by January 12, 1987, at the latest. If the age of the tank is not known, secondary containment must be provided by the time the facility at which the tank is located reaches 15 years of age, or by January 12, 1989, at the latest. New tanks must have secondary containment systems before being put into service.

Permitted T/S/D facilities that use tanks are subject basically to the same standards as interim status facilities.[13] The permanent tank standards assure primary containment through both design and operational controls. For example, EPA has promulgated a design standard which requires sufficient shell strength, compatibility with the wastes to be managed, and, for metal tanks, corrosion protection to prevent tanks from rupturing, corroding or collapsing. The RCRA permit issued to the T/S/D facility will approve the basic tank system design, and also prescribe the foundation, structural support, and pressure controls needed based on published industrial design standards.

For new tanks, the operator must comply with installation standards that are intended to prevent weld breaks, punctures, scrapes of protective coatings, and other damage during installation. The new standards also emphasize proper design, installation, and operation of ancillary equipment such as pipes and pumps.

The operating standards for permitted tanks require waste management procedures that minimize corrosion. Thus, wastes that are incompatible with the construction material of the tank may not be placed in it unless steps are taken to prevent corrosion. These steps might include the installation of a protective liner

---

[12] 40 CFR 265.193(a).

[13] See generally 40 CFR 264.190-264.199.

or coating, the use of a cathodic protection system, or corrosion inhibitors. Operators must also employ controls to prevent tanks from overfilling and overtopping, such as a waste feed cutoff system or sufficient freeboard. The inspection requirements for permitted tanks are the same as for interim status.

At closure, all hazardous waste and residues must be removed from the tank, ancillary equipment, and the foundation structure. EPA has also strengthened the post-closure provisions for tanks without secondary containment by requiring removal of all hazardous residues and contaminated soil at closure, and post-closure care for up to 30 years if all contamination cannot be removed. The operator must also obtain a financial assurance instrument, such as an insurance policy or corporate guarantee, for the costs of any post-closure care.

6.4 Surface Impoundments

A "surface impoundment" is a "natural topographic depression, man-made excavation, or diked area formed primarily of earthen materials (although it may be lined with man-made materials), which is designed to hold an accumulation of liquid wastes or wastes containing free liquids, and which is not an injection well."[14] Surface impoundments include holding ponds, storage impoundments, settling ponds, and aeration pits, ponds, and lagoons.

EPA has identified three different types of problems posed by surface impoundments: (1) leakage of hazardous constituents to groundwater; (2) air emissions from volatile wastes; and (3) overtopping of the impoundment as a result of overfilling, precipitation, or wind. Therefore, the regulations provide that surface impoundments operated under interim status must prevent overtopping by, at a minimum, maintaining two feet of freeboard to

---

[14]   40 CFR 260.10.

protect against overtopping by waves or precipitation.[15] A variance from the two-foot freeboard requirement is allowed if the operator obtains a written certification from a qualified engineer that alternate design features or operating plans will prevent overtopping of the dike.[16] Earthen dikes around the impoundment must have a protective cover such as grass, rocks, or shale to minimize erosion and maintain the structural integrity of the impoundment. Inspections of the freeboard level must be made daily, while weekly inspections of the dikes must be conducted to detect cracks, erosion, or other deterioration.

Special requirements apply when an impoundment is used to chemically treat a waste which is substantially different from previous wastes, including the need for waste analyses and trial tests, or when the impoundment is used to manage ignitable, reactive, or incompatible wastes.

Prior to the 1984 Amendments, EPA did not require that interim status surface impoundments have liners. According to EPA, there were an estimated 200,000 unlined pits, ponds, and lagoons used for the storage, treatment, and disposal of hazardous wastes across the nation. While EPA recognized that these impoundments are a major source of groundwater contamination, the cost of requiring operators to close or retrofit these impoundments with liners was estimated to be very high. In the 1984 Amendments, Congress resolved this controversial issue by requiring companies to retrofit all interim status surface impoundments with double liners, leachate collection systems, and groundwater monitoring by November 1988.[17] EPA can modify these requirements

---

[15] See generally 40 CFR 265.220-265.230. Remember that a discharge from a surface impoundment directly to a river or stream, even if it is caused by rainfall, may constitute a violation of the Clean Water Act's proscription against point source discharges to waters of the United States without an NPDES permit.

[16] 40 CFR 265.222(b).

[17] RCRA § 3005(j).

only if the operator can demonstrate that an impoundment is located, designed, and operated so as to ensure that there will be no migration of any hazardous constituents to the groundwater or surface water at any future time. The retrofit requirements are expected to result in the closing of many existing surface impoundments.

Congress created two carefully limited exemptions to the retrofit requirement. Both of these exemptions were available only to companies that made application to EPA by November 8, 1986. After that time, the exemptions are deemed to be waived. First, a surface impoundment that has at least one liner, is located more than one-quarter mile from an underground source of drinking water, and is in compliance with groundwater monitoring requirements is exempt. The second exemption is for a surface impoundment that is part of a wastewater treatment facility regulated under the Clean Water Act and which meet the following criteria. The impoundment must be used to contain treated wastewater during the secondary or subsequent phases of "aggressive biological treatment" prior to discharge authorized by an NPDES permit.[18] The wastewater treatment facility must be in compliance with any applicable effluent limitations for toxic pollutants or, if no such effluent limitations are contained in the facility's NPDES permit, then the facility must be achieving significant degradation of toxic pollutants and hazardous constituents contained in the untreated waste stream.

EPA's interim status regulations also formerly allowed existing surface impoundments to be replaced or expanded without meeting the permanent standards in Part 264. Congress also changed

---

[18] An "aggressive biological treatment facility" is defined to mean a system of surface impoundments in which the initial impoundment of the secondary treatment segment of the facility utilizes intense mechanical aeration to enhance biological activity to degrade wastewater pollutants. RCRA § 3005(j)(12).

that in the 1984 Amendments. Now each new, replacement, and lateral expansion unit at an existing surface impoundment must have two or more liners and a leachate collection system between the liners.[19] EPA has required that the liners and leachate collection systems be designed and operated in accordance with the permanent standards, discussed below. The operator must also comply with the groundwater protection regulations. See section 6.9 below. Certain exemptions exist for impoundments that use approved alternative design and operating practices and for impoundments that qualify as monofills, as discussed below.

In 1992, EPA increased the level of technological control on land disposal units, including surface impoundments.[20] The required technological control applies to interim status and permitted landfills, surface impoundments, land treatment units and waste piles, and includes:

(1) A leak detection system capable of detecting, collecting and removing leaks "at the earliest practicable time;"[21]

(2) An approved response action plan to prevent hazardous constituent migration out of the unit in excess of EPA-approved health based standards for groundwater protection in the event that the leak detection system exceeds a specified action leakage rate;[22]

---

[19]   RCRA § 3015(b); 40 CFR 265.221.

[20]   57 Fed. Reg. 3462 (January 29, 1992).

[21]   40 CFR 264.221(c), 264.251(c), 264.301(c); 40 CFR 265.221(c), 265.254, 265.301(a).

[22]   40 CFR 264.223, 264.253, 264.304; 40 CFR 265.223, 265.259, 265.303.

(3) Double liners and leachate collection and removal systems for new or expanded surface impoundments, waste piles, and landfills; and[23]

(4) A construction quality assurance program to ensure that land disposal units meet or exceed all construction design requirements.[24]

At closure of an interim status surface impoundment, the operator has the option of either removing all hazardous wastes or closing the impoundment as a landfill. If the operator removes all standing liquids, waste and waste residues, liners, and any contaminated soil, the impoundment is no longer subject to RCRA. Of course, the act of removing the hazardous wastes will constitute generation and the hazardous wastes must then be managed and disposed of properly.

EPA's permanent standards for surface impoundments contain the detailed requirements for the double liner and leachate collection systems required by the 1984 Amendments, as well as more extensive standards regarding inspections, emergency repairs, and closure/post-closure.[25] First, the operator of each new surface impoundment, and each new, replacement, or lateral expansion unit at an existing surface impoundment must install two or more liners, a leachate collection system between the liners, and a groundwater monitoring system.[26] The type of liner to be

---

[23] 40 CFR 264.221(c), 264.251(c), 264.301(c); 40 CFR 265.221(c), 265.254, 265.301(a).

[24] 40 CFR 264.19; 265.19.

[25] See generally 40 CFR 264.220-264.231.

[26] 40 CFR 264.221(c). Although "existing portions" of surface impoundments were exempt under EPA's regulations from the liner requirement, the Congressional mandate to retrofit these impoundments with double liner systems by November 1988 does apply. An "existing portion" is defined as "that land surface area of an existing waste management unit, included in the original Part A permit application, on which wastes
[footnote continued]

installed will be specified on a case-by-case basis in the operator's permit based on the general performance standards set forth in the regulations. These standards require that the top liner be designed, operated, and constructed to prevent the migration of any constituent into the liner during the operating life of the impoundment, including the post-closure period. A lower liner must prevent the migration of any constituents of the hazardous waste through the liner during the same period.

In general, EPA construes the performance standards for surface impoundments to mean that only synthetic liners comply with the regulatory requirements for at least the top liner.[27] EPA believes that clay liners are valuable as a backup to synthetic liners, and in fact has provided in its regulations that a lower liner will be deemed to satisfy the regulations if it is constructed of at least a three foot thick layer of recompacted clay or other natural material with a permeability of no more than 1×10^{-7} centimeter per second.[28] If double liners have been installed at new, replacement, or expansion units at an interim status surface impoundment in accordance with the EPA guidance documents, no different liner or leachate system will be required by EPA when issuing a RCRA permit, provided the liner is not leaking.[29]

EPA can exempt a surface impoundment if the operator can demonstrate that due to the impoundment's alternative design,

---

[continued]
    have been placed prior to the issuance of a permit." 40 CFR 260.10.

[27]   See Permit Applicants' Guidance Manual For Hazardous Waste Land Treatment, Storage, And Disposal Facilities, U.S.EPA, Phase I (Jan. 1985)(NTIS No. PB86-125-580), Phase II (Jan. 1988)(NTIS No. PB88-246-806).

[28]   40 CFR 264.221(c).

[29]   40 CFR 265.221(e).

operating practices, and specific location there will be no migration of hazardous constituents into groundwater or surface water at any future time.[30] In addition, EPA may waive the double liner requirement under both the interim status and permanent standards for monofills that contain only specified hazardous waste.[31] The special requirements for monofills are discussed in section 6.7 on landfills.

The additional permanent standards for permitted surface impoundments augment the basic liner design standards. For example, a surface impoundment must also be designed and operated so as to prevent overtopping that may result from such things as overfilling, wind and wave action, rainfall, malfunctions and human error. This can be done by providing substantial freeboard, carefully controlling inflows and outflows, or using automatic level controllers or alarms. In addition, the surface impoundment must have dikes that are designed, constructed and maintained with sufficient structural integrity to prevent a massive failure, as certified by a qualified engineer.[32]

The operator of a permitted surface impoundment must conduct inspections at specified times during construction and installation of the liner, looking for tight seams, imperfections, tears or punctures, thin spots, etc. Thereafter the impoundment must be inspected weekly and after storms. The operator must also remove the impoundment from operation whenever an emergency situation exists, e.g., when a leaking dike is discovered or when the level of liquids in the impoundment suddenly drops. The operator must then implement a contingency plan to stop any leakage and repair the failure.

---

30   40 CFR 264.221(b), 265.221(c).

31   40 CFR 264.221(e), 265.221(d).

32   40 CFR 264.226(c).

At closure, operators of surface impoundments may choose between two options.[33] The first option is to remove or decontaminate all hazardous wastes (including contaminated structures and subsoil). If this is done, the operator is not required to do any post-closure care or monitoring. The second option allows the operator to leave the wastes in the impoundment, but requires that the operator eliminate all free liquids, stabilize the wastes, place a final cover on the impoundment, and conduct post-closure monitoring and maintenance. Operators of existing portions of surface impoundments that are not fitted with adequate liners and who intend to use the first option must include a contingency plan in their closure plan for complying with the second option in case all wastes cannot be completely removed or decontaminated.[34] Under limited circumstances, surface impoundments, land treatment facilities and landfills may remain open after the final receipt of hazardous wastes in order to receive non-hazardous wastes in that unit.[35]

6.5 Waste Piles

The term "waste pile" is not defined in the regulations. A "pile", however, is defined as "any non-containerized accumulation of solid, nonflowing hazardous waste that is used for treatment or

---

[33] 40 CFR 264.228, 265.228. In 1987 EPA proposed a third type of "hybrid closure" for surface impoundments and landfills which would consist of the removal of the majority of the contaminated materials and would allow covers and post-closure monitoring to be designed based on waste and site characteristics. See 52 Fed. Reg. 8712 (Mar. 19, 1987). The proposal was never finalized and it no longer appears on EPA's regulatory agenda.

[34] EPA has published a Guidance Manual on Closure of Hazardous Waste Surface Impoundments (September 1982), SW-873 (NTIS No. PB87-155-537), which discusses many of the technical aspects of closure.

[35] 54 Fed. Reg. 33376 et seq. (Aug. 14, 1989).

storage."[36]   A waste pile may be used to treat or store hazardous wastes. If the waste pile is utilized as a disposal facility, it must be operated and closed as a landfill.

There are three basic requirements for waste piles operated under interim status.[37] First, the waste pile must be protected from dispersion by the wind. Second, runoff from a waste pile must be adequately contained. If the runoff would be a hazardous waste, then the operator must place the pile on an impermeable base, divert all run-on, and collect and manage any runoff or leachate from the pile as a hazardous waste. Alternatively, the operator can protect the pile from precipitation and run-on by appropriate means (e.g., a roof over the pile and a diversion ditch), and not place liquids and wastes containing free liquids on the pile. Third, a new, replacement, or lateral expansion of a waste pile must have a single liner and a leachate collection system.[38] The liner must prevent any migration of hazardous wastes out of the pile into adjacent subsurface soil and ground or surface water during the active life of the waste pile. The leachate collection and removal system must be designed to assure that not more than one foot of leachate will collect over the liner. The performance standards for both the liner and leachate system are basically the same as for surface impoundments, discussed above, and will be specified in the operator's permit.

Most of these interim status standards for waste piles have been incorporated into the permanent standards.[39] In addition, permitted waste piles must comply with provisions relating to general design and operation, containment systems, groundwater monitoring, and closure. For example, the permanent standards require

---

[36]   40 CFR 260.10.

[37]   See generally 40 CFR 265.250-265.258.

[38]   40 CFR 265.254.

[39]   See generally 40 CFR 264.250-264.259.

operators of waste piles to control run-on and runoff.[40] They must install a run-on control system to minimize leachate generation and a runoff collection system to minimize the environmental danger from contaminated runoff. Certain inspections must also be conducted. The liner must be inspected during construction or installation for uniformity, damage, and imperfections. While the waste pile is in operation, inspections must be conducted weekly and after storms of the run-on and runoff control systems, the leachate collection and removal systems, the wind dispersal control system, and the leak detection system (if applicable).[41] The groundwater monitoring standards discussed in section 6.8 of this Chapter must be met. Existing portions of waste piles are exempt from these permanent standards.[42] A waste pile may also be exempt from the permanent standards if the operator can prove that the facility's design, operating procedures, and location characteristics will prevent the migration of hazardous constituents into ground or surface water at any future time.[43] In addition, dry waste piles located inside structures that are protected from wind dispersal, run-on, and precipitation may be exempt from both the permanent standards for groundwater protection and the requirements for liner and leachate collection systems.[44]

Waste piles may not be used for disposal of hazardous wastes. At closure, therefore, all hazardous wastes and contaminated soil and equipment must be removed.[45] If all contaminated material cannot be removed from a waste pile, the operator must close the

---

[40]   40 CFR 264.251(c)-(e).

[41]   40 CFR 264.254.

[42]   40 CFR 264.251(a).

[43]   40 CFR 264.251(b).

[44]   40 CFR 264.250(c).

[45]   40 CFR 264.258.

waste pile in compliance with the standards applicable to closure of landfills. An operator of an existing waste pile facility that is not fitted with an adequate liner must prepare a contingency closure plan for closing the waste pile in compliance with the landfill standards.

6.6 Land Treatment Facilities

A "land treatment facility" is "a facility or part of a facility at which hazardous waste is applied onto or incorporated into the soil surface; such facilities are disposal facilities if the waste will remain after closure."[46] In a land treatment unit, hazardous wastes are typically applied to the soil in thin layers and traditional farming practices are then utilized, such as discing the material into the soil.   This disposal practice obviously presents high potential risks because the hazardous wastes are directly applied to land surfaces without the liner systems associated with surface impoundments, waste piles and landfills.

The interim status standards basically prohibit land treatment of hazardous wastes unless the operator can demonstrate that biological degradation or chemical reactions in the soil will render the waste sufficiently non-hazardous so that constituents will not be found in the crops grown.[47] The permanent standards for land treatment units require operators to develop a land treatment program designed to ensure that degradation, transformation or immobilization of hazardous constituents will occur through the physical, chemical and biological processes that take

---

[46]   40 CFR 260.10.

[47]   See generally 40 CFR 265.270-265.282. The biological and chemical processes can include degradation of organic waste constituents, transformation which changes constituents to different compounds, and immobilization through precipitation of metals and soil absorption. See 50 Fed. Reg. 16046 (April 23, 1985).

place within a specified treatment zone.[48] Three elements of the treatment program will be specified in a facility's permit: (1) the specific wastes that may be handled at the land treatment unit; (2) a set of design standards and operating procedures (e.g., the waste application rate, the depth of the treatment zone, soil pH); and (3) an unsaturated zone monitoring program to determine the success of treatment within the treatment zone.

Some of the design and operating requirements applicable to land treatment units are similar to those required for surface impoundments, waste piles, and landfills. For example, operators of land treatment units must install run-on and runoff management systems and control wind dispersion. In addition, there are detailed standards for operators growing foodchain crops. Land treatment methods are a highly specialized form of hazardous waste management, and the regulations must be reviewed carefully before such treatment is used.

6.7 Landfills

A "landfill" is defined as "a disposal facility or part of a facility where hazardous waste is placed in or on land and which is not a land treatment facility, a surface impoundment, or an injection well."[49] Historically, landfilling is the most common disposal method for hazardous wastes. Because it presents some of the more serious environmental risks, however, landfill disposal is extensively regulated under RCRA.[50]

Landfills pose basically two types of environmental danger. First, the mismanagement of reactive, ignitable, or incompatible hazardous wastes in a landfill can result in fires, explosions, or

---

[48] See generally 40 CFR 264.270-264.283.

[49] 40 CFR 260.10.

[50] See generally 40 CFR 265.300-265.316, 264.300-264.317.

toxic fumes. Second, leachate and runoff from landfills and wind erosion can contaminate subsoil, groundwater and surface waters.

6.7.1 Prevention of Sudden Releases

Accordingly, both the interim status and permanent regulations provide that ignitable or reactive wastes may not be placed in a landfill unless they are treated before or immediately after placement in the landfill so that the resulting waste no longer meets the definition of ignitable or reactive waste. Solid ignitable wastes in containers may be landfilled without special treatment provided the wastes are disposed of in such a way as to prevent ignition. Incompatible wastes must not be placed in the same landfill cell unless properly treated so as not to present a hazard.

6.7.2 Prevention of Non-Sudden Releases

As required by Congress in the 1984 Amendments, every new landfill, and every new, replacement, and lateral expansion unit at an existing landfill must have a double liner and leachate collection system above and between the liners for all wastes received after May 8, 1985.[51] To facilitate permitting, the operator must give 60 days notice to EPA before accepting waste in such a unit and then file a Part B permit application within six months. The design and operating requirements for the liner and leachate collection system are the same as for surface impoundments, discussed above. Because EPA's prior regulations required only that a landfill have a single liner at the time of permitting, interpretive issues have arisen regarding when a landfill is subject to the new double liner and leachate collection requirements. EPA has taken the position that those units at a landfill that were operational and had received hazardous wastes before November 8, 1984, may continue to satisfy only the single liner

---

[51] RCRA § 3004(o). 40 CFR 264.301, 265.301.

regulation.[52] In order to have been "operational", the unit must have been constructed to comply with all federal, state and local requirements, including licenses and permits, in effect prior to the enactment of the 1984 Amendments.

EPA informally considers a "unit" as a defined or bounded area of land designed to contain waste, with either natural or artificial boundaries.[53] Thus at a landfill, a "unit" will normally be a cell or trench that has been excavated and is bounded by berms or other readily recognizable boundaries. For certain landfills where there are no defined boundaries, EPA will consider the operating record and other objective evidence to determine whether any particular area within the landfill was intended to be an individual unit. Thus, the operator of the landfill may have to retrofit or partition a large cell or trench in order to continue receiving wastes after May 8, 1985. The double liner and leachate collection requirements would then apply to all new, replacement, and expansion units at a landfill which were constructed after November 8, 1984, with respect to all hazardous wastes received after May 8, 1985.

EPA can waive the double liner and leachate collection requirements only if the operator can demonstrate that alternate design and operating practices, together with location characteristics, will prevent the migration of hazardous constituents at least as effectively as such liners and leachate collection systems.[54] In addition, EPA can waive the requirements for certain monofills, which are defined as landfills (also surface impoundments and waste piles) used to treat, store or dispose of inorganic wastes that are hazardous solely because they exhibit the characteristic of EP toxicity.[55] Congress indicated

---

[52]   50 Fed. Reg. 28706-709 (July 15, 1985).

[53]   47 Fed. Reg. 32289 (July 26, 1982).

[54]   40 CFR 264.301(d), 265.301(c).

[55]   47 Fed. Reg. 32281 (July 26, 1982).

in RCRA Section 3004(o) that certain monofills need not meet the minimum technological requirements of the 1984 Amendments. Accordingly, EPA has provided that monofills which contain only EP toxic hazardous wastes from foundry furnace emission controls or metal casting molding sand may be exempt.[56] The monofill must have at least one liner, be located more than one-quarter mile from an underground source of drinking water, and be in compliance with groundwater monitoring requirements. Alternatively, the owner of the monofill may demonstrate that location, design, and operating considerations assure that there will be no migration of hazardous constituents into ground or surface waters at any future time.

The interim status and permanent standards also require all landfill operators to install run-on and runoff control systems.[57] Run-on to the landfill must be diverted to prevent erosion. Run-off from precipitation must be collected and managed to reduce the potential for off-site migration. The operator must, of course, determine whether such runoff is a hazardous waste subject to the RCRA program. An NPDES permit may also be required if the collected runoff is discharged through a point source to waters of the United States.

Landfills may also be subject to wind erosion. The interim and permanent regulations therefore require that landfills be covered or managed so as to control wind dispersal of particulate matter. No particular method of control is specified, but the operator is directed to develop a technique for the particular wastes and/or landfill involved.[58]

---

[56]   40 CFR 264.301(e), 265.301(d). For the parallel provisions for surface impoundments, see 40 CFR 264.221(e) and 265.221(d).

[57]   40 CFR 265.302, 264.301(f) - (h).

[58]   40 CFR 265.302(d), 264.301(i).

6.7.3 Liquids in Landfills

The presence of liquid wastes and free liquids in a landfill poses particular problems because such liquids may become a transport medium and increase the likelihood that hazardous waste constituents will leach into groundwater. EPA initially allowed the disposal of liquids in landfills, provided the landfill was equipped with a single liner and leachate collection system.[59] Congress was dissatisfied with EPA's regulation, however. In the 1984 Amendments, Congress imposed an absolute ban on the disposal in landfills of bulk or non-containerized liquid hazardous waste and hazardous waste containing free liquids.[60] The ban took effect on May 8, 1985, and EPA has amended its regulations accordingly.[61] This ban is closely related to the land disposal restrictions of specific hazardous wastes of 40 CFR Part 268 as discussed in Chapter 7.

The liquids ban encompasses hazardous wastes containing free liquids even if absorbents have been added to such wastes. Moreover, EPA construes the ban on the "placement" of liquids in landfills as prohibiting the practice of solidifying liquid hazardous wastes in a landfill cell.[62] Finally, EPA has also amended its regulations at the direction of Congress to ban the placement of a liquid which is not a hazardous waste in an interim status or permitted landfill.[63]

---

[59]   40 CFR 265.314, 264.314 (1984) (superseded).

[60]   RCRA § 3004(c)(1).

[61]   40 CFR 264.314(b), 265.314(b). EPA has also issued a guidance document entitled "Prohibition on the Placement of Bulk Liquid Hazardous Waste in Landfills - Statutory Interpretative Guidance."   (NTIS No. PB86-212-271) See 51 Fed. Reg. 26008 (July 18, 1986).

[62]   See 50 Fed. Reg. 28705 (July 15, 1985).

[63]   RCRA § 3004(c)(3). 40 CFR 264.314(e), 265.314(f).

Containerized liquid wastes pose the same problems because containers will corrode and leak over time. Consequently, EPA's regulations currently specify that containers of free liquid wastes may not be placed in a landfill unless all freestanding liquid has been removed or the liquid waste has been mixed with absorbent or solidified so that freestanding liquid is eliminated. In addition, containers holding liquids can be placed in landfills if the container itself is designed to hold liquids for a use other than storage (e.g., batteries or capacitors), or if the container meets the regulatory definition of a "lab pack", or if the container is "very small" such as an ampule. Empty containers must be crushed flat or shredded before being placed in a landfill in order to avoid a future problem of collapse and disruption of the final cover. Alternatively, containers must be at least 90 percent full when placed in the landfill.[64] Congress directed EPA to issue regulations that further minimize the disposal of containerized liquid hazardous wastes in landfills, and prohibit the disposal of hazardous wastes mixed with absorbent material that is biodegradable or that will release liquids when compressed under pressures experienced in landfills.[65] In response, EPA adopted the Paint Filter Liquids Test to test whether containerized hazardous waste contains free liquids, listed categories of nonbiodegradable sorbents, such as clay, sand, and synthetic polymers, and identified two tests to determine the nonbiodegradability of sorbents not listed.[66]

6.7.4 Miscellaneous Requirements

While operating a landfill, the operator must record on a map the exact location and dimensions of each landfill cell and the types of hazardous waste deposited there. This requirement is

---

[64] 40 CFR 264.315, 265.315.

[65] RCRA § 3004(c)(2).

[66] 57 Fed. Reg. 54452 (November 18, 1992).

designed to ensure proper operation, closure, and damage assessment. The map must be part of the operating record of the facility. Operators of landfills must also conduct periodic inspections during construction or installation of the liner, and then weekly and after storms.

Operators of interim status and permitted facilities must place a final cover over each cell in the landfill as the cell is closed, and a final cover over the landfill at closure.[67] After closure, the operator must conduct post-closure care. Under limited circumstances, surface impoundments, land treatment facilities and landfills may remain open after the final receipt of hazardous wastes in order to receive non-hazardous wastes in that unit.[68]

6.8 Groundwater Protection and Corrective Action

Protection of groundwater against contamination from releases of hazardous wastes is a major objective of RCRA.[69] The interim and permanent standards for the four types of T/S/D facilities just discussed -- surface impoundments, waste piles (permanent status only), land treatment units, and landfills -- contain extensive groundwater monitoring and response requirements.[70] The interim status standards focus mainly on the installation of monitoring wells, sampling and analysis, and reporting requirements. The permanent standards impose an extensive scheme for detecting leachate plumes at the facility boundary and instituting corrective action when contamination threatens human health or the

---

[67] 40 CFR 264.310, 265.310.

[68] 54 Fed. Reg. 33376 et seq. (Aug. 14, 1989).

[69] S. Rep. No. 94-988, 94th Cong., 2nd Sess. 3 (1976).

[70] 40 CFR Part 265, Subpart F; Part 264, Subpart F. A guidance document concerning the regulations, entitled "RCRA Groundwater Monitoring Technical Enforcement Guidance Document," has been made available by EPA (NTIS No. PB87-107-751). 51 Fed. Reg. 34247 (September 26, 1986).

environment.[71] The corrective action authorities discussed in this chapter are separate from RCRA Section 3004(u) which mandates that all permits issued after 1984 require corrective action for all releases of hazardous waste or constituents from any solid waste management unit ("SWMU"). Corrective action requirements for SWMUs are addressed in Chapter 8. Congress directed that every land disposal facility operating under interim status had to certify to EPA by November 8, 1985, that it was in compliance with applicable groundwater monitoring requirements, or else interim status terminated.[72]

6.8.1 The Interim Status Standards

The interim status regulations provide that the operator of a T/S/D facility that contains a surface impoundment, landfill, or land treatment unit must implement a groundwater monitoring program capable of determining the facility's impact on the quality of groundwater in the uppermost aquifer beneath the facility.[73] The regulations establish specific standards for the installation, operation, and maintenance of the groundwater monitoring system. For example, the regulations specify that there must be at least three monitoring wells installed hydraulically downgradient at the limit of the waste management area and one monitoring well installed hydraulically upgradient from the limit of the waste management area.[74] The siting of the wells and the decision to install more than four is up to the operator, provided the groundwater monitoring system is designed to detect migration of

---

[71] 40 CFR 264.101.

[72] RCRA § 3005(e)(2).

[73] See generally 40 CFR 265.90-265.94.

[74] If the operator knows or is willing to assume that his T/S/D facility is leaching hazardous waste into groundwater, he must develop a plan for an alternative monitoring system on a site-specific basis to determine the extent of groundwater contamination. 40 CFR 265.90(d).

hazardous constituents from the facility to the uppermost aquifer.[75]

During the initial year of the monitoring program, samples of groundwater must be taken and analyzed quarterly for, among other things, suitability of the groundwater as a drinking water supply. The results of the quarterly analysis must be submitted to EPA within 15 days. As part of the report, operators must identify for each well any contaminant that exceeds the EPA Interim Primary Drinking Water Standards.[76] After the first year, sampling and analysis must be conducted annually for the parameters related to groundwater quality and semiannually for the parameters related to groundwater contamination. The groundwater monitoring program must be carried out for the active life of the facility and the records must be maintained throughout the post-closure period.

Once the groundwater monitoring system is installed, the operator must develop and follow a groundwater sampling plan.[77] If by statistical evaluation of groundwater monitoring data, the operator suspects that a hazardous waste discharge is occurring at his facility, he is required to notify EPA and develop a plan to assess the quality of the groundwater. The regulations do not state what immediate remedial steps, if any, EPA might impose during interim status.[78] In the event that an interim status T/S/D

---

[75]   In siting monitoring wells, the operator of an interim status facility should keep in mind the requirements of the permanent program, discussed below, which call for the installation of wells at the boundaries of the waste management area. See 40 CFR 264.95. But see, 40 CFR 265.91 (allowing interim status landfills to site monitoring wells as close to the facility boundary as practical where an existing physical obstacle prevents installing well at limit.)

[76]   On February 23, 1982, EPA suspended the compliance dates for submission of the first two quarterly reports, except where the Drinking Water Standards were exceeded. 47 Fed. Reg. 7841.

[77]   40 CFR 265.92.

[78]   See 45 Fed. Reg. 33161.

facility is found to be contaminating groundwater, EPA will accelerate its review of the facility's permit application. Remedial action required by a permit could require capital-intensive repairs or modifications to the facility and removal of contaminants from the groundwater. EPA's corrective action authority under RCRA Sections 3004(u) and (v) and 3008(h), and its imminent hazard authority under RCRA Section 7003, enable EPA to seek prompt relief if necessary.

6.8.2 The Standards for Permitted Facilities

In the permanent regulations, EPA has established a three-stage program to detect, evaluate, and, if necessary, correct groundwater contamination at permitted land disposal facilities.[79] The first stage is a detection monitoring program designed to monitor groundwater wells for hazardous constituents that would indicate whether a leachate plume has reached the boundary of the waste management area. The second stage, which begins if a plume is detected, consists of a compliance monitoring program designed to track the migration of the hazardous constituents and to compare groundwater samples against a groundwater protection standard. The third stage begins if the groundwater protection standard is violated so that a corrective action program is necessary. Corrective action may consist of the removal or treatment in place of the hazardous constituents. Compliance monitoring and corrective action may continue during the facility's post-closure

---

[79] See generally 40 CFR 264.90-264.100. A limited exemption is provided for any surface impoundment, waste pile, land treatment unit, or landfill unit that EPA finds: (1) is an engineered structure; (2) does not receive or contain liquid waste or waste containing free liquids; (3) is designed and operated to exclude liquid, precipitation, and other run-on and runoff; (4) has both inner and outer layers of containment enclosing the waste; (5) has a leak detection system built into each containment layer which will be continuously operated and maintained; and (6) will not allow hazardous constituents to migrate beyond the outer containment layer. 40 CFR 264.90(b).

care period and, if necessary, even longer. The elements of each of these three programs are discussed below.

All of the important details of an operator's groundwater monitoring program will be developed through the RCRA permitting process, probably after extensive review with EPA (or an authorized state) and the interested public. For most land disposal facilities, the permitting process is likely to be expensive, lengthy, complex, and controversial. EPA's permit procedures, discussed in Chapter 8, provide for public hearings and comment on the terms and conditions of a facility's RCRA permit. The requirements of a groundwater monitoring program will be a highly visible and key aspect of a land disposal facility's RCRA permit.

All land disposal facilities must, at a minimum, institute a detection monitoring program to determine whether the facility is leaking hazardous constituents to groundwater.[80] For existing facilities, if groundwater monitoring during the interim program has revealed that hazardous waste constituents are already leaking from the facility, the operator will have to adopt a compliance monitoring program and corrective action program, if necessary, as part of the initial RCRA permit.[81] In all cases, the operator must install a sufficient number of monitoring wells of an adequate depth at points of compliance specified in the permit to effectively monitor the groundwater.[82] The operator must then monitor the quality of the groundwater passing the compliance points (generally at downgradient wells) and the quality of groundwater that has not been affected by any leakage from the

[80]   40 CFR 264.91(a)(4), 264.98.

[81]   40 CFR 264.91(a)(1), (3).

[82]   40 CFR 264.95, 264.97(a).

facility (generally at upgradient wells). The hazardous constituents or parameters to be monitored will be specified in the facility's permit.[83] As part of the detection monitoring program, the operator must establish a background value for each constituent in the permit based on data from upgradient wells.[84] This background value will be used to compare against monitoring results to determine possible contamination.

In the detection monitoring program, at least twice a year the operator must determine the groundwater quality at each monitoring well.[85] At least once a year the operator must determine the groundwater flow rate and direction in the uppermost aquifer. The procedures and methods for sampling and analysis are set forth in the regulations.[86] Basically they call for the operator to determine whether there is a statistically significant increase over the background value for any constituent or parameter specified in the permit.[87] If so, the operator must move into a more active groundwater protection mode. The operator must first report to EPA within seven days the constituents that have shown statistically significant increases.[88] The operator must also immediately sample groundwater at all monitoring wells and

---

[83] EPA has issued interim guidance on this requirement. See 51 Fed. Reg. 5561 (February 14, 1986).

[84] 40 CFR 264.97(g), 264.98(c).

[85] 40 CFR 264.98(d).

[86] 40 CFR 264.97(d) and (e), and 264.98(f).

[87] At least four samples must be taken from each well to identify any statistically significant evidence of contamination. Due to problems with using the Cochran's Approximation to the Behrens-Fisher Student's T-test, EPA has changed the permanent standards to allow the use of alternative statistical methods to monitor for potential contamination. See 53 Fed. Reg. 39720 (Oct. 11, 1988); 40 CFR 264.97(h),(i).

[88] 40 CFR 264.98(g)(1).

determine the background value and concentration of all constituents identified in Appendix IX to Part 264.[89] Within 90 days, the operator must submit to EPA an application for a permit modification to establish a compliance monitoring program. Within a further 90 days, the operator should submit an engineering feasibility plan for a corrective action program that could be implemented if the contamination continues.[90]

The purpose of the compliance monitoring program is to monitor groundwater to assess compliance with groundwater protection standards and concentration limits for constituents contained in the permit. A groundwater protection standard must be set for each hazardous constituent based on concentration limits proposed by the operator in his application for a permit modification and set by EPA in the permit.[91] The concentration limit will be (1) the maximum limits contained in EPA's Interim Primary Drinking Water Standards, (2) the background level of the constituent in the groundwater if the background level is lower or there is no Interim Primary Drinking Water Standard for that constituent, or (3) an alternate concentration limit which the operator has demonstrated will not pose a substantial present or potential hazard to

---

[89] 40 CFR 264.98(g)(2). Appendix IX is a new list of hazardous constituents developed especially for groundwater monitoring at RCRA land disposal units. See 52 Fed. Reg. 25942 (July 9, 1987).

[90] 40 CFR 264.98(g)(5). The operator may seek a waiver of these requirements if the operator can show, based on adequate monitoring data, that a source other than the operator's facility caused the increase or that the increase resulted from error in sampling, analysis, or evaluation. While the operator may attempt to make this demonstration in lieu of submitting a permit modification, if the requested waiver is rejected by EPA the operator is not relieved from the obligation to seek a timely permit modification and may be found in violation of the permit if the operator does not do so. 40 CFR 264.98(g)(6).

[91] 40 CFR 264.92, 264.99(a).

human health or the environment.[92] Thus, compliance with the groundwater protection standard is intended to preserve the existing best use of the aquifer.

At least twice a year, the operator must determine the concentration of hazardous constituents in the groundwater at each monitoring well and determine whether there is a statistically significant increase.[93] On an annual basis, the operator must analyze samples from all monitoring wells for constituents contained in Appendix IX to determine whether additional hazardous constituents are present in the uppermost aquifer. The compliance period during which the operator must continue to ensure that the groundwater protection standard is not exceeded will be set in the permit. It will generally be equal to the number of years that the waste management area was active (including any period prior to permitting when hazardous waste was disposed of, and the closure period), although this period may be extended in certain circumstances.[94]

Whenever the operator determines as a result of monitoring that a groundwater protection standard is being exceeded, the operator must institute a <u>corrective action</u> program. The EPA regulations do not describe in detail what those corrective measures can be, other than to direct that the operator must remove the hazardous constituent from the groundwater or conduct treatment in place to achieve compliance with the groundwater protec-

---

[92]   40 CFR 264.94. The maximum limits derived from EPA's Interim Primary Drinking Water Standards are set forth in Table 1 to 40 CFR 264.94. EPA has made available a guidance document on this subject entitled, <u>Alternate Concentration Limit Guidance Policy and Information Requirements</u> Part 1 (July 1987) (NTIS No. PB87-206-165); Part 2 (NTIS No. PB88-214-267). 52 <u>Fed. Reg.</u> 27579.

[93]   40 CFR 264.99(d); 40 CFR 264.99(f).

[94]   40 CFR 264.96.

tion standard.[95] Measures to contain or substantially slow down the rate of contamination will not be sufficient.

The operator must file a report in writing with EPA twice a year describing the effectiveness of the corrective action program.[96] If EPA believes that the corrective action program has not resulted in compliance with the groundwater protection standards within a reasonable time, it may seek to modify the facility's permit to impose more extensive requirements. Corrective action may be terminated during the operating life of the facility once the concentration of hazardous constituents is reduced to levels below the limits set in the groundwater protection standards.[97]

6.9 Temporary Part 267 Standards for Land Disposal Facilities

Before EPA issued the permanent Part 264 standards for land disposal activities discussed above, no permits could be issued to new facilities. This effectively resulted in a moratorium on new facility construction at a time when disposal capacity was already scarce. Accordingly, EPA issued temporary Part 267 regulations on February 13, 1981, which established performance standards to allow EPA to issue permits to new land disposal facilities until the final Part 264 standards were issued. These Part 267 regulations expired on January 26, 1983, when the permanent Part 264

---

[95] 40 CFR 264.100.

[96] 40 CFR 264.100(g).

[97] 40 CFR 264.100(e)(4). If the corrective action program extends beyond the compliance period (i.e., the number of years equal to the active life of the waste management area including the closure period), the operator must demonstrate that the groundwater protection standard has not been exceeded for three consecutive years before he is allowed to cease the corrective action measures. 40 CFR 264.100(f).

regulations went into effect.[98] Although they remain in the Code of Federal Regulations, they have no current application.

6.10 Incinerators

An "incinerator" is an "enclosed device using controlled flame combustion that neither meets the criteria for classification as a boiler nor is listed as an industrial furnace."[99] Examples of incinerators are rotary kiln, fluidized bed, and liquid injection incinerators. Properly operated incineration can accomplish the safe destruction of hazardous wastes with very low environmental risk.

The interim status standards for incinerators are "good operating practices" designed to reduce potential hazards.[100] Prior to incinerating a hazardous waste, the operator must conduct a waste analysis to determine the type of pollutants that will be emitted and to establish steady state (normal) operating conditions. The analysis must determine the heating value of the waste, halogen content, sulphur content, and concentrations of lead and mercury. Hazardous waste may not be fed into an incinerator unless it is operating at its steady state condition. The operator must inspect the combustion and emission control instruments every 15 minutes, the outside stack emissions every hour, and the complete incinerator and associated equipment every day.

---

[98]   See 40 CFR 267.3(a).

[99]   40 CFR 260.10(a). An incinerator should be distinguished from a "boiler" and an "industrial furnace" which are elaborately defined in 40 CFR 260.10. The Part 266 standards for burning of hazardous wastes for energy recovery in boilers and furnaces are discussed in section 6.15.3 infra. The standards for burning of used oil in boilers and furnaces are discussed in Chapter 13 of this Handbook. The interim status and permanent standards for incinerators apply to a hazardous waste "incinerator" as defined in the text, and to boilers or industrial furnaces that burn hazardous wastes in order to destroy the wastes, rather than to recover energy.

[100]   See generally 40 CFR 265.340-265.352.

These standards do not apply to wastes that are hazardous only because they are ignitable if the operator can document that the waste feed would not reasonably be expected to contain any of the hazardous constituents listed in 40 CFR Part 261, Appendix VIII.

The permanent standards for incinerators include the "good operating practices" established for interim status facilities and then set forth additional performance and design requirements.[101] Before an incinerator can receive a permit, it must conduct trial burns for waste feeds it proposes to incinerate pursuant to a trial burn permit.[102] Destruction and removal efficiencies can vary greatly for any given waste feed depending on the specific design and operating features of the incinerator. Trial burns must be conducted to determine the operating conditions that must be specified in the incinerator permit to ensure compliance with the applicable performance standards.

To obtain a trial burn permit, the operator of an incinerator must prepare a trial burn plan which includes an extensive amount of information on the waste feed, the design and performance of the incinerator, sampling and monitoring procedures, and the time, waste quantity and operating conditions of the proposed trial burn. The trial burn permit will be of limited duration, generally less than a dozen hours of combustion, spread over operating periods of up to two weeks. A number of trial burns may be required to establish acceptable waste analyses and performance standards.

As part of the trial burn plan, the operator must conduct a detailed analysis of his waste feed which is then submitted with

---

[101] See generally 40 CFR 264.340-264.351. EPA has published a manual that provides guidance to permit writers in designating the facility-specific conditions necessary to comply with the Part 264 incinerator standards. 48 Fed. Reg. 36582 (August 12, 1983). EPA has published a more current guidance document entitled "Permitting Hazardous Waste Incinerators." (EPA LSW 530-SW-88-024, April 15, 1988).

[102] 40 CFR 270.19(b).

Part B of his permit application.[103] The analysis must describe certain physical properties of the waste feed and identify the presence of any hazardous organic constituents listed in 40 CFR Part 261, Appendix VIII. This analysis is necessary to determine the applicability of the destruction and removal performance standards discussed below. In addition, throughout normal operation of the incinerator the operator must conduct sufficient waste analysis tests to verify that the waste feed to the incinerator is within the scope of the permit.

Incinerator permits will be written to specify the waste feeds that are allowed based on the incinerator's demonstrated ability to treat those wastes, and any deviation from the specified waste feed could constitute a permit violation. If an operator wishes to incinerate a waste feed that is not classified in the permit, he must either obtain a modification of the permit or, if the burn is to be of short duration, he may secure a temporary trial burn permit.[104]

The key to the incinerator regulations can be found in three performance standards.[105] The first of these is that incinerators burning hazardous wastes must achieve a destruction and removal efficiency rate of 99.99 percent for each principal organic hazardous constituent ("POHC") designated by EPA for each particular hazardous waste feed. The POHC will be specified in the facility's permit issued by EPA from among those constituents listed in 40 CFR Part 261, Appendix VIII, as determined by the waste analysis. EPA will identify a POHC based upon the degree of

---

[103]   40 CFR 264.341, 270.62.

[104]   40 CFR 264.344.

[105]   40 CFR 264.343. Congress directed in the 1984 Amendments that all incinerators that receive permits must meet these "minimum technological requirements" established by EPA's performance standards. RCRA § 3004(o)(1)(B). The 1984 Amendments simply codified EPA's existing regulations. See 50 Fed. Reg. 28726 (July 15, 1985).

difficulty in incineration of the organic constituents in the waste and their concentration or mass in the waste feed.

The second performance standard is a requirement that incinerators burning hazardous waste containing more than 0.5 percent chlorine must remove 99 percent of the hydrogen chloride from the exhaust gas. Finally, the third performance standard provides that incinerators may not emit particulate matter exceeding 180 milligrams per dry standard cubic meter.

These three performance standards will be implemented largely by the operating requirements set forth in the incinerator's permit. The permit will specify on a case-by-case basis specific operating conditions with respect to each authorized waste feed.[106] In addition, three operating requirements will be applied uniformly. First, during start-up and shutdown of an incinerator, hazardous waste must not be fed unless the incinerator is at a steady state of operation. Second, all operators must control fugitive emissions. Third, incinerators will be required to operate with a system to shut off waste feed to the incinerator when operating requirements are violated.

Finally, the regulations provide that there be continuous monitoring of the incinerator with respect to combustion temperature, waste feed rate, air feed rate and carbon monoxide content of the exhaust. Incinerators and associated equipment must be inspected daily and alarm systems and emergency shutdown controls must be inspected weekly.[107]

6.11 Thermal Treatment Units

Thermal treatment is "the treatment of hazardous waste in a device which uses elevated temperatures as the primary means to

---

[106] 40 CFR 264.345.

[107] 40 CFR 264.347.

change the chemical, physical, or biological character or composition of the hazardous waste."[108] Examples of thermal treatment processes are incineration, molten salt, pyrolysis, calcination, wet air oxidation, and microwave discharge. The permanent technical standards for thermal treatment processes will be promulgated in the future. The existing interim status regulations for thermal treatment facilities are very similar to those for incinerators.[109]

The open burning of wastes is not considered a permissible form of thermal treatment. Open burning of hazardous wastes is prohibited except for the open burning and detonation of waste explosives conducted in accordance with specific requirements in the regulations.

6.12 Chemical, Physical, and Biological Treatment Units

Tanks, surface impoundments, land treatment facilities, and incinerators are the primary methods used by companies to treat hazardous wastes. EPA recognizes, however, that chemical, physical, and biological treatment can be conducted in other types of equipment. At this point, EPA has not developed equipment-specific regulation for treatment processes or types of treatment equipment not discussed above. Therefore, EPA has basically applied the interim status standards for tanks to all chemical, physical, and biological treatment facilities.[110] EPA expects to promulgate more technical standards, including permitted facility standards for chemical, physical, and biological treatment in the future.

---

[108] 40 CFR 260.10.

[109] See generally 40 CFR 265.370-265.383.

[110] See generally 40 CFR 265.400-265.406.

THE RCRA HAZARDOUS WASTES HANDBOOK

6.13 Underground Injection Wells

EPA's regulations exempt those underground injection facilities that are operated pursuant to an Underground Injection Control ("UIC") permit issued in accordance with the Safe Drinking Water Act.[111] That Act establishes a program for the protection of underground sources of drinking water, and authorizes EPA to issue regulations under which states are to establish UIC programs. The states must adopt permit programs to prevent underground injection of pollutants which endanger drinking water supplies. UIC wells are significantly affected by the land disposal restrictions of the 1984 Amendments as discussed in Chapter 7.

EPA's regulations classify injection practices into five categories, or classes of wells, for regulatory treatment. The classes are: (I) wells used for injection of hazardous wastes, other than Class IV wells, and industrial and municipal disposal wells that inject below all underground sources of drinking water; (II) oil and gas production and storage wells; (III) special process injection wells such as are related to mineral mining, energy recovery, and gasification of oil shale; (IV) wells used by generators of hazardous or radioactive waste or hazardous waste management facilities where the waste is injected into or above a formation which, within one-quarter mile of the well, contains an underground source of drinking water; and (V) all other injection wells. Technical criteria and standards are set out for each class of well designed to provide appropriate protection of undergroundwater supplies. EPA has imposed a ban on the injection of

---

[111] See 40 CFR 265.430, 264.1(d). EPA's regulations for the UIC program are set forth at 40 CFR Part 144-147. These regulations were substantially revised in 1988 as part of EPA's implementation of the land disposal restrictions in connection with UIC wells. See 53 Fed. Reg. 28118 et seq. (July 26, 1988). In addition, a new 40 CFR Part 148 was created to address the land ban's application to UIC wells. Id. See discussion in Chapter 7.

hazardous wastes into or above an underground source of drinking water.[112]

In the 1984 Amendments, Congress enacted a new RCRA Section 7010 which bans the injection of hazardous waste into or above any underground formation which contains, within one-quarter mile of the injection well, an underground source of drinking water. This statutory ban on Class IV wells was effective on May 8, 1985, in any state which does not have identical or more stringent prohibitions in effect under the UIC program. Now that Congress has adopted the underground injection ban under RCRA, the statutory prohibition may be enforced under the citizen suit provisions of RCRA Section 7002 and the imminent endangerment authority of RCRA Section 7003.

RCRA Section 7010(b) also provides an exception to the underground injection ban for certain remedial actions taken by EPA. The ban does not apply to the injection of contaminated groundwater into the aquifer from which it was withdrawn if (1) the injection is part of a federally-supervised cleanup action under RCRA or Superfund, (2) the contaminated groundwater is treated to substantially reduce hazardous constituents, and (3) the cleanup will be sufficient to protect human health and the environment.[113]

6.14 Part 266 Standards for the Management of Specific Hazardous Wastes and for Specific Types of Hazardous Waste Facilities

EPA has promulgated a Part 266 to its regulations for special types of T/S/D facilities and hazardous waste management activities. These regulations include standards for facilities that recycle certain hazardous wastes. For the most part they are less extensive than the Part 264 regulation, especially for those types of wastes or management practices that do not pose significant

---

[112]   40 CFR 144.13.

[113]   See discussion at 50 Fed. Reg. 28718-19 (July 15, 1985).

environmental risks. The specific categories covered are: recyclable materials used in a manner constituting disposal (Subpart C); hazardous waste burned for energy recovery (Subpart D); used oil burned for energy recovery (Subpart E); precious metals recovery (Subpart F); and spent lead-acid batteries being reclaimed (Subpart G). EPA plans to add other special regulatory requirements which will govern additional types of T/S/D facilities and/or specific hazardous wastes in the future.

6.14.1 Standards for Recyclable Materials Used in a Manner Constituting Disposal

In EPA's recycling regulations, the Agency has asserted RCRA jurisdiction over hazardous wastes and waste-derived products that are recycled by being applied directly to or placed on the land.[114] In the 1984 Amendments, Congress expected EPA "to devote attention to the dangers posed . . . both with respect to hazardous waste used or re-used directly on the land and with respect to hazardous waste-derived products used or re-used by being applied directly to the land."[115] Congress had in mind the Monument Street Landfill in Baltimore, Maryland, where toxic chromium wastes were used as a landfill cover, resulting in toxic contamination of adjacent soil and surface waters.[116]

In its recycling regulations promulgated in January 1985, EPA provided that spent materials, sludges, by-products, and commercial chemical products which are listed or characteristic hazardous wastes are subject to RCRA when (1) applied to or placed on the land in a manner that constitutes disposal, or (2) contained in products that are applied to the land.[117] Thus,

---

[114] 40 CFR Part 266, Subpart C.

[115] H. Rep. No. 98-198, 98th Cong., 1st Sess. (1983) 46.

[116] Id.

[117] 40 CFR 261.2(c). However, commercial chemical products are
[footnote continued]

STANDARDS FOR SPECIFIC TYPES
OF T/S/D FACILITIES

EPA asserted jurisdiction not only over hazardous wastes used on the land without significant change, but also to all products containing these wastes that continue to qualify as hazardous wastes and are applied to the land. This could include fertilizers, asphalt, and building foundation materials that use hazardous wastes as ingredients and are then applied to the land.[118]

Although EPA has asserted RCRA jurisdiction over waste-derived products that are placed on the land, EPA has temporarily exempted these products from any substantive Part 266 standards. EPA believes that bringing the ultimate users of these waste-derived commercial products, such as farmers and highway construction crews, within the ambit of the RCRA regulatory program is not currently practical. However, the waste-derived product must be a "commercial product" that is marketed for general use in order to be exempted. A generator who adds a hazardous waste to other material, and then applies the waste-derived product to its own land without also selling the product may still be subject to the Part 266 standards.

Accordingly, the Part 266 regulations apply to hazardous wastes, whether mixed or combined with other substances, that are recycled by being applied to or placed directly on the land.[119] In effect, EPA is regulating secondary materials that are hazardous wastes and are recycled in a manner constituting disposal the

---

[continued]
    not considered recycled if they are applied to the land in their ordinary manner of use. _Id_.

[118] _See_ 50 _Fed_. _Reg_. 628 (January 4, 1985).

[119] 40 CFR 266.20(a).

same way as hazardous wastes disposed of in landfills.[120] Operators of facilities that recycle hazardous wastes by land application in a manner constituting disposal are, by virtue of Part 266, subject to the RCRA regulations for landfills in Parts 264 and 265, the RCRA permit provisions in Parts 270 and 124, and the RCRA Section 3010 notification requirement.[121] Generators and transporters of hazardous wastes that will be recycled in this manner are subject to the full requirements of Parts 262 and 263, respectively.[122] Likewise, operators of storage facilities for hazardous wastes that will be used in a manner constituting disposal are subject to the applicable provisions of parts 264 and 265, RCRA permits, and the Section 3010 notification.

In sum, spent materials, sludges, by-products, and commercial chemicals which are hazardous wastes and are recycled by being applied to or placed on the land are essentially regulated like all other hazardous wastes that are landfilled under RCRA.

6.14.2 Hazardous Waste Burned for Energy Recovery

In the 1984 Amendments, Congress demanded immediate action by EPA in regulating the burning and blending of hazardous wastes. Because the burning of hazardous wastes for energy recovery had been exempted by EPA from RCRA regulation, it had become a common practice to burn hazardous waste-derived fuels in commercial, institutional, and industrial boilers resulting in unregulated air emissions of toxic pollutants. Therefore, Congress required all persons who produce, distribute, market, or burn hazardous waste

---

[120] EPA has exempted hazardous wastes that are mixed with other substances and which thereby undergo a chemical reaction so as to become inseparable from the other substance by physical means. EPA intends that this exemption will apply to hazardous wastes that have undergone chemical bonding, so that they are chemically transformed. See 50 Fed. Reg. 646 (January 4, 1985).

[121] 40 CFR 266.23.

[122] 40 CFR 266.21.

fuels to file a notification with EPA or an authorized state by February 8, 1986.[123] Such persons were required to describe their facility, the hazardous waste involved, and the production or energy recovery activity carried out for the facility -- resulting in a "snapshot" of hazardous waste blending and burning activities as the basis for future EPA regulation.

Congress then directed EPA to promulgate regulations for persons that produce, transport, distribute, market, or burn fuel containing hazardous waste.[124] These regulations may include any of the requirements set forth in RCRA Section 3004 for T/S/D facilities (e.g., design, location, construction and operating standards, financial responsibility, permits, etc.) that are necessary to protect human health and the environment. These persons must also maintain records regarding fuel blending, distribution, and use as EPA may require. In the meantime, the 1984 Amendments make it unlawful for any person who is required to file a RCRA Section 3010 notification to distribute or market any hazardous waste-derived fuel after February 7, 1985, without the following legend on the invoice or bill of sale:

> WARNING: THIS FUEL CONTAINS HAZARDOUS WASTES
> [followed by a list of the hazardous wastes]

This legend must appear in conspicuous type which is clearly distinguishable from other printed matter on the invoice or bill of sale.

EPA has defined the entire universe of enclosed devices that use controlled flame combustion to dispose of hazardous wastes as incinerators, boilers, and industrial furnaces. Incinerators have been subject to interim status and permanent standards in 40 CFR Parts 264 and 265, Subpart O, since January 1981. The essential

---

[123] RCRA § 3010(a).

[124] RCRA § 3004(g). EPA has missed the statutory deadline of November 1986 for these rules. See 51 Fed. Reg. 41900 (November 19, 1986).

difference is that incinerators are used to destroy hazardous wastes, while boilers and industrial furnaces are used to burn hazardous waste fuels for energy recovery.

EPA has banned the burning of hazardous wastes as fuels in non-industrial boilers and furnaces. The terms "boilers" and "industrial furnaces" have been elaborately defined to ensure that every other kind of combustion device is regulated as an incinerator requiring a RCRA permit.[125] EPA has defined a "boiler" to mean:

> an enclosed device using controlled flame combustion and having the following characteristics:
>
> (1)(i) the unit must have physical provisions for recovering and exporting thermal energy in the form of steam, heated fluids, or heated gases; and
>
> (ii) the unit's combustion chamber and primary energy recovery section(s) must be of integral design;[126] and
>
> (iii) while in operation, the unit must maintain a thermal energy recovery efficiency of at least 60 percent, calculated in terms of the recovered energy compared with the thermal value of the fuel; and

---

125   40 CFR 260.10.

126   EPA stipulates that to be of "integral design", the combustion chamber and the primary energy recovery section(s), such as water walls and super heaters, must be physically formed into one manufactured or assembled unit. Id. A unit in which the combustion chamber and the primary energy recovery section(s) are joined only by ducts or connections carrying flue gas is not integrally designed. Process heaters and fluidized bed combustion units are not precluded from being boilers, however, solely because they are not of integral design. Id.

(iv) the unit must export and utilize at least 75 percent of the recovered energy, calculated on an annual basis. In this calculation, no credit shall be given for recovered heat used internally in the same unit.[127]

Thus, EPA has relied on physical criteria (integral design, combustion efficiency, and energy recovery) in defining a boiler, supplemented by additional physical standards for continuous and long-term energy recovery. This two-part test is designed to ensure that combustion units which are physically designed as boilers are then actually used for energy recovery and not unregulated and possibly inadequate destruction of hazardous wastes. In addition, EPA has established criteria based on the same design and physical standards for determining on a case-by-case basis whether a combustion device, which does not meet the technical definition of a boiler, nevertheless may be classified as a boiler.[128]

EPA has also promulgated a detailed definition of "industrial furnace" as follows:

any of the following enclosed devices that are integral components of manufacturing processes and that use thermal treatment to accomplish recovery of materials or energy:

(1) cement kilns
(2) lime kilns
(3) aggregate kilns (including light-weight aggregate kilns and aggregate drying kilns used in the asphaltic concrete industry)
(4) phosphate kilns
(5) coke ovens
(6) blast furnaces
(7) smelting, melting, and refining furnaces (including pyrometallurgical devices such as cupolas, reverberator furnaces, sintering machines, roasters, and foundry furnaces)

---

127 Id.

128 40 CFR 260.32.

     (8) titanium dioxide chloride process oxida-
           tion reactors
     (9) methane reforming furnaces
    (10) pulping liquor recovery furnaces
    (11) combustion devices used in the recovery
           of sulfur, values from spent sulfuric
           acid.
    (12) halogen acid furnaces.[129]

In addition, EPA may, after notice and comment, add to this list any other industrial furnaces which are designed and used primarily for energy or materials recovery, in accordance with enumerated criteria.[130]

EPA has promulgated Part 266 standards for any person who generates, transports, or burns hazardous wastes as a fuel in a boiler or industrial furnace.[131] These standards apply to hazardous waste fuels that are produced by processing, blending, or other treatment. These "Phase I" rules require notification to EPA of waste-as-fuel activities, use of the manifest for shipments of hazardous waste fuels, and storage requirements for companies that market and burn hazardous waste fuels.[132]

EPA issued final "Phase II" rules, effective August 21, 1991, that control emissions from the burning of hazardous waste in boilers and industrial furnaces ("BIFs").[133] The rules subject owners/operators of BIF facilities to the general facility standards applicable to all T/S/D facilities and place limits on

---

[129] 40 CFR 260.10, as amended at 56 Fed. Reg. 7206 (Feb. 21, 1991).

[130] Id.

[131] 40 CFR Part 266, Subpart D. These regulations were upheld in Hazardous Waste Treatment Council v. U.S.EPA, 861 F.2d 277 (D.C. Cir. 1988) ("HWTC II"), cert. denied, 490 U.S. 1106 (1989).

[132] Id.

[133] 56 Fed. Reg. 7134 (Feb. 21, 1991). See also 40 CFR Part 266 Appendix IX (Methods Manual for Compliance with BIF Regulations).

the emissions of products of incomplete combustion ("PICs"), toxic metals, particulate matter ("PM"), and hydrogen chloride (HCl), as well as hazardous organic constituents in the waste. BIFs are held to the same destruction and removal efficiency ("DRE") standards as hazardous waste incinerators. PIC emissions are regulated by limits on flue gas concentrations of either carbon monoxide or, when applicable, hydrocarbon concentrations. Toxic metal emissions are regulated by a three-tier approach that allows higher emissions rates as the owner/operator conducts more site-specific testing and analyses. Hazardous waste storage units at regulated BIF facilities are subject to Part 264 permitted facility regulations. Interim status facilities must certify precompliance with emission controls for metals, HCl, particulates and carbon monoxide by August 21, 1991.[134]

For interim status BIFs, these performance standards will be implemented largely through operating restrictions. These operational restrictions mandate that the owner or operator of an interim status BIF 1) submit to the regulatory agency detailed information on the operations of the facility, 2) establish operating parameters regarding feed rate and feed streams, 3) certify that, in the owner's or operator's best engineering judgment, such operating parameters will be sufficient to obtain compliance with the performance standards, 4) notify the public that they have completed the requisite certification, 5) monitor their compliance with the operating parameters, and 6) test to verify compliance with the performance standards.[135]

To obtain a Part B permit, interim status BIFs must also either prepare and submit a trial burn plan and perform a trial burn in accordance with the standards established for new BIFs

---

[134] On September 5, 1991, EPA stayed the application of BIF permitting standards to coke ovens burning hazardous wastes from the coke by-products recovery process. 56 Fed. Reg. 43874 (September 5, 1991).

[135] 40 CFR 266.103.

(outlined below) or submit other data in lieu of a trial burn plan.[136] Data sufficient to qualify for this exemption to the trial burn requirement includes data from previous compliance testing conducted at the facility or data from compliance testing or trial burns at similar BIFs burning similar hazardous wastes under similar conditions.[137]

New BIFs are treated differently. Prior to commencing operation, owners and operators of these facilities must submit permit applications stating operating plans for four defined periods: 1) the pretrial burn period; 2) the trial burn period; 3) the post-trial burn period; and 4) the final permit period.[138] In each of these periods, the owner or operator is required to submit statements indicating operating restrictions believed to be sufficient to meet the applicable performance standards.[139] The EPA will review these statements and, where necessary, will specify additional requirements sufficient to meet the performances standards.

New BIFs must also prepare and submit a trial burn plan and conduct a trial burn.[140] The trial burn plan must include extensive information on the waste feed stream introduced to the boiler, the viscosity and other characteristics of that waste, the engineering design of the BIF and the testing protocol used in the trial burn.[141] Once a trial burn is complete, EPA is directed to make necessary modifications to the operating requirements in the

136 40 CFR 270.66(g).

137 40 CFR 270.22(a)(6).

138 40 CFR 270.66(b)-(f).

139 40 CFR 270.66(b)-(f); 40 CFR 266.104-266.107. The operating restrictions must, at a minimum, meet the operating requirements enumerated for new facilities in 40 CFR 266.102(e).

140 40 CFR 270.66(b)-(f).

141 40 CFR 270.66(c).

final permit to ensure compliance with the performance standards.[142]

Generators of hazardous waste burned as a fuel in boilers and industrial furnaces are subject to full regulation under Part 262, while transporters are subject to Part 263. Marketers of hazardous waste fuels are subject to all applicable provisions of Parts 264 and 265, Subparts A-L, including the need for a RCRA permit.[143] Marketers include generators who market hazardous waste fuel directly to a burner and also persons who receive hazardous waste from generators and then produce, process, or blend the hazardous waste fuel. Before a marketer initiates the first shipment of hazardous waste fuel to a burner, he must obtain a one-time written notice certifying that the burner has notified EPA and will burn the fuel only in an industrial boiler or furnace. Distributors who do not in any way process or blend hazardous waste fuel are not subject to regulation.

Finally, burners who store hazardous waste fuel for more than 90 days are subject to all applicable requirements in Parts 264 and 265, Subparts A-L. Burners can store hazardous waste fuel for less than 90 days without a RCRA permit by complying with the less stringent requirements applicable to generator temporary storage in 40 CFR 262.34. There are no interim status or RCRA permit requirements at this time that apply to burners with respect to the actual burning of the hazardous waste in boilers and industrial furnaces.[144]

Due to the land disposal ban, incineration of hazardous waste has become an increasingly popular form of disposal. As the need for greater incinerator capacity has grown, so has the concern

---

[142]   40 CFR 270.66(b)(4).

[143]   40 CFR 266.34.

[144]   However, "big city" cement kilns (defined as those located in cities with a population of 500,000 or more) may not burn such wastes unless they fully comply with incinerator standards. RCRA § 3004(q)(2)(C).

from neighbors of incinerators over the potential health risks associated with such facilities. On May 18, 1993, EPA announced an 18 month freeze on additional hazardous waste incinerator capacity to give the agency time to propose new waste combustion rules and place greater emphasis on source reduction and waste minimization.[145] During the freeze, interim permits for incinerators and BIFs will be reviewed.

Even before new regulations are proposed, EPA intends to impose several new requirements during the permitting of each interim status incinerator and BIF, including:

°   site-specific risk assessments;

°   more stringent particulate matter ("PM") standards, based upon the technology-based standards currently applicable to municipal waste combustors, to control metals emissions; and

°   more stringent dioxin and furan emission limits.[146]

EPA also intends to enhance public participation in the permitting of incinerators and BIFs, aggressively inspect these facilities for compliance with environmental laws. EPA also announced the start of a national dialog on hazardous waste management to stimulate source reduction.

6.14.3 Recyclable Materials Utilized for Precious Metal Recovery

Limited Part 266 standards have been established for hazardous wastes that are reclaimed to recover economically significant amounts of gold, silver, platinum, palladium, irridium, osmium, rhodium, ruthenium, or any combination of these precious metals.[147]

---

[145]   23 Env. Rptr. 131 (May 21, 1993).

[146]   Id. at 157.

[147]   40 CFR Part 266, Subpart F.

Any person who generates, transports, or stores hazardous wastes utilized for precious metal recovery must file a RCRA Section 3010 notification and comply with the Uniform Manifest System. To facilitate manifesting, the definition of a "designated facility" on the Uniform Manifest was amended to include precious metal recycling facilities.[148] In addition, persons who store such hazardous wastes must keep records showing the volume stored at the beginning of each calendar year, the amount of the waste generated or received during the calendar year, and the amount of waste remaining at the end of the calendar year. These records are necessary to document that the hazardous wastes destined for precious metal recovery are not being speculatively accumulated.

6.14.4 Reclamation of Spent Lead-Acid Batteries

Persons who generate, transport, or collect spent batteries are not subject to any RCRA regulation. Only facilities that store spent batteries before reclaiming them are regulated under Part 266.[149]

Reclamation facilities that store spent batteries must file a RCRA Section 3010 notification and comply with most of the interim status standards for storage facilities in 40 CFR Part 265, Subparts A through L. In addition, such reclamation facilities will have to obtain a RCRA permit in compliance with the permanent standards in 40 CFR Part 264, Subparts A through L.

6.15 Exemption for Wastewater Treatment Units and Elementary Neutralization Units

In 1980 EPA proposed to allow operators of wastewater treatment and elementary neutralization units to obtain national "permits-by-rule" if they would comply with certain basic

---

[148] 40 CFR 260.10.

[149] 40 CFR Part 266, Subpart G.

performance standards.[150] The Agency's rationale was that although RCRA regulation is necessary to protect human health and the environment from the hazards posed by these types of units, a less stringent version of the regular T/S/D facility standards would be adequate for those standard, low risk units.

Under the proposal, operators of eligible units would have been subject to a limited number of simplified performance requirements. The operator would be required to obtain an EPA Identification Number, to complete manifests for any wastes received from off-site sources, to comply with certain recordkeeping and reporting requirements, and to take certain security precautions. Any spills or releases must be reported to EPA within 15 days and all hazardous wastes must be removed at closure. Facility specific permits would not be required. This would save time and expense for owner/operators and regulatory agencies.

Eligible "wastewater treatment units" must meet three criteria:

(1) The units must be part of a wastewater treatment facility, the effluent of which is subject to regulation under either Section 402 (the NPDES program) or Section 307(b) (the pretreatment program) of the Clean Water Act;

(2) The unit must (a) receive, treat or store wastewaters that are hazardous wastes, or (b) generate, accumulate, treat or store wastewater treatment sludges that are hazardous wastes; and

(3) The unit must meet EPA's regulatory definition of a tank.[151]

---

[150] 40 CFR Part 266, Subparts A-B (proposed), 45 Fed. Reg. 76080 (November 17, 1980). See Chapter 8 of this Handbook for a discussion of permits-by-rule.

[151] 40 CFR 260.10.

In order to qualify as an elementary neutralization unit, the facility must meet two criteria:

    (1)   The unit must be used to neutralize wastes which are hazardous only because they exhibit the hazardous waste characteristic of corrosivity or are listed as hazardous wastes because of this characteristic; and

    (2)   The unit must meet EPA's regulatory definition of a tank, container, transport vehicle or vessel.[152]

EPA did not promulgate these regulations in final form, apparently out of concern that they might be inconsistent with the requirement for local comment on each facility-specific permit.[153] Instead, EPA suspended the application of the RCRA hazardous waste program to wastewater treatment and neutralization units. Thus, such facilities are not currently subject to regulation under RCRA.

6.16 Miscellaneous Units: Subpart X

In 1987 EPA promulgated a set of standards under Subpart X of Part 264 that are applicable to owners and operators of new and existing hazardous waste management units not covered under any other specific subpart of Parts 264 or 266.[154] These regulations will enable such "miscellaneous" units to obtain RCRA permits necessary to operate. The most significant requirements in these regulations are the environmental performance standards relating to groundwater and subsurface migration, surface water and quality surface soils, and air quality, which ensure that the facilities are protective of human health and the environment. In some cases a risk assessment will be required.

---

[152]   40 CFR 260.10.

[153]   See RCRA § 7004(b)(2).

[154]   40 CFR 264.600-603; 52 Fed. Reg. 46964 (Dec. 10, 1987).

Special post-closure care requirements for miscellaneous units are provided. The regulations also require that monitoring, testing, analysis, inspections, and reporting procedures and frequencies be specified in the permit to ensure compliance with the environmental protection standards and other Part 264 regulations applicable to T/S/D facilities generally.

6.17 Air Emissions Standards

EPA is currently in the second phase of a three-phased regulatory program to control air emissions from the treatment, storage, and disposal of hazardous waste. These standards are being proposed by EPA under the authority of RCRA sections 3002 and 3004 to reduce organic emissions from certain hazardous waste management units.

The first phase was completed with the promulgation of final standards whereby organic air emissions are limited as a class at T/S/D facilities from: (1) process vents associated with distillation, fractionation, thin film evaporation, solvent extraction, and air or steam stripping operations that manage certain organic hazardous wastes; and (2) leaks from equipment that contains or contacts certain organic hazardous waste streams.[155] The second phase of the program consists of recently proposed new standards and amendments to existing standards that would further reduce air emissions from hazardous waste management units. The new standards proposed for T/S/D facilities require that specific organic emission controls be installed and operated on containers, tanks, and surface impoundments containing hazardous waste with a volatile organic concentration equal to or greater than 500 parts per million by weight.[156]

---

[155] 40 CFR Part 264; 55 Fed. Reg. 25454 et seq. (June 21, 1990); 56 Fed. Reg. 19290 (April 26, 1991) (technical corrections).

[156] 56 Fed. Reg. 33490 et seq. (July 22, 1991). This regulation is scheduled to be finalized in October 1993.

In addition, EPA is proposing amendments that would add the relevant emission control requirements specified by the air emission standards under RCRA for certain T/S/D facility treatment unit process vents (40 CFR 265 Subpart AA), equipment leaks (40 CFR 265 Subpart BB), and tanks, surface impoundments, and containers (proposed as 40 CFR Subpart CC) to the requirements that a hazardous waste generator must comply with pursuant to 40 CFR 262.34(a) in order to exempt certain accumulation tanks and containers from the RCRA Subtitle C permitting requirements.[157] EPA is also proposing an amendment to 40 CFR 270.4 which would require the owner or operator of a T/S/D facility already issued a permit under RCRA Subtitle C to comply with the air emission standards for interim status facilities until the facility's permit is reviewed or reissued by EPA.[158]

For the third phase, EPA will assess the residual risk that remains after implementation of the standards developed in the first two phases and, if necessary, will develop additional standards to protect human health and the environment from T/S/D facility air emissions.[159]

---

157 Id.

158 Id.

159 Id.

CHAPTER 7

LAND DISPOSAL RESTRICTIONS

7.1 Overview

In the 1984 Amendments, Congress significantly amended Section 3004 of RCRA to prohibit the land disposal of untreated hazardous wastes. Congress created a series of scheduled statutory land disposal prohibitions taking effect between 1986 and 1990, and covering specified classes of hazardous wastes.[1] The legislative history reflects Congress' clear intent to dramatically alter existing land disposal practices:

> The Conferees intend to convey a clear and unambiguous message to the regulated community and the Environmental Protection Agency: reliance on land disposal of hazardous waste has resulted in an unacceptable risk to human health and the environment. Consequently, the conferees intend that through the vigorous implementation of the objectives of this Act, land disposal will be eliminated for many wastes and minimized for all others, and that advanced treatment, recycling, incineration and other hazardous waste control technologies should replace land disposal. In other words, land disposal should be used as a last resort and only under conditions which are fully protective of human health and the environment.[2]

The term "land disposal" is broadly defined by statute to include: "any placement of . . . hazardous waste in a landfill, surface impoundment, waste pile, injection well, land treatment facility, salt dome formation, salt bed formation, or underground mine or cave."[3] EPA has promulgated comprehensive regulations implementing the land disposal restrictions in 40 CFR Part 268. Special rules implementing the land disposal restrictions as they

---

[1] RCRA § 3004(d), (e), (f) and (g).

[2] H.R. Rep. No. 1133, 98th Cong., 2d Sess. 80-81, reprinted in 1984 U.S. Code Cong. & Admin. News 5649-51.

[3] RCRA § 3004(k). Accord 40 CFR 268.2(a).

apply to underground injection wells are codified in 40 CFR Part 148.

The first of the phased statutory land disposal prohibition applied to solvent and dioxin wastes and became effective on November 8, 1986.[4] This first phase of the land disposal program is sometimes referred to as the "framework rule." The next phase, effective July 8, 1987, prohibited the so-called "California List" wastes.[5] Prohibitions on the underground injection of solvent, dioxin and California List wastes became effective on August 8, 1988.[6]

All of the remaining listed and characteristic hazardous wastes were addressed under RCRA § 3004(g) one-third at a time according to a prioritization or schedule established by EPA.[7] These are the so-called scheduled wastes. The "First Third" waste

---

[4]   RCRA § 3004(e); 51 Fed. Reg. 40572 et seq. (Nov. 7, 1986).

[5]   RCRA § 3004(d); 52 Fed. Reg. 25760 et seq. (July 8, 1987); 40 CFR 268.32. Section 3004(d) defines the California List wastes to include liquid hazardous wastes containing the following constituent concentrations: Arsenic 500 mg/l; Cadmium 100 mg/l; Chromium 500 mg/l; Cyanides (free) 1,000 mg/l; Lead 500 mg/l; Mercury 20 mg/l; Nickel 134 mg/l; Selenium 100 mg/l; Thallium 130 mg/l; PCBs 50 ppm. In addition, the California List includes liquid hazardous waste having a pH 2.0 or less, and hazardous wastes containing halogenated organic compounds ("HOCs") in concentrations of 1,000 mg/k or more. The California List wastes substantially overlap with the Section 3004(g) scheduled wastes, and they have become increasingly less relevant with the full implementation of the program and promulgation of the Third Third rule in 1990. Nonetheless, EPA has identified some continued applicability of the California List. See 55 Fed. Reg. at 22534 (June 1, 1990).

[6]   RCRA § 3004(f); 53 Fed. Reg. 28118 et seq. (July 26, 1988); 53 Fed. Reg. 30908 et seq. (Aug. 16, 1988).

[7]   RCRA § 3004(g); 40 CFR 268.10-268.13. These scheduled prohibitions apply to land disposal by all methods, including underground injection.

prohibitions took effect on August 8, 1988.[8] The "Second Third" waste prohibitions took effect on June 8, 1989.[9] The "Third Third" waste prohibitions which were the first to apply to characteristic wastes had a statutory effective date of May 8, 1990, but EPA promulgated the Third Third rule with an effective date of August, 8, 1990.[10]

The scheduled waste prohibitions apply to all forms of land disposal, including underground injection. If EPA did not promulgate a treatment standard for a scheduled waste, the waste would have been automatically prohibited from land disposal on May 8, 1990, under RCRA Section 3004(g). Until then, the so-called "soft hammer" provisions allowed First Third and Second Third wastes to be disposed of in landfills or surface impoundments if: (1) the facility (and the individual unit) was in compliance with the minimum technology requirements of RCRA Section 3004(o); and (2) generator certified to EPA that such disposal is the only practical alternative to treatment currently available to the generator.[11] All of the foregoing dates were subject to waste-specific national variances by which EPA could, and often did, postpone, for up to two years, the effective dates of the statutory prohibitions.

Hazardous wastes which are newly identified or listed by EPA are not automatically subject to the land disposal prohibitions. Instead, under RCRA § 3004(g)(4), EPA is required to make separate regulatory determinations regarding the applications of the land

---

[8]   RCRA § 3004(g); 53 Fed. Reg. 31138 et seq. (Aug. 17, 1988); 53 Fed. Reg. 30908 (Aug. 16, 1988).

[9]   The Second Third rule was promulgated on June 23, 1989, 54 Fed. Reg. 26594 et seq.

[10]   See RCRA § 3004(g) and 40 CFR 268.12. 55 Fed. Reg. 22520 et seq. (June 1, 1990) (Third Third rule).

[11]   53 Fed. Reg. 31138, 31179-31186 (Aug. 17, 1988); 40 CFR 268.8.

disposal prohibitions and treatment standards for such wastes.[12] Although RCRA mandates that this determination occur within six months of the new listing or identification, the ban on land disposal does not occur without action by EPA. The Agency has already missed regulatory deadlines pertaining to the 1990 Toxicity Characteristic ("TC") rule.[13] Accordingly, EPA has stated that wastes that exhibit the TC but not the EP are not presently prohibited from land disposal.[14]

7.2   The Treatment Exemption

The principal exemption from the land disposal prohibitions is provided by Section 3004(m) of RCRA. This provision directs EPA to promulgate treatment standards for restricted hazardous wastes so that the health and environmental threats prosed by the waste are minimized. If EPA promulgates such a treatment standard, and if a restricted waste is treated to meet the standard, the land disposal prohibition no longer applies to the treated waste. Section 3004(m) of RCRA provides as follows:

> (1) Simultaneously with the promulgation of regulations under subsection (d), (e), (f), or (g) of this section prohibiting one or more methods of land disposal of a particular hazardous waste, and as appropriate thereafter, the Administrator shall, after notice and an opportunity for hearings and after consultation with appropriate Federal and State agencies, promulgate regulations specifying those levels or methods of treatment, if any, which substantially diminish the toxicity of waste or substantially reduce the likelihood of migration of

---

[12]   For example, EPA recently issued land disposal restrictions and BDAT treatment standards for 20 newly listed hazardous wastes, including some petroleum refining wastes. See 57 Fed. Reg. 37194 (Aug. 18, 1993).

[13]   See 55 Fed. Reg. 26986 (June 29, 1990) (TC rule).

[14]   See 55 Fed. Reg. at 22531 (June 1, 1990).

hazardous constituents from the waste so that short-term and long-term threats to human health and the environment are minimized.

(2) If such hazardous waste has been treated to the level or by a method specified in regulations promulgated under this subsection, such waste or residue thereof shall not be subject to any prohibition promulgated under subsection (d), (e), (f), or (g) of this section and may be disposed of in a land disposal facility which meets the requirements of this subchapter. Any regulation promulgated under this subsection or a particular hazardous waste shall become effective on the same date as any applicable prohibition promulgated under subsection (d), (e), (f), or (g) of this section. [Emphasis added].

EPA has determined that treatment standards under Section 3004(m) should be established based upon the performance achievable by the "Best Demonstrated Available Technologies" ("BDAT").[15] The D.C. Circuit generally upheld EPA's BDAT treatment standard approach against an industry challenge that it was excessively stringent in Hazardous Waste Treatment Council v. U.S. EPA, 886 F.2d 355 (D.C. Cir. 1989), although the court required EPA to provide a further explanation for the regulatory scheme, which EPA has since done.[16] EPA has promulgated treatment standards for the vast majority of the wastes subject to the land disposal restrictions, and these standards are codified at 40 CFR Part 268, Subpart D. The treatment standards are waste-specific, i.e., regardless of whether the waste disposal method involves a landfill or an injection well, the same treatment standard applies. The standards can be expressed as specified technologies, but more commonly are specified as concentrations of hazardous constituents which may not be exceeded in the waste or the waste extract.[17]

---

[15]   See 51 Fed. Reg. 40572, 40578, 40588-92, (Nov. 7, 1986).

[16]   See 55 Fed. Reg. 6640 (Feb. 26, 1990).

[17]   See 40 CFR 268.40-43.

Where a waste "differs significantly from wastes analyzed in developing the treatment standard" such that the waste "cannot be treated to specified levels", EPA has authority to grant a variance from a treatment standard.[18] In recent years, EPA has expressed a willingness to liberally grant such variances in cases involving difficult to treat mixtures, although EPA has stated that variances will not be available where waste streams have been mixed intentionally. In the case of contaminated soil and debris, EPA recently issued new generic alternative treatment standards for contaminated debris (including soil).[19] These new alternative standards were intended to make the land disposal restrictions more flexible with regard to such wastes.

In another challenge to EPA's land disposal program, the D.C. Circuit held that EPA properly decided to not engage in "comparative risk assessments," i.e., comparing the risks to human health and the environment of BDAT waste treatment with those inherent in land disposal of an untreated waste. American Petroleum Inst. v. U.S.EPA, 906 F.2d 729 (D.C. Cir. 1990). The court upheld EPA's approach, in part, because land disposal was presumptively disfavored by RCRA. The court also upheld EPA's determination that the BDAT treatment standard for the petroleum refining wastes (K048-K052) should not be based upon "land treatment," but upon incineration and solvent extraction technologies. The court agreed with EPA that land treatment was itself a form of prohibited "land disposal," as defined by RCRA § 3004(k).

Significantly, with regard to characteristic wastes, EPA asserted in its Third Third rule that it had authority under RCRA to set BDAT treatment standards below the levels at which the characteristic wastes are hazardous.[20] Nonetheless, "for most

---

[18]   40 CFR 268.44.

[19]   57 Fed. Reg. 37194 (Aug. 18, 1992).

[20]   See 55 Fed. Reg. at 22652-22653 (June 1, 1990).

corrosive, reactive, and ignitable characteristic wastes, the Agency . . . determined that the appropriate treatment for these wastes is to remove the characteristic."[21] EPA referred to this as the "deactivation" treatment standard. Moreover, for the EP toxic metals, EPA took the view that, as of the 1990 Third Third rule, it did not possess technical data to justify BDAT treatment standards below the characteristic levels.[22] However, for the EP toxic pesticides and ignitable characteristic wastes with high levels of total organic carbon ("TOC"), EPA did set BDAT treatment standards far below the characteristic levels based upon incineration technology.[23]

In Chemical Waste Management, Inc. v. U.S. EPA, 976 F.2d 2 (D.C. Cir. 1992), cert. denied, ___ U.S. ___ (1993) (hereinafter "Chem-Waste"), the court addressed some of the key issues regarding characteristic wastes under the Third Third rule. First, the court rejected industry claims that EPA lacked authority to mandate treatment of characteristic wastes after their ignitability, corrosiveness, reactivity, or EPA toxicity has been removed. The court held that EPA possessed regulatory authority over wastes from "the moment they are generated," and it concluded that Sections "3004(g)(5) and (m) provide the EPA with authority to bar land disposal of certain wastes unless they have been treated to reduce risks beyond those presented by the characteristics themselves."[24]

Second, the court reviewed EPA's "deactivation" treatment standard as applied to ignitable, corrosive and reactive wastes which were challenged by environmental groups, because EPA authorized dilution of these wastes as opposed to BDAT treatment. The court held that EPA's rules were contrary to RCRA with regard

---

[21]   55 Fed. Reg. at 22655 (June 1, 1990).

[22]   Id. at 22655-22656.

[23]   Id.

[24]   976 F.2d at 14.

to these characteristic wastes, stating as follows: "the deactivation standard, in its present form, is permissible only with regard to corrosive wastes; and then only so long as they do not contain hazardous constituents that, following dilution, would themselves present a continuing danger to human health or the environment." 976 F.2d at 16. The court was particularly concerned with EPA's admissions that hazardous constituents would remain present in deactivated ignitable and reactive wastes (and possibly corrosives) at levels which could pose a risk to human health and the environment.[25] On May 24, 1993, EPA issued an interim final rule to respond to the court's decision[26], and it is discussed immediately below in connection with the dilution rules.

7.3 Dilution Rules

Since the initial 1986 framework rule, EPA has expressly provided that the dilution of wastes is prohibited as a substitute for treatment.[27] What has been reasonably clear is that a waste generator cannot simply add water or absorbents to a listed hazardous waste to dilute it in order to avoid or circumvent a land disposal prohibition and its associated BDAT treatment standard. However, the dilution prohibition has proven to be quite difficult to apply in particular circumstances which are encountered in typical industrial waste generation and management settings. This difficulty has led EPA to provide additional interpretive guidance concerning what activities are, and are not, permissible, although uncertainties remain. For example, EPA has stated that "aggregatation of wastes preceding legitimate treatment is not considered to be impermissible dilution," but that "centralized treatment of incompatible wastestreams [is] not

---

[25]   976 F.2d at 15-19.

[26]   58 Fed. Reg. 29860 (May 24, 1993).

[27]   40 CFR 268.44.

legitimate treatment and constitutes impermissible dilution."[28] EPA has stated further that, "if 'dilution' is a legitimate type of treatment, or a necessary pretreatment step in a legitimate treatment system, such dilution is permissible."[29]

In the case of wastes that are hazardous only because they exhibit a characteristic, the dilution prohibition has become more complicated. First, EPA stated that it is permissible to dilute non-toxic ignitable, reactive and corrosive characteristic wastes,[30] although the D.C. Circuit invalidated this broad position in the 1992 Chem-Waste decision, as discussed above. Second, EPA provided in the Third Third rulemaking that dilution of characteristic wastes is permissible if it occurs in a treatment system regulated under Sections 307 or 402 of the Clean Water Act, 33 U.S.C. §§ 1317, 1342.[31] Third, EPA stated that the dilution prohibition is inapplicable to characteristic wastes that are land disposed via an underground injection well regulated under the Safe Drinking Water Act, 42 U.S.C. §§ 300f et seq.[32]

The Chem-Waste decision also addressed EPA's dilution rules and the interplay between the RCRA land disposal restrictions and the Clean Water Act and the Safe Drinking Water Act. The court reasoned that there needs to be some accommodation between RCRA and these other regulatory programs. However, it nonetheless partially remanded the rules for further rulemaking consistent with the following conclusions:

> The new CWA dilution permission is valid where the waste is decharacterized prior to placement in a CWA

---

[28]   55 Fed. Reg. at 22664 (June 1, 1990).

[29]   Id.

[30]   Id. at 22665-22666. High total organic carbon ("TOC") ignitable nonwastewaters, reactive cyanide wastes, and reactive sulfide wastes, are considered to be toxic characteristic wastes and subject to the dilution prohibition. Id.

[31]   40 CFR 268.3(b).

[32]   See 55 Fed. Reg. at 22665 (June 1, 1990).

surface impoundment and subsequently treated in full conformity with section 3004(m)(1) standards. Aggregation prior to treatment is not per se unacceptable. Aggregation itself occurs in tanks and is, therefore, not "land disposal"; and RCRA does not require treatment before aggregation.

To the extent that aggregation in tanks and dilution results in the removal of the waste's characteristic and the minimization of the toxicity of the constituents as required under section 3004(m), all that RCRA commands has been achieved. However, where aggregation and dilution does not eliminate the characteristic or (more likely) does not minimize the toxicity of the constituents, then RCRA requires further treatment.

In those instances where aggregation and dilution result in the elimination of the characteristic, but the toxicity of the constituents has not been minimized, the required further treatment of the constituents may occur after the waste leaves the CWA tank and enters the surface impoundment . . . . However, in all other respects, treatment of solid wastes in a CWA surface impoundment must meet RCRA requirements prior to ultimate discharge into waters of the United States or publicly owned treatment works ("POTWs"). In other words, what leaves a CWA treatment facility can be no more toxic than if the waste streams were individually treated pursuant to the RCRA treatment standards.

Applying the same principles to the deep injection well rule, we hold that dilution is permissible prior to injection only where dilution itself fully meets the section 3004(m)(1) standards.[33]

On May 24, 1993, EPA issued an interim final rule in response to the Chem-Waste decision.[34] The Agency revised the treatment standards for ignitable and corrosive wastes that are not managed: 1) in centralized wastewater treatment systems subject to the Clean Water Act, or Class I underground injection wells under the Safe Drinking Water Act; or 2) by a zero discharger (a facility that treats wastewater but does not

---

[33] 976 F.2d at 19-20.

[34] 58 Fed. Reg. 29860 (May 24, 1993).

ultimately discharge it to a navigable water or a publicly-owned treatment works) in a wastewater treatment system equivalent to that utilized by Clean Water Act dischargers before land disposal. The interim final rule includes revised treatment standards for certain ignitable and corrosive wastes. EPA retains the requirement for deactivation to remove the hazardous characteristic, but the rule also requires that the waste be treated such that each underlying hazardous constituent in the waste meets the same concentration-based treatment standard promulgated for that constituent in the treatment standards for F039 wastes.[35]

Further, pursuant to the Chem-Waste court's instructions, new precautionary measures are established in the interim final rule to prevent emissions of volatile organic constituents or violent reactions during the process of diluting ignitable and reactive wastes. Thus, the interim final rule incorporates the general facility standards for T/S/D facilities with respect to precautions necessary to prevent reactions which generate: fire, extreme heat or pressure, explosions, uncontrolled toxic mists, fumes, dusts, etc. The interim final rule reflects only EPA's immediate response to the issues addressed by the Chem-Waste decision, and further rulemakings related to these issues are expected in the near future.

7.4 The "No Migration" Exemption

Apart from certain variance provisions which allow postponement of the prohibition effective dates (discussed below), the only other exception to the land disposal prohibitions of Section 3004 is the "no migration" petition procedure, which requires the Administrator to find, in part, that:

---

[35] F039 is the hazardous waste code for liquids that have percolated through land disposed hazardous wastes, i.e., multi-source leachate.

there will be no migration of hazardous constituents from the disposal unit or injection zone for as long as the wastes remain hazardous.[36]

EPA has construed the "no migration" exception to the land ban to be extremely narrow and probably not available for most surface landfills. EPA has stated that a "petitioner should not assume that any man-made barriers or engineered systems will satisfy the 'no migration' standard, because artificial barriers alone cannot be relied upon to provide the long-term assurances that the statutory standard requires."[37] However, the Agency has stated that in the case of underground injection wells that the standard can be more commonly satisfied, and the Agency has granted several no-migration petitions for underground injection wells in recent years.[38]

7.5   Variances From the Prohibition Effective Dates

In addition to the treatment and "no migration" exemptions, there are two variance authorities which have enabled EPA to

---

[36]   40 CFR 268.6. The regulatory provisions is based upon statutory language in RCRA §§ 3004(d), (e), (f), and (g). See also 40 CFR 148.20 (expressing the "no migration" standard for underground injection wells).

[37]   51 Fed. Reg. 40572, 40605 (Nov. 7, 1986). On August 11, 1992, EPA proposed a rule setting forth in more detail its interpretation of the "no migration" variance authority. 57 Fed. Reg. 35940. The proposed rule addresses matters such as how hazardous constituent levels are to be determined, how background concentrations are considered and selecting the appropriate point of compliance.

[38]   In the underground injection well rule proposal, EPA stated its belief that "in most cases deep wells will be able to contain wastes from points of discharge for geologic times." 52 Fed. Reg. 32446, 32452 (Aug. 27, 1987). In the final rule, the Agency retreated somewhat from this optimistic prediction, stating "EPA has no clear idea of the number of demonstrations which might be successful." 53 Fed. Reg. 28118, 28121 (July 26, 1988). See discussion in section 7.9 below.

extend the effective dates of the land disposal prohibitions. Section 3004(h) of RCRA grants EPA limited variance authorities to postpone the prohibition effective dates: (1) on a waste-specific basis based on a national lack of treatment capacity; and (2) on a case-by-case basis based on a commitment to construct or provide needed treatment capacity. National variances may extend a prohibition effective date only to the "earliest date on which adequate alternative treatment, recovery, or disposal capacity will be available," to a maximum of 2 years.[39]

EPA has exercised this national variance extension authority quite extensively since 1986. Case-by-case extensions may be granted for up to one year (renewable for one more year) only where an "applicant demonstrates that there is a binding contractual commitment to construct or otherwise provide such alternative capacity but due to circumstances beyond the control of such applicant such alternative capacity cannot reasonably be made available by such effective date."[40] EPA has promulgated regulations establishing procedures to implement this case-by-case extension authority, 40 CFR 268.5, and has exercised this authority in several cases. However, EPA has stated that it will never grant a case-by-case extension based solely upon the claim that treatment is too costly.

7.6   Storage Prohibition

In the 1984 Amendments, Congress was concerned that the storage of hazardous wastes in barrels and tanks might become a means of evading the requirement that restricted wastes be promptly treated. Accordingly, in Section 3004(j) of RCRA Congress expressly prohibited this storage, stating:

---

[39]   RCRA § 3004(h)(2).

[40]   RCRA § 3004(h)(3).   Accord 40 CFR 268.5.

> In the case of any hazardous waste which is prohibited from one or more methods of land disposal . . . the storage of such hazardous waste is prohibited unless such storage is solely for the purpose of the accumulation of such quantities of hazardous waste as are necessary to facilitate proper recovery, treatment or disposal.[41]

EPA has implemented this prohibition by regulations which specify its application to generators, transporters and T/S/D facilities.[42] Notably, EPA has created a rebuttable presumption that storage for up to one year at a T/S/D facility complies with the storage prohibition. Storage beyond one year is presumptively in violation, although an operator is free to prove that such storage was in fact necessary to facilitate proper recovery, treatment or disposal, of the waste. The D.C. Circuit upheld this EPA interpretation of the storage prohibition in Hazardous Waste Treatment Council v. US. EPA, 886 F.2d 355, 366-68 (D.C. Cir. 1989). Of course, under longstanding requirements, generators are precluded from storing any hazardous waste for more than 90 days without a RCRA permit.[43]

Significantly, EPA has stated that the storage prohibition applies only "to wastes placed in storage after the effective dates" of the land disposal restrictions.[44] Accordingly, under this EPA interpretation, wastes that were placed into storage before the applicable land disposal restrictions are exempt from the storage prohibition and may be stored indefinitely.

In 1991 EPA issued a statement of enforcement policy regarding the storage of "mixed wastes," i.e., wastes that contain both a hazardous waste component regulated under RCRA and a radioactive waste component regulated under the Atomic Energy Act, 42 U.S.C.

---

[41]   RCRA § 3004(j).

[42]   40 C.F.R. 268.50.

[43]   See 40 CFR 262.34.

[44]   See 55 Fed. Reg. at 22525.

§§ 2011 et seq.[45] In the enforcement policy statement, EPA noted that it had "previously concluded that storage of a waste pending development of treatment capacity does not constitute storage to accumulate sufficient quantities to facilitate proper treatment of disposal."[46] As a result, EPA acknowledged that "[g]enerators and storers of [mixed] wastes may find it impossible to comply with the section 3004(j) storage prohibition" because of lack of available treatment and disposal options.[47] Accordingly, EPA stated that for those mixed waste generators who "are operating their storage facilities in an environmentally responsible manner" violations of Section 3004(j) would be considered "reduced priorities among EPA's potential civil enforcement actions."[48] This EPA enforcement policy statement was recently reviewed and upheld by the D.C. Circuit in Edison Electric Institute v. U.S. EPA, 36 E.R.C. 1913 (June 18, 1993).

7.7   Waste Analysis and Recordkeeping

The land disposal restriction rules impose significant additional testing, tracking and recordkeeping obligations on hazardous waste generators, treatment facilities and land disposal facilities.[49] Under 40 CFR 268.7(a), generators are required to determine if their hazardous wastes are subject to the land disposal restrictions, and if so, whether the treatment standards are met. Where treatment standards are not met, the generator must submit a "land ban" notification to the TSD facility which

---

45   See Policy on Enforcement of RCRA Section 3004(J) Storage Prohibition at Facilities Generating Mixed Radioactive/ Hazardous Wastes, 56 Fed. Reg. 42730 (Aug. 29, 1991).

46   Id. at 42732.

47   Id. at 4731.

48   Id. at 42731.

49   See 40 CFR 268.7.

identifies the EPA Hazardous Waste number, the appropriate BDAT treatment standard, the number of the accompanying manifest and available waste analysis data.[50] If the generator determines that the treatment standards are met, he must sign and submit to the TSD a certification so stating under penalty of law along with a land ban notification.[51] Generators must retain on-site copies of all notices, certifications and waste analysis data for at least five years.[52]

Treatment facilities who receive untreated wastes from generators must also sign certifications that the treatment standards are met before the waste or waste residue may be shipped to a land disposal facility.[53] The landfill operator, who must test incoming shipments according to his waste analysis plan, is required to maintain the notifications and certifications that accompany all restricted waste shipments received from generators and treatment facilities.[54]

EPA recently modified the waste analysis and recordkeeping requirements applicable to generators of restricted ignitable and corrosive characteristic wastes to impose a new requirement that such generators "determine what underlying hazardous constituents . . . are reasonably expected to be present in the . . . wastes," and provide such information in the notifications accompanying waste shipments.[55] For characteristic wastes which are treated to the point that they are no longer hazardous and may be land disposed in a Subtitle D facility, EPA has developed a modified

---

[50]   Id.

[51]   40 CFR 268.7(a)(2).

[52]   40 CFR 268.7(a)(6).

[53]   40 CFR 268.7(b).

[54]   40 CFR 268.7(c).

[55]   58 Fed. Reg. at 29884-85 (May 24, 1993)(to be codified at 40 CFR 268.7).

notice and certification requirement.[56] Notably, the tracing documents are not required to be sent to the Subtitle D facility operator, but, instead, to the EPA Regional Administrator or authorized state.

In most cases, testing to determine compliance with the concentration based treatment standards must be done in accordance with the "Toxicity Characteristic Leaching Procedure" or "TCLP", which is set forth in Appendix I to 40 CFR 268.

7.8   Multi-Source Leachate

Until the Second Third rule, the land disposal prohibitions required multi-source leachate, like other mixtures containing more than one hazardous waste, to be treated to meet the most stringent treatment standard applicable to the various hazardous constituents present in the mixture.[57] The D.C. Circuit upheld the legality of EPA's general implementation of the land disposal restrictions as applied to multi-source leachate, and specifically the rule that "leachate which is actively managed after the underlying wastes have been listed as hazardous will itself be deemed a hazardous waste an must be treated to the applicable standards."[58]

Nonetheless, in the Third Third rule, the Agency attempted to solve the severe practical problems with its original rule by promulgating a "fixed set of wastewater treatment standards and a set of nonwastewater treatment standards for all multi-source leachate and residues derived from the treatment of multi-source

---

56   40 CFR 268.9.

57   See Fed. Reg. 8264 (Feb. 27, 1989), and 54 Fed. Reg. 4021 (Jan. 27, 1989).

58   Chemical Waste Management, Inc. v. EPA, 869 F.2d 1526 (D.C. Cir. 1989).

leachate.[59] The BDAT treatment standards for multi-source leachate were promulgated along with a new EPA hazardous waste code number (F039) for these wastes. Leachate from dioxin wastes is considered single-source leachate and not subject to the multi-source standard.

7.9 Underground Injection Wells

As noted above, the disposal of hazardous waste by underground injection wells is also subject to the land disposal prohibitions, specifically those set forth in Section 3004(f) and (g) of RCRA. EPA promulgated the initial regulations implementing the prohibitions, effective on August 8, 1988, applicable to solvents and dioxins, California List wastes and certain First Third wastes.[60] Prohibitions applicable to the remainder of the scheduled wastes took effect in 1989 and 1990, consistent with the schedule for all listed and characteristic wastes. As in the case of the other land disposal restriction, the statutory effective dates for injection wells were subject to national treatment capacity variances.

EPA has promulgated detailed regulations codified at 40 CFR Part 148 implementing the land disposal prohibitions applicable to injection wells. These regulations are closely related to the 40 CFR Part 146 regulations which are the operational requirements for Class I hazardous waste injection wells under the Underground Injection Control ("UIC") program of the Safe Drinking Water Act.[61] The principal focus of the Part 148 regulations is to define the circumstances in which an injection well can satisfy

---

[59] 55 Fed. Reg. at 22523 (June 1, 1990).

[60] 53 Fed. Reg. 28118 et seq. (July 26, 1988); 53 Fed. Reg. 30908 (Aug. 16, 1988); 40 CFR Part 148.

[61] 42 U.S.C. §§ 300f-300j.

the "no migration" demonstration requirement of the 1984 land disposal prohibitions.

EPA has provided that the petitioner must demonstrate that "to a reasonable degree of certainty, there will be no migration of hazardous constituents from the injection zone for as long as the waste remains hazardous."[62] This determination is critical to the continued existence of an injection well. If a restricted waste must be treated to BDAT treatment standards, there is presumable little reason to dispose of it in an injection well since the treated waste or residue may safely be disposed in a landfill. Indeed, the waste treatment process will often change the form of the waste such that underground injection is technically infeasible.

EPA's "no migration" standard for injection wells requires a demonstration that "the waste would not reach a point of discharge, either vertically or horizontally, for a period of 10,000 years."[63] This prediction is based upon computer modeling, using fluid flow techniques developed in the petroleum industry and in the Department of Energy nuclear waste isolation program. The Agency has stated that movement of contaminants by "molecular diffusion" is probably not a significant source of transport, but that it must nonetheless be considered in the "no migration" demonstration.[64] The rules also require a petitioner seeking a "no migration" demonstration to certify that the well is already in compliance with select provisions of the Part 146 UIC operating requirements which were strengthened in 1988.

The D.C. Circuit substantially upheld EPA's regulatory implementation of the land disposal program as it applies to underground injection wells in Natural Resources Defense Council

---

62   40 CFR 148.20.

63   53 Fed. Reg. 28118, 18126 (July 26, 1988). See 40 CFR 148.20.

64   53 Fed. Reg. 28118, 28128 (July 26, 1988).

v. U.S.EPA, 907 F.2d 1146 (1990), against industry claims that the regulations were too stringent and environmental group claims that they were too lenient. The court held the EPA properly considered molecular diffusion to be subject to the no migration standard, and that EPA's selection of 10,000 year time frame to measure compliance through predictive modeling was not unlawful. However, the court did set aside a portion of EPA's rule which would have allowed underground injection of hazardous waste into salt domes, abandoned mines and cave in violation of RCRA § 3004(a), which banned such disposal unless EPA promulgated performance and permitting standards for those unique facilities. In addition, the court reversed EPA's long-standing regulation which held that a UIC permit would constitute a RCRA permit-by-rule under 40 CFR § 270.60, although the court's decision allowed the Agency to demonstrate why the UIC permit was a permissible substitute for a RCRA permit on remand.

7.10   The Land Ban and Superfund Cleanups

The recent full implementation of the land disposal restriction program is having an increasingly significant impact on site remediations under the Comprehensive Environmental Response, Compensation and Liability Act ("CERCLA" or "Superfund"), 42 U.S.C. §§ 6901 et seq., as well as upon RCRA facility closures and corrective actions. Most of the guidance from EPA in this area has focused upon Superfund cleanups, but the general rules should have wide applicability.

EPA guidance is found in the preamble to the 1990 revisions of the Superfund National Contingency Plan rulemaking,[65] and a 1989 guidance document entitled Superfund LDR Guide #5.[66]   EPA has

---

[65]   55 Fed. Reg. at 8759-63 (Mar. 8, 1990).

[66]   The full title to this EPA guidance is Superfund LDR #5 Determining When Land Disposal Restrictions (LDRs) are

(Footnote continued next page)

stated that the definition of "land disposal" and its focus upon "placement" into a land disposal unit is central to determining whether the land disposal restrictions "are applicable to a hazardous waste which is being managed as part of a CERCLA response action, or RCRA closure or corrective action."[67] To apply this definition in the remediation context, EPA has equated the term land disposal unit with individual areas of contamination ("AOCs").[68] With these concepts established, EPA has identified the following guidelines for determining when the land disposal restrictions are triggered.

Placement does occur when wastes are:

o   Consolidated from different AOCs into a single AOC;

o   Moved outside of an AOC (for treatment or storage, for example) and returned to the same or a different AOC; or

o   Excavated from an AOC, placed in a separate unit, such as an incinerator or tank that is within the AOC, and redeposited into the same AOC.

Placement does not occur when wastes are:

o   Treated in situ;

o   Capped in place;

o   Consolidated within the AOC; or

(Footnote continued)
   Applicable to CERCLA Response Actions (OSWER Directive 9347.3, July 1989).

67   55 Fed. Reg. at 8759 (Mar. 8, 1990).

68   55 Fed. Reg. at 8760 (Mar. 8, 1990).

    °   Processed within the AOC (but not in a separate unit, such as a tank) to improve its structural stability (e.g., for capping or to support heavy machinery).[69]

In sum, if placement of a restricted hazardous waste on-site or off-site occurs, the land disposal prohibitions and the corresponding BDAT treatment standards will apply to the Superfund remediation. Of course, it must be kept in mind that the land disposal restrictions only apply to the placement of material that is actually a listed or characteristic hazardous waste. The hazardous waste determination must be made applying the general rules governing the identification of hazardous waste as discussed in Chapter 2. One special consideration which arises in remediations of historic sites is that EPA takes the view that "RCRA requirements apply to any waste materials disposed of prior to 1980 when those materials are managed or disposed of today."[70]

---

[69]   EPA, Superfund LDR Guide #5, supra, at 2 (emphasis added).

[70]   55 Fed. Reg. at 8762-63 (Mar. 8, 1990).

CHAPTER 8

PERMIT REQUIREMENTS UNDER RCRA

8.1 Statutory Requirements for Permitting T/S/D Facilities

8.1.1 Historical Overview

RCRA requires that every owner or operator of a T/S/D facility obtain an operating permit which incorporates performance standards and other requirements set forth at 40 CFR Part 264.[1] To avoid the shortfall in hazardous waste disposal capacity that would have resulted from immediate implementation of the permit requirement before EPA had an opportunity to develop regulations and issue permits, Congress authorized existing facilities to continue operating under "interim status" where certain conditions were met. Construction may not begin on new facilities until they have received a permit. In practice, issuance of permits has been slow, averaging 3 to 5 years or longer from initial application to issuance. The permitting process is also expensive, often costing owners or operators of T/S/D facilities hundreds of thousands or millions of dollars to complete.

Clearly dissatisfied with EPA's pace on permitting, Congress substantially amended Section 3005 in the 1984 Amendments. Interim status land disposal facilities are now subject to greater regulatory control. Interim status for all T/S/D facilities that had it in 1984 was required to be phased out, and permits were required to be issued to such facilities under a statutory timetable. Final permits for both interim status and new facilities with applications pending on November 8, 1984, were to have been issued by statutory deadlines, the latest of which was November 8, 1992.[2]

Final operating permits must contain schedules for corrective action for releases of hazardous waste from any solid waste

---

[1] RCRA § 3005.

[2] RCRA § 3005(c).

management units at the facility. In addition, EPA is now authorized to issue research, demonstration and development permits to promote the use and testing of innovative treatment technology. The permitting process, as modified by the new statutory and regulatory provisions, is discussed in the following sections.

8.1.2 Summary of the Permitting Process

Section 3005(b) provides that an application for a permit must contain such information as EPA specifies in its implementing regulations. At a minimum, Section 3005(b) requires that a permit application:

(1)   identify the site of the T/S/D facility;

(2)   contain estimates of the composition, quantities, and concentrations of hazardous wastes handled by the facility; and

(3)   state the time, frequency, or rate at which the wastes are transported, disposed of, treated, or stored.

The implementing regulations add substantial detail to this brief statutory statement, and create a two-step approach to the permitting process. The Part A application, containing certain basic information about the facility, must be filed as soon as a facility becomes subject to the hazardous waste regulatory program. For most existing facilities, this was November 19, 1980. The Part B application, requiring substantially more detailed information, must be filed after the effective date of the applicable Phase II T/S/D regulations discussed in Chapters 5 and 6 above. Prior to the 1984 amendments, the Part B filing was triggered by EPA or state request. Now, all pending applications are required to be processed by statutory deadlines, and owners or operators of existing T/S/D facilities must submit the Part B by specified dates, unless the Part B is requested earlier by EPA or the state.[3]

Permit applications are requested and final permits are issued by states authorized under RCRA Section 3006 to administer their own programs, or by the EPA Regional Administrator in all other states. Pending state program approval for implementation of the 1984 Amendments, EPA administers those provisions. This has resulted in a temporary dual permitting system.[4] Permit issuance must be based on a determination that the T/S/D facility is in compliance with all requirements of RCRA. RCRA Section 3005(d) expressly provides that any permit may be revoked for noncompliance with applicable standards.

8.2 Interim Status under RCRA

Interim status, as originally envisioned by Congress, was a brief period during which T/S/D facilities which met three statutory conditions would be permitted to operate pending issuance of an operating permit by EPA or an authorized state. These requirements were:

    (1)   the T/S/D facility must have been in existence on November 19, 1980, (the date the RCRA Phase I regulations became effective), or in existence on the effective date of statutory or regulatory changes under RCRA that render the facility subject to Section 3005 permit requirements;

    (2)   the owner or operator must have complied with the RCRA Section 3010(a) notification requirements (as discussed in Chapter 3); and

---

[3]   40 CFR 270.10(e)(4). The deadlines for the Part B submissions are discussed in detail in section 9.2.3 on termination of interim status, infra.

[4]   40 CFR 271.1(f), 271.19, 271.121(f), 271.134; see also EPA guidance document entitled "RCRA Reauthorization and Joint Permitting in Authorized States: RCRA Reauthorizations Statutory Interpretation #5" (July 1, 1985).

> (3)   the owner or operator must have <u>applied</u> for a permit (by filing a Part A permit application). [Emphasis added.][5]

If a unit at a facility has previously been denied a RCRA permit or had its interim status terminated, the owner or operator may not thereafter qualify for interim status for the facility.[6]

In practice, interim status became a more or less permanent condition for facilities which qualified in 1980. In the 1984 Amendments, Congress imposed several additional requirements on existing interim status land disposal facilities to provide a baseline of environmental protection.[7] Such facilities were required to file their Part B applications by November 8, 1985, and to certify compliance with the ground water monitoring and financial responsibility interim status standards.[8]

A facility which newly qualifies for interim status as a result of a change in the regulations must file its Part A within 6 months and meet the interim status standards and certification requirements within twelve months of the change which subjects it to the RCRA permit requirement. Failure to do so results in the termination of interim status.[9] Finally, interim status land-fills, surface impoundments, land treatment units, and waste pile units which received hazardous waste after July 26, 1982, must meet the ground water monitoring, unsaturated zone monitoring, and

---

[5]   RCRA § 3005(e); 40 CFR 270.70(a).

[6]   RCRA § 3005(e)(1); 40 CFR 270.70(c).

[7]   RCRA § 3005(e).

[8]   RCRA § 3005(e)(2); 40 CFR 270.73(c).

[9]   RCRA § 3005(e)(3); 40 CFR 270.10(e)(1)(i); 40 CFR 270.73(d). Under these regulations a facility that qualifies for interim status as a result of a statutory change must file a Part A within 30 days of the effective date of the legislation unless the statute specifies a different date. 40 CFR 270.10(e)(1)(ii).

corrective action standards which apply to _new_ facilities under Section 3004.[10]

8.2.1 _Qualifying for Interim Status Under the Regulations_

EPA's implementing regulations substantially track the statute, and then expand upon it. To qualify for interim status, a T/S/D facility had to have been in existence as of November 19, 1980. EPA has broadly defined "existing hazardous waste management facility" in its regulations to include facilities that were in operation or under construction on November 19, 1980.[11] Construction has commenced when:

> (1)   the owner or operator has obtained all necessary Federal, State, and local approvals or permits [relating to hazardous waste control laws] necessary to begin physical construction; _and_ either
>
> (2)   (a)   a continuous on-site physical construction program has begun; _or_
>
>   (b)   the owner or operator has entered into contractual obligations -- which cannot be cancelled or modified without substantial loss -- for physical construction of the facility to be completed within a reasonable time.

The determination of when a facility "commences construction" has been subject to numerous administrative and judicial interpretations, principally arising under EPA's similarly worded regulations for New Source Performance Standards and Prevention of Significant Deterioration under the Clean Air Act.[12]

---

[10]   RCRA § 3005(i).

[11]   40 CFR 270.2.

[12]   _See_, _e.g._, Determination of Applicability of NSPS to Potomac Electric Power Co. Chalk Point Unit 4, 45 _Fed. Reg._ 20155 (March 27, 1980); _Sierra Pacific Power Co. v. EPA_, 647 F.2d 60 (9th Cir. 1981); _Montana Power Co. v. EPA_, 608 F.2d 334 (9th Cir. 1979); _United States v. City of Painesville_, 431 F. Supp. 496 (N.D. Ohio 1977), _aff'd_, 644 F.2d 1186 (6th Cir.), _cert._ _denied_, 454 U.S. 894 (1981).

In addition, the owner or operator of a facility handling wastes which were hazardous under EPA's regulations of May 19, 1980, must have filed a RCRA Section 3010(a) notification by August 18, 1980, and Part A of its permit application by November 19, 1980. EPA has stated that it may, by regulation, extend this date in situations where ambiguities in its T/S/D performance standards caused confusion as to which facilities were actually covered.[13] EPA will set a new filing deadline by publication in the Federal Register when clarifying or amending the ambiguous regulations. Although such facilities will technically be operating without a permit until they submit their application, EPA will not initiate enforcement action against them if they contact the EPA regional office immediately and file an application within 30 days.

For those facilities that failed to file a Part A permit application and qualify for interim status as a result of their own oversight or excusable neglect, EPA adopted a special enforcement policy.[14] Under this policy, EPA may issue Interim Status Compliance Letters ("ISCLs") to such facilities where their continued operation, despite their failure to qualify for interim status, is determined to be in the public interest.[15] The ISCL will provide assurances to the facility that it will not be prosecuted for operating without a permit, and it will also contain provisions shielding generators and transporters who send their wastes to such unpermitted facilities from federal prosecution. An ISCL, however, would not shield a facility from citizen suits under RCRA Section 7002. In this regard, EPA has expressed the

---

[13]   45 Fed. Reg. 76630 (November 19, 1980).

[14]   45 Fed. Reg. 76632 (November 19, 1980).

[15]   40 CFR 265.1(b) explicitly requires T/S/D facilities that failed to qualify for interim status comply with the interim status regulations, regardless of whether they are eventually allowed to qualify for interim status.

view that federal courts sitting in equity are not likely to close down an otherwise complying facility.

For an existing facility that became subject to RCRA regulation after November 19, 1980, because of revisions to Parts 260, 261, 265 or 266, the deadline for filing a Part A application is 6 months after the date of publication of the RCRA regulations which first require the facility to get a permit.[16] For all other existing T/S/D facilities that may need to qualify for interim status in the future for reasons other than a regulatory change (e.g. statutory change or action by the owner or operator), a Part A application must be filed within 30 days after the facility first becomes subject to RCRA regulation.[17]

Interim status commences once the three statutory prerequisites are satisfied.[18] No approval of the Part A application or action by EPA is required.

8.2.2 Changes to T/S/D Facilities During Interim Status

After a T/S/D facility qualifies for interim status, the operator may wish to manage additional hazardous wastes, or to change the facility's treatment processes or design capacity. In order to handle additional wastes not previously identified, all

---

[16] 40 CFR 270.10(e)(1)(i). For example, T/S/D facilities which became subject to RCRA as a result of the redefinitions of solid waste on January 4, 1985, were required to file a Part A permit application by July 5, 1985. 50 Fed. Reg. 614 (January 4, 1985).

[17] 40 CFR 270.10(e)(1)(ii). A RIM issued on December 10, 1981, states that a generator may belatedly obtain interim status where he exceeds the temporary 90-day storage requirement, if he was in existence as of November 19, 1980, filed a timely Section 3010(a) notification, and files Part A within 30 days of his exceeding the 90-day period. 46 Fed. Reg. 60446 (December 10, 1981).

[18] 40 CFR 270.70(a).

that is required for a facility is to file a revised Part A application prior to handling such wastes.[19]

More significant restrictions, however, are placed on changes in treatment processes or design capacity. EPA has restricted such changes to avoid creating a loophole when modification is tantamount to construction of a new facility requiring a permit. Thus, an increase in the design capacity at a facility may be made only if, after the filing of a revised Part A application, EPA finds that the change is necessary because of either: (1) a lack of available treatment, storage, or disposal capacity at other T/S/D facilities; or (2) the change is necessary to comply with federal, state, or local requirements.[20] Changes in a facility's processes may be made only if EPA finds that such changes are necessary to prevent a threat to human health or the environment because of an emergency situation, or the changes are necessary to comply with federal, state or local requirement.[21] Changes to an existing T/S/D facility which amount to "reconstruction" are prohibited. Reconstruction occurs when the capital investment required for the changes exceeds 50 percent of the capital cost of a comparable new T/S/D facility.[22] Among other things, the reconstruction limit is lifted for changes made: (1) to certain units so long as they are necessary to comply with federal, state, or local requirements; (2) to allow continued handling of newly listed or identified hazardous waste that had previously been handled at the facility prior to the rule establishing the new listing; (3) in accordance with an approved closure plan; or (4) pursuant to a corrective action order.[23]

---

[19]   40 CFR 270.72(a)(1).

[20]   40 CFR 270.72(a)(2).

[21]   40 CFR 270.72(a)(3).

[22]   40 CFR 270.72(b).

[23]   Id.

In addition, any change to an interim status waste pile, landfill or surface impoundment which involves construction of a new unit, replacement of an existing unit, or lateral expansion of an existing unit must meet certain minimum technological requirements.[24] Any such activity at an existing waste pile, which is within the waste management area identified in the Part A application and first received waste after May 8, 1985, must meet the requirements for dual liners and leachate collection systems that currently apply to new facilities and any revisions to those new facility standards adopted under new RCRA Section 3004(o).[25]

Interim status landfills and surface impoundments are subject to the same Section 3004(o) minimum technology requirements with respect to each new unit, replacement, or lateral expansion of an existing unit.[26]

In January 1992, EPA published revised regulations imposing more detailed and more stringent requirements upon these new or expanded units.[27] In particular, these regulations specify that the mandatory leachate collection system between the facility's two required liners must also work as a leak detection system capable of detecting, collection and removing leak residue at the earliest practicable time.[28]

These revised regulations apply to new surface impoundments and landfills on which construction commences after Jan. 29, 1992 and each lateral expansion or replacement commenced after July 29,

---

[24]   RCRA § 3015.

[25]   RCRA § 3015(a); 40 CFR 265.254; 40 CFR 264 Subpart L.

[26]   RCRA § 3015(b); 40 CFR 265.221(a) (surface impoundments), 40 CFR 265.301(a) (landfills).

[27]   See Fed. Reg. 3487, 3489, 3492 and 3494 (Jan. 29, 1992) (codified at 40 CFR 264.221(c), 264.301(c), 265.221(a), 265.301(a)).

[28]   40 CFR 264.221(c), 264.301(c).

1992.[29] Replacement units are exempt from the new requirements if they can demonstrate that the existing unit was constructed in compliance with the design standards of RCRA §§ 3004(o)(1)(A)(i) and (o)(5) and there is no reason to believe that the liner is not functioning as designed.[30]

The owner or operator is required to notify EPA of the expansion at least 60 days prior to receiving waste.[31] EPA or the state must then require a final permit application to be filed within 6 months of that notice. Once a liner and leachate collection system have been installed under this section in "good faith compliance" with EPA regulations and guidance documents, no different liner or leachate collection system shall be required when issuing the first permit for the facility. However, EPA can require a new liner if the first one leaks.[32]

8.2.3 Termination of Interim Status

Generally, interim status will terminate when EPA or an authorized state completes processing of Parts A and B of a facility's permit application and issues a final, effective permit.[33] Special new rules apply, again, to land disposal facilities. Interim status for all land disposal facilities which qualified prior to November 8, 1984, terminated on November 8, 1985, unless the owner or operator applied for a final permit (i.e., filed its Part B application) and certified compliance with ground water monitoring and financial responsibility requirements contained in Part 265.[34] EPA issued an Implementation and Enforcement Policy

---

[29]   40 CFR 265.221(a), 265.301(a).

[30]   40 CFR 265.221(c), 265.301(c).

[31]   RCRA § 3015(b)(2); 40 CFR 265.221(b), 265.301(b).

[32]   RCRA § 3015(b)(3); 40 CFR 265.221(e), 265.301(e).

[33]   40 CFR 270.73(a).

[34]   RCRA § 3005(e); 40 CFR 270.73(c).

and a Guidance Document on these provisions.[35] For a land disposal facility in existence on the effective date of statutory or regulatory changes which first make the facility subject to the requirement after November 8, 1984, these provisions take effect 12 months after the date on which the facility first becomes subject to the permitting requirement.[36]

All interim status facilities must receive final permits either from EPA or an authorized state within the following schedules:[37] (1) all land disposal facility permits must have been issued by November 8, 1988; (2) all incinerator permits must have been issued by November 8, 1989; and (3) all other facilities must have been permitted by November 8, 1992. Interim status for each type of facility except land disposal (discussed above) expires at the time of that deadline unless the owner or operator had a Part B permit application pending in the case of an incinerator as of November 8, 1986, and for all other facilities other than land disposal units, by November 8, 1988.[38] Continuation of interim status is contingent on meeting these Part B filing deadlines. Permitting authority continues for new facilities which come into existence after November 8, 1984.

Interim status may also be revoked, pursuant to RCRA Section 3005(d), for failure to furnish information reasonably required to process a permit application. EPA has interpreted this provision to include failure to respond on time to a request for a Part B application, or failure to submit Part B in an acceptable form.[39]

---

[35]   See 50 Fed. Reg. 38946 (September 25, 1985) (EPA policy) and EPA guidance document entitled "Loss of Interim Status Provision for Land Disposal Facilities - § 3005(e) of the Resource Conservation and Recovery Act" (September 10, 1985).

[36]   40 CFR 270.73(d).

[37]   RCRA § 3005(c).

[38]   40 CFR 270.73(e), (f).

[39]   40 CFR 270.10(e)(5).

Of course, if a Part A application is not submitted in an acceptable form, interim status never starts. An owner or operator of an existing hazardous waste facility who submits an incomplete Part A permit application will first receive notice of the deficiency and an opportunity to cure it before being subject to enforcement for operating without a permit.[40]

8.3   Permit Regulations for the Permanent RCRA Program
8.3.1   Format of the Permit Regulations

Initially, EPA utilized a consolidated permit format to enforce the RCRA permit requirements.[41] These regulations were issued on May 19, 1980, in conjunction with the RCRA Subtitle C regulations and were an attempt by EPA to consolidate permitting and program requirements for five different environmental programs. The consolidated permit regulations applied to the National Pollutant Discharge Elimination System ("NPDES") under the Clean Water Act; the underground injection control ("UIC") program under the Safe Drinking Water Act; the dredge and fill program under Section 404 of the Clean Water Act; the Prevention of Significant Deterioration ("PSD") program under the Clean Air Act (for EPA-issued permits only); and the hazardous waste management program under RCRA.

Although the consolidated permit regulations were intended to be straightforward and to facilitate the permitting process for applicants whose business operations required more than one EPA permit, EPA found that in practice consolidated processing of applications was rare, and the "consolidated" format made the regulations difficult to use because of disagreements over which permitting agency or office would take the lead in setting public notice and comment proceedings, and a perceived inconvenience in having to refer to multiple parts of the regulations to gather all

---

[40]   40 CFR 124.3(c) and (d).

[41]   45 Fed. Reg. 33418, 33484 (May 19, 1980).

the information needed. Accordingly EPA has "deconsolidated" two parts of its consolidated permit regulations at former 40 CFR 122-123.[42]

The definitions and basic permit requirements for RCRA are now contained in 40 CFR Part 270. State program requirements for RCRA are located at 40 CFR Part 271. Although EPA no longer utilizes the "consolidated" format for its regulations, consolidated processing of more than one permit is still permissible.[43] Likewise, EPA's Consolidated Permit Application Forms are still being used for the RCRA permit program.[44]

Many of the regulations in Part 270 are made applicable to approved state programs by reference in Part 271, discussed in Chapter 10 of this Handbook. Most of the information required by Part 270 is requested on standard application forms published by EPA as appendices to the regulations. Applicants for EPA-issued permits under the RCRA program must submit their applications on EPA's forms. These forms include a general form covering all programs and a number of program-specific forms, including one for RCRA. The application forms retain their individual program identities; there never was nor is there now such thing as a "consolidated permit."

Part 124 establishes the procedures for processing and issuing permits under all regulatory programs administered by EPA, including RCRA. It includes procedures for preparing draft permits, public hearings, and final decisions. Part 124 also contains procedures for administrative appeals of EPA permit decisions. Parts 270 and 124 together comprise the complete permit

---

[42] 48 Fed. Reg. 14146 (April 1, 1983); 48 Fed. Reg. 30113 (June 30, 1983).

[43] 40 CFR 124.4.

[44] 40 CFR 270.2.

process for the RCRA program from application, through processing, to issuance, appeal, and final determination.

8.3.2 The Two-Part Permit Application Process

The RCRA permit application process is divided into a Part A application which requires certain basic information to qualify for interim status, and a more extensive Part B application for permanent status.[45] The initial concern to existing T/S/D facilities subject to the RCRA program was to qualify to operate under interim status by filing the Part A application on or before November 19, 1980, or at such later date as any subsequent regulations allowed. Part B applications for all of these interim status facilities must now be filed by the deadlines provided in the statute and regulations, as discussed above. New facilities file both Parts A and B at the same time when applying for a RCRA permit.

Although the permitting requirements are primarily aimed at T/S/D facilities, a generator may become subject to RCRA permit requirements if, for example, it stores hazardous wastes on-site for more than 90 days.[46] A transporter may also become subject to these requirements if it stores hazardous wastes at transportation terminals for more than 10 days, disposes of the residue from an accidental spill of hazardous waste, or otherwise engages in treatment, storage or disposal activities.[47]

8.3.3 Contents of Part A Applications

The Part A application consists of Forms 1 and 3 of the application forms contained in EPA's consolidated permit regulations.[48] Form 1 is a general form required of all applicants for

---

[45]   40 CFR 270.1(b).

[46]   40 CFR 262.34.

[47]   See Chapter 4.

[48]   40 CFR 270.1(b).

permits under the RCRA, NPDES, UIC and PSD programs. It calls for basic identifying information from the applicant, including name, location, nature of business, regulated activities, and a topographic map of the facility site.

An applicant must also identify all other environmental permits he or she has. Applying for a RCRA permit does not trigger a "cross review" of any other environmental permits which a facility may hold.[49] Revision of other permits should be limited to situations which are exceptional, or where for some reason the permitted facility requests it.

T/S/D facilities must check a box on Form 1 indicating that they have also filled out and submitted Form 3. This five page application form calls for more detailed information on the T/S/D facility's hazardous waste activities. Specifically, Form 3 requires:

(1)   the owner's name, address, and telephone number;

(2)   the latitude and longitude of the facility;

(3)   an indication of whether the facility is new or existing;

(4)   for existing facilities, a <u>scale drawing</u> showing past, present, and future treatment, storage, or disposal areas, and <u>photographs</u> delineating existing structures and existing and future areas used for treatment, storage, or disposal;

(5)   a description of the <u>processes</u> used and the design capacity of the processes; and

(6)   a <u>list of the hazardous wastes</u> handled in the facility broken down by EPA code number, the estimated quantity of such wastes handled each year, and a list of the treatment, storage, and disposal processes to be used.

EPA intends to impose legal liability for the accuracy of permit applications on a responsible officer of every company. As

---

[49]   40 CFR 124.10. <u>See</u> discussion of "cross review," which was included in EPA's proposed regulations but deleted in the final promulgation, at 45 <u>Fed</u>. <u>Reg</u>. 33308 (May 19, 1980).

a result, all permit applications must be signed by a responsible corporate officer.[50] A "responsible corporate officer" can be any officer performing policy or decision making functions similar to a vice president, or he or she can be any manager of a manufacturing, production or operating facility who has been delegated the authority to sign permit applications pursuant to corporate procedures, provided that the facility employs more than 250 persons and has gross sales or expenditures in excess of $25 million per year (in 1980 dollars).[51]

The person signing the application form must certify that the information submitted is true, accurate, and complete, and to do this he or she must make inquiries to ascertain that the company has some system of direction or supervision of the qualified individuals who gathered the information and prepared the application. There is no requirement, however, to personally examine and be familiar with all the information in the application form.[52] EPA believes that this standard still maintains an adequate level of corporate involvement and responsibility in the RCRA permit application process. Legal liability may then run both to the corporation and to the individual officer who signs the application. Where the T/S/D facility is owned by one person and operated by another, a responsible officer of both the owner and operator must sign the RCRA permit application.[53]

[50] 40 CFR 270.11.

[51] 40 CFR 270.11(a)(1).

[52] 40 CFR 270.11(d).

[53] 40 CFR 270.10(b), 270.11. EPA has issued a RIM interpreting this requirement which states that the term "owner" does not include persons who hold bare legal title to the T/S/D facility for the purpose of providing security for a financing agreement, and who do not exercise any of the effective incidents of ownership or equitable title, 45 Fed. Reg. 74489 (November 10, 1980).

8.4   Permanent Status and RCRA Permits

8.4.1 Contents of Part B Applications

Existing facilities currently operating under interim status must have submitted a Part B application when requested to do so by EPA or an authorized state or, in any event, prior to November 8, 1985, for land disposal facilities granted interim status prior to November 8, 1984; within twelve months of entry into the RCRA system for any other land disposal facility; by November 8, 1986, for incinerators; and by November 8, 1988, for any other facility. If the Part B application is filed in response to a request, the owner/operator of a T/S/D facility will have at least six months after the request to complete and submit the application.[54]

New T/S/D facilities may not begin physical construction without first filing Part A and Part B of the permit application and receiving a final RCRA permit.[55] The only exception is for PCB incinerators, which may begin construction before a permit is issued.[56]

EPA has not prescribed a form for the Part B application. Instead, the regulations establish extensive information requirements for Part B applications prepared by T/S/D facilities.[57] Each Part B information requirement is tied to a standard in Part 264. These include, among a long list of items, the following:

> (1)   a more complete description of the facility, including detailed information on the facility's location shown on a topographic map, with seismic and flood plain data if required;

---

[54]   45 Fed. Reg. 33321 (May 19, 1980); 40 CFR 270.10(e)(4).

[55]   40 CFR 270.10(f)(1).

[56]   RCRA § 3005(a); 40 CFR 270.10(f)(3).

[57]   40 CFR 270.14 - 270.25. EPA has issued guidance documents on format and content, including model Part B applications.

(2)   the results of chemical and physical analyses of the wastes handled at the facility, and the waste analysis plan;

(3)   the security procedures and inspection schedule to be followed;

(4)   the contingency plan;

(5)   a description of procedures, structures and equipment used to prevent accidents, hazards and harm to the environment;

(6)   the personnel training program;

(7)   information on traffic volume, patterns and control;

(8)   the closure and post-closure plans, including a copy of the most recent closure cost estimate and the financial assurance mechanism adopted by the facility;

(9)   detailed data for each type of treatment, storage, or disposal performed at the site, e.g., containers, surface impoundments, landfills, and so forth; and

(10) information describing the location, type, size and operating history of each solid waste management unit.

EPA has also established specific Part B information requirements for each type of T/S/D facility. The requirements call for a basic description of the design and operation of the facility, and additional information is then specified which EPA will rely on to determine that the facility will be operated in compliance with the applicable Part 264 standards.[58]

One additional category of information required by the 1984 Amendments to be included in the Part B application is exposure information and health assessments.[59] All permit applications for a landfill or surface impoundment filed on or after August 8,

---

[58]   Id.

[59]   RCRA § 3019; 40 CFR 270.10(j).

1985, must be accompanied by information "reasonably ascertainable by the owner or operator" on the potential for the public to be exposed to hazardous wastes or constituents "through releases related to the unit." By regulation EPA has defined such information to include the following:

> (1) Reasonably foreseeable potential releases from normal operations and accidents, including transportation to or from the unit.
>
> (2) Potential pathways of human exposure to hazardous wastes or constituents.
>
> (3) Potential magnitude and nature of human exposure resulting from such releases.[60]

The definition of release that is used is patterned upon the definition of that term in CERCLA which is "any spilling, leaking, pumping, pouring, emitting, emptying, discharging, injecting, escaping, leaching, dumping, or disposing into the environment" without the statutory exclusion.[61]

Owners or operators of landfills or impoundments for which Part B permit applications were submitted prior to the date of enactment of the 1984 Amendments were required to submit the same exposure information not later than August 8, 1985.[62]

EPA or the authorized state which receives the permit application may furnish the exposure information to the Agency for Toxic Substances and Disease Registry ("ATSDR"). EPA or the state may ask ATSDR to conduct a health assessment in connection with any facility which "poses a substantial potential risk to human health due to the existence of releases of hazardous constituents" or a substantial population exposure. Members of

---

60   Id.

61   42 U.S.C. 9601(22); 50 Fed. Reg. 28726 (July 15, 1985). The CERCLA definition excludes releases covered under other regulatory statutes. EPA found the exclusions inappropriate for purposes of the health assessment and did not adopt them.

62   40 CFR 270.10(j)(2).

the public may also submit evidence of releases to EPA, the state or ATSDR.[63] As used in this section, the term "health assessment" includes preliminary assessments of the potential risk to human health to determine whether full scale health or epidemiological studies should be undertaken. EPA has provided, however, that a permit application lacking this information will not be termed incomplete so as not to delay permitting.[64]

8.4.2 RCRA Permit Conditions

Certain standard terms and conditions of a RCRA permit issued to a T/S/D facility are prescribed in 40 CFR Part 270, Subpart C. Section 270.30 sets forth conditions applicable to all permits. The EPA region or the approved state has authority, in certain instances, to establish additional conditions, including any provisions found to be necessary to protect human health and the environment.[65]

Section 270.30 contains a number of "boilerplate" conditions that must be included in all RCRA permits.[66] These include the duty to halt production when necessary to ensure compliance, to "take all reasonable steps to minimize releases to the environment," and to "carry out such measures as are reasonable to prevent significant adverse impacts on human health or the environment."[67] The T/S/D facility must also undertake as a permit condition the responsibility to properly operate and maintain its equipment at all times.[68]

---

[63]   RCRA § 3019(b) and (c).

[64]   40 CFR 270.10(c).

[65]   40 CFR 270.32(a) and (b).

[66]   40 CFR 270.30.

[67]   40 CFR 270.30(c) and (d).

[68]   40 CFR 270.30(e).

Another permit condition requires the T/S/D facility to give advance notice to EPA of any planned changes in the permitted facility or activity which may result in noncompliance with the permit.[69] Although no other information besides notice is required, when planned changes are known sufficiently in advance this notice should be given in time for EPA to modify the permit, if necessary, prior to the occurrence of the event. A modification must undergo the public notice and comment process discussed below. Absent a modification, a T/S/D facility will be acting at its own risk, since a notification of anticipated noncompliance or a request for modification does not operate to stay any permit condition.

With regard to inspection and entry of T/S/D facilities, the standard permit condition provides that an EPA inspector must be admitted to a facility upon presentation of credentials "and other documents as may be required by law."[70] Presumably, this means a search warrant when necessary. EPA recognizes that the inclusion of this condition in a permit does not operate to waive any Fourth Amendment rights a T/S/D facility may have.

In addition to these "boilerplate" conditions, there are a number of other specific provisions that are included in RCRA permits, and these are discussed in the following sections.

8.4.2.1 Special RCRA Requirements

All RCRA permits must include certain special conditions applicable only to RCRA permits. These conditions are in addition to the applicable requirements specified in the technical standards at Parts 264 and 266 which, of course, will also be stated in the permit as enforceable conditions.[71] For example, the RCRA permit must include conditions that specify the waste

---

[69]   40 CFR 270.30(k)(2).

[70]   40 CFR 270.30(i).

[71]   40 CFR 270.32(b)(1).

THE RCRA HAZARDOUS WASTES HANDBOOK

and classes of wastes to be handled at the facility, and a description of the processes to be used, including the design capacities, for each treatment, storage and disposal unit.

Among the permit conditions unique to the RCRA program is the requirement that a new T/S/D facility submit a letter signed by a registered engineer with its permit application stating that the facility has been constructed in compliance with the permit.[72] EPA or the state may then inspect a modified or newly constructed facility prior to operation to determine compliance with all permit conditions. If the T/S/D facility does not receive a notice of intent to inspect from EPA within 15 days from the date the certification is submitted, the inspection authority is waived and operations may begin.[73]

Another important condition in RCRA permits concerns the T/S/D facility's obligation to report any noncompliance that may endanger health or the environment within 24 hours.[74] T/S/D facilities are obligated to make an oral report of any release or discharge of hazardous waste that may endanger public drinking water supplies, result in a fire or explosion, or otherwise threaten the environment outside the facility.

8.4.2.2   The "Shield" Provision

The purpose of a permit is to tell a T/S/D facility exactly what it must do to comply with the law. If an owner or operator could be sued for failing to comply with RCRA, even though he was in full compliance with his permit, business activity could hardly be conducted with any certainty. Therefore, the regulations provide that compliance with a RCRA permit during its term constitutes compliance with Subtitle C of the statute.[75] This

---

72   40 CFR 270.30(1)(2)(i).

73   Id.

74   40 CFR 270.30(1)(6).

75   40 CFR 270.4.

shield provision insulates a permittee from enforcement actions brought by EPA or states as well as suits by citizen groups for failure to comply with regulations. It does not provide a defense, however, to an "imminent hazard" action brought under the emergency provisions of RCRA Section 7003 or Section 7002(a)(1)(B), requirements which become effective by statute, or regulations promulgated to implement the land disposal restrictions.[76]

8.4.2.3 Confidentiality

Information which the T/S/D facility submits to EPA as part of a permit application may be claimed as confidential by asserting such a claim at the time of submission.[77] The permit applicant should place on, or attach to, the confidential information at the time it is submitted to EPA a cover sheet, stamped or typed legend, or other such form of notice indicating that the information is a "trade secret," "proprietary," "company confidential" or similarly deserving of confidential treatment. The information will then be treated in accordance with the procedures in 40 CFR Part 2 which provides for notice to the applicant prior to any public disclosure.

8.4.2.4 Fixed Term Duration

RCRA permits are to be effective for a term not to exceed 10 years.[78] Of course, permits may be issued for less than a 10-year term under appropriate circumstances.[79]

Under EPA's original permit regulations, if an EPA-issued permit expired after a state received authorization to issue RCRA permits, the permit did not continue in force unless state law

---

[76]   Id.

[77]   40 CFR 270.12.

[78]   RCRA § 3005(c)(3); 40 CFR 270.50(a).

[79]   40 CFR 270.50(c).

specifically authorized a continuation. EPA has amended its regulations to provide for an automatic continuation of the EPA-issued permit until the effective date of the state's decision to issue or deny the state RCRA permit, provided that the permittee submits a timely, complete state permit application.[80] Likewise, in non-authorized states, the conditions of an expired EPA permit continue in force if the permittee has submitted a timely application.[81]

8.5 Permitting Procedures

The permit procedures in Part 124, Subpart A, apply to issuance of RCRA permits by EPA. Subpart A contains general procedures for issuing, denying, modifying, revoking and reissuing, or terminating permits, which are discussed briefly below. Many of these permit procedures will also be applicable when a state is administering the RCRA program. EPA has required states to adopt these or comparable procedures as a condition to EPA's granting the states authorization to administer their programs in lieu of the federal program, as discussed in Chapter 10 of this Handbook.

8.5.1 Submission of Application

Where EPA is administering the permit program, the EPA Regional Administrator will initially review the application and notify the T/S/D facility in writing whether the application is complete to his satisfaction.[82] If it is not, EPA must afford the operator an opportunity to submit specified information to complete the application.

For major new T/S/D facilities, EPA will then prepare a "project decision schedule" and send it to the facility.[83] The

---

[80]   40 CFR 270.51(d).

[81]   40 CFR 270.51(a).

[82]   40 CFR 270.10(c), 124.3(c).

[83]   40 CFR 124.3(g).

schedule will specify target dates for preparing a draft permit, completing the public comment process, and issuing a final permit. The project decision schedule is not legally binding on EPA. State procedures are generally similar.

8.5.2 Draft Permit

The next step is the preparation of a draft permit by EPA. The draft permit must incorporate all applicable conditions, compliance schedules, and monitoring requirements.[84] It must be based on an administrative record, publicly noticed, and made available for public comment and hearing. It must also be accompanied either by a "statement of basis" or a "fact sheet."[85]

A statement of basis is a brief document that is used in uncontroversial permit proceedings and for small companies.[86] It serves to meet minimal requirements by describing how the conditions of the draft permit were derived and the reasons for them. The fact sheet, on the other hand, is a more comprehensive and detailed document which is used for major facilities and where there is widespread public interest in the permit.[87] A fact sheet must include the principal facts and significant legal, methodological, and policy issues considered in preparing the draft permit.

8.5.3 Public Comment and Hearing

Public notice must be given of all important permit actions including specifically the preparation of a draft permit.[88] For RCRA permits, a 45-day comment period must be allowed during

---

[84]   40 CFR 124.6.

[85]   40 CFR 124.6(e).

[86]   40 CFR 124.7.

[87]   40 CFR 124.8.

[88]   40 CFR 124.10.

which time any interested person may submit written comments on the draft permit and request a public hearing. EPA must automatically hold a public hearing on a draft RCRA permit whenever anyone submits a written notice of opposition to the permit and requests a hearing. For all other permits subject to the consolidated permit regulations, EPA may hold a hearing at its discretion, but need only hold a hearing when there is "a significant degree of public interest" in a draft permit.[89] All persons submitting comments, including the RCRA permit applicant, must raise all "reasonably ascertainable issues" and submit all "reasonably available arguments and factual grounds" for their position during the public comment period.[90] These limitations on the opportunity for a public hearing have been upheld by the Supreme Court in the context of Clean Water Act permits.[91]

The public hearing applicable to RCRA permit issuance proceedings is basically "legislative" in nature. Interested persons may submit oral and written statements concerning the draft RCRA permit, and a formal record is kept. Cross-examination of witnesses is rarely allowed. EPA has decided that the issuance of RCRA permits will not be subject to the full evidentiary hearing urged by many commentators.

8.5.4 Permit Issuance and Appeal

After the close of the comment period, which will be extended to include any public hearing, EPA must decide whether to issue, deny, modify, revoke, reissue, or terminate a RCRA permit.[92] Neither RCRA Section 3005 nor EPA's consolidated permit regulations specify a deadline by which EPA must make its

---

[89]   40 CFR 124.12.

[90]   40 CFR 124.13.

[91]   Costle v. Pacific Legal Foundation, 445 U.S. 198 (1980).

[92]   40 CFR 124.15.

decision. The final permit decision will normally become effective 30 days after service of the decision on all parties, unless it is challenged.

Before the effective date of the permit, any person who filed comments on the draft permit or who participated in the public hearing may petition EPA's Environmental Appeals Board to review any condition of the permit.[93] If challenged, the effectiveness of the permit is <u>automatically stayed</u>.[94] This means that an unpermitted T/S/D facility may not begin operations, but a facility with a preexisting permit may continue operations under the terms of that prior permit.

Within a "reasonable time" following a petition for review, the Environmental Appeals Board must grant or deny the petition.[95] If granted, briefs will be accepted and the Board will make a final decision on the appeal. A motion to reconsider a final order can be filed with the Board within 10 days after service of a final order.[96] The Board may in its discretion, refer an appeal or motion to the Administrator when it deems it appropriate to do so.[97] A petition for administrative review is a prerequisite to judicial review.[98]

8.5.5 Modification, Reissuance or Termination

In general, a RCRA permit may be modified after issuance only for specified reasons.[99] Major modifications entitle the permittee to the procedural safeguards of notice and comment

---

[93]   40 CFR 124.19.

[94]   40 CFR 124.16.

[95]   40 CFR 124.19(c).

[96]   40 CFR 124.19(g).

[97]   40 CFR 124.2.

[98]   40 CFR 124.19(e)

[99]   40 CFR 270.41(a), 270.42.

proceedings. Chief among these are "material and substantial alterations or additions" to a T/S/D facility, or new information that was not available at the time of permit issuance, which justify different permit conditions. In addition, the permit may be modified when new regulations are issued under RCRA or a T/S/D facility requests modification.[100]

EPA has categorized permit modifications into three classes based upon the degree of alteration proposed in connection with the permit.[101] The purpose of this categorization is to provide owners, operators and EPA more flexibility to change permit conditions, to expand public notification and participation opportunities, and to allow for expedited approval if no public concern exists for a proposed permit modification.

As with many other issues, land disposal facilities have been singled out by the 1984 Amendments for special treatment in the modification area. Permits for these facilities must be reviewed five years after issuance and modified as necessary to ensure compliance with currently applicable regulatory require-ments and any other conditions necessary to protect human health and the environment (including improvements and changes in control and measurement technology).[102]

Class 1 modifications cover routine changes such as typographical errors, replacing equipment with functionally equivalent equipment, and upgrading plans and records maintained by the facility. These changes are generally allowed without prior Agency approval. Owners and operators must, however, notify EPA or the authorized state agency once they have made these changes.

---

[100]   Id.

[101]   40 CFR 270.42, Appendix I. For the reader's convenience, Appendix I is set forth as a separate table at the end of this chapter.

[102]   RCRA § 3005(c)(3); 40 CFR 270.32(b), 270.50(d); 270.41(a)(5).

Class 2 modifications cover common or frequently occurring changes of moderate impact, including those needed to conform to new regulatory requirements. These include changes in the number, location or design of ground water monitoring wells; increases in capacity of up to 25% of the waste that can be treated at specified units; modification of a trial burn plan for an incinerator; and comparable changes that are more significant than the Class 1 changes but which do not require, in EPA's view, the full-scale public participation procedures of the more extensive Class 3 modifications.

Class 2 modification procedures require a request to the permitting agency, public notice of such request by the facility owner, an informal meeting between the owner and the public, and a 60-day comment period.[103] The permitting agency must approve (with or without modifications) or deny the request within 90 days of receipt. The permitting agency may also determine that the request involves significant environment issues and must follow the full Class 3 modification procedures. The permitting agency may also extend this period by 30 days or approve a temporary authorization for up to 180 days.

If the permitting agency does not take action by the end of the 30 day extension, the changes specified in the modification request are automatically authorized for a period of 180 days. If the permitting agency still has not acted by the end of the 180 day period, the requested changes are automatically authorized for the duration of the permit. The owner must notify the public that EPA has not acted 50 days before the end of the 180 day authorization period or the clock on that period is suspended. In other words, the automatic permanent authorization for the duration of the permit will not go into effect until 50 days after the public is notified. This "default" provision is designed to provide reasonable certainty to facility owners

---

[103] 40 CFR 270.42(b).

that Class 2 modification requests will be acted on expeditiously.

Class 3 modifications cover major changes that substantially alter the facility. Full public notice and hearing requirements, similar to procedures for initial permit issuance, apply to these.

Many states are in the process of adopting these more flexible permit modification procedures. Unfortunately, EPA has not required adoption of those procedures, and therefore it is not likely that they will be uniformly adopted in all states.

A RCRA permit may be <u>revoked and reissued</u> (or simply modified) whenever the permit is to be transferred, or when cause exists for termination.[104] When a permit is modified, only the conditions subject to modification are reopened. If a permit is revoked and reissued, the entire permit is reopened and subject to revision to incorporate all new regulatory requirements. The permit is then reissued for a new term.[105]

A RCRA permit may be <u>terminated</u> for noncompliance with any condition of the permit, for failure to disclose fully all relevant facts in the Part A and B applications, or when the treatment, storage, or disposal activity poses a threat to human health or the environment.[106]

The right to terminate a permit for noncompliance with any condition gives EPA extremely broad enforcement discretion. Theoretically, any noncompliance with the permit, whether caused willfully, by neglect, or even without fault may be grounds for termination. Not only will the T/S/D facility be subject to enforcement action, but it no longer will have a permit to conduct its business. EPA has recognized that it should use termination as an enforcement weapon only in extreme

---

[104] 40 CFR 270.41(b).

[105] 40 CFR 270.41.

[106] 40 CFR 270.43.

circumstances.[107] The formal evidentiary hearing procedure in Part 124, Subpart E, must precede any RCRA permit termination.

8.5.6 Corrective Action

As a result of the 1984 Amendments, EPA must, as a condition of any permit, require corrective action as necessary to protect human health and the environment for all releases of hazardous wastes and constituents from any solid waste management unit at a T/S/D facility, regardless of when the waste was placed in the unit.[108] On July 27, 1990, EPA proposed corrective action requirements for solid waste management units at facilities seeking a permit under Subtitle C. Due to the breadth and complexity of these proposal requirements, they are discussed separately in the next chapter.

8.6 Special RCRA Permits
8.6.1 Short Term Permits

An emergency permit may be issued to a facility to allow treatment, storage, or disposal of a hazardous waste when imperative to avoid an imminent and substantial endangerment to human health or the environment.[109] An emergency permit is limited to 90 days in duration, revocable at will, and may be issued orally by the appropriate authorities. If oral, it must be followed within 5 days by a written emergency permit. An emergency permit must also be publicly noticed.[110]

By regulation, EPA has provided that a RCRA permit is not required for activities carried out to contain or treat immediately a spill of hazardous waste, such as a commercial

---

[107]   45 Fed. Reg. 33316 (May 19, 1980).

[108]   RCRA § 3004(u). 40 CFR 264.90(a), 264.101.

[109]   40 CFR 270.61(a).

[110]   40 CFR 270.2.

chemical product listed in 40 CFR 261.33(e) and (f).[111] An emergency permit or other authorization is still needed, however, for any treatment, storage or disposal of spilled material or spill residue or debris.

Short term permits may also be obtained to permit trial burns of incinerators or boilers and industrial furnaces to determine the feasibility of compliance with the applicable performance standards.[112] The trial burn must be conducted in accordance with a detailed trial burn plan which is incorporated into the permit.[113]

8.6.2 Permits-By-Rule

One key feature of the RCRA permit program is the provision for RCRA permits-by-rule. Under this approach, certain types of T/S/D facilities that might otherwise be required to apply for and obtain RCRA permits are exempted, and instead are "deemed" to have a permit if they meet certain listed conditions. Currently, ocean disposal barges with permits issued under the Marine Protection, Research and Sanctuaries Act, operators of underground injection wells with UIC permits issued under the Safe Drinking Water Act, and publicly owned treatment works regulated under the Clean Water Act are deemed by regulation to have a RCRA permit.[114]

Although Section 3005 of RCRA requires that each T/S/D facility eventually have a permit, EPA has considered permits-by-rule for an entire class of facilities. The advantage of such a procedure from the point of view of the regulated community is

---

[111]   40 CFR 270.1(c)(3).

[112]   40 CFR 270.62; 40 CFR 270.66.

[113]   A more detailed description of the operating standards and permit requirements applicable to these units is provided in Section 6.10 (for incinerators) and 6.14 (for boilers and industrial furnaces).

[114]   40 CFR 270.60.

that by complying with stated regulatory requirements, a company can then avoid the procedural burdens of a site-specific permit, as well as certain other detailed facility requirements, which are incumbent upon all facilities that are subject to the Part 264 regulations. Permits-by-rule can simplify the permitting process and reduce regulatory costs where the applicable RCRA requirements can be adequately defined in a national regulation.

From the viewpoint of EPA, there is a similar benefit in terms of conservation of its limited personnel and budgetary resources, since promulgating and monitoring a regulation of general application is far less demanding than processing and enforcing perhaps thousands of site-specific permits. Normally, it is most appropriate where the threat to the environment which could result from the mismanagement of hazardous wastes is comparatively low. Eligibility for a permit-by-rule could be terminated by EPA in an individual case where special environmental concerns or other circumstances warrant.

As discussed in Chapter 6 of this Handbook, standards were proposed in 1980 for elementary neutralization units, which are defined as tanks, containers, transport vehicles, or vessels which are used for neutralizing wastes which are hazardous only because they are corrosive. Standards were also proposed for "wastewater treatment units," which are defined as tanks that are part of a facility that is regulated under the Clean Water Act through either an NPDES permit for a direct discharge or a pretreatment standard for an indirect discharge to a publicly owned treatment works.[115] In an April 19, 1984, notice, EPA indicated that consideration of the proposed Part 266 regulations for wastewater treatment units and elementary neutralization units has been postponed.[116] The principal reason for this seems to be the local notice and comment procedures which the statute

---

[115]   45 Fed. Reg. 76076 (November 17, 1980).

[116]   49 Fed. Reg. 16401 (April 19, 1984).

presently requires for every RCRA permit. For the time being, EPA has exempted elementary neutralization units and wastewater units from compliance with Parts 264, 265 and 270, provided that owners and operators diluting ignitable or corrosive wastes in such units comply with the requirements for these wastes set out in Part 265.[117]

8.6.3 Research, Development and Demonstration Permits

Section 3005(g) authorizes research, development and demonstration ("RD&D") permits to encourage the use of innovative technology. These types of permits may be issued for any treatment facility which proposes to utilize "an innovative and experimental hazardous waste treatment technology or process for which permit standards have not been promulgated."[118] The permit must include conditions to protect human health and the environment. The permit shall allow construction of the facility and operation up to one year, unless renewed. Renewal is authorized for up to three times. The permit authorization is limited to the types and quantities of hazardous waste deemed necessary for determining efficacy and performance capability of the technology. Pilot scale units to test treatment of new waste or alternate operating conditions are envisioned. The permit must include standard safeguards required for all other permits, including monitoring, financial responsibility, closure and remedial action. EPA has developed a manual to provide guidance to permit applicants and writers on preparing and processing RD&D applications and permits.[119]

---

[117] 40 CFR 264.1(g)(6); 40 CFR 265.1(c)(10), 265.17(b); 40 CFR 270.1(c)(2)(v).

[118] 40 CFR 270.65.

[119] The manual is available for purchase from the National Technical Information Service. See 51 Fed. Reg. 30429 (August 26, 1986).

To expedite review and issuance, EPA may modify or waive most substantive permit requirements, except for financial responsibility and public notice and participation. Region III of the EPA proposed the first research, development and demonstration permit in the Spring of 1985.

8.6.4 Mobile Treatment Unit Permits

EPA has recognized that mobile treatment technology could play a valuable role in achieving the goals of RCRA by increasing the treatment options available to industrial generators. EPA has also recognized that is permitting regulations were developed primarily with stationary units in mind and these regulations are extremely burdensome for mobile treatment units ("MTUs") which are designed to move from facility to facility treating wastes. EPA, therefore, in response to a petition from the Hazardous Waste Treatment Council ("HWTC"), has proposed regulations to allow expedited permitting of MTUs. The proposal would allow owners or operators of MTUs to obtain a statewide permit for specific MTUs or groups of identical MTUs. Permits could be issued for a particular unit even if specific sites of operation are not yet identified.

The proposed rule also contains alternative delisting procedures under which delisting can occur as part of the permitting process. This "upfront delisting" would allow the delisting and permitting decisions to be made concurrently. If approved by EPA, the treatment residues from the MTU would be classified as nonhazardous and could be disposed of accordingly. EPA's delisting would be effective nationally. The MTU operator would be required to conduct sampling and analysis to determine that the residues conform to the acceptable hazardous constituent concentration levels specified in the delisting petition. Any residue not complying with those levels would be classified as hazardous waste.

The practical benefit of the upfront delisting by EPA may be lost in those authorized states that have their own delisting programs. Because states can impose requirements that are more stringent than federal requirements, they may decide not to follow the EPA delisting approach. Until those states exercise their own delisting processes consistent with the EPA approach, the MTU residues will still be classified as hazardous waste at the state level unless and until delisted.

Unfortunately these regulations, proposed in 1987, have not become final, largely due to EPA's insistence that site specific conditions be added to the MTU's statewide permit prior to allowing the unit to operate at any facility. HWTC and others have argued these site specific requirements are unduly burdensome and largely eviscerate the benefits of granting statewide permits. EPA has acknowledged that these requirements are burdensome but believes they are mandated by statutory provisions that require local notice of permitting decisions, corrective action at each operating site, and that RCRA permits be issued to a "facility" (which is defined by reference to a site of operation).

8.7   Conclusion

Permitting can be a complicated, expensive and time-consuming process. Owners and operators of T/S/D facilities can limit the potential problems that may arise by filing timely and complete applications, by being thoroughly familiar with the requirements of EPA's regulatory scheme under RCRA, and by consulting the proper EPA personnel, experienced consultants, and legal counsel early in the permitting process.

TABLE 8-1

Classification of Permit Modifications
(Appendix I to 40 CFR 270.42)[120]

Modifications	Class
A. General Permit Provisions..	1
1. Administrative and informational changes..	1
2. Correction of typographical errors...	1
3. Equipment replacement or upgrading with functionally equivalent components (e.g., pipes, valves, pumps, conveyors, controls)........................	1
4. Changes in the frequency of or procedures for monitoring, reporting, sampling, or maintenance activities by the permittee:	
a. To provide for more frequent monitoring, reporting, sampling, or maintenance...........	1
b. Other changes...	2
5. Schedule of compliance:	
a. Changes in interim compliance, with prior approval of the Director....................	1[1]
b. Extension of final compliance date..	3
6. Changes in expiration date of permit to allow earlier permit termination, with prior approval of the Director..	1[1]
7. Changes in ownership or operational control of a facility, provided the procedures of § 270.40(b) are followed....................................	1[1]
B. General Facility Standards	
1. Changes to waste sampling or analysis methods:	
a. To conform with agency guidance or regulations................................	1
b. To incorporate changes associated with F039 (multi-source leachate) sampling or analysis methods..	([1]) 1
b. To incorporate changes associated with F039 (multi-source leachate) sampling or analysis methods...	1
c. Other changes...	2
2. Changes to analytical quality assurance/control plan:	
a. To conform with agency guidance or regulations................................	1
b. Other changes...	2
3. Changes in procedures for maintaining the operating record......................	1
4. Changes in frequency or content of inspection schedules........................	2
5. Changes in the training plan:	
a. That affect the type of decrease the amount of training given to employees...........	2
b. Other changes...	1

---

[120] As amended by 57 Fed. Reg. 37281 (August 18, 1992) (to be codified at 40 CFR 270.42).

   6. Contingency plan:
      a. Changes in emergency procedures (i.e., spill or release response procedures)............. 2
      b. Replacement with functionally equivalent equipment, upgrade, or relocated
          emergency equipment listed.. 1
      c. Removal of equipment from emergency equipment list... 2
      d. Changes in name, address, or phone number of coordinators of other persons
          or agencies identified in the plan... 1
   7. Construction quality assurance plan:
      a. Changes that the CQA officer certifies in the operating record will provide
          equivalent or better certainty that the unit components meet the design
          specifications.. 1
      b. Other changes.. 2

Note: When a permit modification (such as introduction of a new unit) requires a change in facility plans or other general facility standards, that change shall be reviewed under the same procedures as the permit modification.

C. Ground-Water Protection
   1. Changes to wells:
      a. Changes in the number, location, depth, or design of upgradient or downgradient
          wells of permitted groundwater monitoring system................................... 2
      b. Replacement of an existing well that has been damaged or rendered inoperable,
          without change to location, design, or depth of the well................................ 1
   2. Changes in groundwater sampling or analysis procedures or monitoring schedule,
      with prior approval of the Director... ^{1} 1
   3. Changes in statistical procedure for determining whether a statistically significant
      change in groundwater quality between upgradient and downgradient wells has occurred,
      with prior approval of the Director... ^{1} 1
   4. Changes in point of compliance... ^{1} 2
   5. Changes in indicator parameters, hazardous constituents, or concentration limits
      (including ACLs):
      a. As specified in the groundwater protection standard...................................... 3
      b. As specified in the detection monitoring program... 2
   6. Changes to a detection monitoring program as required by § 264.98(j), unless
      otherwise specified in this appendix.. 2
   7. Compliance monitoring program:
      a. Addition of compliance monitoring program as required by §§ 264.98(h)(4) and 264.99...... 3
      b. Changes to a compliance monitoring program as required by § 264.99(k), unless
          otherwise specified in this appendix... 2
   8. Corrective action program:
      a. Addition of a corrective action program as required by §§ 264.99(i)(2) and 264.100....... 3
      b. Changes to a corrective action program as required by § 264.100(h), unless otherwise
          specified in this Appendix... 2

D. Closure
   1. Changes to the closure plan:
      a. Changes in estimate of maximum extent of operations or maximum inventory of waste
          on-site at any time during the active life of the facility, with prior approval
          of the Director... ^{1} 1

3. Storage of different wastes in containers, except as provided in (F)(4) below:
    a. That require additional or different management practices from those authorized in the permit.. **3**
    b. That do not require additional or different management practices from those authorized in the permit.. **2**

Note: See § 270.42(g) for modification procedures to be used for the management of newly listed or identified wastes.

4. Storage of treatment of different wastes in containers:
    a. That require addition of units or change in treatment process or management standards, provided that the wastes are restricted from land disposal and are to be treated to meet some or all of the applicable treatment standards, or that are to be treated to satisfy (in whole or in part) the standard of "use of practically available technology that yields the greatest environmental benefit" contained in § 268.8(a)(2)(ii). This modification is not applicable to dioxin-containing wastes (F020, 021, 022, 023, 026, 027, and 028)........................ **1**
    b. That do not require the addition of units or a change in the treatment process or management standards, and provided that the units have previously received wastes of the same type (e.g., incinerator scrubber water). This modification is not applicable to dioxin-containing wastes (F020, 021, 022, 023, 026, 027, and 028).. **¹ 1**

G. Tanks
  1:
    a. Modification or addition to tank units resulting in greater than 25% increase in the facility's tank capacity, except as provided in G(1)(c), G(1)(d), and G(1)(e) below... **3**
    b. Modification or addition of tank units resulting in up to 25% increase in the facility's tank capacity, except as provided in G(1)(d) and G(1)(e) below................ **2**
    c. Addition of a new tank that will operate for more than 90 days using any of the following physical or chemical treatment technologies: neutralization, dewatering, phase separation, or component separation................................... **2**
    d. After prior approval of the Director, addition of a new tank that will operate for up to 90 days using any of the following physical or chemical treatment technologies: neutralization, dewatering, phase separation, or component separation... **¹ 1**
    e. Modification or addition of tank units or treatment processes necessary to treat wastes that are restricted from land disposal to meet some or all of the applicable treatment standards or to treat wastes to satisfy (in whole or in part) the standard of "use of practically available technology that yields the greatest environmental benefit" contained in § 268.8(a)(2)(ii), with prior approval of the Director. This modification may also involve addition of new waste codes. It is not applicable to dioxin-containing wastes (F020, 021, 022, 023, 026, 027, and 028)... **¹ 1**

2. Modification of a tank unit or secondary containment system without increasing the capacity of the unit... **2**

3. Replacement of a tank with a tank that meets the same design standards and has a capacity within +/- 10% of the replaced tank provided................................... 1
    - The capacity difference is no more than 1500 gallons,
    - The facility's permitted tank capacity is not increased, and
    - The replacement tank meets the same conditions in the permit.
4. Modification of a tank management practices.. 2
5. Management of different wastes in tanks:
    a. That require additional or different management practices, tanks design, different fire protection specifications, or significantly different tank treatment process from that authorized in the permit, except as provided in (G)(5)(c) below.. 3
    b. That do not require additional or different management practices, tank design, different fire protection specifications, or significantly different tank treatment process than authorized in the permit, except as provided in (G)(5)(d)... 2
    c. That require addition of units or change in treatment processes or management standards, provided that the wastes are restricted from land disposal and are to be treated to meet some or all of the applicable treatment standards or that are to be treated to satisfy (in whole or in part) the standard of "use of practically available technology that yields the greatest environmental benefit" contained in § 268.8(a)(2)(ii). The modification is not applicable to dioxin-containing wastes (F020, 021, 022, 023, 026, 027, and 028)............................ 1 1
    d. That do not require the addition of units or a change in the treatment process or management standards, and provided that the units have previously received wastes of the same type (e.g., incinerator scrubber water). This modification is not applicable to dioxin-containing wastes (F020, 021, 022, 023, 026, 027, and 028)............................ 1

Note: See § 270.42(g) for modification procedures to be used for the management of newly listed or identified wastes.

H. Surface Impoundments
1. Modification or addition of surface impoundment units that result in increasing the facility's surface impoundment storage or treatment capacity................. 3
2. Replacement of a surface impoundment unit... 3
3. Modification of a surface impoundment unit without increasing the facility's surface impoundment storage or treatment capacity and without modifying the unit's liner, leak detection system, or leachate collection system..................... 2
4. Modification of a surface impoundment management practice.................................. 2
5. Treatment, storage, or disposal of different wastes in surface impoundments:
    a. That require additional or different management practices or different design of the liner or leak detection system than authorized in the permit 3
    b. That do not require additional or different management practices or different design of the liner or leak detection system than authorized in the permit.. 2

  c. That are wastes restricted from land disposal that meet the applicable
treatment standards or that are treated to satisfy the standard of "use
of practically available technology that yields the greatest environmental benefit" contained in § 269.8(a)(2)(ii), and provided that the
unit meets the minimum technological requirements stated in § 268.5(h)(2).
This modification is not applicable to dioxin-containing wastes (F020,
021, 022, 023, 026, 027, and 028)... 1

  d. That are residues from wastewater treatment or incineration, provided
that disposal occurs in a unit that meets the minimum technological
requirements stated in § 268.5(h)(2), and provided further that the
surface impoundment has previously received wastes of the same type
(for example, incinerator scrubber water). This modification is not
applicable to dioxin-containing wastes (F020, 021, 022, 023, 026,
027, and 028)... 1

 6. Modifications of unconstructed units to comply with §§ 264.221(c),
264.222, 264.223, and 264.226(d)... *1

 7. Changes in response action plan:
  a. Increase in action leakage rate.. 3
  b. Change in a specific response reducing its frequency or effectiveness.................... 3
  c. Other changes... 2

Note: See § 270.42(g) for modification procedures to be used for the management of newly
listed or identified wastes.

I. Enclosed Waste Piles. For all waste piles except those comply with § 264.250(c),
modifications are treated the same as for a landfill. The following modifications
are applicable only to waste piles complying with § 264.250(c).

 1. Modification or addition or waste pile units:
  a. Resulting in greater than 25% increase in the facility's waste pile storage
or treatment capacity... 3
  b. Resulting in up to 25% increase in the facility's waste pile storage or
treatment capacity.. 2

 2. Modification of waste pile unit without increasing the capacity of the unit.................. 2

 3. Replacement of a waste pile unit with another waste pile unit of the same
design and capacity and meeting all waste pile conditions in the permit...................... 1

 4. Modification of a waste pile management practice... 2

 5. Storage or treatment of different wastes in waste piles:
  a. That require additional or different management practices or different
design of the unit.. 3
  b. That do not require additional or different management practices or
different design of the unit.. 2

Note: See § 270.42(g) for modification procedures to be used for the management of newly
listed or identified wastes.

J. Landfills and Unenclosed Waste Piles
 1. Modification or addition of landfill units that result in increasing the facility's
disposal capacity.. 3

§ 270.42

40 CFR Ch 1 (7-1-92 Edition
Appendix I to § 270.42 -
Classification of Permit
Modification

THE RCRA HAZARDOUS WASTES HANDBOOK

40 CFR Ch 1 (7-1-92 Edition
Appendix I to § 270.42 -
Classification of Permit
Modification

6. Modification of a land treatment unit management practice to:
    a. Increase rate or change method of waste application....................................... 3
    b. Decrease rate of waste application.. 1
7. Modification of a land treatment unit management practice to change measures of pH or moisture content, or to enhance microbial or chemical reactions............................ 2
8. Modification of a land treatment unit management practice to grow food chain crops, to add to or replace existing permitted crops with different food chain crops, or to modify operating plans for distribution of animal feeds resulting from such crops........ 3
9. Modification of operating practice due to detection of releases from the land treatment unit pursuant to § 264.278(g)(2)... 3
10. Changes in the unsaturated zone monitoring system, resulting in a change to the location, depth, number of sampling points, or replace unsaturated zone monitoring devices or components of devices with devices or components that have specifications different from permit requirements... 3
11. Changes in the unsaturated zone monitoring system that do not result in a change to the location, depth, number of sampling points, or that replace unsaturated zone monitoring devices or components of devices with devices or components having specifications having specifications different from permit requirements...................... 2
12. Changes in background values for hazardous constituents in soil and soil-pore liquid......... 2
13. Changes in sampling, analysis, or statistical procedure.................................... 2
14. Changes in land treatment demonstration program prior to or during the demonstration........ 2
15. Changes in any condition specified in the permit for a land treatment unit to reflect results of the land treatment demonstration, provided performance standards are met, and the Director's prior approval has been received... 1 [1]
16. Changes to allow a second land treatment demonstration to be conducted when the results of the first demonstration have not shown the conditions under which the wastes can be treated completely, provided the conditions for the second demonstration are substantially the same as the conditions for the first demonstration and have received the prior approval of the Director......................... 1 [1]
17. Changes to allow a second land treatment demonstration to be conducted when the results of the first demonstration have not shown the conditions under which the wastes can be treated completely, where the conditions for the second demonstration are not substantially the same as the conditions for the first demonstration.. 3
18. Changes in vegetative cover requirements for closure.. 2

L. Incinerators, Boilers, and Industrial Furnaces:
    1. Changes to increase by more than 25% any of the following limits authorized in the permit: A thermal feed rate limit, a feedstream feed rate limit, a chlorine/chloride feed rate limit, a metal feed rate limit, or an ash feed rate limit. The Director will require a new trial burn to substantiate compliance with the regulatory performance standards unless this demonstration can be made through other means............. 3
    2. Changes to increase by up to 25% any of the following limits authorized in the permit: A thermal feed rate limit, a feedstream feed rate limit, a chlorine/chloride feed rate limit, a metal feed rate limit, or an ash feed rate limit. The Director will

require a new trial burn to substantiate compliance with the regulatory performance
standards unless this demonstration can be made through other means......................... 2
3. Modification of an incinerator, boiler, or industrial furnace unit by changing the
internal size or geometry of the primary or secondary combustion units, by adding a
primary or secondary combustion unit, by substantially changing the design of any
component used to remove HCI/CI_2, metals, or particulate from the combustion gases,
or by changing other features of the incinerator, boiler, or industrial furnace
that could affect its capacity to meet the regulatory performance standards. The
Director will require a new trial burn to substantiate compliance with the regulatory
performance standards unless this demonstration can be made through other means.............. 3
4. Modification of an incinerator, boiler, or industrial furnace unit in a manner that
would not likely affect the capability of the unit to meet the regulatory performance
standards but which would change the operating conditions or monitoring requirements
specified in the permit. The Director may require a new trial burn to demonstrate
compliance with the regulatory performance standards.. 3
5. Operating requirements:.. 2
   a. Modification of the limits specified in the permit for minimum combustion gas
     temperature, minimum combustion gas residence time, oxygen concentration in the
     secondary combustion chamber, flue gas carbon monoxide and hydrocarbon concentration,
     maximum temperature at the inlet to the particulate matter emission control system,
     or operating parameters for the air pollution control system. The Director will
     require a new trial burn to substantiate compliance with the regulatory performance
     standards unless the demonstration can be made through other means..................... 3
   b. Modification of any stack gas emission limits specified in the permit, or
     modification of any conditions in the permit concerning emergency shutdown or
     automatic waste feed cutoff procedures or controls..................................... 3
   c. Modification of any other operating condition or any inspection or recordkeeping
     requirement specified in the permit.. 2
6. Burning different wastes:...
   a. If the waste contains a POHC that is more difficult to burn than authorized by
     the permit or if burning of the waste requires compliance with different
     performance standards than specified in the permit. The Director will require
     a new trial burn to substantiate compliance with the regulatory performance
     standards unless this demonstration can be made through other means.................... 3
   b. If the waste does not contain a POHC that is more difficult to burn than
     authorized by the permit and if burning of the waste does not require
     compliance with different regulatory performance standards than specified
     in the permit.. 2
NOTE: See § 270.42(g) for modification procedures to be used for the management of newly
listed or identified wastes.
7. Shakedown and trial burn:
   a. Modification of the trial burn plan or any of the permit conditions applicable
     during the shakedown period for determining operational readiness after
     construction, the trial burn period, or the period immediately following
     the trial burn... 2

     b. Authorization of up to an additional 720 hours of waste burning during the shakedown period for determining operational readiness after construction, with the prior approval of the Director.. 1

     c. Changes in the operating requirements set in the permit for conducting a trial burn, provided the change is minor and has received the prior approval of the Director... 1

     d. Changes in the ranges of the operating requirements set in the permit to reflect the results of the trial burn, provided the change is minor and has received the prior approval of the Director.......................... 1

  8. Substitution of an alternative type of nonhazardous waste fuel that is not specified in the permit.. 1

M. Containment Buildings

  1. Modification or addition of containment building units:

     a. Resulting in greater than 25% increase in the facility's containment building storage or treatment capacity.................................... 3

     b. Resulting in up to 25% increase in the facility's containment building storage or treatment capacity.................................... 2

  2. Modification of a containment building unit or secondary containment system without increasing the capacity of the unit...................................... 2

  3. Replacement of a containment building with a containment building that meets the same design standard provided:

     a. The unit capacity is not increased...................................... 1

     b. The replacement containment building meets the same conditions in the permit............ 1

  4. Modification of a containment building management practice.................................. 2

  5. Storage or treatment of different wastes in containment buildings:

     a. That require additional or different management practices................................. 3

     b. That do not require additional or different management practices........................ 2

CHAPTER 9
CORRECTIVE ACTION
FOR SOLID WASTE MANAGEMENT UNITS

As originally enacted, RCRA did not provide EPA with substantial authority to require T/S/D facilities to remediate contamination which had resulted from past operations. Instead, the RCRA program was intended primarily to regulate current treatment, storage and disposal practices. That situation changed with the 1984 Amendments, which not only gave EPA authority but required the Agency to force T/S/D facilities to undertake "corrective action" for contamination which had emanated from any "solid waste management unit" (SWMU) at the facility, regardless of when the wastes were disposed.

9.1. Statutory Overview

Prior to the 1984 Amendments, EPA had to rely on its Section 7003 enforcement authority to require T/S/D facilities to clean up releases of hazardous waste or hazardous constituents which resulted from facility operations. That authority could be evoked only when the Agency could demonstrate that solid or hazardous wastes at a facility presented at least a threat of "imminent and substantial endangerment to human health or the environment." Similarly, under Section 3013 of RCRA, EPA could require facilities to conduct investigations when the presence of hazardous waste or releases of hazardous waste might present a substantial hazard to human health or the environment.

The 1984 Amendments vastly expanded EPA's authority to force T/S/D facilities to conduct corrective action for releases from a facility. In fact, under the new Section 3004(u), the Agency must require:

> [C]orrective action for all releases of hazardous waste or constituents from any solid waste management unit at a treatment, storage, or disposal facility seeking a permit under

> this subchapter, regardless of the time at
> which the waste was placed in such units.

This requirement applies to facilities seeking closure or post-closure permits as well as those seeking ordinary operating permits. The statute does not define the term "solid waste management unit." As discussed _infra_, EPA has interpreted the term very broadly. Furthermore, permits issued to T/S/D facilities must contain both schedules of compliance and "assurances of financial responsibility for completing such corrective action."

Like Section 104 of the Comprehensive Environmental Response, Compensation and Liability Act (CERCLA or Superfund) which authorizes the President to undertake response actions whenever there has been a release of a hazardous substance, Section 3004(u) does not technically require proof of some threat of endangerment before EPA can require corrective action for a release of hazardous wastes or constituents from a SWMU. However, in practical terms, it would be arbitrary and capricious for EPA to require extensive corrective action where no threat to human health or the environment existed. In fact, the regulation implementing this statutory provision states that corrective action will be required "as necessary to protect human health and the environment" -- a significant gloss on the statutory language. _See_ 40 CFR 264.101.

Under Section 3004(v), T/S/D facilities are required to undertake _off-site_ corrective action when necessary to protect human health or the environment. This requirement will not apply if the owner or operator can demonstrate that, despite his best efforts, he was unable to obtain permission from other property owners to conduct such action. Nevertheless, the owner or operator is still required to take such on-site measures as he can to prevent off-site releases.

Sections 3004(v) and 3005(i) apply corrective action requirements to interim status landfills, surface impoundments, land treatment units or waste piles which received hazardous waste after July 26, 1982. Similarly, RCRA Section 3008(h) authorizes EPA to require owners and operators of interim status facilities to perform corrective action when there is or has been a release of hazardous waste from such facility when such action is necessary to protect human health or the environment. Any order issued under Section 3008(h) becomes final after 30 days, unless a public hearing is requested by the person named in the order.[1]

9.2. The Current Regulatory Scheme
9.2.1. The Regulations

The initial regulations implementing these statutory requirements appeared in the First Codification Rule issued in 1985,[2] which added corrective action for solid waste management units to existing rules governing corrective action for ground water.[3] In the preamble to that rule, EPA construed the term "solid waste management unit" to encompass, at least, containers, tanks, surface impoundments, waste piles, land treatment units, landfills, incinerators, and underground injection wells.[4] The term "facility," for purposes of corrective action has been construed by EPA to include the entire piece of real estate, border to border,

---

[1] RCRA § 3008(b). Under the rules governing interim status corrective action orders, the hearing will be more informal than the full adjudicatory hearings governed by 40 CFR Part 22 and include separate requirements for hearings on orders requiring studies and investigations and orders requiring corrective measures. 40 CFR Part 24.

[2] 50 Fed. Reg. at 28702 (July 15, 1985).

[3] EPA's regulations prior to 1984 only required T/S/D facilities to develop programs for addressing releases of hazardous wastes and hazardous constituents from "regulated units" to the ground water. A "regulated unit" was defined as a surface impoundment, waste pile, land treatment unit or landfill which received waste after July 26, 1982. 40 CFR 264.90.

[4] 50 Fed. Reg. 28712. A number of EPA Regions also use the term "area of concern" (AOC) to identify areas at a facility which must be further investigated before they can be identified as SWMUs. As a practical matter, however, there is little difference in how AOCs and SWMUs are treated under the regulations.

under the control of the owner or operator.[5] EPA does not, however, interpret this provision as applicable to spills that cannot be limited to solid waste management units, as for example, from trucks traveling through a facility.[6]

The Second Codification Rule, issued in 1987,[7] added a new provision to existing Part B permit application requirements which requires permit applicants to provide detailed information on releases from SWMUs.[8] The information required consists of the following:

    (1)   the types of existing or closed solid waste management units present at the facility (excluding hazardous waste units shown in the Part B application);

    (2)   a description of the wastes stored, treated or disposed in each unit;

    (3)   available data on prior or current releases (for any solid waste management unit and the hazardous waste management units in the Part B application); and

    (4)   available data concerning the nature and extent of environmental contamination that exists as a result of such releases.

The information provided in response to these questions must be certified as true, accurate and complete by the person supervising the collection of the requested information.

The Second Codification Rule also amended existing corrective action regulations to require off-site action in conformance with Section 3004(v),[9] and included new provisions governing corrective

---

[5]   Id. See United Technologies Corp. v. U.S.E.P.A., 821 F.2d 714, 721 (D.C. Cir. 1987) (upholding EPA's interpretation of the term "facility").

[6]   Id.

[7]   52 Fed. Reg. at 45788 (December 1, 1987).

[8]   40 CFR 270.14(c).

[9]   40 CFR 264.100(e) and 264.101(c).

action requirements through RCRA permits-by-rule for Class 5 hazardous waste injection wells.[10]

9.2.2. Implementation

EPA's implementation of the corrective action requirements has been governed by the National RCRA Corrective Action Strategy.[11] The basic steps in the corrective action process are as follows:

(1) A RCRA Facility Assessment (RFA) is conducted to determine whether there is sufficient evidence of a release to require the owner/operator to undertake additional steps to characterize the release. This step includes a desktop review of available information on solid waste management units at the site, a visual inspection to confirm that information and to identify visual evidence of releases, and, in some cases, a confirmatory sampling visit to develop preliminary evidence regarding possible releases. After completion of the RFA, a schedule of compliance for the remaining steps will be developed, if necessary.

(2) A RCRA Facility Investigation (RFI) is conducted to characterize in detail the nature, extent and rate of migration of potentially significant releases identified in the RFA. The investigation may occur in stages to avoid unnecessary analysis.

(3) A Corrective Measures Study (CMS) will be required in most cases to identify the appropriate corrective measures. Once a remedy has been selected, EPA will either modify the facility's permit or issue a follow up Section 3008(h) order (in the case of interim status facilities) requiring the owner/operator to implement the remedy with Agency oversight.

---

[10]   40 CFR 270.60(b)(3), 144.1(h) and 144.31(g).

[11]   Published by OSWER on October 14, 1985.

(4) <u>Corrective Measures Implementation (CMI)</u> encompasses the design, construction, operation and maintainance of the selected response action.

(5) <u>Interim Measures</u> are short term measures that can be conducted at any time to respond to immediate threats. An RFI or CMS is not required for these measures.

These procedures have been implemented on a case-by-case basis primarily for facilities going through the permit process.[12] The details of the program have been governed by numerous guidance materials issued by the Agency.[13] In general, the present program follows the format which is set forth in detail in the proposed rule described below.

9.3. EPA's Proposed Subpart S RCRA Corrective Action Program

On July 27, 1990, the Environmental Protection Agency proposed a new comprehensive regulatory framework for implementing corrective action requirements.[14] This rule would amend 40 CFR Part 264 to include a new Subpart S. The new framework codifies many of the requirements now found only in guidance materials.

---

[12] 55 <u>Fed. Reg.</u> 30801 (July 27, 1990). Only six states have been authorized to operate the corrective action program on behalf of EPA. <u>Id</u>. at 30802. Consequently, facilities will often have to obtain an operating or closure permit from the state and a separate corrective action permit from the appropriate EPA Region.

[13] <u>RCRA Facility Assessment Guidance</u> (Final, October, 1986); <u>RCRA Facility Investigation Guidance</u> (Interim Final, May, 1989); <u>Corrective Action Plan</u> (Interim Final, May, 1988); and <u>Interim Measures Guidance</u> (Interim Final, May, 1988).

[14] 55 <u>Fed. Reg.</u> 30798 (July 27, 1990). EPA has finalized some key provisions of Subpart S. 58 <u>Fed. Reg.</u> 8658 (February 16, 1993) (discussed <u>infra</u> in Section 9.3.2.8).

9.3.1. Applicability

In accordance with the statutory mandate, the proposed Subpart S generally requires any facility seeking a permit under Subpart C of RCRA to implement corrective action "as necessary to protect human health and the environment." However, the new regulations would not apply to the following four types of RCRA permits: (1) permits for land treatment demonstrations; (2) emergency permits; (3) permits by rule for ocean disposal barges; and (4) research, development and demonstration permits.[15] As the statute also requires, permits will contain schedules of compliance where investigations or corrective action cannot be completed prior to issuance of the permit. In addition, owners/operators will be required to remedy off-site releases as possible.

The regulations will for the first time specifically define the term "solid waste management unit." It includes:

> any discernible unit at which solid wastes have been placed at any time, irrespective of whether the unit was intended for the management of solid or hazardous waste. Such units include any area at a facility at which solid wastes have been routinely and systematically released.[16]

9.3.2. Proposed Corrective Action Program Procedures

9.3.2.1. Preliminary Site Investigations

The proposed rule itself does not specifically distinguish between the RFA and RFI. Instead, it calls for a remedial investigation which "shall characterize the nature, extent, direction, rate, movement and concentration of releases" at the facility.[17] In practice, however, an RFA will precede the more complete RFI.[18] The RFA serves as a screen to eliminate from consideration SWMUs,

---

[15]   55 Fed. Reg. 30874; proposed 40 CFR 264.500(f).

[16]   55 Fed. Reg. 30874; proposed 40 CFR 264.501.

[17]   55 Fed. Reg. 30874; proposed 40 CFR 264.511.

[18]   55 Fed. Reg. 30810.

environmental media or entire facilities which present no evidence of a release posing a threat to human health or the environment. If such a release has occurred or is likely to occur, EPA will require the permittee to conduct a full scale RFI.

At this stage, the owner/operator typically develops a work plan for conducting the RFI, which (upon approval by EPA) becomes a part of the schedule of compliance. The work plan describes the overall approach which will be taken in investigating the facility, including such items as objectives, schedules for performance and the qualifications of personnel conducting the investigations. It will also include the technical methods to be used, and will provide quality assurance plans and data management procedures.[19]

The RFI itself will develop detailed information concerning the environmental characteristics of the facility, including such matters as hydrological and climatological conditions, soil characteristics, surface water and sediment quality, and air quality. Particular SWMUs identified in the RFA will be characterized more fully, and humans or environmental systems which may be exposed to releases from a SWMU will be described. Samples of soil surface water and ground water will be taken and analyzed, and statistical analyses will be used to interpret the data. Laboratory or bench-scale studies may be required to determine the effectiveness of potential treatment technologies.[20]

Eventually, the permittee would be required to submit a final report summarizing the RFI.[21] If it is determined that there have been no releases at a facility, no further action will be required. However, in the vast majority of cases, facilities will move on to the next stage of the corrective action process.

---

[19]   55 Fed. Reg. 30875; proposed 40 CFR 264.512.

[20]   55 Fed. Reg. 30874; proposed 40 CFR 264.511.

[21]   55 Fed. Reg. 30875; proposed 40 CFR 264.513.

9.3.2.2. Action Levels

A "corrective measures study" (CMS) will be required if the RFI shows that certain "action levels" have been exceeded.[22] These "action levels" are established on a site-specific basis for each environmental medium through which exposures may occur. EPA proposes to base them on existing standards, or to derive them from general criteria. For example, "maximum contaminant levels" (MCL) establish drinking water standards under the Safe Drinking Water Act and can be used as action levels for ground water. If an MCL has not been established for the chemical in question, EPA may establish an appropriate concentration level using criteria as set forth in the rule. Similarly, action levels for surface water will be numerical concentrations drawn from the state's water quality standards, but may also be derived by the EPA according to the criteria set forth in the rule.[23] Appendix A to the proposed rulemaking sets out the general criteria for a number of hazardous constituents.

Under limited circumstances, action levels alone would not automatically determine whether a CMS will be required. First, owner/operators could attempt to rebut the presumption that a CMS was required. Second, a permittee may request that EPA modify its permit and require "no further action" because no release poses a threat to human health and the environment, even though releases exceed action levels.[24]

9.3.2.3. Corrective Measure Study

A CMS, which analyzes potential remedies for cleaning up SWMUs, would vary in scope depending on the size of the facility and severity of the contamination. EPA proposes a range of

---

[22] 55 Fed. Reg. 30875; proposed 40 CFR 264.520.

[23] 55 Fed. Reg. 30877; proposed 40 CFR 264.521.

[24] 55 Fed. Reg. 30875; proposed 40 CFR 264.514. The permittee must submit documentation to support its request.

options from analyzing a single remedy to conducting a comprehensive analysis of several alternative remedies. Each potential remedy will be evaluated for performance, reliability, ease of implementation and potential adverse impacts (such as safety concerns and the amount of residual contamination). The remedy's effectiveness, time required for implementation, estimated costs and administrative or institutional requirements (such as state or local permits) will also be examined.[25]

During the course of the CMS, EPA will set "target" cleanup levels as a means of measuring the ability of a remedy to eventually achieve site cleanup to levels protective of human health and the environment. These cleanup concentrations would "serve as preliminary estimates of media cleanup standards to be established in the remedy selection process."[26]

9.3.2.4. Remedy Selection

On the basis of the CMS, EPA will select a remedy that (i) is protective of human health and the environment (ii) achieves the "media cleanup standards" set by EPA for "releases" identified in the RFI, (iii) controls the source of that release and any further releases to the "extent practicable," and (iv) properly manages wastes generated by remedial activity.[27] To assess whether a remedy complies with the standards, EPA would consider the information developed during the CMS to evaluate the following factors:

   (1) the long-term reliability and effectiveness of the remedy, including the amount of wastes left at the site and the need for long-term management;

   (2) the effectiveness of the remedy in reducing the toxicity, mobility or volume of the contaminants;

---

[25]   55 Fed. Reg. 30876; proposed 40 CFR 264.522.

[26]   55 Fed. Reg. 30822.

[27]   55 Fed. Reg. 30877; proposed 40 CFR 264.525(a).

(3) the short-term effectiveness of the remedy, including the magnitude of reduction
of existing risks, short-term risks to
the community or workers, and the time
until full protection is achieved;

(4) the ease of implementation, including
potential technical or administrative
problems and the availability of needed
treatment, storage or disposal services;
and

(5) cost.[28]

After evaluating the proposed remedies according to these
factors and standards, EPA would select a remedy. EPA would also
select "media cleanup standards" (consistent with but perhaps
stricter than target cleanup concentrations) as contaminant concentration limits for each constituent in each environmental
medium. The levels chosen will depend on site-specific factors,
including current, as well as reasonably expected, uses of the
media. For example, contaminated soil limited to industrial uses
would require less stringent levels than soil intended for residential uses. As a starting point, though, cleanup standards for
known or suspected carcinogens will be established at concentration levels representing an excess upperbound lifetime risk to an
individual of between 1×10^{-4} and 1×10^{-6}. For systemic toxicants, the standard shall be the concentration to which a human
may be exposed on a daily basis, without appreciable risk of del-
eterious effect during a lifetime.[29] EPA will establish specific
compliance points where these standards must be met, as discussed
below.

---

[28]   55 Fed. Reg. 30877; proposed 40 CFR 264.525(b).

[29]   55 Fed. Reg. 30878; proposed 40 CFR 264.525(d).

EPA would modify the permit accordingly, subject to public notice and comment and incorporate the selected remedy along with the media cleanup standards into the individual permit.[30]

9.3.2.5. Remedy Implementation And Completion

To implement a corrective action remedy, the owner/operator would be required to prepare a detailed remedy design (including plans, specifications and schedules) which, upon approval, would be incorporated into the permit's schedule of compliance.[31] Through the use of progress reports and on-site inspection, EPA would oversee the remedy implementation.[32] To complete a final remedy, the permittee must comply with media cleanup standards, address the source of contamination and remove all temporary structures required to execute the remedy.[33]

EPA proposes to retain significant flexibility in determining the "point of compliance" ("POC") for measuring completion of a RCRA correction action remedy. For example, in a RCRA corrective action remedy dealing with contaminated ground water, EPA would have discretion to set the POC at the "boundary of the waste management area encompassing the original source(s) of release."[34] Depending on how broadly EPA or the site owner/operator defines the waste management area, this discretion could significantly reduce the quantity of ground water that would need to be cleaned up. The proposed POCs for air, surface water and soil are, respectively, the location of the most exposed individual, the location where the release enters the surface water, and at any

---

[30] 55 Fed. Reg. 30879; proposed 114 CFR 264.526.

[31] 55 Fed. Reg. 30879; proposed 40 CFR 264.527.

[32] 55 Fed. Reg. 30879-80; proposed 40 CFR 264.528.

[33] 55 Fed. Reg. 30880; proposed 40 CFR 264.530.

[34] 55 Fed. Reg. 30878; proposed 40 CFR 264.525(e).

point where direct contact with the soil may occur (_i.e._, near the soil surface).[35]

Once the remedial design is implemented and the remedy goals achieved, the owner/operator will submit to the Regional Administrator a request that the corrective action compliance schedule be terminated.[36] This request must include a certification that the remedy was completed in accordance with the applicable rules and permit requirements. EPA must then determine (subject to public notice and comment) that the remedy is indeed complete.

In appropriate cases, the Regional Administrator may determine that compliance with corrective action requirements for a particular remedy is not technically practicable. In doing so, the Regional Administrator will consider the permittee's efforts to achieve compliance and whether new or innovative technologies exist that could achieve compliance. If compliance is not practicable, the permit will be modified to establish (1) further measures that may be required of the permittee to ensure adequate protection of human health and the environment, and (2) alternate concentration limits which are technically practicable and consistent with the overall goals of the original remedy.[37]

9.3.2.6. Interim Measures

To address sites posing an immediate threat to the human health and the environment, under the proposed rule, EPA can compel an owner/operator to undertake "interim measures" as soon as practicable. These interim measures would be designed to contain contamination until a final remedy can be developed. The threats which justify interim measures include: (i) exposure of populations to hazardous wastes; (ii) contamination of drinking water; (iii) further degradation of the medium absent immediate response;

---

[35] _Id._

[36] 55 _Fed. Reg._ 30880; proposed 40 CFR 264.530.

[37] 55 _Fed. Reg._ 30880; proposed 40 CFR 264.531.

(iv) threat of release from drums; (v) potential migration of hazardous waste; or (vi) risks of fire or explosion. Interim measures do not replace a final remedy, but must be consistent with and a necessary component of any final remedy.[38]

9.3.2.7. Conditional Remedies

EPA could also impose a "conditional remedy" at a site to facilitate cleanup to levels appropriate for current uses of the medium.[39] Where final cleanup appears impracticable, a conditional remedy would primarily allow existing contamination to remain within the facility boundary. The permittee, however, must still: (i) achieve media cleanup levels for contamination beyond the facility boundaries; (ii) control the source of contamination; and (iii) give financial assurances. As long as the risk of exposure remains insignificant and the permittee contains the contamination, then the EPA will defer a final cleanup remedy for the duration of the permit.

9.3.2.8. Corrective Action for Solid Waste Management Units

As noted above on July 27, 1990, EPA proposed a new comprehensive regulatory framework for implementing corrective action requirements.[40] The proposed rule provided for somewhat relaxed management practices to facilitate cleanups and avoid unnecessary regulation. One of these approaches was the Corrective Action Management Unit ("CAMU") which, once so designated, would have allowed hazardous wastes within the CAMU to be moved without being subject to the land disposal restrictions of minimum technology requirements.[41]

---

[38]   55 Fed. Reg. 30880; proposed 40 CFR 264.540.

[39]   55 Fed. Reg. 30879; proposed 40 CFR 264.525(f).

[40]   55 Fed. Reg. 20798.

[41]   55 Fed. Reg. 30851.

On February 16, 1993, EPA promulgated a final rule further expanding the definition of a CAMU.[42]

The new rule defines a CAMU as:

> an area within a facility that is designated by [EPA] . . . for the purpose of implementing corrective action requirements under § 264.101 and RCRA Section 3008(h) [regarding interim status facilities]. A CAMU shall only be used for the management of remediation wastes pursuant to implementing such corrective action requirements at the facility.

One or more CAMUs may be designated at a facility, and non-contained areas may be included within a CAMU if EPA specifically finds that so doing will be more protective than management of such wastes at already-contaminated areas.

"Remediation wastes" include all solid and hazardous wastes, and all media and debris which contain listed hazardous managed for the purpose of implementing corrective action.[43/] Remediation wastes specifically include waste found within the facility boundary (i.e., all contiguous property under the control of the owner or operator) as well as wastes which have migrated beyond that boundary. The definition excludes, however, new or as-generated wastes. In other words, the wastes must result from implementing the corrective action rather than "new" or "as generated" wastes from active processes at the facility.

The effect of this rule is that hazardous wastes, media or debris from non-contiguous areas of a facility (or from areas outside a facility if migration has occurred) undergoing corrective action can now be placed in a CAMU during corrective action without the LDRs becoming applicable. EPA believes that this will

---

[42]   58 Fed. Reg. 8658 (February 16, 1993).

[43/]   58 Fed. Reg. 8683 (codified at 40 CFR 260.10).

encourage alternative treatment technologies since, under the spector of the LDRs, wastes generally were either left in place or incinerated.

Specifically, the rule provides:

- that a regulated unit (landfill, surface impoundment, waste pile, land treatment unit) may be designated as a CAMU or be incorporated into a CAMU if it is closed or closing and such inclusion will enhance the implementation of the remedial action at the facility;

- that non-land based units (e.g., tanks) may be physically located within the boundaries of a CAMU but will not be considered part of the CAMU;

- that the following factors must be evaluated by EPA in designating a CAMU:

    * whether the CAMU will facilitate imple-mentation of a reliable, effective, pro-tective and cost effective remedy;
    * whether the waste management activities at the CAMU will create an unacceptable risk;
    * whether such designation will expedite the remedial activity;
    * whether the designation will enable the use of treatment technologies (including innovative technologies) to enhance the long-term effectiveness of the remedy;
    * whether the CAMU will minimize the land area of a facility upon which wastes will remain after closure:

- that EPA specifies in a permit or order the requirements for the CAMU, including areal configuration, design, operation, ground water monitoring, and closure and post-closure care;

- that EPA document the rationale for designating the CAMU and make such documentation available to the public; and

- that incorporation of a CAMU into an existing permit must be approved according the RCRA permit modification procedures, including public notice and participation.[44]

In conjunction with the CAMU rule, EPA also included provisions identifying another new unit, called a temporary unit ("TU").[45] TUs are temporary tanks and container storage areas used for treatment or storage of remediation wastes during corrective action. Under these provisions, EPA may determine that the design, operating or closure standards generally applicable to such units may be replaced by alternate requirements which are protective of human health and the environment.

In establishing the standards to be applied to a TU, EPA is to consider a number of factors, including the length of time the TU will operate, the volume and characteristics of wastes to be managed in it, potential releases from the TU, and factors which would influence the migration of the wastes if a release occurred. The length of time a TU can operate -- up to one year -- will be specified in a permit or order, although extensions may be

---

[44] 40 CFR 264.552.

[45] 40 CFR 264.553.

granted. Just as in the case of CAMUs, RCRA permit modification procedures will apply to TUs.

Because EPA believes that this final rule is integral to the corrective action program under HSWA, EPA intends to implement it immediately in all States in which the Agency now administers HSWA corrective action authorities, i.e., 1) in States that are unauthorized for the RCRA base program, and 2) States that are authorized for the base program but are not yet authorized for the HSWA corrective action program. Because the rule reduces regulatory requirements for certain types of waste management conducted during corrective action, EPA considers it to be less stringent than existing federal corrective action requirements.[46/] Thus, under Section 3009 of RCRA, the rule does not automatically apply in States that are authorized for the HSWA corrective action requirements until those States adopt comparable provisions under State law. Note, however, that such States are not required to adopt the rule, and States not yet authorized for corrective action are not required to include is provisions in their programs when they seek authorization. Even so, EPA in the preamble to the rule strongly urges such States to adopt it.

9.4 The Philosophy Behind the Corrective Action Program
9.4.1. Relationship to Superfund

Those readers familiar with the Superfund remedial action program as set forth in the National Contingency Plan[47] will recognize many similarities between it and RCRA corrective action. The RFA parallels the Superfund Preliminary Assessment/Site Investigation; the RFI parallels the Superfund Remedial Investigation; the CMS parallels the Superfund Feasibility Study; the Remedy

---

[46/] Various environmental interest groups oppose this rule, arguing that it is either inconsistent with other RCRA provisions or is too broad, e.g., with respect to the reach of the definition of remediation waste. A legal action is expected.

[47] 40 CFR Part 300.

Selection parallels the Superfund Record of Decision; and the CMI parallels the Superfund Remedial Design/Remedial Action.

Indeed, a primary objective of the proposed rule is to achieve substantive consistency with the policies and procedures of the Superfund program.[48] EPA views this consistency as desirable in order "to ensure that the regulated industry can gain no advantage by proceeding under one program rather than the other."[49] Within this overall objective, however, EPA's proposed rule recognizes that significantly more procedural flexibility is appropriate in dealing with RCRA SWMUs, particularly those present at active facilities. As noted in the preamble to the proposed rule, active RCRA sites differ from other Superfund sites in that they represent a controlled use situation where

> [I]t will often be reasonable to require prompt cleanup to levels consistent with current use, but to defer final cleanup as long as the owner/operator remains under a RCRA permit.[50]

In addition, flexibility in setting POCs may allow RCRA corrective action remedies which are less extensive (and, therefore, less costly) than Superfund remedial actions which require compliance with applicable or relevant and appropriate cleanup standards throughout the entire site.[51]

9.4.2. EPA's Management Philosophy

The suggestion of procedural flexibility noted above is further driven by the need to prioritize and rationalize the administrative response to a regulatory burden widely viewed as far outstripping that presented by Superfund. The approximately 5,700 land disposal, incinerator, and treatment and storage facilities

---

[48]   55 Fed. Reg. 30852.

[49]   Id.

[50]   55 Fed. Reg. 30803.

[51]   See Superfund § 121(d).

in existence today are estimated to include as many as 80,000 SWMUs which may need corrective action.[52] EPA estimates based on these data that the number of RCRA facilities that may ultimately need corrective action could be three times the number of sites currently on the NPL.[53] At the national level, however, only 17 work years for developing regulations and guidance for this program are currently budgeted. This compares to 275 work years budgeted for Superfund.[54]

EPA has stated a management philosophy for the RCRA corrective action program which it believes will further its goals.[55] First, the Agency will place its highest priority on "the most environmentally significant facilities and on the most significant problems at specific facilities" -- thus, interim measures may be required even before a final corrective action permit is issued. Second, the Agency may rely on conditional remedies as described above. Third, voluntary cleanup will be encouraged (or, at least, regulatory disincentives will be removed). Fourth, facility investigations "will be streamlined to focus on plausible concerns and likely remedies, and to expedite cleanup decisions." Fifth, the Agency will emphasize early actions and expeditious remedy decisions.

Whether EPA will be able truly to implement this "philosophy" for the RCRA corrective action program and avoid the bureaucratic snarls that have plagued the Superfund program remains, for now, an open question.

---

[52]   55 Fed. Reg. 30802.

[53]   "The Nation's Hazardous Waste Management Program At A Cross-roads: The RCRA Implementation Study," U.S.EPA July 1990, p. 76.

[54]   Id. at 78.

[55]   55 Fed. Reg. 30802-04.

CHAPTER 10

AUTHORIZATION OF STATES TO IMPLEMENT A RCRA SUBTITLE C HAZARDOUS WASTE MANAGEMENT PROGRAM

10.1 Overview

States are authorized by RCRA Section 3006 to develop and carry out their own hazardous waste programs in lieu of the federal program administered by EPA.[1] Authorization requires EPA approval. As of this writing, almost all of the states in the United States have state programs that have received final approval. The status of every state program, however, was significantly affected by the 1984 RCRA Amendments.

Each of the requirements or prohibitions contained in the 1984 Amendments became, or will become, effective on the same date in every state.[2] Authorized states had to go through the state program approval process again before they would administer any of the provisions of the 1984 Amendments. Until such approval was issued, EPA administered the 1984 Amendment provisions in each state and issued the permit provisions required by the Amendments, including requirements for corrective action. This has meant a significant Federal presence in authorized states.

10.2 Historical Perspective on State Program Implementation

Some historical background is necessary to understand the current statutory provisions for state programs. In 1980, Congress determined that some kind of "interim authorization" of state hazardous waste programs was necessary while EPA developed the federal program so that existing progress in the area of state hazardous waste law did not come to an abrupt halt.[3] Congress

---

[1]   RCRA § 3006(a).

[2]   RCRA § 3006(g).

[3]   RCRA § 3006(c); H.R. Rep. No. 1491, 94th Cong., 2d Sess. 29 (1976).

also intended to give those states that had begun developing a hazardous waste program sufficient time after EPA's promulgation of Subtitle C regulations to bring their programs into conformity with the federal minimum standards.

Accordingly, RCRA Section 3006(c) in its pre-1984 form allowed any state that had its own hazardous waste program in existence prior to October 24, 1982, to request interim authorization from EPA to carry out that program under Subtitle C. EPA construed the "in existence" statutory provision to require only that a state have enacted "legislative authority" for such a program by the deadline.[4] The statute permitted interim authorizations where the state's existing program was found to be "substantially equivalent" to the federal program.

EPA complicated the interim authorization process by dividing it into two stages, Phases I and II, and by dividing Phase II into three components, A, B, and C. Phase I interim authorization allowed a state to administer its own hazardous waste program with respect to identification of hazardous waste, standards for generators and transporters, including the manifest system, and preliminary standards for T/S/D facilities.[5] Phase II component A authority became available after EPA issued technical regulations for storage and treatment of hazardous waste in containers, tanks, surface impoundments, and waste piles on January 12, 1981.[6] Component B authority became available after EPA issued technical

---

[4]   45 Fed. Reg. 33387 (May 19, 1980); 47 Fed. Reg. 32375 (July 26, 1982).

[5]   40 CFR 271.128 (July 1, 1986). There was a significant exception to these requirements under which a state with only a partial program (primarily involving the lack of a manifest system) could nevertheless obtain interim authorization. 40 CFR 271.128(d).

[6]   46 Fed. Reg. 2802 (January 12, 1981).

standards for incinerators on January 23, 1981.[7] Component C authority became available after EPA issued technical standards for landfills, land treatment units, waste piles, and surface impoundments on July 26, 1982.[8] Phase II interim authorization allowed a state to permit its own T/S/D facilities.

A complicated set of time schedules applied to the issuance of the various portions of Phase II. For purposes of historical perspective it is sufficient to know that states with Phase I interim authorization were required to apply for the remainder of Phase II by July 26, 1983.[9] Failure to submit an amended application within this time frame terminated the state's interim authorization and responsibility for the entire program within the state reverted to EPA. The Regional Administrator had the authority to, and in several cases did, extend this deadline for good cause.[10]

Once Phase II interim authorization was granted, such authorization could extend until January 26, 1985.[11] At that time, all interim authorizations were to expire automatically, and EPA was to implement a federal program if a state had not received final authorization.

10.3   Statutory Requirements as Amended in 1984

10.3.1 Interim Authorization

Section 3006(c), as amended in 1984, provides for two types of interim authorization. The first is the type of interim authorization provided for in the pre-1984 Amendments and discussed in the preceding section. States still working their way through the

---

[7]   46 Fed. Reg. 7666 (January 23, 1981).

[8]   47 Fed. Reg. 32274 (July 26, 1982).

[9]   40 CFR 271.122(c)(4) (July 1, 1986).

[10]   40 CFR 271.137(a) (July 1, 1986); see, e.g., 48 Fed. Reg. 33018 (August 20, 1984).

[11]   40 CFR 271.122(b) (July 1, 1986).

interim authorization process were given until January 31, 1986, to secure final approval.[12] This required adoption of hazardous waste regulations by the state which were substantially equivalent to the RCRA regulations adopted by EPA in 40 CFR Parts 260-270. Most states accomplished this for both interim and final authorization simply by incorporating by reference EPA's regulations.

The second - and new - type of interim authorization is for all of the provisions of the 1984 Amendments.[13] EPA will administer all of these provisions until a state receives interim or final authorization to do so.[14] Even if a state has provisions in its existing program which meet the requirements of the 1984 Amendments, the state must go through the approval process to administer those provisions itself before EPA can relinquish its duty.[15] Since the statute contains no sunset provision for this type of interim authorization, EPA was directed to adopt such a date by rule.[16] This state of affairs will continue to exist for some time, as EPA interprets the many regulations it is required to issue under the 1984 Amendments as "requirements or prohibitions" which will also take effect at the same time in all states.[17] Federal Register notices accompanying the new requirements will explain their applicability in authorized states.

A T/S/D facility in an authorized state cannot, however, take advantage of the variances and exemptions contained in the

---

[12] RCRA § 3006(c)(1); 40 CFR 271.122(b)(1).

[13] As discussed elsewhere in this Handbook, these provisions include all of the requirements and prohibitions of the 1984 amendments. 50 Fed. Reg. 28729 (July 15, 1985).

[14] RCRA § 3006(c)(4); 40 CFR 271.138.

[15] RCRA § 3006(g)(2); 40 CFR 271.138.

[16] RCRA § 3006(c)(2).

[17] RCRA § 3006(g); see 50 Fed. Reg. 28730 (July 15, 1985).

1984 Amendments if a more stringent state or local requirement exists.[18]

10.3.2 Dual Permitting

One of the most significant consequences of the 1984 HSWA amendments is the dual permitting system. Under this system, authorized states will still conduct permit proceedings and issue permits. In addition, however, EPA will implement the permit-related provisions which were added by the 1984 Amendments, such as the corrective action requirements, until the state gets authorization to implement them.[19] In addition, the shield effect of any existing state permit which runs afoul of any of the 1984 HSWA requirements will be lost with respect to that provision.[20] Section 3006(c)(4) requires EPA to coordinate procedures for issuing such dual permits with the states. EPA is handling this primarily through its regional offices, with oversight from the Permits and State Programs Division of the Office of Solid Waste in Washington, D.C.

A guidance document on the subject of joint permitting has been issued.[21] That document describes two possible procedures:

    (1)   a joint permit signed by EPA and the state; or

    (2)   two separate permits, one state and one federal, which together constitute the RCRA permit.

Where a draft permit has been issued by a state, the guidance provides that the state should complete its permitting process. EPA will give a high priority to the issuance of that permit.

---

[18]   50 Fed. Reg. 28729 (July 15, 1985).

[19]   RCRA § 3006(c); 40 CFR 271.1(f); 271.3(a)(3).

[20]   50 Fed. Reg. 29829 (July 15, 1985).

[21]   EPA Guidance Document "RCRA Reauthorization and Joint Permitting in Authorized States" (July 1, 1985).

Where the state has not issued a draft permit, EPA encourages the use of a joint process. The guidance recognizes that authorized states and EPA regional offices will have to amend their current Memorandum of Understanding and adopt procedures to implement this dual system.

10.3.3 RCRA Section 3006(b) Final Authorization

In providing states with the opportunity under RCRA to implement their own programs equivalent to the federal program, Congress wanted to ensure that there would be as much uniformity as possible among the states regarding how hazardous wastes are controlled.[22] Thus, when final authorization of state programs is fully effective, the standards for generators, transporters, and T/S/D facilities should be "equivalent," whether the regulatory program for hazardous waste is administered by EPA or a state. Congress thereby intended to prevent states with less stringent programs from becoming "dumping grounds" for hazardous waste.

Congress sought to achieve these goals in RCRA Section 3006(b). It provides that a state may seek final authorization to administer its hazardous waste program under Subtitle C, in lieu of the federal program, upon satisfactory application to EPA. The right to seek final authorization exists whether or not the state sought interim authorization. The application must conform to the procedural and substantive requirements established by EPA in its implementing regulations.

The conditions for approval of the state's application are intended to ensure uniformity among the states. To support a grant of final authorization, the Administrator's findings must demonstrate that the state program is "equivalent" to the federal program, that it is "consistent with" federal or state programs in other states, and that it provides adequate enforcement of the requirements of RCRA Subtitle C. The only addition made to Section 3006(b) by the 1984 Amendments was a date of decision for the

---

[22] H.R. Rep. No. 1491, supra at 30.

equivalency determination. The statute now provides that the standard against which the state program is judged is the federal program in effect one year prior to the state's application or in effect on January 26, 1983, whichever is later.[23]

RCRA Section 3009 also expressly provides that state programs may be no less stringent than the federal program. EPA has construed this requirement, however, to apply only to state programs with final authorization.[24] Section 3009 also clearly provides that state hazardous waste management programs may be more stringent than the federal program.[25]

Finally, a state program must have procedures to make information regarding T/S/D facilities publicly available and do it in substantially the same manner, and to the same degree, as would EPA.[26] EPA has interpreted the language "in the same manner and to the same degree", as referring to its Freedom of Information Act procedures concerning how and when to release information and the type and quantity of information released.[27] In addition, EPA interprets the phrase to cover information relating to permitting, compliance, enforcement, and information gathered under the inspection authority of RCRA or its state analogue.

RCRA Section 3006(e) provides that the EPA Administrator may withdraw state authorization whenever he determines that the state is not administering or enforcing its program in accordance with the conditions of approval. To give the state an opportunity to correct its deficiencies, EPA must first notify the state of the intended withdrawal. If appropriate corrective action is not

---

[23]   RCRA § 3006(b).

[24]   45 Fed. Reg. 33391 (May 19, 1980).

[25]   See 40 CFR 271.1(i)(1).

[26]   RCRA § 3006(f); 40 CFR 271.17(c).

[27]   50 Fed. Reg. 28730 (July 15, 1985); see, e.g., 40 CFR Part 2 (EPA Freedom of Information Act procedures issued pursuant to 5 U.S.C. 552).

taken within a reasonable time, EPA may withdraw state authorization based on written reasons and after a public hearing, and establish the federal program in the state.

10.4   EPA's Implementing Regulations, 40 CFR Part 271

EPA's requirements for state RCRA programs are published at 40 CFR Part 271.[28] Part 271 is divided into two Subparts, A and B. Subpart A contains the requirements for states seeking final authorization under RCRA. Subpart B contains all of the requirements applicable to a state's submission for interim authorization. Both Subparts contain general requirements applicable to all state programs, including the elements that must be part of a state submission to EPA for program approval, the substantive provisions that must be included in all state programs, and the procedures EPA will follow in approving, revising, and withdrawing state programs. These are discussed together in the following sections.

10.4.1   Elements of a Program Submission

States applying for interim authorization must develop and send to EPA a "program submission."[29] The elements of a program submission include a letter from the Governor requesting approval, a statement from the Attorney General certifying that the laws of the state provide adequate authority to carry out the program, and copies of all applicable state statutes and regulations.

---

[28]   EPA's requirements for state RCRA programs were originally promulgated as part of EPA's consolidated permit regulations at 40 CFR Part 123. When EPA "deconsolidated" its permit regulations on April 1, 1983, the state RCRA program requirements were placed in a new Part 271 without any substantive changes. See generally 48 Fed. Reg. 14146 (April 1, 1983).

[29]   40 CFR 271.5, 271.123.

In addition, the state must enter into and submit a Memorandum of Agreement ("MOA") with the EPA Regional Administrator.[30] The MOA is the vehicle by which EPA transfers to the state all information obtained in the RCRA Section 3010(a) notifications filed by all generators, transporters, and T/S/D facilities. In return, the state must agree to submit appropriate reports, documents, and other information to EPA. The MOA assures EPA oversight of the state program by allowing EPA to conduct compliance inspections of all generators, transporters, and T/S/D facilities.

Perhaps the most significant element of the state's submission is a comprehensive "program description" of the state's hazardous waste program.[31] This document must describe in narrative form the entire scope, structure, coverage, and procedures of the state program. The state agency with responsibility for administering the program must be described, include an organizational chart of the agency staff, estimates of the costs of administering the program, funding, and a description of applicable state procedures for permitting and judicial review. The program description must include copies of all state forms and a description of the state manifest system, as well as an estimate of the number of generators, transporters, and T/S/D facilities in the state. Regulated companies will find the state's program description a valuable document to obtain when planning business activities in a particular state.

10.4.2 The EPA Approval Process

The approval process for interim authorization requires a state first to submit a complete request to the EPA Regional Administrator.[32] Within 30 days of receipt of the state's program

---

[30] 40 CFR 271.6, 271.8, 271.126.

[31] 40 CFR 271.124.

[32] 40 CFR 271.135.

submission, the Regional Administrator must issue a notice in the Federal Register of a public hearing on the state's application.

Within an additional 90 days, after a public hearing and an opportunity for public comment, the EPA Administrator must make a final determination on whether to approve the state's program. The Administrator's final determination, which will be noticed in the Federal Register, must contain a concise statement of the reasons for his determination.

The chart at the end of this Chapter sets forth the progress made by various states in seeking authorization.

10.5 Final Authorization for Pre-1984 Amendments RCRA Program

A state's interim authorization terminated on January 31, 1986, if it did not receive final authorization.[33] Interim authorization was not a precondition to final authorization.

The elements of a program submission for final authorization, and the procedures EPA follows in approving state applications are substantially similar to those discussed above regarding interim authorization. They are found in 40 CFR Part 271, Subpart A. Briefly stated, a state program must be "equivalent" to the federal program, and must be "consistent" with federal programs and final authorization programs applicable in other states. A state program will be deemed by EPA to be inconsistent if it "unreasonably restricts, impedes, or operates as a ban on the free movement across the State border of hazardous wastes."[34]

A state program for final authorization must contain requirements for identifying and listing hazardous waste,[35] and standards for generators,[36] transporters,[37] and T/S/D facilities[38]

---

[33] See 47 Fed. Reg. 32381 (July 26, 1982).

[34] 40 CFR 271.4(a).

[35] 40 CFR 271.9.

[36] 40 CFR 271.10.

which are practically identical to EPA requirements for the federal program. The state must adopt a list and a set of characteristics for identifying hazardous wastes equivalent to those in 40 CFR Part 261. Thus, the state program must control all the hazardous wastes controlled by EPA. All other requirements for T/S/D facilities imposed by EPA under 40 CFR Part 264 -- including financial responsibility, post-closure measures, personnel training, ground water monitoring, etc. -- must also be imposed in state programs with final authorization. In particular, state law must require permits for T/S/D facilities which require compliance with standards as stringent as EPA's. As noted above, most states have incorporated by reference EPA's regulations. Some states, however, have modified them in the direction of greater stringency.

State programs are judged for equivalency against the federal regulations in effect one year prior to submission of the state's application.[39] Once a state receives final authorization, it must maintain "equivalency" with the federal RCRA program. Thus, state programs must be updated to reflect any amendments to the federal program within one year of the date the federal regulations are promulgated, or, if a state needs to implement statutory changes, within two years.[40] If these time periods are not long enough to accommodate a state's regulatory and legislative schedules, the EPA Regional Administrator may extend these time periods by six months on a case-by-case basis.

10.6 Final Authorization for the 1984 Amendments

In order to ease the burden on states of adopting the new provisions of the 1984 RCRA Amendments, EPA revised 40 CFR Part

---

[37] 40 CFR 271.11.

[38] 40 CFR 271.12.

[39] RCRA § 3006(b).

[40] 40 CFR 271.21(e)(2), 49 Fed. Reg. 21682 (May 22, 1984).

271 to give states substantially more time to amend their programs. Although almost all states now have final authorization under RCRA, they were faced with the problem of revising state statutes and regulations as EPA issued an anticipated 60 new regulations mandated by the 1984 RCRA Amendments. Unless EPA changed the approval process for state programs, the responsibility for enforcing the RCRA program and issuing permits would have bounced back and forth between the states and EPA.

Therefore, EPA made three basic changes to the state program process.[41] First, EPA reviews state program applications based on regulations "in effect" instead of "promulgated" 12 months prior to the submission of the state's application. This allows states more time to make necessary changes in their programs in order to keep final authorization since most federal regulations do not become effective until six months after promulgation.

Second, EPA allows states to "cluster" federal program changes that become effective during the 12-month period from July 1 to June 30 each year. The "one year/two year clock" by which states must amend their programs to adopt EPA regulations begins to run on July 1 for all of the federal program changes that occurred in the prior 12-month period, rather than on the promulgation date of each separate regulation. States can make program modifications for the "cluster" of EPA regulations on an annual basis.

Third, EPA allowed a one-time, multi-year HSWA cluster to encompass all of the federal changes that were promulgated or took effect between November 8, 1984 (the date of enactment of HSWA) and June 30, 1987. States were required to adopt these HSWA provisions by July 1, 1989 (or July 1, 1990 if statutory changes are needed). In addition, EPA created a second multi-year cluster for HSWA rules that were promulgated during the period July 1, 1987, to June 30, 1990. States must have adopted these provisions by July 1, 1991 (or 1992 if statutory changes are needed). To

---

[41]   51 Fed. Reg. 33612 (September 22, 1986).

assist states that could not meet these deadlines, EPA decided to use schedules of compliance to extend the deadlines so that states can avoid having their RCRA programs revert to EPA. These revisions to 40 CFR Part 271 have streamlined the process by which states obtain and maintain final authorizations for the HSWA provisions.

EPA has also codified in 40 CFR Part 272 the list of state programs that have received final authorization. This incorporates by reference the state statutes and regulations that EPA will enforce under RCRA Section 3008 if the state fails to enforce them.[42]

10.7 Cooperative Agreements

States that do not qualify for authorization have an opportunity to enter into cooperative agreements with EPA to administer portions of the program. EPA has published General Guidance on the policies and procedures it follows in developing these cooperative agreements.[43]

A cooperative agreement sets out EPA's and the state's respective responsibilities for implementing a hazardous waste program in the state. The state may administer so much of its program as meets minimum federal standards, and EPA will enforce the federal program in the remaining areas. The state's role could be as limited as providing administrative and informational support to EPA, or as broad as administering the federal manifest system and regulating generators and transporters as EPA's agent.

Procedures for applying for a cooperative agreement and EPA review are set forth in the General Guidance regulations.[44]

---

[42] 51 Fed. Reg. 3955 (Jan. 31, 1986).

[43] 50 Fed. Reg. 7540 (March 4, 1986).

[44] 45 Fed. Reg. 33784-86 (May 20, 1980).

States must provide for public participation, including a public meeting, during development of a cooperative agreement.

10.8 Progress of States in Obtaining RCRA Authorization

As of August 1991, 45 states had final authorization. The table set forth at the end of this chapter, compiled from an informal survey of state environmental offices, identifies the current status of each state's hazardous waste program.

10.9 The New War Between the States: "Equivalency" vs. "Greater Stringency"

When Congress enacted RCRA in 1976, it envisioned a national program controlling the management of hazardous waste. Accordingly, RCRA mandates that a federal program be established by EPA but that states may become authorized to run the RCRA program if the state laws are "consistent" and "equivalent" to the federal program.[45] The federal program establishes minimum standards. In line with the principles of federalism, while states are not permitted to impose requirements which are less stringent than those of the national program, they may impose requirements which are more stringent.[46] This "greater stringency" allowed the

---

[45] RCRA § 3006(b), 42 USC § 6926(b).

[46] RCRA § 3009, 42 USC § 6929. One court has recently held that this provision applies only to states with authorized programs. Hermes Consolidated, Inc. v. Wyoming, 849 p.2d 1302, 1312 (Wyo. 1993). In another recent development, the Fourth Circuit has declined to exercise jurisdiction in a RCRA citizen suit challenging the validity of permits for a hazardous waste incinerator. Palumbo v. Waste Technologies Indus., 989 F.2d 156 (4th Cir. 1993). In Palumbo, plaintiffs had instituted a similar and separate proceeding before a state administrative agency. Id. at 159-60. The Fourth Circuit cited the U.S. Supreme Court's decision in Burford v. Sun Oil Co., 319 U.S. 315 (1943), in holding that federal courts must "abstain[] from review of complex state regulatory scheme[s]" which include specialized review procedures and tribunals. Id.

states has led to conflicts between states concerning interstate shipments of hazardous waste.

Some states and even local governments have recently taken actions under the guise of "greater stringency" which in effect, are aimed at banning the siting of hazardous waste facilities in or the shipment of hazardous waste to their jurisdictions. In doing so, politicians have responded to the "not-in-my-backyard" syndrome (known as the "NIMBY syndrome") exhibited by their constituencies. No one, it seems, wants to have a RCRA treatment, storage or disposal facility in their neighborhood.

The actions taken by various states include bans on the interstate movement of hazardous wastes to commercial T/S/D facilities within the state, indefinite moratoriums on the issuance of pending RCRA permits, absolute local vetos over RCRA permits for commercial facilities, fees which discriminate against out-of-state wastes and regulations (such as excessive fees or dilution requirements or onerous siting requirements) designed to limit the development of new hazardous waste disposal capacity. Most of these measures are directed against out-of-state wastes sent to commercial facilities.

Such measures led to the congressional enactment in 1986 of CERCLA Section 104(c)(9).[47] Pursuant to this provision of the statute, effective in October 1989, the Federal government may not undertake Superfund remedial actions in a state (or otherwise provide Superfund money to that state) unless that state has provided adequate assurances as to the availability of hazardous waste treatment or disposal facilities which have adequate capacity to handle all of the hazardous wastes expected to be generated within the state for the next 20 years. The required facilities may be located outside of the state if there is an appropriate interstate agreement or regional agreement or authority.

EPA published guidance, based largely on recommendations by the National Governors Association, on how states may meet the

---

[47] 42 USC § 9604(c)(9).

requirements of Section 104(c)(9). The guidance addresses such issues as hazardous waste data and future projections, allowances for state waste minimization programs, plans for developing new treatment capacity, and interstate agreements and dispute resolution.

It has been argued that EPA itself has exacerbated the NIMBY problem by not adequately enforcing the RCRA requirements that authorized state programs be consistent with and equivalent to the federal standards. For example, EPA has not required states to adopt the RD&D permit program and other enhanced permit mechanisms, nor has it required states to adopt the 1988 regulatory amendments providing greater flexibility on permit modifications, or the "treatability testing" exemption from RCRA permitting. EPA has stated also that it will not require states to adopt the pending rules for permitting mobile treatment units.

Under RCRA 3006(e), EPA may withdraw authorization from a state program if it determines that the state is not administering and enforcing a program in accordance with RCRA. Pursuant to this authority and in response to petitions from members of the regulated community, EPA initiated withdrawal proceedings for North Carolina's hazardous waste program. 52 Fed. Reg. 43903 (November 17, 1987). The petitions alleged that the state program is inconsistent with the federal program because North Carolina has enacted a law which requires enormous and virtually unattainable dilution of the discharge of wastewater from new commercial hazardous waste treatment facilities. The North Carolina law would effectively prohibit the development of such facilities. In challenging the North Carolina law, EPA raised the ire of certain states rightists and, on August 28, 1988, published a notice indefinitely postponing a hearing in this proceeding. 53 Fed. Reg. 32899. After effectively deferring the issue to a new administration, an EPA Administrative Law Judge denied the petitions on the basis that North Carolina had not "prohibited" the development of all facilities, simply that facility. On judicial review, the D.C. Circuit then affirmed EPA's decision. Hazardous Waste Treatment Council v. Reilly, 938 F.2d 1390 (D.C. Cir. 1991).

In the meantime the Governor of South Carolina, to which wastes from North Carolina are often sent, retaliated by issuing an Executive Order banning as of March 1, 1989, the shipment into South Carolina of any hazardous waste from any other state that does not have reciprocal provisions allowing the disposal of such wastes from South Carolina. At roughly the same time, Alabama enacted a similar "blacklisting law." Thereafter, South Carolina and Alabama both enacted a series of other laws directly interfering with, and discriminating against, interstate commerce. These laws include discriminatory quotas and "caps" on land disposal volume, permitting restrictions on new or expanded treatment facilities, and "additional fees" on imported waste. Ohio and Louisiana also followed this example by imposing discriminatory fees, and Arizona continued to frustrate its own procurement process by not allowing a facility to be constructed after it had contracted to purchase an incinerator to service the needs of its own industry.

Measures such as the North Carolina law, and the South Carolina and Alabama responses highlight the potential conflict between the authority of states to impose "greater stringency" pursuant to RCRA Section 3009 and the requirements of RCRA Section 3006(b) for "consistency" and "equivalency." Such measures also raise at least two constitutional issues: 1) the extent to which RCRA, in fact, preempts state and local regulation of hazardous waste; and 2) the point at which such regulation impermissibly burdens interstate commerce and, therefore, violates the Commerce Clause.

Early in the battle, and in addressing the first of these issues, at least one federal court has invalidated an ordinance which a locality sought to ban the storage, treatment or disposal of certain hazardous wastes within its jurisdictions. The ordinance frustrated the goals of RCRA and, therefore, was in direct conflict with the federal statute. For this reason, it was preempted despite the provisions of RCRA Section 3009.[48] With regard to the second issue, the Supreme Court had ruled over ten years ago that a state statute which operates as a ban on the interstate movement of hazardous waste is unconstitutional because it violates the Commerce Clause.[49]

As these issues made their way to litigation, the federal courts struck down many of these discriminatory laws either because: (1) they violated the Commerce Clause, or (2) were not authorized by Congress either in RCRA or CERCLA.[50] After Alabama's Supreme Court upheld that state's discriminatory "additional fee,"[51] transparently ignoring the 1978 decision in Philadelphia v. New Jersey, the U.S. Supreme Court reversed Alabama's efforts to isolate itself from the rest of the nation.[52]

The regulatory standard for "consistency" reflects these constitutional concerns. First, it states that any aspect of a state program which "unreasonably restricts, impedes, or operates

---

[48] See ENSCO, Inc. v. Dumas, 807 F.2d 743 (8th Cir. 1986); see also Rollins Environmental Services, Inc. v. Parish of St. James, 775 F.2d 627 (5th Cir. 1985) (addressing preemption under Section 18 of the Toxic Substances Control Act).

[49] City of Philadelphia v. New Jersey, 437 U.S. 617 (1978).

[50] See National Solid Waste Management Ass'n v. Alabama Dep't of Environmental Management, 910 F.2d 713, mod. upon denial of rehearing, 924 F.2d 1001 (11th Cir.), cert. denied, 111 S.Ct. 2800 (1991). See also, Hardage v. Atkins, 582 F.2d 1264, 1266 (10th Cir. 1978); Hazardous Waste Treatment Council v. South Carolina, 766 F.Supp. 431 (D.S.C.), aff'd in part, remanded in part, 945 F.2d 781 (4th Cir. 1991); Government Suppliers Consolidating Services v. Bayh, 753 F. Supp. 739 (S.D. Ind. 1990); Industrial Maintenance Service v. Moore, 677 F. Supp. 436 (S.D. W. Va. 1987) (West Virginia import ban).

[51] Chemical Waste Mgt., Inc. v. Hunt, No. 19014 584 S.2d 1367 (Ala. 1991). See also, Bill Kettlewell Excavating, Inc. v. Michigan Department of Natural Resources, 931 F.2d 413 (6th Cir. 1991), rev'd, 112 S.Ct. 2019 (1992) 931 F.2d 413.

[52] 112 S.Ct. 2009 (1992).

as a ban on the free movement across the State border of hazardous wastes from or to other States . . . <u>shall be deemed inconsistent</u>,"[53] and, therefore, impermissible. Second, it states that any aspect of state law or a state program "which has no basis in human health or environmental protection and which acts as a prohibition on the treatment, storage or disposal of hazardous waste in the state <u>may be deemed inconsistent</u>."[54] The phrasing of this latter provision reflects the Constitutional principle that states and localities may prohibit activities which pose a legitimate public health risk. How these conflicts will be resolved over the next several years will have a major impact on waste management, and on Congress' efforts to achieve a national solution to a national problem.

---

[53] 40 CFR § 271.4(a)(emphasis added).

[54] 40 CFR § 271.4(b)(emphasis added).

STATE	CURRENT STATUS OF STATE ASSUMPTION OF RCRA AUTHORITY*/	LEAD AGENCY
ALABAMA	Final Authorization received December 23, 1987	Department of Environmental Management/Land Division/RCRA Compliance Branch Steven O. Jenkins (205) 271-7726
ALASKA	Expect Final Authorization in 1994	Department of Environmental Conservation/Division of Environmental Quality/Solid and Hazardous Waste Section Heather Stockard (907) 465-5150
ARIZONA	Final Authorization received November 20, 1985	Department of Environmental Quality/Office of Waste Programs Steve Johnson (602) 207-2381
ARKANSAS	Final Authorization received January 26, 1985	Department of Pollution Control and Ecology/Hazardous Waste Division Mike Bates (501) 562-6533
CALIFORNIA	Will resubmit Application for Final Authorization December 20, 1991	Environmental Protection Agency ("CalEPA")/Department of Toxic Substance Control William Soo Hoo (916) 323-9723

10-20

*/ Current as of August 1991

STATE	CURRENT STATUS OF STATE ASSUMPTION OF RCRA AUTHORITY	LEAD AGENCY
COLORADO	Final Authorization received November 2, 1984	Department of Health/Hazardous Materials and Waste Management Division/Hazardous Waste Control Joan Sowinski (303) 692-3300
CONNECTICUT	Final Authorization received December 31, 1990	Department of Environmental Protection/Hazardous Waste Management Section Dave Nash (203) 566-5604
DELAWARE	Final Authorization received June 22, 1984	Department of Natural Resources and Environmental Control/ Division of Air and Waste Management/RCRA Branch Nancy Marker (302) 739-3689
DISTRICT OF COLUMBIA	Final Authorization received February 15, 1985	Environmental Regulation Administration/Pesticides, Hazardous Waste and Underground Storage Tank Division Angelo Tompros (202) 404-1167 x3011
FLORIDA	Final Authorization received February 22, 1985	Department of Environmental Protection/Division of Solid & Hazardous Waste Satish Kastury (904) 488-0300

STATE	CURRENT STATUS OF STATE ASSUMPTION OF RCRA AUTHORITY	LEAD AGENCY
GEORGIA	Final Authorization received August 15, 1984	Department of Natural Resources/Environmental Protection Division/Hazardous Waste Management Branch Jennifer Kadack (404) 656-2833
HAWAII	Preliminary stages in applying for Final Authorization. Expect Final Authorization in late 1992	Department of Health/Environmental Management Division/Solid and Hazardous Waste Branch Grace Simmons (808) 586-4226
IDAHO	Final Authorization received April 1990	Department of Health & Welfare/Division of Environmental Quality Mia Crosthwaite (208) 334-5879
ILLINOIS	Final Authorization received January 31, 1986	Environmental Protection Agency/Division of Land Pollution Control Bill Child (217) 782-6762
INDIANA	Final Authorization received January 31, 1986	Department of Environmental Management/Office of Solid and Hazardous Waste/Hazardous Waste Management Branch Tom Linson (317) 232-3292

STATE	CURRENT STATUS OF STATE ASSUMPTION OF RCRA AUTHORITY	LEAD AGENCY
IOWA	Phase I Interim Authorization reverted back to EPA on July 1, 1985	Department of Natural Resources/Solid Waste Section Lavoy Haage (515) 281-4968
KANSAS	Final Authorization received October 17, 1985	Department of Health & Environment/Bureau of Waste Management Bill Bider (913) 296-1600
KENTUCKY	Final Authorization received January 31, 1985	Department for Environmental Protection/Division of Waste Management/Hazardous Waste Branch Michael Welch (502) 564-6716 x246
LOUISIANA	Final Authorization received January 31, 1985	Department of Environmental Quality/Office of Solid and Hazardous Waste/Hazardous Waste Division Glenn Miller (504) 765-0261
MAINE	Final Authorization received April 1988	Department of Environmental Protection/Bureau of Hazardous Materials and Solid Waste Control Scott Whittier (207) 289-2651

STATE	CURRENT STATUS OF STATE ASSUMPTION OF RCRA AUTHORITY	LEAD AGENCY
MARYLAND	Final Authorization received January 25, 1985	Department of Environment/Waste Management Administration Emily Troyer (410) 631-3343
MASSACHUSETTS	Final Authorization received February 7, 1985	Department of Environmental Protection/Bureau of Waste Prevention Patricia Deese Stanton (617) 292-5765
MICHIGAN	Final Authorization received October 30, 1986	Department of Natural Resources/Hazardous Waste Division Jan Adams (517) 373-9875
MINNESOTA	Final Authorization received February 15, 1985	Pollution Control Agency/Hazardous Waste Division Roger Bjork (612) 297-8512
MISSISSIPPI	Final Authorization received June 20, 1984	Department of Natural Resources/Division of Solid Waste Management Leo Barnett (601) 961-5171

STATE	CURRENT STATUS OF STATE ASSUMPTION OF RCRA AUTHORITY	LEAD AGENCY
MISSOURI	Final Authorization received December 4, 1985	Department of Natural Resources/Hazardous Waste Program Ed Sadler (314) 751-3176
MONTANA	Final Authorization received July 25, 1984	Department of Health & Environmental Sciences/ Solid and Hazardous Waste Management Bureau Duane Robertson (406) 444-1430
NEBRASKA	Final Authorization received February 7, 1985	Department of Environmental Control/RCRA Section Bill Imig (402) 471-4217
NEVADA	Final Authorization received November 1, 1985	Department of Conservation & Natural Resources/ Division of Environmental Protection/Bureau of Waste Management Jolaine Johnson (702) 687-5872
NEW HAMPSHIRE	Final Authorization received January 3, 1985	Department of Environmental Services/Division of Waste Management/Waste Management Enforcement Bureau Ken Marschner (603) 271-2900

STATE	CURRENT STATUS OF STATE ASSUMPTION OF RCRA AUTHORITY	LEAD AGENCY
NEW JERSEY	Final Authorization received February 21, 1985	Department of Environmental Protection and Energy/ Hazardous Waste Regulation Program Frank Coolick (609) 633-1418
NEW MEXICO	Final Authorization received January 25, 1985	Health & Environmental Department/Environmental Improvement Division/Hazardous and Radioactive Materials Bureau Benito Garcia (505) 827-4358
NEW YORK	Final Authorization received May 29, 1986	Department of Environmental Conservation/ Hazardous Substances Regulation Norman Nosenchuck (518) 457-6934
NORTH CAROLINA	Final Authorization received December 31, 1984	Department of Human Resources/Division of Health Services/Environmental Health Section/Solid & Hazardous Waste Management Branch Patricia Delaney (919) 733-4996
NORTH DAKOTA	Final Authorization received October 5, 1984	Department of Health/Division of Waste Management Neil Knatterud (701) 221-5166

10-26

STATE	CURRENT STATUS OF STATE ASSUMPTION OF RCRA AUTHORITY	LEAD AGENCY
OHIO	Final Authorization received June 30, 1989	Environmental Protection Agency/Division of Hazardous Waste Management Kit Arthur (614) 644-3174
OKLAHOMA	Final Authorization received January 25, 1985	Department of Environmental Quality/Hazardous Waste Division Damon Wingfield (405) 271-7053
OREGON	Final Authorization received January 29, 1986	Department of Environmental Quality/Solid Waste Management Division Roy Brower (503) 229-6585
PENNSYLVANIA	Final Authorization received January 30, 1986	Department of Environmental Resources/Bureau of Waste Management Jim Snyder (717) 787-9870
RHODE ISLAND	Final Authorization received January 30, 1986	Department of Environmental Management/Division of Waste Management Tom Ebstein (401) 277-2797

STATE	CURRENT STATUS OF STATE ASSUMPTION OF RCRA AUTHORITY	LEAD AGENCY
SOUTH CAROLINA	Final Authorization received November 8, 1985	Department of Health & Environmental Control/ Bureau of Solid & Hazardous Waste Management Suzanne Rhodes (803) 734-5200
SOUTH DAKOTA	Final Authorization received November 2, 1984	Department of Environment & Natural Resources/Division of Environmental Quality/Waste Management Program Vonni Kallemeyn (605) 773-3153
TENNESSEE	Final Authorization received February 5, 1985	Department of Environment and Conservation/Division of Solid Waste Management Tom Tiesler (615) 532-0829
TEXAS	Final Authorization received December 26, 1984	Texas Water Commission/Industrial and Hazardous Waste Division Susie Ferguson (512) 908-2334
UTAH	Final Authorization received October 15, 1984	Department of Environmental Quality/Division of Solid & Hazardous Waste Dennis Downs (801) 538-6170

STATE	CURRENT STATUS OF STATE ASSUMPTION OF RCRA AUTHORITY	LEAD AGENCY
VERMONT	Final Authorization received January 21, 1985	Agency of Natural Resources/Department of Environmental Conservation/Division of Hazardous Materials Bill Ahearn (802) 241-3888
VIRGINIA	Final Authorization received December 17, 1984	Department of Environmental Quality/Waste Division James Adams (804) 225-2667
WASHINGTON	Final Authorization received January 31, 1986	Department of Ecology Hazardous Waste Program: Tom Eaton (206) 459-6316 Solid Waste Program: Mike Wilson (206) 438-7145
WEST VIRGINIA	Final Authorization received May 28, 1986	Department of Environmental Protection/Division of Waste Management G.S. Atwal (304) 558-5393
WISCONSIN	Final Authorization received January 30, 1986	Department of Natural Resources/Bureau of Solid Waste Management/Hazardous Waste Management Section Barb Zellner (608) 266-7055

STATE	CURRENT STATUS OF STATE ASSUMPTION OF RCRA AUTHORITY	LEAD AGENCY
WYOMING	Preliminary stages in applying for Final Authorization	Department of Environmental Quality/Solid and Hazardous Waste Division Dave Finley (307) 777-7752

CHAPTER 11

SUBTITLE D - SOLID WASTE DISPOSAL

11.1 Subtitle D Overview

Subtitle D of RCRA addresses the control and management of nonhazardous solid waste. EPA studies have documented that more than 11 billion tons of solid waste are generated each year, including 7.6 billion tons of industrial nonhazardous waste, 2 to 3 billion tons of oil and gas waste, more than 1.4 billion tons of "non-coal" mining waste, and nearly 160 million tons of municipal solid waste.[1]

Through a ban on "open dumping" that went into effect in 1979, Subtitle D mandated minimum federal standards for state and local (usually municipal) landfills. Subtitle D also establishes an overall regulatory framework for nonhazardous solid waste management, and authorizes EPA to provide technical assistance to states. State and local governments are responsible for the planning and implementation of Subtitle D solid waste programs.

In recent years, EPA has been considering a more expansive role for Subtitle D, with EPA taking the lead, as a vehicle for regulating certain industrial wastes that warrant regulation, not covered under Subtitle C. These "special" wastes, which include mining waste, fly ash, cement kiln dust, and oil and gas production drilling muds and fluids, are discussed below.

11.2 The Ban on "Open Dumping" and the Criteria for
       Sanitary Landfills

Subtitle D establishes a ban on "open dumping".[2] An "open dump" is any nonhazardous solid waste landfill that does not qualify as a "sanitary landfill."[3] The ban on "open dumping" took

---

[1]   See 53 Fed. Reg. 33314, 33317 (Aug. 30, 1988).

[2]   40 CFR 257.1(a)(2) and RCRA § 4005.

[3]   40 CFR 257.1(a)(1).

effect on September 13, 1979, when EPA promulgated criteria for defining a "sanitary landfill." The current "sanitary landfill" criteria ("Criteria for Classification of Solid Waste Disposal Facilities and Practices," 40 CFR Part 257) establish minimum environmental performance standards that address the following areas: (1) flood plains; (2) endangered species; (3) surface water; (4) ground water; (5) land application; (6) disease; (7) air; and (8) safety. These standards are designed to ensure that "no reasonable probability of adverse effects on health or the environment" will result from solid waste disposal facilities or practices.[4]

Appendix I to Part 257 contains a list of maximum contaminant levels ("MCLs") for use in determining whether solid waste disposal activities comply with the ground water criteria. EPA develops MCLs under Section 1412 of the Safe Drinking Water Act, 42 U.S.C. § 300g-1.

On October 9, 1991, EPA amended Part 257 to update the list of applicable MCLs, and make other revisions to the criteria.[5] In the 1991 amendments, EPA stated that a "facility or practice shall not contaminate underground drinking water sources beyond the solid waste boundary," and explained that contamination is defined as concentrations of substances exceeding the MCLs.[6] The 1991 rule also added new definitions of the types of solid waste disposal facilities that are subject to Part 257, such as landfills, surface impoundments, land application units and waste piles.[7] These regulatory amendments were made as a result of the congressionally mandated solid waste study discussed at subsection 11.3 (immediately below).

---

[4] RCRA § 4004(a).

[5] 56 Fed. Reg. 50978, 50998, 51016 (Oct. 9, 1991).

[6] 56 Fed. Reg. at 50998 (Oct. 9, 1991).

[7] Id.

A practice that violates the criteria constitutes "open dump-ing" and is prohibited under Subtitle D. A facility that violates the criteria is classified as an "open dump" for purposes of state solid waste management planning. State plans must provide for the closing or upgrading of all existing "open dumps."[8] As of 1987, the states were also required to develop permit programs to assure compliance with the sanitary landfill criteria by facilities that receive hazardous household waste or hazardous waste from small quantity generators.[9]

States have the primary responsibility for enforcement through their regulatory programs. In addition, citizens may enforce the ban under the citizen suit provision of RCRA. However, if a state fails to implement a permit program to assure compliance with the 1991 revised criteria, EPA may enforce the ban on open dumping directly.[10]

11.3 EPA Study of Municipal Wastes Under Subtitle D

The 1984 Amendments directed EPA to study the existing guide-lines and criteria for solid waste management and disposal facilities.[11] The goal was to determine the adequacy of the guidelines and criteria in preventing ground water contamination. EPA had 36 months after the enactment of the 1984 Amendments to report the results to Congress.[12] After conducting its Subtitle D study, EPA was required to revise the criteria for facilities that may receive hazardous household wastes or hazardous wastes from

---

[8] State plans are developed under the "Guidelines for Develop-ment and Implementation of Solid Waste Management Plans." 40 CFR Part 256.

[9] RCRA § 4005(c)(1)(A).

[10] RCRA § 4005(c)(2)(A); 56 Fed. Reg. 50978 et seq. (Oct. 9, 1991).

[11] RCRA § 4010(a).

[12] RCRA § 4010(b).

small quantity generators[13], and EPA promulgated the revised criteria on October 9, 1991.[14]

EPA completed its Subtitle D study in 1988 and concluded that the existing federal criteria were not adequate to protect human health and the environment, particularly with respect to municipal solid waste landfills ("MSWLFs") that are improperly designed or operated.[15] EPA noted that the criteria lacked several regulatory provisions required by HSWA, including (1) location restrictions, (2) ground water monitoring, and (3) corrective action. EPA also found that other requirements were needed for (1) methane monitoring, (2) closure and postclosure care, and (3) financial assurance.

Accordingly, on October 9, 1991, EPA promulgated new criteria to respond to concerns of the Agency and the public that there are inadequate controls on solid waste disposal.[16] The criteria are designed to address these concerns while providing states the flexibility to take into account the "practicable capability" of the regulated community.[17] The new rules had an effective date of October 9, 1993, except for the financial assurance requirements which had an effective date of April 9, 1994.[18] However, on July 28, 1993, EPA proposed a "one time" six month extension of the rule for certain "small" landfills (receiving up to 100 tons per

---

13 58 Fed. Reg. 50978 et seq.

14 RCRA § 4010(c).

15 53 Fed. Reg. 33321 (August 30, 1988). EPA announced the availability of the "Report to Congress on Solid Waste Disposal in the United States" in October 1988. Copies of the report are available to the public. 53 Fed. Reg. 41615 (Oct. 24, 1988).

16 58 Fed. Reg. 50978 et seq.

17 Id. and RCRA § 4010(c).

18 Id.

day of solid waste), and an additional one year extension of the financial assurance requirements for all regulated landfills.[19]

11.4 New Solid Waste Regulation for Municipal Landfills

EPA revised the criteria at 40 CFR Part 257 by excluding MSWLFs from Part 257 and covering MSWLFs in a new Part 258. As noted above, HSWA directed EPA to revise the Part 257 for solid waste disposal facilities that may receive hazardous household wastes or hazardous wastes from small quantity generators. These facilities include MSWLFs, some industrial solid waste disposal facilities, and certain other Subtitle D facilities. EPA decided to revise the Part 257 criteria in phases. The first phase consists of the Part 258 criteria for MSWLFs. The Part 257 criteria, with minor modifications remains in effect for all solid waste disposal facilities other than MSWLFs. Industrial solid waste disposal facilities and other Subtitle D facilities presumably will be covered in later phases.

To develop its regulatory approach, EPA used a mail survey of state Solid Waste Management programs to gather information on state Subtitle D facilities. EPA also conducted a detailed review of state regulations which showed that states regulate MSWLFs more closely than other Subtitle D facilities. Although many states imposed standards with respect to facility performance and location, the standards varied significantly among the states. The majority of states required ground water monitoring systems and had authority to impose corrective action. About half the states required methane gas monitoring and/or surface water monitoring. Many states had guidelines or requirements for closure and post-closure maintenance, but the stringency of the requirements varied greatly from state to state.

---

[19]   58 Fed. Reg. 40568 et seq. (July 28, 1993).

11.4.1 Scope of Regulation

The new Part 258 sets forth minimum criteria for MSWLFs. Part 258 applies to all new and existing MSWLFs units, which are defined as:

> a discrete area of land or an excavation that receives household waste, and that is not a land application unit, surface impoundment, injection well, or waste pile . . . . A MSWLF unit also may receive other types of RCRA Subtitle D wastes, such as commercial solid waste, nonhazardous sludge, small quantity generator waste and industrial solid waste. Such a landfill may be publicly or privately owned. A MSWLF unit may be a new MSWLF unit, an existing MSWLF unit or a lateral expansion.[20]

The Part 258 regulations are inapplicable to MSWLFs that do not receive waste after October 9, 1991.[21] MSWLF units that receive waste after October 9, 1991, but stop receiving waste before the rule's effective date (i.e., October 9, 1993, unless extended) are exempt from all requirements except the "final cover" closure requirement.[22] Once a landfill becomes subject to Part 258, it must comply with new closure, post-closure care, and corrective action requirements.

11.4.2 Location Restrictions

Part 258 imposes certain restrictions for the following locations: sites near airports, 100-year floodplains, wetland, fault areas, seismic impact zones, and unstable areas.[23] Restrictions on sites in the vicinity of an airport are very similar to the Part 257 restrictions and apply to new and existing MSWLFs. The same is true with respect to floodplain restrictions.

---

[20] 40 CFR § 258.2.

[21] 40 CFR § 258.1.

[22] Id.

[23] 40 CFR § 258.10-16.

Criteria restrictions on siting in wetlands, fault areas and seismic impact zones apply to new MSWLFs. Restrictions on siting in wetlands, fault areas and seismic impact zones apply to new MSWLFs. Restrictions on unstable areas apply to new and existing MSWLFs.

11.4.2.1 Wetlands

Part 258 restricts the siting of new MSWLFs in wetlands unless the owner or operator can demonstrate to the State that the new unit will meet requirements derived from Section 404 of the Clean Water Act.[24] The requirements include showings of (1) no practicable alternative, (2) no significant degradation, and (3) minimization of adverse effects and (4) compliance with other laws. The other laws include state water quality laws, the Clean Water Act, the Endangered Species Act and the Marine Protection, Research, and Sanctuaries Act.

11.4.2.2 Fault Areas

The regulations ban the siting of new MSWLFs in locations within 200 feet of a fault that has had displacement in Holocene time (approximately the last 11,000 years).[25] In 1978 the U.S. Geological Survey mapped the location of Holocene faults in the United States.

11.4.2.3 Seismic Impact Zones

Part 258 requires owners or operators of new MSWLFs in "seismic impact zones" to design the units to resist "the maximum horizontal acceleration in lithified material for the site."[26]

---

[24]   40 CFR § 258.12.

[25]   40 CFR § 258.13.

[26]   40 CFR § 258.14.

The U.S. Geological Survey has prepared maps of potential seismic activity across the United States.

11.4.2.4 Unstable Areas

Owners or operators of new and existing MSWLFs in "unstable areas" must "demonstrate that engineering measures have been incorporated into the unit's design to ensure the stability of the structural components of the unit."[27] Examples of unstable areas include: (1) subsidence-prone areas; (2) areas subject to mass movement due to gravitational influence; (3) weak and unstable soils; and (4) Karst terrains where solution cavities and caverns develop in limestone or dolomitic materials.

11.4.3 Operating Criteria

The operating criteria of Part 258 applies to all new and existing MSWLFs. The criteria address day-to-day as well as long-term procedures such as closure and financial assurance mechanisms.[28] Owners or operators are required to do the following:

(a) Implement a program to detect and prevent attempts to dispose of hazardous wastes and PCB wastes at the facility.

(b) Cover waste at the end of each operating day, or more frequently if needed to control disease vectors, fires, odors, blowing litter, and scavenging. A temporary waiver from the state may be made available if extreme weather conditions make daily cover impractical.

(c) Prevent or control disease vectors (animals, including insects, capable of transmitting disease to humans) using appropriate techniques for the protection of human health and the environment.

---

[27] 40 CFR § 258.15.

[28] See 40 CFR § 258.20–.29.

(d) Implement a routine methane monitoring program for facility structures and property boundaries. If methane concentrations exceed the specified limits the State must be notified of the levels detected and the steps taken to protect human health. Monitoring must be conducted at least quarterly.

(e) Comply with Clean Air Act "state implementation plan" ("SIP") air quality requirements. Part 258 prohibits burning of solid waste except for infrequent burning of specified wastes.

(f) Use artificial or natural barriers to prevent public access, unauthorized vehicular traffic, and illegal dumping.

(g) Design, construct and maintain run-on and runoff control systems.

(h) Control the discharge of pollutants from point and nonpoint sources of pollution, into waters of the U.S., including wetlands.

(i) Prevent bulk or noncontainerized liquid waste from being disposed of in MSWLFs.

(j) Keep records demonstrating compliance with Part 258.

(k) Complete a written plan for closure by the effective date of Part 258, or by the initial receipt of solid waste whichever occurs later. The plan must provide for closure which will minimize the need for further maintenance and minimize the post-closure formation of leachate and explosive gases. The plan must be approved by the State and closure must begin no later than 30 days after the final receipt of wastes, and be completed within 180 days. An extension may be available at the state's discretion if the landfill does not pose a threat to human health and the environment.[29]

---

[29]   40 CFR § 258.60.

(1) During the post-closure period (a minimum of 30 years after closure) maintain and operate the leachate collection system, and maintain and operate the gas monitoring system. A written post-closure plan is required; the timing and approval requirements are identical as those for the closure plan.[30]

(m) Demonstrate that funds for costs of closure and post-closure care and any possible corrective action (based on site-specific cost estimates) will be available in a timely manner when needed, and maintain a financial assurance mechanism.[31] This requirement does not apply to owners or operators who are State or Federal entities.

11.4.4 Design Criteria for New MSWLFs

Part 258 requires that new MSWLFs (and lateral expansions of existing units) be designed with liners, leachate collection systems, and final cover systems, as necessary, to meet the state established design goal.[32] The design must ensure that the concentration of specified contaminants are not exceeded at the "point of compliance," which must be located no more than 150 meters from the waste management unit boundary and on property owned by the MSWLF owner.

The state is required to consider the following factors when establishing the point of compliance: (1) the hydrogeologic characteristics of the facility and surrounding land; (2) the volume and physical characteristics of the leachate; (3) proximity of ground water users; and (4) the existing quality of the ground water.

---

[30]   40 CFR § 258.61.

[31]   40 CFR § 258.70-74.

[32]   40 CFR § 258.40.

11.4.5 Ground Water Monitoring and Corrective Action

The ground water monitoring requirements apply to owners or operators of new and existing MSWLFs.[33] The requirements are suspended, however, for owners or operators who can demonstrate to the state that there is "no potential for migration of hazardous constituents" from the unit to the uppermost aquifer during the unit's active life, closure or post-closure periods.[34] Note that the monitoring requirements effectively prohibit siting of new MSWLFs in areas where effective monitoring is impossible because of subsurface conditions. EPA's regulations phase in the monitoring requirements for existing MSWLFs.

The regulations require owners or operators to install a system of monitoring wells approved by the state at new and existing MSWLFs. The regulations provide procedures for sampling the wells and methods for statistical analysis of data to determine whether the ground water is contaminated. The regulations create a two-phase approach to ground water monitoring and corrective action. Monitoring is to continue through the post-closure period with monitoring frequency set by the state.

Phase I; Detection Monitoring involves monitoring for 62 parameters or constituents referenced in 40 CFR § 258.54. If monitoring indicates contamination or any statistically significant change in the ground water chemistry, Phase II monitoring is triggered. Monitoring frequency is determined by aquifer flow rates and the resource value of the aquifer.

Phase II; Assessment Monitoring involves monitoring an expanded list of hazardous constituents.[35] If any Phase II parameters are detected at statistically significant levels

---

[33]   40 CFR § 258.50.

[34]   40 CFR § 258.50(b).

[35]   40 CFR § 258.55.

above background, the owner or operator must make an assessment of corrective measures.[36] The owner or operator must select a remedy and implement the corrective action program.[37] The remedy must be "protective of human health" and control releases "to the maximum extent practicable."[38] The state retains the authority to: "require the owner or operator to undertake source control measures or other measures that may be necessary to eliminate or minimize further releases to the ground water, to prevent exposure to the ground water, or to remediate the ground water to concentrations that are technically practicable and significantly reduce threats to human health or the environment."[39]

11.5 "Special Study" Wastes

In Section 8002 of RCRA, Congress directed EPA to conduct evaluations of the potential threats to public health and the environment posed by several special categories of wastes including mining wastes, oil and gas wastes, cement kiln dust wastes, and wastes from the combustion of coal such as fly ash and bottom ash.[40]

These studies were intended to assist the Agency's determination under RCRA Section 3001(b) as to whether or not these special wastes should be regulated as hazardous wastes under Subtitle C of RCRA.[41] In addition, these studies were intended to enable the Agency to determine whether changes are needed in the Subtitle D regulatory program to properly

---

[36] 40 CFR § 258.56.

[37] 40 CFR § 258.57-.58.

[38] 40 CFR § 258.57(a).

[39] 40 CFR § 258.57(f).

[40] See RCRA § 8002(f)(m)(n)(o) and (p).

[41] See Chapter 2.

manage these wastes. It now appears likely that new Subtitle D regulatory programs will be developed by EPA, perhaps with supplemental legislative authorization, tailored to the unique waste management concerns associated with a number of these special study wastes. Still in the conceptual stage as of this writing, these are sometimes referred to as the "Subtitle D-plus" programs.

11.5.1 Oil and Gas Wastes

Pursuant to Section 8002(m) of RCRA, in December of 1987 EPA released a Report to Congress on the "Management of Wastes from the Exploration, Development, and Production of Crude Oil, Natural Gas and Geothermal Energy."[42] In July of 1988 EPA determined that regulation of these wastes under Subtitle C is not warranted, but that the Agency will seek to improve existing federal programs under Subtitle D.[43] Specifically, EPA found that the existing federal standards under Subtitle D "provide general environmental performance standards for the disposal of solid wastes, . . . but these standards do not fully address the specific concerns posed by oil and gas wastes."[44]

The volume of wastes subject to this determination is significant. EPA has estimated that 361 million barrels of drilling waste were generated in 1985 from about 70,000 crude oil and natural gas wells. These wastes can contain organic pollutants such as benzene and phenanthrene, and metals such as lead, arsenic and uranium. To ensure proper control over oil and gas waste disposal practices, EPA has stated that it will consider requirements under Subtitle D such as:

---

[42] A notice of the availability of this report was published on January 4, 1988, 53 Fed. Reg. 82.

[43] 53 Fed. Reg. 25446 (July 6, 1988).

[44] Id.

(1) Engineering and operating practices, including runoff controls to minimize releases to surface water and ground water;

(2) Proper procedures for closing facilities;

(3) Monitoring that accommodates site-specific variability; and

(4) Cleanup provisions.[45]

In developing these tailored Subtitle D standards for oil and gas wastes, EPA has stated that it intends to fill gaps in existing state and federal regulations.

11.5.2 Mining and Mineral Processing Wastes

On December 31, 1985, EPA submitted its "Report to Congress on Wastes from the Extraction and Beneficiation of Metallic Ores, Phosphate Rock, Asbestos, Overburden from Uranium Mining, and Oil Shale," pursuant to Section 8002(p) of RCRA.[46] In July of 1986 EPA published its regulatory determination not to regulate these mining wastes (chiefly waste rock and mine tailings) under Subtitle C of RCRA.[47] However, EPA found there was a "lack of Federal oversight and enforcement authority over mining waste controls under Subtitle D," and EPA expressed a commitment to work with Congress to develop an effective regulatory program under

---

[45] 53 Fed. Reg. at 25457 (July 6, 1988).

[46] Wastes from coal mining activities are outside the scope of this report and generally not affected by the Subtitle D regulatory developments. Under Section 3005(f) of RCRA, coal mines permitted through the Surface Mining Control and Reclamation Act of 1977, 30 U.S.C. § 1201 et seq., are not subject to RCRA regulatory requirements.

[47] 51 Fed. Reg. 24496 (July 3, 1986). This determination was upheld in Environmental Defense Fund v. EPA, 852 F.2d 1309 (D.C. Cir. 1988) ("EDF I"). However, EPA's determination to not regulate certain mineral "processing" wastes under Subtitle C was set aside. Environmental Defense Fund v. EPA, 852 F.2d 1316 (D.C. Cir. 1988) ("EDF II").

Subtitle D, and to obtain the necessary oversight and enforcement authority.[48]

On June 13, 1991, EPA published a regulatory determination not to regulate 20 mineral processing wastes that EPA had studied in a 1990 "Report to Congress on Special Wastes from Mineral Processing."[49] These 20 waste streams included wastes such as red and brown muds from bauxite refining, slag from primary lead, zinc and copper processing, iron blast furnace slag, and carbon steel production slag etc. All mineral processing waste streams that were not expressly addressed in the determination and the rules leading to it, are no longer exempt from RCRA hazardous waste regulation.[50] EPA stated that most of these mineral processing wastes warranted regulation under new Subtitle D programs which it hopes to develop, explaining as follows:

> EPA is in the process of developing a RCRA Subtitle D program for mineral extraction and beneficiation wastes. EPA plans to include those mineral processing wastes determined here to warrant regulation under subtitle D under the regulatory "umbrella" for extraction and beneficiation wastes, making it the extraction, beneficiation, and mineral processing wastes program. As the development of this program proceeds, the Agency may find it necessary to control certain mineral processing wastes, such as waste acids, that have little in common with the majority of extraction and beneficiation wastes under a separate regulatory program.[51]

---

[48] 51 Fed. Reg. at 24501 (July 3, 1986).

[49] 56 Fed. Reg. 27300 et seq. (June 13, 1991).

[50] Id. See 55 Fed. Reg. 32135 (Aug. 7, 1990)(notice of availability of report to Congress); 55 Fed. Reg. 2322 (Jan. 23, 1990) (identifying mineral processing wastes to be studied); 54 Fed. Reg. 36592 (Sept. 1, 1989) (final mining waste exclusion criteria).

[51] 56 Fed. Reg. at 27317 (June 13, 1991).

No formal regulatory proposals have yet been published by EPA to implement the Subtitle D mine waste program. This is probably due, in part, to the Agency's belief that it needs additional legislative authority to provide for adequate federal oversight and enforcement. However, during the past few years EPA has circulated to the public unofficial "strawman" proposals of possible Subtitle D mining waste regulatory schemes. The proposals would provide for a jointly administered federal-state program where EPA would approve and oversee the implementation of state mining waste management plans. Federal regulations would establish performance goals, design and operating criteria, monitoring criteria, corrective action criteria, closure and post-closure care criteria and financial responsibility requirements.

The EPA "strawman" proposals have been the subject of substantial debate among the mining industry, other federal agencies such as the Department of the Interior, the states, environmental organizations and Congress. It is likely that further developments will occur in this area in the near future.

11.5.3 Cement Kiln Dust and Coal Combustion Waste

Under Section 8002 of RCRA, EPA was obligated to conduct studies of the adverse effects on human health and the environment, if any, of the disposal of "cement kiln dust" waste and wastes from the combustion of coal other fossil fuels, e.g., fly ash waste, bottom ash waste, flue gas waste and slag waste.[52] These wastes are currently exempted from RCRA Subtitle C regulation,[53] but it is possible that EPA may propose to limit the scope of these exemptions or develop additional regulatory requirements applicable to those wastes under Subtitle D.

In the case of cement kiln dust wastes, EPA has not yet completed its study, and thus, it has not taken any action regarding

---

[52] RCRA § 8002(n)(o).

[53] RCRA § 3001(b)(3).

these wastes. In 1988 EPA issued its Report to Congress on "Wastes from the Combustion of Coal by Electric Utility Power Plants."[54] This report documented that in 1984 coal-fired power plants produced 69 million tons of ash and 16 million tons of flue gas desulfurization wastes. Four-fifths of these wastes were disposed in surface impoundments or landfills. EPA concluded that most coal combustion waste streams generally do not exhibit hazardous characteristics and that the Agency prefers that most of these wastes remain under Subtitle D. On August 9, 1993, EPA issued a formal regulatory determination defining the final scope of the coal combustion waste exemption, consistent with the 1988 Report to Congress.[55] Specifically, EPA concluded that four large-volume coal combustion waste streams -- fly ash, bottom ash, boiler slag, and flue gas emission control waste -- should remain exempt from hazardous waste regulation under Subtitle C of RCRA. EPA stated that it will consider these wastes further during the Agency's ongoing assessment of industrial non-hazardous wastes under Subtitle D of RCRA.

---

[54] EPA published a notice of the availability of this report in March of 1988. 53 Fed. Reg. 9976 (Mar. 28, 1988).

[55] Fed. Reg. 42466 (Aug. 9, 1993).

CHAPTER 12

INSPECTIONS, LIABILITY AND ENFORCEMENT

12.1 Inspection Authority

RCRA Section 3007(a) provides that any officer, employee or representative of EPA, or of a state with an authorized hazardous waste management program, may inspect the premises and records of any person who generates, stores, treats, transports, disposes, or otherwise handles hazardous waste. All privately-operated T/S/D facilities must be inspected at least once every two years. Federally-operated T/S/D facilities and federally-permitted state and local government facilities must be inspected annually.[1]

EPA's inspection authority extends to persons or sites which have handled hazardous wastes in the past but no longer do so. The operator must provide government officials access to records and property relating to the wastes for inspection purposes. Copying and sampling are authorized. Such inspections may be made either to gather information in connection with development of regulations or for purposes related to enforcement.

The inspection program is not limited to persons who manage hazardous wastes identified or listed in EPA's regulations at 40 CFR Part 261 implementing RCRA Section 3001. Congress did not confine the scope of RCRA Section 3007 to "hazardous wastes _identified or listed under this subtitle_" (emphasis added) as it did in RCRA Sections 3002-3004 and 3010. Thus, for purposes of inspection, a waste which has not been listed or identified as

---

[1] RCRA § 3007(c), (d) and (e). The mandatory inspection provisions were adopted in the 1984 Amendments. Congress simultaneously directed EPA to report to it on the feasibility of utilizing a program of private inspections to supplement federal and state inspections by May 8, 1985. RCRA § 3007(e). EPA has missed that deadline but has requested comments on the use of private inspection services, funding mechanisms for such inspections, confidentiality questions and possible conflicts of interest. In addition, this request for comments raises the possibility of certification of an environmental auditing program. 50 _Fed. Reg._ 33103 (August 16, 1985).

hazardous under 40 CFR Part 261 may still be a hazardous waste for Section 3007 inspection purposes if EPA has reason to believe that the material may be hazardous within the broad statutory definition of hazardous waste contained in RCRA Section 1004(5).[2]

Section 3007(a) imposes certain restrictions on inspections. They can only be conducted "at reasonable times," and must be completed "with reasonable promptness." RCRA contains no express requirement that inspectors first obtain a warrant. EPA's inspection activities under RCRA Section 3007 are, however, subject to the Fourth Amendment's protection against unreasonable searches or seizures.[3] The Supreme Court has applied these Fourth Amendment principles in holding that a warrant is generally required for an inspection by an administrative agency. <u>Marshall v. Barlow's, Inc.</u>, 436 U.S. 307 (1978). The Court held that the Fourth Amendment required a warrant for an inspection by an OSHA employee, who was acting under Section 8(a) of the Occupational Safety and Health Act of 1970, in the event that the employer did not voluntarily consent to the inspection. The Supreme Court has, however, stated that legislative schemes authorizing warrantless administrative searches of commercial property do not necessarily violate the Fourth Amendment. In <u>Donovan v. Dewey</u>, 452 U.S. 594 (1981), for example, the Court found that warrantless inspections of mines, as required by the Federal Mine Safety and Health Act (MSHA), do not offend the Fourth Amendment. The Court reasoned that a warrant may not be constitutionally required when Congress has reasonably determined that warrantless searches are necessary

---

[2]   <u>See</u> 40 CFR 261.1(b).

[3]   <u>See</u> <u>In re</u> <u>Order Pursuant to Section 3013(d) RCRA</u>, 550 F. Supp. 1361 (W.D. Wash. 1982) (right of inspection under Section 3007 not unconstitutional where entry by EPA is limited to reasonable times and involves only those activities as are reasonable to ascertain the nature and extent of the potential health hazard).

to further a regulatory scheme and the owner of commercial property must be aware that the owner's property will be subject to periodic inspections under the statute.

Despite the Dewey holding, EPA has recognized the application, by analogy, of the Barlow's case to its own inspection activities under the various statutes administered by it, and has directed its regional offices to be governed accordingly.[4] Like most of EPA's statutory inspection authorities, RCRA Section 3007 is basically similar to the OSHA provision at issue in Barlow's. Thus, EPA has said it will "exercise . . . its Section 3007 authority . . . in a manner consistent with the decision."[5] Presumably, this means EPA will obtain a search warrant when necessary. The Supreme Court has consistently held, however, that the standard for granting a warrant for an "administrative" search is a fairly easy one to meet. The agency requesting the warrant need only show that the inspection bears a reasonable relationship to the regulatory program authorizing the entry.[6]

As originally written, Section 3007(b) was silent as to whether inspections could be conducted by non-EPA employees under contract to conduct such inspections on behalf of EPA. The 1980 Amendments resolved this issue by specifically providing that inspections can be conducted by "representatives" of EPA. The Conference Report accompanying these amendments underscores

---

[4] Memorandum from EPA General Counsel to Assistant Administrators and Regional Administrators, "Effect of Supreme Court Decision in Marshall v. Barlow's, Inc. on EPA Information Gathering and Inspection Activities" (June 29, 1979); Memorandum from EPA Assistant Administrator for Enforcement to Regional Administrators and Others, "Conduct of Inspections After the Barlow's Decision" (April 11, 1979).

[5] 45 Fed. Reg. 33189 (May 19, 1980).

[6] Marshall v. Barlow's Inc., 436 U.S. 307 (1978); Camara v. Municipal Court, 387 U.S. 523 (1967).

Congress' intent that EPA have the option to rely on outside contractors as well as its own employees.[7] The issue has been somewhat clouded by one court's holding that a similar phrase in the Clean Air Act is limited to EPA employees subject to substantive confidentiality and tort liability standards.[8]

RCRA Section 3007(b) provides that all information, records, or reports obtained as a result of an inspection must be made available to the public, unless a claim of confidentiality is asserted pursuant to EPA's business confidentiality regulations, 40 CFR Part 2. EPA employees who divulge information obtained through an inspection that is protected under the confidentiality regulations are liable for criminal penalties under the Federal Trade Secrets Act, 18 U.S.C. Section 1905. Non-federal employees, however, are not subject to this statute. In allowing outside contractors to conduct inspections, Congress also imposed a duty on those persons not to disclose information protected under a valid claim of confidentiality. RCRA Section 3007(b)(2). Willful violation of that duty triggers criminal sanctions. Because this section only applies to willful violations, there still is a valid and important role for written nondisclosure agreements, which EPA contractors have generally been willing to execute before commencing an inspection. A nondisclosure agreement is designed to protect trade secrets from disclosure to unauthorized persons, regardless of whether the disclosure is willful.

EPA may also require monitoring, testing, analysis, and reporting by any present or past owner or operator of a facility where hazardous waste is or has been treated, stored, or disposed

---

[7]   S.Rep. No. 172, 96th Cong., 1st Sess. 3 (1979); H. Conf. Rep. No. 1444, 96th Cong., 2d Sess. 35 (1980).

[8]   In re Stauffer Chemical Co., 14 ERC 1737, 1741 (D. Wyo. 1980), aff'd, 647 F.2d 1075 (10th Cir. 1981); contra In re Clean Air Act Administrative Inspection of the Bunker Hill Co., 15 ERC 1063 (D. Idaho 1980), aff'd, 658 F.2d 1280 (9th Cir. 1981); In re Aluminum Co. of America, 15 ERC 1116 (M.D.N.C. 1980), remanded, 663 F.2d 499 (4th Cir. 1981).

of, when the release of such waste "may present a substantial hazard to human health or the environment."[9] This authority is exercised by administrative order. Normally, the order will be issued to a present owner or operator, but if he or she lacks knowledge concerning the presence of hazardous waste and its potential for release, EPA may issue the order to a previous owner or operator who could reasonably be expected to have such knowledge. Once such an order is issued, the person to whom it is directed has 30 days to respond with a proposal for carrying out the required monitoring, testing, analysis, and reporting. This proposal is then discussed with EPA and, if the proposal is satisfactory to the Agency, the person may proceed to carry out the plan.

If no owner or operator is available, or if the proposal is unsatisfactory, EPA may proceed to carry out the monitoring program itself and require the owner or operator to reimburse the costs. An owner or operator who refuses to cooperate is not only potentially liable for the costs of carrying out the program, but is also liable for a civil penalty of up to $5,000 per day of such refusal.[10] In addition, EPA may secure an ex parte administrative inspection warrant to reasonably carry out the monitoring program.[11]

Orders issued under Section 3013 may be judicially enforced by EPA in any United States District Court. In the case of E.I. duPont de Nemours and Co. v. Daggett, the court held that a recipient of such an order need not wait for the agency to bring such

---

[9] RCRA § 3013.

[10] On September 11, 1981, EPA issued a guidance memorandum to its regional offices prepared by its then Acting Director of Waste Programs Enforcement on the implementation and use of this authority. 12 Env't. Rep. (BNA) 662 (1981).

[11] In re Order Pursuant to Section 3013(d) RCRA, Etc., 550 F. Supp. 1361 (W.D. Wash. 1982).

an enforcement action, but may secure pre-enforcement review of the validity of the order.[12]

12.2   Civil Enforcement

There are several types of enforcement actions available to EPA under RCRA. These include administrative orders, civil and criminal penalties, and injunctive relief. Each is discussed below.

12.2.1   Compliance Orders

Under RCRA Section 3008(a), whenever EPA determines that any person is violating Subtitle C of RCRA (including any regulation or permit issued thereunder), the Agency has two options. First, it may issue an order requiring compliance immediately or within a specified time period. Second, EPA may seek injunctive relief against the violator through a civil action filed in a U.S. District Court. When the violation occurs in a state with an approved hazardous waste program under RCRA Section 3006, EPA must notify the state of the violation 30 days prior to issuing the compliance order or seeking the injunction.

Administrative compliance orders, sometimes called notices of violation, can take several forms. They may be in the form of a letter advising of a violation and requiring compliance, or they may be more formal notices. They may prescribe a period of time for compliance, or require the respondent to advise the agency of the measures it will take to get into compliance.

As discussed elsewhere in the context of "corrective action" at T/S/D facilities, EPA can issue an "interim status corrective

---

[12]   610 F. Supp. 260 (W.D.N.Y. 1985). The court said that since the statute and legislative history clearly divorced § 3013 orders from the imminent and substantial endangerment test, it was not compelled to follow case law under Superfund § 106 holding that pre-enforcement review of such orders was barred. Id. at 263-64.

action order" under Section 3008(h) to any interim status facility, requiring action to abate any releases of hazardous wastes or constituents at such a facility where "necessary to protect human health or the environment." Alternatively, EPA may commence a civil action for appropriate injunctive relief. The order or injunction may include suspension or revocation of interim status, and carries a penalty of up to $25,000 per day for violations.

12.2.2 Administrative Proceedings: Civil Penalties and Permit Suspension or Revocation

Penalties of up to $25,000 per day are authorized for violation of the terms of a compliance order (i.e., failing to abate the violation within the time specified by EPA) or violation of any requirement of Subtitle C.

The issuance of compliance orders and the assessment of civil penalties under RCRA are governed by the procedures in EPA's consolidated rules of practice, 40 CFR Part 22. The process is triggered by the service of a complaint on the alleged violator. The complaint will seek the assessment of a specified civil penalty for the violation and, if the violation is ongoing, will include a compliance order requiring corrective action within a specified time period.

If the alleged violator contests any material facts on which the complaint is based, contends that the proposed penalty is inappropriate, or believes that it is entitled to judgment as a matter of law, a written answer must be filed within 30 days. A hearing, if desired, must be requested in the answer. An evidentiary, trial-type hearing is then conducted, including the right to cross-examine witnesses. An administrative law judge ("ALJ") presides over the hearing. The ALJ has authority to issue subpoenas to require witnesses to appear or to produce documentary evidence. Any party may appeal an adverse order of the ALJ to the Administrator of EPA.

In addition to monetary penalties, EPA may suspend or revoke the permit issued to the violator, whether issued by EPA or a state. If the permittee objects to the suspension or revocation within 30 days, he is entitled to a public hearing. RCRA is silent on whether the permit stays in effect or is suspended during the pendency of the hearing process. However, this process is governed not by the consolidated rules of practice (40 CFR Part 22) but by EPA's consolidated permit regulations, 40 CFR Part 124. Those regulations allow the permit to remain in effect pending revocation procedures. These procedures are more fully discussed in Chapter 9 of this Handbook.

12.2.3 Judicial Proceedings for Civil Penalties

EPA has alternative authority, under Section 3008, to seek civil penalties and injunctive relief for any violation of Sub Title C through a civil action in district court. The courts have held, moreover, that individuals can be held personally liable for the violations committed by their companies. See, e.g., United States v. Conservation Chemical Co. of Illinois, 660 F. Supp. 1236 (N.D. Ind. 1987) (president and principal shareholder of corporation that operated hazardous waste facility were "persons" within meaning of RCRA and could be held personally liable under Section 3008(a)). Section 3008 has also been used as a vehicle for directly enforcing compliance with EPA requests for information under Section 3007.[13] In that context, courts have held that EPA need not issue a compliance order or administrative subpoena prior to seeking civil penalties.[14] The injunctive authority in Section 3008 has also been relied upon to authorize impliedly injunctive

---

[13] United States v. Charles George Trucking Co., 823 F.2d 685 (1st Cir. 1987); United States v. Liviola, 605 F. Supp. 96 (N.D. Ohio 1985).

[14] Charles George Trucking, supra, 823 F.2d at 689-692. Liviola, supra, 605 F. Supp. at 100.

relief in a citizen suit action brought under Section 7002 to enforce provisions of RCRA.[15]

12.2.4 EPA's Civil Penalty Policy

In 1984, EPA developed a written policy governing the assessment of administrative penalties under Section 3008.[16] EPA's policy was recently revised in a document entitled, 1990 Revised RCRA Civil Penalty Policy, issued in October of 1990. The revised policy applies to both administrative settlements and complaints, and for the first time, the penalty policy will apply to civil judicial settlements as well.

EPA's penalty calculation system consists of: (1) a gravity-based penalty established by a penalty assessment matrix; (2) the addition of a "multi-day" component, based upon the duration of the violation; (3) an adjustment of the sum of (1) and (2) up or down, depending upon case-specific circumstances; and (4) the addition of the appropriate economic benefit gained through non-compliance. In both administrative and civil cases, EPA will perform calculations under the policy to explain and document the process by which the Agency arrives at the penalty figure it agrees to accept in settlement.

EPA's base penalty calculation is derived from a matrix which calculates a gravity-based penalty for a particular violation according to the potential for harm and the extent of deviation from a statutory or regulatory requirement. The matrix sets forth the following base penalty ranges:

---

[15] Environmental Defense Fund v. Lamphier, 714 F.2d 331 (4th Cir. 1983); Walls v. Waste Resource Corp., 761 F.2d 311, 316 (6th Cir. 1985).

[16] See RCRA Civil Penalty Policy (May 8, 1984).

		Extent of Deviation from Requirement		
		MAJOR	MODERATE	MINOR
Potential for Harm	MAJOR	$25,000 to 20,000	$19,999 to 15,000	$14,999 to 11,000
	MODERATE	$10,999 to 8,000	$ 7,999 to 5,000	$ 4,999 to 3,000
	MINOR	$ 2,999 to 1,500	$ 1,499 to 500	$ 499 to 100

EPA has the authority, once a base penalty is calculated using the matrix, to seek a separate penalty when an individual or company violates more than one RCRA requirement. In such a case, EPA may seek a penalty for each separate violation that results from independent acts by the violator and that is substantially distinguishable from any other charge in the complaint.

EPA may also seek "multi-day" penalties of up to $25,000 per day of non-compliance for each violation of a Subtitle C requirement. The matrix sets forth when multi-day penalties are to be assessed:

Multi-Day Gravity Based Penalty Matrix

Extent of Deviation from Regulatory Requirement

		MAJOR	MODERATE	MINOR
Potential for Harm	MAJOR	M.	M.	Pr.
	MODERATE	M.	Pr.	Dis.
	MINOR	Pr.	Dis.	Dis.
	Key:	"M." means, "Mandatory" "Pr." means, "Presumed" "Dis." means, "Discretionary"		

For days 2 through 180 of multi-day violations, multi-day penalties could be mandatory, presumed, or discretionary, depending upon the potential for harm and the extent of the deviation of the violations. In assessing multi-day penalties, regions also retain the right to impose penalties of up to $25,000 per day as well as any additional deterrence penalties for days of violation after the first 180.

Once the base penalty and appropriate multi-day penalties have been assessed, EPA will calculate the economic benefit of non-compliance -- i.e., the amount of money saved by the violator as a result of non-compliance -- and will adjust the penalty upwards, as appropriate. Finally, the Agency may further adjust the penalty upwards or downwards to reflect the particular circumstances surrounding a violation. The factors considered in adjusting the penalty include good faith efforts to comply or lack of good faith; degree of willfulness or negligence; history of non-compliance; ability to pay; environmental projects to be undertaken by the violator; or other unique factors. Factors that tend to adjust the penalty downwards, such as good faith and ability to pay, will generally be considered during the settlement stage of a case, after EPA has proposed a penalty in a complaint.

After documenting penalty calculations for proposed penalties and settlement amounts, regions are now required to send the penalty calculation worksheets to EPA Headquarters for review in order to ensure that the penalty policy is properly implemented.

12.2.5 EPA and OSHA Cooperation

In a memorandum of understanding (MOU) issued in November of 1990, the Department of Labor and EPA set forth procedures to establish and improve the working relationship between OSHA and EPA. According to the MOU, the two agencies will cooperate in developing and coordinating training, data and information exchange, referrals of alleged violations, and related compliance and enforcement matters.

EPA and OSHA may also conduct joint inspections as necessary to enforce applicable statutes or on an ad hoc basis, such as in investigations following accidents or injuries in the workplace which result from activities subject to either EPA or OSHA juris- diction. If an EPA or OSHA inspector discovers a potential viola- tion of the other agency's laws or regulations, then the inspector will refer the matter to the other agency. For example, in the course of conducting an EPA inspection, an EPA inspector who receives a complaint about safety or health in the workplace will bring the matter to the attention of OSHA representatives. Both agencies will develop a system to track and manage referral of potential violations, or situations requiring inspection or evalu- ation by either agency. To ensure that valid referrals are made, EPA and OSHA will cooperate in developing and conducting periodic training programs for each other's personnel in the respective laws, regulations, and compliance requirements of each agency.

12.3 Criminal Liability

RCRA Section 3008(d) imposes criminal liability on any person who knowingly:

    (1) transports a hazardous waste to a facility that does not have a permit;

    (2) treats, stores, or disposes of hazardous waste without a permit or in knowing violation of any material condition of a permit or appli- cable interim status standards;

    (3) makes a false statement or representation in any application, label, manifest, record, report, permit, or other document filed, main- tained, or used for purposes of compliance with Subtitle C of RCRA;

    (4) generates, stores, treats, transports, dis- poses of, or otherwise handles any hazardous waste and who knowingly destroys, alters, or conceals any record required to be maintained under Subtitle C;

    (5) transports hazardous waste without a manifest; or

(6) exports a hazardous waste without consent of the receiving country or in violation of an international agreement.

Persons who commit such offenses are subject to a fine of up to $50,000 per day of violation, two years imprisonment (five years in the case of a violation of paragraph (1) or (2)), or both.[17] Subsequent convictions carry a maximum punishment of $100,000 per day and double the terms of imprisonment in the previous sentence.

EPA is not required to issue a notice of violation or an abatement order prior to initiating a criminal prosecution under RCRA section 3008(d). While criminal offenses must be "knowing" violations of RCRA, courts have held that ignorance of the law is no excuse.[18] The precise extent of the defendant's knowledge related to the violation, however, has been extensively litigated.

The court in United States v. Johnson & Towers, Inc., 741 F.2d 662 (3d Cir. 1984, cert. denied, sub nom. Angel v. United States, 469 U.S. 1208 (1985), held that a violation of RCRA section 3008(d)(1) and (2) requires that the defendant knew or should have known that a RCRA permit was required, that a permit had not been obtained, and that the wastes improperly disposed of were hazardous. The defendants in Johnson & Towers were a foreman and a service manager in the trucking department. The court found that these employees were "persons" within the meaning of RCRA and subject to prosecution, and that their professed ignorance of the law was no excuse; by virtue of their position of responsibility

---

[17] On February 23, 1989, a Maryland jury for the first time extended RCRA's criminal liability to three federal employees, high ranking civilian employees of the Army at the Aberdeen Proving Ground outside of Baltimore. The three employees were convicted of various counts of illegally storing, transporting and disposing of hazardous wastes generated by the chemical weapons on the site, and now face terms of imprisonment of up to 15 years and civil penalties of up to $750,000.

[18] United States v. Dean, 969 F.2d 187 (6th 1992); United States v. Hayes Int'l Corp. and Louis Beasley, 786 F.2d 1499 (11th Cir. 1986).

in the company they should have known the applicable law and relevant facts.[19]

Other courts have rejected the "should have known" standard, requiring the government to show affirmatively that the defendant knew that the facility receiving the hazardous waste did not have a permit. United States v. Speach, 968 F.2d 795 (9th Cir. 1992); United States v. White, 1991 U.S. Dist. LEXIS 5567 (E.D. Wash. 1991). In White, the court held that for a RCRA conviction, some "actual knowledge" (such as knowledge of the hazardousness of the waste) of the conduct in question is required. The court also stated that a "should have known" standard or the application of the "responsible corporate officer" doctrine may not be substituted for the statute's requirement of some actual knowledge. A similar conclusion was reached in United States v. MacDonald & Watson Waste Oil Co., 933 F.2d 35 (1st Cir. 1991).

There have also been a number of state court criminal prosecutions for illegal disposal of hazardous waste, some with inventive sanctions. The Los Angeles, California, County Special District Attorney has obtained several orders requiring corporate officers convicted of environmental violations to pay for full page advertisements in the Los Angeles Times and Wall Street Journal warning others of the risks of violating environmental laws. One such full page advertisement which ran in the Times in February, 1985, blared in bold capitals:

---

[19] Accord United States v. Hoflin, 880 F.2d 1033 (9th Cir. 1989), cert. denied, 111 S. Ct. 1143 (1990). See also United States v. Dee, 912 F.2d 741 (4th Cir. 1990) (upholding conviction of civilian employees of Army base, rejecting the defense that supervisors knew of and directed their unlawful conduct), cert. denied, 111 S. Ct. 1307 (1991); United States v. Hayes Int'l Corp. and Louis Beasley, 786 F.2d 1499 (11th Cir. 1986) (lack of knowledge that waste was "hazardous" or that the defendant did not know that a permit was required for its disposal was no defense to Section 3008 liability).

WARNING
THE ILLEGAL DISPOSAL OF
TOXIC WASTES WILL
RESULT IN JAIL.
WE SHOULD KNOW.
WE GOT CAUGHT.

The advertisement identified the company and continued: "We are paying the price. Today, while you read this ad our President and Vice President are serving time in JAIL and we were forced to place this ad."

Criminal liability is also imposed upon any person for "knowing endangerment." The purpose of this sanction, found at RCRA Section 3008(e), is to provide substantial felony penalties for certain life-threatening conduct. The endangerment offense has two elements. First, the person charged must have violated one of the provisions of Section 3008(d) listed above. Second, at the time of the offense, the person charged must have known that he was placing another in imminent danger of death or serious bodily injury.

An individual convicted of violating Section 3008(e) faces a fine of up to $250,000 and/or up to fifteen years imprisonment. An organizational defendant is subject to a maximum fine of $1 million. Individuals convicted in federal court of RCRA violations that occurred after November 1, 1987 must be sentenced according to guidelines issued by the United States Sentencing Commission. The base offense level for an individual convicted of knowing endangerment under RCRA section 3008(e) would result in a sentence of between 51 and 125 months imprisonment, depending on the defendant's prior criminal history and various mitigating and aggravating circumstances.[20] Although the Sentencing Commission has issued guidelines for sentencing corporate offenders, these guidelines are not mandatory for environmental crimes.

In fiscal year 1992, the Department of Justice issued 89 indictments alleging violations of RCRA and/or CERCLA, bringing

---

[20] U.S. Sentencing Guidelines § 2Q1.1.

the ten year total to 488.[21] Prosecutions for violations of RCRA and CERCLA accounted for 47 percent of all environmental indictments in fiscal year 1992. One quarter of these were indictments against corporations and slightly more than one quarter were indictments against individuals who did not serve in a supervisory capacity. Convictions for environmental offenses during fiscal year 1992 resulted in fines of $163,647,344 and prison terms totalling over 37 years.

12.4   Imminent Hazard Liability

RCRA Section 7003(a) provides that EPA may bring suit for injunctive relief upon receipt of evidence that any person's past or present handling, storage, treatment, transportation, or disposal of hazardous waste may present an "imminent and substantial endangerment to health or the environment." The 1984 Amendments to the statutory language, which specifically include past conduct, have laid to rest the issue of whether Section 7003 covers past, off-site non-negligent activities, an issue which haunted enforcement of this provision prior to the 1984 Amendments.[22]

Like EPA's inspection authority under RCRA Section 3007, EPA's authority under RCRA Section 7003(a) is not limited to hazardous wastes identified in 40 CFR Part 261. A waste which is not listed or identified as hazardous is nevertheless hazardous for purposes

---

[21] DOJ Memorandum to Neil S. Cartusciello from Peggy Hutchins (October 27, 1992).

[22] Compare, United States v. Solvents Recovery Service of New England, 496 F. Supp. 1127 (D.Conn. 1980) (holding pre-RCRA conduct was covered) and United States v. Waste Industries, Inc., 734 F.2d 159 (4th Cir. 1984) (holding RCRA applies to leaking resulting from pre-RCRA disposal), with United States v. Northeastern Pharmaceutical & Chemical Co., ("NEPACCO") 579 F. Supp. 823 (W.D. Mo. 1984) (questioning application to past conduct of non-negligent off-site generators); aff'd in part, rev'd in part, 810 F.2d 726 (8th Cir. 1986), on reh., 842 F.2d 977 (8th Cir. 1988) (en banc), cert. denied, 109 S. Ct. 66 (1988).

of RCRA Section 7003 if the statutory elements for an imminent hazard action are established.[23]

Action under this Section is authorized against any "person", including any past or present generator, past or present transporter, or past or present owner or operator of a T/S/D facility, who has contributed or is contributing to the endangerment. The term "person", in turn, is broadly defined to include "an individual, trust, firm, joint stock company, corporation (including a governmental corporation), partnership, association, State, municipality, commission, political subdivision of a State, or any interstate body."[24]

EPA issued a memorandum on January 25, 1980, defining "imminent and substantial endangerment" as posing a "risk of harm" or "potential harm" but not requiring proof of actual harm.[25] This interpretation was upheld in United States v. Vertac Chemical Corp., 489 F. Supp. 870 (E.D. Ark. 1980), the first published decision interpreting RCRA Section 7003. In issuing a preliminary injunction to contain the migration of dioxin from landfills and a treatment basin into a creek, the court held that under the endangerment provisions of both RCRA and the Clean Water Act, harm need only be threatened rather than actually occurring. Accord United States v. Midwest Solvent Recovery, Inc., 484 F. Supp. 138 (N.D. Ill. 1980); United States v. Price, 688 F.2d 204 (3d Cir. 1982); United States v. Reilly Tar and Chemical Corp., 546 F. Supp. 1100 (D. Minn. 1982); United States v. Waste Industries Inc., 734 F.2d 159 (4th Cir. 1984). As the court noted in NEPACCO, supra, 579 F. Supp. at 832, application of the standard requires a

---

[23] 40 CFR 261.1(b)(2).

[24] RCRA § 1004(15), NEPACCO, supra, 810 F.2d at 745-46 (shareholders and officers of chemical manufacturer individually liable for contributing to imminent and substantial endangerment).

[25] Memorandum dated January 25, 1980, from Douglas MacMillan, Acting Director of EPA's Hazardous Waste Enforcement Task Force, to Regional Enforcement Division Directors and others.

case-by-case assessment of the relationship between the magnitude of risk and harm arising from the presence of the hazardous waste.

A broad spectrum of relief is available to EPA under Section 7003. It includes injunctive relief restraining the defendant from the activities causing the imminent and substantial endangerment and directing him to take such other action as may be necessary. Pursuant to this provision, EPA has secured either by court order or consent agreement the following types of relief:

(1) surface cleanup of drums, tanks, etc.;

(2) restricted public access to site;

(3) provision of alternate water supply where ground water is contaminated;

(4) development and implementation of a plan to prevent further contamination;[26]

(5) financial guarantees, often in the form of trust funds, to insure implementation;

(6) restoration of ground water and other contaminated resources;

(7) ongoing monitoring programs to determine the adequacy of cleanup;

(8) site restoration; and

---

[26] EPA memoranda may indicate in advance agency plan preferences. See, e.g., Memorandum dated January 31, 1985, from Jack McGraw, Acting Assistant Administrator, entitled "Draft Interpretation of Minimum Technology Requirements for Hazardous Waste Liner, Leachate Collection Systems Under RCRA," dated February 15, 1985, 16 Env't. Rep. (BNA) 1678 (1985).

(9) reimbursement of EPA funds expended in connection with a site.[27]

EPA is now required by statute to provide for public notice and comment and an opportunity for a public meeting in the affected area prior to entering into a settlement or covenant not to sue with a defendant in a Section 7003 action.[28] This codifies the previous policy of EPA and the Department of Justice ("DOJ") under 28 CFR 50.7 of allowing a 30-day public comment period prior to entry of consent agreements involving injunctive relief.

EPA is also authorized to "take any other action under this section including, but not limited to, issuing such orders as may be necessary to protect public health and the environment." This empowers EPA itself to mandate specific action to deal with an imminent danger. The Agency need not wait for a court to order such remedies. For failure to obey such an order, Section 7003(b) allows EPA to seek a fine in a U.S. District Court of up to $5,000 per day of violation. Where EPA chooses to issue a Section 7003 administrative order, EPA must give prior notice to the affected State. No statutory period for such prior notice is specified. EPA guidance on the issuance of administrative orders suggests that the notice be given at least one week in advance of issuance of the order. The advantage of an administrative order, in EPA's

---

[27] NEPACCO, supra; United States v. Conservation Chemical Co., 619 F. Supp. 162 (D.C. Mo. 1985); United States v. Hooker Chemicals and Plastics, 749 F.2d 968 (2d Cir. 1984), aff'd, 776 F.2d 410 (2d Cir. 1985); United States v. Seymour Recycling Corp., 554 F. Supp. 1334 (S.D. Ind. 1982); United States v. Kin-Buc, Inc., 17 ERC 1934 (D.N.J. 1982); United States v. Midwest Solvent Recovery, Inc., 484 F. Supp. 138 (N.D. Ind. 1980); see, e.g., United States v. Waste Industries, Inc., 734 F.2d 159 (4th Cir. 1984). In joint CERCLA/RCRA enforcement actions EPA has been successful in recovering its RCRA oversight costs. United States v. Rohm & Haas Corp., 790 F. Supp. 1255 (E.D. Pa. 1992).

[28] RCRA § 7003(b).

view, is that it can be issued as soon as EPA has evidence satisfying the statutory criteria. An enforcement action is more time-consuming, as it involves referral to the DOJ and filing of a complaint.[29] EPA's Hazardous Waste Enforcement policy, which applies to Section 7003 cases, addresses criteria for settlement, covenants not to sue, contribution protection, exchange of documents and information, timing of negotiations, and other matters.[30]

As a practical matter, RCRA imminent hazard authority is usually coordinated with enforcement authority under another statute, such as Superfund Section 106. There are three situations in which a RCRA 7003 order will be issued where a Superfund order cannot. These are:

(1) where the imminent hazard is caused by a RCRA solid waste, but not a hazardous waste;

(2) where a waste is a hazardous waste under Section 1004(5) of RCRA but not a hazardous waste under 40 CFR Part 261; and

(3) where the waste involved is excluded from regulation under Superfund because it is a petroleum product.

For example, administrative orders have been issued under Section 7003 to owners of underground storage tanks that were leaking gasoline or other petroleum products.[31]

---

[29] U.S.EPA, "Issuance of Final Revised Guidance on the Use and Issuance of Administrative Orders Under § 7003 of RCRA" (September 21, 1984).

[30] 50 Fed. Reg. 5034 (Feb. 5, 1985).

[31] "Final Revised Guidance on the Use and Issuance of § 7003 Administrative Orders." U.S.EPA, September 21, 1984 at p.8.

12.5 Hazardous Waste Enforcement Litigation

The DOJ is actively working with EPA to compel the cleanup of existing and abandoned hazardous waste sites using the RCRA Section 7003 imminent hazard authority and, where appropriate, similar provisions of other federal statutes.[32] As a practical matter, this activity can be expected to increase now that Congress has clarified the application of Section 7003 to past practices. The DOJ's Environment and Natural Resources Division has an Environmental Enforcement Section to provide the necessary legal resources to handle civil hazardous waste enforcement cases. This includes an Environmental Crimes Section to prosecute criminal cases, in conjunction with an EPA/FBI program, to investigate possible criminal violations. That program is aimed at curbing midnight dumping and other attempts to evade the hazardous waste regulations. A parallel unit exists in EPA's Office of Enforcement. As reflected by the foregoing discussion of Section 7003, numerous cases have been successfully prosecuted or settled as a result of the government's vigorous enforcement of these provisions.

Perhaps the most publicized litigation has involved Hooker Chemicals and Plastics Corp. DOJ filed four separate lawsuits against Hooker seeking damages in excess of $100 million in order to clean up chemical waste disposed of in four sites in the Niagara Falls, New York area. A settlement of just one of those suits, the so-called "S" Area Landfill suit, United States v. Hooker Chemicals and Plastics Corp. (W.D.N.Y. Civil No. 79-988, filed 12/20/79) requires Hooker to do the following:

> (1) conduct surveys and studies to determine the nature and extent of migration of toxic chemicals from S-Area into the Niagara River and underlying bedrock;

---

[32] These include Clean Water Act § 504; Superfund § 106; Safe Drinking Water Act § 1431; Clean Air Act § 303; Toxic Substances Control Act § 7; and the Rivers and Harbors Act of 1899.

(2) install a barrier wall, drain tile collection system, barrier plugs and a cap at the S-Area landfill;

(3) install a drain tile collection system around the Niagara Falls Drinking Water Treatment Plant ("Plant");

(4) construct a new intake system to protect the integrity of the public drinking water supply and share maintenance costs with the city; and

(5) guarantee $20 million over a 35-year period to cover the costs of these remedial programs.[33]

12.6 EPA's Enforcement Approach

EPA has established a classification system for RCRA violations.[34] Class I violations include significant deviations from regulations, compliance orders, permit conditions or other requirements which could result in improper disposal or release of hazardous waste to the environment; failures to assure early detection of such releases; or other circumstances that could involve environmental harm. All other violations are Class II violations.

There are also three classes of violators: A High Priority Violator is one whose violation has caused actual exposure or a substantial likelihood of exposure to hazardous waste, one who is a chronic or recalcitrant violator, or one whose violation reflects a substantial deviation from RCRA requirements. A Medium Priority Violator is one who has one or more Class I violations, but does not meet the criteria for a High Priority Violator. One

---

[33] See also United States v. Hooker Chemicals & Plastics Corp., 749 F.2d 968 (2d Cir. 1984), aff'd, 776 F.2d 410 (2d Cir. 1985).

[34] Memorandum from EPA Assistant Administrator for Solid Waste and Emergency Response, J. Winston Porter addressing the Agency's RCRA Enforcement Response Policy (December 21, 1987) OSWER Directive 9900.00-1A. This policy document, effective October 1, 1988, revised and superseded the December 21, 1984, RCRA Enforcement Response Policy.

who has only Class II violations may also, under some circumstances (if, for example, compliance could be achieved more appropriately through an administrative order than a lesser notice of violation), be classified as a Medium Priority Violator. A Low Priority Violator is a waste handler who has only Class II violations and who is not a High Priority or Medium Priority Violator. Depending on the class of violation and the classification of the violator, the policy memorandum prescribes various appropriate enforcement responses, ranging from warning letters and notices of violation to administrative orders, and civil or criminal actions.

This enforcement approach is designed to concentrate the agency's attention and resources on what it considers the most serious actions, and so match its enforcement response to the gravity of the offense. In particular, the policy reflects EPA's expanded focus and emphasis on corrective action requirements, land disposal restrictions and permitting violations.

Criminal indictments for violations of environmental laws increased from 40 in fiscal year 1985 to 191 in fiscal year 1992 -- an increase of 478 percent. EPA and the Department of Justice publish annual enforcement statistics that detail the number of indictments, convictions and penalties imposed. The emphasis, it seems, is to seek to impose criminal penalties, including jail time, on responsible corporate officers and employees. But as a measure of the trend in corporate compliance with environmental regulations, the "body count" of criminal enforcement measures is an increasingly irrelevant yardstick. More relevant is the fact that U.S. industry each year spends over $70 billion on pollution control technology and related environmental protection costs in order to comply with environmental regulations and avoid becoming an enforcement statistic.

12.7 Citizen Suits

Persons who violate their duties under RCRA are subject not only to federal enforcement action, but may also be sued in a private civil action. RCRA Section 7002 allows any person to commence a civil action in U.S. District Court on his own behalf against any other person including the United States alleged to be in violation of any permit, regulation, or provision of the Act. The 1984 Amendments expand this authority to include imminent and substantial endangerment actions against past and present generators, transporters and owners or operators of T/S/D facilities.[35] Before commencing such a "citizen suit," the plaintiff must give 60 days notice to EPA, the state involved, and the alleged violator, charging that a violation is being committed.[36] Ninety days notice is required for imminent and substantial endangerment cases. The courts are authorized to issue injunctive relief and appropriate penalties in any such action.[37]

A citizen can also bring an action against EPA charging that it has failed to perform a nondiscretionary duty under RCRA. This generally involves failure to issue regulations required to be issued by a statutory deadline. The district court may order EPA to execute the action or actions at issue.

Citizen suits are prohibited in the following instances:

---

[35] RCRA § 7002(a), (1)(B). In _Jones v. Inmont Corp._, 584 F. Supp. 1425 (S.D. Ohio 1984) the court held that the prior version of § 7002 also authorized imminent and substantial endangerment suits by citizens on the theory that 7003 was a substantive requirement of RCRA. Congress apparently agreed.

[36] The giving of timely notice is a prerequisite of jurisdiction, and failure to comply results in dismissal of the suit. _Hallstrom v. Tillamook County_, 844 F.2d 598 (9th Cir. 1987), _aff'd_, 493 U.S. 20 (1989).

[37] RCRA § 7002(a); _Environmental Defense Fund v. Lamphier_, 714 F.2d 331 (4th Cir. 1983); _Jones v. Inmont Corp., supra_.

(1) with respect to siting and permitting of T/S/D
    facilities;[38]

(2) where EPA is prosecuting an action under RCRA
    or Superfund;

(3) while EPA or a state is engaged in a Superfund
    removal or has incurred costs to engage in a
    remedial action; and

(4) where the responsible party is conducting a
    removal or remedial action pursuant to EPA
    order.

In any citizen suit, attorneys' fees may be awarded to the
prevailing or substantially prevailing party. Citizen suits can
have a very substantial impact on a company's operations. In
United States v. Environmental Waste Control, Inc., 710 F. Supp.
1172 (N.D. Ind. 1989), aff'd, 917 F.2d 327 (7th Cir. 1990), an
environmental group which intervened in an EPA enforcement action
convinced the court to order permanent closure of a non-complying
RCRA facility. Additionally, the court assessed a civil penalty
of $2.78 million based on factors such as: (1) the landfill
operated after it lost interim status; (2) the operator did not
make a good-faith attempt to meet ground water monitoring
standards, and the landfill operated without a proper system for
three years; and (3) the operator placed waste in unlined cells,
which was likely to cause ground water contamination.

EPA sought the assessment of penalties, but not a permanent
closure order. EPA also sought injunctive relief to require the
defendant to remedy the multitude of problems at the facility.
The citizens group sought penalties and permanent closure. The

---

[38] The federal appeals courts have exclusive jurisdiction to hear
appeals brought by citizens against the issuance of a RCRA
permit. RCRA § 7006(b). District courts lack jurisdiction to
hear a collateral attack on an agency permitting decision
brought in a citizens suit. Palumbo v. Waste Technologies
Inc., 989 F.2d 156 (4th Cir. 1993).

court held that the facility operator was afforded repeated opportunities to comply with RCRA requirements, but responded by developing a "dismal history of delay, misperformance, and noncompliance." Accordingly, the court granted the citizen's group request for injunctive relief permanently enjoining the defendants from operating a hazardous waste facility at the site.

Thus under RCRA, as under the other major federal environmental statutes, a business manager must be sensitive to the power that Congress has vested in private citizens and environmental groups under these provisions.

CHAPTER 13

THE USED OIL RECYCLING ACT OF 1980

13.1 Overview

In 1980, Congress enacted the Used Oil Recycling Act as an amendment to RCRA.[1] The purposes of this Act are to: 1) provide incentives for the recycling of used oil; 2) provide comprehensive management standards for recycling facilities; and 3) require EPA to determine what, if any, RCRA regulations should apply to recycled used oil. EPA has estimated that 1.1 billion gallons of waste oil are generated each year. EPA believes that over 464 million gallons of used automotive oil and another 380 million gallons of used industrial oil are disposed of annually in this country. In 1980, most of that used oil was burned for fuel, but about 15 percent was used as a road oil or dust suppressant, and 30 percent was disposed of in landfills.[2]

Although Congress recognized that used oil is a valuable source of increasingly scarce energy and materials, and that the technology exists to reclaim and otherwise recycle used oil, Congress also determined that used oil constituted a threat to public health and the environment when used or disposed of improperly.[3] Used oil contains toxic constituents that are motile, persistent, bioaccumulative, and capable of migrating in hazardous concentrations. It is therefore capable of causing substantial harm when mismanaged. Thus, Congress directed EPA in the Used Oil Recycling Act to study and report back to Congress on the market supply and demand for used oil, and the environmental problems

---

[1] RCRA § 3012, Pub. L. No. 96-463, 94 Stat. 2055 (1980), renumbered as RCRA § 3014 by Section 502 of the Hazardous and Solid Waste Amendments of 1984, Pub. L. No. 98-616, 98 Stat. 3221, 3277 (1984).

[2] Franklin Associated, Ltd., Composition and Management of Used Oil Generated in the United States (September 1984) at 1-9.

[3] Used Oil Recycling Act, § 2.

associated with the improper reuse or disposal of used oil.[4] Based on the study, EPA was to decide whether to list used oil as a hazardous waste under RCRA by 1981, and then to develop regulations establishing performance standards and other requirements for the recycling of used oil.[5]

When EPA failed to make a decision on the listing of used oil under RCRA or to promulgate any standards, Congress sought to spur EPA action in the Hazardous and Solid Waste Amendments of 1984. Congress imposed new deadlines on EPA for identifying whether used oil is a hazardous waste, and directed EPA to establish a special regulatory scheme for companies that generate, transport, and recycle used oil. Congress also imposed a ban on the application of used oil that has been contaminated with hazardous wastes as a dust suppressant or for road treatment.[6] The statutory scheme and EPA's efforts thus far to implement Congress' mandate are discussed in this Chapter.

13.2   The Listing Of Used Oil as a Hazardous Waste

The Used Oil Recycling Act defines used oil as "any oil that has been - (A) refined from crude oil, (B) used, and (C) as a result of such use, [becomes] contaminated by physical or chemical impurities."[7] Used oil may become contaminated with additives from automotive motors, lead from gasoline, and other heavy metals from contact with industrial machinery.[8]

---

[4]   Used Oil Recycling Act, § 9.

[5]   Used Oil Recycling Act, § 8. EPA had previously proposed to list certain waste oils, mainly waste lubricating, hydraulic, and cutting oils, as hazardous wastes under RCRA, but EPA had not gone forward with the proposal. See 43 Fed. Reg. 58946 (December 18, 1979).

[6]   RCRA § 3004(1).

[7]   RCRA § 1004(36).

[8]   H.R. Rep. No. 96-1415, 96th Cong., 2nd Sess. 6 (1980).

Although EPA has not yet listed any type of used oil as a RCRA hazardous waste in 40 CFR Part 261, used oil is regulated as a hazardous waste under RCRA if it exhibits a hazardous characteristic and is disposed of. Used oil that is mixed with a characteristic hazardous waste is not regulated if the resulting mixture does not exhibit the hazardous characteristic.[9] Moreover, used oil that is a household waste is not regulated.[10] Used oil that is recycled (other than by being burned for energy recovery), however, is a solid waste and is not currently regulated as a hazardous waste.[11]

EPA was directed in the Used Oil Recycling Act to report to Congress by January 1981 concerning the applicability of the RCRA hazardous waste criteria and regulations to used oil, and to indicate EPA's position with respect to the listing of used oil.[12] EPA submitted to Congress a report entitled Listing of Waste Oil as a Hazardous Waste (January 1981) in which EPA indicated its intention to list the following categories of waste oil as hazardous under RCRA:

(1) oil spilled on the land and oily debris generated from cleaning up spills to land or surface water;

(2) used automotive oil; and

(3) used industrial oils.

EPA determined that these used oils usually contain benzene, phenols, naphthalene, trace metals and other hazardous constituents in Part 261, Appendix VIII.

---

[9] 40 CFR 261.3(a)(2)(iii).

[10] 40 CFR 261.4(b)(1).

[11] 40 CFR 261.6(a)(3)(iii). Used oil burned for energy recovery is regulated under 40 CFR Part 266, as discussed below.

[12] Used Oil Recycling Act, § 8.

EPA's study caused widespread concern, and the Office of Management and Budget ("OMB") requested that EPA conduct a regulatory impact analysis on the cost of listing used oil pursuant to Executive Order No. 12291 issued by President Reagan which requires that new federal regulations be subject to a cost/benefit analysis and to OMB review. The EPA analysis demonstrated that the listing of used oil under RCRA would impose very high costs on industry, particularly for the permitting of an estimated 500,000 used oil storage facilities.[13] EPA's development of a listing proposal for used oil became stalled.

In the 1984 Amendments, Congress sought to spur EPA action by directing that the Agency decide whether to propose the listing of used automobile and truck crankcase oil and other used oil as RCRA hazardous wastes by November 19, 1985, and to finalize its proposal by November 19, 1986.[14] EPA did propose the listing of all petroleum derived and synthetic used oil as hazardous wastes on November 29, 1985.[15] The proposal would have included all used oil from motor vehicles and industrial manufacturing processes, such as lubricants (e.g., engine oils), hydraulic fluid, metal working fluids (e.g., cutting, grinding, and machining fluids), and transformer fluids.

In addition, EPA proposed to amend the mixture rule to exclude from RCRA regulation wastewaters containing small amounts of used oil from small leaks, spills or drips from pumps, machinery and equipment due to normal operations. Although no de minimis concentration limit was set, EPA stated that the exemption would not apply to used oil that is discarded as a result of abnormal manufacturing operations, such as plant shutdowns or malfunctions that result in substantial spills. The used oil recovered from

---

[13] PEDCO Environmental, Inc., A Risk Assessment of Waste Oil (1983).

[14] RCRA § 3014(b).

[15] 50 Fed. Reg. 49258 (November 29, 1986).

wastewater, _e.g._, from an oil/water separator, would be regulated as a hazardous waste if disposed of, or as a recycled oil if recycled. EPA's proposal also would have exempted oily rags and similar "industrial wipers" that become contaminated with used oil from wiping machinery, tools, the user's hands, and the like.

The RCRA listing of used oil as a hazardous waste would also have meant that any spill of used oil in a reportable quantity to the environment would have to be reported under CERCLA. EPA proposed a reportable quantity of 100 pounds. Any spill residue, absorbants, etc. resulting from a spill of used oil would have had to be disposed of as hazardous waste.

EPA's proposed listing of used oil drew extensive public comment, including critical comments from EPA's own Office of the Ombudsman on behalf of small business. Subsequently, EPA requested additional public comment on a regulatory option suggested at public hearings of listing only used oil that is disposed of as a RCRA hazardous waste.[16] Used oil that is recycled would then be subject to management standards, as discussed below, based on RCRA Section 3014 (the Used Oil Recycling Act), and recycled oil would not be listed as a hazardous waste.

As the statutory deadline for a final determination drew near, on November 19, 1986 EPA promulgated a final determination not to list used oil that is recycled as a hazardous waste under RCRA Section 3001.[17] On October 7, 1988, however, the D.C. Circuit Court of Appeals held that EPA's basis, which included the stigma of such listing, was contrary to RCRA. Hazardous Waste Treatment Council v. EPA, 861 F.2d 270 (D.C. Cir. 1988), cert. denied, 490 U.S. 1106 (1989). The court held that Section 3014(b) of RCRA requires EPA to determine whether used oil meets the technical criteria for listing as hazardous and that consideration of the

---

[16] 51 Fed. Reg. 8206 (March 10, 1986).

[17] 51 Fed. Reg. 41900 (November 19, 1986).

"stigmatic effects" of such a listing was not a factor permitted by the statute.[18]

In response to the court's ruling in Hazardous Waste Treatment Council v. EPA, EPA agreed to the entry of a consent decree that required it to issue a proposed determination of whether to list or identify used oil as a hazardous waste by September 1991, and to make a final determination by May 1992. Accordingly, on September 23, 1991, EPA announced the availability of additional data on the composition of used oil and used oil residuals, and its intention to consider the new data in arriving at a final decision as to whether to list used oils as hazardous wastes.[19] At the same time, EPA also indicated it would consider amending its regulations under RCRA to include the listing of four wastes (distillation bottoms, gravity and mechanical separation waste streams, lube polishing media, and waste-water and treatment residues) from the re-refining and reprocessing of used oils.

On May 20, 1992, EPA issued a final rule in which it decided not to list used oil from gasoline-powered engine crankcases which is destined for disposal as hazardous waste.[20] This decision was based on the finding that some used oils do not typically or frequently meet the technical criteria for listing. In effect, the rule preserved the status quo for such oil.[21]

---

[18] Id. at 277.

[19] 56 Fed. Reg. 48000 (September 23, 1991).

[20] 57 Fed. Reg. 21524 (May 20, 1992).

[21] At the same time, EPA modified the exclusions to the definition of hazardous waste to provide an exemption for non-terne-plated used oil filters (terne is an alloy of tin and lead) which have been gravity "hot-drained" (i.e., at or near engine operating temperature) to remove used oil. Terne-plated used oil filters are not included in the exclusion because the terne plating makes the filter exhibit the characteristic of toxicity for lead. Although the language of the exclusion does not specify the use to which such filters were put, the preamble to the rule appears to confine the exclusion to oil filters used in light and heavy duty

The Agency did not take final action on a listing determination with respect to the listing of the four wastes noted above from the re-refining and reprocessing of used oils.

13.3 Standards for Recycling of Used Oil

In the 1984 Amendments, Congress directed EPA to establish a special regulatory scheme by November 1986 for companies that generate and transport used oil that is a hazardous waste under Section 3001 and is recycled.[22] The new standards may not include a manifest requirement or RCRA recordkeeping and reporting (except for records of agreements for delivery of used oil) for generators that send used oil to qualified recycling facilities. In addition, EPA was also to promulgate comprehensive standards for used oil recycling facilities, which would then be deemed to have a RCRA permit if they complied with the standards.

On November 29, 1985, EPA proposed comprehensive management standards for generators, transporters, and used oil recycling facilities in conjunction with the listing proposal.[23] For example, under the proposal, generators of used oil destined for recycling would have been allowed to store the used oil on site for up to 90 days in tanks and containers that met RCRA standards, similar to 90-day on-site storage of hazardous wastes by generators discussed in Chapter 3 of this Handbook. Used oil sent off-site for recycling or re-refining would have had to be packaged and labeled in accordance with the RCRA generator standards. Generators would not have been required to use the Uniform Manifest if they arranged to send the used oil to a permitted recycling facility.

---

vehicles.

[22] RCRA § 3014(c).

[23] 50 Fed. Reg. 49212 (November 29, 1985).

In addition, transporters of used oil would have had to obtain an EPA Identification Number and comply with requirements for reporting spills and accidental releases of used oil. Under the proposal, used oil recycling facilities would have been regulated through a permit-by-rule approach, unless a facility already had a RCRA permit.

EPA decided to delay final promulgation of these proposed standards for recycled oil until a final decision was made on the listing of used oil that is disposed of, so that all new regulations for used oil would be put into effect at the same time.[24] Accordingly, on September 10, 1992, EPA issued a final rule in which it determined that recycled used oil is not a hazardous waste.[25] EPA claimed that the decision not to list recycled used oil as a hazardous waste was designed to encourage recycling and that extensive new used oil management standards, which are discussed below, would be adequately protective of human health and the environment without the need to require used oil generators and transporters to meet RCRA's hazardous waste regulations.

Under the rule, recycled used oil must be handled as a hazardous waste only in the following circumstances:

°   used oil that has been mixed with listed hazardous waste is subject to regulation as a hazardous waste;

°   used oil that has been mixed with a characteristic hazardous waste is subject to regulation as a hazardous waste if the resulting mixture exhibits a hazardous characteristic (otherwise, it will be regulated under 40 CFR Part 279);

°   used oil that contains more than 1000 ppm total halogens is presumed to be mixed with a hazardous waste (this presumption does not apply to some metalworking oils/fluids containing chlorinated paraffins and used

---

24   51 Fed. Reg. 41900 (November 19, 1986).

25   57 Fed. Reg. 41566 (September 10, 1992). Technical corrections to the final rule were issued on May 3, 1993. 58 Fed. Reg. 26420.

oil contaminated with chlorofluorocarbons ("CFCs") removed from refrigeration units where the CFCs are destined for reclamation); and

° used oil contaminated with pslychlorinated biphmyls ("PCBs") is subject to regulation as a hazardous waste under 40 CFR Part 761.

To make the handling of used oil simpler, EPA presumes all used oil is destined for recycling, thereby making all used oil (with the above-limited exceptions) subject to the regulations contained in 40 CFR Part 279 regardless of whether the oil exhibits a hazardous waste characteristic. The recycling presumption will no longer apply, however, once a person disposes of used oil or sends it for disposal. In those situations, the disposal of the used oil must meet the current requirements of RCRA if the used oil meets the definition of hazardous waste.

Used oil generated by households and "do-it-yourselfers" is not subject to the used oil management standards until it is collected and aggregated at individual privately-owned or company-owned service stations or other state or local government-approved collection centers. Service station dealers collecting used oil from do-it-yourselfers are exempt from Superfund liability for any response costs associated with the release of collected used oil, provided they comply with all applicable used oil management standards and do not mix the collected used oil with hazardous waste.

The rule provides detailed management standards for used oil generators (§§ 279.20-24), collection centers and aggregate points (§§ 279.30-32), transporter and transfer facilities (§§ 279.40-47), processors and re-refiners (§§ 279.50-59), oil burners who burn off-specification used oil for energy recovery (§§ 279.60-67), fuel marketers (§§ 279.70-75), and used oil used as a dust suppressant (§§ 279.80-82). The standards are primarily good housekeeping measures designed to prevent improper storage, leaks, spills, and adulteration with hazardous waste. For example, while transporters of used oil need not prepare manifests for shipments, they must maintain records of the quantity, generator, and delivery of all shipments of used oil. Similarly, used oil storage containers must be maintained in "good condition" and storage must include secondary containment, although the provisions are considerably less onerous than RCRA's hazardous waste standards. It is important to note, however, that storage of used oil must comply with all spill containment and control ("SPCC") regulations[26] as well as underground storage tank regulations, where applicable.[27]

13.3.1 Burning and Blending of Used Oil

One form of recycling, which was a particular concern to Congress, is the burning and blending of used oil as a fuel. EPA studies have shown that the burning of contaminated used oil in residential, commercial, and institutional boilers and furnaces causes high emissions of PCBs, dioxins, toxic metals and other hazardous constituents. In the 1984 Amendments, Congress directed EPA to regulate on an expedited schedule the burning and blending of used oil fuels.[28] Congress also required all persons who produce, distribute, market or burn used oil as a fuel to file a notification with EPA by February 8, 1986. This notification provided EPA with a "snapshot" of the burning and blending of used oil fuels by U.S. industry, similar to the RCRA Section 3010(a) notification of hazardous waste management activities in August 1980 (see, e.g., Chapter 3).

In November, 1985, EPA took the first step in implementing Congress' directive in final rules for used oil that is burned for energy recovery.[29] At the outset, the regulations significantly

---

[26] (cite) 40 CFR Part 112.

[27] 40 CFR Part 280.

[28] RCRA § 3010(a)(1).

[29] 40 CFR Part 266, Subpart E, 50 Fed. Reg. 49212 (November 29,

distinguish between contaminated used oil that will be regulated as a hazardous waste under RCRA and used oil fuel which, when blended and burned, will be regulated under the Used Oil Recycling Act. This distinction is important because EPA views its regulatory authorities created by the Used Oil Recycling Act as independent of RCRA, and thus used oil recyclers, generators, marketers, and transporters would not be subject to RCRA permit and enforcement sanctions.[30] Thus, used oil that is mixed with a hazardous waste (except small quantity generator hazardous waste) is subject to full RCRA regulation. Used oil that contains more than 1000 ppm total halogens is presumed to be a hazardous waste, unless rebutted by evidence that the used oil has not been adulterated with any hazardous spent solvents or other hazardous wastes.[31] Used oil that exhibits a hazardous characteristic, but which is not mixed with any hazardous waste, is regulated as a used oil.

Under the Used Oil Recycling Act EPA regulates the blending and burning of "off-specification" used oil.[32] A used oil is "off-specification" if it exceeds any of the following criteria or has a flash point below 100°F:[33]

Constituent/Property	Allowable Level
Arsenic	5 ppm maximum
Cadmium	2 ppm maximum
Chromium	10 ppm maximum
Lead	100 ppm maximum
Flash Point	100°F minimum
Total Halogens	4,000 ppm maximum

1985). At the same time, EPA also promulgated rules at 40 CFR Part 266, Subpart D, for the burning and blending of hazardous waste-derived fuels, as discussed in Chapter 7 of this Handbook.

30 See 50 Fed. Reg. 1691 (January 11, 1985).

31 40 CFR 266.40(c).

32 40 CFR 266.40(e).

33 Id.

Under the rules, off-specification used oil can be burned only in industrial furnaces, utility boilers, or industrial boilers.[34] It is unlawful for any person to produce, market, or burn off-specification oil in a residential, commercial or institutional boiler or other unauthorized facility. Used oil that meets the fuel specifications set forth above, however, can continue to be burned in non-industrial boilers as well as any industrial facility, pending further study by EPA. Off-specification used oil can also be processed or blended to meet the specifications and then burned in non-industrial boilers.

Any person who markets a used oil must notify EPA stating the location and general description of used oil management facilities.[35] Even if a marketer has previously notified EPA of his hazardous waste activities under RCRA Section 3010, he must renotify to identify his used oil management activities.[36] The marketer is also responsible for analyzing the used oil fuel to determine if it is off-specification.[37] If so, the marketer is subject to the prohibition against burning the off-specification used oil in non-industrial boilers or furnaces. The marketer must use an invoice system for documenting the names, addresses, and EPA ID Numbers of the shipping and receiving facilities.[38] Before a marketer initiates the first shipment of off-specification used

---

[34] 40 CFR 266.41. Off-specification used oil can also be burned in certain oil-fired space heaters provided that the heater burns only used oil that the owner or operator generates or used oil received from do-it-yourself oil changes who generate used oil as household waste; the heater is designed to have a maximum capacity of not more than 0.5 million Btu per hour; once the combustion gases from the heaters are vented to the ambient air. 40 CFR 266.41(b)(2)(iii)(A)-(C).

[35] 40 CFR 266.43(b)(3).

[36] Id.

[37] 40 CFR 266.43(b)(1).

[38] Id.

oil to a burner or other marketer, he must obtain a one-time written certification from the burner or marketer certifying that the burner or marketer has filed its notification with EPA and will burn the off-specification used oil fuel only in an approved boiler or furnace.[39]

Similarly, a burner of used oil must file a RCRA Section 3010 notification, provide the required notices to marketers, maintain records of all invoices, and adhere to the prohibition against burning off-specification used oil fuel in other than an industrial or utility boiler or furnace. Generators and transporters of used oil are not subject to these regulations unless they are also marketers or burners of used oil fuel.[40]

13.4 Conclusion

Used oil is a valuable resource because the technology exists to recycle it. However, when used oil is disposed of improperly it becomes a threat to public health and the environment. EPA studies have found extremely high concentrations of toxic contaminants, such as lead, arsenic, cadium, halogens, and even PCB's in used oil. Such studies have found that used oil has been burned improperly, resulting in the release of these hazardous substances directly into the atmosphere, thereby causing serious air pollution problems. Moreover, those who have improperly stored or handled used oil have caused serious pollution of ground water supplies. For these reasons, EPA's recent regulations are necessary to assure protection of human health and the environment.

---

[39] 40 CFR 266.43(b)(5)(A), (B).

[40] 40 CFR 266.43(a)(1).

CHAPTER 14
UNDERGROUND STORAGE TANKS

14.1 Overview of the Underground Storage Tank Program

Industry and environmental experts have only recently recognized the important role underground storage tanks ("USTs") play in environmental contamination. Surveys by EPA discovered that USTs are a major source of ground water contamination, and EPA estimates that up to 200,000 tanks may develop leaks before 1994.[1]

To address this problem, Congress added Subtitle I ("eye") to RCRA in 1984, creating a new and comprehensive program for USTs.[2] In addition to establishing some basic parameters regarding UST ownership and operation, Subtitle I authorized EPA to promulgate regulations implementing the program. EPA has essentially completed the process, having published final regulations governing technical standards (53 Fed. Reg. 37082, codified at 40 CFR Part 280) and state program approval (53 Fed. Reg. 37212, codified at 40 CFR Part 281) for all USTs on September 23, 1988, and financial responsibility requirements for USTs containing petroleum products on October 26, 1988 (53 Fed. Reg. 43322, codified at 40 CFR Part 280, Subpt. H).[3] The emphasis has now shifted to the development and approval by EPA of state UST programs.

EPA's UST program covers virtually every aspect of tank ownership and operation. Regulations provide for notifying state agencies of the existence of tanks. Design, construction, and installation of tanks are required to conform to selected industry

---

[1]   53 Fed. Reg. 37095 (September 23, 1988).

[2]   RCRA §§ 9001-9010, 42 U.S.C. § 6991 (Supp. 1988).

[3]   The only remaining substantial piece of the regulatory program, financial responsibility regulations for hazardous substance USTs, was the subject of an Advance Notice of Proposed Rulemaking on February 9, 1988 (53 Fed. Reg. 3818). The most recent EPA regulatory agenda set September 1993 as a deadline for a proposed rulemaking. 58 Fed. Reg. 24996, 25049 (Apr. 26, 1993).

codes and the repair and closure of tanks must meet regulatory standards. To address the problem of leaking tanks, the regulations contain performance standards for new tanks to control corrosion and spills, requirements for upgrading existing tanks to new tank standards within ten years, and corrective action requirements in the event of a leak.

Lead agencies have response and enforcement options that are similar to other environmental programs, including the power to inspect sites, issue compliance orders, seek civil penalties for non-compliance, and take corrective action and recover costs from owners and operators.

Subtitle I requires owners and operators of USTs to demonstrate financial responsibility for taking corrective action and compensating third parties for damage caused by UST leaks. EPA's regulations establish financial assurance limits, describe the available assurance mechanisms, and determine when owners and operators must demonstrate responsibility.

The state program approval regulations place great emphasis on the enforcement of UST regulations by state and local agencies. EPA felt that local enforcement was the only feasible option due to the vast number of USTs and the fact that most UST owners are small enterprises unused to dealing with federal agencies. To encourage states to take the lead role, EPA will approve state programs that meet broad federal objectives rather than the line-by-line comparison familiar to other environmental programs.

The UST program has had a major impact on the petroleum marketing business as well as others. Many major companies are engaged in upgrading their tank systems and establishing leak detection and corrective action programs. The financial impact on small operations is expected to be severe, with some experts predicting that up to half of the outlets owned by independent marketers will be forced to close.[4]

14.2 Technical Standards and Corrective Action Requirements for UST Owners and Operators

RCRA Subtitle I established a number of technical standards and corrective action requirements for owners and operators of USTs. Most of these, however, were interim standards to be superseded by the promulgation of release detection, prevention, and correction regulations mandated by section 9003.[5]

The regulations developed by EPA are an exhaustive, cradle-to-grave system designed to prevent releases or minimize their damage. In most instances they rely heavily on industrial codes promulgated by recognized national organizations to provide the minute detail required for safe construction, ownership, and operation of USTs. Reflecting EPA's desire to provide flexibility and encourage new innovation, most provisions give implementing agencies the option to approve any technology that is "no less protective of human health and the environment" than the methods specified by the regulations. In general, the regulations for tanks containing petroleum and for tanks containing hazardous substances are the same, except for release detection, release reporting, and financial responsibility requirements.

---

[4] See "Underground Tank Insurance Requirements Will Cause Large-Scale Shutdowns, PMAA Says," 19 BNA Env't Rep. 2053 (Feb. 3, 1989).

[5] RCRA § 9003, 42 U.S.C. § 6991b.

14.2.1 Coverage of UST Technical Standards and Corrective Action Requirements

The scope of the technical standards and corrective action requirements encompasses "all owners and operators of a UST system."[6] The definitions of these terms -- "owner," "operator," and "UST" -- together with a number of statutory and regulatory exclusions and deferrals, determine the types of facilities that must conform to the regulations.

14.2.1.1 "Owners and Operators"

For the most part, the regulations apply to present owners and operators of USTs. But the statutory definition of "owner" has an unexpected twist: the "owner" of a UST may not be the entity who presently owns the tank and surrounding property. If a tank was not "in use" on November 8, 1984, the "owner" under the regulations is the entity that owned the tank when it was last used.[7] This distinction is important to present owners of not-in-use tanks who are faced with civil liability or tank closure requirements.[8]

The definition of "operator" is more straightforward: an operator under the statute is "any person in control of, or having responsibility for, the daily operation of" the UST.[9] EPA's regulations codify the statutory definitions without comment.

14.2.1.2 "Underground Storage Tank"

Unless a tank is excluded or deferred from the regulations, a tank is an "underground storage tank" if the volume of the tank

---

[6]   40 CFR 280.10(a).

[7]   RCRA § 9001(3), 42 U.S.C. § 6991(3).

[8]   See RCRA § 9006(d), 42 U.S.C. § 6991e(d) (civil liability attaches to "owners and operators" of tanks); 40 CFR 280.73 ("owner or operator" of systems closed before December 22, 1988, may be required to conform to closure requirements).

[9]   RCRA § 9001(4), 42 U.S.C. § 6991(3)(B).

and its piping is at least ten percent underground and it contains "regulated substances."[10] "Regulated substances" include any substance defined in CERCLA section 9601(14) -- a very broad category of hazardous substances -- and "petroleum."[11] Included in "petroleum" are petroleum-based substances derived from crude oil, such as motor fuels, jet fuels, distillate fuel oils, residual fuel oils, lubricants, petroleum solvents, and used oils.[12]

A number of types of tanks are excluded from the definition of a UST by both Subtitle I and the regulations. Among these are:

° farm or residential tanks of 1100 gallon capacity or less used for storing motor fuel for noncommercial purposes;

° tanks used for storing heating oil for consumptive use on the premises;

° septic tanks;

° regulated pipeline facilities;

° surface impoundments, pits, ponds, and lagoons;

° storm-water or wastewater collection systems;

° flow-through process tanks; and

° tanks in underground areas (such as a basement or tunnel) but sitting on a floor.[13]

In addition, some types of tanks are excluded from the technical standard and corrective action provisions. These include:

---

[10]   RCRA § 9001(1), 42 U.S.C. § 6991(1).

[11]   Id. at (2).

[12]   40 CFR 280.12.

[13]   RCRA § 9001(1)(A)-(I), 42 U.S.C. § 6991(1)(A)-(I), 40 CFR 280.11.

- ° tanks holding hazardous wastes regulated under RCRA Subtitle C or any mixture of hazardous wastes and regulated substances;

- ° tanks used for operational purposes, such as hydraulic lift tanks and electrical equipment tanks;

- ° tanks with a capacity of 110 gallons or less;

- ° tanks containing a de minimis concentration of regulated substances;[14] and

- ° emergency tanks that are emptied expeditiously after use.[15]

Tanks containing RCRA Subtitle C hazardous wastes are regulated under that program, e.g., Parts 260-271, rather than Subtitle I.

EPA also deferred several types of tanks from the regulations pending further study. These tanks, however, must still meet interim requirements governing release prevention, cathodic protection, and substance compatibility.[16] Deferred tanks include:

- ° wastewater treatment tank systems;

- ° tanks containing radioactive material;

- ° tanks that are part of emergency generators at nuclear power facilities;

- ° airport hydrant fuel systems; and

- ° field-constructed tanks.[17]

---

[14] The regulations do not prescribe a percentage cutoff for de minimis concentrations. Instead, EPA will determine on a case-by-case basis whether the concentration is "very low," poses a minimal threat, and would impose an excessive regulatory burden if included. Examples noted are storm and wastewater treatment tanks, tanks that store potable water treated with chlorine, and in-ground swimming pools.

[15] 40 CFR 280.10(b).

[16] 40 CFR 280.11.

[17] 40 CFR 280.10(c).

Some types of tanks are partially covered, excluded, or deferred. The list includes wastewater treatment tanks, emergency power generator tanks, and sumps.[18]

14.2.2 Notice Requirements

Subtitle I required owners who brought a new tank into service after May 8, 1986, to notify the appropriate state or local agency within 30 days.[19] EPA's regulations codify this requirement and include a notification form in Appendix I and a list of state agencies designated to receive notices in Appendix II.[20] Owners must provide information on a tank's ownership, age, size, type, location, uses, construction, internal and external protection, piping, installation, and release detection method.

In addition, Subtitle I required all owners of existing USTs, whether in use or not, to notify the appropriate agency of the existence of their tanks by May 8, 1986.[21] The only exceptions provided were for tanks taken out of use before January 1, 1974, for tanks that the owner knows have been removed from the ground, and for tanks already reported under CERCLA Section 103(c) (hazardous substance facilities).[22] Information required included age, size, type, location, uses, and if the tank was not in use, the date the tank was taken out of operation and the type and quantity of substances left in the tank. Owners of existing tanks who failed to meet the statutory deadline should report the existence of their tanks as soon as possible on the form provided in

---

[18]   See discussion at 53 Fed. Reg. 37108-10 (September 23, 1988).

[19]   RCRA § 9002(a)(3), 42 U.S.C. § 6991a(a)(3).

[20]   See 40 CFR 280.22. States may use forms different from EPA's as long as they contain the information required in RCRA § 9002 (42 U.S.C. § 6991a).

[21]   RCRA § 9002(a), 42 U.S.C. § 6991a(a).

[22]   RCRA § 9002(a)(2)(A), (a)(4), 42 U.S.C. § 6991a(a)(2)(A), (a)(4).

Appendix I of the regulations.[23] Knowing failure to report a tank is punishable under RCRA Section 9006(d)(1) by a fine of $10,000 per tank.

The statute and regulations include one other significant notice requirement. Beginning October 24, 1988, any person who sells an UST must notify the purchaser of the owner's obligation to notify the appropriate state agency of the tank's existence.[24] In Appendix III, EPA has provided boilerplate notice language that sellers can include in shipping tickets and invoices.

14.2.3 Requirements for New USTs

EPA's regulations establish extensive requirements that owners of new USTs must follow when purchasing, installing, and using a new tank. A UST is considered a "new tank system" if installation has commenced after December 22, 1988.[25] The following requirements must be satisfied for new tanks as long as the system is used to store regulated substances.

14.2.3.1 Design and Construction

Under the technical standards regulations, all new tanks and piping must be properly designed, constructed, and protected from

---

[23] EPA's regulations allow the use of this form to report tanks that should have been reported by May 8, 1984. See 40 CFR 280.22(a). Although these owners could be assessed a fine of up to $10,000 per tank if they knowingly failed to report, it is doubtful EPA will attempt to collect such fines from owners who voluntarily come forth at this point to report their tanks. Owners who continue to withhold information on their tanks are more likely targets of a civil penalty.

[24] RCRA § 9002(a)(6), 42 U.S.C. § 6991a(a)(6); 40 CFR 280.22(g). A similar requirement directed towards persons who deposited materials in USTs expired on May 8, 1987. See RCRA § 9002(a)(5), 42 U.S.C. § 6991a(a)(5).

[25] Installation has commenced if the owner or operator has obtained all permits and either begun construction or signed binding construction contracts. See definitions of "new tank system" and "existing tank system" under 40 CFR 280.11.

corrosion.[26] To meet these requirements, owners and operators can install one of three types of tanks that EPA found were virtually leakproof when constructed and installed properly. They include:

- fiberglass-reinforced plastic ("FRP") tanks;

- steel tanks that are cathodically protected with either a dielectric coating, a field-installed cathodic protection system, or an impressed current system; and

- a composite tank consisting of steel and FRP.

Industry codes govern the specifics for each of these options.[27]

A fourth option allows the use of a steel tank without corrosion protection, but only if a corrosion expert determines that the site is not corrosive enough to cause any corrosion leaks in the lifetime of the tank.[28] A final option is the catch-all provision that allows any other tank construction and protection that is no less protective of human health and the environment.[29]

Piping requirements are similar, except that the use of a steel-FRP composite is not included.[30]

14.2.3.2 Spill and Overfill Prevention

The regulations require owners and operators to install spill and overfill prevention equipment on all new UST systems.[31] Spill prevention equipment must prevent release of the product to the environment when the transfer hose is detached. Overfill prevention equipment must either (1) automatically shut off flow when

---

[26] 40 CFR 280.20(a), (b).

[27] See 40 CFR 280.20(a)(1)-(3).

[28] 40 CFR 280.12(a)(4).

[29] 40 CFR 280.12(a)(5).

[30] 40 CFR 280.12(b).

[31] 40 CFR 280.20(c).

THE RCRA HAZARDOUS WASTES HANDBOOK

the tank is no more than 95 percent full, or (2) alert the operator when the tank is 90 percent full by an alarm or flow restriction. These requirements are waived if the owner or operator
installs alternative but equally protective equipment or if the
UST system is filled by transfers of no more than 25 gallons at
one time.

14.2.3.3 Installation

All new UST systems must be installed in accordance with
recognized industry codes and the manufacturer's instructions.[32]
Owners and operators must supply a certification of installation
compliance with the notification form (see section 14.2.2) identifying the method used to ensure appropriate installation.[33]

14.2.3.4 Leak Detection for New UST Systems

In general, the leak detection requirements in the regulations provide for the use of regular monitoring to discover any
leaks before they cause substantial harm to the environment.
Because new tanks must meet strict design, construction, and corrosion protection standards (see section 14.2.3.1), and as a
result are essentially leakproof for at least ten years, the
requirements for new tanks are much less stringent than those
applied to existing tanks. Leak detection requirements for new
tanks are effective immediately upon installation.

In addition to the distinction between new and existing
tanks, the regulations establish more stringent leak detection
requirements for tanks containing hazardous substances than for
tanks containing petroleum substances. The former are considered
more dangerous because petroleum substances are more predictable,

---

[32] 40 CFR 280.20(d).

[33] 40 CFR 280.20(e). Owners and operators can certify appropriate installation by using a certified installer or registered
installation engineer, inspection by the implementing agency,
completion of a manufacturer's installation checklist, or any
other method equally protective.

create well-known risks, and are subject to more widely available release detection and correction equipment.[34]

14.2.3.4.1 Petroleum UST Systems

New UST systems containing petroleum require a combination of two methods of leak detection for the first ten years: monthly inventory control and tank tightness testing.[35] Monthly inventory control requires reconciliation of deliveries with withdrawals[36] while tank tightness testing involves pressure testing a tank for holes and must be performed once every five years.[37] After ten years, new tanks must be monitored every thirty days using automatic tank gauging or vapor, ground water, or interstitial monitoring.[38]

New petroleum UST system piping must also have leak detection equipment. If the piping is pressurized, it must have an automatic line leak detector attached[39] and also receive either annual tightness testing or monthly vapor, ground water, or interstitial monitoring.[40] Suction piping requires only a line tightness test

---

[34] See 53 Fed. Reg. 37116.

[35] 40 CFR 280.41.

[36] 40 CFR 280.43(a).

[37] 40 CFR 280.42(c).

[38] 40 CFR 280.41(a).

[39] EPA delayed until September 22, 1991 the deadlines for attaching automatic leak detectors that meet two of the regulatory criteria, the probability of detection and probability of false alarm requirements, to allow manufacturers more time to produce such equipment. 56 Fed. Reg. 24. Owners and operators were still required to have in place leak detection devices that met other requirements as of December 11, 1990.

[40] 40 CFR 280.41(b), 280.44. For a description of these monitoring methods, see 40 CFR 280.43; 53 Fed. Reg. 37147-51, 37157-66.

every three years or monthly monitoring, and even these are excused if the leaking substances will drain back into the tank.[41]

14.2.3.4.2 Hazardous Substance UST Systems

The periodic monitoring and tightness testing approved for new petroleum USTs were not deemed adequate to prevent harm from leaking UST systems containing hazardous substances. As a result, new hazardous substance tank systems must have either secondary containment systems, double-walled tanks, or external liners. Each of these must contain leaking substances and either detect the failure of the inner tank or be checked for evidence of a leak, as well as meet other requirements.[42] Hazardous substance UST piping must also have secondary containment and, if pressurized, have an automatic line leak detector.[43]

14.2.4 Technical Standards for Existing UST Systems

EPA has established a regulatory program designed to convert the existing inadequately designed and monitored UST universe to one in which all tanks will have leak protection and detection. The conversion will take place over a ten year period between 1988 and 1998. In the interim, leak detection is phased in based on the age of the tank.

14.2.4.1 Upgrading of Existing UST Systems

By December 22, 1998, all existing UST systems (all systems for which installation has commenced on or after December 22, 1988) must either meet new UST performance standards described in

---

[41]   40 CFR 280.41(b)(2).

[42]   40 CFR 280.42.

[43]   40 CFR 280.42(b)(4).

section 14.2.3, be upgraded as described below, or be closed permanently.[44] Some existing tanks may already meet new tank standards if they are FRP or steel-FRP composite. Most, however, are unprotected bare steel, the type of tank that is most prone to leak and which cannot easily be modified to meet the new tank requirements. The upgrading requirements in the regulations are therefore directed towards steel tanks.

The regulations provide three options for upgrading an existing steel tank. The first requires internal lining and inspection of the lining at ten years and every five years thereafter.[45] This option is not practical for many tanks because they are not designed for internal access.

The second option requires installation of cathodic protection to prevent corrosion.[46] If the tank is more than ten years old, this option is not available unless the tank can be internally inspected to ensure the integrity of the tank. Cathodic protection must be combined with an assessment for corrosion holes by either monthly monitoring (through automatic tank gauging or vapor, ground, or interstitial monitoring) or two tightness tests, one performed before installing cathodic protection, and one three

---

[44] 40 CFR 280.21(a).

[45] 40 CFR 280.21(b)(1).

[46] 40 CFR 280.21(b)(2). Cathodic protection prevents corrosion of metal tanks by overrriding the natural electrical current that flows through and corrodes underground tanks. Left to itself, a bare metal tank becomes a sort of battery, with current flowing out of one end (the anode) and into the other (the cathode). Corrosion occurs where the current leaves the tank. Cathodic protection prevents this by supplying a source of electricity to the tank, converting the entire tank into a noncorroding cathode. Two types of cathodic protection are in common use. The first is the sacrificial anode method, in which a more active block of metal is buried next to the tank to displace the tank as the anode. The second is the impressed current method, in which a source of current from the surface is delivered to the tank.

to six months afterwards.[47] The owner or operator may use an alternative method of assessing for corrosion holes if approved by the implementing agency.

The third option requires both internal lining of the tank and installation of cathodic protection.[48] No monitoring or testing (other than leak detection requirements discussed below) is required for upgrading under this option.

Metal piping must also be upgraded through installation of cathodic protection.[49] No other options are available. The regulations list codes that may be used to comply with the upgrading requirements. In addition, all existing tanks must meet the spill and overfill protection requirements for new tanks (see section 14.2.3.2) by December 22, 1998, or be closed.[50]

14.2.4.2 Leak Detection Requirements for Upgraded Tanks

In addition to the requirement that existing tanks meet new or upgraded standards in ten years, all existing tanks must meet permanent leak detection standards by December 22, 1998. These standards require monitoring for leaks every thirty days by use of automatic tank gauging, vapor monitoring, ground water monitoring, interstitial monitoring, or another equally effective method. The requirements for existing petroleum and hazardous substance tanks are the same.[51]

Both petroleum and hazardous substance existing tanks must also install temporary leak detection methods within one to five years, whether they are upgraded or not. If the tanks meet new or upgraded tank standards, they may satisfy the temporary leak

---

[47] 40 CFR 280.21(b).

[48] 40 CFR 280.21(b)(3).

[49] 40 CFR 280.21(c).

[50] 40 CFR 280.21(d).

[51] 40 CFR 280.42(a).

detection requirements by using monthly inventory control or automatic tank gauging coupled with tank tightness testing every five years.[52] This method is satisfactory until December 22, 1998, or if the tank is upgraded after December 22, 1988, for ten years after the upgrading.

If the tank does not meet new or upgraded standards, the owner or operator must use monthly inventory control or manual tank gauging and _annual_ tightness testing.[53] This method must be implemented based on the date the tank was installed as follows:[54]

Date of Installation	Date Release Detection Required
before 1965 or unknown	1989
1965-1969	1990
1970-1974	1991
1975-1979	1992
1980-1988	1993

The temporary leak detection method is satisfactory until December 22, 1998, when the owner must have upgraded the tank and installed permanent leak detection equipment or must close the tank.

Leak detection requirements for existing system piping is the same as that for new UST piping (_see_ section 14.2.3.4) and must have been installed by 1990 for all pressurized piping or, according to the above schedule, for all suction piping.[55]

14.2.5 Operational and Recordkeeping Requirements

EPA's UST regulations contain provisions governing the operation and maintenance of UST systems, as well as reporting and recordkeeping. Corrosion protection systems must be operated and

---

[52]   40 CFR 280.41(a)(1).

[53]   40 CFR 280.41(a)(2).

[54]   40 CFR 280.41(c).

[55]   40 CFR 280.41(b).

maintained appropriately and inspected periodically.[56] Substances used in USTs must be compatible with the tank liner.[57] Repairs are allowed, but only if they are performed according to industry codes, if they will prevent a release as long as the tank is in use, and if the tank is tightness tested, internally inspected, or monitored after the repair.[58] Corrosion-damaged metal piping, however, cannot be repaired and must be replaced.

Owners and operators must report to the implementing agency the existence of an UST system (see section 14.2.2), any release of product (see section 14.3.1), any corrective action taken (see section 14.3.2), and permanent closure of a tank or change in service (see section 14.2.6). In addition, owners and operators must keep documentation of corrosion protection system installation and operation, UST repairs, compliance with leak detection requirements, and the site investigation at permanent closure.[59]

14.2.6 UST Closure and Change in Service

A tank owner or operator who temporarily or permanently takes a tank out of use must comply with regulations regarding closure of a tank. The owner or operator of a tank closed temporarily for less than three months must meet all requirements governing corrosion protection, equipment maintenance, release detection, and release reporting and response.[60] If the tank is empty, release detection is not required. If the tank is closed for three to twelve months, the owner or operator must meet the above requirements, leave vent lines open and cap all other lines.[61] If the

---

[56]   40 CFR 280.31.

[57]   40 CFR 280.32.

[58]   40 CFR 280.33.

[59]   40 CFR 280.34.

[60]   40 CFR 280.70(a).

[61]   40 CFR 280.70(b).

tank is closed for more than twelve months, it must be permanently closed unless it meets new or upgraded tank standards (except spill and overfill requirements).[62]

Permanent closure of a tank requires notifying the implementing agency before closure, emptying, and cleaning the tank, removing the tank or filling it with inert material (if taking the tank out of use permanently), assessing the site for any leaked product, and completing and maintaining closure records.[63] UST systems closed prior to December 22, 1988, may have to assess the site for leakage and perform permanent closure requirements if the implementing agency decides that releases from the UST may pose a threat to human health or the environment.[64]

An owner or operator that changes the material stored in a tank from regulated to non-regulated substances must meet the requirements for a change in service. Before a change in service owners and operators must notify the agency, clean the tank, and conduct a site assessment.[65]

14.3 Release Reporting, Investigation, and Response

Owners and operators are required to respond to any actual or suspected leaks by investigating, cleaning up free product, and in most cases reporting the leak to the implementing agency. In addition, corrective action may be required to alleviate the damage caused by a leak. Specific requirements generally depend upon the results of the initial investigation.

[62] 40 CFR 280.70(c).

[63] 40 CFR 280.71.

[64] 40 CFR 280.73.

[65] 40 CFR 280.71.

14.3.1 Initial Reporting and Investigation

The owner or operator of a UST must respond immediately to all actual or suspected leaks.[66] The discovery of an actual leak (for example, by finding free product at the site or in the surrounding area) must be reported within 24 hours. A suspected leak, discovered through unusual operating conditions or monitoring equipment, must be investigated to determine whether equipment is defective.[67] Confirmed leaks must be reported within 24 hours. If further monitoring uncovers no evidence of a leak, however, no action is required.

If a leak is confirmed or suspected after further monitoring, within seven days the owner or operator must conduct tightness testing to determine whether the tank is leaking.[68] No further action is required if the test proves negative unless environmental contamination is the basis for suspecting a leak. In the event of either environmental contamination or a positive tightness test, the owner or operator must perform a site check by investigating the area around the tank where contamination is most likely to be present. If contamination is discovered, the owner or operator must begin corrective action as described below in section 14.4.2.[69]

Investigation may be required by the implementing agency if regulated substances are discovered off-site, even if the owner's UST monitoring equipment shows no evidence of a leak.[70] If so, the owner must perform both a tank tightness test and a site investigation, even if the tightness test is negative.

---

[66]   40 CFR 280.50.

[67]   40 CFR 280.50(b), (c).

[68]   40 CFR 280.52.

[69]   40 CFR 280.52.

[70]   40 CFR 280.51.

One type of leak, spills and overfills, requires special action. Any spill or overfill must be contained and cleaned up. In addition, the owner or operator must notify the implementing agency if a spill or overfill exceeds 25 gallons of petroleum product or the reportable quantity of a particular hazardous substance under CERCLA (40 CFR Part 302), or if the product cannot be cleaned up in 24 hours. Spills in excess of 25 gallons or the reportable quantity also require initiation of corrective action.[71]

14.3.2 Corrective Action

Within 24 hours of the confirmation of a release, owners and operators must report the release, take action to prevent further release, and mitigate immediate hazards such as fire or explosion.[72] Other actions are also required, unless the implementing agency directs otherwise, including initial abatement measures, site characterization, free product removal, and investigation of soil and ground water contamination.[73]

At any time during this investigation, a corrective action plan may be required by the implementing agency or submitted voluntarily by the owner or operator. The plan must provide for adequate protection of human health and the environment, but cleanup standards will be determined on a case-by-case basis. Owners and operators may begin cleanup actions before the corrective action plan is complete as long as they notify the agency and comply with any agency-imposed conditions.[74]

If a corrective action plan is required by the agency, the public has a chance to get involved. The agency must provide

---

[71]   40 CFR 280.53.

[72]   40 CFR 280.61.

[73]   40 CFR 280.62-65.

[74]   40 CFR 280.66.

notice of the release, make information available, and hold a public hearing before approving a corrective action plan.[75]

EPA has proposed a rule that would exclude petroleum contaminated soils subject to Subtitle I corrective action from the Toxicity Characteristics Rule under RCRA. 58 Fed. Reg. 8504 (Feb. 12, 1993). Without such an exclusion, soil from hundreds of thousands of UST spills would be subject to RCRA hazardous waste rules, overwhelming the hazardous waste treatment and disposal system. Id. at 8504. EPA had earlier deferred decision on UST-contaminated soils under the TC Rule (55 Fed. Reg. 11862 (March 29, 1990)), and the proposed rule would simply adopt that deferral as an exclusion.

14.4   Inspection and Enforcement Authority

Owners and operators must look first to state programs and authority to determine the extent of inspection and enforcement authority. EPA intends to rely heavily on the states to implement and enforce the UST program. States may enforce federal provisions through a cooperative agreement with EPA,[76] including recovery of expended federal trust fund moneys.[77] States may also enforce their own provisions through an EPA-approved state program that "provides for adequate enforcement of compliance."[78] If the

---

[75]   40 CFR 280.67.

[76]   See RCRA § 9003(h)(7), 42 U.S.C. § 6991b(h)(7) (state cooperative agreement program for corrective actions).

[77]   EPA plans to allow states to recover money spent from the Leaking Underground Storage Tank trust fund and keep the money to use on future cleanups. See "Cost Recovery Policy for the Leaking Underground Storage Tank Trust Fund," Office of Solid Waste and Emergency Response Directive No. 9610.10 (Oct. 7, 1988).

[78]   RCRA § 9004(a), (d), 42 U.S.C. § 6991c(a), (d).

program is approved, the state has "primary enforcement responsibility with respect to requirements of its program."[79]

EPA's authority under Subtitle I, therefore, will serve as the basis for a state cooperative agreement action, as a model for state programs, and as independent authority for EPA to act if it so chooses.[80] This section describes the types of inspection and enforcement authorities possessed by EPA and likely to be possessed at a minimum by states.

14.4.1 Inspection, Monitoring, Testing, and Corrective Action

EPA and state representatives have authority under RCRA 9005(a) to access owner and operator records, enter facilities, inspect and obtain samples, conduct monitoring and testing, and take corrective action. In addition, owners and operators must furnish any information regarding their tanks and conduct monitoring as required. Section 9005 includes a confidentiality provision designed to make records available to the public unless shown to be entitled to protection under 18 U.S.C. § 1905 (penalties for disclosure of confidential information).[81]

14.4.2 Corrective Action Authority

Under Subtitle I, EPA has authority to undertake corrective action in certain circumstances for petroleum releases[82] using

---

[79]   RCRA § 9004(d)(2), 42 U.S.C. § 6991c(d)(2).

[80]   See RCRA § 9006(a)(2), 42 U.S.C. § 6991e(a)(2) (EPA required only to give notice to state with approved program before enforcing provisions of Subtitle I in that state).

[81]   The inspection authority under this provision probably grants EPA (and state authorities operating under similar provisions) the right in an emergency to enter property, inspect, and obtain samples without a court order or warrant. See V-1 Oil Co. v. Wyoming Department of Environmental Quality, 696 F. Supp. 578 (D. Wyo. 1988).

[82]   RCRA § 9003(h)(1), 42 U.S.C. § 6991(b)(h)(1). This authority is limited to petroleum releases because hazardous substance releases are already covered by CERCLA.

funds from the Leaking Underground Storage Tank Trust Fund created by the 1986 Superfund Amendments. EPA may not undertake corrective action on its own, however, unless it is necessary to protect human health or the environment and no responsive or capable owner or operator can be found, prompt action is required to protect human health or the environment, or corrective action costs exceed the amount of financial responsibility an owner or operator is required to maintain.[83]

Because of these limits on EPA's ability to act itself, EPA's primary corrective action authority is to issue corrective action orders to owners and operators.[84] These orders may be in respect to any petroleum release and may be enforced in the same manner as compliance orders, discussed below in section 14.4.3. EPA has established a proposed rule for a streamlined internal procedure for issuing corrective action orders, similar to those used under 40 C.F.R. Part 24, that eliminate the examination of witnesses and other steps to ensure rapid response to UST releases. 55 Fed. Reg. 33430. The proposed rule has come under fire and as of this date has not been issued in final form.

States have authority under Section 9003(h)(7) to perform corrective action pursuant to a cooperative agreement with EPA whereby the state assumes EPA's enforcement role. In addition, a state can issue corrective action orders to private parties pursuant to a cooperative agreement, but only until the state's own UST program is approved.[85]

14.4.3 Compliance Orders and Civil Penalties

EPA has authority to issue compliance orders to "any person [who] is in violation of any requirement" of Subtitle I or file civil actions for "appropriate relief, including a temporary or

---

[83]   RCRA § 9003(h)(2), 42 U.S.C. § 6991(b)(h)(2).

[84]   See RCRA § 9003(h)(2), (4), 42 U.S.C. § 6991b(h)(2), (4).

[85]   RCRA § 9003(h)(4), 42 U.S.C. § 6991b(h)(4).

permanent injunction."[86] If the violation occurs in a state with an approved program, EPA must notify the state. Failure to comply with an order may result in civil penalties of up to $25,000 per day.

In addition, owners and operators are liable for other penalties. Knowing failure to report the existence of a UST may result in a fine of up to $10,000 per tank. Failure to comply with any federal UST regulation or with any approved state program standard may result in a fine of up to $10,000 for each tank for each day of violation.[87] EPA has authority to enhance the penalty if the liable party has a history of noncompliance or is uncooperative.[88]

14.4.4 Citizens Suits and Private Liability

Owners and operators of USTs may find themselves in a position to seek reimbursement of cleanup costs from other private parties who might have owned or operated the UST when the leaking occurred. Two courts have now held that the mechanism for doing so is the general citizen suit provision in RCRA Section 7002 (42 U.S.C. § 6972).

In Zands v. Nelson, 779 F. Supp. 1254 (S.D. Cal. 1991), the court held that the leaking of petroleum product from a UST is tantamount to the creation of solid waste under RCRA. As such, the disposal of such waste in the surrounding soil and groundwater requires a RCRA permit and is in violation of federal law if it occurs without a permit. As a result, leaking petroleum product will support a citizen suit under Section 7002 as a "violation of any . . . prohibition" effective pursuant to RCRA. 42 U.S.C. § 6972(1)(A). The court also held that the absence of a specific citizen suit provision in Subtitle I was no bar to such a claim

---

[86] RCRA § 9006(a), 42 U.S.C. § 6991e(a).

[87] RCRA § 9006(a)(3), (d), 42 U.S.C. § 6991e(a)(3), (d).

[88] See U.S.EPA Penalty Guidance for Violations of UST Regulations (Nov. 14, 1990).

under Section 7002. These holdings were followed in <u>Pantry, Inc.</u> <u>v. Stop-N-Go Foods</u>, No. IP 88-1345-C (S.D. Ind. June 29, 1992). would support a citizen suit, based on Stop-N-Go's violation of Kentucky's RCRA laws.

CERCLA can also provide a basis for a private right of action if the substance that leaked from the UST is a hazardous substance rather than a petroleum product. CERCLA provides a private right of cost recovery for cleanup of hazardous substances under certain circumstances. <u>See</u> 42 U.S.C. § 9607(a); <u>Amoco Oil Co. v. Borden,</u> <u>Inc.</u>, 889 F.2d 664, 668 (5th Cir. 1989). CERCLA was used in this manner in <u>Nurad, Inc. v. William E. Hooper & Sons Co.</u>, 966 F.2d 837 (4th Cir. 1992) to recover for the costs of removing leaking USTs from previous site owners and operators, including some operators who never used the tanks but were responsible for the facility when the tanks were present and leaking. <u>Id</u>. at 844-46. Because CERCLA's coverage excludes petroleum products, however (<u>see</u> 42 U.S.C. § 9601(14)), its usefulness is limited to USTs containing non-petroleum products.

14.5 Financial Responsibility Requirements

To ensure that a fund is available to pay for corrective actions and injuries to third parties, Subtitle I required EPA to promulgate regulations requiring owners and operators to maintain evidence of financial responsibility.[89] EPA published final regulations for owners and operators of petroleum tanks on October 26, 1988 (53 <u>Fed. Reg.</u> 43322, codified at 40 CFR Part 280).[90]

---

[89] RCRA § 9003(d), 42 U.S.C. § 6991b(d). The financial responsibility requirements were enacted under the Superfund Amendments and Reauthorization Act ("SARA") of 1986.

[90] The financial responsibility regulations for owners and operators of hazardous substance tanks have not yet been made final; an Advanced Notice of Public Rulemaking was issued on February 9, 1988 (53 <u>Fed. Reg.</u> 3818).

14.5.1 Applicability and Compliance Dates

Many of these smaller operators must depend on state assurance funds, but many states have not yet developed such funds. The financial responsibility requirements apply to all owners and operators of petroleum USTs that are subject to the technical standards requirements, see section 14.2.1.1, except state and federal government entities whose debts and liabilities are those of the state or the United States. USTs excluded under § 280.10(b) and (c) are also excluded from the financial responsibility requirements. See section 14.2.1.2. If the owner and operator are two entities, only one must supply evidence of financial responsibility, although both remain liable for noncompliance.

Owners of 1,000 or more petroleum USTs or with a net worth of $20 million or more must have complied by January 24, 1989. All petroleum marketing firms owning 100-999 USTs must comply by October 26, 1989. All petroleum marketing firms owning 1-12 USTs at all facilities or less than 100 at a single facility, or non-marketers whose net worth is less than $20 million (generally including small retail gasoline stations and state and local government) originally were required to comply by October 26, 1990, but EPA extended the deadline several times, most recently to December 31, 1993, due to the difficulty these smaller operators were having in obtaining insurance (56 Fed. Reg. 66369).

14.5.2 Amount and Scope of Coverage

Owners and operators must demonstrate financial responsibility for both corrective action costs and for compensating third parties for bodily injury or property damage that results from any sudden or nonsudden accidental releases from a UST.[91] The regulations establish a $500,000 per occurrence limit, except petroleum marketing facilities or other facilities that handle an average of more than 10,000 gallons per month must provide $1 million per

---

[91] 40 CFR 280.93(a).

occurrence. Annual aggregate limits are set at $1 million for owners or operators of 1 to 100 USTs and $2 million for owners or operators of 101 or more USTs.[92]

14.5.3 <u>Mechanisms of Demonstrating Financial Responsibility</u>

Owners and operators may use one or a combination of several mechanisms of demonstrating financial responsibility. The regulations list a number of options and provide limits and restrictions on the use of each. In addition, each option is accompanied by form language for the legal agreements necessary to bind a provider.

The options included in the regulations are self-insurance, obtaining a guarantee, using traditional insurance or a risk retention group, obtaining a surety bond, obtaining an irrevocable letter of credit, or establishing a trust fund. The self-insurance option is subject to the owner or operator's ability to pass a strict financial test and a guarantor must also meet the financial test.

In addition, owners and operators may use state-approved mechanisms in some cases. If the state does not have an EPA-approved UST program, and the state requires evidence of financial responsibility, a state-required financial responsibility mechanism may suffice if it is equivalent to the financial mechanisms in the federal regulations.[93] The regulations also approve the use of a state fund if it is equivalent to federally-approved mechanisms.[94] Most states now have assurance funds available to assist with cleanups.[95]

---

[92] 40 CFR 280.93(b).

[93] 40 CFR 280.100.

[94] 40 CFR 280.101.

[95] <u>See</u> "Financial Assurance Funds in Place for Most State Storage Tank Programs; Leak Detection, Prevention, Corrective Action in Formative Stages," -- BNA Env't Rp. 1882, 1883 (Nov. 20, 1992).

EPA has created four additional financial assurance mechanisms for local governments to comply. These include a bond rating test, a local government financial test, a governmental guarantee, and a maintenance of a fund balance (or any combination of the above). 58 Fed. Reg. 9026 (Feb. 18, 1993).

14.5.4 Drawing on Financial Assurance Mechanism Funds

EPA's approach to obtaining funds from a financial assurance mechanism will vary depending on the mechanism. Self-insured owners or operators are subject to cost recovery actions under RCRA § 9003(h)(6). For owners and operators who are not self-insured, Subtitle I provides broad authority for EPA to assert claims directly against "any person . . . who provides evidence of financial responsibility" if the owner or operator is insolvent.[96] EPA can require guarantors and the issuers of surety bonds and letters of credit to deposit any amount up to the occurrence or aggregate limits into a standby trust fund, accessible by EPA, to cover corrective action costs or third-party liability claims under certain circumstances.

When giving notice of cancellation, providers of assurance must allow time for owners and operators to obtain alternate mechanisms.[97] EPA may force certain providers to place necessary funds into the standby trust even after notice of cancellation if the owner or operator cannot find an alternative mechanism.[98]

14.5.5 Records and Notice of Financial Responsibility

Owners and operators must at all times maintain records demonstrating adequate financial responsibility. In addition, owners and operators must describe the method of financial assurance used when notifying the agency of a new or existing tank.

---

[96]   RCRA § 9003(d)(2), (4), 42 U.S.C. § 6991b(d)(2), (4).

[97]   40 CFR 280.105.

[98]   40 CFR 280.108.

Submission of actual documentation is required after a known or suspected release, when a provider becomes incapable of providing assurance, when a provider revokes the assurance and the owner or operator is unable to obtain alternate coverage, or when requested by the agency.

14.5.6 Failure to Assure Financial Responsibility

An owner or operator who fails to demonstrate adequate financial responsibility is subject to penalties for noncompliance.[99] These penalties can be quite severe and according to some industry experts, the inability of small operators to obtain financial assurance mechanisms will force many out of business.[100]

In addition, EPA is prohibited from expending Leaking Underground Storage Tank trust funds for cleanup activities at any site where the owner or operator failed to maintain evidence of financial responsibility.[101] EPA and the states are limited to corrective action orders issued against the owners and operators in this situation. The only exceptions are for certain limited response actions to releases that threaten human health or the environment or for full corrective actions when no solvent owner or operator can be found and the agency must respond to an imminent and substantial endangerment.

EPA has authority to suspend financial responsibility requirements in the event financial assurance mechanisms are not

---

[99]   See RCRA § 9006, 42 U.S.C. § 6991e.

[100] See "Underground Tank Insurance Requirements Will Cause Large-Scale Shutdowns, PMAA Says," 19 BNA Env't Rep. 2053 (Feb. 3, 1989).

[101] RCRA § 9003(h)(11), 42 U.S.C. § 6991b(h)(11).

available for a particular class.[102] EPA did not promulgate regulations providing for suspension along with the rest of the financial responsibility regulations but intends to do so in the future.

14.6 State Program Approval

In general, EPA established a flexible state program approval system designed to encourage states to adopt programs and to utilize methods and technology different from those in the federal program as long as they are equally protective. The regulations include both substantive standards and procedural requirements for program approval.

Subtitle I created the option of either interim or final approval. Interim approval is appropriate for states whose programs require legislative or regulatory activity to complete. States do not need "no less stringent" regulations for some parts of the program, but interim approval is good for only one to three years.

Final approval requires a "no less stringent" program of regulations and "adequate enforcement of compliance" capabilities. The technical standard requirements for "no less stringent" generally track the federal regulations but establish only minimum standard "objectives" that "do not dictate the methods the states can use in reaching these standards."[103] State enforcement provisions must include inspection, monitoring, and testing authority as well as legal authority to obtain interim relief and recover penalties.

EPA requires a Memorandum of Agreement with each approved-program state that delineates the state and federal roles.[104] States may adopt partial programs covering only petroleum tanks or

---

[102] RCRA § 9003(d)(5)(D), 42 U.S.C. § 6991b(d)(5)(D).

[103] 53 Fed. Reg. 37217.

[104] 40 CFR 281.24.

hazardous substance tanks if they choose.[105]   To date, Mississippi, New Mexico, New Hampshire, Georgia, North Dakota, Vermont, Maine, Louisiana, Maryland, Oklahoma, Rhode Island, and Washington have approved programs, and many other applications are pending.

UST owners and operators should keep in mind that all 50 states have independent UST regulatory programs that apply to UST management, even if those programs have not yet been approved by EPA.

---

[105]   RCRA § 9004(a), 42 U.S.C. § 6991c(a); 40 CFR 280.12.

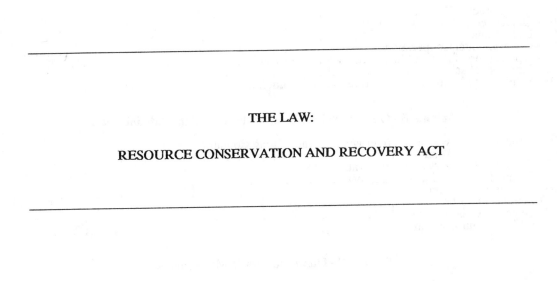

THE LAW:

RESOURCE CONSERVATION AND RECOVERY ACT

RESOURCE CONSERVATION AND RECOVERY ACT

TITLE II - Solid Waste Disposal

Subtitle A - General Provisions

Subtitle B - Office of Solid Waste; Authorities of the Administrator

Subtitle C - Hazardous Waste Management

Subtitle D - State or Regional Solid Waste Plans

Provisions That Do Not Amend RCRA

HAZARDOUS AND SOLID WASTE AMENDMENTS OF 1984

Provisions That Do Not Amend RCRA

FEDERAL FACILITY COMPLIANCE ACT

Public Law 102-386, October 6, 1992

Provisions That Do Not Amend RCRA

RESOURCE CONSERVATION AND RECOVERY ACT
(SOLID WASTE DISPOSAL ACT)

42 U.S.C. § 6901 et seq.

as amended[1]

SUBTITLE A--GENERAL PROVISIONS

CONGRESSIONAL FINDINGS

42 USC 6901

Sec. 1002. (a) Solid Waste.--The Congress finds with respect to solid waste

(1) that the continuing technological progress and improvement in methods of manufacture, packaging, and marketing of consumer products has resulted in an evermounting increase, and in a change in the characteristics, of the mass material discarded by the purchaser of such products;

(2) that the economic and population growth of our Nation, and the improvements in the standard of living enjoyed by our population, have required increased industrial production to meet our needs, and have made necessary the demolition of old buildings, the construction of new buildings, and the provision of highways and other avenues of transportation, which, together with related industrial, commercial, and agricultural operations, have resulted in a rising tide of scrap, discarded, and waste materials;

(3) that the continuing concentration of our population in expanding metropolitan and other urban areas has presented these communities with serious financial, management, intergovernmental, and technical problems in the disposal of solid wastes resulting from the industrial, commercial, domestic, and other activities carried on in such areas;

(4) that while the collection and disposal of solid wastes should continue to be primarily the function of State, regional, and local agencies, the problems of waste disposal as set forth above have become a matter national in scope and in concern and necessitate Federal action through financial and technical assistance and leadership in the development, demonstration, and application of new and improved methods and processes to reduce the amount of waste and unsalvageable materials and to provide for proper and economical solid waste disposal practices.

(b) Environment and Health.--The Congress finds with respect to the environment and health, that

(1) although land is too valuable a national resource to be needlessly polluted by discarded materials, most solid waste is disposed of on land in open dumps and sanitary landfills;

(2) disposal of solid waste and hazardous waste in or on the land without careful planning and management can present a danger to human health and the environment;

---

[1] PL 94-580, October 21, 1976, as amended by PL 95-609, the Quiet Communities Act of 1978; PL 96-463, the Used Oil Recycling Act of 1980; PL 96-482, the Solid Waste Disposal Act of 1980; PL 96-510, the Comprehensive Environmental Response, Compensation and Liability Act of 1980; PL 97-272, September 30, 1982; PL 97-375, December 21, 1982; PL 98-45, July 12, 1983; PL 98-371, July 18, 1984; 1984 Hazardous and Solid Waste Amendments, PL 98-616, November 9, 1984; PL 99-160, November 25, 1985; PL 99-339, June 19, 1986; PL 99-499, October 17, 1986; PL 100-202, December 22, 1987; PL 100-582, November 1, 1988; PL 102-386, October 6, 1992; and PL 102-389, October 6, 1992.

(3) as a result of the Clean Air Act, the Water Pollution Control Act, and other Federal and State laws respecting public health and the environment, greater amounts of solid waste (in the form of sludge and other pollution treatment residues) have been created. Similarly, inadequate and environmentally unsound practices for the disposal or use of solid waste have created greater amounts of air and water pollution and other problems for the environment and for health;

(4) open dumping is particularly harmful to health, contaminates drinking water from underground and surface supplies, and pollutes the air and the land;

(5) the placement of inadequate controls on hazardous waste management will result in substantial risks to human health and the environment;

(6) if hazardous waste management is improperly performed in the first instance, corrective action is likely to be expensive, complex, and time consuming;

(7) certain classes of land disposal facilities are not capable of assuring longterm containment of certain hazardous wastes, and to avoid substantial risk to human health and the environment, reliance on land disposal should be minimized or eliminated, and land disposal, particularly landfill and surface impoundment, should be the least favored method for managing hazardous wastes; and

(8) alternatives to existing methods of land disposal must be developed since many of the cities in the United States will be running out of suitable solid waste disposal sites within five years unless immediate action is taken.

(c) Materials.--The Congress finds with respect to materials, that

(1) millions of tons of recoverable material which could be used are needlessly buried each year;

(2) methods are available to separate usable materials from solid waste; and

(3) the recovery and conservation of such materials can reduce the dependence of the United States on foreign resources and reduce the deficit in its balance of payments.

(d) Energy.--The Congress finds with respect to energy, that

(1) solid waste represents a potential source of solid fuel, oil, or gas that can be converted into energy;

(2) the need exists to develop alternative energy sources for public and private consumption in order to reduce our dependence on such sources as petroleum products, natural gas, nuclear and hydroelectric generation; and

(3) technology exists to produce usable energy from solid waste.

CONGRESSIONAL FINDINGS: USED OIL RECYCLING

The Congress finds and declares that

(1) used oil is a valuable source of increasingly scarce energy and materials;

(2) technology exists to rerefine, reprocess, reclaim, and otherwise recycle used oil;

(3) used oil constitutes a threat to public health and the environment when reused or disposed of improperly; and that, therefore, it is in the national interest to recycle used oil in a manner which does not constitute a threat to public health and the environment and which conserves energy and materials.

OBJECTIVES AND NATIONAL POLICY

42 USC 6902

Sec. 1003. (a) Objectives.--The objectives of this Act are to promote the protection of health and the environment and to conserve valuable material and energy resources by

(1) providing technical and financial assistance to State and local governments and interstate agencies for the development of solid waste management plans (including resource recovery and resource conservation systems) which will promote improved solid waste management techniques (including more effective organizational arrangements), new and improved methods of collection, separation, and recovery of solid waste, and the environmentally safe disposal of nonrecoverable residues;

(2) providing training grants in occupations involving the design, operation, and maintenance of solid waste disposal systems;

(3) prohibiting future open dumping on the land and requiring the conversion of existing open dumps to facilities which do not pose a danger to the environment or to health;

(4) assuring that hazardous waste management practices are conducted in a manner which protects human health and the environment;

(5) requiring that hazardous waste be properly managed in the first instance thereby reducing the need for corrective action at a future date;

(6) minimizing the generation of hazardous waste and the land disposal of hazardous waste by encouraging process substitution, materials recovery, properly conducted recycling and reuse, and treatment;

(7) establishing a viable FederalState partnership to carry out the purposes of this Act and insuring that the Administrator will, in carrying out the provisions of subtitle C of this Act, give a high priority to assisting and cooperating with States in obtaining full authorization of State programs under subtitle C;

(8) providing for the promulgation of guidelines for solid waste collection, transport, separation, recovery, and disposal practices and systems;

(9) promoting a national research and development program for improved solid waste management and resource conservation techniques, more effective organizational arrangements, and new and improved methods of collection, separation, and recovery, and recycling of solid wastes and environmentally safe disposal of nonrecoverable residues;

(10) promoting the demonstration, construction, and application of solid waste management, resource recovery, and resource conservation systems which preserve and enhance the quality of air, water, and land resources; and

(11) establishing a cooperative effort among the Federal, State, and local governments and private enterprise in order to recover valuable materials and energy from solid waste.

(b) National Policy.--The Congress hereby declares it to be the national policy of the United States that, wherever feasible, the generation of hazardous waste is to be reduced or eliminated as expeditiously as possible. Waste that is nevertheless generated should be treated, stored, or disposed of so as to minimize the present and future threat to human health and the environment.

DEFINITIONS

42 USC 6903

Sec. 1004. As used in this Act:

(1) The term "Administrator" means the Administrator of the Environmental Protection Agency.

(2) The term "construction," with respect to any project of construction under this Act, means (A) the erection or building of new structures and acquisition of lands or interests therein, or the acquisition, replacement, expansion, remodeling, alteration, modernization, or extension of existing structures, and (B) the acquisition and installation of initial equipment of, or required in connection with, new or newly acquired structures or the expanded, remodeled, altered, modernized or extended part of existing structures (including trucks and other motor vehicles, and tractors, cranes, and other machinery) necessary for the proper utilization and operation of the facility after completion of the project; and includes preliminary planning to determine the economic and engineering feasibility and the public health and safety aspects of the project, the engineering, architectural, legal, fiscal, and economic investigations and studies, and any surveys, designs, plans, working drawings, specifications, and other action necessary for the carrying out of the project, and (C) the inspection and supervision of the process of carrying out the project to completion.

(2A) The term "demonstration" means the initial exhibition of a new technology process or practice or a significantly new combination or use of technologies, processes or practices, subsequent to the development stage, for the purpose of proving technological feasibility and cost effectiveness.

(3) The term "disposal" means the discharge, deposit, injection, dumping, spilling, leaking, or placing of any solid waste or hazardous waste into or on any land or water so that such solid waste or hazardous waste or any constituent thereof may enter the environment or be emitted into the air or discharged into any waters, including ground waters.

(4) The term "Federal agency" means any department, agency, or other instrumentality of the Federal Government, and any independent agency or establishment of the Federal Government including any Government corporation, and the Government Printing Office.

(5) The term "hazardous waste" means a solid waste, or combination of solid wastes, which because of its quantity, concentration, or physical, chemical or infectious characteristics may

(A) cause, or significantly contribute to an increase in mortality or an increase in serious irreversible, or incapacitating reversible, illness; or

(B) pose a substantial present or potential hazard to human health or the environment when improperly treated, stored, transported, or disposed of, or otherwise managed.

(6) The term "hazardous waste generation" means the act or process of producing hazardous waste.

(7) The term "hazardous waste management" means the systematic control of the collection, source separation, storage, transportation, processing, treatment, recovery, and disposal of hazardous wastes.

(8) For purposes of Federal financial assistance (other than rural communities assistance), the term "implementation" does not include the acquisition, leasing, construction, or modification of facilities or equipment or the acquisition, leasing, or improvement of land.

(9) The term "intermunicipal agency" means an agency established by two or more municipalities with responsibility for planning or administration of solid waste.

(10) The term "interstate agency" means an agency of two or more municipalities in different States, or an agency established by two or more States, with authority to provide for the management of solid wastes and serving two or more municipalities located in different States.

(11) The term "long term contract" means, when used in relation to solid waste supply, a contract of sufficient duration to assure the viability of a resource recovery facility (to the extent that such viability depends upon solid waste supply).

(12) The term "manifest" means the form used for identifying the quantity, composition, and the origin, routing, and destination of hazardous waste during its transportation from the point of generation to the point of disposal, treatment, or storage.

(13) The term "municipality" (A) means a city, town, borough, county, parish, district, or other public body created by or pursuant to State law, with responsibility for the planning or administration of solid waste management, or an Indian tribe or authorized tribal organization or Alaska Native village or organization, and (B) includes any rural community or unincorporated town or village or any other public entity for which an application for assistance is made by a State or political subdivision thereof.

(14) The term "open dump" means any facility or site where solid waste is disposed of which is not a sanitary landfill which meets the criteria promulgated under section 4004 and which is not a facility for disposal of hazardous waste.

(15) The term "person" means an individual, trust, firm, joint stock company, corporation (including a government corporation), partnership, association, State, municipality, commission, political subdivision of a State, or any interstate body and shall include each department, agency, and instrumentality of the United States.

(16) The term "procurement item" means any device, good, substance, material, product, or other item whether real or personal property which is the subject of any purchase, barter, or other exchange made to procure such an item.

(17) The term "procuring agency" means any Federal agency, or any State agency or agency of a political subdivision of a State which is using appropriated Federal funds for such procurement, or any person contracting with any such agency with respect to work performed under such contract.

(18) The term "recoverable" refers to the capability and likelihood of being recovered from solid waste for a commercial or industrial use.

(19) The term "recovered material" means waste material and byproducts which have been recovered or diverted from solid waste, but such term does not include those materials and byproducts generated from, and commonly reused within, an original manufacturing process.

(20) The term "recovered resources" means material or energy recovered from solid waste.

(21) The term "resource conservation" means reduction of the amounts of solid waste that are generated, reduction of overall resource consumption, and utilization of recovered resources.

(22) The term "resource recovery" means the recovery of material or energy from solid waste.

(23) The term "resource recovery system" means a solid waste management system which provides for collection, separation, recycling, and recovery of solid wastes, including disposal of nonrecoverable waste residues.

(24) The term "resource recovery facility" means any facility at which solid waste is processed for the purpose of extracting, converting to energy, or otherwise separating and preparing solid waste for reuse.

(25) The term "regional authority" means the authority established or designated under section 4006.

(26) The term "sanitary landfill" means a facility for the disposal of solid waste which meets the criteria published under section 4004.

(26A) The term "sludge" means any solid, semisolid or liquid waste generated from a municipal, commercial, or industrial wastewater treatment plant, water supply treatment plant, or air pollution control facility or any other such waste having similar characteristics and effects.

(27) The term "solid waste" means any garbage, refuse, sludge, from a waste treatment plant, water supply treatment plant, or air pollution control facility and other discarded material, including solid, liquid, semisolid, or contained gaseous material resulting from industrial, commercial, mining, and agricultural operations, and from community activities, but does not include solid or dissolved material in domestic sewage, or solid or dissolved materials in irrigation return flows or industrial discharges which are point sources subject to permits under section 402 of the Federal Water Pollution Control Act, as amended (86 Stat. 880), or source, special nuclear, or byproduct material as defined by the Atomic Energy Act of 1954, as amended (68 Stat. 923).

(28) The term "solid waste management" means the systematic administration of activities which provide for the collection, source separation, storage, transportation, transfer, processing, treatment, and disposal of solid waste.

(29) The term "solid waste management facility" includes

(A) any resource recovery system or component thereof,

(B) any system, program, or facility for resource conservation, and

(C) any facility for the collection, source separation, storage, transportation, transfer, processing, treatment, or disposal of solid wastes, including hazardous wastes, whether such facility is associated with facilities generating such wastes or otherwise.

(30) The term "solid waste planning", "solid waste management", and "comprehensive planning" include planning or management respecting resource recovery and resource conservation.

(31) The term "State" means any of the several States, the District of Columbia, the Commonwealth of Puerto Rico, the Virgin Islands, Guam, American Samoa, and the Commonwealth of the Northern Mariana Islands.

(32) The term "State authority" means the agency established or designated under section 4007.

(33) The term "storage", when used in connection with hazardous waste, means the containment of hazardous waste, either on a temporary basis or for a period of years, in such a manner as not to constitute disposal of such hazardous waste.

(34) The term "treatment", when used in connection with hazardous waste, means any method, technique, or process, including neutralization, designed to change the physical, chemical, or biological character or composition of any hazardous waste so as to neutralize such waste or so as to render such waste nonhazardous, safer for transport, amenable for recovery, amenable for storage, or reduced in volume. Such term includes any activity or processing designed to change the physical form or chemical composition of hazardous waste so as to render it nonhazardous.

(35) The term "virgin material" means a raw material, including previously unused copper, aluminum, lead, zinc, iron, or other metal or metal ore, any undeveloped resource that is, or with new technology will become a source of raw materials.

(36) The term "used oil" means any oil which has been

(A) refined from crude oil,

(B) used, and

(C) as a result of such use, contaminated by physical or chemical impurities.

(37) The term "recycled oil" means any used oil which is reused, following its original use, for any purpose (including the purpose for which the oil was originally used). Such term includes oil which is rerefined, reclaimed, burned, or reprocessed.

(38) The term "lubricating oil" means the fraction of crude oil which is sold for purposes of reducing friction in any industrial or mechanical device. Such term includes rerefined oil.

(39) The term "rerefined oil" means used oil from which the physical and chemical contaminants acquired through previous use have been removed through a refining process.

(40) Except as otherwise provided in this paragraph, the term "medical waste" means any solid waste which is generated in the diagnosis, treatment, or immunization of human beings or animals, in research pertaining thereto, or in the production or testing of biologicals. Such term does not include any hazardous waste identified or listed under subtitle C or any household waste as defined in regulations under subtitle C.

(41) The term "mixed waste" means waste that contains both hazardous waste and source, special nuclear, or by-product material subject to the Atomic Energy Act of 1954 (42 U.S.C. 2011 et seq.).

GOVERNMENTAL COOPERATION

42 USC 6904

Sec. 1005. (a) Interstate Cooperation.--The provisions of this Act to be carried out by States may be carried out by interstate agencies and provisions applicable to States may apply to interstate regions where such agencies and regions have been established by the respective States and approved by the Administrator. In such case, action required to be taken by the Governor of a State, respecting regional designation shall be required to be taken by the Governor of each of the respective States with respect to so much of the interstate region as is within the jurisdiction of that State.

(b) Consent of Congress to Compacts.--The consent of the Congress is hereby given to two or more states to negotiate and enter into agreements or compacts, not in conflict with any law or treaty of the United States, for
(1) cooperative effort and mutual assistance for the management of solid waste or hazardous waste (or both) and the enforcement of their respective laws relating thereto, and
(2) the establishment of such agencies, joint or otherwise, as they deem desirable for making effective such agreements or compacts.
No such agreement or compact shall be binding or obligatory upon any State a party thereto unless it is agreed upon by all parties to the agreement and until it has been approved by the Administrator and the Congress.

APPLICATION OF ACT AND INTEGRATION
WITH OTHER ACTS

42 USC 6905

Sec. 1006. (a) Application of Act.--Nothing in this Act shall be construed to apply to (or to authorize any State, interstate, or local authority to regulate) any activity or substance which is subject to the Federal Water Pollution Control Act (33 U.S.C. 1151 and following), the Safe Drinking Water Act (42 U.S.C. 300f and following), the Marine Protection, Research and Sanctuaries Act of 1972 (33 U.S.C. 1401 and following), or the Atomic Energy Act of 1954 (42 U.S.C. 2011 and following) except to the extent that such application (or regulation) is not inconsistent with the requirements of such Acts.

(b) Integration with Other Acts.
(1) The Administrator shall integrate all provisions of this Act for purposes of administration and enforcement and shall avoid duplication, to the maximum extent practicable, with the appropriate provisions of the Clean Air Act (42 U.S.C. 1857 and following), the Federal Water Pollution Control Act (33 U.S.C. 1151 and following), the Federal Insecticide, Fungicide, and Rodenticide Act (7 U.S.C. 135 and following), the Safe Drinking Water Act (42 U.S.C. 300f and following), the Marine Protection, Research and Sanctuaries Act of 1972 (33 U.S.C. 1401 and following) and such other Acts of Congress as grant regulatory authority to the Administrator. Such integration shall be effected only to the extent that it can be done in a manner consistent with the goals and policies expressed in this Act and in other acts referred to in this subsection.
(2)(A) As promptly as practicable after the date of the enactment of the Hazardous and Solid Waste Amendments of 1984, the Administrator shall submit a report describing
(i) the current data and information available on emissions of polychlorinated dibenzo-p-dioxins from resource recovery facilities burning municipal solid waste;
(ii) any significant risks to human health posed by these emissions; and
(iii) operating practices appropriate for controlling these emissions.
(B) Based on the report under subparagraph (A) and on any future information on such emissions, the Administrator may publish advisories or guidelines regarding the control of dioxin emissions from such facilities. Nothing in this paragraph shall be construed to preempt or otherwise affect the authority of the Administrator to promulgate any regulations under the Clean Air Act regarding emissions of polychlorinated dibenzo-p-dioxins.

(3) Notwithstanding any other provisions of law, in developing solid waste plans, it is the intention of this Act that in determining the size of a waste-to-energy facility, adequate provisions shall be given to the present and reasonably anticipated future needs, including those needs created by thorough implementation of section 6002(h), of the recycling and resource recovery interests within the area encompassed by the solid waste plan.

(c) Integration with the Surface Mining Control and Reclamation Act of 1977.--

(1) No later than 90 days after the date of enactment of the Solid Waste Disposal Act Amendments of 1980, the Administrator shall review any regulations applicable to the treatment, storage, or disposal of any coal mining wastes or overburden promulgated by the Secretary of the Interior under the Surface Mining and Reclamation Act of 1977. If the Administrator determines that any requirement of final regulations promulgated under any section of subtitle C relating to mining wastes or overburden is not adequately addressed in such regulations promulgated by the Secretary, the Administrator shall promptly transmit such determination, together with suggested revisions and supporting documentation, to the Secretary.

(2) The Secretary of the Interior shall have exclusive responsibility for carrying out any requirement of subtitle C of this Act with respect to coal mining wastes or overburden for which a surface coal mining and reclamation permit is issued or approved under the Surface Mining Control and Reclamation Act of 1977. The Secretary shall, with the concurrence of the Administrator, promulgate such regulations as may be necessary to carry out the purposes of this subsection and shall integrate such regulations with regulations promulgated under the Surface Mining Control and Reclamation Act of 1977.

FINANCIAL DISCLOSURE

42 USC 6906

Sec. 1007. (a) Statement.--Each officer or employee of the Administrator who

(1) performs any function or duty under this Act; and

(2) has any known financial interest in any person who applies for or receives financial assistance under this Act

shall, beginning on February 1, 1977, annually file with the Administrator a written statement concerning all such interests held by such officer or employee during the preceding calendar year. Such statement shall be available to the public.

(b) Action By Administrator.--The Administrator shall

(1) act within ninety days after the date of enactment of this Act

(A) to define the term 'known financial interest' for purposes of subsection (a) of this section; and

(B) to establish the methods by which the requirement to file written statements specified in subsection (a) of this section will be monitored and enforced, including appropriate provision for the filing by such officers and employees of such statements and the review by the Administrator of such statements; and

(2) report to the Congress on June 1, 1978, and of each succeeding calendar year with respect to such disclosures and the actions taken in regard thereto during the preceding calendar year.

(c) Exemption.--In the rules prescribed under subsection (b) of this section, the Administrator may identify specific positions within the Environmental Protection Agency which are of a nonpolicymaking nature and provide that officers or employees occupying such positions shall be exempt from the requirements of this section.

(d) Penalty.--Any officer or employee who is subject to, and knowingly violates this section shall be fined not more than $2,500 or imprisoned not more than one year, or both.

SOLID WASTE MANAGEMENT INFORMATION AND GUIDELINES

42 USC 6907

Sec. 1008. (a) Guidelines.--Within one year of enactment of this section, and from time to time thereafter, the Administrator shall, in cooperation with appropriate Federal, State, municipal, and intermunicipal agencies, and in consultation with other interested persons, and after public hearings, develop and publish suggested guidelines for solid waste management. Such suggested guidelines shall

(1) provide a technical and economic description of the level of performance that can be attained by various available solid waste management practices (including operating practices) which provide for the protection of public health and the environment;

(2) not later than two years after the enactment of this section, describe levels of performance, including appropriate methods and degrees of control, that provide at a minimum for (A) protection of public health and welfare; (B) protection of the quality of ground waters and surface waters from leachates; (C) protection of the quality of surface waters from runoff through compliance with effluent limitations under the Federal Water Pollution Control Act, as amended; (D) protection of ambient air quality through compliance with new source performance standards or requirements of air quality implementation plans under the Clear Air Act, as amended; (E) disease and vector control; (F) safety; and (G) esthetics; and

(3) provide minimum criteria to be used by the States to define those solid waste management practices which constitute the open dumping of solid waste or hazardous waste and are to be prohibited under subtitle D of this Act.

Where appropriate, such suggested guidelines also shall include minimum information for use in deciding the adequate location, design, and construction of facilities associated with solid waste management practices, including the consideration of regional, geographic, demographic, and climatic factors.

(b) Notice.--The Administrator shall notify the Committee on Public Works of the Senate and the Committee on Interstate and Foreign Commerce of the House of Representatives a reasonable time before publishing any suggested guidelines or proposed regulations under this Act, of the content of such proposed suggested guidelines or proposed regulations under this Act.

SUBTITLE B OFFICE OF SOLID WASTE; AUTHORITIES OF THE ADMINISTRATOR

OFFICE OF SOLID WASTE AND INTERAGENCY COORDINATING COMMITTEE

42 USC 6911

Sec. 2001. (a) Office of Solid Waste.--The Administrator shall establish within the Environmental Protection Agency an Office of Solid Waste (hereinafter referred to as the 'Office') to be headed by an Assistant Administrator of the Environmental Protection Agency. The duties and responsibilities (other than duties and responsibilities relating to research and development) of the Administrator under this Act (as modified by applicable reorganization plans) shall be carried out through the Office.

(b) Interagency Coordinating Committee.--

(1) There is hereby established an Interagency Coordinating Committee on Federal Resource Conservation and Recovery Activities which shall have the responsibility for coordinating all activities dealing with resource conservation and recovery from solid waste carried out by the Environmental Protection Agency, the Department of Energy, the Department of Commerce, and all other Federal agencies which conduct such activities pursuant to this or any other Act. For purposes of this subsection, the term "resource conservation and recovery activities" shall include, but not be limited to, all research, development and demonstration projects on resource conservation or energy, or material, recovery from solid waste, and all technical or financial assistance for State or local planning for, or implementation of, projects related to resource conservation or energy or material, recovery from solid waste. The committee shall be chaired by the Administrator of the Environmental Protection Agency or such person as the Administrator may designate. Members of the Committee shall include representatives of the Department of Energy, the Department of Commerce, the Department of the Treasury, and each other Federal agency which the Administrator determines to have programs or responsibilities affecting resource conservation or recovery.

(2) The Interagency Coordinating Committee shall include oversight of the implementation of

(A) the May 1979 Memorandum of Understanding on Energy Recovery from Municipal Solid Waste between the Environmental Protection Agency and the Department of Energy;

(B) the May 30, 1978, Interagency Agency Agreement between the Department of Commerce and the Environmental Protection Agency on the Implementation of the Resource Conservation and Recovery Act; and

(C) any subsequent agreements between these agencies or other Federal agencies which address Federal resource recovery or conservation activities.

(3) The Interagency Coordinating Committee shall submit to the Congress by March 1, 1981, and on March 1 each year thereafter, a five-year action plan for Federal resource conservation or recovery activities which shall identify means and propose programs to encourage resource conservation or material and energy recovery and increase private municipal investment in resource conservation or recovery systems, especially those which provide for material conservation or recovery as well as energy conservation or recovery. Such plan shall describe, at a minimum, a coordinated and nonduplicatory plan for resource recovery and conservation activities for the Environmental Protection Agency, the Department of Energy, the Department of Commerce, and all other Federal agencies which conduct such activities.

AUTHORITIES OF ADMINISTRATOR

42 USC 6912

Sec. 2002. (a) Authorities.--In carrying out this Act, the Administrator is authorized to

(1) prescribe, in consultation with Federal, State, and regional authorities, such regulations as are necessary to carry out his functions under this Act;

(2) consult with or exchange information with other Federal agencies undertaking research, development, demonstration projects, studies, or investigations relating to solid waste;

(3) provide technical and financial assistance to states or regional agencies in the development and implementation of solid waste plans and hazardous waste management programs;

(4) consult with representatives of science, industry, agriculture, labor, environmental protection and consumer organizations, and other groups, as he deems advisable;

(5) utilize the information, facilities, personnel and other resources of Federal agencies, including the National Bureau of Standards and the National Bureau of the Census, on a reimbursable basis, to perform research and analyses and conduct studies and investigations related to resource recovery and conservation and to otherwise carry out the Administrator's functions under this Act, and;

(6) to delegate to the Secretary of Transportation the performance of any inspection or enforcement function under this Act relating to the transportation of hazardous waste where such delegation would avoid unnecessary duplication of activity and would carry out the objectives of this Act and of the Hazardous Materials Transportation Act.

(b) Revision of Regulations.--Each regulation promulgated under this Act shall be reviewed and, where necessary, revised not less frequently than every three years.

(c) Criminal Investigations.--In carrying out the provisions of this Act, the Administrator, and duly-designated agents and employees of the Environmental Protection Agency, are authorized to initiate and conduct investigations under the criminal provisions of this Act, and to refer the results of these investigations to the Attorney General for prosecution in appropriate cases.

RESOURCE RECOVERY AND CONSERVATION PANELS

42 USC 6913

Sec. 2003. The Administrator shall provide teams of personnel, including Federal, State, and local employees or contractors (hereinafter referred to as 'Resource Conservation and Recovery Panels') to provide Federal agencies, States and local governments upon request with technical assistance on solid waste management, resource recovery, and resource conservation. Such teams shall include technical, marketing, financial, and institutional specialists, and the services of such teams shall be provided without charge to States or local governments.

[Editor's note: Public Law 97-272, an appropriations bill for the Department of Housing and Urban Development and independent agencies, provides the following concerning funds for EPA compliance activities:

ABATEMENT, CONTROL AND COMPLIANCE

For abatement, control and compliance activities, $369,075,000, to remain available until September 30, 1984: Provided, That none of these funds may be expended for purposes of Resource Conservation and Recovery Panels established under section 2003 of the Resource Conservation and Recovery Act, as amended (42 U.S.C. 6913) or for support to State, regional, local and interstate agencies in accordance with subtitle D of the Solid Waste Disposal Act, as amended, other than section 4008(a)(2) or 4009"...]

GRANTS FOR DISCARDED TIRE DISPOSAL

42 USC 6914

Sec. 2004. (a) Grants.--The Administrator shall make available grants equal to 5 percent of the purchase price of tire shredders (including portable shredders attached to tire collection trucks) to those eligible applicants best meeting criteria promulgated under this section. An eligible applicant may be any private purchaser, public body, or public-private joint venture. Criteria for receiving grants shall be promulgated under this section and shall include the policy to offer any private purchaser the first option to receive a grant, the policy to develop widespread geographic distribution of tire shredding facilities, the need for such facilities within a geographic area, and the projected risk and viability of any such venture. In the case of an application under this section from a public body, the Administrator shall first make a determination that there are no private purchasers interested in making an application before approving a grant to a public body.

(b) Authorization.--There is authorized to be appropriated $750,000 for each of the fiscal years 1978 and 1979 to carry out this section.

LABELING OF CERTAIN OIL

42 USC 6914a

Sec. 2005. For purposes of any provision of law which requires the labeling of commodities, lubricating oil shall be treated as lawfully labeled only if it bears the following statement, prominently displayed:

"DON'T POLLUTE--CONSERVE RESOURCES; RETURN USED
OIL TO COLLECTION CENTERS."

ANNUAL REPORT

42 USC 6915

Sec. 2006. The Administrator shall transmit to the Congress and the President, not later than ninety days after the end of each fiscal year, a comprehensive and detailed report on all activities of the Office during the preceding fiscal year. Each such report shall include

(1) a statement of specific and detailed objectives for the activities and programs conducted and assisted under this Act;

"(2) statements of the Administrator's conclusions as to the effectiveness of such activities and programs in meeting the stated objectives and the purposes of this Act, measured through the end of such fiscal year;

(3) a summary of outstanding solid waste problems confronting the Administrator, in order of priority;

(4) recommendations with respect to such legislation which the Administrator deems necessary or desirable to assist in solving problems respecting solid waste;

(5) all other information required to be submitted to the Congress pursuant to any other provision of this Act; and

(6) the Administrator's plans for activities and programs respecting solid waste during the next fiscal year.

GENERAL AUTHORIZATION

42 USC 6916

Sec. 2007. (a) General Administration.--There are authorized to be appropriated to the Administrator for the purpose of carrying out the provision of this Act, $35,000,000 for the fiscal year ending September 30, 1977, $38,000,000 for the fiscal year ending September 30, 1978, $42,000,000 for the fiscal year ending September 30, 1979, $70,000,000 for the fiscal year ending September 30, 1980, $80,000,000 for the fiscal year ending September 30, 1981, $80,000,000 for the fiscal year ending September 30, 1982, $70,000,000 for the fiscal year ending September 30, 1985, $80,000,000 for the fiscal year ending September 30, 1986, $80,000,000 for the fiscal year ending September 30, 1987, and $80,000,000 for the fiscal year 1988.

(b) Resource Recovery and Conservation Panels.--Not less than 20 percent of the amount appropriated under subsection (a), or $5,000,000 per fiscal year, whichever is less, shall be used only for purposes of Resource Recovery and Conservation Panels established under section 2003 (including travel expenses incurred by such panels in carrying out their functions under this Act).

(c) Hazardous Waste.--Not less than 30 percent of the amount appropriated under subsection (a) shall be used only for purposes of carrying out subtitle C of this Act (relating to hazardous waste) other than section 3011.

(d) State and Local Support.--Not less than 25 per centum of the total amount appropriated under this title, up to the amount authorized in section 4008(a)(1), shall be used only for purposes of support to State, regional, local, and interstate agencies in accordance with subtitle D of this Act other than section 4008(a)(2) or 4009.

(e) Criminal Investigators.--There is authorized to be appropriated to the Administrator $3,246,000 for the fiscal year 1985, $2,408,300 for the fiscal year 1986, $2,529,000 for the fiscal year 1987, and $2,529,000 for the fiscal year 1988 to be used

(1) for additional officers or employees of the Environmental Protection Agency authorized by the Administrator to conduct criminal investigations (to investigate, or supervise the investigation of, any activity for which a criminal penalty is provided) under this Act; and

(2) for support costs for such additional officers or employees.

(f) Underground Storage Tanks.--

(1) There are authorized to be appropriated to the Administrator for the purpose of carrying out the provisions of subtitle I (relating to regulation of underground storage tanks), $10,000,000 for each of the fiscal years 1985 through 1988.

(2) There is authorized to be appropriated $25,000,000 for each of the fiscal years 1985 through 1988 to be used to make grants to the States for purposes of assisting the States in the development and implementation of approved State underground storage tank release detection, prevention, and correction programs under subtitle I.

OFFICE OF OMBUDSMAN

42 USC 6917

Sec. 2008. (a) Establishment; Functions.--The Administrator shall establish an Office of Ombudsman, to be directed by an Ombudsman. It shall be the function of the Office of Ombudsman to receive individual complaints, grievances, requests for information submitted by any person with respect to any program or requirement under this Act.

(b) Authority to Render Assistance.--The Ombudsman shall render assistance with respect to the complaints, grievances, and requests submitted to the Office of Ombudsman, and shall make appropriate recommendations to the Administrator.

(c) Effect on Procedures for Grievances, Appeals, or Administrative Matters.--The establishment of the Office of Ombudsman shall not affect any procedures for grievances, appeals, or administrative matters in any other provision of this Act, any other provision of law, or any Federal regulation.

(d) Termination.--The Office of the Ombudsman shall cease to exist 4 years after the date of enactment of the Hazardous and Solid Waste Amendments of 1984.

SUBTITLE C--HAZARDOUS WASTE MANAGEMENT

IDENTIFICATION AND LISTING OF HAZARDOUS WASTE

42 USC 6921

Sec. 3001. (a) Criteria for Identification or Listing.--Not later than eighteen months after the date of the enactment of this Act, the Administrator shall, after notice and opportunity for public hearing, and after consultation with appropriate Federal and State agencies, develop and promulgate criteria for identifying the characteristics of hazardous waste, and for listing hazardous waste, which should be subject to the provisions of this subtitle, taking into account toxicity, persistence, and degradability in nature, potential for accumulation in tissue, and other related factors such as flammability corrosiveness, and other hazardous characteristics. Such criteria shall be revised from time to time as may be appropriate.

(b) Identification and Listing.--

(1) Not later than eighteen months after the date of enactment of this section, and after notice and opportunity or public hearing, the Administrator shall promulgate regulations identifying the characteristics of hazardous waste, and listing particular hazardous wastes (within the meaning of section 1004(5), which shall be subject to the provisions of this subtitle. Such regulations shall be based on the criteria promulgated under subsection (a) and shall be revised from time to time thereafter as may be appropriate. The Administrator, in cooperation with the Agency for Toxic Substances and Disease Registry and the National Toxicology Program, shall also identify or list those hazardous wastes which shall be subject to the provisions of this subtitle solely because of the presence in such wastes of certain constituents (such as identified carcinogens, mutagens, or teratogens) at levels in excess of levels which endanger health.

(2)(A) Notwithstanding the provisions of paragraph (1) of this subsection, drilling fluids, produced waters, and other wastes associated with the exploration, development, or production of crude oil or natural gas or geothermal energy shall be subject only to existing State or Federal regulatory programs in lieu of subtitle C until at least 24 months after the date of enactment of the Solid Waste Disposal Act Amendments of 1980 and after promulgation of the regulations in accordance with subparagraphs (B) and (C) of this paragraph. It is the sense of the Congress that such State or Federal programs should include, for waste disposal sites which are to be closed, provisions requiring at least the following:

(i) The identification through surveying, platting, or other measures, together with recordation of such information on the public record, so as to assure that the location where such wastes are disposed of can be located in the future; except however, that no such surveying, platting, or other measure identifying the location of a disposal site for drilling fluids and associated wastes shall be required if the distance from the disposal site to the surveyed or platted location to the associated well is less than two hundred linear feet; and

(ii) A chemical and physical analysis of a produced water and a composition of a drilling fluid suspected to contain a hazardous material, with such information to be acquired prior to closure and to be placed on the public record.

(B) Not later than six months after completion and submission of the tudy required by section 8002(m) of this Act, the Administrator shall, after public hearings and opportunity for comment, determine either to promulgate regulations under this subtitle for drilling fluids, produced waters, and other wastes associated with the exploration, development, or production of crude oil or natural gas or geothermal energy or that such regulations are unwarranted. The Administrator shall publish his decision in the Federal Register accompanied by an explanation and justification of the reasons for it. In making the decision under this paragraph, the Administrator shall utilize the information developed or accumulated pursuant to the study required under section 8002(m).

(C) The Administrator shall transmit his decision, along with any regulations, if necessary, to both Houses of Congress. Such regulations shall take effect only when authorized by Act of Congress.

(3)(A) Notwithstanding the provisions of paragraph (1) of this subsection, each waste listed below shall, except as provided in subparagraph (B) of this paragraph, be subject only to regulation under other applicable provisions of Federal or State law in lieu of this subtitle until at least six months after the date of submission of the applicable study required to be conducted under subsection (f), (n), (o), or (p) of section 8002 of this Act and after promulgation of regulations in accordance with subparagraph (C) of this paragraph:

(i) Fly ash waste, bottom ash waste, slag waste, and flue gas emission control waste generated primarily from the combustion of coal or other fossil fuels.

(ii) Solid waste from the extraction, beneficiation, and processing of ores and minerals, including phosphate rock and overburden from the mining of uranium ore.

(iii) Cement kiln dust waste.

(B)(i) Owners and operators of disposal sites for wastes listed in subparagraph (A) may be required by the Administrator, through regulations prescribed under authority of section 2002 of this Act--

(I) as to disposal sites for such wastes which are to be closed, to identify the locations of such sites through surveying, platting, or other measures, together with recordation of such information on the public record, to assure that the locations where such wastes are disposed of are known and can be located in the future, and

(II) to provide chemical and physical analysis and composition of such wastes, based on available information, to be placed on the public record.

(ii)(I) In conducting any study under subsection (f), (n), (o), or (p), of section 8002 of this Act, any officer, employee, or authorized representative of the Environmental Protection Agency, duly designated by the Administrator, is authorized, at reasonable times and as reasonably necessary for the purposes of such study, to enter any establishment where any waste subject to such study is generated, stored, treated, disposed of, or transported from; to inspect, take samples, and conduct monitoring and testing; and to have access to and copy records relating to such waste. Each such inspection shall be commenced and completed with reasonable promptness. If the officer, employee, or authorized representative obtains any samples prior to leaving the premises, he shall give to the owner, operator, or agent in charge a receipt describing the sample obtained and if requested a portion of each such sample equal in volume or weight to the portion retained. If any analysis is made of such samples, or monitoring and testing performed, a copy of the results shall be furnished promptly to the owner, operator, or agent in charge.

(II) Any records, reports, or information obtained from any person under subclause (I) shall be available to the public, except that upon a showing satisfactory to the Administrator by any person that records, reports, or information, or particular part thereof, to which the Administrator has access under this subparagraph if made public, would divulge information entitled to protection under section 1905 of title 18 of the United States Code, the Administrator shall consider such information or particular portion thereof confidential in accordance with the purposes of that section, except that such record, report, document, or information may be disclosed to other officers, employees, or authorized representatives of the United States concerned with carrying out this Act. Any person not subject to the provisions of section 1905 of title 18 of the United States Code who knowingly and willfully divulges or discloses any information entitled to protection under this subparagraph shall, upon conviction, be subject to a fine of not more than $5,000 or to imprisonment not to exceed one year, or both.

(iii) The Administrator may prescribe regulations, under the authority of this Act, to prevent radiation exposure which presents an unreasonable risk to human health from the use in construction or land reclamation (with or without revegetation) of (I) solid waste from the extraction, beneficiation, and processing of phosphate rock or (II) overburden from the mining of uranium ore.

(iv) Whenever on the basis of any information the Administrator determines that any person is in violation of any requirement of this subparagraph, the Administrator shall give notice to the violator of his failure to comply with such requirement. If such violation extends beyond the thirtieth day after the Administrator's notification, the Administrator may issue an order requiring compliance within a specified time period or the Administrator may commence a civil action in the United States district court in the district in which the violation occurred for appropriate relief, including a temporary or permanent injunction.

(C) not later than six months after the date of submission of the applicable study required to be conducted under subsection (f), (n), (o), or (p), of section 8002 of this Act, the Administrator shall, after public hearings and opportunity for comment, either determine to promulgate regulations under this subtitle for each waste listed in subparagraph (A) of this paragraph or determine that such regulations are unwarranted. The Administrator shall publish his determination, which shall be based on information developed or accumulated pursuant to such study, public hearings, and comment, in the Federal Register accompanied by an explanation and justification of the reasons for it.

(c) Petition by State Governor.--At any time after the date eight-
een months after the enactment of this title, the Governor of any State may petition the Administrator to identify or list a material as a hazardous waste. The Administrator shall act upon such petition within ninety days following his receipt thereof and shall notify the Governor of such action. If the Administrator denies such petition because of financial considerations, in providing such notice to the Governor, he shall include a statement concerning such considerations.

(d) Small Quantity Generator Waste.--

(1) By March 31, 1986, the Administrator shall promulgate standards under sections 3002, 3003, and 3004 for hazardous waste generated by a generator in a total quantity of hazardous waste greater than 100 kilograms but less than 1,000 kilograms during a calendar month.

(2) The standards referred to in paragraph (1), including standards applicable to the legitimate use, reuse, recycling, and reclamation of such wastes, may vary from the standards applicable to hazardous waste generated by larger quantity generators, but such standards shall be sufficient to protect human health and the environment.

(3) Not later than 270 days after the enactment of the Hazardous and Solid Waste Amendments of 1984 any hazardous waste which is part of a total quantity generated by a generator generating greater than 100 kilograms but less than 1,000 kilograms during one calendar month and which is shipped off the premises on which such waste is generated shall be accompanied by a copy of the Environmental Protection Agency Uniform Hazardous Waste Manifest form signed by the generator. This form shall contain the following information:

(A) the name and address of the generator of the waste;

(B) the United States Department of Transportation description of the waste, including the proper shipping name, hazard class, and identification number (UN/NA), if applicable;

(C) the number and type of containers;

(D) the quantity of waste being transported; and

(E) the name and address of the facility designated to receive the waste.

If subparagraph (B) is not applicable, in lieu of the description referred to in such subparagraph (B), the form shall contain the Environmental Protection Agency identification number, or a generic description of the waste, or a description of the waste by hazardous waste characteristic. Additional requirements related to the manifest form shall apply only if determined necessary by the Administrator to protect human health and the environment.

(4) The Administrator's responsibility under this subtitle to protect human health and the environment may require the promulgation of standards under this subtitle for hazardous wastes which are generated by any generator who does not generate more than 100 kilograms of hazardous waste in a calendar month.

(5) Until the effective date of standards required to be promulgated under paragraph (1), any hazardous waste identified or listed under section 3001 generated by any generator during any calendar month in a total quantity greater than 100 kilograms but less than 1,000 kilograms, which is not treated, stored, or disposed of at a hazardous waste treatment, storage, or disposal facility with a permit under section 3005, shall be disposed of only in a facility which is permitted, licensed, or registered by a State to manage municipal or industrial solid waste.

(6) Standards promulgated as provided in paragraph (1) shall, at a minimum, require that all treatment, storage, or disposal of hazardous wastes generated by generators referred to in paragraph (1) shall occur at a facility with interim status or a permit under this subtitle, except that onsite storage of hazardous waste generated by a generator generating a total quantity of hazardous waste greater than 100 kilograms, but less than 1,000 kilograms during a calendar month, may occur without the requirement of a permit for up to 180 days. Such onsite storage may occur without the requirement of a permit for not more than 6,000 kilograms for up to 270 days if such generator must ship or haul such waste over 200 miles.

(7)(A) Nothing in this subsection shall be construed to affect or impair the validity of regulations promulgated by the Secretary of Transportation pursuant to the Hazardous Materials Transportation Act.

(B) Nothing in this subsection shall be construed to affect, modify, or render invalid any requirements in regulations promulgated prior to January 1, 1983 applicable to any acutely hazardous waste identified or listed under section 3001 which is generated by any generator during any calendar month in a total quantity less than 1,000 kilograms.

(8) Effective March 31, 1986, unless the Administrator promulgates standards as provided in paragraph (1) of this subsection prior to such date, hazardous waste generated by any generator in a total quantity greater than 100 kilograms but less than 1,000 kilograms during a calendar month shall be subject to the following requirements until the standards referred to in paragraph (1) of this subsection have become effective:

(A) the notice requirements of paragraph (3) of this subsection shall apply and in addition, the information provided in the form shall include the name of the waste transporters and the name and address of the facility designated to receive the waste;

(B) except in the case of the onsite storage referred to in paragraph (6) of this subsection, the treatment, storage, or disposal of such waste shall occur at a facility with interim status or a permit under this subtitle;

(C) generators of such waste shall file manifest exception reports as required of generators producing greater amounts of hazardous waste per month except that such reports shall be filed by January 31, for any waste shipment occurring in the last half of the preceding calendar year, and by July 31, for any waste shipment occurring in the first half of the calendar year; and

(D) generators of such waste shall retain for 3 years a copy of the manifest signed by the designated facility that has received the waste.

Nothing in this paragraph shall be construed as a determination of the standards appropriate under paragraph (1).

(9) The last sentence of section 3010(b) shall not apply to regulations promulgated under this subsection.

[Ed. Note: Section 2(j) of the Hazardous and Solid Waste Amendments of 1984 authorizes the following appropriation:

There is authorized to be appropriated for purposes of section 221(b) of this Act (entitled "Small Quantity Generator Waste") $500,000 for each of the fiscal years 1985 through 1987."]

(e) Specified Wastes.--

(1) Not later than 6 months after the date of enactment of the Hazardous and Solid Waste Amendments of 1984, the Administrator shall, where appropriate, list under subsection (b)(1), additional wastes containing chlorinated dioxins or chlorinated-dibenzofurans. Not later than one year after the date of enactment of the Hazardous and Solid Waste Amendments of 1984, the Administrator shall, where appropriate, list under subsection (b)(1) wastes containing remaining halogenated dioxins and halogenated-dibenzofurans.

(2) Not later than 15 months after the date of enactment of the Hazardous and Solid Waste Amendments of 1984, the Administrator shall make a determination of whether or not to list under subsection (b)(1) the following wastes: Chlorinated Aliphatics, Dioxin, Dimethyl Hydrazine, TDI (toluene diisocyanate), Carbamates,

Bromacil, Linuron, Organo-bromines, solvents, refining wastes, chlorinated aromatics, dyes and pigments, inorganic chemical industry wastes, lithium batteries, coke byproducts, paint production wastes, and coal slurry pipeline effluent.

(f) Delisting Procedures.--

(1) When evaluating a petition to exclude a waste generated at a particular facility from listing under this section, the Administrator shall consider factors (including additional constituents) other than those for which the waste was listed if the Administrator has a reasonable basis to believe that such additional factors could cause the waste to be a hazardous waste. The Administrator shall provide notice and opportunity for comment on these additional factors before granting or denying such petition.

(2)(A) To the maximum extent practicable the Administrator shall publish in the Federal Register a proposal to grant or deny a petition referred to in paragraph (1) within 12 months after receiving a complete application to exclude a waste generated at a particular facility from being regulated as a hazardous waste and shall grant or deny such a petition within 24 months after receiving a complete application.

(B) The temporary granting of such a petition prior to the enactment of the Hazardous and Solid Waste Amendments of 1984 without the opportunity for public comment and the full consideration of such comments shall not continue for more than 24 months after the date of enactment of the Hazardous and Solid Waste Amendments of 1984. If a final decision to grant or deny such a petition has not been promulgated after notice and opportunity for public comment within the time limit prescribed by the preceding sentence, any such temporary granting of such petition shall cease to be in effect.

(g) EP Toxicity.--Not later than 28 months after the date of enactment of the Hazardous and Solid Waste Amendments of 1984 the Administrator shall examine the deficiencies of the extraction procedure toxicity characteristic as a predictor of the leaching potential of wastes and make changes in the extraction procedure toxicity characteristic, including changes in the leaching media, as are necessary to insure that it accurately predicts the leaching potential of wastes which pose a threat to human health and the environment when mismanaged.

(h) Additional Characteristics.--Not later than 2 years after the date of enactment of the Hazardous and Solid Waste Amendments of 1984, the Administrator shall promulgate regulations under this section identifying additional characteristics of hazardous waste, including measures or indicators of toxicity.

(i) Clarification of Household Waste Exclusion.---A resource recovery facility recovering energy from the mass burning of municipal solid waste shall not be deemed to be treating, storing, disposing of, or otherwise managing hazardous wastes for the purposes of regulation under this subtitle, if-

(1) such facility--

(A) receives and burns only--

(i) household waste (from single and multiple dwellings, hotels, motels, and other residential sources), and

(ii) solid waste from commercial or industrial sources that does not contain hazardous waste identified or listed under this section, and

(B) does not accept hazardous wastes identified or listed under this section, and

(2) the owner or operator of such facility has established contractual requirements or other appropriate notification or inspection procedures to assure that hazardous wastes are not received at or burned in such facility.

STANDARDS APPLICABLE TO GENERATORS
OF HAZARDOUS WASTE

42 USC 6922

Sec. 3002. (a) In General.--Not later than eighteen months after the date of the enactment of this section, and after notice and opportunity for public hearings and after consultation with appropriate Federal and State agencies, the Administrator shall promulgate regulations establishing such standards, applicable to generators of hazardous waste identified or listed under this subtitle, as may be necessary to protect human health and the environment. Such standards shall establish requirements respecting--

(1) recordkeeping practices that accurately identify the quantities of such hazardous waste generated, the constituents thereof which are significant in quantity or in potential harm to human health or the environment, and the disposition of such wastes;

(2) labeling practices for any containers used for the storage, transport, or disposal of such hazardous waste such as will identify accurately such waste;

(3) use of appropriate containers for such hazardous waste;

(4) furnishing of information on the general chemical composition of such hazardous waste to persons transporting, treating, storing, or disposing of such wastes;

(5) use of a manifest system and any other reasonable means necessary to assure that all such hazardous waste generated is designated for treatment, storage, or disposal in, and arrives at treatment, storage, or disposal facilities (other than facilities on the premises where the waste is generated) for which a permit has been issued as provided in this subtitle, or pursuant to title I of the Marine Protection, Research, and Sanctuaries Act (86 Stat. 1052); and

(6) submission of reports to the Administrator (or the State agency in any case in which such agency carries out a permit program pursuant to this subtitle) at least once every 2 years, setting out--

(A) the quantities and nature of hazardous waste identified or listed under this subtitle that he has generated during the year;

(B) the disposition of all hazardous waste reported under subparagraph (A);

(C) the efforts undertaken during the year to reduce the volume and toxicity of waste generated; and

(D) the changes in volume and toxicity of waste actually achieved during the year in question in comparison with previous years, to the extent such information is available for years prior to enactment of the Hazardous and Solid Waste Amendments of 1984.

(b) Waste Minimization.--Effective September 1, 1985, the manifest re-quired by subsection (a)(5) shall contain a certification by the generator that--

(1) the generator of the hazardous waste has a program in place to reduce the volume or quantity and toxicity of such waste to the degree determined by the generator to be economically practicable; and

(2) the proposed method of treatment, storage, or disposal is that practicable method currently available to the generator which minimizes the present and future threat to human health and the environment.

STANDARDS APPLICABLE TO TRANSPORTERS OF HAZARDOUS WASTE

42 USC 6923

Sec. 3003. (a) Standards.--Not later than eighteen months after the date of enactment of this section, and after opportunity for public hearings, the Administrator, after consultation with the Secretary of Transportation and the States, shall promulgate regulations establishing such standards, applicable to transporters of hazardous waste identified or listed under this subtitle, as may be necessary to protect human health and the environment. Such standards shall include but need not be limited to requirements respecting--

(1) recordkeeping concerning such hazardous waste transported, and their source and delivery points;

(2) transportation of such waste only if properly labeled;

(3) compliance with the manifest system referred to in section 3002(5); and

(4) transportation of all such hazardous waste only to the hazardous waste treatment, storage, or disposal facilities which the shipper designates on the manifest form to be a facility holding a permit issued under this subtitle, or pursuant to title I of the Marine Protection, Research, and Sanctuaries Act (86 Stat. 1052).

(b) Coordination with Regulations of Secretary of Transportation.--In case of any hazardous waste identified or listed under this subtitle which is subject to the Hazardous Materials Transportation Act (88 Stat. 2156; 49 U.S.C. 1801 and following), the regulations promulgated by the Administrator under this section shall be consistent with the require-ments of such Act and the regulations thereunder. The Administrator is authorized to make recommendations to the Secretary of Transportation respecting the regulations of such hazardous waste under the Hazardous Materials Transportation Act and for addition of materials to be covered by such Act.

(c) Fuel from Hazardous Waste.--Not later than 2 years after the date of enactment of the Hazardous and Solid Waste Amendments of 1984, and after opportunity for public hearing, the Administrator shall promulgate regulations establishing standards, applicable to transporters of fuel produced (1) from any hazardous waste identified or listed under section 3001, or (2) from any hazardous waste identified or listed under section 3001 and any other material, as may be necessary to protect human health and the environment. Such standards may include any of the requirements set forth in paragraphs (1) through (4) of subsection (a) as may be appropriate.

STANDARDS APPLICABLE TO OWNERS AND OPERATORS OF HAZARDOUS WASTE TREATMENT, STORAGE, AND DISPOSAL FACILITIES

42 USC 6924

Sec. 3004. (a) In General.--Not later than eighteen months after the date of enactment of this section, and after opportunity for public hearings and after consultation with appropriate Federal and State agencies, the Administrator shall promulgate regulations establishing such performance standards, applicable to owners and operators of facilities for the treatment, storage, or disposal of hazardous waste identified or listed under this subtitle, as may be necessary to protect human health and the environment. In establishing such standards the Administrator shall, where appropriate, distinguish in such standards between requirements appropriate for new facilities and for facilities in existence on the date of promulgation of such regulations. Such standards shall include, but need not be limited to, requirements respecting--

(1) maintaining records of all hazardous wastes identified or listed under this title which is treated, stored, or disposed of, as the case may be, and the manner in which such wastes were treated, stored, or disposed of;

(2) satisfactory reporting, monitoring, and inspection and compliance with the manifest system referred to in section 3002(5);

(3) treatment, storage, or disposal of all such waste received by the facility pursuant to such operating methods, techniques, and practices as may be satisfactory to the Administrator;

(4) the location, design, and construction of such hazardous waste treatment, disposal, or storage facilities;

(5) contingency plans for effective action to minimize unanticipated damage from any treatment, storage, or disposal of any such hazardous waste;

(6) the maintenance of operation of such facilities and requiring such additional qualifications as to ownership, continuity of operation, training for personnel, and financial responsibility (including financial responsibility for corrective action) as may be necessary or desirable; and

(7) compliance with the requirements of section 3005 respecting permits for treatment, storage, or disposal.

No private entity shall be precluded by reason of criteria established under paragraph (6) from the ownership or operation of facilities providing hazardous waste treatment, storage, or disposal services where such entity can provide assurances of financial responsibility and continuity of operation consistent with the degree and duration of risks asso-ciated with the treatment, storage, or disposal of specified hazardous waste.

(b) Salt Dome Formations, Salt Bed Formations, Underground Mines and Caves.--

(1) Effective on the date of the enactment of the Hazardous and Solid Waste Amendments of 1984, the placement of any noncontainerized or bulk liquid hazardous waste in any salt dome formation, salt bed formation, underground mine, or cave is prohibited until such time as--

(A) the Administrator has determined, after notice and opportunity for hearings on the record in the affected areas, that such placement is protective of human health and the environment;

(B) the Administrator has promulgated performance and permitting standards for such facilities under this subtitle; and

(C) a permit has been issued under section 3005 (c) for the facility concerned.

(2) Effective on the date of enactment of the Hazardous and Solid Waste Amendments of 1984, the placement of any hazardous waste other than a hazardous waste referred to in paragraph (1) in a salt dome formation, salt bed formation, underground mine, or cave is prohibited until such time as a permit has been issued under section 3005(c) for the facility concerned.

(3) No determination made by the Administrator under subsection (d), (e), or (g) of this section regarding any hazardous waste to which such subsection (d), (e), or (g) applies shall affect the prohibition contained in paragraph (1) or (2) of this subsection.

(4) Nothing in this subsection shall apply to the Department of Energy Waste Isolation Pilot Project in New Mexico.

(c) Liquids in Landfills.--

(1) Effective 6 months after the date of the enactment of the Hazardous and Solid Waste Amendments of 1984, the placement of bulk or noncontainerized liquid hazardous waste or free liquids contained in hazardous waste (whether or not absorbents have been added) in any landfill is prohibited. Prior to such date the requirements (as in effect on April 30, 1983) promulgated under this section by the Administrator regarding liquid hazardous waste shall remain in force and effect to the extent such requirements are applicable to the placement of bulk or noncontainerized liquid hazardous waste, or free liquids contained in hazardous waste, in landfills.

(2) Not later than 15 months after the date of the enactment of the Hazardous and Solid Waste Amendments of 1984, the Administrator shall promulgate final regulations which--

(A) minimize the disposal of containerized liquid hazardous waste in landfills, and

(B) minimize the presence of free liquids in containerized hazardous waste to be disposed of in landfills.

Such regulations shall also prohibit the disposal in landfills of liquids that have been absorbed in materials that biodegrade or that release liquids when compressed as might occur during routine landfill operations. Prior to the date on which such final regulations take effect, the requirements (as in effect on April 30, 1983) promulgated under this section by the Administrator shall remain in force and effect to the extent such requirements are applicable to the disposal of containerized liquid hazardous waste, or free liquids contained in hazardous waste, in landfills.

(3) Effective 12 months after the date of the enactment of the Hazardous and Solid Waste Amendments of 1984, the placement of any liquid which is not a hazardous waste in a landfill for which a permit is required under section 3005(c) or which is operating pursuant to interim status granted under section 3005(e) is prohibited unless the owner or operator of such landfill demonstrates to the Administrator, or the Administrator determines, that--

(A) the only reasonably available alternative to the placement in such landfill is placement in a landfill or unlined surface impoundment, whether or not permitted under section 3005(c) or operating pursuant to interim status under section 3005(e), which contains, or may reasonably be anticipated to contain, hazardous waste; and

(B) placement in such owner or operator's landfill will not present a risk of contamination of any underground source of drinking water.

As used in subparagraph (B), the term "underground source of drinking water" has the same meaning as provided in regulations under the Safe Drinking Water Act (title XIV of the Public Health Service Act).

(4) No determination made by the Administrator under subsection (d), (e), or (g) of this section regarding any hazardous waste to which such subsection (d), (e), or (g) applies shall affect the prohibition contained in paragraph (1) of this subsection.

(d) Prohibitions on Land Disposal of Specified Wastes.--

(1) Effective 32 months after the enactment of the Hazardous and Solid Waste Amendments of 1984 (except as provided in subsection (f) with respect to underground injection into deep injection wells), the land disposal of the hazardous wastes referred to in paragraph (2) is prohibited unless the Administrator determines the prohibition on one or more methods of land disposal of such waste is not required in order to protect human health and the environment for as long as the waste remains hazardous, taking into account--

(A) the long-term uncertainties associated with land disposal,

(B) the goal of managing hazardous waste in an appropriate manner in the first instance, and

(C) the persistence, toxicity, mobility, and propensity to bioaccumulate of such hazardous wastes and their hazardous constituents.

For the purposes of this paragraph, a method of land disposal may not be determined to be protective of human health and the environment for a hazardous waste referred to in paragraph (2) (other than a hazardous waste which has complied with the pretreatment regulations promulgated under section (m)), unless, upon application by an interested person, it has been demonstrated to the Administrator, to a reasonable degree of certainty, that there will be no migration of hazardous constituents from the disposal unit or injection zone for as long as the wastes remain hazardous.

(2) Paragraph (1) applies to the following hazardous wastes listed or identified under section 3001:

(A) Liquid hazardous wastes, including free liquids associated with any solid or sludge, containing free cyanides at concentrations greater than or equal to 1,000 mg/l.

(B) Liquid hazardous wastes, including free liquids associated with any solid or sludge, containing the following metals (or elements) or compounds of these metals (or elements) at concentrations greater than or equal to those specified below:

(i) arsenic and/or compounds (as As) 500 mg/l;

(ii) cadmium and/or compounds (as Cd) 100 mg/l;

(iii) chromium (VI and/or compounds (as Cr VI)) 500 mg/l;

(iv) lead and/or compounds (as Pb) 500 mg/l;

(v) mercury and/or compounds (as Hg) 20 mg/l;

(vi) nickel and/or compounds (as Ni) 134 mg/l;

(vii) selenium and/or compounds (as Se) 100 mg/l; and

(viii) thallium and/or compounds (as Th) 130 mg/l.

(C) Liquid hazardous waste having a pH less than or equal to two (2.0).

(D) Liquid hazardous wastes containing polychlorinated biphenyls at concentrations greater than or equal to 50 ppm.

(E) Hazardous wastes containing halogenated organic compounds in total concentration greater than or equal to 1,000 mg/kg.

When necessary to protect human health and the environment, the Administrator shall substitute more stringent concentration levels than the levels specified in subparagraphs (A) through (E).

(3) During the period ending 48 months after the date of the enactment of the Hazardous and Solid Waste Amendments of 1984, this subsection shall not apply to any disposal of contaminated soil or debris resulting from a response action taken under section 104 or 106 of the Comprehensive Environmental Response, Compensation, and Liability Act of 1980 or a corrective action required under this subtitle.

(e) Solvents and Dioxins.--

(1) Effective 24 months after the date of enactment of the Hazardous and Solid Waste Amendments of 1984 (except as provided in subsection (f) with respect to underground injection into deep injection wells), the land disposal of the hazardous wastes referred to in paragraph (2) is prohibited unless the Administrator determines the prohibition of one or more methods of land disposal of such waste is not required in order to protect human health and the environment for as long as the waste remains hazardous, taking into account the factors referred to in subparagraph (A) through (C) of subsection (d)(1). For the purposes of this paragraph, a method of land disposal may not be determined to be protective of human health and the environment for a hazardous waste referred to in paragraph (2) (other than a hazardous waste which has complied with the pretreatment regulations promulgated under subsection (m)), unless upon application by an interested person it has been demonstrated to the Administrator, to a reasonable degree of certainty, that there will be no migration of hazardous constituents from the disposal unit or injection zone for as long as the wastes remain hazardous.

(2) The hazardous wastes to which the prohibition under paragraph (1) applies are as follows--

(A) dioxin-containing hazardous wastes numbered F020, F021, F022, and F023 (as referred to in the proposed rule published by the Administrator in the Federal Register for April 4, 1983), and

(B) those hazardous wastes numbered F001, F002, F003, F004, and F005 in regulations promulgated by the Administrator under section 3001 (40 C.F.R. 261.31 (July 1, 1983)), as those regulations are in effect on July 1, 1983.

(3) During the period ending 48 months after the date of the enactment of the Hazardous and Solid Waste Amendments of 1984, this subsection shall not apply to any disposal of contaminated soil or debris resulting from a response action taken under section 104 or 106 of the Comprehensive Environmental Response, Compensation, and Liability Act of 1980 or a corrective action required under this subtitle.

(f) Disposal Into Deep Injection Wells; Specified
      Subsection (d) Wastes; Solvents and Dioxins.--

(1) Not later than 45 months after the date of enactment of the Hazardous and Solid Waste Amendments of 1984, the Administrator shall complete a review of the disposal of all hazardous wastes referred to in paragraph (2) of subsection (d) and in paragraph (2) of subsection (e) by underground injection into deep injection wells.

(2) Within 45 months after the date of the enactment of the Hazardous and Solid Waste Amendments of 1984, the Administrator shall make a determination regarding the disposal by underground injection into deep injection wells of the hazardous wastes referred to in paragraph (2) of subsection (d) and the hazardous wastes referred to in paragraph (2) of subsection (e). The Administrator shall promulgate final regulations prohibiting the disposal of such wastes into such wells if it may reasonably be determined that such disposal may not be protective of human health and the environment for as long as the waste remains hazardous, taking into account the factors referred to in subparagraphs (A) through (C) of subsection (d)(1). In promulgating such regulations, the Administrator shall consider each hazardous waste referred to in paragraph (2) of subsection (d) or in paragraph (2) of subsection (e) which is prohibited from disposal into such wells by any State.

(3) If the Administrator fails to make a determination under paragraph (2) for any hazardous waste referred to in paragraph (2) of subsection (d) or in paragraph (2) of subsection (e) within 45 months after the date of enactment of the Hazardous and Solid Waste Amendments of 1984, such hazardous waste shall be prohibited from disposal into any deep injection well.

(4) As used in this subsection, the term "deep injection well" means a well used for the underground injection of hazardous waste other than a well to which section 7010(a) applies.

(g) Additional Land Disposal Prohibition
      Determinations

(1) Not later than 24 months after the date of enactment of the Hazardous and Solid Waste Amendments of 1984, the Administrator shall submit a schedule to Congress for--

    (A) reviewing all hazardous wastes listed (as of the date of the enactment of the Hazardous and Solid Waste Amendments of 1984) under section 3001 other than those wastes which are referred to in subsection (d) or (e); and

    (B) taking action under paragraph (5) of this subsection with respect to each such hazardous waste.

(2) The Administrator shall base the schedule on a ranking of such listed wastes considering their intrinsic hazard and their volume such that decisions regarding the land disposal of high volume hazardous wastes with high intrinsic hazard shall, to the maximum extent possible, be made by the date 45 months after the date of enactment of the Hazardous and Solid Waste Amendments of 1984. Decisions regarding low volume hazardous wastes with lower intrinsic hazard shall be made by the date 66 months after such date of enactment.

(3) The preparation and submission of the schedule under this subsection shall not be subject to the Paperwork Reduction Act of 1980. No hearing on the record shall be required for purposes of preparation or submission of the schedule. The schedule shall not be subject to judicial review.

(4) The schedule under this subsection shall require that the Administrator shall promulgate regulations in accordance with paragraph (5) or make a determination under paragraph (5)

    (A) for at least one-third of all hazardous wastes referred to in paragraph (1) by the date 45 months after the date of enactment of the Hazardous and Solid Waste Amendments of 1984;

    (B) for at least two-thirds of all such listed wastes by the date 55 months after the date of enactment of such Amendments; and

    (C) for all such listed wastes and for all hazardous wastes identified under 3001 by the date 66 months after the date of enactment of such Amendments.

In the case of any hazardous waste identified or listed under section 3001 after the date of enactment of the

Hazardous and Solid Waste Amendments of 1984, the Administrator shall determine whether such waste shall be prohibited from one or more methods of land disposal in accordance with paragraph (5) within 6 months after the date of such identification or listing.

(5) Not later than the date specified in the schedule published under this subsection, the Administrator shall promulgate final regulations prohibiting one or more methods of land disposal of the hazardous wastes listed on such schedule except for methods of land disposal which the Administrator determines will be protective of human health and the environment for as long as the waste remains hazardous, taking into account the factors referred to in subparagraph (A) through (C) of subsection (d)(1). For the purposes of this paragraph, a method of land disposal may not be determined to be protective of human health and the environment (except with respect to a hazardous waste which has complied with the pretreatment regulations promulgated under subsection (m)) unless, upon application by an interested person, it has been demonstrated to the Administrator, to a reasonable degree of certainty, that there will be no migration of hazardous constituents from the disposal unit or injection zone for as long as the wastes remain hazardous.

(6)(A) If the Administrator fails (by the date 45 months after the date of enactment of the Hazardous and Solid Waste Amendments of 1984) to promulgate regulations or make a determination under paragraph (5) for any hazardous waste which is included in the first one-third of the schedule published under this subsection, such hazardous waste may be disposed of in a landfill or surface impoundment only if--

(i) such facility is in compliance with the requirements of subsection (o) which are applicable to new facilities (relating to minimum technological requirements); and

(ii) prior to such disposal, the generator has certified to the Administrator that such generator has investigated the availability of treatment capacity and has determined that the use of such landfill or surface impoundment is the only practical alternative to treatment currently available to the generator.

The prohibition contained in this subparagraph shall continue to apply until the Administrator promulgates regulations or makes a determination under paragraph (5) for the waste concerned.

(B) If the Administrator fails (by the date 55 months after the date of enactment of the Hazardous and Solid Waste Amendments of 1984) to promulgate regulations or make a determination under paragraph (5) for any hazardous waste which is included in the first two-thirds of the schedule published under this subsection, such hazardous waste may be disposed of in a landfill or surface impoundment only if--

(i) such facility is in compliance with the requirements of subsection (o) which are applicable to new facilities (relating to minimum technological requirements); and

(ii) prior to such disposal the generator has certified to the Administrator that such generator has investigated the availability of treatment capacity and has determined that the use of such landfill or surface impoundment is the only practical alternative to treatment currently available to the generator.

The prohibition contained in this subparagraph shall continue to apply until the Administrator promulgates regulations or makes a determination under paragraph (5) for the waste concerned.

(C) If the Administrator fails to promulgate regulations, or make a determination under paragraph (5) for any hazardous waste referred to in paragraph (1) within 66 months after the date of enactment of the Hazardous and Solid Waste Amendments of 1984, such hazardous waste shall be prohibited from land disposal.

(h) Variances From Land Disposal Prohibitions.--

(1) A prohibition in regulations under subsection (d), (e), (f), or (g) shall be effective immediately upon promulgation.

(2) The Administrator may establish an effective date different from the effective date which would otherwise apply under subsection (d), (e), (f), or (g) with respect to a specific hazardous waste which is subject to a prohibition under subsection (d), (e), (f), or (g) or under regulations under subsection (d), (e), (f), or (g). Any such other effective date shall be established on the basis of the earliest date on which adequate alternative treatment, recovery, or disposal capacity which protects human health and the environment will be available. Any such other effective date shall in no event be later than 2 years after the effective date of the prohibition which would otherwise apply under subsection (d), (e), (f), or (g).

(3) The Administrator, after notice and opportunity for comment and after consultation with appropriate State agencies in all affected States, may on a case-by-case basis grant an extension of the effective date

which would otherwise apply under subsection (d), (e), (f), or (g) or under paragraph (2) for up to one year, where the applicant demonstrates that there is a binding contractual commitment to construct or otherwise provide such alternative capacity but due to circumstances beyond the control of such applicant such alternative capacity cannot reasonably be made available by such effective date. Such extension shall be renewable once for no more than one additional year.

(4) Whenever another effective date (hereinafter referred to as a "variance") is established under paragraph (2), or an extension is granted under paragraph (3), with respect to any hazardous waste, during the period for which such variance or extension is in effect, such hazardous waste may be disposed of in a landfill or surface impoundment only if such facility is in compliance with the requirements of subsection (o).

(i) Publication of Determination.--If the Administrator determines that a method of land disposal will be protective of human health and the environment, he shall promptly publish in the Federal Register notice of such determination, together with an explanation of the basis for such determination.

(j) Storage of Hazardous Waste Prohibited From Land Disposal.--In the case of any hazardous waste which is prohibited from one or more methods of land disposal under this section (or under regulations promulgated by the Administrator under any provision of this section) the storage of such hazardous waste is prohibited unless such storage is solely for the purpose of the accumulation of such quantities of hazardous waste as are necessary to facilitate proper recovery, treatment or disposal.

(k) Definition of Land Disposal.--For the purposes of this section, the term "land disposal", when used with respect to a specified hazardous waste, shall be deemed to include, but not be limited to, any placement of such hazardous waste in a landfill, surface impoundment, waste pile, injection well, land treatment facility, salt dome formation, salt bed formation, or underground mine or cave.

(l) Ban on Dust Suppression.--The use of waste or used oil or other material, which is contaminated or mixed with dioxin or any other hazardous waste identified or listed under section 3001 (other than a waste identified solely on the basis of ignitibility), for dust suppression or road treatment is prohibited.

(m) Treatment Standards for Wastes Subject to Land
    Disposal Prohibition.--
    (1) Simultaneously with the promulgation of regulations under subsection (d), (e), (f), or (g) prohibiting one or more methods of land disposal of a particular hazardous waste, and as appropriate thereafter, the Administrator shall, after notice and an opportunity for hearings and after consultation with appropriate Federal and State agencies, promulgate regulations specifying those levels or methods of treatment, if any, which substantially diminish the toxicity of the waste or substantially reduce the likelihood of migration of hazardous constituents from the waste so that short-term and long-term threats to human health and the environment are minimized.
    (2) If such hazardous waste has been treated to the level or by a method specified in regulations promulgated under this subsection, such waste or residue thereof shall not be subject to any prohibition promulgated under subsection (d), (e), (f), or (g) and may be disposed of in a land disposal facility which meets the requirements of this subtitle. Any regulation promulgated under this subsection for a particular hazardous waste shall become effective on the same date as any applicable prohibition promulgated under subsection (d), (e), (f), or (g).

(n) Air Emissions.--Not later than 30 months after the date of enactment of the Hazardous and Solid Waste Amendments of 1984, the Administrator shall promulgate such regulations for the monitoring and control of air emissions at hazardous waste treatment, storage, and disposal facilities, including but not limited to open tanks, surface impoundments, and landfills, as may be necessary to protect human health and the environment.

(o) Minimum Technological Requirements.--
    (1) The regulations under subsection (a) of this section shall be revised from time to time to take into account improvements in the technology of control and measurement. At a minimum, such regulations shall

require, and a permit issued pursuant to a section 3005(c) after the date of enactment of the Hazardous and Solid Waste Amendments of 1984 by the Administrator or a State shall require--

(A) for each new landfill or surface impoundment, each new landfill or surface impoundment unit at an existing facility, each replacement of an existing landfill or surface impoundment unit, and each lateral expansion of an existing landfill or surface impoundment unit, for which an application for a final determination regarding issuance of a permit under section 3005(c) is received after the date of enactment of the Hazardous and Solid Waste Amendments of 1984--

(i) the installation of two or more liners and a leachate collection system above (in the case of a landfill) and between such liners; and

(ii) ground water monitoring; and

(B) for each incinerator which receives a permit under section 3005(c) after the date of enactment of the Hazardous and Solid Waste Amendments of 1984, the attainment of the minimum destruction and removal efficiency required by regulations in effect on June 24, 1982.

The requirements of this paragraph shall apply with respect to all waste received after the issuance of the permit.

(2) Paragraph (1)(A)(i) shall not apply if the owner or operator demonstrates to the Administrator, and the Administrator finds for such landfill or surface impoundment, that alternative design and operating practices, together with location characteristics, will prevent the migration of any hazardous constituents into the ground water or surface water at least as effectively as such liners and leachate collection systems.

(3) The double-liner requirement set forth in paragraph (1)(A)(i) may be waived by the Administrator for any monofill, if--

(A) such monofill contains only hazardous wastes from foundry furnace emission controls or metal casting molding sand,

(B) such wastes do not contain constituents which would render the wastes hazardous for reasons other than the Extraction Procedure ("EP") toxicity characteristics set forth in regulations under this subtitle, and

(C) such monofill meets the same requirements as are applicable in the case of a waiver under section 3005(j) (2) or (4).

(4)(A) Not later than 30 months after the date of enactment of the Hazardous and Solid Waste Amendments of 1984, the Administrator shall promulgate standards requiring that new landfill units, surface impoundment units, waste piles, underground tanks and land treatment units for the storage, treatment, or disposal of hazardous waste identified or listed under section 3001 shall be required to utilize approved leak detection systems.

(B) For the purposes of subparagraph (A)

(i) the term "approved leak detection system" means a system or technology which the Administrator determines to be capable of detecting leaks of hazardous constituents at the earliest practicable time; and

(ii) the term "new units" means units on which construction commences after the date of promulgation of regulations under this paragraph.

(5)(A) The Administrator shall promulgate regulations or issue guidance documents implementing the requirements of paragraph (1)(A) within 2 years after the date of the enactment of the Hazardous and Solid Waste Amendments of 1984.

(B) Until the effective date of such regulations or guidance documents, the requirement for the installation of two or more liners may be satisfied by the installation of a top liner designed, operated, and constructed of materials to prevent the migration of any constituent into such liner during the period such facility remains in operation (including any post-closure monitoring period), and a lower liner designed, operated and constructed to prevent the migration of any constituent through such liner during such period. For the purpose of the preceding sentence, a lower liner shall be deemed to satisfy such requirement if it is constructed of at least a 3-foot thick layer of recompacted clay or other natural material with a permeability of no more than 1×10^{-1} centimeter per second.

(6) Any permit under section 3005 which is issued for a landfill located within the State of Alabama shall require the installation of two or more liners and a leachate collection system above and between such liners, notwithstanding any other provision of this Act.

(7) In addition to the requirements set forth in this subsection, the regulations referred to in paragraph

(1) shall specify criteria for the acceptable location of new and existing treatment, storage, or disposal facilities as necessary to protect human health and the environment. Within 18 months after the enactment of the Hazardous and Solid Waste Amendments of 1984, the Administrator shall publish guidance criteria identifying areas of vulnerable hydrogeology.

(p) Ground Water Monitoring.--The standards under this section concerning ground water monitoring which are applicable to surface impoundments, waste piles, land treatment units, and landfills shall apply to such a facility whether or not--
    (1) the facility is located above the seasonal high water table;
    (2) two liners and a leachate collection system have been installed at the facility; or
    (3) the owner or operator inspects the liner (or liners) which has been installed at the facility.
This subsection shall not be construed to affect other exemptions or waivers from such standards provided in regulations in effect on the date of enactment of the Hazardous and Solid Waste Amendments of 1984 or as may be provided in revisions to those regulations, to the extent consistent with this subsection. The Administrator is authorized on a case-by-case basis to exempt from ground water monitoring requirements under this section (including subsection (o)) any engineered structure which the Administrator finds does not receive or contain liquid waste (nor waste containing free liquids), is designed and operated to exclude liquid from precipitation or other runoff, utilizes multiple leak detection systems within the outer layer of containment, and provides for continuing operation and maintenance of these leak detection systems during the operating period, closure, and the period required for post-closure monitoring and for which the Administrator concludes on the basis of such findings that there is a reasonable certainty hazardous constituents will not migrate beyond the outer layer of containment prior to the end of the period required for post-closure monitoring."

(q) Hazardous Waste Used as Fuel.--
    (1) Not later than two years after the date of the enactment of the Hazardous and Solid Waste Amendments of 1984, and after notice and opportunity for public hearing, the Administrator shall promulgate regulations establishing such--
        (A) standards applicable to the owners and operators of facilities which produce a fuel--
            (i) from any hazardous waste identified or listed under section 3001, or
            (ii) from any hazardous waste identified or listed under section 3001 and any other material;
        (B) standards applicable to the owners and operators of facilities which burn, for purposes of energy recovery, any fuel produced as provided in subparagraph (A) or any fuel which otherwise contains any hazardous waste identified or listed under section 3001; and
        (C) standards applicable to any person who distributes or markets any fuel which is produced as provided in subparagraph (A) or any fuel which otherwise contains any hazardous waste identified or listed under section 3001
as may be necessary to protect human health and the environment. Such standards may include any of the requirements set forth in paragraph (1) through (7) of subsection (a) as may be appropriate. Nothing in this subsection shall be construed to affect or impair the provisions of section 3001(b)(3). For purposes of this subsection, the term hazardous waste listed under section 3001 includes any commercial chemical product which is listed under section 3001 and which, in lieu of its original intended use, is (i) produced for use as (or as a component of) a fuel, (ii) distributed for use as a fuel, or (iii) burned as a fuel.
    (2)(A) This subsection, subsection (r), and subsection (s) shall not apply to petroleum refinery wastes containing oil which are converted into petroleum coke at the same facility at which such wastes were generated, unless the resulting coke product would exceed one or more characteristics by which a substance would be identified as a hazardous waste under section 3001.
        (B) The Administrator may exempt from the requirements of this subsection, subsection (r), or subsection (s) facilities which burn de minimis quantities of hazardous waste as fuel, as defined by the Administrator, if the wastes are burned at the same facility at which such wastes are generated; the waste is burned to recover useful energy, as determined by the Administrator on the basis of the design and operating characteristics of the facility and the heating value and other characteristics of the waste; and the waste is burned in a type of device determined by the Administrator to be designed and operated at a destruction and removal efficiency sufficient such that protection of human health and environment is assured.

(C)(i) After the date of the enactment of the Hazardous and Solid Waste Amendments of 1984 and until standards are promulgated and in effect under paragraph (2) of this subsection, no fuel which contains any hazardous waste may be burned in any cement kiln which is located within the boundaries of any incorporated municipality with a population greater than 500,000 (based on the most recent census statistics) unless such kiln fully complies with regulations (as in effect on the date of the enactment of the Hazardous and Solid Waste Amendments of 1984) under this subtitle which are applicable to incinerators.

(ii) Any person who knowingly violates the prohibition contained in clause (i) shall be deemed to have violated section 3008(d)(2).

(r) Labeling.--

(1) Notwithstanding any other provision of law, until such time as the Administrator promulgates standards under subsection (q) specifically superceding this requirement, it shall be unlawful for any person who is required to file a notification in accordance with paragraph (1) or (3) of section 3010 to distribute or market any fuel which is produced from any hazardous waste identified or listed under section 3001, or any fuel which otherwise contains any hazardous waste identified or listed under section 3001 if the invoice or the bill of sale fails--

(A) to bear the following statement: "WARNING: THIS FUEL CONTAINS HAZARDOUS WASTES", and

(B) to list the hazardous wastes contained therein.

Beginning ninety days after the enactment of the Hazardous and Solid Waste Amendments of 1984, such statement shall be located in a conspicuous place on every such invoice or bill of sale and shall appear in conspicuous and legible type in contrast by typography, layouts, or color with other printed matter on the invoice or bill of sale.

(2) Unless the Administrator determines otherwise as may be necessary to protect human health and the environment, this subsection shall not apply to fuels produced from petroleum refining waste containing oil if-

(A) such materials are generated and reinserted on site into the refining process;

(B) contaminants are removed; and

(C) such refining waste containing oil is converted along with normal process streams into petroleum-derived fuel products at a facility at which crude oil is refined into petroleum products and which is classified as a number SIC 2911 facility under the Office of Management and Budget Standard Industrial Classification Manual.

(3) Unless the Administrator determines otherwise as may be necessary to protect human health and the environment, this subsection shall not apply to fuels produced from oily materials, resulting from normal petroleum refining, production and transportation practices, if (A) contaminants are removed; and (B) such oily materials are converted along with normal process streams into petroleum-derived fuel products at a facility at which crude oil is refined into petroleum products and which is classified as a number SIC 2911 facility under the Office of Management and Budget Standard Classification Manual.

(s) Recordkeeping.--Not later than 15 months after the date of enactment of the Hazardous and Solid Waste Amendments of 1984, the Administrator shall promulgate regulations requiring that any person who is required to file a notification in accordance with subparagraph (1), (2), or (3), or section 3010(a) shall maintain such records regarding fuel blending, distribution, or use as may be necessary to protect human health and the environment.

(t) Financial Responsibility Provisions.--

(1) Financial responsibility required by subsection (a) of this section may be established in accordance with regulations promulgated by the Administrator by any one, or any combination, of the following: insurance, guarantee, surety bond, letter of credit, or qualification as a self-insurer. In promulgating requirements under this section, the Administrator is authorized to specify policy or other contractual terms, conditions, or defenses which are necessary or are unacceptable in establishing such evidence of financial responsibility in order to effectuate the purposes of this Act.

(2) In any case where the owner or operator is in bankruptcy, reorganization, or arrangement pursuant to the Federal Bankruptcy Code or where (with reasonable diligence) jurisdiction in any State court or any Federal Court cannot be obtained over an owner or operator likely to be solvent at the time of judgement, any claim arising from conduct for which evidence of financial responsibility must be provided under this

section may be asserted directly against the guarantor providing such evidence of financial responsibility. In the case of any action pursuant to this subsection, such guarantor shall be entitled to involve all rights and defenses which would have been available to the owner or operator if any action had been brought against the owner or operator by the claimant and which would have been available to the guarantor if an action had been brought against the guarantor by the owner or operator.

(3) The total liability of any guarantor shall be limited to the aggregate amount which the guarantor has provided as evidence of financial responsibility to the owner or operator under this Act. Nothing in this subsection shall be construed to limit any other State or Federal statutory, contractual or common law liability of a guarantor to its owner or operator including, but not limited to, the liability of such guarantor for bad faith either in negotiating or in failing to negotiate the settlement of any claim. Nothing in this subsection shall be construed to diminish the liability of any person under section 107 or 111 of the Comprehensive Environmental Response, Compensation and Liability Act of 1980 or other applicable law.

(4) For the purpose of this subsection, the term "guarantor" means any person, other than the owner or operator, who provides evidence of financial responsibility for an owner or operator under this section.

(u) Continuing Releases at Permitted Facilities.--Standards promulgated under this section shall require, and a permit issued after the date of enactment of the Hazardous and Solid Waste Amendments of 1984 by the Administrator or a State shall require, corrective action for all releases of hazardous waste or constituents from any solid waste management unit at a treatment, storage, or disposal facility seeking a permit under this subtitle, regardless of the time at which waste was placed in such unit. Permits issued under section 3005 shall contain schedules of compliance for such corrective action (where such corrective action cannot be completed prior to issuance of the permit) and assurances of financial responsibility for completing such corrective action.

(v) Corrective Actions Beyond Facility Boundary.-- As promptly as practicable after the date of the enactment of the Hazardous and Solid Waste Amendments of 1984, the Administrator shall amend the standards under this section regarding corrective action required at facilities for the treatment, storage, or disposal, of hazardous waste listed or identified under section 3001 to require that corrective action be taken beyond the facility boundary where necessary to protect human health and the environment unless the owner or operator of the facility concerned demonstrates to the satisfaction of the Administrator that, despite the owner or operator"s best efforts, the owner or operator was unable to obtain the necessary permission to undertake such action. Such regulations shall take effect immediately upon promulgation, notwithstanding section 3010(b), and shall apply to--

(1) all facilities operating under permits issued under subsection (c), and

(2) all landfills, surface impoundments, and waste pile units (including any new units, replacements of existing units, or lateral expansions of existing units) which receive hazardous waste after July 26, 1982.

Pending promulgation of such regulations, the Administrator shall issue corrective action orders for facilities referred to in paragraph (1) and (2), on a case-by-case basis, consistent with the purposes of this subsection.

(w) Underground Tanks.--Not later than March 1, 1985, the Adminis-trator shall promulgate final permitting standards under this section for underground tanks that cannot be entered for inspection. Within 48 months after the date of the enactment of the Hazardous and Solid Waste Amendments of 1984, such standards shall be modified, if necessary, to cover at a minimum all requirements and standards described in section 9003.

(x) Mining and Other Special Wastes.--If (1) solid waste from the extraction, beneficiation or processing of ores and minerals, including phosphate rock and overburden from the mining of uranium, (2) fly ash waste, bottom ash waste, slag waste, and flue gas emission control waste generated primarily from the combustion of coal or other fossil fuels, or (3) cement kiln dust waste, is subject to regulation under this subtitle, the Administrator is authorized to modify the requirements of subsections (c), (d), (e), (f), (g), (o), and (u) and section 3005(j), in the case of landfills or surface impoundments receiving such solid waste, to take into account the special characteristics of such wastes, the practical difficulties associated with implementation of such requirements, and site-specific characteristics, including but not limited to the climate, geology, hydrology and soil chemistry at the site, so long as such modified requirements assure protection of human health and the environment.

(y) Munitions.--(1) Not later than 6 months after the date of the enactment of the Federal Facility Compliance Act of 1992, the Administrator shall propose, after consulting with the Secretary of Defense and appropriate State officials, regulations identifying when military munitions become hazardous waste for purposes of this subtitle and providing for the safe transportation and storage of such waste. Not later than 24 months after such date, and after notice and opportunity for comment, the Administrator shall promulgate such regulations. Any such regulations shall assure protection of human health and the environment.

(2) For purposes of this subsection, the term "military munitions" includes chemical and conventional munitions.

PERMITS FOR TREATMENT, STORAGE, OR DISPOSAL OF HAZARDOUS WASTE

42 USC 6925

Sec. 3005. (a) Permit Requirements.--Not later than eighteen months after the date of the enactment of this section, the Administrator shall promulgate regulations requiring each person owning or operating an existing facility or planning to construct a new facility for the treatment, storage, or disposal of hazardous waste identified or listed under this subtitle to have a permit issued pursuant to this section. Such regulations shall take effect on the date provided in section 3010 and upon and after such date the treatment, storage, or disposal of any such hazardous waste and the construction of any new facility for the treatment, storage, or disposal of any such hazardous waste is prohibited except in accordance with such a permit. No permit shall be required under this section in order to construct a facility if such facility is constructed pursuant to an approval issued by the Administrator under section 6(e) of the Toxic Substances Control Act for the incineration of polychlorinated biphenyls and any person owning or operating such a facility may, at any time after operation or construction of such facility has begun, file an application for a permit pursuant to this section authorizing such facility to incinerate hazardous waste identified or listed under this subtitle.

(b) Requirements of Permit Application.--Each application for a permit under this section shall contain such information as may be required under regulations promulgated by the Administrator, including information respecting--

(1) estimates with respect to the composition, quantities, and concentrations of any hazardous waste identified or listed under this subtitle, or combinations of any such hazardous waste and any other solid waste, proposed to be disposed of, treated, transported, or stored, and the time, frequency, or rate of which such waste is proposed to be disposed of, treated, transported, or stored; and

(2) the site at which such hazardous waste or the products of treatment of such hazardous waste will be disposed of, treated, transported to, or stored.

(c) Permit Issuance.--

(1) Upon a determination by the Administrator (or a State, if applicable), of compliance by a facility for which a permit is applied for under this section with the requirements of this section and section 3004, the Administrator (or the State) shall issue a permit for such facilities. In the event permit applicants propose modification of their facilities, or in the event the Administrator (or the State) determines that modifications are necessary to conform to the requirements under this section and section 3004, the permit shall specify the time allowed to complete the modifications.

(2)(A)(i) Not later than the date 4 years after the enactment of the Hazardous and Solid Waste Amendments of 1984, in the case of each application under this subsection for a permit for a land disposal facility which was submitted before such date, the Administrator shall issue a final permit pursuant to such application or issue a final denial of such application.

(ii) Not later than the date 5 years after the enactment of the Hazardous and Solid Waste Amendments of 1984, in the case of each application for a permit under this subsection for an incinerator facility which was submitted before such date, the Administrator shall issue a final permit pursuant to such application or issue a final denial of such application.

(B) Not later than the date 8 years after the enactment of the Hazardous and Solid Waste Amendments of 1984, in the case of each application for a permit under this subsection for any facility (other than a facility referred to in subparagraph (A)) which was submitted before such date, the Administrator shall issue a final permit pursuant to such application or issue a final denial of such application.

(C) The time periods specified in this paragraph shall also apply in the case of any State which is administering an authorized hazardous waste program under section 3006. Interim status under subsection (e) shall terminate for each facility referred to in subparagraph (A)(ii) or (B) on the expiration of the 5 or 8 year period referred to in subparagraph (A) or (B), whichever is applicable, unless the owner or operator of the facility applies for a final determination regarding the issuance of a permit under this subsection within--

(i) 2 years after the date of the enactment of the Hazardous and Solid Waste Amendments of 1984 (in the case of a facility referred to in subparagraph (A)(ii), or

(ii) 4 years after such date of enactment (in the case of a facility referred to in subparagraph (B)).

(3) Any permit under this section shall be for a fixed term, not to exceed 10 years in the case of any land disposal facility, storage facility, or incinerator or other treatment facility. Each permit for a land disposal facility shall be reviewed 5 years after date of issuance or reissuance and shall be modified as necessary to assure that the facility continues to comply with the currently applicable requirements of this section and section 3004. Nothing in this subsection shall preclude the Administrator from reviewing and modifying a permit at any time during its term. Review of any application for a permit renewal shall consider improvements in the state of control and measurement technology as well as changes in applicable regulations. Each permit issued under this section shall contain such terms and conditions as the Administrator (or the State) determines necessary to protect human health and the environment.

(d) Permit Revocation.-- Upon a determination by the Administrator (or by a State, in the case of a State having an authorized hazardous waste program under section 3006) of noncompliance by a facility having a permit under this title with the requirements of this section or section 3004, the Administrator (or State, in the case of a State having an authorized hazardous waste program under section 3006) shall revoke such permit.

(e) Interim Status.

(1) Any person who--

(A) owns or operates a facility required to have a permit under this section which facility--

(i) was in existence on November 19, 1980, or

(ii) is in existence on the effective date of statutory or regulatory changes under this Act that render the facility subject to the requirement to have a permit under this section,

(B) has complied with the requirements of section 3010(a), and

(C) has made an application for a permit under this section shall be treated as having been issued such permit until such time as final administrative disposition of such application is made, unless the Administrator or other plaintiff proves that final administrative disposition of such application has not been made because of the failure of the applicant to furnish information reasonably required or requested in order to process the application.

This paragraph shall not apply to any facility which has been previously denied a permit under this section or if authority to operate the facility under this section has been previously terminated.

(2) In the case of each land disposal facility which has been granted interim status under this subsection before the date of enactment of the Hazardous and Solid Waste Amendments of 1984, interim status shall terminate on the date 12 months after the date of the enactment of such Amendments unless the owner or operator of such facility--

(A) applies for a final determination regarding the issuance of a permit under subsection (c) for such facility before the date 12 months after the date of the enactment of such Amendments; and

(B) certifies that such facility is in compliance with all applicable groundwater monitoring and financial responsibility requirements.

(3) In the case of each land disposal facility which is in existence on the effective date of statutory or regulatory changes under this Act that render the facility subject to the requirement to have a permit under this section and which is granted interim status under this subsection, interim status shall terminate on the date 12 months after the date on which the facility first becomes subject to such permit requirement unless the owner or operator of such facility--

(A) applies for a final determination regarding the issuance of a permit under subsection (c) for such facility before the date 12 months after the date on which the facility first becomes subject to such permit requirement; and

(B) certifies that such facility is in compliance with all applicable groundwater monitoring and financial responsibility requirements.

(f) Coal Mining Wastes and reclamation Permits.--Notwithstanding subsection (a) through (e) of this section, any surface coal mining and reclamation permit covering any coal mining wastes or overburden which has been issued or approved under the Surface Mining Control and Reclamation Act of 1977 shall be deemed to be a permit issued pursuant to this section with respect to the treatment, storage, or disposal of such wastes or overburden. Regulations promulgated by the Administrator under this subtitle shall not be applicable to treatment, storage, or disposal of coal mining wastes and overburden which are covered by such a permit.

(g) Research, Development, and Demonstration Permits.--

(1) The Administrator may issue a research, development, and demonstration permit for any hazardous waste treatment facility which proposes to utilize an innovative and experimental hazardous waste treatment technology or process for which permit standards for such experimental activity have not been promulgated under this subtitle. Any such permit shall include such terms and conditions as will assure protection of human health and the environment. Such permits--

(A) shall provide for the construction of such facilities, as necessary, and for operation of the facility for not longer than one year (unless renewed as provided in paragraph (4)), and

(B) shall provide for the receipt and treatment by the facility of only those types and quantities of hazardous waste which the Administrator deems necessary for purposes of determining the efficacy and performance capabilities of the technology or process and the effects of such technology or process on human health and the environment, and

(C) shall include such requirements as the Administrator deems necessary to protect human health and the environment (including, but not limited to, requirements regarding monitoring, operation, insurance or bonding, financial responsibility, closure, and remedial action), and such requirements as the Administrator deems necessary regarding testing and providing of information to the Administrator with respect to the operation of the facility.

The Administrator may apply the criteria set forth in this paragraph in establishing the conditions of each permit without separate establishment of regulations implementing such criteria.

(2) For the purpose of expediting review and issuance of permits under this subsection, the Administrator may, consistent with the protection of human health and the environment, modify or waive permit application and permit issuance requirements established in the Administrator's general permit regulations except that there may be no modification or waiver of regulations regarding financial responsibility (including insurance) or of procedures established under section 7004(b)(2) regarding public participation.

(3) The Administrator may order an immediate termination of all operations at the facility at any time he determines that termination is necessary to protect human health and the environment.

(4) Any permit issued under this subsection may be renewed not more than 3 times. Each such renewal shall be for a period of not more than 1 year.

(h) Waste Minimization.--Effective September 1, 1985, it shall be a condition of any permit issued under this section for the treatment, storage, or disposal of hazardous waste on the premises where such waste was generated that the permittee certify, no less often than annually, that--

(1) the generator of the hazardous waste has a program in place to reduce the volume or quantity and toxicity of such waste to the degree determined by the generator to be economically practicable; and

(2) the proposed method of treatment, storage, or disposal is that practicable method currently available to the generator which minimizes the present and future threat to human health and the environment.

(i) Interim Status Facilities Receiving Wastes After July 26, 1982.--The standards concerning ground water monitoring, unsaturated zone monitoring, and corrective action, which are applicable under section 3004 to new landfills, surface impoundments, land treatment units, and waste-pile units required to be permitted under subsection (c) shall also apply to any landfill, surface impoundment, land treatment unit, or waste-pile unit qualifying for the authorization to operate under subsection (e) which receives hazardous waste after July 26, 1982.

(j) Interim Status Surface Impoundments.

(1) Except as provided in paragraph (2), (3), or (4), each surface impoundment in existence on the date of enactment of the Hazardous and Solid Waste Amendments of 1984 and qualifying for the authorization to operate under subsection (e) of this section shall not receive, store, or treat hazardous waste after the date 4 years after such date of enactment unless such surface impoundment is in compliance with the requirements of section 3004(o)(1)(A) which would apply to such impoundment if it were new.

(2) Paragraph (1) of this subsection shall not apply to any surface impoundment which (A) has at least one liner, for which there is no evidence that such liner is leaking; (B) is located more than 1/4 mile from an underground source of drinking water; and (C) is in compliance with generally applicable ground water monitoring requirements for facilities with permits under subsection (c) of this section.

(3) Paragraph (1) of this subsection shall not apply to any surface impoundment which (A) contains treated waste water during the secondary or subsequent phases of an aggressive biological treatment facility subject to a permit issued under section 402 of the Clean Water Act (or which holds such treated waste water after treatment and prior to discharge); (B) is in compliance with generally applicable ground water monitoring requirements for facilities with permits under subsection (c) of this section; and (C)(i) is part of a facility in compliance with section 301(b)(2) of the Clean Water Act, or (ii) in the case of a facility for which no effluent guidelines required under section 304(b)(2) of the Clean Water Act are in effect and no permit under section 402(a)(1) of such Act implementing section 301(b)(2) of such Act has been issued, is part of a facility in compliance with a permit under section 402 of such Act, which is achieving significant degradation of toxic pollutants and hazardous constituents contained in the untreated waste stream and which has identified those toxic pollutants and hazardous constituents in the untreated waste stream to the appropriate permitting authority.

(4) The Administrator (or the State, in the case of a State with an authorized program), after notice and opportunity for comment, may modify the requirements of paragraph (1) for any surface impoundment if the owner or operator demonstrates that such surface impoundment is located, designed and operated so as to assure that there will be no migration of any hazardous constituent into ground water or surface water at any future time. The Administrator or the State shall take into account locational criteria established under section 3004(o)(7).

(5) The owner or operator of any surface impoundment potentially subject to paragraph (1) who has reason to believe that on the basis of paragraph (2), (3), or (4) such surface impoundment is not required to comply with the requirements of paragraph (1), shall apply to the Administrator (or the State, in the case of a State with an authorized program) not later than twenty-four months after the date of enactment of the Hazardous and Solid Waste Amendments of 1984 for a determination of the applicability of paragraph (1) (in the case of paragraph (2) or (3)) or for a modification of the requirements of paragraph (1) (in the case of paragraph (4)), with respect to such surface impoundment. Such owner or operator shall provide, with such application, evidence pertinent to such decision, including:

(A) an application for a final determination regarding the issuance of a permit under subsection (c) of this section for such facility, if not previously submitted;

(B) evidence as to compliance with all applicable ground water monitoring requirements and the information and analysis from such monitoring;

(C) all reasonably ascertainable evidence as to whether such surface impoundment is leaking; and

(D) in the case of applications under paragraph (2) or (3), a certification by a registered professional engineer with academic training and experience in ground water hydrology that--

(i) under paragraph (2), the liner of such surface impoundment is designed, constructed, and operated in accordance with applicable requirements, such surface impoundment is more than 1/4 mile from an underground source of drinking water and there is no evidence such liner is leaking; or

(ii) under paragraph (3), based on analysis of those toxic pollutants and hazardous constituents that are likely to be present in the untreated waste stream, such impoundment satisfies the conditions of paragraph (3).

In the case of any surface impoundment for which the owner or operator fails to apply under this paragraph within the time provided by this paragraph or paragraph (6), such surface impoundment shall comply with paragraph (1) notwithstanding paragraph (2), (3), or (4). Within twelve months after receipt of such application and evidence and not later than thirty-six months after such date of enactment, and after notice and opportunity to comment, the Administrator (or, if appropriate, the State) shall advise such owner or operator on the applicability of paragraph (1) to such surface impoundment or as to whether and how the requirements of paragraph (1) shall be modified and applied to such surface impoundment.

(6)(A) In any case in which a surface impoundment becomes subject to paragraph (1) after the date of enactment of the Hazardous and Solid Waste Amendments of 1984 due to the promulgation of additional listings or characteristics for the identification of hazardous waste under section 3001, the period for compliance in paragraph (1) shall be four years after the date of such promulgation, the period for demonstrations under paragraph (4) and for submission of evidence under paragraph (5) shall be not later than twenty-four months after the date of such promulgation, and the period for the Administrator (or if appropriate, the State) to advise such owners or operators under paragraph (5) shall be not later than thirty-six months after the date of promulgation.

(B) In any case in which a surface impoundment is initially determined to be excluded from the requirements of paragraph (1) but due to a change in condition (including the existence of a leak) no longer satisfies the provisions of paragraph (2), (3), or (4) and therefore becomes subject to paragraph (1), the period for compliance in paragraph (1) shall be two years after the date of discovery of such change of condition, or in the case of a surface impoundment excluded under paragraph (3) three years after such date of discovery.

(7)(A) The Administrator shall study and report to the Congress on the number, range of size, construction, likelihood of hazardous constituents migrating into ground water, and potential threat to human health and the environment of existing surface impoundments excluded by paragraph (3) from the requirements of paragraph (1). Such report shall address the need, feasibility, and estimated costs of subjecting such existing surface impoundments to the requirements of paragraph (1).

(B) In the case of any existing surface impoundment or class of surface impoundments from which the Administrator (or the State, in the case of a State with an authorized program) determines hazardous constituents are likely to migrate into ground water, the Administrator (or if appropriate, the State) is authorized to impose such requirements as may be necessary to protect human health and the environment, including the requirements of section 3004(o) which would apply to such impoundments if they were new.

(C) In the case of any surface impoundment excluded by paragraph (3) from the requirements of paragraph (1) which is subsequently determined to be leaking, the Administrator (or, if appropriate, the State) shall require compliance with paragraph (1), unless the Administrator (or, if appropriate, the State) determines that such compliance is not necessary to protect human health and the environment.

(8) In the case of any surface impoundment in which the liners and leak detection system have been installed pursuant to the requirements of paragraph (1) and in good faith compliance with section 3004(o) and the Administrator's regulations and guidance documents governing liners and leak detection systems, no liner or leak detection system which is different from that which was so installed pursuant to paragraph (1) shall be required for such unit by the Administrator when issuing the first permit under this section to such facility. Nothing in this paragraph shall preclude the Administrator from requiring installation of a new liner when the Administrator has reason to believe that any liner installed pursuant to the requirements of this subsection is leaking.

(9) In the case of any surface impoundment which has been excluded by paragraph (2) on the basis of a liner meeting the definition under paragraph (12)(A)(ii), at the closure of such impoundment the Administrator shall require the owner or operator of such impoundment to remove or decontaminate all waste residues, all contaminated liner material, and contaminated soil to the extent practicable. If all contaminated soil is not removed or decontaminated, the owner or operator of such impoundment shall be required to comply with

appropriate post-closure requirements, including but not limited to ground water monitoring and corrective action.

(10) Any incremental cost attributable to the requirements of this subsection or section 3004(o) shall not be considered by the Administrator (or the State, in the case of a State with an authorized program under section 402 of the Clean Water Act)

(A) in establishing effluent limitations and standards under section 301, 304, 306, 307, or 402 of the Clean Water Act based on effluent limitations guidelines and standards promulgated any time before twelve months after the date of enactment of the Hazardous and Solid Waste Amendments of 1984; or

(B) in establishing any other effluent limitations to carry out the provisions of section 301, 307, or 402 of the Clean Water Act on or before October 1, 1986.

(11)(A) If the Administrator allows a hazardous waste which is prohibited from one or more methods of land disposal under subsection (d), (e), or (g) of section 3004 (or under regulations promulgated by the Administrator under such subsections) to be placed in a surface impoundment (which is operating pursuant to interim status) for storage and treatment, such impoundment shall meet the requirements that are applicable to new surface impoundments under section 3004(o)(1), unless such impoundment meets the requirements of paragraph (2) or (4).

(B) In the case of any hazardous waste which is prohibited from one or more methods of land disposal under subsection (d), (e), or (g) of section 3004 (or under regulations promulgated by the Administrator under such subsection) the placement or maintenance of such hazardous waste in a surface impoundment for treatment is prohibited as of the effective date of such prohibition unless the treatment residues which are hazardous are, at a minimum, removed for subsequent management within one year of the entry of the waste into the surface impoundment.

(12)(A) For the purposes of paragraph (2)(A) of this subsection, the term "liner" means--

(i) a liner designed, constructed, installed, and operated to prevent hazardous waste from passing into the liner at any time during the active life of the facility; or

(ii) a liner designed, constructed, installed, and operated to prevent hazardous waste from migrating beyond the liner to adjacent subsurface soil, ground water, or surface water at any time during the active life of the facility.

(B) For the purposes of this subsection, the term "aggressive biological treatment facility" means a system of surface impoundments in which the initial impoundment of the secondary treatment segment of the facility utilizes intense mechanical aeration to enhance biological activity to degrade waste water pollutants and

(i) the hydraulic retention time in such initial impoundment is no longer than 5 days under normal operating conditions, on an annual average basis;

(ii) the hydraulic retention time in such initial impoundment is no longer than 30 days under normal operating conditions, on an annual average basis: PROVIDED, That the sludge in such impoundment does not constitute a hazardous waste as identified by the extraction procedure toxicity characteristic in effect on the date of enactment of the Hazardous and Solid Waste Amendments of 1984; or

(iii) such system utilizes activated sludge treatment in the first portion of secondary treatment.

(C) For the purposes of this subsection, the term "underground source or drinking water" has the same meaning as provided in regulations under the Safe Drinking Water Act (title XIV of the Public Health Service Act).

(13) The Administrator may modify the requirements of paragraph (1) in the case of a surface impoundment for which the owner or operator, prior to October 1, 1984, has entered into, and is in compliance with, a consent order, decree, or agreement with the Administrator or a State with an authorized program mandating corrective action with respect to such surface impoundment that provides a degree of protection of human health and the environment which is at a minimum equivalent to that provided by paragraph (1).

AUTHORIZED STATE HAZARDOUS WASTE PROGRAMS

42 USC 6926

Sec. 3006. (a) Federal Guidelines.--Not later than eighteen months after the date of enactment of this Act, the Administrator, after consultation with State authorities, shall promulgate guidelines to assist States in the development of State hazardous waste programs.

(b) Authorization of State Program.--Any State which seeks to administer and enforce a hazardous waste program pursuant to this subtitle may develop and, after notice and opportunity for public hearing, submit to the Administrator an application, in such form as he shall require, for authorization of such program. Within ninety days following submission of an application under this subsection, the Administrator shall issued a notice as to whether or not he expects such program to be authorized, and within ninety days following such notice (and after opportunity for public hearing) he shall publish his findings as to whether or not the conditions listed in item (1), (2), and (3) below have been met. Such State is authorized to carry out such program in lieu of the Federal program under this subtitle in such State and to issue and enforce permits for the storage, treatment, or disposal of hazardous waste (and to enforce permits deemed to have been issued under section 3012(d)(1)) unless, within ninety days following submission of the application the Administrator notifies such State that such program may not be authorized and, within ninety days following such notice and after opportunity for public hearing, he finds that (1) such State program is not equivalent to the Federal program under this subtitle, (2) such program is not consistent with the Federal or State programs applicable in other States, or (3) such program does not provide adequate enforcement of compliance with the requirements of this subtitle. In authorizing a State program, the Administrator may base his findings on the Federal program in effect one year prior to submission of a State's application or in effect on January 26, 1983, whichever is later.

(c) Interim Authorization.--

(1) Any State which has in existence a hazardous waste program pursuant to State law before the date ninety days after the date of promulgation of regulations under sections 3002, 3003, 3004, and 3005, may submit to the Administrator evidence of such existing program and may request a temporary authorization to carry out such program under this subtitle. The Administrator shall, if the evidence submitted shows the existing State program to be substantially equivalent to the Federal program under this subtitle, grant an interim authorization to the State to carry out such program in lieu of the Federal program pursuant to this subtitle for a period ending no later than January 31, 1986.

(2) The Administrator shall, by rule, establish a date for the expiration of interim authorization under this subsection.

(3) Pending interim or final authorization of a State program for any State which reflects the amendments made by the Hazardous and Solid Waste Amendments of 1984, the State may enter into an agreement with the Administrator under which the State may assist in the administration of the requirements and prohibitions which take effect pursuant to such Amendments.

(4) In the case of a State permit program for any State which is authorized under subsection (b) or under this subsection, until such program is amended to reflect the amendments made by the Hazardous and Solid Waste Amendments of 1984 and such program amendments receive interim or final authorization, the Administrator shall have the authority in such State to issue or deny permits or those portions of permits affected by the requirements and prohibitions established by the Hazardous and Solid Waste Amendments of 1984. The Administrator shall coordinate with States the procedures for issuing such permits.

(d) Effect of State Permit.--Any action taken by a State under a hazardous waste program authorized under this section shall have the same force and effect as action taken by the Administrator under this subtitle.

(e) Withdrawal of Authorization.--Whenever the Administrator determines after public hearing that a State is not administering and enforcing a program authorized under this section in accordance with requirements of this section, he shall so notify the State and, if appropriate corrective action is not taken within a reasonable time, not to exceed ninety days, the Administrator shall withdraw authorization of such program and establish a Federal program pursuant to this subtitle. The Administrator shall not withdraw authorization of any such program unless he shall first have notified the State, and made public, in writing, the reasons for such withdrawal.

(f) Availability of Information.--No State program may be authorized by the Administrator under this section unless--

(1) such program provides for the public availability of information obtained by the State regarding facilities and sites for the treatment, storage, and disposal of hazardous waste; and

(2) such information is available to the public in substantially the same manner, and to the same degree, as would be the case if the Administrator was carrying out the provisions of this subtitle in such State.

[Ed. Note: Section 226(b) of the Hazardous and Solid Waste Amendments of 1984 includes the following amendment that does not amend:

"The amendment made by subsection (a) [226(a)-referring to Section 3006(f) Availability of Information] shall apply with respect to State programs authorized under section 3006 before, on, or after the date of enactment of the Hazardous and Solid Waste Amendments of 1984."]

"(g) Amendments Made by 1984 Act.--

"(1) Any requirement or prohibition which is applicable to the generation, transportation, treatment, storage, or disposal of hazardous waste and which is imposed under this subtitle pursuant to the amendments made by the Hazardous and Solid Waste Amendments of 1984 shall take effect in each State having an interim or finally authorized State program on the same date as such requirement takes effect in other States. The Administrator shall carry out such requirement directly in each such State unless the State program is finally authorized (or is granted interim authorization as provided in paragraph (2) with respect to such requirement.

"(2) Any State which, before the date of the enactment of the Hazardous and Solid Waste Amendments of 1984 has an existing hazardous waste program which has been granted interim or final authorization under this section may submit to the Administrator evidence that such existing program contains (or has been amended to include) any requirement which is substantially equivalent to a requirement referred to in paragraph (1) and may request interim authorization to carry out that requirement under this subtitle. The Administrator shall, if the evidence submitted shows the State requirement to be substantially equivalent to the requirement referred to in paragraph (1), grant an interim authorization to the State to carry out such requirement in lieu of direct administration in the State by the Administrator of such requirement.

"(h) State Programs for Used Oil.--In the case of used oil which is not listed or identified under this subtitle as a hazardous waste but which is regulated under 3014, the provisions of this section regarding State programs shall apply in the same manner and to the same extent as such provisions apply to hazardous waste identified or listed under this subtitle.

INSPECTIONS

42 USC 6927

Sec. 3007. (a) Access Entry.--For purposes of developing or assisting in the development of any regulation or enforcing the provisions of this title, any person who generates, stores, treats, transports, disposes of, or otherwise handles or has handled hazardous wastes shall, upon request of any officer, employee or representative of the Environmental Protection Agency, duly designated by the Administrator, or upon request of any duly designated officer, employee or representative of a State having an authorized hazardous waste program, furnish information relating to such wastes and permit such person at all reasonable times to have access to, and to copy all records relating to such wastes. For the purposes of developing or assisting in the development of any regulation or enforcing the provisions of this title, such officers, employees or representatives are authorized--

"(1) to enter at reasonable times any establishment or other place where hazardous wastes are or have been generated, stored, treated, disposed of, or transported from;

"(2) to inspect and obtain samples from any person of any such wastes and samples of any containers or labeling for such wastes.

Each such inspection shall be commenced and completed with reasonable promptness. If the officer, employee or representative obtains any samples, prior to leaving the premises, he shall give to the owner, operator, or agent in charge a receipt describing the sample obtained and if requested a portion of each such sample equal in volume or weight to the portion retained. If any analysis is made of such samples, a copy of the results of such analysis shall be furnished promptly to the owner, operator, or agent in charge.

(b) Availability to Public.--

(1) Any records, reports, or information (including records, reports, or information obtained by representatives of the Environmental Protection Agency) obtained from any person under this section shall be available to the public, except that upon a showing satisfactory to the Administrator (or the State, as the case may be) by any person that records, reports, or information, or particular part thereof, to which the Administrator (or the State, as the case may be) or any officer, employee or representative thereof has access under this section if made public, would divulge information entitled to protection under section 1905 of title 18 of the United States Code, such information or particular portion thereof shall be considered confidential in accordance with the purposes of that section, except that such record, report, document, or information may be disclosed to other officers, employees, or authorized representatives of the United States concerned with carrying out this Act, or when relevant in any proceeding under this Act.

(2) Any person not subject to the provisions of section 1905 of title 18 of the United States Code who knowingly and willfully divulges or discloses any information entitled to protection under this subsection shall, upon conviction, be subject to a fine of not more than $5,000 or to imprisonment not to exceed one year, or both.

(3) In submitting data under this Act, a person required to provide such data may--

(A) designate the data which such person believes is entitled to protection under this subsection, and

(B) submit such designated data separately from other data submitted under this Act.

A designation under this paragraph shall be made in writing and in such manner as the Administrator may prescribe.

(4) Notwithstanding any limitation contained in this section or any other provision of law, all information reported to, or otherwise obtained by, the Administrator (or any representative of the Administrator) under this Act shall be made available, upon written request of any duly authorized committee of the Congress, to such committee (including records, reports, or information obtained by representatives of the Environmental Protection Agency).

(c) Federal Facility Inspections.--The Administrator shall undertake on an annual basis a thorough inspection of each facility for the treatment, storage, or disposal of hazardous waste which is owned or operated by a department, agency, or instrumentality of the United States to enforce its compliance with this subtitle and the regulations promulgated thereunder. Any State with an authorized hazardous waste program also may conduct an inspection of any such facility for purposes of enforcing the facility's compliance with the State hazardous waste program. The records of such inspections shall be available to the public as provided in subsection (b). The department, agency, or instrumentality owning or operating each such facility shall reimburse the Environmental Protection Agency for the costs of the inspection of the facility. With respect to the first inspection of each such facility occurring after the date of the enactment of the Federal Facility Compliance Act of 1992, the Administrator shall conduct a comprehensive ground water monitoring evaluation at the facility, unless such an evaluation was conducted during the 12-month period preceding such date of enactment.

(d) State-Operated Facilities.--The Administrator shall annually undertake a thorough inspection of every facility for the treatment, storage, or disposal of hazardous waste which is operated by a State or local government for which a permit is required under section 3005 of this title. The records of such inspection shall be available to the public as provided in subsection (b).

(e) Mandatory Inspections.--

(1) The Administrator (or the State in the case of a State having an authorized hazardous waste program under this subtitle) shall commence a program to thoroughly inspect every facility for the treatment, storage, or disposal of hazardous waste for which a permit is required under section 3005 no less often than every 2 years as to its compliance with this subtitle (and the regulations promulgated under this subtitle). Such inspections shall commence not later than 12 months after the date of enactment of the Hazardous and Solid Waste Amendments of 1984. The Administrator shall, after notice and opportunity for public comment, promulgate regulations governing the minimum frequency and manner of such inspections, including the manner in which records of such inspections shall be maintained and the manner in which reports of such inspections shall be filed. The Administrator may distinguish between classes and categories of facilities commensurate with the risks posed by each class or category.

(2) Not later than 6 months after the date of enactment of the Hazardous and Solid Waste Amendments of 1984, the Administrator shall submit to the Congress a report on the potential for inspections of hazardous waste treatment, storage, or disposal facilities by nongovernmental inspectors as a supplement to inspections conducted by officers, employees, or representatives of the Environmental Protection Agency or States having authorized hazardous waste programs or operating under a cooperative agreement with the Administrator. Such report shall be prepared in cooperation with the States, insurance companies offering environmental impairment insurance, independent companies providing inspection services, and other such groups as appropriate. Such report shall contain recommendations on provisions and requirements for a program of private inspections to supplement governmental inspections.

FEDERAL ENFORCEMENT

42 USC 6928

Sec. 3008. (a) Compliance Orders.--

(1) Except as provided in paragraph (2), whenever on the basis of any information the Administrator determines that any person has violated or is in violation of any requirement of this subtitle, the Administrator may issue an order assessing a civil penalty for any past or current violation, requiring compliance immediately or within a specified time period, or both, or the Administrator may commence a civil action in the United States district court in the district in which the violation occurred for appropriate relief, including a temporary or permanent injunction.

(2) In the case of a violation of any requirement of this subtitle where such violation occurs in a State which is authorized to carry out a hazardous waste program under section 3006, the Administrator shall give notice to the State in which such violation has occurred prior to issuing an order or commencing a civil action under this section.

(3) Any order issued pursuant to this subsection may include a suspension or revocation of any permit issued by the Administrator or a State under this subtitle and shall state with reasonable specificity the nature of the violation. Any penalty assessed in the order shall not exceed $25,000 per day of noncompliance for each violation of a requirement of this subtitle. In assessing such a penalty, the Administrator shall take into account the seriousness of the violation and any good faith efforts to comply with applicable requirements.

(b) Public Hearing.--Any order issued under this section shall become final unless, no later than thirty days after the order is served, the person or persons named therein request a public hearing. Upon such request the Administrator shall promptly conduct a public hearing. In connection with any proceeding under this section the Administrator may issue subpoenas for the attendance and testimony of witnesses and the production of relevant papers, books, and documents, and may promulgate rules for discovery procedures.

(c) Violation of Compliance Orders.--If a violator fails to take corrective action within the time specified in a compliance order, the Administrator may assess a civil penalty of not more than $25,000 for each day of continued noncompliance with the order and the Administrator may suspend or revoke any permit issued to the violator (whether issued by the Administrator or the State).

(d) Criminal Penalties.--Any person who--

(1) knowingly transports or causes to be transported any hazardous waste identified or listed under this subtitle to a facility which does not have a permit under section this subtitle, or pursuant to title I of the Marine Protection, Research, and Sanctuaries Act (86 Stat. 1052),

(2) knowingly treats, stores, or disposes of any hazardous waste identified or listed under this subtitle--

(A) without a permit under this subtitle or pursuant to title I of the Marine Protection, Research, and Sanctuaries Act (86 Stat. 1052); or

(B) in knowing violation of any material condition or requirement of such permit; or

(C) in knowing violation of any material condition or requirement of any applicable interim status regulations or standards;

(3) knowingly omits material information or makes any false material statement or representation in any application, label, manifest, record, report, permit, or other document filed, maintained, or used for purposes of compliance with regulations promulgated by the Administrator (or by a State in the case of an authorized State program) under this subtitle;

(4) knowingly generates, stores, treats, transports, disposes of, exports, or otherwise handles any hazardous waste or any used oil not identified or listed as a hazardous waste under this subtitle (whether such activity took place before or takes place after the date of the enactment of this paragraph) and who knowingly destroys, alters, conceals, or fails to file any record, application, manifest, report, or other document required to be maintained or filed for purposes of compliance with regulations promulgated by the Administrator (or by a State in the case of an authorized State program) under this subtitle;

(5) knowingly transports without a manifest, or causes to be transported without a manifest, any hazardous waste or any used oil not identified or listed as a hazardous waste under this subtitle required by regulations promulgated under this subtitle (or by a State in the case of a State program authorized under this subtitle) to be accompanied by a manifest;

(6) knowingly exports a hazardous waste identified or listed under this subtitle

(A) without the consent of the receiving country or,

(B) where there exists an international agreement between the United States and the government of the receiving country establishing notice, export, and enforcement procedures for the transportation, treatment, storage, and disposal of hazardous wastes, in a manner which is not in conformance with such agreement; or

(7) knowingly stores, treats, transports, or causes to be transported, disposes of, or otherwise handles any used oil not identified or listed as a hazardous waste under subtitle C of the Solid Waste Disposal Act--

(A) in knowing violation of any material condition or requirement of a permit under this subtitle C; or

(B) in knowing violation of any material condition or requirement of any applicable regulations or standards under this Act;

shall, upon conviction, be subject to a fine of not more than $50,000 for each day of violation, or imprisonment not to exceed two years (five years in the case of a violation of paragraph (1) or (2)), or both. If the conviction is for a violation committed after a first conviction of such person under this paragraph, the maximum punishment under the respective paragraph shall be doubled with respect to both fine and imprisonment.

(e) Knowing Endangerment.--Any person who knowingly transports, treats, stores, disposes of, or exports any hazardous waste identified or listed under this subtitle or used oil not identified or listed as a hazardous waste under this subtitle in violation of paragraph (1), (2), (3), (4), (5), (6), or (7) of subsection (d) of this section who knows at that time that he thereby places another person in imminent danger of death or serious bodily injury, shall, upon conviction, be subject to a fine of not more than $250,000 or imprisonment for not more than 15 years, or both. A defendant that is an organization shall, upon conviction of violating this subsection, be subject to a fine of not more than $1,000,000.

(f) Special Rules.--For the purposes of subsection (e)

(1) A person's state of mind is knowing with respect to--

(A) his conduct, if he is aware of the nature of his conduct;

(B) an existing circumstance, if he is aware or believes that the circumstance exists; or

(C) a result of his conduct, if he is aware or believes that his conduct is substantially certain to cause danger of death or serious bodily injury.

(2) In determining whether a defendant who is a natural person knew that his conduct placed another person in imminent danger of death or serious bodily injury--

(A) the person is responsible only for actual awareness or actual belief that he possessed; and

(B) knowledge possessed by a person other than the defendant but not by the defendant himself may not be attributed to the defendant;

Provided, That in proving the defendant's possession of actual knowledge, circumstantial evidence may be used, including evidence that the defendant took affirmative steps to shield himself from relevant information.

(3) It is an affirmative defense to prosecution that the conduct charged was consented to by the person endangered and that the danger and conduct charged were reasonably foreseeable hazards of

(A) an occupation, a business, or a profession; or

(B) medical treatment or medical or scientific experimentation conducted by professionally approved methods and such other person had been made aware of the risks involved prior to giving consent.

The defendant may establish an affirmative defense under this subsection by a preponderance of the evidence.

(4) All general defenses, affirmative defenses, and bars to prosecution that may apply with respect to other Federal criminal offenses may apply under subsection (e) and shall be determined by the courts of the United States according to the principles of common law as they may be interpreted in the light of reason and experience. Concepts of justification and excuse applicable under this section may be developed in the light of reason and experience.

(5) The term 'organization' means a legal entity, other than a government, established or organized for any purpose, and such term includes a corporation, company, association, firm, partnership, joint stock company, foundation, institution, trust, society, union, or any other association of persons.

(6) The term 'serious bodily injury' means--

(A) bodily injury which involves a substantial risk of death;

(B) unconsciousness;

(C) extreme physical pain;

(D) protracted and obvious disfigurement; or

(E) protracted loss or impairment of the function of a bodily member, organ, or mental faculty.

(g) Civil Penalty.--Any person who violates any requirement of this subtitle shall be liable to the United States for a civil penalty in an amount not to exceed $25,000 for each such violation. Each day of such violation shall, for purposes of this subsection, constitute a separate violation.

(h) Interim Status Corrective Action.

(1) Whenever on the basis of any information the Administrator determines that there is or has been a release of hazardous waste into the environment from a facility authorized to operate under section 3005(e) of this subtitle, the Administrator may issue an order requiring corrective action or such other response measure as he deems necessary to protect human health or the environment or the Administrator may commence a civil action in the United States district court in the district in which the facility is located for appropriate relief, including a temporary or permanent injunction.

(2) Any order issued under this subsection may include a suspension or revocation of authorization to operate under section 3005(e) of this subtitle, shall state with reasonable specificity the nature of the required corrective action or other response measure, and shall specify a time for compliance. If any person named in an order fails to comply with the order, the Administrator may assess, and such person shall be liable to the United States for, a civil penalty in an amount not to exceed $25,000 for each day of noncompliance with the order.

RETENTION OF STATE AUTHORITY

42 USC 6929

Sec. 3009. Upon the effective date of regulations under this subtitle no State or political subdivision may impose any requirements less stringent than those authorized under this subtitle respecting the same matter as governed by such regulations, except that if application of a regulation with respect to any matter under this subtitle is postponed or enjoined by the action of any court, no State or political subdivision shall be prohibited from acting with respect to the same aspect of such matter until such time as such regulation takes effect. Nothing in this title shall be construed to prohibit any State or political subdivision thereof from imposing any requirements, including those for site selection, which are more stringent than those imposed by such regulations. Nothing in this title (or in any regulation adopted under this title) shall be construed to prohibit any State from requiring that the State be provided with a copy of each manifest used in connection with hazardous waste which is generated within that State or transported to a treatment, storage, or disposal facility within that State.

EFFECTIVE DATE

42 USC 6930

Sec. 3010. (a) Preliminary Notification.--Not later than ninety days after promulgation of regulations under section 3001 identifying by its characteristics or listing any substance as hazardous waste subject to this subtitle, any person generating or transporting such substance or owning or operating a facility for treatment, storage, or disposal of such substance shall file with the Administrator (or with States having authorized hazardous waste permit programs under section 3006) a notification stating the location and general description of such activity and the identified or listed hazardous wastes handled by such person. Not later than 15 months after the date of enactment of the Hazardous and Solid Waste Amendments of 1984--

(1) the owner or operator of any facility which produces a fuel (A) from any hazardous waste identified or listed under section 3001, (B) from such hazardous waste identified or listed under section 3001 and any other material, (C) from used oil, or (D) from used oil and any other material;

(2) the owner or operator of any facility (other than a single or two-family residence) which burns for purposes of energy recovery any fuel produced as provided in paragraph (1) or any fuel which otherwise contains used oil or any hazardous waste identified or listed under section 3001; and

(3) any person who distributes or markets any fuel which is produced as provided in paragraph (1) or any fuel which otherwise contains used oil or any hazardous waste identified or listed under section 3001 shall file with the Administrator (and with the State in the case of a State with an authorized hazardous waste program) a notification stating the location and general description of the facility, together with a description of the identified or listed hazardous waste involved and, in the case of a facility referred to in paragraph (1) or (2), a description of the production or energy recovery activity carried out at the facility and such other information as the Administrator deems necessary. For purposes of the preceding provisions, the term "hazardous waste listed under section 3001" also includes any commercial chemical product which is listed under section 3001 and which, in lieu of its original intended use, is (i) produced for use as (or as a component of) a fuel, (ii) distributed for use as a fuel, or (iii) burned as a fuel. Notification shall not be required under the second sentence of this subsection in the case of facilities (such as residential boilers) where the Administrator determines that such notification is not necessary in order for the Administrator to obtain sufficient information respecting current practices of facilities using hazardous waste for energy recovery. Nothing in this subsection shall be construed to affect or impair the provisions of section 3001(b)(3). Nothing in this subsection shall affect regulatory determinations under section 3014". In revising any regulation under section 3001 identifying additional characteristics of hazardous waste or listing any additional substance as hazardous waste subject to this subtitle, the Administrator may require any person referred to in the preceding provisions to file with the Administrator (or with States having authorized hazardous waste permit programs under section 3006) the notification described in the preceding provisions. Not more than one such notification shall be required to be filed with respect to the same substance. No identified or listed hazardous waste subject to this subtitle may be transported, treated, stored, or disposed of unless notification has been given as required under this subsection.

(b) Effective Date of Regulation.--The regulations under this subtitle respecting requirements applicable to the generation, transportation, treatment, storage, or disposal of hazardous waste (including requirements respecting permits for such treatment, storage, or disposal) shall take effect on the date six months after the date of promulgation thereof (or six months after the date of revision in the case of any regulation which is revised after the date required for promulgation thereof). At the time a regulation is promulgated, the Administrator may provide for a shorter period prior to the effective date, or an immediate effective date for:

(1) a regulation with which the Administrator finds the regulated community does not need 6 months to come into compliance;

(2) a regulation which responds to an emergency situation; or

(3) other good cause found and published with the regulation.

AUTHORIZATION OF ASSISTANCE TO STATES

42 USC 3031

Sec. 3011. (a) Authorization.--There is authorized to be appropriated $25,000,000 for each of the fiscal years

1978 and 1979, $20,000,000 for fiscal year 1980, $35,000,000 for fiscal year 1981, $40,000,000 for the fiscal year 1982, $55,000,000 for the fiscal year 1985, $60,000,000 for the fiscal year 1986, $60,000,000 for the fiscal year 1987, and $60,000,000 for the fiscal year 1988 to be used to make grants to the States for purposes of assisting the States in the development and implementation of authorized State hazardous waste programs.

(b) Allocation.--Amounts authorized to be appropriated under subsection (a) shall be allocated among the States on the basis of regulations promulgated by the Administrator, after consultation with the States, which take into account, the extent to which hazardous waste is generated, transported, treated, stored, and disposed of within such State, the extent of exposure of human beings and the environment within such State to such waste, and such other factors as the Administrator deems appropriate.

(c) Activities Included.--State hazardous waste programs for which grants may be made under subsection (a) may include (but shall not be limited to) planning for hazardous waste treatment, storage and disposal facilities, and the development and execution of programs to protect health and the environment from inactive facilities which may contain hazardous waste.

HAZARDOUS WASTE SITE INVENTORY

42 USC 6932

Sec. 3012. (a) State Inventory Programs.--Each State shall, as expeditiously as practicable, undertake a continuing program to compile, publish, and submit to the Administrator an inventory describing the location of each site within such State at which hazardous waste has at any time been stored or disposed of. Such inventory shall contain--

(1) a description of the location of the sites at which any such storage or disposal has taken place before the date on which permits are required under section 3005 for such storage or disposal;

(2) such information relating to the amount, nature, and toxicity of the hazardous waste at each such site as may be practicable to obtain and as may be necessary to determine the extent of any health hazard which may be associated with such site;

(3) the name and address, or corporate headquarters of, the owner of each site, determined as of the date of preparation of the inventory;

(4) an identification of the types or techniques of waste treatment or disposal which have been used at each such site; and

(5) information concerning the current status of the site, including information respecting whether or not hazardous waste is currently being treated or disposed of at such site (and if not, the date on which such activity ceased) and information respecting the nature of any other activity currently carried out at such site.

For purposes of assisting the States in compiling information under this section, the Administrator shall make available to each State undertaking a program under this section such information as is available to him concerning the items specified in paragraphs (1) through (5) with respect to the sites within such State, including such information as the Administrator is able to obtain from other agencies or departments of the United States and from surveys and studies carried out by any committee or subcommittee of the Congress. Any State may exercise the authority of section 3007 for purposes of this section in the same manner and to the same extent as provided in such section in the case of States having an authorized hazardous waste program, and any State may by order require any person to submit such information as may be necessary to compile the data referred to in paragraphs (1) through (5).

(b) Environmental Protection Agency Program.--If the Administrator determines that any State program under subsection (a) is not adequately providing information respecting the sites in such State referred to in subsection (a) the Administrator shall notify the State. If within ninety days following such notification, the State program has not been revised or amended in such manner as will adequately provide such information, the Administrator shall carry out the inventory program in such State. In any such case--

(1) the Administrator shall have the authorities provided with respect to State programs under subsection (a);

(2) the funds allocated under subsection (c) for grants to states under this section may be used by the Administrator for carrying out such program in such State; and

(3) no further expenditure may be made for grants to such State under this section until such time as the Administrator determines that such State is carrying out, or will carry out, an inventory program which meets the requirements of this section.

(c) Grants.

(1) Upon receipt of an application submitted by any State to carry out a program under this section, the Administrator may make grants to the States for purposes of carrying out such a program. Grants under this section shall be allocated among the several States by the Administrator based upon such regulations as he prescribes to carry out the purposes of this section. The Administrator may make grants to any State which has conducted an inventory program which effectively carried out the purposes of this section before the date of the enactment of the Solid Waste Disposal Act Amendments of 1980 to reimburse such State for all, or any portion of, the costs incurred by such State in conducting such program.

(2) There are authorized to be appropriated to carry out this section $25,000,000 for each of the fiscal years 1985 through 1988.

(d) No Impediment to Immediate Remedial Action.--Nothing in this sec-tion shall be construed to provide that the Administrator or any State should, pending completion of the inventory required under this section, postpone undertaking any enforcement or remedial action with respect to any site at which hazardous waste has been treated, stored, or disposed of.

MONITORING, ANALYSIS, AND TESTING

42 USC 6934

Sec. 3013. (a) Authority of Administrator.--If the Administrator determines, upon receipt of any information, that--

(1) the presence of any hazardous waste at a facility or site at which hazardous waste is, or has been, stored, treated, or disposed of, or

(2) the release of any such waste from such facility or site may present a substantial hazard to human health or the environment, he may issue an order requiring the owner or operator of such facility or site to conduct such monitoring, testing, analysis, and reporting with respect to such facility or site as the Administrator deems reasonable to ascertain the nature and extent of such hazard.

(b) Previous Owners and Operators.-- In the case of any facility or site not in operation at the time a determination is made under subsection (a) with respect to the facility or site if the Administrator finds that the owner of such facility or site, could not reasonably be expected to have actual knowledge of the presence of hazardous waste at such facility or site and of its potential for release, he may issue an order requiring the most recent previous owner or operator of such facility or site who could reasonably be expected to have such actual knowledge to carry out the actions referred to in subsection (a).

(c) Proposal.--Any order under subsection (a) or (b) shall require the person to whom such order is issued to submit to the Administrator within 30 days from the issuance of such order a proposal for carrying out the required monitoring, testing, analysis, and reporting. The Administrator may, after providing such person with an opportunity to confer with the Administrator respecting such proposal, require such person to carry out such monitoring, testing, analysis, and reporting in accordance with such proposal, and such modifications in such proposal as the Administrator deems reasonable to ascertain the nature and extent of the hazard.

(d) Monitoring, Etc., Carried Out by Administrator.--(1) If the Administrator determines that no owner or operator referred to in subsection (a) or (b) is able to conduct monitoring, testing, analysis, or reporting satisfactory to the Administrator, if the Administrator deems any such action carried out by an owner or operator to be unsatisfactory, or if the Administrator cannot initially determine that there is an owner or operator referred to in subsection (a) or (b) who is able to conduct such monitoring, testing, analysis, or reporting, he may--

(A) conduct monitoring, testing, or analysis (or any combination thereof) which he deems reasonable to ascertain the nature and extent of the hazard associated with the site concerned, or

(B) authorize a State or local authority or other person to carry out any such action, and require, by order, the owner or operator referred to in subsection (a) or (b) to reimburse the Administrator or other authority or person for the costs of such activity.

(2) No order may be issued under this subsection requiring reimbursement of the costs of any action carried out by the Administrator which confirms the results of an order issued under subsection (a) or (b).

(3) For purposes of carrying out this subsection, the Administrator or any authority or other person authorized under paragraph (1) may exercise the authorities set forth in section 3007.

(e) Enforcement.--The Administrator may commence a civil action against any person who fails or refuses to comply with any order issued under this section. Such action shall be brought in the United States district court in which the defendant is located, resides, or is doing business. Such court shall have jurisdiction to require compliance with such order and to assess a civil penalty of not to exceed $5,000 for each day during which such failure or refusal occurs.

RESTRICTIONS ON RECYCLED OIL

42 USC 6935

Sec. 3014. (a) In General.--Not later than one year after the date of the enactment of this section, the Administrator shall promulgate regulations establishing such performance standards and other requirements as may be necessary to protect the public health and the environment from hazards associated with recycled oil. In developing such regulations, the Administrator shall conduct an analysis of the economic impact of the regulations on the oil recycling industry. The Administrator shall ensure that such regulations do not discourage the recovery or recycling of used oil, consistent with the protection of human health and the environment.

(b) Identification or Listing of Used Oil as Hazardous Waste.--Not later than 12 months after the date of enactment of the Hazardous and Solid Waste Amendments of 1984 the Administrator shall propose whether to list or identify used automobile and truck crankcase oil as hazardous waste under section 3001. Not later than 24 months after such date of enactment, the Administrator shall make a final determination whether to list or identify used automobile and truck crankcase oil and other used oil as hazardous wastes under section 3001.

(c) Used Oil Which is Recycled.--(1) With respect to generators and transporters of used oil identified or listed as a hazardous waste under section 3001, the standards promulgated under section 3001(d), 3002, and 3003 of this subtitle shall not apply to such used oil if such used oil is recycled.

(2)(A) In the case of used oil which is exempt under paragraph (1), not later than 24 months after the date of enactment of the Hazardous and Solid Waste Amendments of 1984, the Administrator shall promulgate such standards under this subsection regarding the generation and transportation of used oil which is recycled as may be necessary to protect human health and the environment. In promulgating such regulations with respect to generators, the Administrator shall take into account the effect of such regulations on environmentally acceptable types of used oil recycling and the effect of such regulations on small quantity generators and generators which are small businesses (as defined by the Administrator).

(B) The regulations promulgated under this subsection shall provide that no generator of used oil which is exempt under paragraph (1) from the standards promulgated under section 3001(d), 3002, and 3003 shall be subject to any manifest requirement or any associated recordkeeping and reporting requirement with respect to such used oil if such generator--

(i) either--

(I) enters into an agreement or other arrangement (including an agreement or arrangement with an independent transporter or with an agent of the recycler) for delivery of such used oil to a recycling facility which has a permit under section 3005(c) (or for which a valid permit is deemed to be in effect under subsection (d)), or

(II) recycles such used oil at one or more facilities of the generator which has such a permit under section 3005 of this subtitle (or for which a valid permit is deemed to have been issued under subsection (d) of this section);

(ii) such used oil is not mixed by the generator with other types of hazardous wastes; and

(iii) the generator maintains such records relating to such used oil, including records of agreements or other arrangements for delivery of such used oil to any recycling facility referred to in clause (i)(I), as the Administrator deems necessary to protect human health and the environment.

(3) The regulations under this subsection regarding the transportation of used oil which is exempt from the standards promulgated under sections 3001(d), 3002, and 3003 under paragraph (1) shall require the transporters of such used oil to deliver such used oil to a facility which has a valid permit under section 3005 of this subtitle or which is deemed to have a valid permit under subsection (d) of this section. The Administrator shall also establish other standards for such transporters as may be necessary to protect human health and the environment.

(d) Permits.--(1) The owner or operator of a facility which recycles used oil which is exempt under subsection (c)(1), shall be deemed to have a permit under this subsection(1) for all such treatment or recycling (and any associated tank or container storage) if such owner and operator comply with standards promulgated by the Administrator under section 3004; except that the Administrator may require such owners and operators to obtain an individual permit under section 3005(c) if he determines that an individual permit is necessary to protect human health and the environment.

(2) Notwithstanding any other provision of law, any generator who recycles used oil which is exempt under subsection (c)(1) shall not be required to obtain a permit under section 3005(c) with respect to such used oil until the Administrator has promulgated standards under section 3004 regarding the recycling of such used oil.

EXPANSION DURING INTERIM STATUS

42 USC 6936

Sec. 3015. (a) Waste Piles.--The owner or operator of a waste pile qualifying for the authorization to operate under section 3005(e) shall be subject to the same requirements for liners and leachate collection systems or equivalent protection provided in regulations promulgated by the Administrator under section 3004 before October 1, 1982, or revised under section 3004(o) (relating to minimum technological requirements), for new facilities receiving individual permits under subsection (c) of section 3005, with respect to each new unit, replacement of an existing unit, or lateral expansion of an existing unit that is within the waste management area identified in the permit application submitted under section 3005, and with respect to waste received beginning 6 months after the date of enactment of the Hazardous and Solid Waste Amendments of 1984.

(b) Landfills and Surface Impoundments.--(1) The owner or operator of a landfill or surface impoundment qualifying for the authorization to operate under section 3005(e) shall be subject to the requirements of section 3004(o) relating to minimum technological requirements), with respect to each new unit, replacement of an existing unit, or lateral expansion of an existing unit that is within the waste management area identified in the permit application submitted under this section, and with respect to waste received beginning 6 months after the date of enactment of the Hazardous and Solid Waste Amendments of 1984.

(2) The owner or operator of each unit referred to in paragraph (1) shall notify the Administrator (or the State, if appropriate) at least 60 days prior to receiving waste. The Administrator (or the State) shall require the filing, within 6 months of receipt of such notice, of an application for a final determination regarding the issuance of a permit for each facility submitting such notice.

(3) In the case of any unit in which the liner and leachate collection system has been installed pursuant to the requirements of this section and in good faith compliance with the Administrator's regulations and guidance documents governing liners and leachate collection systems, no liner or leachate collection system which is different from that which was so installed pursuant to this section shall be required for such unit by the Administrator when issuing the first permit under section 3005 to such facility, except that the Administrator shall not be precluded from requiring installation of a new liner when the Administrator has reason to believe that any liner installed pursuant to the requirements of this section is leaking. The Administrator may, under section 3004, amend the requirements for liners and leachate collection systems required under this section as may be necessary to provide additional protection for human health and the environment.

INVENTORY OF FEDERAL AGENCY HAZARDOUS
WASTE FACILITIES

42 USC 6937

Sec. 3016. (a) Program Requirement; Submission; Availability; Contents.--Each Federal agency shall undertake a continuing program to compile, publish, and submit to the Administrator (and to the State in the case of sites in States having an authorized hazardous waste program) an inventory of each site which the Federal agency owns or operates or has owned or operated at which hazardous waste is stored, treated, or disposed of or has been disposed of at any time. The inventory shall be submitted every 2 years beginning January 31, 1986. Such inventory shall be available to the public as provided in section 3007(b). Information previously submitted by a Federal agency under section 103 of the Comprehensive Environmental Response, Compensation, and Liability Act of 1980, or under section 3005 or 3010 of this Act, or under this section need not be resubmitted except that the agency shall update any previous submission to reflect the latest available data and information. The inventory shall include each of the following:

(1) A description of the location of each site at which any such treatment, storage, or disposal has taken place before the date on which permits are required under section 3005 for such storage, treatment, or disposal, and where hazardous waste has been disposed, a description of hydrogeology of the site and the location of withdrawal wells and surface water within one mile of the site.

(2) Such information relating to the amount, nature, and toxicity of the hazardous waste in each site as may be necessary to determine the extent of any health hazard which may be associated with any site.

(3) Information on the known nature and extent of environmental contamination at each site, including a description of the monitoring data obtained.

(4) Information concerning the current status of the site, including information respecting whether or not hazardous waste is currently being treated, stored, or disposed of at such site (and if not, the date on which such activity ceased) and information respecting the nature of any other activity currently carried out at such site.

(5) A list of sites at which hazardous waste has been disposed and environmental monitoring data has not been obtained, and the reasons for the lack of monitoring data at each site.

(6) A description of response actions undertaken or contemplated at contaminated sites.

(7) An identification of the types of techniques of waste treatment, storage, or disposal which have been used at each site.

(8) The name and address and responsible Federal agency for each site, determined as of the date of preparation of the inventory.

(b) Environmental Protection Agency Program.--If the Administrator determines that any Federal agency under subsection (a) is not adequately providing information respecting the sites referred to in subsection (a), the Administrator shall notify the chief official of such agency. If within 90 days following such notification, the Federal agency has not undertaken a program to adequately provide such information, the Administrator shall carry out the inventory program for such agency.

EXPORT OF HAZARDOUS WASTE

42 USC 6938

Sec. 3017. (a) In General.--Beginning 24 months after the date of enactment of the Hazardous and Solid Waste Amendments of 1984, no person shall export any hazardous waste identified or listed under this subtitle unless

(1)(A) such person has provided the notification required in subsection (c) of this section,

(B) the government of the receiving country has consented to accept such hazardous waste,

(C) a copy of the receiving country's written consent is attached to the manifest accompanying each waste shipment, and

(D) the shipment conforms with the terms of the consent of the government of the receiving country required pursuant to subsection (e), or

(2) the United States and the government of the receiving country have entered into an agreement as provided for in subsection (f) and the shipment conforms with the terms of such agreement.

(b) Regulations.--Not later than 12 months after the date of enactment of the Hazardous and Solid Waste Amendments of 1984, the Administrator shall promulgate the regulations necessary to implement this section. Such regulations shall become effective 180 days after promulgation.

(c) Notification.--Any person who intends to export a hazardous waste identified or listed under this subtitle beginning 12 months after the date of enactment of the Hazardous and Solid Waste Amendments of 1984, shall, before such hazardous waste is scheduled to leave the United States, provide notification to the Administrator. Such notification shall contain the following information:
    (1) the name and address of the exporter;
    (2) the types and estimated quantities of hazardous waste to be exported;
    (3) the estimated frequency or rate at which such waste is to be exported; and the period of time over which such waste is to be exported;
    (4) the ports of entry;
    (5) a description of the manner in which such hazardous waste will be transported to and treated, stored, or disposed in the receiving country; and
    (6) the name and address of the ultimate treatment, storage or disposal facility.

(d) Procedures for Requesting Consent of the Receiving Country.--Within 30 days of the Administrator's receipt of a complete notification under this section, the Secretary of State, acting on behalf of the Administrator, shall--
    (1) forward a copy of the notification to the government of the receiving country;
    (2) advise the government that United States law prohibits the export of hazardous waste unless the receiving country consents to accept the hazardous waste;
    (3) request the government to provide the Secretary with a written consent or objection to the terms of the notification; and
    (4) forward to the government of the receiving country a description of the Federal regulations which would apply to the treatment, storage, and disposal of the hazardous waste in the United States.

(e) Conveyance or Written Consent to Exporter.--Within 30 days of receipt by the Secretary of State of the receiving country's written consent or objection (or any subsequent communication withdrawing a prior consent or objection), the Administrator shall forward such a consent, objection, or other communication to the exporter.

(f) International Agreements.--Where there exists an international agreement between the United States and the government of the receiving country establishing notice, export, and enforcement procedures for the transportation, treatment, storage, and disposal of hazardous wastes, only the requirements of subsections (a)(2) and (g) shall apply.

(g) Reports.--After the date of enactment of the Hazardous and Solid Waste Amendments of 1984, any person who exports any hazardous waste identified or listed under section 3001 of this subtitle shall file with the Administrator no later than March 1 of each year, a report summarizing the types, quantities, frequency, and ultimate destination of all such hazardous waste exported during the previous calendar year.

(h) Other Standards.--Nothing in this section shall preclude the Administrator from establishing other standards for the export of hazardous wastes under section 3002 or section 3003 of this subtitle.

DOMESTIC SEWAGE

42 USC 6939

Sec. 3018. (a) Report.--The Administrator shall, not later than 15 months after the date of enactment of the Hazardous and Solid Waste Amendments of 1984, submit a report to the Congress concerning those substances identified or listed under section 3001 which are not regulated under this subtitle by reason of the exclusion for mixtures of domestic sewage and other wastes that pass through a sewer system to a publicly owned treatment works. Such report shall include the types, size and number of generators which dispose of such substances in this manner, the types and quantities disposed of in this manner, and the identification of significant generators, wastes, and waste constituents not regulated under existing Federal law or regulated in a manner sufficient to protect human health and the environment.

(b) Revisions of Regulations.--Within 18 months after submitting the report specified in subsection (a), the Administrator shall revise existing regulations and promulgate such additional regulations pursuant to this subtitle (or any other authority of the Administrator, including section 307 of the Federal Water Pollution Control Act) as are necessary to assure that substances identified or listed under section 3001 which pass through a sewer system to a publicly owned treatment works are adequately controlled to protect human health and the environment.

(c) Report on Wastewater Lagoons.--The Administrator shall, within 36 months after the date of the enactment of the Hazardous and Solid Waste Amendments of 1984, submit a report to Congress concerning wastewater lagoons at publicly owned treatment works and their effect on groundwater quality. Such report shall include--

(1) the number and size of such lagoons;
(2) the types and quantities of waste contained in such lagoons;
(3) the extent to which such waste has been or may be released from such lagoons and contaminate ground water; and
(4) available alternatives for preventing or controlling such releases.

The Administrator may utilize the authority of sections 3007 and 3013 for the purpose of completing such report.

(d) Application of Section 3010 and Section 3007.--The provisions of sections 3007 and 3010 shall apply to solid or dissolved materials in domestic sewage to the same extent and in the same manner as such provisions apply to hazardous waste.

EXPOSURE INFORMATION AND HEALTH ASSESSMENTS

42 USC 6939a

Sec. 3019. (a) Exposure Information.--Beginning on the date nine months after the enactment of the Hazardous and Solid Waste Amendments of 1984, each application for a final determination regarding a permit under section 3005(c) for a landfill or surface impoundment shall be accompanied by information reasonably ascertainable by the owner or operator on the potential for the public to be exposed to hazardous wastes or hazardous constituents through releases related to the unit. At a minimum, such information must address:

(1) reasonably foreseeable potential releases from both normal operations and accidents at the unit, including releases associated with transportation to or from the unit;
(2) the potential pathways of human exposure to hazardous wastes or constituents resulting from the releases described under paragraph (1); and
(3) the potential magnitude and nature of the human exposure resulting from such releases.

The owner or operator of a landfill or surface impoundment for which an application for such a final determination under section 3005(c) has been submitted prior to the date of enactment of the Hazardous and Solid Waste Amendments of 1984 shall submit the information required by this subsection to the Administrator (or the State, in the case of a State with an authorized program) no later than the date 9 months after such date of enactment.

(b) Health Assessments.--(1) The Administrator for the State, in the case of a State with an authorized program) shall make the information required by subsection (a), together with other relevant information, available to the Agency for Toxic Substances and Disease Registry established by section 104(i) of the Comprehensive Environmental Response, Compensation and Liability Act of 1980.

(2) Whenever in the judgment of the Administrator, or the State (in the case of a State with an authorized program), a landfill or a surface impoundment poses a substantial potential risk to human health, due to the existence of releases of hazardous constituents, the magnitude of contamination with hazardous

constituents which may be the result of a release, or the magnitude of the population exposed to such release or contamination, the Administrator or the State (with the concurrence of the Administrator) may request the Administrator of the Agency for Toxic Substances and Disease Registry to conduct a health assessment in connection with such facility and take other appropriate action with respect to such risks as authorized by section 104(b) and (i) of the Comprehensive Environmental Response, Compensation and Liability Act of 1980. If funds are provided in connection with such request the Administrator of such Agency shall conduct such health assessment.

(c) Members of the public.--Any member of the public may submit evidence of releases of or exposure to hazardous constituents from such a facility, or as to the risks or health effects associated with such releases or exposure, to the Administrator of the Agency for Toxic Substances and Disease Registry, the Administrator, or the State (in the case of a State with an authorized program).

(d) Priority.--In determining the order in which to conduct health assessments under this subsection, the Administrator of the Agency for Toxic Substances and Disease Registry shall give priority to those facilities or sites at which there is documented evidence of release of hazardous constituents, at which the potential risk to human health appears highest, and for which in the judgment of the Administrator of such Agency existing health assessment data is inadequate to assess the potential risk to human health as provided in subsection (f).

(e) Periodic Reports.--The Administrator of such Agency shall issue periodic reports which include the results of all the assessments carried out under this section. Such assessments or other activities shall be reported after appropriate peer review.

(f) Definition.--For the purposes of this section, the term 'health assessments' shall include preliminary assessments of the potential risk to human health posed by individual sites and facilities subject to this section, based on such factors as the nature and extent of contamination, the existence of potential for pathways of human exposure (including ground or surface water contamination, air emissions, and food chain contamination), the size and potential susceptibility of the community within the likely pathways of exposure, the comparison of expected human exposure levels to the short-term and long-term health effects associated with identified contaminants and any available recommended exposure or tolerance limits for such contaminants, and the comparison of existing morbidity and mortality data on diseases that may be associated with the observed levels of exposure. The assessment shall include an evaluation of the risks to the potentially affected population from all sources of such contaminants, including known point or nonpoint sources other than the site or facility in question. A purpose of such preliminary assessments shall be to help determine whether full-scale health or epidemiological studies and medical evaluations of exposed populations shall be undertaken.

(g) Cost Recovery.--In any case in which a health assessment performed under this section discloses the exposure of a population to the release of a hazardous substance, the costs of such health assessment may be recovered as a cost of response under section 107 of the Comprehensive Environmental Response, Compensation, and Liability Act of 1980 from persons causing or contributing to such release of such hazardous substance or, in the case of multiple releases contributing to such exposure, to all such releases.

INTERIM CONTROL OF HAZARDOUS WASTE INJECTION

42 USC 6979a

Sec. 3020. (a) Underground Source of Drinking Water.--No hazardous waste may be disposed of by underground injection--

(1) into a formation which contains (within one-quarter mile of the well used for such underground injection) an underground source of drinking water; or

(2) above such a formation.

The prohibitions established under this section shall take effect 6 months after the enactment of the Hazardous and Solid Waste Amendments of 1984 except in the case of any State in which identical or more stringent prohibitions are in effect before such date under the Safe Drinking Water Act.

(b) Actions Under CERCLA.--Subsection (a) shall not apply to the injection of contaminated ground water into the aquifer from which it was withdrawn, if--

(1) such injection is--

(A) a response action taken under section 104 or 106 of the Comprehensive Environmental Response, Compensation and Liability Act of 1980, or

(B) part of corrective action required under this title

intended to clean up such contamination;

(2) such contaminated ground water is treated to substantially reduce hazardous constituents prior to such injection; and

(3) such response action or corrective action will, upon completion, be sufficient to protect human health and the environment.

(c) Enforcement.--In addition to enforcement under the provisions of this Act, the prohibitions established under paragraphs (1) and (2) of subsection (a) shall be enforceable under the Safe Drinking Water Act in any State--

(1) which has adopted identical or more stringent prohibitions under part C of the Safe Drinking Water Act and which has assumed primary enforcement responsibility under that Act for enforcement of such prohibitions; or

(2) in which the Administrator has adopted identical or more stringent prohibitions under the Safe Drinking Water Act and is exercising primary enforcement responsibility under that Act for enforcement of such prohibitions.

(d) The terms "primary enforcement responsibility", "underground source of drinking water", "formation" and "well" have the same meanings as provided in regulations of the Administrator under the Safe Drinking Water Act. The term "Safe Drinking Water Act" means title XIV of the Public Health Service Act.

MIXED WASTE INVENTORY REPORTS AND PLANS

Sec. 3021. (a) Mixed Waste Inventory Reports.--

(1) Requirement.--Not later than 180 days after the date of the enactment of the Federal Facility Compliance Act of 1992, the Secretary of Energy shall submit to the Administrator and to the Governor of each State in which the Department of Energy stores or generates mixed wastes the following reports:

(A) A report containing a national inventory of all such mixed wastes, regardless of the time they were generated, on a State-by-State basis.

(B) A report containing a national inventory of mixed waste treatment capacities and technologies.

(2) Inventory of Wastes.--The report required by paragraph (1)(A) shall include the following:

(A) A description of each type of mixed waste at each Department of Energy facility in each State, including, at a minimum, the name of the waste stream.

(B) The amount of each type of mixed waste currently stored at each Department of Energy facility in each State, set forth separately by mixed waste that is subject to the land disposal prohibition requirements of section 3004 and mixed waste that is not subject to such prohibition requirements.

(C) An estimate of the amount of each type of mixed waste the Department expects to generate in the next 5 years at each Department of Energy facility in each State.

(D) A description of any waste minimization actions the Department has implemented at each Department of Energy facility in each State for each mixed waste stream.

(E) The EPA hazardous waste code for each type of mixed waste containing waste that has been characterized at each Department of Energy facility in each State.

(F) An inventory of each type of waste that has not been characterized by sampling and analysis at each Department of Energy facility in each State.

(G) The basis for the Department's determination of the applicable hazardous waste code for each type of mixed waste at each Department of Energy facility and a description of whether the determination is based on sampling and analysis conducted on the waste or on the basis of process knowledge.

(H) A description of the source of each type of mixed waste at each Department of Energy facility in each State.

(I) The land disposal prohibition treatment technology or technologies specified for the hazardous waste component of each type of mixed waste at each Department of Energy facility in each State.

(J) A statement of whether and how the radionuclide content of the waste alters or affects use of the technologies described in subparagraph (1).

(3) Inventory of Treatment Capacities and Technologies.--The report required by paragraph (1)(B) shall include the following:

(A) An estimate of the available treatment capacity for each waste described in the report required by paragraph (1)(A) for which treatment technologies exist.

(B) A description, including the capacity, number and location, of each treatment unit considered in calculating the estimate under subparagraph (A).

(C) A description, including the capacity, number and location, of any existing treatment unit that was not considered in calculating the estimate under subparagraph (A) but that could, alone or in conjunction with other treatment units, be used to treat any of the wastes described in the report required by paragraph (1)(A) to meet the requirements of regulations promulgated pursuant to section 3004(m).

(D) For each unit listed in subparagraph (C), a statement of the reasons why the unit was not included in calculating the estimate under subparagraph (A).

(E) A description, including the capacity, number, location, and estimated date of availability, of each treatment unit currently proposed to increase the treatment capacities estimated under subparagraph (A).

(F) For each waste described in the report required by paragraph (1)(A) for which the Department has determined no treatment technology exists, information sufficient to support such determination and a description of the technological approaches the Department anticipates will need to be developed to treat the waste.

(4) Comments and Revisions.--Not later than 90 days after the date of the submission of the reports by the Secretary of Energy under paragraph (1), the Administrator and each State which received the reports shall submit any comments they may have concerning the reports to the Department of Energy. The Secretary of Energy shall consider and publish the comments prior to publication of the final report.

(5) Requests for Additional Information.--Nothing in this subsection limits or restricts the authority of States or the Administrator to request additional information from the Secretary of Energy.

(b) Plan for Development of Treatment Capacities and Technologies.--

(1) Plan Requirement.--(A)(i) For each facility at which the Department of Energy generates or stores mixed wastes, except any facility subject to a permit, agreement, or order described in clause (ii), the Secretary of Energy shall develop and submit, as provided in paragraph (2), a plan for developing treatment capacities and technologies to treat all of the facility's mixed wastes, regardless of the time they were generated, to the standards promulgated pursuant to section 3004(m).

(ii) Clause (i) shall not apply with respect to any facility subject to any permit establishing a schedule for treatment of such wastes, or any existing agreement or administrative or judicial order governing the treatment of such wastes, to which the State is a party.

(B) Each plan shall contain the following:

(i) For mixed wastes for which treatment technologies exist, a schedule for submitting all applicable permit applications, entering into contracts, initiating construction, conducting systems testing, commencing operations, and processing backlogged and currently generated mixed wastes.

(ii) For mixed wastes for which no treatment technologies exist, a schedule for identifying and developing such technologies, identifying the funding requirements for the identification and development of such technologies, submitting treatability study exemptions, and submitting research and development permit applications.

(iii) For all cases where the Department proposes radionuclide separation of mixed wastes, or materials derived from mixed wastes, it shall provide an estimate of the volume of waste generated by each case of radionuclide separation, the volume of waste that would exist or be generated without radionuclide separation, the estimated costs of waste treatment and disposal if radionuclide separation is used compared to the estimated costs if it is not used, and the assumptions underlying such waste volume and cost estimates.

(C) A plan required under this subsection may provide for centralized, regional, or on-site treatment of mixed wastes, or any combination thereof.

(2) Review and Approval of Plan.--(A) For each facility that is located in a State (i) with authority under State law to prohibit land disposal of mixed waste until the waste has been treated and (ii) with both authority under State law to regulate the hazardous components of mixed waste and authorization from the Environmental Protection Agency under section 3006 to regulate the hazardous components of mixed waste, the Secretary of Energy shall submit the plan required under paragraph (1) to the appropriate State regulatory officials for their review and approval, modification, or disapproval. In reviewing the plan, the State shall consider the need for regional treatment facilities. The State shall consult with the Administrator and any other State in which a facility affected by the plan is located and consider public comments in making its determination on the plan. The State shall approve, approve with modifications, or disapprove the plan within 6 months after receipt of the plan.

(B) For each facility located in a State that does not have the authority described in subparagraph (A), the Secretary shall submit the plan required under paragraph (1) to the Administrator of the Environmental Protection Agency for review and approval, modification, or disapproval. A copy of the plan also shall be provided by the Secretary to the State in which such facility is located. In reviewing the plan, the Administrator shall consider the need for regional treatment facilities. The Administrator shall consult with the State or States in which any facility affected by the plan is located nd consider public comments in making a determination on the plan. The Administrator shall approve, approve with modifications, or disapprove the plan within 6 months after receipt of the plan.

(C)Upon the approval of a plan under this paragraph by the Administrator or a State, the Administrator shall issue an order under appropriate State authority, requiring compliance with the approved plan.

(3) Public Participation.--Upon submission of a plan by the Secretary of Energy to the Administrator or a State, and before approval of the plan by the Administrator or a State, the Administrator or State shall publish a notice of the availability of the submitted plan and make such submitted plan available to the public on request.

(4) Revisions of Plan.--If any revisions of an approved plan are proposed by the Secretary of Energy or required by the Administrator or a State, the provisions of paragraphs (2) and (3) shall apply to the revisions in the same manner as they apply to the original plan.

(5) Waiver of Plan Requirement.--(A) A State may waive the require-ment for the Secretary of Energy to develop and submit a plan under this subsection for a facility located in the State if the State (i) enters into an agreement with the Secretary of Energy that addresses compliance at that facility with section 3004(j) with respect to mixed waste, and (ii) issues an order requiring compliance with such agreement and which in effect.

(B) Any violation of an agreement or order referred to in subparagraph (A) is subject to the waiver of sovereign immunity contained in section 6001(a).

(c) Schedule and Progress Reports.--

(1) Schedule.--Not later than 6 months after the date of the enactment of the Federal Facility Compliance Act of 1992, the Secretary of Energy shall publish in the Federal Register a schedule for submitting the plans required under subsection (b).

(2) Progress Reports.--(A) Not later than the deadlines specified in subparagraph (B), the Secretary of Energy shall submit to the Committee on Environment and Public Works of the Senate and the Committee on Energy and Commerce of the House of Representatives a progress report containing the following:

(i) An identification, by facility, of the plans that have been submitted to States or the Administrator of the Environmental Protection Agency pursuant to subsection (b).

(ii) The status of State and Environmental Protection Agency review and approval of each such plan.

(iii) The number of orders requiring compliance with such plans that are in effect.

(iv) For the first 2 reports required under this paragraph, an identification of the plans required under such subsection (b) that the Secretary expects to submit in the 12-month period following submission of the report.

(B) The Secretary of Energy shall submit a report under subparagraph (A) not later than 12 months after the date of the enactment of the Federal Facility Compliance Act of 1992, 24 months after such date, and 36 months after such date.

PUBLIC VESSELS

Sec. 3022.--(a)Waste Generated on Public Vessels.--Any hazardous waste generated on a public vessel shall not be subject to the storage, mani-fest, inspection, or recordkeeping requirements of this Act until such waste is transferred to a shore facility, unless--

(1) the waste is stored on the public vessel for more than 90 days after the public vessel is placed in reserve or is otherwise no longer in service; or

(2) the waste is transferred to another public vessel within the territorial waters of the United States and is stored on such vessel or another public vessel for more than 90 days after the date of transfer.

(b) Computation of Storage Period.--For purposes of subsection (a), the 90-day period begins on the earlier of--

(1) the date on which the public vessel on which the waste was generated is placed in reserve or is otherwise no longer in service; or

(2) the date on which the waste is transferred from the public vessel on which the waste was generated to another public vessel within the territorial waters of the United States;

and continues, without interruption, as long as the waste is stored on the original public vessel (if in reserve or not in service) or another public vessel.

(c) Definitions.--For purposes of this section:

(1) The term "public vessel" means a vessel owned or bareboat chartered and operated by the United States, or by a foreign nation, except when the vessel is engaged in commerce.

(2) The terms "in reserve" and "in service" have the meanings applicable to those terms under section 7293 and sections 7304 through 7308 of title 10, United States Code, and regulations prescribed under those sections.

(d) Relationship to Other Law.--Nothing in this section shall be construed as altering or otherwise affecting the provisions of section 7311 of title 10, United States Code.

FEDERALLY OWNED TREATMENT WORKS

Sec. 3023.--(a) In General.--For purposes of section 1004(27), the phrase "but does not include solid or dissolved material in domestic sewage" shall apply to any solid or dissolved material introduced by a source into a federally owned treatment works if--

(1) such solid or dissolved material is subject to a pretreatment standard under section 307 of the Federal Water Pollution Control Act (33 U.S.C. 1317), and the source is in compliance with such standard;

(2) for a solid or dissolved material for which a pretreatment standard has not been promulgated pursuant to section 307 of the Federal Water Pollution Control Act (33 U.S.C. 1317), the Administrator has promulgated a schedule for establishing such a pretreatment standard which would be applicable to such solid or dissolved material not later than 7 years after the date of enactment of this section, such standard is promulgated on or before the date established in the schedule, and after the effective date of such standard the source is in compliance with such standard;

(3) such solid or dissolved material is not covered by paragraph (1) or (2) and is not prohibited from land disposal under subsections (d), (e), (f), or (g) of section 3004 because such material has been treated in accordance with section 3004 (m); or

(4) notwithstanding paragraphs (1), (2), or (3), such solid or dissolved material is generated by a household or person which generates less than 100 kilograms of hazardous waste per moth unless such solid or dissolved material would otherwise be an acutely hazardous waste and subject to standards, regulations, or other requirements under this Act notwithstanding the quantity generated.

(b) Prohibition.--It is unlawful to introduce into a federally owned treatment works any pollutant that is a hazardous waste.

(c) Enforcement.--(1) Actions taken to enforce this section shall not require closure of a treatment works if the hazardous waste is removed or decontaminated and such removal or decontamination is adequate, in the discretion of the Administrator or, in the case of an authorized State, of the State, to protect human health and the environment.

(2) Nothing in this subsection shall be construed to prevent the Administrator or an authorized State from ordering the closure of a treatment works if the Administrator or State determines such closure is necessary for protection of human health and the environment.

(3) Nothing in this subsection shall be construed to affect any other enforcement authorities available to the Administrator or a State under this subtitle.

(d) Definition.--For purposes of this section, the term "federally owned treatment works" means a facility that is owned and operated by a department, agency, or instrumentality of the Federal Government treating wastewater, a majority of which is domestic sewage, prior to discharge in accordance with a permit issued under section 402 of the Federal Water Pollution Control Act.

(e) Savings Clause.--Nothing in this section shall be construed as affecting any agreement, permit, or administrative or judicial order, or any condition or requirement contained in such an agreement, permit, or order, that is in existence on the date of the enactment of this section and that requires corrective action or closure at a federally owned treatment works or solid waste management unit or facility related to such a treatment works.

SUBTITLE D--STATE OR REGIONAL SOLID WASTE PLANS

OBJECTIVES OF SUBTITLE

42 USC 6941

Sec. 4001. The objectives of this subtitle are to assist in developing and encouraging methods for the disposal of solid waste which are environmentally sound and which maximize the utilization of valuable resources including energy and materials which are recoverable from solid waste and to encourage resource conservation. Such objectives are to be accomplished through Federal technical and financial assistance to States or regional authorities for comprehensive planning pursuant to federal guidelines designed to foster cooperation among Federal, State, and local governments and private industry. In developing such comprehensive plans, it is the intention of this Act that in determining the size of the waste-to-energy facility, adequate provision shall be given to the present and reasonably anticipated future needs, including those needs created by thorough implementation of section 6002(h), of the recycling and resource recovery interest within the area encompassed by the planning process.

FEDERAL GUIDELINES FOR PLANS

42 USC 6942

Sec. 4002. (a) Guidelines for Identification of Regions.--For purposes of encouraging and facilitating the development of regional planning for solid waste management, the Administrator, within one hundred and eighty days after the date of enactment of this section and after consultation with appropriate Federal, State, and local authorities, shall by regulation publish guidelines for the identification of those areas which have common solid waste management problems and are appropriate units for planning regional solid waste management services. Such guidelines shall consider

(1) the size and location of areas which should be included,

(2) the volume of solid waste which should be included, and

(3) the available means of coordinating regional planning with other related regional planning and for coordination of such regional planning into the State plan.

(b) Guidelines for State Plans.--Not later than eighteen months after the date of enactment of this section and after notice and hearing, the Administrator shall, after consultation with appropriate Federal, State, and local authorities, promulgate regulations containing guidelines to assist in the development and implementation of State solid waste management plans (hereinafter in this title referred to as "State plans"). The guidelines shall contain methods for achieving the objectives specified in section 4001. Such guidelines shall be reviewed from time to time, but not less frequently than every three years, and revised as may be appropriate.

(c) Considerations for State Plan Guidelines.--The guidelines promulgated under subsection (b) shall consider

(1) the varying regional, geologic, hydrologic, climatic, and other circumstances under which different solid waste practices are required in order to insure the reasonable protection of the quality of the ground and surface waters from leachate contamination, the reasonable protection of the quality of the surface waters from surface runoff contamination, and the reasonable protection of ambient air quality;

(2) characteristics and conditions of collection, storage, processing, and disposal operating methods, techniques and practices, and location of facilities where such operating methods, techniques, and practices are conducted, taking into account the nature of the material to be disposed;

(3) methods for closing or upgrading open dumps for purposes of eliminating potential health hazards;

(4) population density, distribution, and projected growth;

(5) geographic, geologic, climatic, and hydrologic characteristics;

(6) the type and location of transportation;

(7) the profile of industries;

(8) the constituents and generation rates of waste;

(9) the political, economic, organizational, financial, and management problems affecting comprehensive solid waste management;

(10) types of resource recovery facilities and resource conservation systems which are appropriate; and

(11) available new and additional markets for recovered material and energy and energy resources recovered from solid waste as well as methods for conserving such materials and energy.

REQUIREMENTS FOR APPROVAL OF PLANS

42 USC 6943

Sec. 4003. (a) Minimum Requirements.--In order to be approved under section 4007, each State plan must comply with the following minimum requirements

(1) The plan shall identify (in accordance with section 4006(b) (A) the responsibilities of State, local, and regional authorities in the implementation of the State plan, (B) the distribution of Federal funds to the authorities responsible for development and implementation of the State plan, and (C) the means for coordinating regional planning and implementation under the State plan.

(2) The plan shall, in accordance with section 4004 (b) and 4005(a), prohibit the establishment of new open dumps within the State, and contain requirements that all solid waste (including solid waste originating in other States, but not including hazardous waste) shall be (A) utilized for resource recovery or (B) disposed of in sanitary landfills (within the meaning of section 4004 (a)) or otherwise disposed of in an environmentally sound manner.

(3) The plan shall provide for the closing or upgrading of all existing open dumps with the State pursuant to the requirements of section 4005.

(4) The plan shall provide for the establishment of such State regulatory powers as may be necessary to implement the plan.

(5) The plan shall provide that no State or local government within the State shall be prohibited under State or local law from negotiating and entering into long-term contracts for the supply of solid waste to resource recovery facilities, from entering into long-term contracts for the operation of such facilities, or from securing long-term markets for material and energy recovered from such facilities or for conserving materials or energy by reducing the volume of waste.

(6) The plan shall provide for such resource conservation or recovery and for the disposal of solid waste in sanitary landfills or any combination of practices so as may be necessary to use or dispose of such waste in a manner that is environmentally sound.

(b) Discretionary Plan Provisions Relating to Recycled Oil.--
Any State plan submitted under this subtitle may include, at the option of the State, provisions to carry out each of the following:

(1) Encouragement, to the maximum extent feasible and consistent with the protection of the public health and the environment, of the use of recycled oil in all appropriate areas of State and local government.

(2) Encouragement of persons contracting with the State to use recycled oil to the maximum extent feasible, consistent with protection of the public health and the environment.

(3) Informing the public of the uses of recycled oil.

(4) Establishment and implementation of a program (including any necessary licensing of persons and including the use, where appropriate, of manifests) to assure that used oil is collected, transported, treated, stored, reused, and disposed of, in a manner which does not present a hazard to the public health or the environment.

Any plan submitted under this title before the date of the enactment of the Used Oil Recycling Act of 1980 may be amended, at the option of the State, at any time after such date to include any provision referred to in this subsection.

(c) Energy and Materials Conservation and Recovery
Feasibility Planning and Assistance.--
(1) A State which has a plan approved under this subtitle or which has submitted a plan for such approval shall be eligible for assistance under section 4008(a)(3) if the Administrator determines that under such plan the State will

(A) analyze and determine the economic and technical feasibility of facilities and programs to conserve resources which contribute to the waste stream or to recover energy and materials from municipal waste;

(B) analyze the legal, institutional, and economic impediments to the development of systems and facilities for conservation of energy or materials which contribute to the waste stream or for the recovery of energy and materials from municipal waste and make recommendations to appropriate governmental authorities for overcoming such impediments;

(C) assist municipalities within the State in developing plans, programs, and projects to conserve resources or recover energy and materials from municipal waste; and

(D) coordinate the resource conservation and recovery planning under subparagraph (C).

(2) The analysis referred to in paragraph (1)(A) shall include

(A) the evaluation of, and establishment of priorities among, market opportunities for industrial and commercial users of all types (including public utilities and industrial parks) to utilize energy and materials recovered from municipal waste;

(B) comparisons of the relative costs of energy recovered from municipal waste in relation to the costs of energy derived from fossil fuels and other sources;

(C) studies of the transportation and storage problems and other problems associated with the development of energy and materials recovery technology, including curbside source separation;

(D) the evaluation and establishment of priorities among ways of conserving energy or materials which contribute to the waste stream;

(E) comparison of the relative total costs between conserving resources and disposing of or recovering such waste; and

(F) studies of impediments to resource conservation or recovery, including business practices, transportation requirements, or storage difficulties.

Such studies and analyses shall also include studies of other sources of solid waste from which energy and materials may be recovered or minimized.

(d) Size of Waste-to-Energy Facilities.--Notwithstanding any of the above requirements, it is the intention of this Act and the planning process developed pursuant to this Act that in determining the size of the waste-to-energy facility, adequate provision shall be given to the present and reasonably anticipated future needs of the recycling and resource recovery interest within the area encompassed by the planning process.

CRITERIA FOR SANITARY LANDFILLS; SANITARY LANDFILLS REQUIRED FOR ALL DISPOSAL

42 USC 6944

Sec. 4004. (a) Criteria for Sanitary Landfills.--Not later than one year after the date of enactment of this section, after consultation with the States, and after notice and public hearings, the Administrator shall promulgate regulations containing criteria for determining which facilities shall be classified as sanitary landfills and which shall be classified as open dumps within the meaning of this Act. At a minimum, such criteria shall provide that a facility may be classified as a sanitary landfill and not an open dump only if there is no reasonable probability of adverse effects on health or the environment from disposal of solid waste at such facility. Such regulations may provide for the classification of the types of sanitary landfills.

(b) Disposal Required to be in Sanitary Landfills, etc.--For purposes of complying with section 4003(2) each State plan shall prohibit the establishment of open dumps and contain a requirement that disposal of all solid waste within the State shall be in compliance with such section 4003(2).

(c) Effective Date.--The prohibition contained in subsection (b) shall take effect on the date six months after the date of promulgation of regulations under subsection (a).

UPGRADING OF OPEN DUMPS

42 USC 6945

Sec. 4005. (a) Closing or Upgrading of Existing Open Dumps.--Upon promulgation of criteria under section 1008(a)(3), any solid waste management practice or disposal of solid waste or hazardous waste which constitutes the open dumping of solid waste or hazardous waste is prohibited, except in the case of any practice or disposal of solid waste under a timetable or schedule for compliance established under this section. The prohibition contained in the preceding sentence shall be enforceable under section 7002 against persons engaged in the act of open dumping. For purposes of complying with section 4003(2) and 4003(3), each State plan shall contain a requirement that all existing disposal facilities or sites for solid waste in such State which are open dumps listed in the inventory under subsection (b) shall comply with such measures as may be promulgated by the Administrator to eliminate health hazards and minimize potential health hazards. Each such plan shall establish, for any entity which demonstrates that it has considered other public or private alternatives for solid waste management to comply with the prohibition on open dumping and is unable to utilize such alternatives to so comply, a timetable or schedule for compliance for such practice or disposal of solid waste which specifies a schedule of remedial measures, including an enforceable sequence of actions or operations, leading to compliance with the prohibition on open dumping of solid waste within a reasonable time (not to exceed 5 years from the date of publication of the criteria under section 1008(a)(3)).

(b) Inventory.--To assist the States in complying with section 4003(3), not later than one year after promulgation of regulations under section 4004, the Administrator, with the cooperation of the Bureau of the Census shall publish an inventory of all disposal facilities or sites in the United States which are open dumps within the meaning of this Act.

(c) Control of Hazardous Disposal.--

(1)(A) Not later than 36 months after the date of enactment of the Hazardous and Solid Waste Amendments of 1984, each State shall adopt and implement a permit program or other system of prior approval and conditions to assure that each solid waste management facility within such State which may receive hazardous household waste or hazardous waste due to the provision of section 3001(d) for small quantity generators (otherwise not subject to the requirement for a permit under section 3005) will comply with the applicable criteria promulgated under section 4004(a) and section 1008(a)(3).

(B) Not later than 18 months after the promulgation of revised criteria under subsection 4004(a) (as required by section 4010(c)), each State shall adopt and implement a permit program or other system or prior approval and conditions, to assure that each solid waste management facility within such State which may receive hazardous household waste or hazardous waste due to the provision of section 3001(d) for small quantity generators (otherwise not subject to the requirement for a permit under section 3005) will comply with the criteria revised under section 4004(a).

(C) The Administrator shall determine whether each State has developed an adequate program under this paragraph. The Administrator may make such a determination in conjunction with approval, disapproval or partial approval of a State plan under section 4007.

(2)(A) In any State that the Administrator determines has not adopted an adequate program for such facilities under paragraph (1}(B) by the date provided in such paragraph, the Administrator may use the authorities available under sections 3007 and 3008 of this title to enforce the prohibition contained in subsection (a) of this section with respect to such facilities.

(B) For purposes of this paragraph, the term "requirement of this subtitle" in section 3008 shall be deemed to include criteria promulgated by the Administrator under sections 1008(a)(3) and 4004(a) of this title, and the term "hazardous wastes" in section 3007 shall be deemed to include solid waste at facilities that may handle hazardous household wastes or hazardous wastes from small quantity generators.

PROCEDURE FOR DEVELOPMENT AND IMPLEMENTATION
OF STATE PLAN

42 USC 6946

Sec. 4006. (a) Identification of Regions.--Within one hundred and eighty days after publication of guidelines under section 4002(a)(relating to identification of regions), the Governor of each State, after consultation with local elected officials, shall promulgate regulations based on such guidelines identifying the boundaries of each area within the State which, as a result of urban concentrations, geographic conditions, markets, and other factors, is appropriate for carrying out regional solid waste management. Such regulations may be modified from time to time (identifying additional or different regions) pursuant to such guidelines.

(b) Identification of State and Local
Agencies and Responsibilities.--

(1) Within one hundred and eighty days after the Governor promulgates regulations under subsection (a), for purposes of facilitating the development and implementation of a State plan which will meet the minimum requirements of section 4003, the State, together with appropriate elected officials of general purpose units of local government, shall jointly (A) identify an agency to develop the State plan and identify one or more agencies to implement such plan, and (B) identify which solid waste management activities will, under such State plan, be planned for and carried out by the State and which such management activities will, under such State plan, be planned for and carried out by a regional or local authority or a combination of regional or local and State authorities. If a multifunctional regional agency authorized by State law to conduct solid waste planning and management (the members of which are appointed by the Governor) is in existence on the date of enactment of this Act, the Governor shall identify such authority for purposes of carrying out within such region clause (A) of this paragraph. Where feasible, designation of the agency for the affected area designated under section 208 of the Federal Water Pollution Control Act (86 Stat. 839) shall be considered. A State agency identified under this paragraph shall be established or designated by the Governor of such State. Local or regional agencies identified under this paragraph shall be composed of individuals at least a majority of whom are elected local officials.

(2) If planning and implementation agencies are not identified and designated or established as required under paragraph (1) for any affected area, the governor shall, before the date two hundred and seventy days

after promulgation of regulations under subsection (a), establish or designate a State agency to develop and implement the State plan for such area.

(c) Interstate Regions.--

(1) In the case of any region which, pursuant to the guidelines published by the Administrator under section 4002(a) (relating to identification of regions), would be located in two or more States, the Governors of the respective States, after consultation with local elected officials, shall consult, cooperate, and enter into agreements identifying the boundaries of such region pursuant to subsection (a).

(2) Within one hundred and eighty days after an interstate region is identified by agreement under paragraph (1), appropriate elected officials of general purpose units of local government within such region shall jointly establish or designate an agency to develop a plan for such region. If no such agency is established or designated within such period by such officials, the Governors of the respective States may, by agreement, establish or designate for such purpose a single representative organization including elected officials of general purpose units of local government within such region.

(3) Implementation of interstate regional solid waste management plans shall be conducted by units of local government, for any portion of a region within their jurisdiction, or by multijurisdictional agencies or authorities designated in accordance with State law, including those designated by agreement by such units of local government for such purpose. If no such unit, agency, or authority is so designated, the respective Governors shall designate or establish a single interstate agency to implement such plan.

(4) For purposes of this subtitle, so much of an interstate regional plan as is carried out within a particular State shall be deemed part of the State plan for such State.

APPROVAL OF STATE PLAN; FEDERAL ASSISTANCE

42 USC 6947

Sec. 4007. (a) Plan Approval.--The Administrator shall, within six months after a State plan has been submitted for approval, approve or disapprove the plan. The Administrator shall approve a plan if he determines that

(1) it meets the requirements of paragraphs (1), (2), (3), and (5) of section 4003; and

(2) it contains provision for revision of such plan, after notice and public hearing, whenever the Administrator, by regulation determines

(A) that revised regulations respecting minimum requirements have been promulgated under paragraphs (1), (2), (3), and (5) of section 4003 with which the State plan is not in compliance;

(B) that information has become available which demonstrates the inadequacy of the plan to effectuate the purposes of this subtitle; or

(C) that such revision is otherwise necessary.

The Administrator shall review approved plans from time to time and if he determines that revision or corrections are necessary to bring such plan into compliance with the minimum requirements promulgated under section 4003 (including new or revised requirements), he shall, after notice and opportunity for public hearing, withdraw his approval of such plan. Such withdrawal of approval shall cease to be effective upon the Administrator's determination that such complies with such minimum requirements.

(b) Eligibility of States for Federal Financial Assistance.--

(1) The Administrator shall approve a State application for financial assistance under this subtitle, and make grants to such State, if such State and local and regional authorities within such State have complied with the requirements of section 4006 within the period required under such section and if such State has a State plan which has been approved by the Administrator under this subtitle.

(2) The Administrator shall approve a State application for financial assistance under this subtitle, and make grants to such State, for fiscal years 1978 and 1979 if the Administrator determines that the State plan continues to be eligible for approval under subsection (a) and is being implemented by the State.

(3) Upon withdrawal of approval of a State plan under subsection (a), the Administrator shall withhold

Federal financial and technical assistance under this subtitle (other than such technical assistance as may be necessary to assist in obtaining the reinstatement of approval) until such time as such approval is reinstated.

(c) Existing Activities.   Nothing in this subtitle shall be construed to prevent or affect any activities respecting solid waste planning or management which are carried out by the State, regional, or local authorities unless such activities are inconsistent with a State plan approved by the Administrator under this subtitle.

FEDERAL ASSISTANCE

42 USC 6948

Sec. 4008. (a) Authorization of Federal Financial Assistance.--

(1) There are authorized to be appropriated $30,000,000 for the fiscal year 1978, $40,000,000 for fiscal year 1979, $20,000,000 for fiscal year 1980, $15,000,000 for fiscal year 1981, $20,000,000 for the fiscal year 1982, and $10,000,000 for each of the fiscal years 1985 through 1988 for purposes of financial assistance to States and local, regional, and interstate authorities for the development and implementation of plans approved by the Administrator under this subtitle (other than the provisions of such plans referred to in section 4003(b), relating to feasibility planning for municipal waste energy and materials conservation and recovery).

(2)(A) The Administrator is authorized to provide financial assistance to States, counties, municipalities, and intermunicipal agencies and State and local public solid waste management authorities for implementation of programs to provide solid waste management, resource recovery, and resource conservation services and hazardous waste management.   Such assistance shall include assistance for facility planning and feasibility studies; expert consultation; surveys and analyses of market needs; marketing of recovered resources; technology assessments; legal expenses; construction feasibility studies; source separation projects; and fiscal or economic investigations or studies; but such assistance shall not include any other element of construction, or any acquisition of land or interest in land, or any subsidy for the price of recovered resources.   Agencies assisted under this subsection shall consider existing solid waste management and hazardous waste management services and facilities as well as facilities proposed for construction.

(B) An applicant for financial assistance under this paragraph must agree to comply with respect to the project or program assisted with the applicable requirements of section 4005 and Subtitle C of this Act and apply applicable solid waste management practices, methods, and levels of control consistent with any guidelines published pursuant to section 1008 of this Act.   Assistance under this paragraph shall be available only for programs certified by the State to be consistent with any applicable State or area-wide solid waste management plan or program.   Applicants for technical and financial assistance under this section shall not preclude or foreclose consideration of programs for the recovery of recyclable materials through source separation or other resource recovery techniques.

(C) There are authorized to be appropriated $15,000,000 for each of the fiscal years 1978 and 1979 for the purposes of this section.   There are authorized to be appropriated $10,000,000 for fiscal year 1980, $10,000,000 for fiscal year 1981, $10,000,000 for fiscal year 1982, and $10,000,000 for each of the fiscal years 1985 through 1988 for purposes of this paragraph.

(D) There are authorized

(i) to be made available $15,000,000 out of funds appropriated for fiscal year 1985, and

(ii) to be appropriated for each of the fiscal years 1986 through 1988, $20,000,000   f o r grants to States (and where appropriate to regional, local, and interstate agencies) to implement programs requiring compliance by solid waste management facilities with the criteria promulgated under section 4004(a) and section 1008(a)(3) and with the provisions of section 4005.   To the extent practicable, such programs shall require such compliance not later than 36 months after the date of the enactment of the Hazardous and Solid Waste Amendments of 1984.

(3)(A) There is authorized to be appropriated for the fiscal year beginning October 1, 1981, and for each fiscal year thereafter before October 1, 1986, $4,000,000 for purposes of making grants to States to carry out section 4003(b).   No amount may be appropriated for such purposes for the fiscal year beginning on October 1, 1986, or for any fiscal year thereafter.

(B) Assistance provided by the Administrator under this paragraph shall be used only for the purposes specified in section 4003(b). Such assistance may not be used for purposes of land acquisition, final facility design, equipment purchase, construction, startup or operation activities.

(C) Where appropriate, any State receiving assistance under this paragraph may make all or any part of such assistance available to municipalities within the State to carry out the activities specified in section 4003(b)(1)(A) and (B).

(b) State Allotment.--The sums appropriated in any fiscal year under subsection (a)(1) shall be allotted by the Administrator among all States, in the ratio that the population in each State bears to the population in all of the States, except that no State shall receive less than one-half of 1 per centum of the sums so allotted in any fiscal year. No State shall receive any grant under this section during any fiscal year when its expenditures of nonFederal funds for other than nonrecurrent expenditures for solid waste management control programs will be less than its expenditures were for such programs during fiscal year 1975, except that such funds may be reduced by an amount equal to their proportionate share of any general reduction of State spending ordered by the Governor or legislature of such State. No State shall receive any grant for solid waste management programs unless the Administrator is satisfied that such grant will be so used as to supplement and, to the extent practicable, increase the level of State, local, regional, or other nonFederal funds that would in the absence of such grant be made available for the maintenance of such programs.

(c) Distribution of Federal Financial Assistance within the State.--The Federal assistance allotted to the States under subsection (b) shall be allocated by the State receiving such funds to State, local, regional, and interstate authorities carrying out planning and implementation of the State plan. Such allocation shall be based upon the responsibilities of the respective parties as determined pursuant to section 4006(b).

(d) Technical Assistance.--

(1) The Administrator may provide technical assistance to State and local governments for purposes of developing and implementing State plans. Technical assistance respecting resource recovery and conservation may be provided through resource recovery and conservation panels, established in the Environmental Protection Agency under subtitle B, to assist the State and local governments with respect to particular resource recovery and conservation projects under consideration and to evaluate their effect on the State plan.

(2) In carrying out this subsection, the Administrator may, upon request, provide technical assistance to States to assist in the removal or modification of legal, institutional, economic, and other impediments to the recycling of used oil. Such impediments may include laws, regulations, and policies, including State procurement policies, which are not favorable to the recycling of used oil.

(3) In carrying out this subsection, the Administrator is authorized to provide technical assistance to States, municipalities, regional authorities, and intermunicipal agencies upon request, to assist in the removal or modification of legal, institutional, and economic impediments which have the effect of impeding the development of systems and facilities to recover energy and materials from municipal waste or to conserve energy or materials which contribute to the waste stream. Such impediments may include

(A) laws, regulations, and policies, including State and local procurement policies, which are not favorable to resource conservation and recovery policies, systems, and facilities.

(B) impediments to the financing of facilities to conserve or recover energy and materials from municipal waste through the exercise of State and local authority to issue revenue bonds and the use of State and local credit assistance; and

(C) impediments to institutional arrangements necessary to undertake projects for the conservation or recovery of energy and materials from municipal waste, including the creation of special districts, authorities, or corporations where necessary having the power to secure the supply of waste of a project, to conserve resources, to implement the project, and to undertake related activities.

(e) Special Communities.--

(1) The Administrator, in cooperation with State and local officials, shall identify local governments within the United States

(A) having a solid waste disposal facility

(i) which is owned by the unit of local government,

(ii) for which an order has been issued by the State to cease receiving solid waste for treatment, storage, or disposal, and

(iii) which is subject to a State-approved end-use recreation plan;

(B) which are located over an aquifer which is the source of drinking water for any person or public water system and which has serious environmental problems resulting from the disposal of such solid waste, including possible methane migration;

(2) There is authorized to be appropriated to the Administrator $2,500,000 for the fiscal year 1980, $1,500,000 for each of the fiscal years 1981 and 1982, and $500,000 for each of the fiscal years 1985 through 1988 to make grants to be used for the containment and stabilization of solid waste located at the disposal sites referred to in paragraph (1). Not more than one community in any State shall be eligible for grants under this paragraph and not more than one project in any State shall be eligible for such grants. No unit of local government shall be eligible for grants under this paragraph with respect to any site which exceeds 65 acres in size.

(f) Assistance to States for Discretionary Program for Recycled Oil.--

(1) The Administrator may make grants to States, which have a State plan approved under section 4007, or which have submitted a State plan for approval under such section, if such plan includes the discretionary provisions described in section 4003(b). Grants under this subsection shall be for purposes of assisting the State in carrying out such discretionary provisions. No grant under this subsection may be used for construction or for the acquisition of land or equipment.

(2) Grants under this subsection shall be allotted among the States in the same manner as provided in the first sentence of subsection (b).

(3) No grant may be made under this subsection unless an application therefor is submitted to, and approved by, the Administrator. The application shall be in such form, be submitted in such manner, and contain such information as the Administrator may require.

(4) For purposes of making grants under this subsection, there are authorized to be appropriated $5,000,000 for fiscal year 1982, $5,000,000 for fiscal year 1983, and $5,000,000 for each of the fiscal years 1985 through 1988.

(g) Assistance to Municipalilties for Energy and Materials Conservation and Recovery Planning Activities.--

(1) The Administrator is authorized to make grants to municipalities, regional authorities, and intermunicipal agencies to carry out activities described in subparagraphs (A) and (B) of section 4003(b)(1). Such grants may be made only pursuant to an application submitted to the Administrator by the municipality which application has been approved by the State and determined by the State to be consistent with any State plan approved or submitted under this subtitle or any other appropriate planning carried out by the State.

(2) There is authorized to be appropriated for the fiscal year beginning October 1, 1981, and for each fiscal year thereafter before October 1, 1986, $8,000,000 for purposes of making grants to municipalities under this subsection. No amount may be appropriated for such purposes for the fiscal year beginning on October 1, 1986, or for any fiscal year thereafter.

(3) Assistance provided by the Administrator under this subsection shall be used only for the purposes specified in paragraph (1). Such assistance may not be used for purposes of land acquisition, final facility design, equipment purchase, construction, startup or operation activities.

RURAL COMMUNITIES ASSISTANCE

42 USC 6949

Sec. 4009. (a) In General.--The Administrator shall make grants to States to provide assistance to municipalities with a population of five thousand or less, or counties with a population of ten thousand or less or less than twenty persons per square mile and not within a metropolitan area, for solid waste management facilities (including equipment) necessary to meet the requirements of section 4005 of this Act or restrictions on open burning or other requirements arising under the Clean Air Act or the Federal Water Pollution Control Act. Such assistance shall only be available (1) to any municipality or county which could not feasibly be included in a solid waste management system or facility serving an urbanized, multijurisdictional area because of its distance from such systems;

(2) where existing or planned solid waste management services or facilities are unavailable or insufficient to comply with the requirements of section 4005 of this Act; and

(3) for systems which are certified by the State to be consistent with any plans or programs established under any State or area-wide planning process.

(b) Allotment.--The Administrator shall allot the sums appropriated to carry out this section in any fiscal year among the States in accordance with regulations promulgated by him on the basis of the average of the ratio which the population of rural areas of each State bears to the total population of rural areas of all the States the ratio which the population of counties in each State having less than twenty persons per square mile bears to the total population of such counties in all the States, and the ratio which the population of such low-density counties in each State having 33 per centum or more of all families with incomes not in excess of 125 per centum of the poverty level bears to the total population of such counties in all of the States.

(c) Limit.--The amount of any grant under this section shall not exceed 75 per centum of the costs of the project. No assistance under this section shall be available for the acquisition of land or interests in land.

(d) Appropriations.--There are authorized to be appropriated $25,000,000 for each of the fiscal years 1978 and 1979 to carry out this section. There are authorized to be appropriated $10,000,000 for the fiscal year 1980 and $15,000,000 for each of the fiscal years 1981 and 1982 to carry out this section.

ADEQUACY OF CERTAIN GUIDELINES AND CRITERIA

42 USC 6949a

Sec. 4010. (a) Study.--The Administrator shall conduct a study of the extent to which the guidelines and criteria under this Act (other than guidelines and criteria for facilities to which subtitle C applies) which are applicable to solid waste management and disposal facilities, including, but not limited to landfills and surface impoundments, are adequate to protect human health and the environment from ground water contamination. Such study shall include a detailed assessment of the degree to which the criteria under section 1008(a) and the criteria under section 4004 regarding monitoring, prevention of contamination, and remedial action are adequate to protect ground water and shall also include recommendation with respect to any additional enforcement authorities which the Administrator, in consultation with the Attorney General, deems necessary for such purposes.

(b) Report.--Not later than 36 months after the date of enactment of the Hazardous and Solid Waste Amendments of 1984, the Administrator shall submit a report to the Congress setting forth the results of the study required under this section, together with any recommendations made by the Administrator on the basis of such study.

(c) Revisions of Guidelines and Criteria.--Not later than March 31, 1988, the Administrator shall promulgate revisions of the criteria promulgated under paragraph (1) of section 4004(a) and under section 1008(a)(3) for facilities that may receive hazardous household wastes or hazardous wastes from small quantity generators under section 3001(d). The criteria shall be those necessary to protect human health and the environment and may take into account the practicable capability of such facilities. At a minimum such revisions for facilities potentially receiving such wastes should require ground water monitoring as necessary to detect contamination, establish criteria for the acceptable location of new or existing facilities, and provide for corrective action as appropriate.

SUBTITLE E-DUTIES OF THE SECRETARY OF COMMERCE
IN RESOURCE AND RECOVERY

FUNCTIONS

42 USC 6951

Sec. 5001. The Secretary of Commerce shall encourage greater commercialization of proven resource recovery technology by providing

(1) accurate specifications for recovered materials;

(2) stimulation of development of markets for recovered materials;

(3) promotion of proven technology; and

(4) a forum for the exchange of technical and economic data relating to resource recovery facilities.

DEVELOPMENT OF SPECIFICATIONS
OR SECONDARY MATERIALS

42 USC 6952

Sec. 5002. The Secretary of Commerce, acting through the National Bureau of Standards, and in conjunction with national standards-setting organizations in resource recovery, shall, after public hearings, and not later than two years after September 1, 1979, publish guidelines for the development of specifications for the classification of materials recovered from waste which were destined for disposal. The specifications shall pertain to the physical and chemical properties and characteristics of such materials with regard to their use in replacing virgin materials in various industrial, commercial, and governmental uses. In establishing such guidelines the Secretary shall also, to the extent feasible, provide such information as may be necessary to assist Federal agencies with procurement of items containing recovered materials. The Secretary shall continue to cooperate with national standards-setting organizations, as may be necessary, to encourage the publication, promulgation and updating of standards for recovered materials and for the use of recovered materials in various industrial, commercial, and governmental uses.

DEVELOPMENT OF MARKETS FOR RECOVERED MATERIALS

42 USC 6953

Sec. 5003. The Secretary of Commerce shall within two years after September 1, 1979 take such actions as may be necessary to

(1) identify the geographical location of existing or potential markets for recovered materials;

(2) identify the economic and technical barriers to the use of recovered materials; and

(3) encourage the development of new uses for recovered materials.

TECHNOLOGY PROMOTION

42 USC 6954

Sec. 5004. The Secretary of Commerce is authorized to evaluate the commercial feasibility of resource recovery facilities and to publish the results of such evaluation, and to develop a data base for purposes of assisting persons in choosing such a system.

MARKETING POLICIES, ESTABLISHMENT;
NONDISCRIMINATION REQUIREMENT

42 USC 6955

Sec. 5005. In establishing any policies which may affect the development of new markets for recovered materials and in making any determination concerning whether or not to impose monitoring or other controls on any marketing or transfer of recovered materials, the Secretary of Commerce may consider whether to establish the same or similar policies or impose the same or similar monitoring or other controls on virgin materials.

AUTHORIZATION OF APPROPRIATIONS

42 USC 6956

Sec. 5006. There are authorized to be appropriated to the Secretary of Commerce $5,000,000 for each of fiscal years 1980, 1981, and 1982 and $1,500,000 for each of the fiscal years 1985 through 1988 to carry out the purposes of this subtitle.

SUBTITLE F-FEDERAL RESPONSIBILITIES

APPLICATION OF FEDERAL, STATE, AND LOCAL LAW
TO FEDERAL FACILITIES

42 USC 6961

Sec. 6001. (a) In General.-- Each department, agency, and instrumentality of the executive, legislative, and judicial branches of the Federal Government (1) having jurisdiction over any solid waste management facility or disposal site, or (2) engaged in any activity resulting, or which may result, in the disposal or management of solid waste or hazardous waste shall be subject to and comply with, all Federal, State, interstate, and local requirements, both substantive and procedural (including any requirement for permits or reporting or any provisions for injunctive relief and such sanctions as may be imposed by a court to enforce such relief), respecting control and abatement of solid waste or hazardous waste disposal and management in the same manner, and to the same extent, as any person is subject to such requirements, including the payment of reasonable service charges. The Federal, State, interstate, and local substantive and procedural requirements referred to in this subsection include, but are not limited to, all administrative orders and all civil and administrative penalties and fines, regardless of whether such penalties or fines are punitive or coercive in nature or are imposed for isolated, intermittent, or continuing violations. The United States hereby expressly waives any immunity otherwise applicable to the United States with respect to any such substantive or procedural requirement (including, but not limited to, any injunctive relief, administrative order or civil or administrative penalty or fine referred to in the preceding sentence, or reasonable service charge). The reasonable service charges referred to in this subsection include, but are not limited to, fees or charges assessed in connection with the processing and issuance of permits, renewal of permits, amendments to permits, review of plans, studies, and other documents, and inspection and monitoring of facilities, as well as any other nondiscriminatory charges that are assessed in connection with a Federal, State, interstate, or local solid waste or hazardous waste regulatory program. Neither the United States, nor any agent, employee, or officer thereof, shall be immune or exempt from any process or sanction of any State or Federal Court with respect to the enforcement of any such injunctive relief. No agent, employee, or officer of the United States shall be personally liable for ny civil penalty under any Federal, State, interstate, or local solid or hazardous waste law with respect to any act or omission within the scope of the official duties of the agent, employee, or officer. An agent, employee, or officer of the United States shall be subject to any criminal sanction (including, but not limited to, any fine or imprisonment) under any Federal or State solid or hazardous waste law, but no department, agency, or instrumentality of the executive, legislative, or judicial branch of the Federal Government shall be subject to any such sanction. The President may exempt any solid waste management facility of any department, agency, or instrumentality in the executive branch from compliance with such a requirement if he determines it to be in the paramount interest of the United States to do so. No such exemption shall be granted due to lack of appropriation unless the President shall have specifically requested such appropriation as a part of the budgetary process and the Congress shall have failed to make available such requested appropriation. Any exemption shall be for a period not in excess of one year, but additional exemptions may be granted for periods not to exceed one year upon the President's making a new determination. The President shall report each January to the Congress all exemptions from the requirements of this section granted during the preceding calendar year, together with his reason for granting each such exemption.

(b) Administrative Enforcement Actions.--(1) The Administrator may commence an administrative enforcement action against any department, agency, or instrumentality of the executive, legislative, or judicial branch of the

Federal Government pursuant to the enforcement authorities contained in this Act. The Administrator shall initiate an administrative enforcement action against such a department, agency, or instrumentality in the same manner and under the same circumstances as an action would be initiated against another person. Any voluntary resolution or settlement of such an action shall be set forth in a consent order.

(2) No administrative order issued to such a department, agency, or instrumentality shall become final until such department, agency, or instrumentality has had the opportunity to confer with the Administrator.

(c) Limitation on State Use of Funds Collected from Federal Government.--Unless a State law in effect on the date of the enactment of the Federal Facility Compliance Act of 1992 or a State constitution requires the funds to be used in a different manner, all funds collected by a State from the Federal Government from penalties and fines imposed for violation of any substantive or procedural requirement referred to in subsection (a) shall be used by the State only for projects designed to improve or protect the environment or to defray the costs of environmental protection or enforcement.

FEDERAL PROCUREMENT

42 USC 6962

Sec. 6002. (a) Application of Section.--Except as provided in subsection (b), a procuring agency shall comply with the requirements set forth in this section and any regulations issued under this section, with respect to any purchase or acquisition of a procurement item where the purchase price of the item exceeds $10,000 or where the quantity of such items or of functionally equivalent items purchased or acquired in the course of the preceding fiscal year was $10,000 or more.

(b) Procurement Subject to Other Law.--Any procurement, by any procuring agency, which is subject to regulations of the Administrator under section 6004 (as promulgated before the date of enactment of this section under comparable provisions of prior law) shall not be subject to the requirements of this section to the extent that such requirements are inconsistent with such regulations.

(c) Requirements.--

(1) After the date specified in applicable guidelines prepared pursuant to subsection (e) of this section, each procuring agency which procures any items designated in such guidelines shall procure such items composed of the highest percentage of recovered materials practicable (and in the case of paper, the highest percentage of the post-consumer recovered materials referred to in subsection (h)(1) practicable), consistent with maintaining a satisfactory level of competition, considering such guidelines. The decision not to procure such items shall be based on a determination that such procurement items

(A) are not reasonably available within a reasonable period of time;

(B) fail to meet the performance standards set forth in the applicable specifications or fail to meet the reasonable performance standards of the procuring agencies; or

(C) are only available at an unreasonable price. Any determination under subparagraph (B) shall be made on the basis of the guidelines of the Bureau of Standards in any case in which such material is covered by such guidelines.

(2) Agencies that generate heat, mechanical, or electrical energy from fossil fuel in systems that have the technical capacity of using energy or fuels derived from solid waste as a primary or supplementary fuel shall use such capability to the maximum extent practicable.

(3) After the date specified in any applicable guidelines prepared pursuant to subsection (e) of this section, contracting officers shall require that vendors:

(A) certify that the percentage of recovered materials to be used in the performance of the contract will be at least the amount required by applicable specifications or other contractual requirements and

(B) estimate the percentage of the total material utilized for the performance of the contract which is recovered materials.

(d) Specifications.--All Federal agencies that have the responsibility for drafting or reviewing specifications for procurement items procured by Federal agencies shall

(1) as expeditiously as possible but in any event no later than 18 months after the date of enactment of the Hazardous and Solid Waste Amendments of 1984, eliminate from such specifications
    (A) any exclusion of recovered materials and
    (B) any requirement that items be manufactured from virgin materials; and
(2) within one year after the date of publication of applicable guidelines under subsection (e), or as otherwise specified in such guidelines, assure that such specifications require the use of recovered materials to the maximum extent possible without jeopardizing the intended end use of the item.

(e) Guidelines.--The Administrator, after consultation with the Administrator of General Services, the Secretary of Commerce (acting through the Bureau of Standards), and the Public Printer, shall prepare, and from time to time revise, guidelines for the use of procuring agencies in complying with the requirements of this section. Such guidelines shall
(1) designate those items which are or can be produced with recovered materials and whose procurement by procuring agencies will carry out the objectives of this section, and in the case of paper, provide for maximizing the use of post consumer recovered materials referred to in subsection (h)(1) and
(2) set forth recommended practices with respect to the procurement of recovered materials and items containing such materials and with respect to certification by vendors of the percentage of recovered materials used, and shall provide information as to the availability, relative price, and performance of such materials and items and where appropriate shall recommend the level of recovered material to be contained in the procured product. The Administrator shall prepare final guidelines for paper within 180 days after the enactment of the Hazardous and Solid Waste Amendments of 1984, and for three additional product categories (including tires) by October 1, 1985. In making the designation under paragraph (1), the Administrator shall consider, but is not limited in his considerations, to
    (A) the availability of such items;
    (B) the impact of the procurement of such items by procuring agencies on the volume of solid waste which must be treated, stored or disposed of;
    (C) the economic and technological feasibility of producing and using other items; and
    (D) other uses for such recovered materials.

(f) Procurement of Services.--A procuring agency shall, to the maximum extent practicable, manage or arrange for the procurement of solid waste management services in a manner which maximizes energy and resource recovery.

(g) Executive Office.--The Office of Procurement Policy in the Executive Office of the President, in cooperation with the Administrator, shall implement the requirements of this section. It shall be the responsibility of the Office of Procurement Policy to coordinate this policy with other policies for Federal procurement, in such a way as to maximize the use of recovered resources.

(h) Definition.--As used in this section, in the case of paper products, the term "recovered materials" includes
(1) post-consumer materials such as
    (A) paper, paperboard, and fibrous wastes from retail stores, office buildings, homes, and so forth, after they have passed through their end-usage as a consumer item, including: used corrugated boxes, old newspapers; old magazines; mixed waste paper, tabulating cards; and used cordage; and
    (B) all paper, paperboard, and fibrous wastes that enter and are collected from municipal solid waste, and
(2) manufacturing, forest residues, and other wastes such as
    (A) dry paper and paperboard waste generated after completion of the papermaking process (that is, those manufacturing operations up to and including the cutting and trimming of the paper machine reel into smaller rolls or rough sheets) including: envelope cuttings, bindery trimmings, and other paper and paperboard waste, resulting from printing, cutting, forming, and other converting operations; bag, box, and carton manufacturing wastes; and butt rolls, mill wrappers, and rejected unused stock; and
    (B) finished paper and paperboard from obsolete inventories of paper and paperboard manufacturers, merchants, wholesalers, dealers, printers, converters, or others;

(C) fibrous byproducts of harvesting, manufacturing, extractive, or woodcutting processes, flax, straw, linters, bagasse, slash, and other forest residues;

(D) wastes generated by the conversion of goods made from fibrous material (that is, waste rope from cordage manufacture, textile mill waste, and cuttings); and

(E) fibers recovered from waste water which otherwise would enter the waste stream.

(i) Procurement Program.--

(1) Within 1 year after the date of publication of applicable guidelines under subsection (e), each procuring agency shall develop an affirmative procurement program which will assure that items composed of recovered materials will be purchased to the maximum extent practicable and which is consistent with applicable provisions of Federal procurement law.

(2) Each affirmative procurement program required under this subsection shall, at a minimum, contain

(A) a recovered materials preference program;

(B) an agency promotion program to promote the preference program adopted under subparagraph (A);

(C) a program for requiring estimates of the total percentage of recovered material utilized in the performance of a contract; certification of minimum recovered material content actually utilized, where appropriate; and reasonable verification procedures for estimates and certifications; and

(D) annual review and monitoring of the effectiveness of an agency's affirmative procurement program.

In the case of paper, the recovered materials preference program required under subparagraph (A) shall provide for the maximum use of the post consumer recovered materials referred to in subsection (h)(1).

(3) In developing the preference program, the following options shall be considered for adoption:

(A) Case-by-Case Policy Development: Subject to the limitations of subsection (c)(1)(A) through (C), a policy of awarding contracts to the vendor offering an item composed of the highest percentage of recovered materials practicable (and in the case of paper, the highest percentage of the post consumer recovered materials referred to in subsection (h)(1)). Subject to such limitations, agencies may make an award to a vendor offering items with less than the maximum recovered materials content.

(B) Minimum Content Standards: Minimum recovered materials content specifications which are set in such a way as to assure that the recovered materials content (and in the case of paper, the content of post consumer materials referred to in subsection (h)(1)) required is the maximum available without jeopardizing the intended end use of the item, or violating the limitations of subsection (c)(1)(A) through (C).

Procuring agencies shall adopt one of the options set forth in subparagraphs (A) and (B) or a substantially equivalent alternative, for inclusion in the affirmative procurement program.

COOPERATION WITH THE ENVIRONMENTAL PROTECTION AGENCY

42 USC 6963

Sec. 6003. (a) General Rule.--All Federal agencies shall assist the Administrator in carrying out his functions under this Act and shall promptly make available all requested information concerning past or present Agency waste management practices and past or present Agency owned, leased, or operated solid or hazardous waste facilities. This information shall be provided in such format as may be determined by the Administrator.

(b) Information Relating to Energy and Materials Conservation and Recovery.--The Administrator shall collect, maintain, and disseminate information concerning the market potential of energy and materials recovered from solid waste, including materials obtained through source separation, and information concerning the savings potential of conserving resources contributing to the waste stream. The Administrator shall identify the regions in which the increased substitution of such energy for energy derived from fossil fuels and other sources is most likely to be feasible, and provide information on the technical and economic aspects of developing integrated resource conservation or recovery systems which provide for the recovery of source-separated materials to be recycled or the conservation of resources. The Administrator shall utilize the authorities of subsection (a) in carrying out this subsection.

APPLICABILITY OF SOLID WASTE DISPOSAL GUIDELINES
TO EXECUTIVE AGENCIES

42 USC 6964

Sec. 6004. (a) Compliance.--

(1) If

(A) an Executive agency (as defined in section 105 of title 5, United States Code) or any unit of the legislative branch of the Federal Government has jurisdiction over any real property or facility the operation or administration of which involves such agency in solid waste management activities, or

(B) such an agency enters into a contract with any person for the operation by such person of any Federal property or facility, and the performance of such contract involves such person in solid waste management activities, then such an agency shall insure compliance with the guidelines recommended under section 1008 and the purposes of this Act in the operation or administration of such property or facility, or the performance of such contract, as the case may be.

(2) Each Executive agency or any unit of the legislative branch of the Federal Government which conducts any activity

(A) which generates solid waste, and

(B) which, if conducted by a person other than such agency, would require a permit or license from such agency in order to dispose of such solid waste, shall insure compliance with such guidelines and the purposes of this Act in conducting such activity.

(3) Each Executive agency which permits the use of Federal property for purposes of disposal of solid waste shall insure compliance with such guidelines and the purposes of this Act in the disposal of such waste.

(4) The President or the Committee on House Administration of the House of Representatives and the Committee on Rules and Administration of the Senate with regard to any unit of the legislative branch of the Federal Government shall prescribe regulations to carry out this subsection.

(b) Licenses and Permits.--Each Executive agency which issues any license or permit for disposal of solid waste shall, prior to the issuance of such license or permit, consult with the Administrator to insure compliance with guidelines recommended under section 1008 and the purposes of this Act.

SUBTITLE G-MISCELLANEOUS PROVISIONS

EMPLOYEE PROTECTION

42 USC 6971

Sec. 7001. (a) General.--No person shall fire, or in any other way discriminate against, or cause to be fired or discriminated against, any employee or any authorized representative of employees by reason of the fact that such employee or representative has filed, instituted, or caused to be filed or instituted any proceeding under this Act or under any applicable implementation plan, or has testified or is about to testify in any proceeding resulting from the administration or enforcement of the provisions of this Act or of any applicable implementation plan.

(b) Remedy.--Any employee or a representative of employees who believes that he has been fired or otherwise discriminated against by any person in violation of subsection (a) of this section may, within thirty days after such alleged violation occurs, apply to the Secretary of Labor for a review of such firing or alleged discrimination. A copy of the application shall be sent to such person who shall be the respondent. Upon receipt of such application, the Secretary of Labor shall cause such investigation to be made as he deems appropriate. Such investigation shall provide an opportunity for a public hearing at the request of any party to such review to enable the parties to present information relating to such alleged violation. The parties shall be given written notice of the time and place of the hearing at least five days prior to the hearing. Any such hearing shall be of record and shall be subject to section 554 of title 5 of the United States Code. Upon receiving the report of such investigation, the Secretary of Labor shall make findings of fact. If he finds that such violation did occur, he shall issue a decision, incorporating an order therein and his findings, requiring the party committing such violation to take such affirmative action to abate the violation as the Secretary of Labor deems appropriate, including, but not limited to, the rehiring or reinstatement of the employee or representative of employees to his former position with compensation. If he finds that there was no such violation, he shall issue an order denying the application. Such order issued by the Secretary of Labor under this subparagraph shall be subject to judicial review in the same manner as orders and decisions of the Administrator or subject to judicial review under this Act.

(c) Costs.--Whenever an order is issued under this section to abate such violation, at the request of the applicant, a sum equal to the aggregate amount of all costs and expenses (including the attorney's fees) as determined by the Secretary of Labor, to have been reasonably incurred by the applicant for, or in connection with, the institution and prosecution of such proceedings, shall be assessed against the person committing such violation.

(d) Exception.--This section shall have no application to any employee who, acting without direction from his employer (or his agent) deliberately violates any requirement of this Act.

(e) Employment Shifts and Loss.--The Administrator shall conduct continuing evaluations of potential loss or shifts of employment which may result from the administration or enforcement of the provisions of this Act and applicable implementation plans, including where appropriate, investigating threatened plant closures or reductions in employment allegedly resulting from such administration or enforcement. Any employee who is discharged, or laid off, threatened with discharge or layoff, or otherwise discriminated against by any person because of the alleged results of such administration or enforcement, or any representative of such employee, may request the Administrator to conduct a full investigation of the matter. The Administrator shall thereupon investigate the matter and, at the request of any party, shall hold public hearings on not less than five days' notice, and shall at such hearings require the parties, including the employer involved, to present information relating to the actual or potential effect of such administration or enforcement on employment and on any alleged discharge, layoff, or other discrimination and the detailed reasons or justification therefor. Any such hearing shall be of record and shall be subject to section 554 of title 5 of the United States Code. Upon receiving the report of such investigation, the Administrator shall make findings of fact as to the effect of such administration or enforcement on employment and on the alleged discharge, layoff, or discrimination and shall make such recommendations as he deems appropriate. Such report, findings, and recommendations shall be available to the public. Nothing in this subsection shall be construed to require or authorize the Administrator or any State to modify or withdraw any standard, limitation, or any other requirement of this Act or any applicable implementation plan.

(f) Occupational Safety and Health.--In order to assist the Secretary of Labor and the Director of the National Institute for Occupational Safety and Health in carrying out their duties under the Occupational Safety and Health Act of 1970, the Administrator shall

(1) provide the following information, as such information becomes available, to the Secretary and the Director:

(A) the identity of any hazardous waste generation, treatment, storage, disposal facility or site where cleanup is planned or underway;

(B) information identifying the hazards to which persons working at a hazardous waste generation, treatment, storage, disposal facility or site or otherwise handling hazardous waste may be exposed, the nature and extent of the exposure, and methods to protect workers from such hazards; and

(C) incidents of worker injury or harm at a hazardous waste generation, treatment, storage or disposal facility or site; and

(2) notify the Secretary and the Director of the Administrator's receipt of notifications under section 3010 or reports under sections 3002, 3003, and 3004 of this title and make such notifications and reports available to the Secretary and the Director.

CITIZEN SUITS

42 USC 6972

Sec. 7002. (a) In General.--Except as provided in subsection (b) or (c) of this section, any person may commence a civil action on his own behalf

(1)(A) against any person (including (a) the United States, and (b) any other governmental instrumentality or agency, to the extent permitted by the eleventh amendment to the Constitution) who is alleged to be in violation of any permit, standard, regulation, condition, requirement, prohibition, or order which has become effective pursuant to this Act; or

(B) against any person, including the United States and any other governmental instrumentality or agency, to the extent permitted by the eleventh amendment to the Constitution, and including any past or present generator, past or present transporter, or past or present owner or operator of a treatment, storage, or disposal facility, who has contributed or who is contributing to the past or present handling, storage, treatment, transportation, or disposal of any solid or hazardous waste which may present an imminent and substantial endangerment to health or the environment; or

(2) against the Administrator where there is alleged a failure of the Administrator to perform any act or duty under this Act which is not discretionary with the Administrator.

Any action under paragraph (a) (1) of this subsection shall be brought in the district court for the district in which the alleged violation occurred or the alleged endangerment may occur. Any action brought under paragraph (a) (2) of this subsection may be brought in the district court for the district in which the alleged violation occurred or in the District Court of the District of Columbia. The district court shall have jurisdiction, without regard to the amount in controversy or the citizenship of the parties, to enforce the permit, standard, regulation, condition, requirement, prohibition, or order, referred to in paragraph (1)(A), to restrain any person who has contributed or who is contributing to the past or present handling, storage, treatment, transportation, or disposal of any solid or hazardous waste referred to in paragraph (1)(B), to order such person to take such other action as may be necessary, or both, or to order the Administrator to perform the act or duty referred to in paragraph (2), as the case may be, and to apply any appropriate civil penalties under section 3008 (a) and (g).

(b) Actions Prohibited.--
(1) No action may be commenced under subsection (a)(1) (A) of this section
(A) prior to 60 days after the plaintiff has given notice of the violation to
(i) the Administrator;
(ii) the State in which the alleged violation occurs; and
(iii) to any alleged violator of such permit, standard, regulation, condition, requirement, prohibition, or order,
except that such action may be brought immediately after such notification in the case of an action under this section respecting a violation of subtitle C of this Act; or
(B) if the Administrator or State has commenced and is diligently prosecuting a civil or criminal action in a court of the United States or a State to require compliance with such permit, standard, regulation, condition, requirement, prohibition, or order.

In any action under subsection (a)(1)(A) in a court of the United States, any person may intervene as a matter of right.

(2) No action may be commenced under subsection (a)(1)(B) of this section prior to 90 days after the plaintiff has given notice of the endangerment to
(A) the Administrator;
(B) the State in which the alleged endangerment may occur;
(C) any person alleged to have contributed or to be contributing to the past or present handling, storage, treatment, transportation, or disposal of any solid or hazardous waste referred to in subsection (a)(1)(B), except that such action may be brought immediately after such notification in the case of an action under this section respecting a violation of subtitle C of this Act.
(B) No action may be commenced under subsection (a)(1)(B) of this section if the Administrator, in order to restrain or abate acts or conditions which may have contributed or are contributing to the activities which may present the alleged endangerment
(i) has commenced and is diligently prosecuting an action under section 7003 of this Act or under section 106 of the Comprehensive Environmental Response, Compensation and Liability Act of 1980,
(ii) is actually engaging in a removal action under section 104 of the Comprehensive Environmental Response, Compensation and Liability Act of 1980;

(iii) has incurred costs to initiate a Remedial Investigation and Feasibility Study under section 104 of the Comprehensive Environmental Response, Compensation and Liability Act of 1980 and is diligently proceeding with a remedial action under that Act; or

(iv) has obtained a court order (including a consent decree) or issued an administrative order under section 106 of the Comprehensive Environmental Response, Compensation and Liability Act of 1980 or section 7003 of this Act pursuant to which a responsible party is diligently conducting a removal action, Remedial Investigation and Feasibility Study (RIFS), or proceeding with a remedial action.

In the case of an administrative order referred to in clause (iv), actions under subsection (a)(1)(B) are prohibited only as to the scope and duration of the administrative order referred to in clause (iv).

(C) No action may be commenced under subsection (a)(1)(B) of this section if the State, in order to restrain or abate acts or conditions which may have contributed or are contributing to the activities which may present the alleged endangerment

(i) has commenced and is diligently prosecuting an action under subsection (a)(1)(B);

(ii) is actually engaging in a removal action under section 104 of the Comprehensive Environmental Response, Compensation and Liability Act of 1980; or

(iii) has incurred costs to initiate a Remedial Investigation and Feasibility Study under section 104 of the Comprehensive Environmental Response, Compensation and Liability Act of 1980 and is diligently proceeding with a remedial action under that Act.

(D) No action may be commenced under subsection (a)(1)(B) by any person (other than a State or local government) with respect to the siting of a hazardous waste treatment, storage, or a disposal facility, nor to restrain or enjoin the issuance of a permit for such facility.

(E) In any action under subsection (a)(1)(B) in a court of the United States, any person may intervene as a matter of right when the applicant claims an interest relating to the subject of the action and he is so situated that the disposition of the action may, as a practical matter, impair or impede his ability to protect that interest, unless the Administrator or the State shows that the applicant's interest is adequately represented by existing parties.

(F) Whenever any action is brought under subsection (a)(1)(B) in a court of the United States, the plaintiff shall serve a copy of the complaint on the Attorney General of the United States and with the Administrator.

(c) Notice.--No action may be commenced under paragraph (a)(2) of this section prior to sixty days after the plaintiff has given notice to the Administrator that he will commence such action, except that such action may be brought immediately after such notification in the case of an action under this section respecting a violation of Subtitle C of this Act. Notice under this subsection shall be given in such manner as the Administrator shall prescribe by regulation. Any action respecting a violation under this Act may be brought under this section only in the judicial district in which such alleged violation occurs.

(d) Intervention.--In any action under this section the Administrator, if not a party, may intervene as a matter of right.

(e) Costs.--The court, in issuing any final order in any action brought pursuant to this section or section 7006 may award costs of litigation (including reasonable attorney and expert witness fees) to the prevailing or substantially prevailing party whenever the court determines such an award is appropriate. The court may, if a temporary restraining order or preliminary injunction is sought, require the filing of a bond or equivalent security in accordance with the Federal Rules of Civil Procedure.

(f) Other Rights Preserved.--Nothing in this section shall restrict any right which any person (or class of persons) may have under any statute or common law to seek enforcement of any standard or requirement relating to the management of solid waste or hazardous waste, or to seek any other relief (including relief against the Administrator or a State agency).

(g) Transporters.--A transporter shall not be deemed to have contributed or to be contributing to the handling, storage, treatment, or disposal, referred to in subsection (a)(1)(B) taking place after such solid waste or hazardous waste has left the possession or control of such transporter, if the transportation of such waste was under a sole contractual arrangement arising from a published tariff and acceptance for carriage by common carrier by rail and such transporter has exercised due care in the past or present handling, storage, treatment, transportation and disposal of such waste.

IMMINENT HAZARD

42 USC 6973

Sec. 7003. (a) Authority of Administrator.--Notwithstanding any other provision of this Act, upon receipt of evidence that the past or present handling, storage, treatment, transportation or disposal of any solid waste or hazardous waste may present an imminent and substantial endangerment to health or the environment, the Administrator may bring suit on behalf of the United States in the appropriate district court against any person (including any past or present generator, past or present transporter, or past or present owner or operator of a treatment, storage, or disposal facility) who has contributed or who is contributing to such handling, storage, treatment, transportation or disposal to restrain such person from such handling, storage, treatment, transportation, or disposal, to order such person to take such other action as may be necessary, or both. A transporter shall not be deemed to have contributed or to be contributing to such handling, storage, treatment, or disposal taking place after such solid waste or hazardous waste has left the possession or control of such transporter if the transportation of such waste was under a sole contractual arrangement arising from a published tariff and acceptance for carriage by common carrier by rail and such transporter has exercised due care in the past or present handling, storage, treatment, transportation and disposal of such waste. The Administrator shall provide notice to the affected State of any such suit. The Administrator may also, after notice to the affected State, take other action under this section including, but not limited to, issuing such orders as may be necessary to protect public health and the environment.

(b) Violations.--Any person who willfully violates, or fails or refuses to comply with, any order of the Administrator under subsection (a) may, in an action brought in the appropriate United States district court to enforce such order, be fined not more than $5,000 for each day in which such violation occurs or such failure to comply continues.

(c) Immediate Notice.--Upon receipt of information that there is hazardous waste at any site which has presented an imminent and substantial endangerment to human health or the environment, the Administrator shall provide immediate notice to the appropriate local government agencies. In addition, the Administrator shall require notice of such endangerment to be promptly posted at the site where the waste is located.

(d) Public Participation in Settlements.--Whenever the United States or the Administrator proposes to covenant not to sue or to forbear from suit or to settle any claim arising under this section, notice, and opportunity for a public meeting in the affected area, and a reasonable opportunity to comment on the proposed settlement prior to its final entry shall be afforded to the public. The decision of the United States or the Administrator to enter into or not to enter into such Consent Decree, covenant or agreement shall not constitute a final agency action subject to judicial review under this Act or the Administrative Procedure Act.

PETITION FOR REGULATIONS; PUBLIC PARTICIPATION

42 USC 6974

Sec. 7004. (a) Petition.--Any person may petition the Administrator for the promulgation, amendment, or repeal of any regulation under this Act. Within a reasonable time following receipt of such petition, the Administrator shall take action with respect to such petition and shall publish notice of such action in the Federal Register, together with the reasons therefor.

(b) Public Participation.--

(1) Public participation in the development, revision, implementation, and enforcement of any regulation, guideline, information, or program under this Act shall be provided for, encouraged, and assisted by the

Administrator and the States. The Administrator, in cooperation with the States, shall develop and publish minimum guidelines for public participation in such processes.

(2) Before the issuing of a permit to any person with any respect to any facility for the treatment, storage, or disposal of hazardous wastes under section 3005, the Administrator shall

(A) cause to be published in major local newspapers of general circulation and broadcast over local radio stations notice of the agency's intention to issue such permit, and

(B) transmit in writing notice of the agency's intention to issue such permit to each unit of local government having jurisdiction over the area in which such facility is proposed to be located and to each State agency having any authority under State law with respect to the construction or operation of such facility.

If within 45 days the Administrator receives written notice of opposition to the agency's intention to issue such permit and a request for a hearing, or if the Administrator determines on his own initiative, he shall hold an informal public hearing (including an opportunity for presentation of written and oral views) on whether he should issue a permit for the proposed facility. Whenever possible the Administrator shall schedule such hearing at a location convenient to the nearest population center to such proposed facility and give notice in the aforementioned manner of the date, time, and subject matter of such hearing. No State program which provides for the issuance of permits referred to in this paragraph may be authorized by the Administrator under section 3006 unless such program provides for the notice and hearing required by the paragraph.

SEPARABILITY

42 USC 6975

Sec. 7005. If any provision of this Act, or the application of any provision of this Act to any person or circumstance, is held invalid, the application of such provision to other persons or circumstances, and the remainder of this Act, shall not be affected thereby.

JUDICIAL REVIEW

42 USC 6976

Sec. 7006. (a) Review of Final Regulations and Certain Petitions.--Any judicial review of final regulations promulgated pursuant to this Act and the Administrator's denial of any petition for the promulgation, amendment, or repeal of any regulation under this Act shall be in accordance with sections 701 through 706 of title 5 of the United States Code, except that

(1) a petition for review of action of the Administrator in promulgating any regulation, or requirement under this Act or denying any petition for the promulgation, amendment or repeal of any regulation under this Act may be filed only in the United States Court of Appeals for the District of Columbia, and such petition shall be filed within ninety days from the date of such promulgation or denial, or after such date if such petition for review is based solely on grounds arising after such ninetieth day; action of the Administrator with respect to which review could have been obtained under this subsection shall not be subject to judicial review in civil or criminal proceedings for enforcement; and

(2) in any judicial proceeding brought under this section in which review is sought of a determination under this Act required to be made on the record after notice and opportunity for hearing, if a party seeking review under this Act applied to the court for leave to adduce additional evidence, and shows to the satisfaction of the court that the information is material and that there were reasonable grounds for the failure to adduce such evidence in the proceeding before the Administrator, the court may order such additional evidence (and evidence in rebuttal thereof) to be taken before the Administrator, and to be adduced upon the hearing in such manner and upon such terms and conditions as the court may deem proper; the Administrator may modify his findings as to the facts, or make new findings, by reason of the additional evidence so taken, and he shall file with the court such modified or new findings and his recommendation, if any, for the modification or setting aside of his original order, with the return of such additional evidence.

(b) Review of Certain Actions Under Sections 3005 and 3006.

--Review of the Administrator's action

(1) in issuing, denying, modifying, or revoking any permit under section 3005 (or in modifying or revoking any permit which is deemed to have been issued under section 3012(d)(1), or

(2) in granting, denying, or withdrawing authorization or interim authorization under section 3006, may be had by any interested person in the Circuit Court of Appeals of the United States for the Federal judicial district in which such person resides or transacts such business upon application by such person. Any such application shall be made within ninety days from the date of such issuance, denial, modification, revocation, grant, or withdrawal, or after such date only if such application is based solely on grounds which arose after such ninetieth day. Action of the Administrator with respect to which review could have been obtained under this subsection shall not be subject to judicial review in civil or criminal proceedings for enforcement. Such review shall be in accordance with sections 701 through 706 of title 5 of the United States Code.

GRANTS OR CONTRACTS FOR TRAINING PROJECTS

42 USC 6977

Sec. 7007. (a) General Authority.--The Administrator is authorized to make grants to, and contracts with any eligible organization. For purposes of this section the term eligible organization means a State or interstate agency, a municipality, educational institution, and any other organization which is capable of effectively carrying out a project which may be funded by grant under subsection (b) of this section.

(b) Purposes.--

(1) Subject to the provisions of paragraph (2), grants or contracts may be made to pay all or a part of the costs, as may be determined by the Administrator, of any project operated or to be operated by an eligible organization, which is designed

(A) to develop, expand, or carry out a program (which may combine training, education, and employment) for training persons for occupations involving the management, supervision, design, operation, or maintenance of solid waste management and resource recovery equipment and facilities; or

(B) to train instructors and supervisory personnel to train or supervise persons in occupations involving the design, operation, and maintenance of solid waste management and resource recovery equipment and facilities.

(2) A grant or contract authorized by paragraph (1) of this subsection may be made only upon application to the Administrator at such time or times and containing such information as he may prescribe, except that no such application shall be approved unless it provides for the same procedures and reports (and access to such reports and to other records) as required by section 207(b) (4) and (5) (as in effect before the date of the enactment of Resource Conservation and Recovery Act of 1976) with respect to applications made under such section (as in effect before the date of the enactment of Resource Conservation and Recovery Act of 1976).

(c) Study.--The Administrator shall make a complete investigation and study to determine

(1) the need for additional trained State and local personnel to carry out plans assisted under this Act and other solid waste and resource recovery programs;

(2) means of using existing training programs to train such personnel; and

(3) the extent and nature of obstacles to employment and occupational advancement in the solid waste management and resource recovery field which may limit either available manpower or the advancement of personnel in such field.

He shall report the results of such investigation and study, including his recommendations to the President and the Congress.

PAYMENTS

42 USC 6978

Sec. 7008. (a) General Rule.--Payments of grants under this Act may be made (after necessary adjustment on account of previously made underpayments or overpayments) in advance or by way of reimbursements, and in such installments and on such conditions as the Administrator may determine.

(b) Prohibition.--No grant may be made under this Act to any private profitmaking organization.

LABOR STANDARDS

42 USC 6979

Sec. 7009. No grant for a project of construction under this Act shall be made unless the Administrator finds that the application contains or is supported by reasonable assurance that all laborers and mechanics employed by contractors or subcontractors on projects of the type covered by the Davis-Bacon Act, as amended (40 U.S.C. 276a276a5), will be paid wages at rates not less than those prevailing on similar work in the locality as determined by the Secretary of Labor in accordance with that Act; and the Secretary of Labor shall have with respect to the labor standards specified in this section the authority and functions set forth in Reorganization Plan Numbered 14 of 1950 (15 F.R. 3176; 5 U.S.C. 133z5) and section 2 of the Act of June 13, 1934, as amended (40 U.S.C. 276c).

LAW ENFORCEMENT AUTHORITY

Sec. 7010. The Attorney General of the United States shall, at the request of the Administrator and on the basis of a showing of need, deputize qualified employees of the Environmental Protection Agency to serve as special Deputy United States Marshals in criminal investigations with respect to violations of the criminal provisions of this Act.

SUBTITLE H-RESEARCH, DEVELOPMENT, DEMONSTRATION, AND INFORMATION

RESEARCH, DEMONSTRATIONS, TRAINING, AND OTHER ACTIVITIES

42 USC 6981

Sec. 8001. (a) General Authority.--The Administrator, alone or after consultation with the Administrator of the Federal Energy Administration, the Administrator of the Energy Research and Development Administration, or the Chairman of the Federal Power Commission shall conduct, and encourage, cooperate with, and render financial and other assistance to appropriate public (whether Federal, State, interstate, or local) authorities, agencies, and institutions, private agencies and institutions, and individuals in the conduct of, and promote the coordination of, research, investigations, experiments, training, demonstrations, surveys, public education programs, and studies relating to

(1) any adverse health and welfare effects of the release into the environment of material present in solid waste, and methods to eliminate such effects;

(2) the operation and financing of solid waste management programs;

(3) the planning, implementation, and operation of resource recovery and resource conservation systems and hazardous waste management systems, including the marketing of recovered resources;

(4) the production of usable forms of recovered resources, including fuel, from solid waste;

(5) the reduction of the amount of such waste and unsalvageable waste materials;

(6) the development and application of new and improved methods of collecting and disposing of solid waste and processing and recovering materials and energy from solid wastes;

(7) the identification of solid waste components and potential materials and energy recoverable from such waste components;

(8) small scale and low technology solid waste management systems, including but not limited to, resource recovery source separation systems;

(9) methods to improve the performance characteristics of resources recovered from solid waste and the relationship of such performance characteristics to available and potentially available markets for such resources;

(10) improvements in land disposal practices for solid waste (including sludge) which may reduce the adverse environmental effects of such disposal and other aspects of solid waste disposal on land, including

means for reducing the harmful environmental effects of earlier and existing landfills, means for restoring areas damaged by such earlier or existing landfills, means for rendering landfills safe for purposes of construction and other uses, and techniques of recovering materials and energy from landfills;

(11) methods for the sound disposal of, or recovery of resources, including energy, from, sludge (including sludge from pollution control and treatment facilities, coal slurry pipelines, and other sources);

(12) methods of hazardous waste management, including methods of rendering such waste environmentally safe; and

(13) any adverse effects on air quality (particularly with regard to the emission of heavy metals) which result from solid waste which is burned (either alone or in conjunction with other substances) for purposes of treatment, disposal or energy recovery.

(b) Management Program.--

(1)(A) In carrying out his functions pursuant to this Act, and any other Federal legislation respecting solid waste or discarded material research, development, and demonstrations, the Administrator shall establish a management program or system to insure the coordination of all such activities and to facilitate and accelerate the process of development of sound new technology (or other discoveries) from the research phase, through development, and into the demonstration phase.

(B) The Administrator shall

(i) assist, on the basis of any research projects which are developed with assistance under this Act or without Federal assistance, the construction of pilot plant facilities for the purpose of investigating or testing the technological feasibility of any promising new fuel, energy, or resource recovery or resource conservation method or technology; and

(ii) demonstrate each such method and technology that appears justified by an evaluation at such pilot plant stage or at a pilot plant stage developed without Federal assistance. Each such demonstration shall incorporate new or innovative technical advances or shall apply such advances to different circumstances and conditions, for the purpose of evaluating design concepts or to test the performance, efficiency, and economic feasibility of a particular method or technology under actual operating conditions. Each such demonstration shall be so planned and designed that, if successful, it can be expanded or utilized directly as a full-scale operational fuel, energy, or resource recovery or resource conservation facility.

(2) Any energy-related research, development, or demonstration project for the conversion including bioconversion, of solid waste carried out by the Environmental Protection Agency or by the Energy Research and Development Administration pursuant to this or any other Act shall be administered in accordance with the May 7, 1976, Interagency Agreement between the Environmental Protection Agency and the Energy Research and Development Administration on the Development of Energy from Solid Wastes and specifically, that in accordance with this agreement,

(A) for those energy-related projects of mutual interest, planning will be conducted jointly by the Environmental Protection Agency and the Energy Research and Development Administration, following which project responsibility will be assigned to one agency;

(B) energy-related portions of projects for recovery of synthetic fuels or other forms of energy from solid waste shall be the responsibility of the Energy Research and Development Administration;

(C) the Environmental Protection Agency shall retain responsibility for the environmental, economic, and institutional aspects of solid waste projects and for assurance that such projects are consistent with any applicable suggested guidelines published pursuant to section 1008, and any applicable State or regional solid waste management plan; and

(D) any activities undertaken under provisions of sections 8002 and 8003 as related to energy; as related to energy or synthetic fuels recovery from waste; or as related to energy conservation shall be accomplished through coordination and consultation with the Energy Research and Development Administration.

(c) Authorities.--

(1) In carrying out subsection (a) of this section respecting solid waste research, studies, development, and demonstration, except as otherwise specifically provided in section 8004(d), the Administrator may make

grants to or enter into contracts (including contracts for construction) with, public agencies and authorities or private persons.

(2) Contracts for research, development, or demonstrations or for both (including contracts for construction) shall be made in accordance with and subject to the limitations provided with respect to research contracts of the military departments in title 10, United States Code, section 2353, except that the determination, approval, and certification required thereby shall be made by the Administrator.

(3) Any invention made or conceived in the course of, or under, any contract under this Act shall be subject to section 9 of the Federal Nonnuclear Energy Research and Development Act of 1974 to the same extent and in the same manner as inventions made or conceived in the course of contracts under such Act, except that in applying such section, the Environmental Protection Agency shall be substituted for the Energy Research and Development Administration and the words "solid waste" shall be substituted for the word "energy" where appropriate.

(4) For carrying out the purpose of this Act the Administrator may detail personnel of the Environmental Protection Agency to agencies eligible for assistance under this section.

SPECIAL STUDIES; PLANS FOR RESEARCH,
DEVELOPMENT, AND DEMONSTRATIONS

42 USC 6982
Sec. 8002. (a) Glass and Plastic.--The Administrator shall undertake a study and publish a report on resource recovery from glass and plastic waste, including a scientific, technological, and economic investigation of potential solutions to implement such recovery.

(b) Composition of Waste Stream.--The Administrator shall undertake a systematic study of the composition of the solid waste stream and of anticipated future changes in the composition of such stream and shall publish a report containing the results of such study and quantitatively evaluating the potential utility of such components.

(c) Priorities Study.--For purposes of determining priorities for research on recovery of materials and energy from solid waste and developing materials and energy recovery research, development, and demonstration strategies, the Administrator shall review, and make a study of, the various existing and promising techniques of energy recovery from solid waste (including, but not limited to, waterwall furnace incinerators, dry shredded fuel systems, pyrolysis, densified refuse-derived fuel systems, anerobic digestion, and fuel and feedstock preparation systems). In carrying out such study the Administrator shall investigate with respect to each such technique
(1) the degree of public need for the potential results of such research, development, or demonstration,
(2) the potential for research, development, and demonstration without Federal action, including the degree of restraint on such potential posed by risks involved, and
(3) the magnitude of effort and period of time necessary to develop the technology to the point where Federal assistance can be ended.

(d) Small-Scale and Low Technology Study.--The Administrator shall undertake a comprehensive study and analysis of, and publish a report on, systems of small-scale and low technology solid waste management, including household resource recovery and resource recovery systems which have special application to multiple dwelling units and high density housing and office complexes. Such study and analysis shall include an investigation of the degree to which such systems could contribute to energy conservation.

(e) Front-End Source Separation.--The Administrator shall undertake research and studies concerning the compatibility of front-end source separation systems with high technology resource recovery systems and shall publish a report continuing the results of such research and studies.
(f) Mining Waste.--The Administrator, in consultation with the Secretary of the Interior, shall conduct a detailed and comprehensive study on the adverse effects of solid wastes from active and abandoned surface and underground mines on the environment, including, but not limited to, the effects of such wastes on humans, water, air, health, welfare, and natural resources, and on the adequacy of means and measures currently employed by the mining industry, Government agencies, and others to dispose of and utilize such solid wastes and to prevent or substantially mitigate such adverse effects. Such study shall include an analysis of

(1) the sources and volume of discarded material generated per year from mining;

(2) present disposal practices;

(3) potential dangers to human health and the environment from surface runoff of leachate and air pollution by dust;

(4) alternatives to current disposal methods;

(5) the cost of those alternatives in terms of the impact on mine product costs; and

(6) potential for use of discarded material as a secondary source of the mine product.

Not later than thirty-six months after the date of the enactment of the Solid Waste Disposal Act Amendments of 1980 the Administrator shall publish a report of such study and shall include appropriate findings and recommendations for Federal and nonFederal actions concerning such effects. Such report shall be submitted to the Committee on Environment and Public Works of the United States Senate and the Committee on Interstate and Foreign Commerce of the United States House of Representatives.

(g) Sludge.--The Administrator shall undertake a comprehensive study and publish a report on sludge. Such study shall include an analysis of

(1) what types of solid waste (including but not limited to sewage and pollution treatment residues and other residues from industrial operations such as extraction of oil from shale, liquefaction and gasification of coal and coal slurry pipeline operations) shall be classified as sludge:

(2) the effects of air and water pollution legislation on the creation of large volumes of sludge;

(3) the amounts of sludge originating in each State and in each industry producing sludge;

(4) methods of disposal of such sludge, including the cost, efficiency, and effectiveness of such methods;

(5) alternative methods for the use of sludge, including agricultural applications of sludge and energy recovery from sludge; and

(6) methods to reclaim areas which have been used for the disposal of sludge or which have been damaged by sludge.

(h) Tires.--The Administrator shall undertake a study and publish a report respecting discarded motor vehicle tires which shall include an analysis of the problems involved in the collection, recovery of resources including energy, and use of such tires.

(i) Resource Recovery Facilities.--The Administrator shall conduct research and report on the economics of, and impediments, to the effective functioning of resource recovery facilities.

(j) Resource Conservation Committee.--

(1) The Administrator shall serve as Chairman of a Committee composed of himself, the Secretary of Commerce, the Secretary of Labor, the Chairman of the Council on Environmental Quality, the Secretary of Treasury, the Secretary of the Interior, the Secretary of Energy, the Chairman of the Council of Economic Advisors, and a representative of the Office of Management and Budget, which shall conduct a full and complete investigation and study of all aspects of the economic, social, and environmental consequences of resource conservation with respect to

(A) the appropriateness of recommended incentives and disincentives to foster resource conservation;

(B) the effect of existing public policies (including subsidies and economic incentives and disincentives, percentage depletion allowances, capital gains treatment and other tax incentives and disincentives) upon resource conservation, and the likely effect of the modification or elimination of such incentives and disincentives upon resource conservation;

(C) the appropriateness and feasibility of restricting the manufacture or use of categories of consumer products as a resource conservation strategy;

(D) the appropriateness and feasibility of employing as a resource conservation strategy the imposition of solid waste management charges on consumer products, which charges would reflect the costs of solid waste management services, litter pickup, the value of recoverable components of such product, final disposal, and any social value associated with the nonrecycling or uncontrolled disposal of such product; and

(E) the need for further research, development, and demonstration in the area of resource conservation.

(2) The study required in paragraph (1)(D) may include pilot scale projects, and shall consider and evaluate alternative strategies with respect to

(A) the product categories on which such charges would be imposed;

(B) the appropriate state in the production of such consumer product at which to levy such charge;

(C) appropriate criteria for establishing such charges for each consumer product category;

(D) methods for the adjustment of such charges to reflect actions such as recycling which would reduce the overall quantities of solid waste requiring disposal; and

(E) procedures for amending, modifying, or revising such charges to reflect changing conditions.

(3) The design for the study required in paragraph (1) of this subsection shall include timetables for the completion of the study. A preliminary report putting forth the study design shall be sent to the President and the Congress within six months following enactment of this section and followup reports shall be sent six months thereafter. Each recommendation resulting from the study shall include at least two alternatives to the proposed recommendation.

(4) The results of such investigation and study, including recommendations, shall be reported to the President and the Congress not later than two years after enactment of this subsection.

(5) There are authorized to be appropriated not to exceed $2,000,000 to carry out this subsection.

(k) Airport Landfills.--The Administrator shall undertake a comprehensive study and analysis of and publish a report on systems to alleviate the hazards to aviation from birds congregating and feeding on landfills in the vicinity of airports.

(l) Completion of Research and Studies.--The Administrator shall complete the research and studies, and submit the reports, required under subsection (b), (c), (d), (e), (f), (g), and (k) not later than October 1, 1978. The Administrator shall complete the research and studies, and submit the reports, required under subsections (a), (h), and (i) not later than October 1, 1979. Upon completion, each study specified in subsections (a) through (k) of this section, the Administrator shall prepare a plan for research, development, and demonstration respecting the findings of the study and shall submit any legislative recommendations resulting from such study to appropriate committees of Congress.

(m) Drilling Fluids, Produced Waters, and Other Wastes Associated with the Exploration, Development, or Production of Crude Oil or Natural Gas or Geothermal Energy.--

(1) The Administrator shall conduct a detailed and comprehensive study and submit a report on the adverse effects, if any, of drilling fluids, produced waters, and other wastes associated with the exploration, development, or production of crude oil or natural gas or geothermal energy on human health and the environment, including, but not limited to, the effects of such wastes on humans, water, air, health, welfare, and natural resources and on the adequacy of means and measures currently employed by the oil and gas and geothermal drilling and production industry, Government agencies, and others to dispose of and utilize such wastes and to prevent or substantially mitigate such adverse effects. Such study shall include an analysis of

(A) the sources and volume of discarded material generated per year from such wastes;

(B) present disposal practices;

(C) potential danger to human health and the environment from the surface runoff or leachate;

(D) documented cases which prove or have caused danger to human health and the environment from surface runoff or leachate;

(E) alternatives to current disposal methods;

(F) the cost of such alternatives; and

(G) the impact of those alternatives on the exploration for, and development and production of, crude oil and natural gas or geothermal energy. In furtherance of this study, the Administrator shall, as he deems appropriate, review studies and other actions of other Federal agencies concerning such wastes with a view toward avoiding duplication of effort and the need to expedite such study. The Administrator shall publish a report of such study and shall include appropriate findings and recommendations for Federal and non-Federal actions concerning such effects.

(2) The Administrator shall complete the research and study and submit the report required under paragraph (1) not later than twenty-four months from the date of enactment of the Solid Waste Disposal Act Amendments of 1980. Upon completion of the study, the Administrator shall prepare a summary of the findings of the study, a plan for research, development, and demonstration respecting the findings of the study, and shall submit the findings and the study, along with any recommendations resulting from such study, to the Committee on Environment and Public Works of the United States Senate and the Committee on Interstate and Foreign Commerce of the United States House of Representatives.

(3) There are authorized to be appropriated not to exceed $1,000,000 to carry out the provisions of this subsection.

(n) Materials Generated from the Combustion of Coal and Other Fossil Fuels.--The Administrator shall conduct a detailed and comprehensive study and submit a report on the adverse effects on human health and the environment, if any, of the disposal and utilization of fly ash waste, bottom ash waste, slag waste, flue gas emission control waste, and other byproduct materials generated primarily from the combustion of coal or other fossil fuels. Such study shall include an analysis of

(1) the source and volumes of such material generated per year;

(2) present disposal and utilization practices;

(3) potential danger, if any, to human health and the environment from the disposal and reuse of such materials;

(4) documented cases in which danger to human health or the environment from surface runoff or leachate has been proved;

(5) alternatives to current disposal methods;

(6) the costs of such alternatives;

(7) the impact of those alternatives on the use of coal and other natural resources; and

(8) The current and potential utilization of such materials.

In furtherance of this study, the Administrator shall, as he deems appropriate, review studies and other actions of other Federal and State agencies concerning such material and invite participation by other concerned parties, including industry and other Federal and State agencies, with a view toward avoiding duplication of effort. The Administrator shall publish a report on such study, which shall include appropriate findings, not later than twenty-four months after the enactment of the Solid Waste Disposal Act Amendments of 1980. Such study and findings shall be submitted to the Committee on Environment and Public Works of the United States Senate and the Committee on Interstate and Foreign Commerce of the United States House of Representatives.

(o) Cement Kiln Dust Waste.--The Administrator shall conduct a detailed and comprehensive study of the adverse effects on human health and the environment, if any, of the disposal of cement kiln dust waste. Such study shall include an analysis of

(1) the source and volumes of such materials generated per year;

(2) present disposal practices;

(3) potential danger, if any, to human health and the environment from the disposal of such materials;

(4) documented cases in which danger to human health or the environment has been proved;

(5) alternatives to current disposal methods;

(6) the costs of such alternatives;

(7) the impact of those alternatives on the use of natural resources; and

(8) the current and potential utilization of such materials.

In furtherance of this study, the Administrator shall, as he deems appropriate, review studies and other actions of other Federal and State agencies concerning such waste or materials and invite participation by other concerned parties, including industry and other Federal and State agencies, with a view toward avoiding duplication of effort. The Administrator shall publish a report of such study, which shall include appropriate findings, not later than thirty-six months after the date of enactment of the Solid Waste Disposal Act Amendments of 1980. Such report shall be submitted to the Committee on Environment and Public Works of the United States Senate and the Committee on Interstate and Foreign Commerce of the United States House of Representatives.

(p) Materials Generated from the Extraction, Beneficiation, and Processing of Ores and Minerals, Including Phosphate Rock and Overburden from Uranium Mining.--The Administrator shall conduct a detailed and comprehensive study on the adverse effects on human health and the environment, if any, of the disposal and utilization of solid waste from the extraction, beneficiation, and processing of ores and minerals, including phosphate rock and overburden from uranium mining. Such study shall be conducted in conjunction with the study of mining wastes required by subsection (f) of this section and shall include an analysis of

  (1) the source and volumes of such materials generated per year;
  (2) present disposal and utilization practices;
  (3) potential danger, if any, to human health and the environment from the disposal and reuse of such materials;
  (4) documented cases in which danger to human health or the environment has been proved;
  (5) alternatives to current disposal methods;
  (6) the costs of such alternatives;
  (7) the impact of those alternatives on the use of phosphate rock and uranium ore, and other natural resources; and
  (8) the current and potential utilization of such materials.

In furtherance of this study, the Administrator shall, as he deems appropriate, review studies and other actions of other Federal and State agencies concerning such waste or materials and invite participation by other concerned parties, including industry and other Federal and State agencies, with a view toward avoiding duplication of effort. The Administrator shall publish a report of such study, which shall include appropriate findings, in conjunction with the publication of the report of the study of mining wastes required to be conducted under subsection (f) of this section. Such report and findings shall be submitted to the Committee on Environment and Public Works of the United States Senate and the Committee on Interstate and Foreign Commerce of the United States House of Representatives.

(q) Authorization of Appropriations.--There are authorized to be appropriated not to exceed $8,000,000 for the fiscal years 1978 and 1979 to carry out this section other than subsection (j).

(r) Minimization of Hazardous Waste.--The Administrator shall compile, and not later than October 1, 1986, submit to the Congress, a report on the feasibility and desirability of establishing standards of performance or of taking other additional actions under this Act to require the generators of hazardous waste to reduce the volume or quantity and toxicity of the hazardous waste they generate, and of establishing with respect to hazardous wastes required management practices or other requirements to assure such wastes are managed in ways that minimize present and future risks to human health and the environment. Such report shall include any recommendations for legislative changes which the Administrator determines are feasible and desirable to implement the national policy established by section 1003.

(s) Extending the Useful Life of Sanitary Landfills.--The Administrator shall conduct detailed, comprehensive studies of methods to extend the useful life of sanitary landfills and to better use sites in which filled or closed landfills are located. Such studies shall address

  (1) methods to reduce the volume of materials before placement in landfills;
  (2) more efficient systems for depositing waste in landfills;
  (3) methods to enhance the rate of decomposition of solid waste in landfills, in a safe and environmentally acceptable manner;
  (4) methane production from closed landfill units;
  (5) innovative uses of closed landfill sites, including use for energy production such as solar or wind energy and use for metals recovery;
  (6) potential for use of sewage treatment sludge in reclaiming landfilled areas; and
  (7) methods to coordinate use of a landfill owned by one municipality by nearby municipalities, and to establish equitable rates for such use, taking into account the need to provide future landfill capacity to replace that so used.

The Administrator is authorized to conduct demonstrations in the areas of study provided in this subsection. The Administrator shall periodically report on the results of such studies, with the first such report not later than

October 1, 1986. In carrying out this subsection, the Administrator need not duplicate other studies which have been completed and may rely upon information which has previously been compiled.

COORDINATION, COLLECTION, AND DISSEMINATION
OF INFORMATION

42 USC 6983

Sec. 8003. (a) Information.--The Administrator shall develop, collect, evaluate, and coordinate information on

(1) methods and costs of the collection of solid waste;

(2) solid waste management practices, including data on the different management methods and the cost, operation, and maintenance of such methods;

(3) the amounts and percentages of resources (including energy) that can be recovered from solid waste by use of various solid waste management practices and various technologies;

(4) methods available to reduce the amount of solid waste that is generated;

(5) existing and developing technologies for the recovery of energy or materials from solid waste and the costs, reliability, and risks associated with such technologies;

(6) hazardous solid waste, including incidents of damage resulting from the disposal of hazardous solid wastes; inherently and potentially hazardous solid wastes; methods of neutralizing or properly disposing of hazardous solid wastes; facilities that properly dispose of hazardous wastes;

(7) methods of financing resource recovery facilities or, sanitary landfills, or hazardous solid waste treatment facilities, whichever is appropriate for the entity developing such facility or landfill (taking into account the amount of solid waste reasonably expected to be available to such entity);

(8) the availability of markets for the purchase of resources, either materials or energy, recovered from solid waste; and

(9) research and development projects respecting solid waste management.

(b) Library.--

(1) The Administrator shall establish and maintain a central reference library for

(A) the materials collected pursuant to subsection (a) of this section and

(B) the actual performance and cost effectiveness records and other data and information with respect to

(i) the various methods of energy and resource recovery from solid waste,

(ii) the various systems and means of resource conservation,

(iii) the various systems and technologies for collection, transport, storage, treatment, and final disposition of solid waste, and

(iv) other aspects of solid waste and hazardous solid waste management.

Such central reference library shall also contain, but not be limited to, the model codes and model accounting systems developed under this section, the information collected under subsection (d), and, subject to any applicable requirements of confidentiality, information respecting any aspect of solid waste provided by officers and employees of the Environmental Protection Agency which has been acquired by them in the conduct of their functions under this Act and which may be of value to Federal, State, and local authorities and other persons.

(2) Information in the central reference library shall, to the extent practicable, be collated, analyzed, verified, and published and shall be made available to State and local governments and other persons at reasonable times and subject to such reasonable charges as may be necessary to defray expenses of making such information available.

(c) Model Accounting System.--In order to assist State and local governments in determining the cost and revenues associated with the collection and disposal of solid waste and with resource recovery operations, the Administrator shall develop and publish a recommended model cost and revenue accounting system applicable to the solid waste management functions of State and local governments. Such system shall be in accordance with generally accepted accounting principles. The Administrator shall periodically, but not less frequently than once every five years, review such accounting system and revise it as necessary.

R-85

(d) Model Codes.--The Administrator is authorized, in cooperation with appropriate State and local agencies, to recommend model codes, ordinances, and statutes, providing for sound solid waste management.

(e) Information Programs.--

(1) The Administrator shall implement a program for the rapid dissemination of information on solid waste management, hazardous waste management, resource conservation, and methods of resource recovery from solid waste, including the results of any relevant research, investigations, experiments, surveys, studies, or other information which may be useful in the implementation of new or improved solid waste management practices and methods and information on any other technical, managerial, financial, or market aspect of resource conservation and recovery facilities.

(2) The Administrator shall develop and implement educational programs to promote citizen understanding of the need for environmentally sound solid waste management practices.

(f) Coordination.--In collecting and disseminating information under this section, the Administrator shall coordinate his actions and cooperate to the maximum extent possible with State and local authorities.

(g) Special Restriction.--Upon request, the full range of alternative technologies, programs or processes deemed feasible to meet the resource recovery or resource conservation needs of a jurisdiction shall be described in such a manner as to provide a sufficient evaluative basis from which the jurisdiction can make its decisions, but no officer or employee of the Environmental Protection Agency shall, in an official capacity, lobby for or otherwise represent an agency position in favor of resource recovery or resource conservation, as a policy alternative for adoption into ordinances, codes, regulations, or law by any State or political subdivision thereof.

FULL-SCALE DEMONSTRATION FACILITIES

42 USC 6984

Sec. 8004. (a) Authority.--The Administrator may enter into contracts with public agencies or authorities or private persons for the construction and operation of a full-scale demonstration facility under this Act, or provide financial assistance in the form of grants to a full-scale demonstration facility under this Act only if the Administrator finds that

(1) such facility or proposed facility will demonstrate at full scale a new or significantly improved technology or process, a practical and significant improvement in solid waste management practice, or the technological feasibility and cost effectiveness of an existing, but unproven technology, process, or practice, and will not duplicate any other Federal, State, local, or commercial facility which has been constructed or with respect to which construction has begun (determined as of the date action is taken by the Administrator under this Act),

(2) such contract or assistance meets the requirements of section 8001 and meets other applicable requirements of the Act,

(3) such facility will be able to comply with the guidelines published under section 1008 and with other laws and regulations for the protection of health and the environment,

(4) in the case of a contract for construction or operation, such facility is not likely to be constructed or operated by State, local, or private persons or in the case of an application for financial assistance, such facility is not likely to receive adequate financial assistance from other sources, and

(5) any Federal interest in, or assistance to, such facility will be disposed of or terminated, with appropriate compensation, within such period of time as may be necessary to carry out the basic objectives of this Act.

(b) Time Limitation.--No obligation may be made by the Administrator for financial assistance under this subtitle for any full-scale demonstration facility after the date ten years after the enactment of this section. No expenditure of funds for any such full-scale demonstration facility under this subtitle may be made by the Administrator after the date fourteen years after such date of enactment.

(c) Cost Sharing.--

(1) Wherever practicable, in constructing, operating, or providing financial assistance under this subtitle to a full-scale demonstration facility, the Administrator shall endeavor to enter into agreements and make other arrangements for maximum practicable cost sharing with other Federal, State, and local agencies, private persons, or any combination thereof.

(2) The Administrator shall enter into arrangements, wherever practicable and desirable, to provide monitoring of full-scale solid waste facilities (whether or not constructed or operated under this Act) for purposes of obtaining information concerning the performance, and other aspects, of such facilities. Where the Administrator provides only monitoring and evaluation instruments or personnel (or both) or funds for such instruments or personnel and provides no other financial assistance to a facility, notwithstanding section 8001(c)(3), title to any invention made or conceived of in the course of developing, constructing, or operating such facility shall not be required to vest in the United States and patents respecting such invention shall not be required to be issued to the United States.

(d) Prohibition.--After the date of enactment of this section, the Administrator shall not construct or operate any full-scale facility (except by contract with public agencies or authorities or private persons).

SPECIAL STUDY AND DEMONSTRATION PROJECTS ON RECOVERY OF USEFUL ENERGY AND MATERIALS

42 USC 6985

Sec. 8005. (a) Studies.--The Administrator shall conduct studies and develop recommendations for administrative or legislative action on

(1) means of recovering materials and energy from solid waste, recommended uses of such materials and energy for national or international welfare, including identification of potential markets for such recovered resources, the impact of distribution of such resources on existing markets, and potentials for energy conservation through resource conservation and resource recovery;

(2) actions to reduce waste generation which have been taken voluntarily or in response to governmental action, and those which practically could be taken in the future, and the economic, social, and environmental consequences of such actions;

(3) methods of collection, separation, and containerization which will encourage efficient utilization of facilities and contribute to more effective programs of reduction, reuse, or disposal of wastes;

(4) the use of Federal procurement to develop market demand for recovered resources;

(5) recommended incentives (including Federal grants, loans and other assistance) and disincentives to accelerate the reclamation or recycling of materials from solid wastes, with special emphasis on motor vehicle hulks;

(6) the effect of existing public policies, including subsidies and economic incentives and disincentives, percentage depletion allowances, capital gains treatment and other tax incentives and disincentives, upon the recycling and reuse of materials, and the likely effect of the modification or elimination of such incentives and disincentives upon the reuse, recycling and conservation of such materials;

(7) the necessity and method of imposing disposal or other charges on packaging, containers, vehicles, and other manufactured goods, which charges would reflect the cost of final disposal, the value of recoverable components of the item, and any social costs associated with nonrecycling or uncontrolled disposal of such items; and

(8) the legal constraints and institutional barriers to the acquisition of land needed for solid waste management, including land for facilities and disposal sites;

(9) in consultation with the Secretary of Agriculture, agricultural waste management problems and practices, the extent of reuse and recovery of resources in such wastes, the prospects for improvement, Federal, State, and local regulations governing such practices, and the economic, social, and environmental consequences of such practices; and

(10) in consultation with the Secretary of the Interior, mining waste management problems, and practices, including an assessment of existing authorities, technologies, and economics, and the environmental and public health consequences of such practices.

(b) Demonstration.--The Administrator is also authorized to carry out demonstration projects to test and demonstrate methods and techniques developed pursuant to subsection (a).

(c) Application of Other Sections.--Section 8001(b) and (c) shall be applicable to investigations, studies, and projects carried out under this section.

GRANTS FOR RESOURCE RECOVERY SYSTEMS AND IMPROVED SOLID WASTE DISPOSAL FACILITIES

42 USC 6986

Sec. 8006. (a) Authority.--The Administrator is authorized to make grants pursuant to this section to any State, municipal, or interstate or intermunicipal agency for the demonstration of resource recovery systems or for the construction of new or improved solid waste disposal facilities.

(b) Conditions.--

(1) Any grant under this section for the demonstration of a resource recovery system may be made only if it (A) is consistent with any plans which meet the requirements of subtitle D of this Act; (B) is consistent with the guidelines recommended pursuant to section 1008 of this Act; (C) is designed to provide area-wide resource recovery systems consistent with the purposes of this Act, as determined by the Administrator, pursuant to regulations promulgated under subsection (d) of this section; and (D) provides an equitable system for distributing the costs associated with construction, operation, and maintenance of any resource recovery system among the users of such system.

(2) The Federal share for any project to which paragraph (1) applies shall not be more than 75 percent.

(c) Limitations.--

(1) A grant under this section for the construction of a new or improved solid waste disposal facility may be made only if

(A) a State or interstate plan for solid waste disposal has been adopted which applies to the area involved, and the facility to be constructed (i) is consistent with such plan, (ii) is included in a comprehensive plan for the area involved which is satisfactory to the Administrator for the purposes of this Act, and (iii) is consistent with the guidelines recommended under section 1008, and

(B) the project advances the state of the art by applying new and improved techniques in reducing the environmental impact of solid waste disposal, in achieving recovery of energy or resources, or in recycling useful materials.

(2) The Federal share for any project to which paragraph (1) applies shall not be more than 50 percent in the case of a project serving an area which includes only one municipality, and not more than 75 percent in any other case.

(d) Regulations.--

(1) The Administrator shall promulgate regulations establishing a procedure for awarding grants under this section which

(A) provides that projects will be carried out in communities of varying sizes, under such conditions as will assist in solving the community waste problems of urban-industrial centers, metropolitan regions, and rural areas, under representative geographic and environmental conditions; and

(B) provides deadlines for submission of, and action on, grant requests.

(2) In taking action on applications for grants under this section, consideration shall be given by the Administrator (A) to the public benefits to be derived by the construction and the propriety of Federal aid in making such grant; (B) to the extent applicable, to the economic and commercial viability of the project (including contractual arrangements with the private sector to market any resources recovered); (C) to the potential of such project for general application to community solid waste disposal problems; and (D) to the use by the applicant of comprehensive regional or metropolitan area planning.

(e) Additional Limitations.--A grant under this section

(1) may be made only in the amount of the Federal share of (A) the estimated total design and construction costs, plus (B) in the case of a grant to which subsection (b)(1) applies, the first-year operation and maintenance costs;

(2) may not be provided for land acquisition or (except as otherwise provided in paragraph (1) (B)) for operating or maintenance costs;

(3) may not be made until the applicant has made provision satisfactory to the Administrator for proper and efficient operation and maintenance of the project (subject to paragraph (1) (B)); and

(4) may be made subject to such conditions and requirements, in addition to those provided in this section, as the Administrator may require to properly carry out his functions pursuant to this Act.

For purposes of paragraph (1), the nonFederal share may be in any form, including, but not limited to, lands or interests therein needed for the project or personal property or services, the value of which shall be determined by the Administrator.

(f) Single State.--

(1) Not more than 15 percent of the total of funds authorized to be appropriated for any fiscal year to carry out this section shall be granted under this section for projects in any one State.

(2) The Administrator shall prescribe by regulation the manner in which this subsection shall apply to a grant under this section for a project in an area which includes all or part of more than one State.

AUTHORIZATION OF APPROPRIATIONS

42 USC 6987

Sec. 8007. There are authorized to be appropriated not to exceed $35,000,000 for the fiscal year 1978 to carry out the purposes of this subtitle (except for section 8002).

SUBTITLE I-REGULATION OF UNDERGROUND STORAGE TANKS

DEFINITIONS AND EXEMPTIONS

42 USC 6991

Sec. 9001. For the purposes of this subtitle

(1) The term "underground storage tank" means any one or combination of tanks (including underground pipes connected thereto) which is used to contain an accumulation of regulated substances, and the volume of which (including the volume of the underground pipes connected thereto) is 10 percent or more beneath the surface of the ground. Such term does not include any

(A) farm or residential tank of 1,100 gallons or less capacity used for storing motor fuel for noncommercial purposes.

(B) tank used for storing heating oil for consumptive use on the premises where stored..

(C) septic tank,

(D) pipeline facility (including gathering lines) regulated under

(i) the Natural Gas Pipeline Safety Act of 1968, (49 U.S.C.App. 1671, et seq.),

(ii) the Hazardous Liquid Pipeline Safety Act of 1979 (49 U.S.C.App. 2001, et seq.), or

(iii) which is an intrastate pipeline facility regulated under State laws comparable to the provisions of law referred to in clause (i) or (ii) of this subparagraph;

(E) surface impoundment, pit, pond, or lagoon,

(F) storm water or waste water collection system.

(G) flowthrough process tank;

(H) liquid trap or associated gathering lines directly related to oil or gas production and gathering operations; or

(I) storage tank situated in an underground area (such as a basement, cellar, mineworking, drift, shaft, or tunnel) if the storage tank is situated upon or above the surface of the floor.

The term "underground storage tank" shall not include any pipes connected to any tank which is described in subparagraphs (A) through (I).

(2) The term "regulated substance" means

(A) any substance defined in section 101(14) of the Comprehensive Environmental Response, Compensation, and Liability Act of 1980 (but not including any substance regulated as a hazardous waste under subtitle C), and

(B) petroleum. The term "petroleum" means petroleum, including crude oil or any fraction thereof which is liquid at standard conditions of temperature and pressure (60 degrees Fahrenheit and 14.7 pounds per square inch absolute).

(3) The term "owner" means

(A) in the case of an underground storage tank in use on the date of enactment of the Hazardous and Solid Waste Amendments of 1984, or brought into use after that date, any person who owns an underground storage tank used for the storage, use, or dispensing of regulated substances, and

(B) in the case of any underground storage tank in use before the date of enactment of the Hazardous and Solid Waste Amendments of 1984, but no longer in use on the date of enactment of such Amendments, any person who owned such tank immediately before the discontinuation of its use.

(4) The term "operator" means any person in control of, or having responsibility for, the daily operation of the underground storage tank.

(5) The term "release" means any spilling, leaking, emitting, discharging, escaping, leaching, or disposing from an underground storage tank into ground water, surface water or subsurface soils.

(6) The term "person" has the same meaning as provided in section 1004(15), except that such term includes a consortium, a joint venture, and a commercial entity, and the United States Government.

(7) The term "nonoperational storage tank" means any underground storage tank in which regulated substances will not be deposited or from which regulated substances will not be dispensed after the date of the enactment of the Hazardous and Solid Waste Amendments of 1984.

(8) The term "petroleum" means petroleum, including crude oil or any fraction thereof which is liquid at standard conditions of temperature and pressure (60 degrees Fahrenheit and 14.7 pounds per square inch absolute)

NOTIFICATION

42 USC 6991a

Sec. 9002. (a) Underground Storage Tanks.--

(1) Within 18 months after the date of enactment of the Hazardous and Solid Waste Amendments of 1984, each owner of an underground storage tank shall notify the State or local agency or department designated pursuant to subsection (b)(1) of the existence of such tank, specifying the age, size, type, location, and uses of such tank.

(2)(A) For each underground storage tank taken out of operation after January 1, 1974, the owner of such tank shall, within 18 months after the date of enactment of the Hazardous and Solid Waste Amendments of 1984, notify the State or local agency, or department designated pursuant to subsection (b)(1) of the existence of such tanks (unless the owner knows the tank subsequently was removed from the ground). The owner of a tank taken out of operation on or before January 1, 1974, shall not be required to notify the State or local agency under this subsection.

(B) Notice under subparagraph (A) shall specify, to the extent known to the owner

(i) the date the tank was taken out of operation,

(ii) the age of the tank on the date taken out of operation,

(iii) the size, type and location of the tank, and

(iv) the type and quantity of substances left stored in such tank on the date taken out of operation.

(3) Any owner which brings into use an underground storage tank after the initial notification period specified under paragraph (1), shall notify the designated State or local agency or department within 30 days of the existence of such tank, specifying the age, size, type, location and uses of such tank.

(4) Paragraphs (1) through (3) of this subsection shall not apply to tanks for which notice was given

pursuant to section 103(c) of the Comprehensive Environmental Response, Compensation, and Liability Act of 1980.

(5) Beginning 30 days after the Administrator prescribes the form of notice pursuant to subsection (b)(2) and for 18 months thereafter, any person who deposits regulated substances in an underground storage tank shall reasonably notify the owner or operator of such tank of the owner's notification requirements pursuant to this subsection.

(6) Beginning 30 days after the Administrator issues new tank performance standards pursuant to section 9003(e) of this subtitle, any person who sells a tank intended to be used as an underground storage tank shall notify the purchaser of such tank of the owner's notification requirements pursuant to this subsection.

(b) Agency Designation.--

(1) Within 180 days after the enactment of the Hazardous and Solid Waste Amendments of 1984, the Governors of each State shall designate the appropriate State agency or department or local agencies or departments to receive the notifications under subsection (a)(1), (2), or (3).

(2) Within 12 months after the date of enactment of the Hazardous and Solid Waste Amendments of 1984, the Administrator, in consultation with State and local officials designated pursuant to subsection (b)(1), and after notice and opportunity for public comment, shall prescribe the form of the notice and the information to be included in the notifications under subsection (a)(1), (2), or (3). In prescribing the form of such notice, the Administrator shall take into account the effect on small businesses and other owners and operators.

(c) State Inventories.--Each State shall make 2 separate inventories of all underground storage tanks in such State containing regulated substances. One inventory shall be made with respect to petroleum and one with respect to the other regulated substances. In making such inventories, the State shall utilize and aggregate the data in the notification forms submitted pursuant to subsections (a) and (b) of this section. Each State shall submit such aggregated data to the Administrator not later than 270 days after the enactment of the Superfund Amendments and Reauthorization Act of 1986.

RELEASE DETECTION, PREVENTION, AND CORRECTION REGULATIONS

42 USC 6991b

Sec. 9003. (a) Regulations.--The Administrator, after notice and opportunity for public comment, and at least 3 months before the effective dates specified in subsection (f), shall promulgate release detection, prevention, and correction regulations applicable to all owners and operators of underground storage tanks, as may be necessary to protect human health and the environment.

(b) Distinctions in Regulations.--In promulgating regulations under this section, the Administrator may distinguish between types, classes, and ages of underground storage tanks. In making such distinctions, the Administrator may take into consideration factors, including, but not limited to: location of the tanks, soil and climate conditions, uses of the tanks, history of maintenance, age of the tanks, current industry recommended practices, national consensus codes, hydrogeology, water table, size of the tanks, quantity of regulated substances periodically deposited in or dispensed from the tank, the technical capability of the owners and operators, and the compatibility of the regulated substance and the materials of which the tank is fabricated.

(c) Requirements.--The regulations promulgated pursuant to this section shall include, but need not be limited to, the following requirements respecting all underground storage tanks

(1) requirements for maintaining a leak detection system, an inventory control system together with tank testing, or a comparable system or method designed to identify releases in a manner consistent with the protection of human health and the environment;

(2) requirements for maintaining records of any monitoring or leak detection system or inventory control system or tank testing or comparable system;

(3) requirements for reporting of releases and corrective action taken in response to a release from an underground storage tank;

(4) requirements for taking corrective action in response to a release from an underground storage tank;

(5) requirements for the closure of tanks to prevent future releases of regulated substances into the environment; and

(6) requirements for maintaining evidence of financial responsibility for taking corrective action and compensating third parties for bodily injury and property damage caused by sudden and nonsudden accidental releases arising from operating an underground storage tank.

(d) Financial Responsibility.--(1) Financial responsibility required by this subsection may be established in accordance with regulations promulgated by the Administrator by any one, or any combination, of the following: insurance, guarantee, surety bond, letter of credit, qualification as a selfinsurer or any other method satisfactory to the Administrator. In promulgating requirements under this subsection, the Administrator is authorized to specify policy or other contractual terms, conditions, or defenses which are necessary or are unacceptable in establishing such evidence of financial responsibility in order to effectuate the purposes of this subtitle.

(2) In any case where the owner or operator is in bankruptcy, reorganization, or arrangement pursuant to the Federal Bankruptcy Code or where with reasonable diligence jurisdiction in any State court of the Federal Courts cannot be obtained over an owner or operator likely to be solvent at the time of judgement, any claim arising from conduct for which evidence of financial responsibility must be provided under this subsection may be asserted directly against the guarantor providing such evidence of financial responsibility. In the case of any action pursuant to this paragraph such guarantor shall be entitled to invoke all rights and defenses which would have been available to the owner or operator if any action had been brought against the owner or operator by the claimant and which would have been available to the guarantor if an action had been brought against the guarantor by the owner or operator.

(3) The total liability of any guarantor shall be limited to the aggregate amount which the guarantor has provided as evidence of financial responsibility to the owner or operator under this section. Nothing in this subsection shall be construed to limit any other State or Federal statutory, contractual or common law liability of a guarantor to its owner or operator including, but not limited to, the liability of such guarantor for bad faith either in negotiating or in failing to negotiate the settlement of any claim. Nothing in this subsection shall be construed to diminish the liability of any person under section 107 or 111 of the Comprehensive Environmental Response, Compensation and Liability Act of 1980 or other applicable law.

(4) For the purpose of this subsection, the term "guarantor" means any person, other than the owner or operator, who provides evidence of financial responsibility for an owner or operator under this subsection.

(5)(A) The Administrator, in promulgating financial responsibility regulations under this section, may establish an amount of coverage for particular classes or categories of underground storage tanks containing petroleum which shall satisfy such regulations and which shall not be less than $1,000,000 for each occurrence with an appropriate aggregate requirement.

(B) The Administrator may set amounts lower than the amounts required by subparagraph (A) of this paragraph for underground storage tanks containing petroleum which are at facilities not engaged in petroleum production, refining, or marketing and which are not used to handle substantial quantities of petroleum.

(C) In establishing classes and categories for purposes of this paragraph, the Administrator may consider the following factors:

(i) The size, type, location, storage, and handling capacity of underground storage tanks in the class or category and the volume of petroleum handled by such tanks.

(ii) The likelihood of release and the potential extent of damage from any release from underground storage tanks in the class or category.

(iii) The economic impact of the limits on the owners and operators of each such class or category, particularly relating to the small business segment of the petroleum marketing industry.

(iv) The availability of methods of financial responsibility in amounts greater than the amount established by this paragraph.

(v) Such other factors as the Administrator deems pertinent.

(D) The Administrator may suspend enforcement of the financial responsibility requirements for a particular class or category of underground storage tanks or in a particular State, if the Administrator makes a determination that methods of financial responsibility satisfying the requirements of this subsection are not generally available for underground storage tanks in that class or category and

(i) steps are being taken to form a risk retention group for such class of tanks; or

(ii) such State is taking steps to establish a fund pursuant to section 9004(c)(1) of this Act to be submitted as evidence of financial responsibility.

A suspension by the Administrator pursuant to this paragraph shall extend for a period not to exceed 180 days. A determination to suspend may be made with respect to the same class or category or for the same State at the end of such period, but only if substantial progress has been made in establishing a risk retention group, or the owners or operators in the class or category demonstrate, and the Administrator finds, that the formation of such a group is not possible and that the State is unable or unwilling to establish such a fund pursuant to clause (ii).

(e) New Tank Performance Standards.--The Administrator shall, not later than 3 months prior to the effective date specified in subsection (f), issue performance standards for underground storage tanks brought into use on or after the effective date of such standards. The performance standards for new underground storage tanks shall include, but need not be limited to, design, construction, installation, release detection, and compatibility standards.

(f) Effective Dates.--

(1) Regulations issued pursuant to subsection (c) and (d) of this section, and standards issued pursuant to subsection (e) of this section, for underground storage tanks containing regulated substances defined in section 9001(2)(B) (petroleum, including crude oil or any fraction thereof which is liquid at standard conditions of temperature and pressure) shall be effective not later than 30 months after the date of enactment of the Hazardous and Solid Waste Amendments of 1984.

(2) Standards issued pursuant to subsection (e) of this section (entitled "New Tank Performance Standards") for underground storage tanks containing regulated substances defined in section 9001(2)(A) shall be effective not later than 36 months after the date of enactment of the Hazardous and Solid Waste Amendments of 1984.

(3) Regulations issued pursuant to subsection (c) of this section (entitled "Requirements") and standards issued pursuant to subsection (d) of this section (entitled "Financial Responsibility") for underground storage tanks containing regulated substances defined in section 9001(2)(A) shall be effective not later than 48 months after the date of enactment of the Hazardous and Solid Waste Amendments of 1984.

(g) Interim Prohibition.--

(1) Until the effective date of the standards promulgated by the Administrator under subsection (e) and after 180 days after the date of the enactment of the Hazardous and Solid Waste Amendments of 1984, no person may install an underground storage tank for the purpose of storing regulated substances unless such tank (whether of single or double wall construction)

(A) will prevent releases due to corrosion or structural failure for the operational life of the tank;

(B) is cathodically protected against corrosion, constructed of noncorrosive material, steel clad with a noncorrosive material, or designed in a manner to prevent the release or threatened release of any stored substance; and

(C) the material used in the construction or lining of the tank is compatible with the substance to be stored.

(2) Notwithstanding paragraph (1), if soil tests conducted in accordance with ASTM Standard G5778, or another standard approved by the Administrator, show that soil resistivity in an installation location is 12,000 ohm/cm or more (unless a more stringent standard is prescribed by the Administrator by rule), a storage tank without corrosion protection may be installed in that location during the period referred to in paragraph (1).

(h) EPA Response Program for Petroleum.--

(1) Before Regulations.Before the effective date of regulations under subsection (c), the Administrator (or a State pursuant to paragraph (7)) is authorized to

(A) require the owner or operator of an underground storage tank to undertake corrective action with respect to any release of petroleum when the Administrator (or the State) determines that such corrective action will be done properly and promptly by the owner or operator of the underground storage tank from which the release occurs; or

(B) undertake corrective action with respect to any release of petroleum into the environment from an underground storage tank if such action is necessary, in the judgment of the Administrator (or the State), to protect human health and the environment.

The corrective action undertaken or required under this paragraph shall be such as may be necessary to protect human health and the environment. The Administrator shall use funds in the Leaking Underground Storage Tank Trust Fund for payment of costs incurred for corrective action under subparagraph (B), enforcement action under subparagraph (A), and cost recovery under paragraph (6) of this subsection. Subject to the priority requirements of paragraph (3), the Administrator (or the State) shall give priority in undertaking such actions under subparagraph (B) to cases where the Administrator (or the State) cannot identify a solvent owner or operator of the tank who will undertake action properly.

(2) After Regulations.Following the effective date of regulations under subsection (c), all actions or orders of the Administrator (or a State pursuant to paragraph (7)) described in paragraph (1) of this subsection shall be in conformity with such regulations. Following such effective date, the Administrator (or the State) may undertake corrective action with respect to any release of petroleum into the environment from an underground storage tank only if such action is necessary, in the judgment of the Administrator (or the State) to protect human health and the environment and one or more of the following situations exists:

(A) No person can be found, within 90 days or such shorter period as may be necessary to protect human health and the environment, who is

(i) an owner or operator of the tank concerned,

(ii) subject to such corrective action regulations, and

(iii) capable of carrying out such corrective action properly.

(B) A situation exists which requires prompt action by the Administrator (or the State) under this paragraph to protect human health and the environment.

(C) Corrective action costs at a facility exceed the amount of coverage required by the Administrator pursuant to the provisions of subsection (c) and (d)(5) of this section and, considering the class or category of underground storage tank from which the release occurred, expenditures from the Leaking Underground Storage Tank Trust Fund are necessary to assure an effective corrective action.

(D) The owner or operator of the tank has failed or refused to comply with an order of the Administrator under this subsection or section 9006 or with the order of a State under this subsection to comply with the corrective action regulations.

(3) Priority of Corrective Actions.The Administrator (or a State pursuant to paragraph (7)) shall give priority in undertaking corrective actions under this subsection, and in issuing orders requiring owners or operators to undertake such actions, to releases of petroleum from underground storage tanks which pose the greatest threat to human health and the environment.

(4) Corrective Action Orders.The Administrator is authorized to issue orders to the owner or operator of an underground storage tank to carry out subparagraph (A) of paragraph (1) or to carry out regulations issued under subsection (c)(4). A State acting pursuant to paragraph (7) of this subsection is authorized to carry out subparagraph (A) of paragraph (1) only until the State's program is approved by the Administrator under section 9004 of this subtitle. Such orders shall be issued and enforced in the same manner and subject to the same requirements as orders under section 9006.

(5) Allowable Corrective Actions.The corrective actions undertaken by the Administrator (or a State pursuant to paragraph (7)) under paragraph (1) or (2) may include temporary or permanent relocation of residents and alternative household water supplies. In connection with the performance of any corrective action under paragraph (1) or (2), the Administrator may undertake an exposure assessment as defined in paragraph (10) of this subsection or provide for such an assessment in a cooperative agreement with a State pursuant to paragraph (7) of this subsection. The costs of any such assessment may be treated as corrective action for purposes of paragraph (6), relating to cost recovery.

(6) Recovery of Costs.--

(A) In General.--Whenever costs have been incurred by the Administrator, or by a State pursuant to paragraph (7), for undertaking corrective action or enforcement action with respect to the release of petroleum from an underground storage tank, the owner or operator of such tank shall be liable to the

Administrator or the State for such costs. The liability under this paragraph shall be construed to be the standard of liability which obtains under section 311 of the Federal Water Pollution Control Act.

(B) Recovery.--In determining the equities for seeking the recovery of costs under subparagraph (A), the Administrator (or a State pursuant to paragraph (7) of this subsection) may consider the amount of financial responsibility required to be maintained under subsections (c) and (d)(5) of this section and the factors considered in establishing such amount under subsection (d)(5).

(C) Effect on Liability.--

(i) No Transfers of Liability.--No indemnification, hold harmless, or similar agreement or conveyance shall be effective to transfer from the owner or operator of any underground storage tank or from any person who may be liable for a release or threat of release under this subsection, to any other person the liability imposed under this subsection. Nothing in this subsection shall bar any agreement to insure, hold harmless, or indemnify a party to such agreement for any liability under this section.

(ii) No Bar to Cause of Action.--Nothing in this subsection, including the provision of clause (i) of this subparagraph, shall bar a cause of action that an owner or operator or any other person subject to liability under this section, or a guarantor, has or would have, by reason of subrogation or otherwise against any person.

(D) Facility.--For purposes of this paragraph, the term facility means, with respect to any owner or operator, all underground storage tanks used for the storage of petroleum which are owned or operated by such owner or operator and located on a single parcel of property (or on any contiguous or adjacent property).

(7) State Authorities.--

(A) General.--A State may exercise the authorities in paragraphs (1) and (2) of this subsection, subject to the terms and conditions of paragraphs (3), (5), (9), (10), and (11), and including the authorities of paragraphs (4), (6), and (8) of this subsection if

(i) the Administrator determines that the State has the capabilities to carry out effective corrective actions and enforcement activities; and

(ii) The Administrator enters into a cooperative agreement with the State setting out the actions to be undertaken by the State.

The Administrator may provide funds from the Leaking Underground Storage Tank Trust Fund for the reasonable costs of the State's actions under the cooperative agreement.

(B) Cost Share.--Following the effective date of the regulations under subsection (c) of this section, the State shall pay 10 per centum of the cost of corrective actions undertaken either by the Administrator or by the State under a cooperative agreement, except that the Administrator may take corrective action at a facility where immediate action is necessary to respond to an imminent and substantial endangerment to human health or the environment if the State fails to pay the cost share.

(8) Emergency Procurement Powers.--Notwithstanding any other provision of law, the Administrator may authorize the use of such emergency procurement powers as he deems necessary.

(9) Definition of Owner.--As used in this subsection, the term "owner" does not include any person who, without participating in the management of an underground storage tank and otherwise not engaged in petroleum production, refining, and marketing, holds indicia of ownership primarily to protect the owner's security interest in the tank.

(10) Definition of Exposure Assessment.--As used in this subsection, the term "exposure assessment" means an assessment to determine the extent of exposure of, or potential for exposure of, individuals to petroleum from a release from an underground storage tank based on such factors as the nature and extent of contamination and the existence of or potential for pathways of human exposure (including ground or surface water contamination, air emissions, and food chain contamination), the size of the community within the likely pathways of exposure, and the comparison of expected human exposure levels to the shortterm and longterm health effects associated with identified contaminants and any available recommended exposure or tolerance limits for such contaminants. Such assessment shall not delay corrective action to abate immediate hazards or reduce exposure.

(11) Facilities Without Financial Responsibility.--At any facility where the owner or operator has failed to maintain evidence of financial responsibility in amounts at least equal to the amounts established by subsection (d)(5)(A) of this section (or a lesser amount if such amount is applicable to such facility as a

result of subsection (d)(5)(B) of this section) for whatever reason the Administrator shall expend no monies from the Leaking Underground Storage Tank Trust Fund to clean up releases at such facility pursuant to the provisions of paragraph (1) or (2) of this subsection. At such facilities the Administrator shall use the authorities provided in subpargraph (A) of paragraph (1) and para-graph (4) of this subsection and section 9006 of this subtitle to order corrective action to clean up such releases. States acting pursuant to paragraph (7) of this subsection shall use the authorities provided in subparagraph (A) of paragraph (1) and paragraph (4) of this subsection to order corrective action to clean up such releases. Notwithstanding the provisions of this paragraph, the Administrator may use monies from the fund to take the corrective actions authorized by paragraph (5) of this subsection to protect human health at such facilities and shall seek full recovery of the costs of all such actions pursuant to the provisions of paragraph (6)(A) of this subsection and without consider-ation of the factors in paragraph (6)(B) of this subsection. Nothing in this paragraph shall prevent the Administrator (or a State pursuant to paragraph (7) of this subsection) from taking corrective action at a facility where there is no solvent owner or operator or where immedi-ate action is necessary to respond to an immediate and substantial endangerment of human health or the environment.

APPROVAL OF STATE PROGRAMS

42 USC 6991c

Sec. 9004. (a) Elements of State Program.--

(1) Beginning 30 months after the date of enactment of the Hazardous and Solid Waste Amendments of 1984, any State may submit an underground storage tank release detection, prevention, and correc-tion program for review and approval by the Administrator. The program may cover tanks used to store regulated substances referred to in 9001(2)(A) or (B) or both.

(2) A State program may be approved by the Administrator under this section only if the State demonstrates that the State program includes the following requirements and standards and provides for adequate enforcement of compliance with such requirements and standards

(1) requirements for maintaining a leak detection system, an inventory control system together with tank testing, or a comparable system or method designed to identify releases in a manner consistent with the protection of human health and the environment;

(2) requirements for maintaining records of any monitoring or leak detection system or inventory control system or tank testing system;

(3) requirements for reporting of any releases and corrective action taken in response to a release from an underground storage tank;

(4) requirements for taking corrective action in response to a release from an underground storage tank;

(5) requirements for the closure of tanks to prevent future releases of regulated substances into the environment;

(6) requirements for maintaining evidence of financial responsibility for taking corrective action and compensating third parties for bodily injury and property damage caused by sudden and nonsudden accidental releases arising from operating an underground storage tank;

(7) standards of performance for new underground storage tanks; and

(8) requirements

(A) for notifying the appropriate State agency or department (or local agency or department) designated according to section 9002(b)(1) of the existence of any operational or nonoperational underground storage tank; and

(B) for providing the information required on the form issued pursuant to section 9002(b)(2).

(b) Federal Standards.--

(1) A State program submitted under this section may be approved only if the requirements under paragraphs (1) through (7) of subsection (a) are no less stringent than the corresponding requirements standards promulgated by the Administrator pursuant to section 9003(a).

(2)(A) A State program may be approved without regard to whether or not the requirements referred to in paragraphs (1), (2), (3), and (5) of subsection (a) are less stringent than the corresponding standards under section 9003(a) during the 1year period commencing on the date of promulgation of regulations under section 9003(a) if State regulatory action but no State legislative action is required in order to adopt a State program.

(B) If such State legislative action is required, the State program may be approved without regard to whether or not the requirements referred to in paragraph (1), (2), (3), and (5) of subsection (a) are less stringent than the corresponding standards under section 9003(a) during the 2-year period commencing on the date of promulgation of regulations under section 9003(a) (and during an additional 1-year period after such legislative action if regulations are required to be promulgated by the State pursuant to such legislative action).

(c) Financial Responsibility.--

(1) Corrective action and compensation programs administered by State or local agencies or departments may be submitted for approval under subsection (a)(6) as evidence of financial responsibility.

(2) Financial responsibility required by this subsection may be established in accordance with regulations promulgated by the Administrator by any one, or any combination of the following: insurance, guarantee, surety bond, letter of credit, qualification as a selfinsurer, or any other method satisfactory to the Administrator. In promulgating requirements under this subsection, the Administrator is authorized to specify policy or other contractual terms including the amount of coverage required for various classes and categories of underground storage tanks pursuant to section 9003(d)(5), conditions, or defenses which are necessary or are unacceptable in establishing such evidence of financial responsibility in order to effectuate the purposes of this subtitle.

(3) In any case where the owner or operator is in bankruptcy, reorganization, or arrangement pursuant to the Federal Bankruptcy Code or where with reasonable diligence jurisdiction in any State court of the Federal Courts cannot be obtained over an owner or operator likely to be solvent at the time of judgement, any claim arising from conduct for which evidence of financial responsibility must be provided under this subsection may be asserted directly against the guarantor providing such evidence of financial responsibility. In the case of any action pursuant to this paragraph such guarantor shall be entitled to invoke all rights and defenses which would have been available to the owner or operator if any action had been brought against the owner or operator by the claimant and which would have been available to the guarantor if an action had been brought against the guarantor by the owner or operator.

(4) The total liability of any guarantor shall be limited to the aggregate amount which the guarantor has provided as evidence of financial responsibility to the owner or operator under this section. Nothing in this subsection shall be construed to limit any other State or Federal statutory, contractual or common law liability of a guarantor to its owner or operator including, but not limited to, the liability of such guarantor for bad faith either in negotiating or in failing to negotiate the settlement of any claim. Nothing in this subsection shall be construed to diminish the liability of any person under section 107 or 111 of the Comprehensive Environmental Response, Compensation and Liability Act of 1980 or other applicable law.

(5) For the purpose of this subsection, the term "guarantor" means any person, other than the owner or operator, who provides evidence of financial responsibility for an owner or operator under this subsection.

(d) EPA Determination.--

(1) Within 180 days of the date of receipt of a proposed State program, the Administrator shall, after notice and opportunity for public comment, make a determination whether the State's program complies with the provisions of this section and provides for adequate enforcement of compliance with the requirements and standards adopted pursuant to this section.

(2) If the Administrator determines that a State program complies with the provisions of this section and provides for adequate enforcement of compliance with the requirements and standards adopted pursuant to this section, he shall approve the State program in lieu of the Federal program and the State shall have primary enforcement responsibility with respect to requirements of its program.

(e) Withdrawal of Authorization.--Whenever the Administrator determines after public hearing that a State is not administering and enforcing a program authorized under this subtitle in accordance with the provisions of this section, he shall so notify the State. If appropriate action is not taken within a reasonable time, not to exceed 120 days after such notification, the Administrator shall withdraw approval of such program and reestablish the Federal program pursuant to this subtitle.

INSPECTIONS, MONITORING, TESTING
AND CORRECTIVE ACTION

Sec. 9005. (a) Furnishing Information.--For the purposes of developing or assisting in the development of any regulations, conducting any study, taking any corrective action, enforcing the provisions of this subtitle, any owner or operator of an underground storage tank (or any tank subject to study under section 9009 that is used for storing regulated substances) shall, upon request of any officer, employee or representative of the Environmental Protection Agency, duly designated by the Administrator, or upon request of any duly designated officer, employee, or representa-tive of a State acting pursuant to subsection (h)(7) of section 9003 or with an approved program, furnish information relating to such tanks, their associated equipment, their contents, conduct monitoring or testing, permit such officer at all reasonable times to have access to, and to copy all records relating to such tanks and permit such officer to have access for corrective action. For the purposes of developing or assisting in the development of any regulation, conducting any study, taking corrective action, or enforcing the provisions of this subtitle, such officers, employees, or representatives are authorized

(1) to enter at reasonable times any establishment or other place where an underground storage tank is located;

(2) to inspect and obtain samples from any person of any regulated substances contained in such tank;

(3) to conduct monitoring or testing of the tanks, associated equipment, contents, or surrounding soils, air, surface water or ground water; and

(4) to take corrective action.

Each such inspection shall be commenced and completed with reasonable promptness.

(b) Confidentiality.--

(1) Any records, reports, or information obtained from any persons under this section shall be availabe to the public, except that upon a showing satisfactory to the Administrator (or the State, as the case may be) by any person that records, reports, or information, or a particular part thereof, to which the Administrator (or the State, as the case may be) or any officer, employee, or representative thereof has access under this section if made public, would divulge information entitled to protection under section 1905 of title 18 of the United States Code, such information or particular portion thereof shall be considered confidential in accordance with the purposes of that section, except that such record, report, document, or information may be disclosed to other officers, employees, or authorized representatives of the United States concerned with carrying out this Act, or when relevant in any proceeding under this Act.

(2) Any person not subject to the provisions of section 1905 of title 18 of the United States Code who knowingly and willfully divulges or discloses any information entitled to protection under this subsection shall, upon conviction, be subject to a fine of not more than $5,000 or to imprisonment not to exceed one year, or both.

(3) In submitting data under this subtitle, a person required to provide such data may

(A) designate the data which such person believes is entitled to protection under this subsection, and

(B) submit such designated data separately from other data submitted under this subtitle.

A designation under this paragraph shall be made in writing and in such manner as the Administrator may prescribe.

(4) Notwithstanding any limitation contained in this section or any other provision of law, all information reported to, or otherwise obtained, by the Administrator (or any representative of the Administrator) under this Act shall be made available, upon written request of any duly authorized committee of the Congress, to such committee (including records, reports, or information obtained by representatives of the Environmental Protection Agency).

FEDERAL ENFORCEMENT

42 USC 6991e

Sec. 9006. (a) Compliance Orders.--

(1) Except as provided in paragraph (2), whenever on the basis of any information, the Administrator determines that any person is in violation of any requirement of this subtitle, the Administrator may issue an order requiring compliance within a reasonable specified time period or the Administrator may commence a civil action in the United States district court in which the violation occurred for appropriate relief, including a temporary or permanent injunction.

(2) In the case of a violation of any requirement of this subtitle where such violation occurs in a State with a program approved under section 9004, the Administrator shall give notice to the State in which such violation has occurred prior to issuing an order or commencing a civil action under this section.

(3) If a violator fails to comply with an order under this subsection within the time specified in the order, he shall be liable for a civil penalty of not more than $25,000 for each day of continued noncompliance.

(b) Procedure.--Any order issued under this section shall become final unless, no later than 30 days after the order is served, the person or persons named therein request a public hearing. Upon such request the Administrator shall promptly conduct a public hearing. In connection with any proceeding under this section the Administrator may issue subpoenas for the attendance and testimony of witnesses and the pro-duction of relevant papers, books, and documents, and may promulgate rules for discovery procedures.

(c) Contents of Order.--Any order issued under this section shall state with reasonable specificity the nature of the violation, specify a reasonable time for compliance, and assess a penalty, if any, which the Administrator determines is reasonable taking into account the seriousness of the violation and any good faith efforts to comply with the applicable requirements.

(d) Civil Penalties.--

(1) Any owner who knowingly fails to notify or submits false information pursuant to section 9002(a) shall be subject to a civil penalty not to exceed $10,000 for each tank for which notification is not given or false information is submitted.

(2) Any owner or operator of an underground storage tank who fails to comply with

(A) any requirement or standard promulgated by the Administrator under section 9003;

(B) any requirement or standard of a State program approved pursuant to section 9004, or

(C) the provisions of section 9003(g) (entitled "Interim Prohibition")

shall be subject to a civil penalty not to exceed $10,000 for each tank for each day of violation.

FEDERAL FACILITIES

42 USC 6991f

Sec. 9007. (a) Application of Subtitle.--Each department, agency, and instrumentality of the executive, legislative, and judicial branches of the Federal Government having jurisdiction over any underground storage tank shall be subject to and comply with all Federal, State, interstate, and local requirements, applicable to such tank, both substantive and procedural, in the same manner, and to the same extent, as any other person is subject to such requirements, including payment of reasonable service charges. Neither the United States, nor any agent, employee, or officer thereof, shall be immune or exempt from any process or sanction of any State or Federal court with respect to the enforcement of any such injunctive relief.

(b) Presidential Exemption.--The President may exempt any under-ground storage tanks of any department, agency, or instrumentality in the executive branch from compliance with such a requirement if he deter-mines it to be in the paramount interest of the United States to do so. No such exemption shall be granted due to lack of appropriation unless the President shall have specifically requested such appropriation as a part of the budgetary process and the Congress shall have failed to make available such requested appropriations. Any exemption shall be for a period not in excess of one year, but additional exemptions may be granted for periods not to exceed one year upon the President's making a new determination. The President shall report each January to the Congress all exemptions from the requirements of this section granted during the preceding calendar year, together with his reason for granting each such exemption.

STATE AUTHORITY

42 USC 6991g

Sec. 9008. Nothing in this subtitle shall preclude or deny any right of any State or political subdivision thereof to adopt or enforce any regulation, requirement, or standard of performance respecting underground storage tanks that is more stringent than a regulation, requirement, or standard of performance in effect under this subtitle or to impose any additional liability with respect to the release of regulated substances within such State or political subdivision.

STUDY OF UNDERGROUND STORAGE TANKS

42 USC 6991h

Sec. 9009. (a) Petroleum Tanks.--Not later than 12 months after the date of enactment of the Hazardous and Solid Waste Amendments of 1984, the Administrator shall complete a study of underground storage tanks used for the storage of regulated substances defined in section 9001(2)(B).

(b) Other Tanks.--Not later than 36 months after the date of enactment of the Hazardous and Solid Waste Amendments of 1984, the Administrator shall complete a study of all other underground storage tanks.

(c) Elements of Studies.--The studies under subsections (a) and (b) shall include an assessment of the ages, types (including methods of manufacture, coatings, protection systems, the compatibility of the construction materials and the installation methods) and locations (including the climate of the locations) of such tanks; soil conditions, water tables, and the hydrogeology of tank locations; the relationship between the foregoing factors and likelihood of releases from underground storage tanks; the effectiveness and costs of inventory systems, tank testing, and leak detection systems; and such other factors as the Administrator deems appropriate.

(d) Farm and Heating Oil Tanks.--Not later than 36 months after the date of enactment of the Hazardous and Solid Waste Amendments of 1984, the Administrator shall conduct a study regarding the tanks referred to in section 9001(1)(A) and (B). Such study shall include estimates of the number and location of such tanks and an analysis of the extent to which there may be releases or threatened releases from such tanks into the environment.

(e) Reports.--Upon completion of the studies authorized by this section, the Administrator shall submit reports to the President and to the Congress containing the results of the studies and recommendations respecting whether or not such tanks should be subject to the preceding provisions of this subtitle.

(f) Reimbursement.--

(1) If any owner or operator (excepting an agency, department, or instrumentality of the United States Government, a State or a political subdivision thereof) shall incur costs, including the loss of business opportunity, due to the closure or interruption of operation of an underground storage tank solely for the purpose of conducting studies authorized by this section, the Administrator shall provide such person fair and equitable reimbursement for such costs.

(2) All claims for reimbursement shall be filed with the Administrator not later than 90 days after the closure or interruption which gives rise to the claim.

(3) Reimbursements made under this section shall be from funds appropriated by the Congress pursuant to the authorization contained in section 2007(g).

(4) For purposes of judicial review, a determination by the Administrator under this subsection shall be considered final agency action.

AUTHORIZATION OF APPROPRIATIONS

42 USC 6991i

Sec. 9010. For authorization of appropriations to carry out this subtitle, see section 2007(g).

SUBTITLE J-DEMONSTRATION MEDICAL WASTE TRACKING PROGRAM

SCOPE OF DEMONSTRATION PROGRAM FOR MEDICAL WASTE

42 USC 6992

Sec. 11001. (a) Covered States.--The States within the demonstration program established under this subtitle for tracking medical wastes shall be New York, New Jersey, Connecticut, the States contiguous to the Great Lakes and any State included in the program through the petition procedure described in subsection (c), except for any of such States in which the Governor notifies the Administrator under subsection (b) that such State shall not be covered by the program.

(b) Opt Out.--

(1) If the Governor of any State covered under subsection (a) which is not contiguous to the Atlantic Ocean notifies the Administrator that such State elects not to participate in the demonstration program, the Administrator shall remove such State from the program.

(2) If the Governor of any other State covered under subsection (a) notifies the Administrator that such State has implemented a medical waste tracking program that is no less stringent than the demonstration program under this subtitle and that such State elects not to participate in the demonstration program, the Administrator shall, if the Administrator determines that such State program is no less stringent than the demonstration program under this subtitle, remove such State from the demonstration program.

(3) Notifications under paragraphs (1) or(2) shall be submitted to the Administrator no later than 30 days after the promulgation of regulations implementing the demonstration program under this subtitle.

(c) Petition In.--The Governor of any State may petition the Administrator to be included in the demonstration program and the Administrator may, in his discretion, include any such State. Such petition may not be made later than 30 days after promulgation of regulations establishing the demonstration program under this subtitle, and the Administrator shall determine whether to include the State within 30 days after receipt of the State's petition.

(d) Expiration of Demonstration Program.--The demonstration program shall expire on the date 24 months after the effective date of the regulations under this subtitle.

LISTING OF MEDICAL WASTES

42 USC 6992a

Sec. 11002. (a) List.--Not later than 6 months after the enactment of this subtitle, the Administrator shall promulgate regulations listing the types of medical waste to be tracked under the demonstration program. Except as provided in subsection (b), such list shall include, but need not be limited to, each of the following types of solid waste:

(1) Cultures and stocks of infectious agents and associated biologicals, including cultures from medical and pathological laboratories, cultures and stocks of infectious agents from research and industrial laboratories, wastes from the production of biologicals, discarded live and attenuated vaccines, and culture dishes and devices used to transfer, inoculate, and mix cultures.

(2) Pathological wastes, including tissues, organs, and body parts that are removed during surgery or autopsy.

(3) Waste human blood and products of blood, including serum, plasma, and other blood components.

(4) Sharps that have been used in patient care or in medical, research, or industrial laboratories, including hypodermic needles, syringes, pasteur pipettes, broken glass, and scalpel blades.

(5) Contaminated animal carcasses, body parts, and bedding of animals that were exposed to infectious agents during research, production of biologicals, or testing of pharmaceuticals.

(6) Wastes from surgery or autopsy that were in contact with infectious agents, including soiled dressings, sponges, drapes, lavage tubes, drainage sets, underpads, and surgical gloves.

(7) Laboratory wastes from medical, pathological, pharmaceutical, or other research, commercial, or industrial laboratories that were in contact with infectious agents, including slides and cover slips, disposable gloves, laboratory coats, and aprons.

(8) Dialysis wastes that were in contact with the blood of patients undergoing hemodialysis, including contaminated disposable equipment and supplies such as tubing, filters, disposable sheets, towels, gloves, aprons, and laboratory coats.

(9) Discarded medical equipment and parts that were in contact with infectious agents.

(10) Biological waste and discarded materials contaminated with blood, excretion, excudates or secretion from human beings or animals who are isolated to protect others from communicable diseases.

(11) Such other waste material that results from the administration of medical care to a patient by a health care provider and is found by the Administrator to pose a threat to human health or the environment.

(b) Exclusions from List.--The Administrator may exclude from the list under this section any categories or items described in paragraphs (6) through (10) of subsection (a) which he determines do not pose a substantial present or potential hazard to human health or the environment when improperly treated, stored, transported, disposed of, or otherwise managed.

TRACKING OF MEDICAL WASTE

42 USC 6992b

Sec. 11003. (a) Demonstration Program.--Not later than 6 months after the enactment of this subtitle, the Administrator shall promulgate regulations establishing a program for the tracking of the medical waste listed in section 11002 which is generated in a State subject to the demonstration program. The program shall (1) provide for tracking of the transportation of the waste from the generator to the disposal facility, except that waste that is incinerated need not be tracked after incinera-tion, (2) include a system for providing the generator of the waste with assurance that the waste is received by the disposal facility, (3) use a uniform form for tracking in each of the demonstration States, and (4) include the following requirements:

(A) A requirement for segregation of the waste at the point of generation where practicable.

(B) A requirement for placement of the waste in containers that will protect waste handlers and the public from exposure.

(C) A requirement for appropriate labeling of containers of the waste.

(b) Small Quantities.--In the program under subsection (a), the Administrator may establish an exemption for generators of small quantities of medical waste listed under section 11002, except that the Administrator may not exempt from the program any person who, or facility that, generates 50 pounds or more of such waste in any calendar month.

(c) Onsite Incinerators.--Concurrently with the promulgation of regulations under subsection (a), the Administrator shall promulgate a recordkeeping and reporting requirement for any generator in a demonstration State of medical waste listed in section 11002 that (1) incinerates medical waste listed in section 11002 on site and (2) does not track such waste under the regulations promulgated under subsection (a). Such requirement shall require the generator to report to the Adminis-trator on the volume and types of medical waste listed in section 11002 that the generator incinerated on site during the 6 months following the effective date of the requirements of this subsection.

(d) Type of Medical Waste and Types of Generators.--For each of the requirements of this section, the regulations may vary for different types of medical waste and for different types of medical waste generators.

INSPECTIONS

42 USC 6992c

Sec. 11004. (a) Requirements of Access.--For purposes of developing or assisting in the development of any regulation or report under this subtitle or enforcing any provision of this subtitle, any person who generates, stores, treats, transports, disposes of, or otherwise handles or has handled medical waste shall, upon request of any officer, employee, or representative of the Environmental Protection Agency duly desig-nated by the Administrator, furnish information relating to such waste, including any tracking forms required to be maintained under section 11003, conduct monitoring or testing, and permit such person at all reasonable times to have access to, and to copy, all records relating to such waste. For such purposes, such officers, employees, or representatives are authorized to

(1) enter at reasonable times any establishment or other place where medical wastes are or have been generated, stored, treated, disposed of, or transported from;

(2) conduct monitoring or testing; and

(3) inspect and obtain samples from any person of any such wastes and samples of any containers or labeling for such wastes.

(b) Procedures.--Each inspection under this section shall be commenced and completed with reasonable promptness. If the officer, employee, or representative obtains any samples, prior to leaving the premises he shall give to the owner, operator, or agent in charge a receipt describing the sample obtained and, if requested, a portion of each such sample equal in volume or weight to the portion retained if giving such an equal portion is feasible. If any analysis is made of such samples, a copy of the results of such analysis shall be furnished promptly to the owner, operator, or agent in charge of the premises concerned.

(c) Availability to Public.--The provisions of section 3007(b) of this Act shall apply to records, reports, and information obtained under this section in the same manner and to the same extent as such provisions apply to records, reports, and information obtained under section 3007.

ENFORCEMENT

42 USC 6992d

Sec. 11005. (a) Compliance Orders.--

(1) Violations.Whenever on the basis of any information the Administrator determines that any person has violated, or is in violation of, any requirement or prohibition in effect under this subtitle (including any requirement or prohibition in effect under regulations under this subtitle) (A) the Administrator may issue an order (i) assessing a civil penalty for any past or current violation, (ii) requiring compliance immediately or within a specified time period, or (iii) both, or (B) the Administrator may commence a civil action in the United States district court in the district in which the violation occurred for appropriate relief, including a temporary or permanent injunction. Any order issued pursuant to this subsection shall state with reasonable specificity the nature of the violation.

(2) Orders Assessing Penalties.Any penalty assessed in an order under this subsection shall not exceed $25,000 per day of noncompliance for each violation of a requirement or prohibition in effect under this subtitle. In assessing such a penalty, the Administrator shall take into account the seriousness of the violation and any good faith efforts to comply with applicable requirements.

(3) Public Hearing.Any order issued under this subsection shall become final unless, not later than 30 days after issuance of the order, the persons named therein request a public hearing. Upon such request, the Administrator shall promptly conduct a public hearing. In connection with any proceeding under this section, the Administrator may issue subpoenas for the production of relevant papers, books, and documents, and may promulgate rules for discovery procedures.

(4) Violation of Compliance Orders.In the case of an order under this subsection requiring compliance with any requirement of or regulation under this subtitle, if a violator fails to take corrective action within the time specified in an order, the Administrator may assess a civil penalty of not more than $25,000 for each day of continued noncompliance with the order.

(b) Criminal Penalties.--Any person who

(1) knowingly violates the requirements of or regulations under this subtitle;

(2) knowingly omits material information or makes any false material statement or representation in any label, record, report, or other document filed, maintained, or used for purposes of compliance with this subtitle or regulations thereunder; or

(3) knowingly generates, stores, treats, transports, disposes of, or otherwise handles any medical waste (whether such activity took place before or takes place after the date of the enactment of this paragraph) and who knowingly destroys, alters, conceals, or fails to file any record, report, or other document required to be maintained or filed for purposes of compliance with this subtitle or regulations thereunder

shall, upon conviction, be subject to a fine of not more than $50,000 for each day of violation, or imprisonment not to exceed 2 years (5 years in the case of a violation of paragraph (1)). If the conviction is for a violation committed after a first conviction of such person under this paragraph, the maximum punishment under the respective paragraph shall be doubled with respect to both fine and imprisonment.

(c) Knowing Endangerment.--Any person who knowingly violates any provision of subsection (b) who knows at that time that he thereby places another person in imminent danger of death or serious bodily injury, shall upon conviction be subject to a fine of not more than $250,000 or imprisonment for not more than 15 years, or both. A defen-dant that is an organization shall, upon conviction under this subsection, be subject to a fine of not more than $1,000,000. The terms of this paragraph shall be interpreted in accordance with the rules provided under section 3008(f) of this Act.

(d) Civil Penalties.--Any person who violates any requirement of or regulation under this subtitle shall be liable to the United States for a civil penalty in an amount not to exceed $25,000 for each such violation. Each day of such violation shall, for purposes of this section, constitute a separate violation.

(e) Civil Penalty Policy.--Civil penalties assessed by the United States or by the States under this subtitle shall be assessed in accordance with the Administrator's "RCRA Civil Penalty Policy," as such policy may be amended from time to time.

FEDERAL FACILITIES

42 USC 6992e

Sec. 11006. (a) In General.--Each department, agency, and instrumentality of the executive, legislative, and judicial branches of the Federal Government in a demonstration State (1) having jurisdiction over any solid waste management facility or disposal site at which medical waste is disposed of or otherwise handled, or (2) engaged in any activity resul-ting, or which may result, in the disposal, management, or handling of medical waste shall be subject to, and comply with, all Federal, State, interstate, and local requirements, both substantive and procedural (including any requirement for permits or reporting or any provisions for injunctive relief and such sanctions as may be imposed by a court to enforce such relief), respecting control and abatement of medical waste disposal and management in the same manner, and to the same extent, as any person is subject to such requirements, including the payment of reasonable service charges. The Federal, State, interstate, and local substantive and procedural requirements referred to in this subsection include, but are not limited to, all administrative orders, civil, criminal, and administrative penalties, and other sanctions, including injunctive relief, fines, and imprisonment. Neither the United States, nor any agent, employee, or officer thereof, shall be immune or exempt from any process or sanction of any State or Federal court with respect to the enforcement of any such order, penalty, or other sanction. For purposes of enforcing any such substantive or procedural requirement (including, but not limited to, any injunctive relief, administrative order, or civil, criminal, administrative penalty, or other sanction), against any such department, agency, or instrumentality, the United States hereby expressly waives any immunity otherwise applicable to the United States. The President may exempt any department, agency, or instrumentality in the executive branch from compliance with such a requirement if he deter-mines it to be in the paramount interest of the United States to do so. No such exemption shall be granted due to lack of appropriation unless the President shall have specifically requested such appropriation as a part of the budgetary process and the Congress shall have failed to make available such requested appropriation. Any exemption shall be for a period not in excess of one year, but additional exemptions may be granted for periods not to exceed one year upon the President's making a new determination. The President shall report each January to the Congress all exemptions from the requirements of this section granted during the preceding calendar year, together with his reason for granting each such exemption.

(b) Definition of Person.--For purposes of this Act, the term "person" shall be treated as including each department, agency, and instrumen-tality of the United States.

RELATIONSHIP TO STATE LAW

42 USC 6992f

Sec. 11007. (a) State Inspections and Enforcement.--A State may con-duct inspections under 11004 and take enforcement actions under section 11005 against any person, including any person who has imported medical waste into a State in violation of the requirements of, or regulations under, this subtitle, to the same extent as the Administrator. At the time a State initiates an enforcement action under section 11005 against any person, the State shall notify the Administrator in writing.

(b) Retention of State Authority.--Nothing in this subtitle shall
(1) preempt any State or local law; or
(2) except as provided in subsection (c), otherwise affect any State or local law or the authority of any State or local government to adopt or enforce any State or local law.

(c) State Forms.--Any State or local law which requires submission of a tracking form from any person subject to this subtitle shall require that the form be identical in content and format to the form required under section 11003, except that a State may require the submission of other tracking information which is supplemental to the information required on the form required under section 11003 through additional sheets or such other means as the State deems appropriate.

REPORT TO CONGRESS

42 USC 6992g

Sec 11008. (a) Final Report. Not later than 3 months after the expiration of the demonstration program, the Administrator shall report to Congress on the following topics:

(1) The types, number, and size of generators of medical waste (including small quantity generators) in the United States, the types and amounts of medical waste generated, and the onsite and offsite methods currently used to handle, store, transport, treat, and dispose of the medical waste, including the extent to which such waste is disposed of in sewer systems.

(2) The present or potential threat to human health and the environment posed by medical waste or the incineration thereof.

(3) The present and potential costs (A) to local economies, persons, and the environment from the improper handling, storage, transportation, treatment or disposal of medical waste and (B) to generators, transporters, and treatment, storage, and disposal facilities from regulations establishing requirements for tracking, handling, storage, transportation, treatment, and disposal of medical waste.

(4)(A) The success of the demonstration program established under this subtitle in tracking medical waste,

(B) changes in incineration and storage practices attributable to the demonstration program, and

(C) other available and potentially available methods for tracking medical waste and their advantages and disadvantages of extending tracking requirements to (i) rural areas and (ii) small quantity generators.

(5) Available and potentially available methods for handling, storing, transporting, and disposing of medical waste and their advantages and disadvantages.

(6) Available and potentially available methods for treating medical waste, including the methods of incineration, sterilization, chemical treatment, and grinding, and their advantages, including their ability to render medical waste noninfectious or less infectious, and unrecog-nizable and otherwise protect human health and the environment, and disadvantages.

(7) Factors affecting the effectiveness of the treatment methods identified in subsection (a)(5), including quality control and quality assurance procedures, maintenance procedures, and operator training.

(8) Existing State and local controls on the handling, storage, transportation, treatment, and disposal of medical waste, including the enforcement and regulatory supervision thererof.

(9) The appropriateness of using any existing State requirements or the requirements contained in subtitle C as nationwide requirements to monitor and control medical waste.

(10) The appropriateness of the penalties provided in section 11006 for insuring compliance with the requirements of this subtitle, including a review of the level of penalties imposed under this subtitle.

(11)(A) The effect of excluding households and small quantity generators from any regulations governing the handling, storage, transportation, treatment, and disposal of medical waste, and

(B) potential guidelines for the handling, storage, treatment, and disposal of medical waste by households and small quantity generators.

(12) Available and potentially available methods for the reuse or reduction of the volume of medical waste generated.

(b) Interim Reports.--The Administrator shall submit two interim reports to Congress on the topics listed in subsection (a). The interim reports shall contain the information on the topics available to the Administrator at the time of submission. One interim report shall be due 9 months after enactment of this subtitle and one shall be due 12 months after the effective date of regulations under this subtitle.

(c) Consultation.--In preparing the reports under this section, the Administrator shall consult with appropriate State and local agencies.

HEALTH IMPACTS REPORT

42 USC 6992h

Sec. 11009. Within 24 months after the enactment of this section, the Administrator of the Agency for Toxic Substances and Disease Registry shall prepare for Congress a report on the health effects of medical waste, including each of the following

(1) A description of the potential for infection or injury from the segregation, handling, storage, treatment, or disposal of medical wastes.

(2) An estimate of the number of people injured or infected annually by sharps, and the nature and seriousness of those injuries or infections.

(3) An estimate of the number of people infected annually by other means related to waste segregation, handling, storage, treatment, or disposal, and the nature and seriousness of those infections.

(4) For diseases possibly spread by medical waste, including Acquired Immune Deficiency Syndrome and hepatitis B, an estimate of what percentage of the total number of cases nationally may be traceable to medical wastes.

GENERAL PROVISIONS

42 USC 6992i

Sec. 11010. (a) Consultation.--(1) In promulgating regulations under this subtitle, the Administrator shall consult with the affected States and may consult with other interested parties.

(2) The Administrator shall also consult with the International Joint Commission to determine how to monitor the disposal of medical waste emanating from Canada.

(b) Public Comment.--In the case of the regulations required by this subtitle to be promulgated within 9 months after the enactment of this subtitle, the Administrator may promulgate such regulations in interim final form without prior opportunity for public comment, but the Administrator shall provide an opportunity for public comment on the interim final rule. The promulgation of such regulations shall not be subject to the Paperwork Reduction Act of 1980.

(c) Relationship to Subtitle C.--Nothing in this subtitle shall affect the authority of the Administrator to regulate medical waste, including medical waste listed under section 11002, under subtitle C of this Act.

EFFECTIVE DATE

42 USC 6992j

Sec. 11011. The regulations promulgated under this subtitle shall take effect within 90 days after promulgation, except that, at the time of promulgation, the Administrator may provide for a shorter period prior to the effective date if he finds the regulated community does not need 90 days to come into compliance.

AUTHORIZATION OF APPROPRIATIONS

42 USC 6992k

Sec. 11012. There are authorized to be appropriated to the Administrator such sums as may be necessary for each of the fiscal years 1989 through 1991 for purposes of carrying out activities under this subtitle.

*　　*　　*

PROVISIONS THAT DO NOT AMEND

FROM PUBLIC LAW 96-463, OCTOBER 15, 1980 USED OIL RECYCLING ACT OF 1980

Sections That Do Not Amend

FINDINGS

Sec. 2. The Congress finds and declares that

(1) used oil is a valuable source of increasingly scarce energy and materials;

(2) technology exists to rerefine, reprocess, reclaim, and otherwise recycle used oil;

(3) used oil constitutes a threat to public health and the environment when reused or disposed of improperly; and that, therefore, it is in the national interest to recycle used oil in a manner which does not constitute a threat to public health and the environment and which conserves energy and materials.

Sec. 4. (c) Before the effective date of the labeling standards required to be prescribed under section 383(d)(1)(A) of the Energy Policy and Conservation Act, no requirement of any rule or order of the Federal Trade Commission may apply, or remain applicable, to any container of recycled oil (as defined in section 383(b) of such Act) if such requirement provides that the container must bear any label referring to the fact that it has been derived from previously used oil. Nothing in this subsection shall be construed to affect any labeling requirement applicable to recycled oil under any authority of law to the extent such requirement relates to fitness for intended use or any other performance characteristic of such oil or to any characteristic of such oil other than that referred to in the preceding sentence.

USED OIL AS A HAZARDOUS WASTE

Sec. 8. Not later than ninety days after the date of the enactment of this Act, the Administrator of the Environmental Protection Agency shall

(1) make a determination as to the applicability to used oil of the criteria and regulations promulgated under subsections (a) and (b) of section 3001 of the Solid Waste Disposal Act relating to characteristics of hazardous wastes, and

(2) report to the Congress the determination together with a detailed statement of the data and other information upon which the determination is based.

In making a determination under paragraph (1), the Administrator shall ensure that the recovery and reuse of used oil are not discouraged.

STUDY

Sec. 9. The Administrator of the Environmental Protection Agency, in cooperation with the Secretary of Energy, the Federal Trade Commission, and the Secretary of Commerce, shall conduct a study

(1) assessing the environmental problems associated with the improper disposal or reuse of used oil;

(2) addressing the collection cycle of used oil prior to recycling;

(3) analyzing supply and demand in the used oil industry, including (A) estimates of the future supply and quality of used oil feedstocks for purpose of refining and (B) estimates of the future supply of virgin crude oil available for refining for purposes of producing lubricating oil;

(4) comparing the energy savings associated with rerefining used oil and the energy savings associated with other uses of used oil; and

(5) recommending Federal, State, and local policies to encourage methods for environmentally sound and economically feasible recycling of used oil.

Where appropriate, for purposes of the study under this section, the Administrator may utilize and update information and data previously collected by the administrator and by other agencies, departments, and instrumentalities of the United States. The Administrator shall submit to Congress a report containing the results of the study under this section not later than one year after the date of the enactment of this Act.

PUBLIC LAW 96–482, OCTOBER 20, 1980

SOLID WASTE DISPOSAL ACT AMENDMENTS OF 1980

Sections That Do Not Amend

Sec. 4. (a) In order to demonstrate effective means of dealing with contamination of public water supplies by leachate from abandoned or other landfills, the Administrator of the Environmental Protection Agency is authorized to provide technical and financial assistance for a research program to control leachate from the Llangollen Landfill in New Castle County, Delaware.

(b) The research program authorized by this section shall be designed by the New Castle County areawide waste treatment management program, in cooperation with the Environmental Protection Agency, to develop methods for controlling leachate contamination from abandoned and other landfills that may be applied at the Llangollen Landfill and other landfills throughout the Nation. Such research program shall investigate all alternative solutions or corrective actions, including

(1) hydrogeologic isolation of the landfill combined with the collection and treatment of leachate;

(2) excavation of the refuse, followed by some type of incineration;

(3) excavation and transportation of the refuse to another landfill; and

(4) collection and treatment of contaminated leachate or ground water.

Such research program shall consider the economic, social, and environmental consequences of each such alternative.

(c) The Administrator of the Environmental Protection Agency shall make available personnel of the Agency, including those of the Solid and Hazardous Waste Research Laboratory (Cincinnati, Ohio), and shall arrange for other Federal personnel to be made available, to provide technical assistance and aid in such research. The

Administrator may provide up to $250,000, of the sums appropriated under the Solid Waste Disposal Act, to the New Castle County areawide waste treatment management program to conduct such research, including obtaining consultant services.

(d) In order to prevent further damage to public water supplies during the period of this study, the Administrator of the Environmental Pro-tection Agency shall provide up to $200,000 in each of fiscal years 1977 and 1978, of the sums appropriated under the Solid Waste Disposal Act for the operating costs of a counterpumping program to contain the leachate from the Llangollen Landfill.

ENERGY AND MATERIALS CONSERVATION AND RECOVERY

Sec. 32. (a) --The Congress finds that
(1) significant savings could be realized by conserving materials in order to reduce the volume or quantity of material which ultimately becomes waste;
(2) solid waste contains valuable energy and material resources which can be recovered and used thereby conserving increasingly scarce and expensive fossil fuels and virgin materials;
(3) the recovery of energy and materials contributing to such waste streams, can have the effect of reducing the volume of the municipal waste stream and the burden of disposing of increasing volumes of solid waste;
(4) the technology to conserve resources exists and is commercially feasible to apply;
(5) the technology to recover energy and materials from solid waste is of demonstrated commercial feasibility; and
(6) various communities throughout the nation have different needs and different potentials for conserving resources and for utilizing techniques for the recovery of energy and materials from waste, and Federal assistance in planning and implementing such energy and materials conservation and recovery programs should be available to all communities on an equitable basis in relation to their needs and potential.

NATIONAL ADVISORY COMMISSION ON RESOURCE CONSERVATION AND RECOVERY

Sec. 33. (a)(1) There is hereby established in the executive branch of the United States the National Advisory Commission on Resource Conservation and Recovery, hereinafter in this section referred to as the Commission.

(2) The Commission shall be composed of nine members to be appointed by the President. Such members shall be qualified by reason of their education, training, or experience to represent the view of consumer groups, industry associations, and environmental and other groups concerned with resource conservation and recovery and at least two shall be elected or appointed State or local officials. Members shall be appointed for the life of the Commission.
(3) A vacancy in the Commission shall be filled in the manner in which the original appointment was made.
(4) Five members of the Commission shall constitute a quorum for transacting business of the Commission except that a lesser number may hold hearings and conduct informationgathering meetings.
(5) The Chairperson of the Commission shall be designated by the President from among the members.
(6) Upon the expiration of the twoyear period beginning on (A) the date when all initial members of the Commission have been appointed or when (B) the date when initial funds become available to carry out this section, whichever is later, the Commission shall transmit to the President, and to each House of the Congress, a final report containing a detailed statement of the findings and conclusions of the Commission, together with such recommendations as it deems advisable.
(7) The Commission shall submit an interim report on February 15, 1982, and the Commission may also submit, for legislative and administrative actions relating to the Solid Waste Disposal Act, other interim reports prior to the submission to its final report.
(8) The Commission shall cease to exist 30 days after the submission of its final report.

THE LAW: RESOURCE CONSERVATION AND RECOVERY ACT

(b) The Commission shall

(1) after consultation with the appropriate Federal agencies, review budgetary priorities relating to resource conservation and recovery, determine to what extent program goals relating to resource conservation and recovery are being realized, and make recommendations concerning the appropriate program balance and priorities.

(2) review any existing or proposed resource conservation and recovery guidelines or regulations;

(3) determine the economic development or savings potential of resource conservation and recovery, including the availability of markets for recovered energy and materials, for economic materials savings through conservation, and make recommendations concerning the utilization of such potential;

(4) identify, and make recommendations addressing, institutional obstacles impeding the development of resource conservation and resource recovery; and

(5) evaluate the status of resource conservation and recovery technology and systems including both materials and energy recovery technologies, recycling methods, and other innovative methods for both conserving energy and materials extractable from solid waste.

The review referred to in paragraph (1) should include but not be limited to an assessment of the effectiveness of the technical assistance panels, the public participation program and other program activities under the Solid Waste Disposal Act.

(c)(1) Members of the Commission while serving on business of the Commission, shall be compensated at a rate not to exceed the rate specified at the time of such service for grade GS16 of the General Schedule for each day they are engaged in the actual performance of Commission duties, including travel time; and while so serving away from their homes or regular places of business, all members of the Commission may be allowed travel expenses, including per diem in lieu of subsistence, as authorized by section 5703 of title 5, United States Code, for persons in Government service employed intermittently.

(2) Subject to such rules as may be adopted by the Commission, the Chairperson, without regard to the provisions of title 5, United States Code, governing appointments in the competitive service and without regard to the provisions of chapter 51 and subchapter III of chapter 53 of such title relating to classification and General Schedule pay rates, shall have the power to

(A) appoint a Director, who shall be paid at a rate not to exceed the rate of basic pay for level I, GS16 of the General Schedule; and

(B) appoint and fix the compensation of not more than 5 additional staff personnel.

(3) This Commission is authorized to procure temporary and intermittent services of experts and consultants as are necessary to the extent authorized by section 3109 of title 5, United States Code, but at rates not to exceed the rate specified at the time of such service for grade GS16 in section 5332 of such title. Experts and consultants may be employed without compensation if they agree to do so in advance.

(4) Upon request of the Commission, the head of any Federal agency is authorized to detail on a reimbursable or nonreimbursable basis any of the personnel of such agency to the Commission to assist the Commission in carrying out its duties under this section.

(5) The Commission is exempt from the requirements of sections 4301 through 4308 of title 5, United States Code.

(6) The Commission is authorized to enter into contracts with Federal and State agencies, private firms, institutions, and individuals for the conduct of research or surveys, the preparation of reports, and other activities necessary to the discharge of its duties and responsibilities.

(7) In order to expedite matters pertaining to the planning for, and work of, the Commission, the Commission is authorized to make purchases and contracts without regard to section 252 of title 41 of the United States Code, pertaining to advertising and competitive bidding, and may arrange for the printing of any material pertaining to the work of the Commission without regard to the Government Printing and Binding Regulations and any related laws or regulations.

(8) The Commission may use the United States mail in the same manner and under the same conditions as other departments and agencies of the United States.

(9) The Commission may secure directly from any department or agency of the United States information necessary to enable it to carry out its duties and functions. Upon request of the Chairperson, the head of any such Federal agency shall furnish such information to the Commission subject to applicable law.

(10) Financial and administrative services (including those related to budget and accounting, financial reporting, personnel, and procurement) shall be provided to the Commission by the General Services Administration for which payment shall be made in advance or by reimbursement, from funds of the Commission, in such amounts as may be agreed upon by the Chairperson of the Commission and the Administrator of General Services.

(d) In carrying out its duties under this section the Commission, or any duly authorized committee thereof, is authorized to hold such hearings and take testimony, with respect to matters to which it has a responsi-bility under this section as the Commission may deem advisable. The Chairperson of the Commission or any member authorized by him may administer oaths or affirmations to witnesses appearing before the Commission or before any committee thereof.

(e) From the amounts authorized to be appropriated under the Solid Waste Disposal Act for the fiscal years 1981 and 1982, not more than $1,000,000 may be used to carry our the provisions of this section.

PROVISIONS FROM PUBLIC LAW 98-616, NOVEMBER 9, 1984

THE HAZARDOUS AND SOLID WASTE AMENDMENTS OF 1984

Sections That Do Not Amend

Sec. 221. (b) The Administrator of the Environmental Protection Agency shall undertake activities to inform and educate the waste generators of their responsibilities under the amendments made by this section during the period within 30 months after the enactment of the Hazardous and Solid Waste Amendments of 1984 to help assure compliance.

(c) The Administrator of the Environmental Protection Agency in cooperation with the States shall conduct a study of hazardous waste identified or listed under section 3001 of the Solid Waste Disposal Act which is generated by individual generators in total quantities for each generator during any calendar month of less than 1,000 kilograms. The Administrator may require from such generators information as may be necessary to conduct the study. Such study shall include a characterization of the number and type of such generators, the quantity and characteristics of hazardous waste generated by such generators, State requirements applicable to such generators, the individual and industry waste management practices of such generators, the potential costs of modifying those practices and the impact of such modifications on national treatment and disposal facility capacity, and the threat to human health and the environment and the employees of transporters or others involved in solid waste management posed by such hazardous wastes or such management practices. Such study shall be submitted to the Congress not later than April 1, 1985.

(d) The Administrator of the Environmental Protection Agency shall cause to be studied the existing manifest system for hazardous wastes as it applies to small quantity generators and recommend whether the current system shall be retained or whether a new system should be introduced. The study shall include an analysis of the cost versus the benefits of the system studied as well as an analysis of the ease of retrieving and collating information and identifying a given substance. Finally, any new proposal shall include a list of those standards that are necessary to protect human health and the environment. Such study shall be submitted to the Congress not later than April 1, 1987.

(e) The Administrator of the Environmental Protection Agency, in conjunction with the Secretary of Transportation, shall prepare and submit to the Congress a report on the feasibility of easing the adminis-trative burden on small quantity generators, increasing compliance with statutory and regulatory requirements, and simplifying enforcement efforts through a program of licensing hazardous waste transporters to assume the responsibilities of small quantity generators relating to the preparation of manifests and associated recordkeeping and reporting requirements. The report shall examine the appropriate licensing requirements under such a program including the need for financial assurances by licensed transporters and shall make recommendations on provisions and requirements for such a program including the appropriate division of responsibilities between the Department of Transportation and the Environmental Protection Administration. Such report shall be submitted to the Congress not later than April 1, 1987.

(f)(1) The Administrator of the Environmental Protection Agency shall, in consultation with the Secretary of Education, the States, and appro-priate educational associations, conduct a comprehensive study of problems associated with the accumulation, storage and disposal of hazardous wastes from educational institutions. The study shall include an investigation of the feasibility and availability of environmentally sound methods for the treatment, storage or disposal of hazardous waste from such institutions, taking into account the types and quantities of such waste which are generated by these institutions, and the nonprofit nature of these institutions.

(2) The Administrator shall submit a report to the Congress containing the findings of the study carried out under paragraph (1) not later than April 1, 1987.

(3) For purposes of this subsection

(A) the term "hazardous waste" means hazardous waste which is listed or identified under Section 3001 of the Solid Waste Disposal Act;

(B) the term "educational institution" includes, but shall not be limited to,

(i) secondary schools as defined in section 198(a)(7) of the Elementary and Secondary Education Act of 1965; and

(ii) institutions of higher education as defined in section 1201(a) of the Higher Education Act of 1965.

REPORT TO CONGRESS ON INJECTION OF HAZARDOUS WASTE

Sec. 701. (a) The Administrator, in cooperation with the States, shall compile and, not later than 6 months after the date of enactment of the Hazardous and Solid Waste Amendments of 1984, submit to the Committee on Environment and Public Works of the United States Senate and the Committee on Energy and Commerce of the United States House of Representatives, an inventory of all wells in the United States which inject hazardous wastes. The inventory shall include the following information:

(1) the location and depth of each well;

(2) engineering and construction details of each, including the thickness and composition of its casing, the width and content of the annulus, and pump pressure and capacity;

(3) the hydrogeological characteristics of the overlying and underlying strata, as well as that into which the waste is injected;

(4) the location and size of all drinking water aquifers penetrated by the well, or within a one-mile radius of the well, or within two hundred feet below the well injection point;

(5) the location, capacity, and population served by each well providing drinking or irrigation water which is within a fivemile radius of the injection well;

(6) the nature and volume of the waste injected during the one-year period immediately preceding the date of the report;

(7) the dates and nature of the inspections of the injection well conducted by independent third parties or agents of State, Federal, or local government;

(8) the name and address of all owners and operators of the well and any disposal facility associated with it;

(9) the identification of all wells at which enforcement actions have been initiated under this Act (by reason of well failure, operator error, groundwater contamination or for other reasons) and an identification of the wastes involved in such enforcement actions; and

(10) such other information as the Administrator may, in his discretion, deem necessary to define the scope and nature of hazardous waste disposal in the United States through underground injection.

(b) In fulfilling the requirements of paragraphs (3) through (5) of subsection (a), the Administrator need only submit such information as can be obtained from currently existing State records and from site visits to at least 20 facilities containing wells which inject hazardous waste.

(c) The States shall make available to the Administrator such information as he deems necessary to accomplish the objectives of this section.

URANIUM MILL TAILINGS

Sec. 703. Nothing in the Hazardous and Solid Waste Amendments of 1984 shall be construed to affect, modify, or amend the Uranium Mill Tailings Radiation Control Act of 1978.

NATIONAL GROUND WATER COMMISSION

Sec. 704. (a) There is established a commission to be known as the National Ground Water Commission (hereinafter in this section referred to as the "Commission").

(b) The duties of the Commission are to:

(1) Assess generally the amount, location, and quality of the Nation's ground water resources.

(2) Identify generally the sources, extent, and types of ground water contamination.

(3) Assess the scope and nature of the relationship between ground water contamination and ground water withdrawal and develop projections of available, usable ground water in future years on a nationwide basis.

(4) Assess the relationship between surface water pollution and ground water pollution.

(5) Assess the need for a policy to protect ground water from degradation caused by contamination.

(6) Assess generally the extent of overdrafting of ground water resources, and the adequacy of existing mechanisms for preventing such overdrafting.

(7) Assess generally the engineering and technological capability to recharge aquifers.

(8) Assess the adequacy of the present understanding of ground water recharge zones and sole source aquifers and assess the adequacy of knowledge regarding the interrelationship of designated aquifers and recharge zones.

(9) Assess the role of landuse patterns as these relate to protecting ground water from contamination.

(10) Assess methods for remedial abatement of ground water contamination as well as the costs and benefits of cleaning up polluted ground water and compare cleanup costs to the costs of substitute water supply methods.

(11) Investigate policies and actions taken by foreign governments to protect ground water from contamination.

(12) Assess the use and effectiveness of existing interstate compacts to address ground water protection from contamination.

(13) Analyze existing legal rights and remedies regarding contamination of ground water.

(14) Assess the adequacy of existing standards for ground water quality under State and Federal law.

(15) Assess monitoring methodologies of the States and the Federal Government to achieve the level of protection of the resource as required by State and Federal law.

(16) Assess the relationship between ground water flow systems (and associated recharge areas) and the control of sources of contamination.

(17) Assess the role of underground injection practices as a means of disposing of waste fluids while protecting ground water from contami-nation.

(18) Assess methods for abatement and containment of ground water contamination and for aquifer restoration including the costs and benefits of alternatives to abatement and containment.

(19) Assess State and Federal ground water law and mechanisms with which to manage the quality of the ground water resource.

(20) Assess the adequacy of existing ground water research and determine future ground water research needs.

(21) Assess the roles of State, local, and Federal Governments in managing ground water quality.

(c)(1) The Commission shall be composed of 19 members as follows:

(A) 6 appointed by the Speaker of the United States House of Representatives from among the Members of the House of Represen-tatives, 2 of whom shall be members of the Committee on Energy and Commerce, 2 of whom shall be members of the Committee on Public Works and Transportation, and 2 of whom shall be members of the Committee on Interior and Insular Affairs;

(B) 4 appointed by the majority leader of the United States Senate from among the Members of the United States Senate;

(C) 8 appointed by the President as follows:

(i) 4 from among a list of nominations submitted to the President by the National Governors Association, 2 of whom shall be repre-sentatives of ground water appropriation States and 2 of whom shall be representatives of ground water riparian States;

(ii) one from among a list of nominations submitted to the President by the National League of Cities and the United States Conference of Mayors;

(iii) one from among a list of nominations submitted to the President by the National Academy of Sciences;

(iv) one from among a list of nominations submitted to the President by groups, organizations, or associations of industries the activities of which may affect ground water; and

(v) one from among a list of nominations submitted to the President from groups, organizations, or associations of citizens which are representative of persons concerned with pollution and environmental issues and which have participated, at the State or Federal level, in studies, administrative proceedings, or litigation (or any combination thereof) relating to ground water; and

(D) the Director of the Office of Technology Assessment.

A vacancy in the Commission shall be filled in the manner in which the original appointment was made. Appointments may be made under this subsection without regard to section 5311(b) of title 5, United States Code. Not more than three of the six members appointed under subparagraph (A) and not more than two of the four members appointed under subparagraph (B) may be of the same political party. No member appointed under paragraph (c) may be an officer or employee of the Federal Government.

(2) If any member of the Commission who was appointed to the Commission as a Member of the Congress leaves that office, or if any member of the Commission who was appointed from persons who are not officers or employees of any government becomes an officer or employee of a government, he may continue as a member of the Commission for not longer than the ninetyday period beginning on the date he leaves that office or becomes such an officer or employee, as the case may be.

(3) Members shall be appointed for the life of the Commission.

(4)(A) Except as provided in subparagraph (B), members of the Commission shall each be entitled (subject to appropriations provided in advance) to receive the daily equivalent of the maximum annual rate of basic pay in effect for grade GS18 of the General Schedule for each day (including travel time) during which they are engaged in the actual performance of duties vested in the Commission. While away from their homes or regular places of business in the performance of services for the Commission, members of the Commission shall be allowed travel expenses, including per diem in lieu of subsistence, in the same manner as persons employed intermittently in Government service are allowed expenses under section 5703 of title 5 of the United State Code.

(B) Members of the Commission who are Members of the Congress shall receive no additional pay, allowances, or benefits by reason of their service on the Commission.

(5) Five members of the Commission shall constitute a quorum but two may hold hearings.

(6) The Chairman of the Commission shall be appointed by the Speaker of the House of Representatives from among members appointed under paragraph (1)(A) of this subsection and the Vice Chairman of the Commission shall be appointed by the majority leader of the Senate from among members appointed under paragraph (1)(B) of this sub-section. The Chairman and the Vice Chairman of the Commission shall serve for the life of the Commission unless they cease to be members of the Commission before the termination of the Commission.

(7) The Commission shall meet at the call of the Chairman or a majority of its members.

(d)(1) The Commission shall have a Director who shall be appointed by the Chairman, without regard to section 5311(b) of title 5, United States Code.

(2) The Chairman may appoint and fix the pay of such additional personnel as the Chairman considers appropriate.

(3) With the approval of the Commission, the Chairman may procure temporary and intermittent services under section 3109(b) of title 5 of the United States Code.

(4) The Commission shall request, and the Chief of Engineers and the Director of the Geological Survey are each authorized to detail, on a reimbursable basis, any of the personnel of their respective agencies to the Commission to assist it in carrying out its duties under this section. Upon request of the Commission, the head of any other Federal agency is authorized to detail, on a reimbursable basis, any of the personnel of such agency to the Commission to assist it in carrying out its duties under this section.

(e)(1) The Commission may, for the purpose of carrying out this section, hold such hearings, sit and act at such times and places, take such testimony, and receive such evidence, as the Commission considers appropriate.

(2) Any member or agent of the Commission may, if so authorized by the Commission, take any action which the Commission is authorized to take by this section.

(3) The Commission may use the United States mails in the same manner and under the same conditions as other departments and agencies of the United States.

(4) The Administrator of General Services shall provide to the Commission on a reimbursable basis such administrative support services as the Commission may request.

(5) The Commission may secure directly from any department or agency of the United States information necessary to enable it to carry out this section. Upon request of the Chairman of the Commission, the head of such department or agency shall furnish such information to the Commission.

(f)(1) The Commission shall transmit to the President and to each House of the Congress a report not later than October 30, 1986. The report shall contain a detailed statement of the findings and conclusions of the Commission with respect to each item listed in subsection (b), together with its recommendations for such legislation; and administrative actions, as it considers appropriate.

(2) Not later than one year after the enactment of the Hazardous and Solid Waste Amendments of 1984, the Commission shall complete a pre-liminary study concerning ground water contamination from hazardous and other solid waste and submit to the President and to the Congress a report containing the findings and conclusions of such preliminary study. The study shall be continued thereafter, and final findings and conclusions shall be incorporated as a separate chapter in the report required under paragraph (1). The preliminary study shall include an analysis of the extent of ground water contamination caused by hazardous and other solid waste, the regions and major water supplies most significantly affected by such contamination, and any recommen-dations of the Commission for preventive or remedial measures to protect human health and the environment from the effects of such contamination.

(g) The Commission shall cease to exist on January 1, 1987.

(h) Nothing in this section and no recommendation of the Commission shall affect any rights to quantities of water established under State law, interstate compact, or Supreme Court decree.

(i) There is authorized to be appropriated for the fiscal years 1985 through 1987 not to exceed $7,000,000 to carry out this section.

FROM PUBLIC LAW 100-582 NOVEMBER 1, 1988

POWERS OF THE ENVIRONMENTAL PROTECTION AGENCY

Sec. 4. (a) Upon designation by the Administrator of the Environmental Protection Agency, any law enforcement officer of the Environmental Protection Agency with responsibility for the investigation of criminal violations of a law administered by the Environmental Protection Agency, may

(1) carry firearms;

(2) execute and serve any warrant or any other processes issued under the authority of the United States; and

(3) make arrests without warant for

(A) any offense against the United States committed in such officer's presence; or

(B) any felony offense against the United States if such officer has probably cause to believe that the person to be arrested has committed or is committing that felony offense.

(b) The powers granted under subsection (a)of this section shall be exercised in accordance with guidelines approved by the Attorney General.

FROM PUBLIC LAW 102-389, OCTOBER 6, 1992

EXTENDING COMMENT PERIOD FOR REVISIONS TO CERTAIN HAZARDOUS WASTE RULES

Funds appropriated or transferred to EPA may be used to develop revisions to 40 CFR 261.3, as reissued on March 3, 1992, published at 57 Fed. Reg. 7628 et seq. EPA shall promulgate revisions to paragraphs (a)(2)(iv) and (c)(2)(i) of 40 CFR 261.3, as reissued on March 3, 1992, by October 1, 1994, but any revisions to such paragraphs shall not be promulgated or become effective prior to October 1, 1993. Notwith-standing paragraph (e) of 40 CFR 261.3, as reissued on March 3, 1992, paragraphs (a)(2)(iv) and (c)(2)(i) of such regulations shall not be terminated or withdrawn until revisions are promulgated and become effective in accordance with the preceding sentence. The deadline of October 1, 1994 shall be enforceable under section 7002 of the Solid Waste Disposal Act.

PROVIDING FOR A STUDY OF METALS RECOVERY

Funds appropriated or transferred to the Environmental Protection Agency shall be used in part to conduct a study on the effect of existing regulations on efforts to recover metals from the nation's wastes, how such metals recovery can be best encouraged, and how the materials should be regulated in order to protect human health and the environ-ment and to effectuate the resource conservation and recovery goals of the Resource Conservation and Recovery Act. In doing so, EPA shall consult with the Secretary of Commerce, the Secretary of the Interior, the metals recovery industry, and other interested parties.

The Administrator seal complete the study not later than April 28, 1993. Upon completion of the study, the Administrator shall prepare a summary of the findings of the study and any recommendations resulting from such study, to the Committee on Environment and Public Works of the United States Senate and the Committee on Energy and Commerce of the United States House of Representatives.

SOLID WASTE DISPOSAL ACT

No funds appropriated to the Environmental Protection Agency for fiscal year 1993 may be expended for the promulgation, implementation, or enforcement of any regulation under the Solid Waste Disposal Act (42 U.S.C. 6901 et seq.) concerning process wastewater from phosphoric acid production and phosphogypsum from phosphoric acid production. The preceding sentence shall not apply to the regulation of those wastes under sections 3007, 3013, and 7003 of that Act (42 U.S.C. 6927, 6934, and 6973, respectively).

PROVISIONS THAT DO NOT AMEND
FROM PUBLIC LAW 102-386, OCTOBER 6, 1992

FEDERAL FACILITY COMPLIANCE ACT

(c) Effective Dates.--

(1) In General.--Except as otherwise provided in paragraphs (2) and (3), the amendments made by

subsection (a) [*of this Act to Sec. 6001 of the Solid Waste Disposal Act*] shall take effect upon the date of the enactment of this Act.

(2) Delayed Effective Date for Certain Mixed Waste.--Until the date that is 3 years after the date of the enactment of this Act, the waiver of sovereign immunity contained in section 6001(a) of the Solid Waste Disposal Act with respect to civil, criminal, and administrative penalties and fines (as added by the amendments made by subsection (a)[*of this Act*]) shall not apply to departments, agencies, and instrumentalities of the executive branch of the Federal Government for violations of section 3004(j) of the Solid Waste Disposal Act involving storage of mixed waste that is not subject to an existing agreement, permit, or administrative or judicial order, so long as such waste is managed in compliance with all other applicable requirements.

(3) Effective Date for Certain Mixed Waste.--(A) Except as provided in subparagraph (B), after the date that is 3 years after the date of enactment of this Act, the waiver of sovereign immunity contained in section 6001(a) of the Solid Waste Disposal Act with respect to civil, criminal, and administrative penalties and fines (as added by the amendments made by subsection (a) [*of this Act*]) shall apply to departments, agencies, and instrumentalities of the executive branch of the Federal Government for violations of section 3004(j) of the Solid Waste Disposal Act involving storage of mixed waste.

(B) With respect of the Department of Energy, the waiver of sovereign immunity referred to in subparagraph (A) shall not apply after the date that is 3 years after the date of the enactment of this Act for violations of section 3004(j) of such Act involving storage of mixed waste, so long as the Department of Energy is in compliance with both--

(i) a plan that has been submitted and approved pursuant to section 3021(b) of the Solid Waste Disposal Act and which is in effect; and

(ii) an order requiring compliance with such plan which has been issued pursuant to such section 3021(b) and which is in effect.

(4) Application of Waiver to Agreements and Orders.--The waiver of sovereign immunity contained in section 6001(a) of the Solid Waste Disposal Act (as added by the amendments made by subsection (a) [*of this Act*]) shall take effect on the date of the enactment of this Act with respect to any agreement, permit, or administrative or judicial order existing on such date of enactment (and any subsequent modifi-cations to such an agreement, permit, or order), including, without limitation, any provision of an agreement, permit, or order that addresses compliance with section 3004(j) of such Act with respect to mixed waste.

(5) Agreement or Order.--Except as provided in paragraph (4), nothing in this Act shall be construed to alter, modify, or change in any manner any agreement, permit, or administrative or judicial order, including, without limitation, any provision of an agreement, permit, or order--

(i) that addresses compliance with section 3004(j) of the Solid Waste Disposal Act with respect to mixed waste;

(ii) that is in effect on the date of enactment of this Act; and

(iii) to which a department, agency, or instrumentality of the executive branch of the Federal Government is a party.

* * * * *

(c) GAO Report.--

(1) Requirement.--Not later than 18 months after the date of the enactment of this Act, the Comptroller General shall submit to Congress a report on the Department of Energy's progress in complying with section 3021(b) of the Solid Waste Disposal Act.

(2) Matters to be Included.--The report required under paragraph (1) shall contain, at a minimum, the following:

(A) The Department of Energy's progress in submitting to the States or the Administrator of the Environmental Protection Agency a plan for each facility for which a plan is required under section 3021(b) of the Solid Waste Disposal Act and the status of State or Environmental Protection Agency review and approval of each such plan.

(B) The Department of Energy's progress in entering into orders requiring compliance with any such plans that have been approved.

(C) An evaluation of the completeness and adequacy of each such plan as of the date of submission of the report required under paragraph (1).

(D) An identification of any recurring problems among the Department of Energy's submitted plans.

(E) A description of treatment technologies and capacity that have been developed by the Department of Energy since the date of the enactment of this Act and a list of the wastes that are expected to be treated by such technologies and the facilities at which the wastes are generated or stored.

(F) The progress made by the Department of Energy in characterizing its mixed waste streams at each such facility by sampling and analysis.

(G) An identification and analysis of additional actions that the Department of Energy must take to--

(i) complete submission of all plans required under such section 3021(b) for all such facilities;

(ii) obtain the adoption of orders requiring compliance with all such plans; and

(iii) develop mixed waste treatment capacity and technologies.

* * * * *

SMALL TOWN ENVIRONMENTAL PLANNING

Sec. 109. (a) Establishment.--The Administrator of the Environmental Protection Agency (hereafter referred to as the "Administrator") shall establish a program to assist small communities in planning and financing environmental facilities. The program shall be known as the "Small Town Environmental Planning Program".

(b) Small Town Environmental Planning Task Force.--(1) The Adminis-trator shall establish a Small Town Environmental Planning Task Force which shall be composed of representatives of small towns from different areas of the United States, Federal and State governmental agencies, and public interest groups. The Administrator shall terminate the Task Force not later than 2 years after the establishment of the Task Force.

(2) The Task Force shall--

(A) identify regulations developed pursuant to Federal environmental laws which pose significant compliance problems for small towns;

(B) identify means to improve the working relationship between the Environmental Protection Agency (hereafter referred to as the Agency) and small towns;

(C) review proposed regulations for the protection of the environmental and public health and suggest revisions that could improve the ability of small towns to comply with such regulations;

(D) identify means to promote regionalization of environmental treatment systems and infrastructure serving small towns to improve the economic condition of such systems and infrastructure; and

(E) provide such other assistance to the Administrator as the Administrator deems appropriate.

(c) Identification of Environmental Requirements.--(1) Not later than 6 months after the date of the enactment of this Act, the Administrator shall publish a list of requirements under Federal environmental and public health statutes (and the regulations developed pursuant to such statutes) applicable to small towns. Not less than annually, the Administrator shall make such additions and deletions to and from the list as the Administrator deems appropriate.

(2) The Administrator shall, as part of the Small Town Environmental Planning Program under this section, implement a program to notify small communities of the regulations identified under paragraph (1) and of future regulations and requirements through methods that the Administrator determines to be effective to provide information to the greatest number of small communities, including any of the following:

(A) Newspapers and other periodicals.

(B) Other news media.

(C) Trade, municipal, and other associations that the Administrator determines to be appropriate.

(D) Direct mail.

About Government Institutes

Government Institutes, Inc. was founded in 1973 to provide continuing education and practical information for your professional development. Specializing in environmental, health and safety concerns, we recognize that you face unique challenges presented by the ever-increasing number of new laws and regulations and the rapid evolution of new technologies, methods and markets.

Our information and continuing education efforts include a Videotape Distribution Service, over 140 courses held nation-wide throughout the year, and over 150 publications, making us the world's largest publisher in these areas.

Government Institutes, Inc.
4 Research Place, Suite 200
Rockville, MD 20850
(301) 921-2300

Other related books published by Government Institutes:

Current Developments in RCRA: 1993 Report - This report covers developments in: the Definitions of Solid & Hazardous Waste; RCRA Reauthorization; the Mixture Rule & Derived From Wastes; RCRA Enforcement Trends; What You Sould Be Doing With Used Oil; TSD Regulations; Land Disposal Restrictions; RCRA Corrective Action; RCRA/CERCLA Interaction; and more! Softcover/219 pages/Mar '93/ $59   ISBN: 0-86587-339-9

Managing Your Hazardous Waste: A Step-by-step Guide - The detailed checklists in this guide will help you accurately identify your RCRA requirements, and then tell you the actual steps to take toward compliance. This manual clearly explains the procedures for handling contingency plans, permits, labeling, EPA Notification, employee training, and much more. Softcover/ 220 pages/Sept '92/$65   ISBN: 0-86587-311-9

RCRA Inspection Manual, 2nd Edition - Covers all details of a RCRA inspection, from facility entry to closing discussion with the owner/operator, including a synopsis of the regulations and the corresponding inspection procedures. Softcover/370 pages/ Feb '89/$69   ISBN: 0-86587-762-9

Underground Storage Tank Management: A Practical Guide, 4th Edition - This guide will help you develop or maintain UST management programs that will minimize the risk of a release and reduce the potential for costly repurcussions. Brings you up-to-date on the latest in tank design, how to predict tank leaks, test tank integrity, avoid costly tank replacement, and more. Softcover/420 pages/Nov '91/$79   ISBN: 0-86587-271-6

Aboveground Storage Tank Management: A Practical Guide - Explains how to cost-effectively design, build, manage, operate and maintain an aboveground tank system that meets your storage needs and complies with all federal and state codes and regulations. Softcover/220 pages/Feb '90/$59   ISBN: 0-86587-202-3

Call the above number for our current book/video catalog and course schedule.